THE SEPTUAGINT IN CONTEXT

THE SEPTUAGINT
IN CONTEXT

Introduction to the Greek Version of the Bible

BY

NATALIO FERNÁNDEZ MARCOS

TRANSLATED BY WILFRED G.E. WATSON

BRILL

LEIDEN · BOSTON · KÖLN

2000

BS
38
.F4713
2000

This book is printed on acid-free paper.

Published with financial support from the Dirección General del Libro, Archivos y Bibliotecas del Ministerio de Educación y Cultura, Spain

Library of Congress Cataloging-in Publication data

Fernández Marcos, Natalio, 1940-
  [Introduccíon a las versiones griegas de la Biblia. English]
  The Septuagint in context : introduction to the Greek version of the Bible /
  by Natalio Fernández Marcos ; translated by Wilfred G.E. Watson.
       p.   cm.
  Includes bibliographical references and index.
  ISBN 9004115749
  1. Bible. Greek—Versions. I. Title.

  BS38.F4713 2000
  221.4'8—dc21   00–041378
                                                                      CIP

Deutsche Bibliothek – CIP-Einheitsaufnahme

Fernández Marcos, Natalio :
The Septuagint in context : introduction to the Greek version of the
bible / by Natalio Fernández Marcos. Transl. by Wilfred G.E.Watson.
– Leiden ; Boston ; Köln : Brill, 2000
   ISBN 90-04-11574-9

ISBN   90 04 11574 9

PRINTED IN THE NETHERLANDS

CONTENTS

PART FOUR

THE SEPTUAGINT IN CHRISTIAN TRADITION

PART FIVE

THE SEPTUAGINT AND CHRISTIAN ORIGINS

FOREWORD

When the first edition of this work, published in 1979, ran out it seemed like a good opportunity to prepare a second edition, revised and brought up to date. Every field of biblical research, but particularly the history of the biblical text, has undergone profound changes over the last twenty years as a result of the new information provided by the documents from Qumran. In addition, recent studies on the Septuagint as a literary work have helped to give vital stimulus to study of the Greek versions of the Bible.

The title of this book expresses the main concern that, as a selective criterion, has been my guide during the course of its production. I am aware that the Septuagint is not a translation but a "collection of translations", but I also think that an introduction of this kind should include other translations of the Bible into Greek – some better known, others preserved only as fragments – whose authors turned to the Hebrew text with more or less success but with the firm resolve of transmitting the original better than their predecessors. This activity of correcting and improving the first version of the Bible, the Septuagint, began the day after the translation, as can be conjectured judging by the Jewish papyri we have, and went on until the Byzantine era. We can even extend this process to the publication of the trilingual Pentateuch of Constantinople in 1547. The special history of the text of the Greek Bible, which culminated in the production of Origen's Hexapla, precludes separating these two sources of a single channel of transmission.

It is mandatory to mention here two classics in this area of research: H. B. Swete, *An Introduction to the Old Testament in Greek* (revised by R. R. Ottley, Cambridge 1914), which is a mine of information and assimilated knowledge, indispensable even today as a reference work, although, of course, obsolete in many respects; and S. Jellicoe, *The Septuagint and Modern Study* (Oxford 1968), produced to complement and update the previous work. To these must be added the recent publication by the French specialist scholars M. Harl, G. Dorival and O. Munnich, *La Bible grecque des Septante: Du judaïsme hellénistique au christianisme ancien* (Paris 1988). These three works are present in this *Introduction*. Hence it often refers to them for information and aspects of research which they include, whereas I am more expansive in those chapters that include either recent achievements or the questions most discussed in recent years. A mere glance at the list of contents is enough to give some idea of the new topics or those points which, while not completely new, are tackled from a different perspective.

Nor should there any need to say that this *Introduction* claims to be selective rather than exhaustive. It does not treat systematically such important topics as the language of the Septuagint, the manuscripts, the papyri and the principal editions of the Greek Bible, the problems peculiar to each book or the history of research on the Septuagint. Most of these points are studied extensively in the introductions by Swete, Jellicoe or Harl *et al.* mentioned above. On the other hand, the specialised bibliographies by S. P. Brock, Ch. T. Fritsch, S. Jellicoe, *A Classified Bibliography of the Septuagint* (Leiden 1973), and C. Dogniez, *Bibliography of the Septuagint: Bibliographie de la Septante 1970-1993* (Leiden 1995), can be used for guidance on most of these topics (I will refer to these two works respectively as CB and Dogniez *BS* throughout this volume). However, in the last chapter I have inserted a short guide to the secondary versions, some of which, like the Old Latin or the Coptic versions, are of primary importance for restoring the Old Greek.

I could also have tackled in a more systematic way such significant topics as the translation techniques of the various books, the manuscript illustrations, or the Greek Bible and information technology. However, it was necessary to circumscribe in some way the frame of reference of this *Introduction* in order to keep to a logical plan and to remain within reasonable limits, particularly with regard to the length of the book. Instead, space has been given to material that, in my opinion, has so far not been properly discussed, such as the double texts of the Greek Bible and Targumism, the Jewish versions into mediaeval and modern Greek, and several chapters in section IV such as those on other revisions, biblical quotations, the commentaries, and the *catenae*. Also, I have considered it useful to include two new chapters in this second edition, one on the Septuagint and the Hebrew text and other on the Septuagint and early Christian literature, in view of the special attention given to these topics in recent publications.

To conclude, I hope that this modest contribution to the study of the Greek text of the Bible will be useful not only to a small and select group of Septuagintalists but also to biblical scholars in general, philologists and historians of antiquity, and for all those interested in this important cultural legacy.

I would like to thank Mª Isabel Tejero, research assistant in the Departamento de Filología Bíblica y de Oriente Antiguo in the Instituto de Filología del CSIC, for her work in putting the first edition of this book into computerised format.

Natalio Fernández Marcos

ACKNOWLEDGEMENTS

I wish to thank Wilfred G. E. Watson for his willingness to translate this *Introduction* from the Spanish. During the translation process we have been in frequent contact in order to clarify the meaning of difficult passages. Kristin De Troyer read the English manuscript and made some valuable suggestions. Although the original manuscript was completed in 1996, some subsequently published titles have been incorporated into the English edition, especially in the notes and bibliography.

I am grateful to Brill Academic Publishers, especially to Mr Hans van der Meij and Anniek Meinders-Durksz, for their interest in this translation and their friendly cooperation to carry it out.

Madrid, January 2000
Natalio Fernández Marcos

PART ONE

THE LINGUISTIC AND CULTURAL SETTING

CHAPTER ONE

BIBLICAL GREEK AND ITS POSITION WITHIN *KOINĒ*

a) *History of Research*

Until the close of the 19th century, biblical Greek was understood to be the Greek of the Bible as opposed to secular Greek. Some theologians, impressed by the peculiarities of these texts, the Semitic loans, the Hebraising constructions etc., had reached the conclusion that it was a special language of the Bible, which in some way had come under divine inspiration.[1] And although since Deissmann's studies this expression has fallen into disfavour, it continues to be used to indicate in a concise way some typical elements of the language of the LXX, the pseudepigraphic writings preserved in Greek and the New Testament, such as syntactic Semitisms, and the neologisms coined to express Jewish–Christian concepts. In any event, it would be preferable to speak of translation Greek since although not all the writings included are strictly translations, they arose conditioned by the bilingualism of their authors or are influenced to a different extent by a translation language, the language of the LXX.

The New Testament writings began to appear in the second half of the 1st century CE[2] at the same time as the apogee of the Attic movement[3] and of the literary *koinē* of a Plutarch or the historian Flavius Arrianus. Attention was only paid to the past as the literature of the golden century and the literary writers of the Hellenistic

---

[1] See, for example, R. Rothe, *Zur Dogmatik*, Gotha 1863, 238: "Therefore we can with reason speak of a language of the Holy Spirit. Because in the Bible it is evident how the divine Spirit operating in revelation takes the language of a particular people, chosen to be the recipient and makes it a characteristic religious variety by transforming linguistic elements and existing concepts in a mould specially suited for the Holy Spirit. This process is clearly evident in NT Greek." An idea which the theologian H. Cremer promotes in the foreword to his *Biblisch-theologisches Wörterbuch der neutestamentlichen Gracität*, Gotha 1893, 8.

[2] See P. Feine, J. Behm and W. Kümmel, *Einleitung in das Neue Testament*, Heidelberg 1964.

[3] See W. Schmid, *Der Attizismus in seinen Hauptvertretern*, 1–5, Stuttgart 1887–97, 1, Vff., and M. Michaelis, "Der Attizismus und das Neue Testament", *ZNW* 22 (1923), 90–121.

period such as Polybius.[4] It is not surprising therefore that the Greek of the Bible would look like a foreign body and the attacks on Christianity by Celsus, Porphyrius, Hierocles and Julian were frequently peppered with contemptuous allusions to the barbaric language of the Bible.

The Fathers of the Church reacted in different ways to this uncomfortable fact. Most of them accepted the differences between the New Testament works and the literary works of contemporary pagan authors, and attempted to justify theologically the low artistic level of the language of the Greek Bible. According to them this simple and plain language was chosen so that the whole world, without exception, could understand it, since the Christian message is directed to all men without distinction of culture or social class.[5] Slightly different arguments were adopted by Origen in his *Contra Celsum*.[6] Finally, the resort to the simple language of scripture would become one of the most recurrent topics in the rhetorical prologues of the works of the Fathers.[7] Another movement among Christian writers, the minority, tried to defend the artistic perfection and elegance of biblical language and some even claimed to see applied to biblical compositions not only the rules of classical metrics but even various stylistic devices.[8]

The distance between the Fathers and biblical Greek is evident not only in their statements about the language of scripture but pri-

---

[4] On the channelling of culture from antiquity along lines which today are known to us, see L. Gil, *Censura en el mundo antiguo*, Madrid 1961, and W. Speyer, "Büchervernichtung", *JAC* 13 (1970), 122–53.

[5] For example, Isidore of Pelusia: Δι' ὃ καὶ ἡ Γραφὴ τὴν ἀλήθειαν πεζῷ λόγῳ ἡρμήνευσεν, ἵνα καὶ ἰδιῶται καὶ σοφοὶ καὶ παῖδες καὶ γυναῖκες μάθοιεν (*PG* 78,1124). Jerome appeals to the example of the Romans who in translating Greek coined very many neologisms without anybody being scandalised, even though in translating Greek into Latin there is less difference than in translating Hebrew to Greek (see *PL* 26, 347ff.).

[6] *Contra Celsum* I, chap. LXII. If the apostles had used the rhetorical and dialectical devices of the Greeks they would have given the impression that Jesus Christ was the founder of a new school of philosophy. However, in this way it is proved that the force of persuasion comes from something superior and divine.

[7] It has been called "die christliche Unfähigkeitstopik" (see K. Thraede, "Untersuchungen zum Ursprung und zur Geschichte der christlichen Poesie" II, in *JAC* 5 [1962] 138), which means that these authors in the prologues to their works constantly make decisive pronouncements about not using the rhetorical and brilliant language of the classics keeping instead to the simple language of Scripture. Nevertheless, after this declaration of principles they automatically use in their writings all the figures of literary language.

[8] See, for example, Augustine, *De doctrina Christiana* I, IV, 14.

marily from analysing their own writings, in particular their explanations of *voces biblicae* which claim most attention. This new perspective provoked by recent studies stresses the unease they felt with a translation language that, to some extent detached from the original, has been made unintelligible within the Greek system.[9]

During the Middle Ages the use of the Vulgate became general in the West. In Eastern Christianity, instead, the LXX remained in force, but we have no information that studies of its language were a concern. It should not be forgotten however, that this is a period in which most of the biblical manuscripts we now have were copied and that around this activity of transmission, the avatars of the texts can be seen and also the impact made upon it by the linguistic development of Greek, in variants, glosses and all kinds of comments.

With the advent of Humanism, we can appreciate a renaissance first of classical studies and somewhat later of biblical Hebrew studies. In 1520 the main edition of the Greek Bible was published in the inner column of the Alcalá Polyglot.[10] Yet again the differences from the Greek of the classics make the debate on biblical Greek leap onto the literary stage, to continue latent in the dispute between Hellenists and Hebraisers. The division deepened through dogmatic questions and inspirationist theories, in that one would be a purist or Hebraiser depending on whether or not one considered the presence of Hebraisms in biblical Greek irreconcilable with the dignity of scripture. Prominently for the Hebraist camp are J. Drusius and D. Heinsius, and for the Hellenist, S. Pfochen and Ch. S. Georgius, one of the most fanatical purists. The writings of the Hebraists were published by J. Rhenferd in Leenwarden (1702), and the writings of the Hellenists by T. van der Honert in Amsterdam (1703).[11]

---

[9] See M. Harl, "Y-a-t-il une influence du 'grec biblique' sur la langue spirituelle des chrétiens?", in *La Bible et les Pères*, Strasbourg 1971, 243–63, and N. Fernández Marcos, "En torno al estudio del griego de los cristianos", *Emerita* 41 (1973), 45–56. The linguistic information that patristic literature transmits to us about biblical Greek is very meagre; see G. J. M. Bartelink, "Observations de Saint Basile sur la langue biblique et théologique", *VC* 17 (1963), 85–105. Hadrian's *Eisagogué*, the first treatise on biblical semantics, merits more attention.

[10] It had already been printed in 1517. It took four years to publish due to the negotiations for obtaining papal approval. The *Aldina*, printed in February 1518, is later than the printing of the Complutensian, although published earlier.

[11] For further details on these two schools, see J. Ros, *De studie van het bijbelgrieksch*, 52 and 54. Apart from the dogmatic conditioning of this era, this controversy is a good example of the sterility of such discussions if no attempt is made to lower the horizon of one's own discipline. Even today there are phenomena of biblical Greek

Unfortunately, so many years of controversy did not produce the results one would have expected at the level of language, since the first attempts at a systematic approach to a grammar of biblical Greek were by Wyss and Pasor.[12] Even though there was a wait lasting two centuries for a grammar of the New Testament, the one by Winer applied the new methods of linguistics to biblical Greek. In less than a century this grammar ran to eight editions and it was translated into various European languages.[13] In the area of the LXX, the 18th century produced a very valuable work for its time, the concordance by Trom,[14] undoubtedly the best forerunner to the one by Hatch – Redpath and in some respects preferable to it, as for example in the distribution of the passages according to the various Hebrew meanings to which the Greek word in question corresponds. This century also saw the start of the great edition by Holmes – Parsons.[15]

b) *Comparison with the Papyri*

However, marginal to this work, an event was taking place that was to revolutionise the study of biblical Greek: the successive discoveries of papyri. Although the excavation of Herculaneum had already begun in 1752, the first finds of papyri in Egypt did not appear until 1778, and this happened by chance. At all events, these isolated discoveries did not capture the attention of scholars until the Napoleonic expedition to Egypt in 1798, an expedition which included many scholars. From this period come the collections of papyri that are

that a Hebraist would explain as the influence of Hebrew–Aramaic, whereas a Hellenist would explain them as due to the diachronic development of his own *koiné*, since probably both influences were concurrent at a particular moment in the history of Greek.

  [12] Wyssius Casparus, *Dialectologia Sacra*, Zurich 1650; Georgii Pasoris and Gr. L. Professoris, *Grammatica Graeca Sacra Novi Testamenti*, Groningen 1655.

  [13] G. B. Winer, *Grammatik des neutestamentlichen Sprachidioms als sichere Grundlage der neutestamentlichen Exegese*, Leipzig 1822.

  [14] A. Trom, *Concordantiae Graecae versionis vulgo dictae LXX interpretum*, 2 vols, Amsterdam 1718.

  [15] R. Holmes and J. Parsons, *Vetus Testamentum Graecum cum variis lectionibus* I–V, Oxford 1798–1827. Important works from the beginning of the 19th century, before the use of papyri for linguistic purposes, that are worth mentioning are F. G. Sturz, *De dialecto macedonica et alexandrina liber*, Leipzig 1808, and the lexicon by J. Fr. Schleusner, *Novus Thesaurus philologico-criticus, sive lexicon in LXX et reliquos interpretes graecos ac scriptores apocryphos Veteris Testamenti*, Leipzig 1920, the only one of its kind even today (reprint: Turnhout, Brepols 1994).

now to be found in the museums of Paris, Berlin, Leiden, Rome and Turin. However, only in 1877 did the real period of papyrology begin. In that year, in the ancient city of Arsinoe, in the Fayyum, thousands of fragments appeared. Other places in Egypt were just as productive: Oxyrhynchus, Hermopolis, Aphroditopolis, Panopolis (Akhmim), Elephantine and, more recently, Nag-Hammadi. From the close of the 19th century the biblical papyri were constantly being added to European collections. Probably the most sensational find was in the excavations of Oxyrhynchus, carried out systematically from 1896 to 1906 by P. B. Grenfell and A. S. Hunt, students from Oxford. Today we have a considerable collection of papyri both of the LXX and of the New Testament, which, in addition, is continually growing.[16]

In this heap of finds, next to unknown texts by ancient writers there was a storehouse of letters, wills, administrative documents and other writings which have put us in contact with unknown sectors of life and society in ancient times. Hence they were primarily used for historical and socio-economic study. It was Deissmann who, for the first time, used them systematically for linguistic purposes, and in this sense his *Bibelstudien* (Marburg 1895) caused a transcendental change of direction in the approach to biblical Greek.[17] He compared the Greek of the LXX and the New Testament with the language of the inscriptions, papyri and ostraca of the Hellenistic period, and obtained surprising results. On the one hand he showed the presence in secular documents of terms considered to be specifically Christian, like those called *voces biblicae*: ἀγάπη, ἀντιλήμπτωρ, ἐπίσκοπος, πρεσβύτερος, προφήτης, κατήγωρ, ἀναθεματίζειν, ἱερατεύειν, νεόφυτος, etc.[18] Even words that Jerome considered peculiar to Scripture such as ἀποκάλυψις are due to error or lack of perspective by the Christian writers, since this term and others similar terms are found in Plutarch.[19] As knowledge of the *koiné* and especially of the papyri and inscriptions grew, it could be shown how the percentage of *voces biblicae*

---

[16] See J. O'Callaghan, "Lista de los papiros de los LXX", *Bib* 66, 1 (1975), 74–93; K. Aland, *Repertorium der Griechischen Christlichen Papyri. I Biblische Papyri. Altes Testament, Neues Testament, Varia, Apokryphen*, Berlin–New York 1976; J. van Haelst, *Catalogue des papyrus littéraires juifs et chrétiens*, Paris 1976; O. Montevecchi, *La Papirologia*, Turin 1973 (2nd edition, Milan 1988), and F. T. Gignac, *A Grammar of the Greek Papyri of the Roman and Byzantine Periods*, 2 vols, Milan 1976 and 1982.

[17] To be followed by *Neue Bibelstudien* in 1897 and *Licht vom Osten* in 1908.

[18] A. Deissmann, *Licht vom Osten*, 58ff.

[19] Jerome, *Comm. in Gal.* 1, 12 (*PL* 26, 347ff.) and A. Deissmann, *Licht vom Osten*, 61.

noted by ancient philologists decreased. The clearest example is to be found in the Dictionary by W. Bauer: if we compare the lists in the introduction to those of the second edition, which appeared in 1928, with the lists in the introduction to the fourth edition of 1952, we can see that the number of *voces biblicae* has been considerably reduced.[20]

Deissmann was also opposed to the existence of Jewish-Greek as a special language of Hellenised Jews. The introduction of certain technical terms from the new religion does not justify speaking of a new language and the syntactic Semitisms are due more to the influence of a translation language than to linguistic peculiarities of the group. Each cultural movement, the Stoics, Gnosticism, neo-Platonism, etc., brings lexical neologisms but no-one would consider describing a new language or writing a grammar of neo-Platonic writings.

The analyses of the lexicon carried out by Deissman were extended by A. Thumb to the field of syntax.[21] Besides helping to spread his ideas, Thumb set biblical Greek decidedly within the development of *koiné*. He noted how quite a number of the constructions held to be Semitisms also occur in the papyri. As a result there was no other solution than the distinction between popular *koiné* on the one hand and literary, written *koiné* on the other. This literary *koiné* was the only one known until the discovery of papyri and inscriptions. The Greek Bible and the papyri belong to popular *koiné*; both sets of documents comprised a sort of advance party within the diachronic development of the language until modern Greek strengthened Thumb's idea that these phenomena were due to the normal development of Greek and not to the influence of a foreign language.[22] In this hypothesis the LXX and the New Testament would be the first writings intended for the people in a plain language that everyone could understand.

---

[20] W. Bauer, *Zur Einführung in das Wörterbuch zum Neuen Testament*. Coniectanea Neotestamentica 15, Lund 1955. See now the sixth edition of W. Bauer, *Griechisch–deutsches Wörterbuch zu den Schriften des Neuen Testaments und der frühchristlichen Literatur*, edited by K. Aland and B. Aland, Berlin–New York 1988.

[21] A. Thumb, *Die griechische Sprache im Zeitalter des Hellenismus*.

[22] A. Thumb, "On the Value of the Modern Greek for the Study of Ancient Greek", *CQ* 8 (1914), 181–205. For the development of Greek in the papyri, see O. Montevecchi, "Dal Paganesimo al Cristianesimo. Aspetti dell'evoluzione della lingua greca nei papiri dell'Egitto", *Aegyptus* 37 (1957), 41–59.

c) *The New Approach of Bilingualism*

The reaction against Deissmann–Thumb began in the sphere of the New Testament. A series of specialists set out to find the Aramaic sources of the gospels, starting precisely from the syntactic anomalies of Greek: the most prominent of these specialists were J. Wellhausen and G. Dalman.[23] The latter focused his analyses on the distinction between Hebraisms and Aramaisms in the New Testament. However, apart from other studies that attempt to emphasise the rabbinic roots in the expressions and composition techniques of the gospels, the school most energetically opposed to Deissmann was that of C. C. Torrey and C. F. Burney. On the basis of Aramaisms they tried to prove that a large part of the New Testament (Acts 1:1-15:35; the Gospel of John; and the Apocalypse) is translated from Aramaic, attributing the mistakes in translation to inconsistencies and obscurities in the Greek text.[24] This theory had J. A. Montgomery, R. B. Y. Scott and M. Burrows among its followers, but there were also important professors who opposed it, including H.-J. Cadbury, E.-J. Goodspeed and F.-C. Burkitt. However, in my view the best refutation of this hypothesis is by D.-W. Riddle,[25] because he insists on the lack of objective criteria for distinguishing a real translation from something written by a bilingual person in a language less familiar to him.

In spite of Deissmann's results, biblical philologists continued to look for Semitisms in the New Testament. For even though the data from the papyri had been decisive in the area of the lexicon, the constructions that diverged from classical Greek were so important that the explanation of a few sporadic agreements with the Greek of the papyri was not explanation enough. Moreover, the discussion took on a new twist, turning the argument from the papyri against Deissmann himself: the many Jews residing in the Nile Valley could have influenced the peculiarities of the Greek of Egypt.

Are the non-classical expressions of the papyri not actually Semitisms?

---

[23] J. Wellhausen, *Einleitung in die drei ersten Evangelien*, Berlin 1911, and G. Dalman, *Die Worte Jesu, mit Berücksigtigung des nachkanonischen jüdischen Schriftums und der aramäischen Sprache erörtert*, Leipzig 1930.

[24] Especially C. C. Torrey, *The Four Gospels: A New Translation*, New York 1933.

[25] In "The Logic of the Theory of Translation Greek", *JBL* 51 (1932), 13–30.

To this new direction of study authors such as H.-A. Redpath,[26] R. R. Ottley,[27] C.-F. Burney,[28] A.-T. Robertson,[29] P. Joüon[30] and others seem to rally.

J. Vergote emphasised the impact and productive nature of this evocative hypothesis which has a precise theoretical formulation in the review by Lefort of Abel's grammar of biblical Greek.[31] He starts from the fact of bilingualism in Ptolemaic, Roman and Byzantine Egypt. There is no need, therefore, to resort – as did the authors quoted above – to the presence of Semitisms, which is less probable for the Greek of Egypt. What happens is that the same syntactic phenomena which in biblical Greek are due to the influence of Hebrew–Aramaic occur in the Greek of the papyri due to the influence of Coptic–Egyptian. In fact the strong linguistic affinity between Egyptian and Hebrew–Aramaic is proved not only in syntax but also in the way reality is structured. Bilingualism, therefore, is responsible both for the syntactic peculiarities of the Greek of the Old and New Testaments, and of the papyri. Some biblical books are too well written to think of vulgarisms or that they express spoken *koiné*. Some of them, such as the Apocalypse (Revelation), belong rather to the class of esoteric literature. And as for the vulgarisms of the papyri, there should be no exaggeration since their authors, at least, knew how to write, which amounted to something in the society of that time. Vergote notes accurately how in all the cases where a Semitism of biblical Greek has been denied due to the same construction having been found in the papyri, there is an exact parallel in a Coptic construction: for example, the *casus pendens*, the construction with καί and finite verb after a participle or infinitive, the pleonastic use of the personal pronoun in oblique cases, the use of the numeral εἷς instead of the indefinite τις, the repetition of the same word with a distributive meaning, ἰδού meaning 'from', ἐν with an instrumental meaning, the expression of the vocative by means of the nominative with the article.[32]

---

[26] In "The Present Position of the Study of the Septuagint", *AJT* 7 (1903), 11.

[27] In *A Handbook to the Septuagint*, New York 1920, 165.

[28] In *The Aramaic Origin of the Fourth Gospel*, Oxford 1922, 4.

[29] In *A Grammar of the Greek New Testament*, New York 1923, 91.

[30] In *L'Evangile de Notre-Seigneur Jésus-Christ*, Paris 1930, XIII.

[31] J. Vergote, "Grec Biblique", 1354ff., and F.-M. Abel, *Grammaire du grec biblique suivie d'un choix de papyrus*, Paris 1927; L.-T. Lefort, "Pour une grammaire des LXX", *Le Muséon* 41 (1928), 152–60.

[32] J. Vergote, "Grec Biblique", 1355–59. A study of the papyri from this aspect

In recent years the problem of Semitisms has again been in the foreground and the expression 'Jewish-Greek' recurs in both its meanings, as literary language and as spoken or colloquial language.[33] The deeply Semitised nature of translation Greek has again raised old problems as the Hebrew–Aramaic sources from the times of biblical Greek become better known (especially through Qumran and the Targums) and more books of Jewish intertestamental literature are published, written in the same Semitised Greek as the canonical books. In the 1950s a new reaction against Deissmann is noticeable both from Septuagintalists and New Testament philologists.[34] N. Turner insists that no-one is completely convinced of Deissmann's hypothesis, even though so many specialists have followed it, including his predecessor in New Testament grammar, J. H. Moulton. Some specifically Semitic syntactic uses stand out in contrast to the language of the papyri, and he defends the existence of Jewish-Greek in the first centuries shared by the LXX, the New Testament and the pseudepigraphic and apocalyptic writers. He sets out these ideas in the introduction to the third volume of his grammar of the New Testament, on syntax.[35] The peculiarity of biblical Greek was to become a characteristic feature in the first place in the translation Greek of the LXX and which later was transmitted to other intertestamental writers and to the New Testament – even if they are not translations – as a sort of sacred language that had to be imitated. At a later stage a distinction has to be made between global Semitisms, Hebraisms and Aramaisms, and Septuagintisms proper. Within this

---

reveals many other peculiarities of the Greek of Egypt which can be explained by their closeness to Coptic constructions.

[33] M. Black, "The Semitic Element in the New Testament", *ET* 77 (1965–66), 20–23: "And this language, like the Hebrew of the Old Testament which moulded it, was a language apart from the beginning; Biblical Greek is a peculiar language, the language of a peculiar people" (p. 23).

[34] See P. Katz, "Zur Übersetzungstechnik der Septuaginta", *Die Welt des Orients* II (1956), 272ff.; H. S. Gehman, "The Hebraic Character of the Septuagint", *VT* 1 (1951), 81–90: "If the LXX made sense to Hellenistic Jews, we may infer that there was a Jewish Greek which was understood apart from the Hebrew language", p. 90; Gehman, "Hebraisms of the Old Greek Version of Genesis", *VT* III (1953), 141–48; Gehman, "Ἅγιος in the Septuagint, and its Relation to the Hebrew Original", *VT* IV (1954), 337–48; N. Turner, "The Unique Character of Biblical Greek", *VT* V (1955), 208–13; Turner, "The Testament of Abraham: Problems in Biblical Greek", *NTS* I (1955), 222ff.

[35] J. H. Moulton, *A Grammar of New Testament Greek. Vol. III: Syntax* by N. Turner, Edinburgh 1963, 4: biblical Greek as a whole "is a unique language with a unity and character of its own".

tendency must be included recent philological works on the New Testament by Beyer,[36] Black[37] and Wilcox.[38]

d) *The Technical Language of Hellenistic Prose*

From a different perspective, better knowledge of Hellenistic prose has contributed to modifying the conclusions of Deissmann about popular and literary *koiné* in relation to biblical Greek. This starts with the monographs devoted to the language of a particular Hellenistic author such as the one by Durham on Menander,[39] or the one by Bonhoeffer on Epictetus,[40] up to more recent studies on late literary and popular Greek carried out chiefly by the Swedish school of Uppsala and Lund. Some of this research is the result of doctoral theses that were never published, such as Arnim's study of Philo of Byzantium.[41] Others have had more success, such as Meecham's work on the *Letter of Aristeas*[42] or the study by Adrados on Aesop's Fables.[43]

In the 1946 Tyndale Lecture, E. K. Simpson proposed a series of words from the Greek Bible that the papyri did not illustrate but which instead were explained by comparison with literary usage in

---

[36] K. Beyer, *Semitische Syntax im Neuen Testament. Band I, Satzlehre Teil 1*, Göttingen 1962, 11. For bilingualism in the field of phonology, see F. T. Gignac, *A Grammar of the Greek Papyri of the Roman and Byzantine Periods. Volume I: Phonology*, Milan 1975, 46ff.

[37] M. Black, *An Aramaic Approach to the Gospels and Acts*, Oxford 1954.

[38] M. Wilcox, *The Semitisms of Acts*, Oxford 1965. Recent publications such as J. Amstutz, Ἁπλότης. *Eine begriffsgeschichtliche Studie zum jüdisch–christlichen Griechisch*. Theophaneia 9, Bonn 1968, while not discussing Jewish-Greek, presuppose at least a certain linguistic unity in this material due to the chronological limitations and the selection of texts that they make (Greek Bible, Jewish–Hellenistic literature, Jewish–Palestinian literature, New Testament and early Christian writings). However, the results make biblical Greek an integral part of *koiné*, since the only new meaning of ἁπλότης in the synagogue–church which was not already represented in the *koiné* is "simplicity–totality or integrity", ibid. 14.

[39] D. B. Durham, *The Vocabulary of Menander considered in its relation to the koiné*, Princeton 1913 (reprint Amsterdam 1969), where the relationship of the LXX lexicon with the lexicon of middle and new comedy is clear (p. 103).

[40] A. Bonhoeffer, *Epiktet und das Neue Testament*, Giessen 1911, for the linguistic closeness between Stoic and Pauline parenesis. In this sense the monographs in the series *Corpus Hellenisticum Novi Testamenti* published in Leiden, especially G. Mussies, *Dio Chrysostom and the New Testament* (1972), and P. W. Van der Horst, *Aelius Aristides and the New Testament* (1980), can provide interesting comparative data.

[41] M. Arnim, "De Philonis Byzantii dicendi genere". Diss. Greifswald 1912.

[42] H. G. Meecham, *The Letter of Aristeas: A Linguistic Study with Special Reference to the Greek Bible*, Manchester 1935.

[43] F. Rodríguez-Adrados, *Estudio sobre el léxico de las fábulas esópicas. En torno a los problemas de la koiné literaria*, Salamanca 1948.

Hellenistic prose.[44] And in 1955, J. Palm devoted an impeccable study to the language and style of Diodorus Siculus.[45] In Palm's opinion, the term *koiné* should be reserved for the popular language of the post-classical period, and the expression 'normal Hellenistic prose' for the language used by authors such as Philo of Byzantium, Apollonius of Perge, Polybius and Diodorus Siculus, a prose which became widespread with the flowering and diffusion of the various sciences in the Hellenistic period, consistent and logical, a suitable and functional tool for practical purposes, not very different from the modern prose of administrative language with its own pros and cons.[46] This movement culminated in a monograph of Rydbeck, who formulated the thesis that the language of the New Testament is closer to the specialised, scientific and technical prose of its period than to the language of the papyri.[47]

e) *Conclusions*

The outright achievement of Deissmann – Thumb, definitive in terms of methodology, has been to rescue biblical Greek from the domain of theology, in order to study it not on its own but as an integral part of Hellenistic Greek. The secular and sterile discussion between Hellenists and Hebraisers has been resolved, as has the idea of biblical Greek as a special language, a suitable vehicle for the expression of a religious movement. Today, in the paths opened up by Deissmann and Thumb, belong projects such as Horsley's on the new documents to illustrate primitive Christianity, or studies such as Silva's which uses the analysis of bilingualism and the approaches of modern linguistics.[48]

However, the various approaches that we have seen from the close of the 19th century, such as inscriptions, papyri, bilingualism or the

---

[44] E. K. Simpson, *Words Worth Weighing in the Greek NT*. Tyndale Lecture, 1946.

[45] J. Palm, *Über Sprache und Stil des Diodoros von Sizilien. Ein Beitrag zur Beleuchtung der hellenistischen Prosa*, Lund 1955. The language of Diodorus has many features in common with the second book of Maccabees, p. 199, and L. Gil, "Sobre el estilo del libro segundo de los Macabeos", *Emerita* 26 (1958), 11–32.

[46] J. Palm, *Über Sprache und Stil*, 206–207.

[47] L. Rydbeck, *Fachprosa, vermeintliche Volkssprache und Neues Testament*.

[48] G. H. R. Horsley, *New Documents Illustrating Early Christianity* 1–5, Macquarie University, 1981–89, and Horsley, "Divergent Views on the Nature of the Greek Bible", *Bib* 65 (1984), 393–403; M. Silva, "Bilinguism and the Character of Palestinian Greek", *Bib* 61 (1980), 198–219.

literary works of *koiné*, came to the fore in research. They show us
that we are only beginning to know post-classical Greek. Each monograph discovers new contacts between biblical Greek and the linguistic area being explored, and as a result shifts the perspective to
that particular area of comparison.

Thus a systematic study of all the documentation of the Hellenistic
period is required, popular as well as literary, to be able to place
the Greek of the Bible in its correct location. In reality, the language of the LXX has not yet been examined thoroughly in the
light of the enormous number of papyrus documents. Although we
know enough about the popular Greek of Egypt in the Ptolemaic
period, our knowledge of the literary use of Greek in the same period
is very inexact; the lack of studies of the language of post-classical
Greek is too obvious a fact to be stressed. The *koiné* does not have
to be as uniform as the manuals insist. Today it is increasingly
accepted that most of the morphological innovations of modern Greek
go back to the period of *koiné*.[49] It is also possible that there were
greater degrees of dialectal differentiation than we know through the
process of linguistic uniformity imposed by a great section of literary *koiné* and the way of speaking well and writing well spread by
the Atticist movement.[50]

---

[49] A. Meillet, *Aperçu d'une histoire de la langue grecque*, Paris 1965, 334; S. G.
Kapsomenos, "Die griechische Sprache zwischen Koiné und Neugriechisch", 19ff.;
A. Mirambel, *La langue grecque moderne. Description et analyse*, Paris 1959, 8. The problem of biblical Greek is to some extent linked with the way *koiné* spread, about
which there is as yet no agreement among historians of the Greek language.
Kretschmer puts this expansion within the domain of spoken language, as spread
by Alexander's conquests. The soldiers carried with them elements of the various
dialects of the countries from which they came and as a result the *koiné* is an amalgam or mosaic of dialects (see "Die Entstehung der koiné"). However, according
to Meillet, *Aperçu d'une histoire*, 249–54, the *koiné* spread as a modern language through
the conquering spread of Attic, which as a superior cultural language, imposed its
ways of speaking and writing. This theory is also defended by E. Mayser, *Grammatik
der griechischen Papyri aus der Ptolemäerzeit* I,1 Berlin, 1970 1–4. Depending on which
theory specialists hold, they will explain the anomalies in the Greek of the papyri
and the Bible as a reflex of popular usage or as the literary influence of a foreign
language. On the impact of the social and political history of Athens on the language, see A. López Eire, "Historia antigua e historia de la lengua griega: el origen del griego helenístico", *Studia Historica* I,1 (1983), 5–19.
[50] S.G. Kapsomenos, "Die griechische Sprache zwischen koiné und neugriechisch";
Kapsomenos, "Das Griechische in Aegypten", *Museum Helveticum* 10 (1953), 248–63,
and N. Fernández Marcos, "¿Rasgos dialectales en la koiné tardía de Alejandría?",
Emerita 39 (1971), 33–47.

Alongside this deepening at all levels of the production of *koiné*, more attention should be paid to the phenomenon of bilingualism and its repercussions in the area of syntax. Most of the peculiar features of the Greek of Egypt can usually be explained by the influence of Coptic. One should not speak of the vulgarisms of the papyri (some of which also have literary merit) but in each case it needs to be determined which phenomenon is due to the inner development of Hellenistic Greek and which depends on or has traces of the influence of Coptic. And given the difficulty of this distinction in many cases, since Coptic is a language with a very simple construction, it has to be determined in which cases a particular linguistic phenomenon could be the result of both tendencies combined. This same analysis has to be applied to the Greek of the Bible. It is necessary for studies of the language of the New Testament to be extended, to the same level and to the same degree, to the Greek of the LXX. It is also necessary to use all the linguistic information provided by the intertestamental pseudepigraphic writings to trace as far as possible the successive stages in the development of biblical Greek. This is because the Greek of the Pentateuch, a translation Greek written in the 3rd century BCE in Egypt is not the same as New Testament Greek or the Palestinian Greek of the *Lives of the Prophets* of the 1st–2nd centuries CE. Even so, the many common features allow it to be studied as a single linguistic complex that has its own identity, in spite of the differences in detail, for the influence of the first translation of the LXX extends even to the books that were not translated from Hebrew–Aramaic, such as the New Testament or certain pseudepigraphic writings.[51]

At the close of this long survey of the history of biblical Greek, from the first reactions by the Fathers of the Church until the present, it would seem that there has been little progress if we consider that the problem of the existence or not of a Jewish Greek, around which at various stages the discussion has revolved, although it is

---

[51] Apparently this translation Greek imposed its own linguistic categories on a series of later religious writers since it was considered to be a sacred language. It is sufficient to see how the translator of the book of Sira, capable of writing Greek adorned with rhetorical figures as shown by the prologue, turned to channels of Semitised Greek or translation Greek to begin his version of the Hebrew text. On the other hand, if we compare passages from the LXX (Exodus, Kings, Chronicles) with parallel passages from Josephus, there is a clear shift from the semantic calque of Hebrew in translating the LXX, to an imitation of classical Greek which chiefly affected style.

dismissed today in most publications, continues to some extent latent under the name of translation Greek.[52] However, the question of biblical Greek is not banal, even though it has remained hidden and has comprised the background to impassioned discussions not only in the Reformation and post-Renaissance periods but even in our own day. Melancthon's statement that *Scriptura non potest intelligi theologice nisi antea intellecta sit grammatice*[53] continues to be valid. It must be clearly understood that the only way to come close to ancient thinking is inductively through language and not the reverse. And we can only understand this language through analysis – as complete as possible – of all the documents (in the widest sense) of the past that are available to us.[54] Although the impact on the language of any important cultural or religious movement must be taken into account,[55] Barr's comments on Kittel's lexicon of the New Testament should keep us alert to the constant danger of going beyond the limits of semantics, inserting into the text elements of interpretation that really belong to biblical theology.[56]

SELECT BIBLIOGRAPHY

Abel, F.-M., "Coup d'oeil sur la koiné". *RB* 23 (1926), 5–26.
Debrunner, A., *Geschichte der griechischen Sprache. II Grundfragen und Grundzüge des nach-klassischen Griechisch*, Berlin 1954.
Deissmann, A., *Bibelstudien*, Marburg 1895.
———, *Licht vom Osten. Das Neue Testament und die neuentdeckten Texte der hellenistisch-römischen Welt*, Tübingen 1923⁴.
———, *Neue Bibelstudien*, Marburg 1897.
Frösén, J., *Prolegomena to a Study of the Greek Language in the First Century AD: The Problem of Koiné and Atticism*, Helsinki 1974.
Gehman, H. S., "The Hebraic Character of LXX". *VT* 1 (1951), 81–90.
Hadrianus, *Eisagogué*, ed. F. Gössling, Berlin 1887.

---

[52] Using the terminology of Sephiha for calque-languages, we would say that there is no evidence for spoken Jewish-Greek; instead there must have been a translation Greek in which some peculiar syntactic features emerged due to the source language, Hebrew–Aramaic; see H. V. Sephiha, *Le ladino, judéo-espagnol calque. Deutéronome. Versions de Constantinople (1547) et de Ferrara (1553). Édition, étude linguistique et lexique*, Paris 1973, 42ff.

[53] Taken from J. Ros, *De studie van het bijbelgrieksch*, 9.

[54] See J. Z. Smith, "The Social Description of Early Christianity", *RSR* I, 1 (1975), 19–25: "The second option is to take seriously the notion that man creates his world primarily through language . . . not by theological and philosophical speculation on 'hermeneutics'" (p. 21).

[55] C. Mohrmann, "Transformations linguistiques et évolution sociale et spirituelle", *VC* 11 (1957), 11–37.

[56] J. Barr, *The Semantics of Biblical Language*, Oxford 1961, 206ff.

Harl, M., "La langue de la Septante". M. Harl *et al.*, *La Bible grecque des Septante*, 223–66.

Kapsomenos, S. G., "Die griechische Sprache zwischen koiné und neugriechisch". *Berichte zum XI Intern. Byzantinisten-Kongress*, Munich 1958, 1–39 (with a lengthy bibliography on the inscriptions, papyri and modern Greek as an indirect source for the linguistic phenomena of *koiné*).

Kretschmer, P., "Die Entstehung der Koiné". *Sitzungsbericht der Wiener Akad. Phil.-Hist. Klasse*, 144, X, Vienna 1900.

Mussies, G., "Greek in Palestine and the Diaspora". *The Jewish People in the First Century*, ed. S. Safrai and M. Stern, I, 2, Assen–Amsterdam 1976, 1040–64.

———, *The Morphology of koiné Greek as Used in the Apocalypse of St. John: A Study in Bilingualism*. *NTS* 27, Leiden 1971.

Orlinsky, H.-M., "Current Progress and Problems in Septuagint Research". *The Study of the Bible Today and Tomorrow*, ed. H. R. Willoughby, Chicago 1947, 144–61.

Psichari, J., "Essai sur le grec de la Septante". *REJ* 1908, 161–208.

Ros, J., *De studie van het bijbelgrieksch van Hugo Grotius tot Adolf Deissmann*, Nijmegen 1940.

Rydbeck, L., *Fachprosa, vermeintliche Volkssprache und Neues Testament. Zur Beurteilung der sprachlichen Niveauunterschiede in nachklassischen Griechisch*, Uppsala 1967.

Thackeray, H. St J., *A Grammar of the Old Testament in Greek According to the Septuagint. Vol. I: Introduction, Orthography and Accidence*, Cambridge 1909.

Thumb, A., *Die griechische Sprache im Zeitalter des Hellenismus. Beiträge zur Geschichte und Beurteilung der Koiné*, Strasbourg 1901 (reprinted by De Gruyter, Berlin–New York 1974).

Turner, E. G., *Greek Papyri: An Introduction*, Oxford 1968.

Turner, N., "The Unique Character of Biblical Greek". *VT* 5 (1955) 208–13.

Vergote, J., "Grec Biblique". *DBS* III, 1938, 1320–69.

The select bibliography can be complemented by referring to *CB* 21–34 and C. Dogniez, *BS*, 27–46.

CHAPTER TWO

THE SEPTUAGINT AS A TRANSLATION

a) *An Unprecedented Event*

Although today it is taken for granted that the Bible had to be translated and even has the distinction of being the book translated into the largest number of languages,[1] nevertheless the LXX, the first biblical translation, was an unusual and unparalleled event in the ancient world. In the West, the translating tradition really began with the Romans when faced with the Greek literary legacy which they considered to be culturally superior. However, the Greeks thought that their literature was completely self-sufficient and the curiosity aroused by countries such as Egypt or by oriental religious movements such as Zoroastrianism never caused them to learn those languages. Herodotus spread the image of an enigmatic Egypt among the Greeks, and in the Hellenistic period there arose a whole pseude-pigraphic literature composed in Greek, but none of these works went back to the original by translating the *Gathas*,[2] for example. Thus the translation of the Jewish Pentateuch into Greek in the 3rd century BCE can be considered an event without precedent in the ancient world, of extreme importance for the history of our civilisation. For it to happen, several determinative processes of very different character had to converge. It could only arise from within a common cultural background created over centuries, with some particular ideological foundations and with the confluence of favourable historical circumstances. There existed from ancient times a common

---

[1] Translated into about 2,000 languages, and in the last fifty years into over 200 pre-literary primitive languages.

[2] Hymns dedicated to the exaltation of Zoroaster's reform in Persia in the 7th–6th centuries BCE. See S. P. Brock, *The Phenomenon of the Septuagint*, 14, and E. J. Bickermann, *The LXX as a Translation*, 174. At the same time that the translators of the LXX were beginning their enterprise, the Babylonian priest Berossus was writing the history of his people, dedicating it to Antiochus I of Syria, and the Egyptian high priest Manetho was compiling a history of the pharaohs. Thus *c.* 280–260 BCE, under royal auspices, representatives of the Oriental peoples decided to provide the Greek public with authentic information instead of the fables that were circulating about their origins and history.

Mediterranean culture, and contacts with the East go back to very much earlier than the Hellenistic period and are revealed not only through the many borrowings from Semitic into ancient Greek but even through finds of Mycenaean pottery in Ugarit and in the analysis of mythological constellations.[3] To the point that in some sense one can agree with Astour's words: "Long before Hellenism imposed itself over the ancient civilisations of the East, Semitism had exercised no less impact upon the young civilisation of Greece. Hellenism became the epilogue of the Oriental civilisations, but Semitism was the prologue of Greek civilisation".[4]

However, the ideological background that made the translation of the LXX possible was in germ in Jewish thought itself, as the Torah which Israel received on Sinai was originally considered to be a guide for the whole of humankind, since 'God did not speak in secret' (Isa. 45:19). In fact – according to a rabbinic tradition – it was offered first to the gentiles but they gave it the cold shoulder. The rabbis also state that Joshua had buried the Law under the stones of the altar (Josh. 8:30) not only in the original but in all the languages of the world; the nations received a copy of the Law, but after reading it they paid it no attention.[5]

In respect of the LXX, in the Talmud we find the statement that the only foreign language allowed for the transcription of the Law scroll is Greek, as it is proved to be the one that translates it best.[6] Even so, as we shall see in the next chapter, there is no lack of negative judgements in rabbinic literature about that translation.

On the other hand, for the Jews of the diaspora, once they had abandoned the language of their fathers, the only way to preserve the religious legacy of their ancestors was to translate it into the foreign language that they used. The danger of losing this cultural

---

[3] See E. Masson, *Recherches sur les plus anciens emprunts sémitiques en grec*, Paris, 1967; E. Haag, *Homer, Ugarit und das Alte Testament*, Tübingen, 1962; M. C. Astour, *Hellenosemitica*, Leiden 1965; J. P. Brown, *Literary Contexts*; H. B. Rosén, *L'hébreu et ses rapports avec le monde classique. Éssai d'une évaluation culturelle*, Paris 1979.

[4] Astour, *Hellenosemitica*, 361.

[5] M. L. Margolis, *The Story of Bible Translation*, 9–10. The Jewish tradition concerning the revelation on Sinai is universalist. According to that tradition the Law was presented there to the pagan peoples in several languages; seventy, says Rabbi Yohanan. See J. Potin, *La fête juive de la Pentecôte, I Commentaire; II Textes (targumiques)*, Paris 1971, 311ff.

[6] *Jerusalem Talmud* (ed. M. Schwass, Paris 1930), Meg. I, 9(8): "Selon R. Simon b. Gamaliel, est-il dit, la seule langue étrangère permise pour la transcription du rouleau de la Loi est le grec; car, après examen, on a observé que le texte de la Loi peut le mieux être traduit suffisamment en grec."

inheritance had been felt earlier in the communities of Hellenistic Judaism than in those in Palestine; the latter defended themselves ideologically from Hellenism by producing apocalyptic literature; whereas in the diaspora, the Hellenistic communities reacted by taking the battle to their own camp through the translation of the Torah into Greek.[7] This explains why the translation of the LXX was made by Jews and for Jews, meaning that it was done by bilingual orientals and not by Greeks. It arose therefore due to the religious needs of the Jews of Alexandria; liturgical needs on the one hand and educational needs on the other, due to the special position of Judaism in the Greek world with a high proportion of Greek-speaking Jews who did not know the original language of their own scriptures. Thus the picture painted by the *Letter of Aristeas* of the circumstances surrounding the translation of the LXX in the court of king Ptolemy is deceptive.[8] Its purpose was probably to guarantee the authenticity of the Greek version of the Pentateuch against the criticism, which had already begun to be voiced, that this translation did not reflect exactly the Palestinian Hebrew text. These differences caused theological problems in Hellenistic Judaism which the *Letter of Aristeas* was trying to confront by stating that the translators used the best Hebrew manuscripts brought from Jerusalem.

A process of idealising the LXX began which culminated in the requirement for inspiration which first Philo and later Augustine claim for the Greek translation.[9] In this way the differences from the Hebrew text are safeguarded, since revelation itself could take

---

[7] R. Hanhart, "Zum Wesen der makedonisch-hellenistischen", 55–57

[8] See F. J. Foakes and Kirsopp Lake, *The Beginnings of Christianity*, London 1920, 153: "As the Alexandrian grammarians were the interpreters of the classics of Greece to the world, so the Alexandrian Jews expounded their own literature . . . The venerable names of Orpheus and of the mysterious Sibyls were attached to hymns and oracles designed to glorify Judaism in the eyes of the Greeks; and literary frauds of this description were for a considerable time practised at Alexandria by Jews and Christians alike." In various places a whole rang of literary fiction arose with the aim of showing that the most revered teachers of antiquity were imbued with the spirit by Hebrew sages. On Hellenistic interpretation or rewriting of the history of Israel, see N. Fernández Marcos, "Interpretaciones helenísticas del pasado de Israel", *CFC* 8 (1975), 157–86.

[9] *Vita Mosis*, II, 37–40. The translators state, καθάπερ ἐνθουσιῶντες προεφήτευον οὐκ ἄλλα ἄλλοι, τὰ δ' αὐτὰ πάντες ὀνόματα καὶ ῥήματα, ὥσπερ ὑποβολέως ἑκάστοις ἀοράτως ἐνηχοῦντος ("they prophesied like enthusiasts, not some [saying] one thing and others another but all the same names and words as if an invisible prompter were whispering to each"). And he even compares them to Moses, . . . οὐχ ἑρμηνέας ἐκείνους ἀλλ' ἱεροφάντας καὶ προφήτας προσαγορεύοντες, οἷς ἐξεγένετο

on different forms: one form being the Hebrew text and another the Greek translation. However, within Judaism and before Philo, the shortcomings of the translation were noticed and interpreted in a very different way. The author of the prologue to Sira (132 BCE) apologises for the inadequacy of his translation and adds that often the Law and the Prophets in Greek are different when compared with the original.[10] Evidence of this unease due to the difference between the two Bibles, Hebrew and Greek, are: the traces of correction of the Greek text to fit it to the Hebrew text in use which can be detected in some pre-Christian papyri and especially in the fragments of Twelve Prophets from Naḥal Ḥever;[11] the new revisions and translations of the LXX started within Judaism; and the critical work of Origen in his Hexapla and of Jerome in his new translation, the Vulgate.[12]

Independently of these aims that guided the Jews of the diaspora in starting the translation of the sacred Hebrew books, the cultural importance of the LXX also lies in its becoming the best tool for spreading Christianity, acting as a *praeparatio evangelica* through the many proselytes already converted to Jewish monotheism. Beyond the expectations of the translators, by being adopted by the Church as the official Bible, it became the main vehicle for the expansion into the West of oriental Semitic thought.

συνδραμεῖν λογισμοῖς εἰλικρινέσι τῷ Μωυσέως καθαρωτάτῳ πνεύματι ("not calling them interpreters but hierophants and prophets due to the flawless reasoning by which they emulated the purest spirit of Moses"). See also, Augustine, *De Civ. Dei*, XVIII, 42–43. On the hypothesis of the inspiration of the LXX as discussed by modern scholars, see *CB*, 13, and C. Dogniez, *BS*, 25.

[10] οὐ γὰρ ἰσοδυναμεῖ αὐτὰ ἐν ἑαυτοῖς Ἑβραϊστὶ λεγόμενα καὶ ὅταν μεταχθῇ εἰς ἑτέραν γλῶσσαν, οὐ μόνον δὲ ταῦτα, ἀλλὰ καὶ αὐτὸς ὁ νόμος καὶ αἱ προφητεῖαι καὶ τὰ λοιπὰ τῶν βιβλίων οὐ μικρὰν ἔχει διαφορὰν ἐν ἑαυτοῖς λεγόμενα ("for these things said in Hebrew do not have the same force when translated into another language; and not only that, but even the Law, the Prophecies and the other books differ not a little when said in their own language").

[11] D. Barthélemy, *Les Devanciers d'Aquila*. VTS 10 (1963), and the critical and diplomatic edition by E. Tov, *The Greek Minor Prophets Scroll from Naḥal Ḥever (8 ḤevXIIgr): The Seiyâl Collection* I, with the collaboration of R. A. Kraft and a contribution by P. J. Parsons, DJD VIII, Oxford 1990.

[12] The dispute between the philological principle and the inspirationist principle has persisted in key moments of the rebirth of biblical studies and not only in the dispute between Jerome and Augustine, the latter being a staunch defender of the LXX against the Vulgate, but later in the positions of Erasmus and Luther. Augustine describes the disturbances that broke out (in Tripoli) the first time that the book of Jonah was read according to Jerome's version, because the Old Latin, following the LXX had translated the plant in Jon. 4:6 as a coloquinth, whereas the Vulgate identifies it as the ivy, see W. Schwartz, *Principles and Problems*, 38ff.

b) *A Range of Translation Techniques*

However, the LXX is not a uniform translation that can be judged by modern criteria but the result of much trial and error. At first different equivalents were tried until the most suitable Greek words prevailed as the most suited for the various Hebrew expressions. The Greek Pentateuch came to be a rudimentary lexicon for books translated later, such as Isaiah.[13] Something similar was to happen, centuries later, with the decanting to Latin of concepts from the new Christian religion; first several terms were tried, many of them imported from Greek, for the technical terms of Christianity until one of them prevailed and was standardised as the only Latin equivalent.[14]

Rather than a single translation, in the LXX one should speak of a collection of translations depending on the book; even within a single book, different literary units reflect different translation techniques. Studies of these techniques indicate more than one translator for each book, although the total number did not come to seventy or seventy-two as the *Letter of Aristeas* says.[15] For this same reason, although Swete's remarks on the LXX as a version[16] or Thackeray's in the grammar on Semitisms[17] continue to be valid, today their conclusions need to be refined, since, for lack of precedents and being the work of several translators, we find reflected in the LXX a whole

---

[13] See J. Ziegler, *Untersuchungen zur Septuaginta des Buches Isaias*, Münster 1934, and E. Tov, "The Impact of the LXX Translation of the Pentateuch on the Translation of Other Books", *Mélanges D. Barthélemy*, ed. P. Casetti, Freiburg–Göttingen 1981, 577–92.

[14] This is what happens with various Christian terms such as "baptism", "baptist", "saviour" (see Ch. Mohrmann, *Latin vulgaire, latin des chrétiens, latin médiéval*, Paris 1955, 18ff., and in general the works of the Nijmegen School), or with the first romanced bibles in Castilian, see G. M. Verd, "Las Biblias romanzadas. Criterios de traducción", *Sefarad* 31, 1 (1971), 319–51, and M. Morreale, "Vernacular Scriptures in Spain", *The Cambridge History of the Bible* II, ed. G. W. H. Lampe, Cambridge 1969, 465–92.

[15] The theory defended by H. St J. Thackeray, "The Bisection of Books in primitive Septuagint manuscripts", *JTS* 9 (1908), 88–98, and by J. Herrmann and Fr. Baumgärtel, *Beiträge zur Entstehungsgeschichte der Septuaginta*. BWAT 5, Berlin 1923, who propose two different translators for Isaiah and even three for the Twelve Prophets and Ezekiel, finds few followers today. A large part of the arguments used by these authors evaporates, since they used manual editions in their studies which attributed to the original LXX material belonging to later stages of transmission, see J. Ziegler, "Die Einheit der Septuaginta zum Zwölfprophetenbuch", *Beilage zum Vorlesungsverzeichnis der Staatl. Akademie zu Braunsberg-Ostpr.* 1934–35, 1–16.

[16] H. B. Swete, *An Introduction to the Old Testament in Greek*, 315–41.

[17] H. St J. Thackeray, *A Grammar of the Old Testament in Greek I*, Cambridge 1909, 32ff.

gamut of translation techniques which run from literal translation (including transliteration) to paraphrase, especially in the later writings, although the usual midrashic expansions and procedures of the Targums were never used. A global judgement of the LXX translation, besides being deceptive as the LXX does not reflect this unity of translation, also has the danger of being conditioned by the kind of translation for which the researcher is looking. The extreme position is taken by those defining the LXX as a targumic paraphrase conceived for the majority of the Jews who did not know Hebrew. Taking this line, R. Kittel even stated that the LXX is not a real translation but a theological commentary.[18] However this is only true at the primary level of the distribution of the material, the titles of the books of the Pentateuch, the grouping of Samuel–Kings, the retitling of Chronicles and Lamentations and the introduction of a new chronological sequence that places Ruth after Judges and Lamentations after Jeremiah, and the reinterpretation it presupposes.[19] Once we get into the actual text, as a general rule the translation of the Pentateuch is faithful to the Hebrew text, more than was thought at the beginning of the century. And in the light of recent discoveries at Qumran, the great divergences in the historical books between the LXX and the Hebrew have to be interpreted more as a witness of the pluralism of the Hebrew text before its consonantal fixation at the synod of Yamnia, *c.* 100 CE, than as the result of the exegetical preferences of the translators. Ch. Rabin has insisted on this literal nature of the LXX translation by noting the relative frequency with which the authors use translations of perplexity (*Verlegenheitsübersetzungen*), even though they make no sense, leaving it up to the reader to divine or intuit the meaning of the passage. This procedure is not used in the Targum, and if the translators had really had contact with the Targums they would have adopted midrashic solutions or theological interpretations for many of these *aporiai* of the original text, some of which continue to be real enigmas for the translator even today.[20] Another matter is that the translators of books

---

[18] In a lecture given at the *Orientalentag* in Leipzig, 1921; see A. Bentzen, *Introduction to the Old Testament*, Copenhagen 1952, 76.

[19] For the main differences between the LXX and the Masoretic Text, see O. Munnich, "Le texte de la Septante", M. Harl *et al.*, *La Bible grecque des Septante*, 173–82.

[20] Ch. Rabin, "The Translation Process", 24, and J. Ziegler, *Untersuchungen zur LXX des Buches Isaias*, 13.

after the Pentateuch used it as a sort of elementary lexicon for Hebrew–Greek equivalents, as noted above.[21] And in general it can be stated that the biblical Greek adopted by the translators of the Pentateuch became a sort of sub-language which later translators or the authors of pseudepigrapha, if they were bilingual, imitated.[22] This has to be taken into account for its direct repercussion on the recent discussion about Semitisms in the New Testament and in biblical Greek in general.[23]

The analysis of the translation techniques of each book or of each unit of translation has to precede any study of syntax, for often it has been shown that a different translation of certain Hebrew expressions does not always argue for different translators, since the different styles, psychologies and tastes for variety of the various authors come into play.[24] The extent of Semitic influence on the translation Greek is evident in the many transcriptions of proper names and toponyms even in the Pentateuch, in the many neologisms from the institutions and the religious practices of Israel, in the tendency to use in Greek a word similar in sound to the Hebrew word, and in the many syntactic Semitisms. The translation into Greek of polysemic Hebrew words often produces an extension of the semantic field of the Greek word in question, creating new meanings: for example, ἀφόρισμα = 'what is set apart' comes to denote 'the offering of first-fruits' (Ex. 29:24); τὰ ἔθνη as a translation of *goyyîm* comes to mean 'non-Jews'; ἄγγελος = 'messenger' is used for the heavenly intermediary beings that abound in apocalyptic literature, just as ἐγρή-γορος = 'watcher' denotes a particular type of angel, the *'îrîm*.[25]

We also come across Greek words that take on non-Greek meanings due to a confusion of homonyms in Hebrew; this happens with the verb ἀγχιστεύειν = 'to be the closest', a translation of Hebrew

---

[21] J. L. Seeligmann, *The Septuagint Version of Isaiah*, 45ff. and note 13.

[22] Ch. Rabin, "The Translation Process", 25.

[23] The discussion is based on the analysis of Semitisms (Hebraisms and Aramaisms) that can be found in works that have only been transmitted in Greek. It is also possible (or sometimes certain, as there is no Hebrew–Aramaic construction to support it) that they are Septuagintisms, i.e. analogical formations that have been absorbed by the New Testament through LXX Greek which became the standard language for religious Jewish-Hellenistic writers.

[24] See J. Ziegler, "Die Einheit der Septuaginta".

[25] See Dan. 4:10 according to θ' in the Alexandrian ms.; Lam. 4:14 and 1 Enoch 1:5ff.

gā'al I, but in some cases in the passive, according to the dictionary of Liddell–Scott/Jones, = 'to be excluded by descent'. As Katz[26] has noted, what happens is that the translator of Esdras B[1] confused the two Hebrew homonyms *gā'al* I and II, the second of which means precisely 'to be disqualified, to be excluded'. And there are cases of Semitic loans that through homophony take on the form of existing Greek words but with a different meaning. Thus in 1 Kgs 18:32, 35, 38 the word *t^{ec}alâ* = 'channel', translated correctly by ὑδραγωγός in other Old Testament passages,[27] is interpreted as θάλασσα probably through homophony with *tal'ata'* in the Aramaic spoken by the translators.[28] And these are only a few lexical examples. Thackeray studied various aspects of syntax by which the translators tried to establish a meaning within the Greek system. Possibly one of the more successful guesses is the translation of a Hebrew syntagm as alien to the Greek system as the infinitive absolute to indicate the inevitable aspect of an action. The first attempts go from literal translation of the infinitive to translation by an adverb or periphrastic translation or even omission. However, after these initial attempts, the translators, in general, opted for one of the following two solutions: (1) dative of the noun corresponding to the verb in question: θανάτῳ ἀποθανεῖσθε for *môt tāmût* of Gen. 2:17 and (2) participle of the same verb or of a verb close in meaning: πληθύνων πληθυνῶ for the *harbâ 'arbê* of Gen. 3:16.

---

[26] P. Walters (formerly Katz), *The Text of the Septuagint: Its Corruptions and their Emendation*, ed. D. Gooding, Cambridge 1973, 149.

[27] See Is. 36:2.

[28] P. Walters, *The Text of the Septuagint*, 191. The influence of homophony in the translation of the LXX is a topic discussed in current research. Caird holds that homophony was one of the translation techniques used by the translators which influenced the choice of words. At other times it was an ingenious procedure for extracting a plausible meaning from an otherwise unintelligible text, see G. B. Caird, "Homoeophony in the Septuagint", *Essays in Honor of W. D. Davies*, ed. R. Hammerton-Kelly and R. Scroggs, Leiden 1976, 74–88. Although there are undeniable traces of this procedure, not all the cases presented by Caird are convincing; see J. Barr, "Doubts about Homoeophony in the Septuagint", *Textus* 12 (1985), 1–77. On the relationship between lexicography and translation techniques, E. Tov, "Three Dimensions of LXX Words", *RB* 83 (1976), 529–44; Tov, "Loan-words, Homophony and Transliteration in the Septuagint", *Bib* 60 (1979), 216–36; N. Fernández Marcos, "Nombres propios y etimologías populares en la Septuaginta", *Sefarad* 37 (1977), 239–59; and J. A. L. Lee, "Equivocal and Stereotyped Renderings in the LXX", *RB* 87 (1980), 104–17, can be consulted. Lee insists that at times the translators are aware of the polysemy of certain words and do not attempt to resolve the ambiguity, so that more than one reading of the same text is possible.

This last procedure is the one that prevailed in the historical books. However, the two syntagms that ultimately imposed themselves already enjoyed some authority in classical Greek.[29]

c) *Modern Linguistics and the Translation Process*

In the history of research on the LXX there is no lack of monographs on the translation technique of certain books, especially around the theory of a double translator for each book, as set out by Thackeray in 1903;[30] works devoted to various sections of the lexicon include those by S. Daniel, Jellicoe, Skehan, Zlotowitz, Heater, Olofsson[31] and others such as those by Orlinsky, Fritsch and Soffer on the anthropomorphisms, with the aim of uncovering the true theology of the LXX;[32] finally there are some syntactic analyses particularly by the Helsinki school.[33] However, there are no comprehensive structural studies, based on modern linguistics, on the bilingualism of the translators, which would throw light with new perspectives on the translation process, one of the more complex phenomena of linguistic expression. And this even though in recent years we have seen several events that have contributed to the development of this area of language: the emergence of structuralism in Europe at the beginning of the century with F. de Saussure, the

---

[29] H. St J. Thackeray, *A Grammar of the Old Testament*, 47–48.

[30] H. St J. Thackeray, "The Translators of Jeremiah", *JTS* 4 (1903), 245–66; Thackeray, "The Translators of Ezekiel", *JTS* 4 (1903), 398–411; Thackeray, "The Translators of the Prophetical Book", *JTS* 4 (1903), 578–85; Thackeray, "The Greek Translators of the Four Books of Kings", *JTS* 8 (1907), 262–78; Thackeray, "The Bisection of Books in Primitive LXX Manuscripts", *JTS* 9 (1908), 88–98. And more particularly see *CB* 34–37.

[31] S. Daniel, *Recherches sur le vocabulaire du culte dans la Septante*, Paris 1966; S. Jellicoe, "Hebrew–Greek Equivalents for the Nether World: Its Milieu and Inhabitants in the Old Testament", *Textus* 8 (1973), 1–20; P. W. Skehan, "The Divine Name at Qumran, in the Masada Scroll and in the Septuagint", *BIOSCS* 13 (1980), 14–44; B. M. Zlotowitz, *The Septuagint Translation of the Hebrew Terms in Relation to God in the Book of Jeremiah*, New York 1981; H. Heater, *A Septuagint Translation Technique in the Book of Job*, Washington 1982 (he discovers the technique of interpolating material from elsewhere in the LXX, usually another part of Job, in the passage being translated); S. Olofsson, *God is my Rock: A Study of Translation Technique and Theological Exegesis in the Septuagint*, Stockholm 1990.

[32] See *CB* 20.

[33] I. Soisalon-Soininen, *Die Infinitive in der Septuaginta*, Helsinki 1965, and R. Sollamo, "Some 'Improper' Prepositions in the Septuagint and Early koiné Greek", *VT* 25, 4 (1975), 773–83. See also I. Soisalon-Soininen, *Studien zur Septuaginta-Syntax*, and A. Aejmelaeus, *On the Trail of the Septuagint Translators*.

Prague circle and the Copenhagen school; and in the United States the coincidence of a large number of linguists interested in the relationship between language and culture; and the transformational–generative linguistics of N. Chomsky. All the linguistic theories mentioned have repercussions for the problem of translation. They have been applied to the translation of the Bible with surprising results as shown by publications by E. Nida and others.[34] Beyond the excessive publicity and the practical results achieved, there is no doubt that the exercise of translation by using computers has produced important results in semantic theory and greater precision in the analysis and evaluation of linguistic equivalences.[35]

However, prescinding from our opinion concerning the various linguistic schools of our century, from a functional aspect it seems clear that the structural and transformational–generative are the most productive approaches to be applied to the phenomenon of translation. The dynamic and generative aspects of the language are of prime importance for the translator who tries to describe the decoding processes of the message in the source language to adapt them to the structures of the target language. As the linguistic sign is arbitrary and free in nature, some languages make more distinctions than others in ordering the totality of experience. There are no two languages that completely agree in the linguistic categories by which they structure reality. Furthermore, these structures differ much more radically than do the cultural worlds that transmit these extralinguistic referents to us. Hence even in the most literal translation there is an inevitable shortfall or discrepancy between the message of the source language and what reaches the target language. When the LXX translates *'elohim* by θεός and *yahweh* by κύριος, it has only reproduced in an approximate way and for the Greek-speaking world what the Jews understood by the name of their God. In the same way, Ulfilas used Gothic *Guþ* to translate the θεός of the LXX not because the Goths understood *Guþ* to mean what Jewish Christians understood by θεός but because this Germanic term could be adopted as a rough equivalent of the Greek term.

---

[34] E. A. Nida, *Towards a Science of Translating*; J.-C. Margot, *Traducir sin traicionar. Teoría de la traducción aplicada a los textos bíblicos*, Madrid 1987, and V. García Yebra, *Traducción: Historia y Teoría*, Madrid 1994.

[35] See C. Dogniez, *BS* 9–11, especially E. Tov and B. G. Wright, "Computer-Assisted Study of the Criteria for Assessing the Literalness of Translation Units in the LXX", *Textus* 12 (1985), 149–87.

Of course this discrepancy, which is inherent to every translation, is in some way alleviated by the capacity of the context to reabsorb the semantic discrepancy due to the different areas of meaning (oligosemy–polysemy) of the corresponding words in one or other language especially when one translates mechanically. In any case, all that has been said, together with the various techniques of making the implicit explicit, but which adds no new information, and still with great reservations about the hypothesis of a different *Vorlage*, forces us to look at the debated problem of the theological variants or the value judgements on the competence of the translators.[36]

These linguistic theories have been fruitful in the translations of the Bible into modern languages, especially pre-literary primitive languages, where the technique of dynamic equivalents has its maximum application. In the LXX only timid attempts have so far been made, such as the one by de Waard for the book of Ruth[37] and by Rabin for the indefinite subject,[38] and especially by Heller applied to categories of inflection.[39] Prior to any study of the theology of the translation or any induction about the possible different Hebrew *Vorlage* that the translators had in front of them, one has to ask oneself to what extent the divergences from the Hebrew text are conditioned by the linguistic possibilities of Greek as compared to Hebrew. These requirements of the linguistic expression no doubt have theological consequences, but primarily they are linguistic and do not in themselves imply a concrete exegetic tendency on the part of the translators. And they have to be taken into account if one wishes to avoid any type of generalisation that contrasts Semitic thought with Greek thought or the repeated digressions about Greek anthropocentrism

---

[36] For example, it is not possible to ascribe to the translators' incompetence or dilettantism the scarce agreement we notice in the LXX between Greek and Hebrew tenses. It should be noted, instead, that the tenses in Greek correspond only very vaguely to the Hebrew tenses. And Rabin has examined the particular case of the indefinite subject in the ancient versions, reaching the conclusion that the differences in translation are due to stylistic preferences of the target languages in question, not because the translators had a different *Vorlage*; Ch. Rabin, "The Ancient Versions and the Indefinite Subject", *Textus* 2 (1962), 60–76. On the other hand, statistical analysis confirms that the principle of semantic equivalence is retained with a very high percentage except in those cases where the polysemy of the Hebrew word allows multiple translations; see B. Kedar-Kopfstein, "Zum lexicalischen Äquivalenzprinzip in Bibelübersetzungen", *ZAH* 2 (1994), 133–44.

[37] J. de Waard, "Translation Techniques Used by the Greek Translators of Ruth", *Bib* 54, 4 (1973), 499–515.

[38] Ch. Rabin, "The Ancient Versions".

[39] J. Heller, "Grenzen sprachlicher Entsprechung".

against Hebrew theocentrism.[40] From an examination of the basic grammatical structures of the language, Heller concludes that the translators of the LXX had hardly any difficulty in the translation of pronouns; the obstacles to translating nouns increase in proportion the more abstract they are. However, where the discrepancy acquires alarming proportions is in the translation of verbs. The precision in translating the 1st person singular pronoun (*'anî*) in the Pentateuch is in excess of 99%; and this even though in Greek it is not necessary to make the personal pronoun explicit as the subject. Nor did they find particular difficulty in translating the person. As a result, where there is a change of person within respect to the Hebrew, the passage has to be examined with greater accuracy as it can reflect an exegetical tendency of the translators and need not be due exclusively to linguistic change.

After the categories of person and number, the active and passive are reproduced more faithfully. Most of the changes observed are due to the fact that Greek lacks the causative form of the verb; but other cases are due to a different *Vorlage* or the exegetical attitude of the translator.

The translation of verbal inflection is much freer than for inflected nouns. In Indo-European languages, the intensive and the causative are not morphological categories but semantic; hence the *hiphil* and *hophal* cause the translators particular confusion. Even so, what can be stated from this analysis of the structures of both languages is that the translators were not amateurs but did their best to reach all the precision allowed them in the shift from one linguistic system to such a different one. Hasty judgements, such as that the translators gave clear signals of incompetence, have to be revised in the light of these criteria. In each passage where we find one of the translations called free or paraphrastic the reasons for that translation have to be examined, whether a particular expression can be

---

[40] See T. Boman, *Das hebräische Denken im Vergleich mit dem Griechischen*, Göttingen 1968; C. Tresmontant, *Essai sur la pensée hébraïque*, Paris 1962, or the studies by G. Bertram, especially "Die religiöse Umdeutung altorientalischer Lebensweisheit in der griechischen Übersetzung des AT", *ZAW* 54 (1936), 153–67; Bertram, "Von Wesen der LXX-Frömmigkeit", *WO* II, 3 (1956), 274–84; Bertram, "Zur Bedeutung der Religion der LXX in der hellenistischen Welt", *TLZ* 92 (1967), 245–50. Recent studies make it clear that the chasm that some have wished to mark out between Semitic and Greek thought never actually existed: N. P. Bratsiotis, "Nephes-psyché. Ein Beitrag zur Erforschung der Sprache und der Theologie der LXX", *VTS* 15 (1966), 58–89, and L. M. Pasinya, *La notion de 'nomos' dans le Pentateuque grec*, Rome 1973.

translated literally within the range of possibilities of the language or whether the interpreter had a different *Vorlage* before his eyes. Only in those cases where the two previous explanations fail is it permissible to consider intentional change by the translator, as the reflection and crystallisation of the actual theology of the LXX.

SELECT BIBLIOGRAPHY

Aejmelaeus, A., *On the Trail of the Septuagint Translators: Collected Essays*, Kampen 1993.
Astour, M. C., *Hellenosemitica*, Leiden 1965.
Bardy, G., *La question des langues dans l'église ancienne*, Paris 1948, 1–78.
Barr, J., *The Typology of Literalism in Ancient Biblical Translations*. MSU XV, Göttingen 1979.
Bickermann, E. J., "The LXX as a Translation". *PAAJR* 28 (1959), 1–39 (reprinted in Bickermann, *Studies in Jewish and Christian History*, Leiden 1976, 167–201).
Brock, S. P., "Aspects of Translation Technique in Antiquity". *GRBS* 20 (1979), 69–87.
———, "The Phenomenon of the Septuagint". *OS* XVII (1972), 11–36.
———, "Translating the Old Testament". *It is Written*, ed. D. A. Carson, 1988, 87–98.
Brown, J. P., "Literary Contexts of Hebrew–Greek Vocabulary". *JSS* (1968), 163–91.
Cook, J., "Were the Persons Responsible for the Septuagint Translators and/or Scribes and/or Editors?". *JNSL* 21 (1995), 45–58.
Coste, J., "La première expérience de traduction biblique: La Septante". *La Maison Dieu* 53 (1958), 96–102.
Frankel, Z., *Vorstudien zu der Septuaginta*, Leipzig 1841, 163–203.
Hanhart, R., "Die Übersetzungstechnik der Septuaginta als Interpretation". *Mélanges D. Barthélemy*, ed. P. Casetti, 1981, 135–57.
———, "Zum Wesen der makedonisch-hellenistischen Zeit Israels". *Wort, Lied und Gottesspruch. Beiträge zur Septuaginta. Festschrift für Joseph Ziegler* II, Würzburg 1972, 49–59.
Harl, M., "Les divergences entre la Septante et le texte massorétique". M. Harl et al., *La Bible grecque des Septante*, 1988, 201–22.
Heller, J., "Grenzen sprachlicher Entsprechung der LXX. Ein Beitrag zur Übersetzungstechnik der LXX auf dem Gebiet der Flexionskategorien". *MIOF* 15 (1969), 234–48.
Jellicoe, S., *SMS*, 314–29.
Katz, P., "Zur Übersetzungstechnik der Septuaginta". *WO* II (1956), 267–73.
Lee, J. A. L., *A Lexical Study of the Septuagint Version of the Pentateuch*, SCS 14, Chico, Calif. 1983.
Margolis, M. L., *The Story of Bible Translation*, Philadelphia 1917 (reprinted in Israel 1970).
Martin, R. A., "Some Syntactical Criteria of Translation Greek". *VT* 10 (1960), 295–310.
———, *Syntactical Evidence of Semitic Sources in Greek Documents*. SCS 3, Missoula, Mont. 1974.
Mounin, G., *Les problèmes théoriques de la traduction*, Paris 1963.
Nida, E. A., *Towards a Science of Translating*, Leiden 1964.
Nida, E. A., and Ch. R. Taber, *The Theory and Practice of Translation*, Leiden 1969.
Olofsson, S., *The LXX Version: A Guide to the Translation Technique of the Septuagint*, Stockholm 1990.

Rabin, Ch., "The Ancient Versions and the Indefinite Subject". *Textus* 2 (1962), 60–76.

——, "The Translation Process and the Character of the Septuagint". *Textus* 6 (1968), 1–27.

Rife, J. M., "The Mechanics of Translation Greek". *JBL* 52 (1933), 244–52.

Roberts, B. J., *The Old Testament Text and Versions*, Cardiff 1951, 172–88.

Schwarz, W., *Principles and Problems of Biblical Translation*, Cambridge 1955.

Seeligmann, J. L., *The Septuagint Version of Isaiah: A Discussion of its Problems*, Leiden 1948.

Soisalon-Soininen, I., *Studien zur Septuaginta-Syntax*, eds. A. Aejmelaeus and R. Sollamo, Helsinki 1987.

Sollamo, R., *Renderings of Hebrew Semiprepositions in the Septuagint*, Helsinki 1979.

Swete, H. B., *An Introduction to the Old Testament in Greek*, Cambridge 1914, 315–41.

Talshir, Z., "Linguistic Development and the Evaluation of Translation Technique in the Septuagint". Scripta Hierosolymitana 33, Jerusalem 1986, 301–20.

Tov, E., "The Nature and Study of the Translation Technique of the LXX in the Past and Present". *VI Congress of the IOSCS*, 1987, 337–59.

Waard, J. de, "La Septante: une traduction". *Études sur le judaïsme hellénistique*, eds. R. Kuntzmann and J. Schlosser, Paris 1984, 133–45.

Weissert, D., "Alexandrinian Analogical Word Analysis and Septuagint Translation Techniques". *Textus* 8 (1973), 31–44.

For further bibliography, see *CB* 16–20 and C. Dogniez, *BS* 47–52.

PART TWO

THE ORIGINS OF THE SEPTUAGINT

CHAPTER THREE

THE *LETTER OF PSEUDO-ARISTEAS* AND OTHER ANCIENT SOURCES

a) *The Jews of Alexandria*

The diaspora or voluntary dispersion of the Jews had already started at the beginning of the 6th century BCE in connection with the Babylonian exile. Some Jews fought as mercenaries on the side of Psammeticus II (594–589) against Nebuchadnezzar and afterwards fled to Egypt for fear of the Jews (see Jeremiah 42–43). In Egypt, they founded the military colony in Elephantine in the southern part of a small island in the Nile, a few kilometres north of the first cataract. This Jewish settlement became famous for the many legal papyri found there in 1906–07, among them the oldest translation into Aramaic (end of the 5th century BCE) of the *Book of Aḥiqar*. However, the diaspora only gained importance in the Hellenistic period. Shortly after the conquest by Alexander (332 BCE) and the foundation of Alexandria (331 BCE) the presence of many Jews is already noticeable in Egypt and particularly in that city. According to the *Letter of Aristeas* (§§12–13), when Ptolemy I Lagos (323–283) occupied Palestine in 312 BCE, he took to Egypt as slaves many Jewish prisoners of war. His son Ptolemy II Philadelphus (283–246) granted them freedom. Philo of Alexandria (*Contra Flaccum*, 43) speaks of a million Jews resident in Egypt. However, this figure seems to be exaggerated and historians calculate about two hundred thousand, half of them residing in Alexandria. They were not ruled by the law of the *polis* but were organised as their own ethnic group within the state, presided over by an ethnarch and governed by the *gerousia* or Council of Elders, a senate with seventy-one members. Hellenisation occurred not only at the level of language but also with respect to culture as can be seen from the onomasticon and the offices and professions they carried out.[1] Whereas contacts with their original

---

[1] D. Rokeah, "Prosopography of the Jews in Egypt", *Appendix II*, CPJ III, 1964, 167–96. See also V. Tcherikover, "The Ptolemaic Period (323–30 BC)", CPJ I, 1957, 1–47; H. Hegermann, "The Diaspora in the Hellenistic Age", *The Cambridge*

homeland by means of pilgrimages to Jerusalem on the chief feasts and the annual tribute to the Temple kept their traditions alive, the opening to Hellenistic Judaism and its oriental attraction captivated many proselytes from the Hellenistic surroundings.

In imitation of the Greeks, the Jews of the Hellenistic period also cultivated a series of new literary forms such as writing history and even publicity with the purpose of presenting Judaism to a Hellenised society, philosophy and epic, tragedy and even the novel.[2] However, of all the Jewish-Hellenistic production preserved, without any doubt whatsoever the main contribution was the translation of the Hebrew Bible into Greek. A result of this unique event was also the production of new books in Greek, Greek expansions of some Hebrew books, and a whole series of pseudepigraphic literature in Greek which grew in the shadow of the Bible translated into Greek.[3]

b) *Description and Contents of the* Letter

The document that claims to describe the origin and circumstances surrounding the translation of the LXX is the *Letter of Aristeas*. It is a pseudepigraphic writing in the form of a letter by the supposed author, Aristeas, to his friend Philocrates. However, as in so many cases in antiquity,[4] it is in fact a literary fiction that conceals a treatise with several topics on events of the past with a strong dose of indoctrination about the Jewish people. The situation of Jews in the diaspora, living in Alexandria in a hostile environment, very soon gave rise to a whole range of propaganda literature against the

---

History of Judaism, 1989, 115–66, and P. M. Fraser, *Ptolemaic Alexandria* I–III, Oxford 1972.

[2] N. Walter, "Jewish-Greek Literature of the Greek Period", *Cambridge History of Judaism*, 1989, 385–408.

[3] Those books which do not appear in the Hebrew Bible are called 'apocrypha' in Protestant tradition and 'deuterocanonical' by Catholics. However, it is not easy to agree on either the name or the classification of this literature and even less on parabiblical literature commonly called pseudepigrapha or intertestamental since the boundaries between the various literary forms and the actual manuscript transmission are not always clear. A good example is provided by the treatment this literature receives in two recent works: M. Delcor, "The Apocrypha and Pseudepigrapha of the Hellenistic period", *The Cambridge History of Judaism*, 1989, 409–503, and M. E. Stone (ed.), *Jewish Writings of the Second Temple Period*, Assen–Philadelphia 1984, 33–184 and 283–442.

[4] For example, the letters of Seneca and Cicero, which are really treatises on relevant topics in the form of a letter; see N. Fernández Marcos, "Letter of Aristeas", 13.

Hellenistic world, among which our letter must be included.[5] This work, which has reached us in twenty-three manuscripts, has no *superscriptio*. It usually appears as a prologue in a series of Byzantine minuscule manuscripts that contain a *catena* (biblical text and continuous commentary by various Fathers) to the Octateuch. Josephus calls it τὸ ᾿Αρισταίου βιβλίον ('the book of Aristeas')[6] and Eusebius refers to it in the following terms: περὶ τῆς ἑρμηνείας τοῦ τῶν ᾿Ιουδαίων νόμου ('on the translation of the Law of the Jews').[7] The word ἐπιστολή occurs for the first time in ms. *Parisinus* 950 of the Paris National Library (14th century). In book 12 of the *Antiquities* Josephus paraphrases two-fifths of the letter, rewriting the story in Attic style;[8] and Eusebius, in books 8 and 9 of the *Praeparatio Evangelica*, extracts about a quarter of the content of the letter. The indirect tradition of Eusebius is valuable in transmitting to us virtually the same text as in the manuscripts but several centuries earlier, given that the oldest date to the 11th century.

It is not easy to summarise the contents of the letter. It describes the origin, purpose and result of the mission of the writer Aristeas (one of the three envoys) together with the high priest of Jerusalem, Eleazar. The king of Egypt, Ptolemy Philadelphus, commissions his librarian Demetrius of Phalerum to collect in Alexandria, by purchase or translation, all the books of the world. Aristeas is present at the interview between the king and the librarian and can prove how the former expresses his wish to include in this great collection a copy of the Jewish Law translated into Greek. With this aim he orders a letter to be written to the high priest of the Jews to draw up a team of competent translators (§§1–21). To win the high priest's favour, Aristeas suggests that the king concede freedom to 100,000 Jewish slaves, prisoners of war, and in the letter includes a document of manumission (§§22–25).[9] There is an exchange of letters and credentials between Ptolemy and Eleazar with a detailed description of

---

[5] See H. Willrich, "Urkundenfälschung", and N. Fernández Marcos, "Interpretaciones helenísticas del pasado de Israel", *CFC* 8 (1975), 157–86.

[6] Josephus, *Ant.* XII, 100.

[7] Eusebius, *Praeparatio Evang.* IX, 38.

[8] A. Pelletier, *Flavius Josèphe adaptateur*.

[9] H. Liebesny has published, translated and commented on one of the documents which might have been a source for the redactor of the letter in this passage: see "Ein Erlass des Königs Ptolomaios II Philadelphos über die Deklaration von Vieh und Sklaven in Syrien und Phönikien (PER Inv. N. 24. 552 gr.)", *Aegyptus* 16 (1936), 257–91.

each gift; the texts of the letters are also included in the writing. Ptolemy's letter to the high priest asks him to send six old men from each tribe (6 × 12 = 72), men of exemplary life and versed in the Law. Next, the list of translators is given in which the predominance of Semitic but Hellenised names is evident (§§47–50).[10] Ptolemy's delegation describes their impressions of Jerusalem, the temple, the cult, the city and the whole of Judah (§§83–120). Aristeas questions the high priest on some Jewish laws and he explains their deeper meaning (§§128–70).[11]

Text, translators and delegation return successfully to Egypt where they are immediately received by the king, contrary to every custom in Greek courts. Ptolemy prepares a seven-day banquet for his Jewish guests. Here the author uses the genre of the symposium to describe the banquet in the royal court; this symposium takes up most of the letter (§§187–292). The king questions them on the scriptures and proposes an enigma (ḥidâ) to each of the old men, which they solve brilliantly, to the surprise and joy of the audience.[12] Next come short paragraphs devoted to the actual translation and its results (§§301–16). The worthy guests, who are taken to an island, surrounded by silence and provided with everything necessary, complete the translation in seventy-two days as a sign of remarkable coincidence.[13] Every morning they wash their hands in the sea following Jewish usage, as testimony that they had done nothing wrong.[14]

At the close, Demetrius gathers together the whole Jewish community

---

[10] Isserlin wishes to see in this predominance of Palestinian names over Egyptian an indication that perhaps there is a basis of truth and that the description of the delegation is not a complete invention: see "The Names of the 72 Translators". However, the use of Palestinian names belonging to the twelve tribes could be quite intentional within the literary fiction to which the letter belongs.

[11] On this part of the *Letter*, see N. Fernández Marcos, "El 'sentido profundo' de las prescripciones dietéticas judías".

[12] A procedure which was very common the in Oriental Hellenistic courts, as can be seen in the passage about the three bodyguards of King Darius (I Ezra 3–5). On the connection between questions about wisdom and courtly education, see F. Cantera and M. Iglesias, *Sagrada Biblia*, Madrid 1975, 603–604, and L. M. Wills, *The Jew in the Court of the Foreign King*, Minneapolis 1990.

[13] συνέτυχε δὲ οὕτως, ὥστε ἐν ἡμέραις ἑβδομήκοντα δυσὶ τελειωθῆναι τὰ τῆς μεταγραφῆς, οἱονεὶ κατὰ πρόθεσίν τινα τοῦ τοιούτου γεγενημένου ("The outcome was such that in seventy-two days the business of translation was completed, just as if such a result was achieved by some deliberate design carried out as if it were according to a goal previously fixed," *Letter of Aristeas* §307).

[14] διεσάφουν δὲ ὅτι μαρτύριόν ἐστι τοῦ μηδὲν εἰργάσθαι κακόν ("They explained that it is evidence that they have done no evil," *Letter of Aristeas* §306).

and reads the translation aloud and it is greeted with general acclaim, everyone promising to utter a curse – as was the custom – against anyone who removed anything from the text or added anything.[15]

c) *Historicity*

Since the letter as a whole was accepted as historical in antiquity, in successive versions legendary elements were added. It was not until the modern age that the first doubts arose concerning the letter's authenticity. The first to voice reservations about it was the Spanish humanist Luis Vives (1492–1540), commenting on the passage in Augustine (*De Civ. Dei* XVIII, 42) on the translation of the LXX.[16] In 1606, J. Justus Scaliger (1540–1609) had the same doubts and a century later, H. Hody was indifferent to the statements in the letter.[17]

Editions and translations into modern languages are listed exhaustively in A. Pelletier's introduction, the most complete and most recent edition of this text.[18] All the same it is worth noting the edition by L. Mendelsohn and P. Wendland in the Teubner collection (Leipzig 1900), to whom we owe the division of the letter into 322 paragraphs, generally accepted today, and the edition by H. St John Thackeray, printed as an appendix to Swete's Greek Old Testament, also in 1900.[19] As for translations into modern languages, there are several in Italian, French, English, German and one in Spanish, in Modern Hebrew and in Japanese.[20]

---

[15] ἐκέλευσαν διαράσασθαι, καθὼς ἔθος αὐτοῖς ἐστιν, εἴ τις διασκευάσει προστιθεὶς ἢ μεταφέρων τι τὸ σύνολον τῶν γεγραμμένων ἢ ποιούμενος ἀφαίρεσιν, καλῶς τοῦτο πράσσοντες, ἵνα διὰ παντὸς ἀέννα καὶ μένοντα φυλάσσηται ("they commanded that a curse should be laid, as was their custom, on anyone who should alter the version by any addition or change to any part of the written text, or any deletion either. This was a good step taken, to ensure that the words were preserved completely and permanently in perpetuity," *Letter of Aristeas* §311).

[16] L. Vives, *In XXII libros de Civitate Dei Commentaria*, Basel 1522, on book XVIII, 42.

[17] J. J. Scaliger, *Animadversiones in Chronologica Eusebii*, Leiden 1606, 122–25, and H. Hody, "Contra historiam LXX interpretum Aristeae nomine inscriptum dissertatio", in *De Bibliorum Textibus Originalibus, Versionibus Graecis, et Latina Vulgata*, Oxford 1705, 1–89.

[18] A. Pelletier, *Lettre d'Aristée à Philocrate*.

[19] H. B. Swete, *An Introduction to the Old Testament in Greek*, 531–606.

[20] By N. Fernández Marcos, "Letter of Aristeas"; by A. Kahana, in *Ha-sefarîm Ha-ḥisonîm*, 1–71; and by Y. Sakon in *Apocrypha and Pseudepigrapha V*, Tokyo 1975, 15–85 and 283–301. See C. Dogniez, *BS* 18.

Today the pseudepigraphic genre of the letter and its legendary nature are accepted without question. But the literary fiction is not without historical elements however difficult it may be to extract them by sound source criticism: the date of the translation of the Pentateuch cannot be put back too far (in fact before direct or indirect association with Ptolemy II Philadelphus in the first half of the 3rd century BCE seems likely, although the work itself was begun by the Jews of the diaspora and for the Jews and was not an official undertaking of the Egyptian court). The translation was made basically for liturgical and didactic, but not expressly literary, reasons, as can be gathered from a simple comparison of the Pentateuch with the style of Josephus, Philo and even of the letter we are discussing. The language of the Pentateuch belongs to the first half of the 3rd century BCE in Alexandria, as the studies by A. Deissmann have shown. Furthermore, there are the witnesses of *Pap Rylands* 458 (with fragments of Deuteronomy 23–28) which comes from the 2nd century BCE, and of *Pap Fouad* 266 (Dt. 31:36–32:7) from the 1st century BCE. To these indications can be added the fact that the Jewish-Hellenistic historian Demetrius, from the end of the 3rd century BCE, certainly knew Genesis in Greek.[21] The knowledge that we have from other sources of the reign of Ptolemy II make this hypothesis likely, and in 132 BCE the translator of the book of Sira already alludes in the prologue to the Torah, the Prophecies and other writings as integral parts of the Alexandrian Bible.[22]

---

[21] See J. Freudenthal, *Hellenistiche Studien*, 185ff. According to Meecham ("The Letter of Aristeas", 316–24) the author of this letter was familiar with the Greek Pentateuch as can be shown from a series of allusions and reminiscences. Wevers however stresses that he *only* knows the Pentateuch and that no relationship between *Letter of Aristeas* §§57–82 and I Kings 6–7 can be established. Instead, the relationship of Aristeas with Ex. 25:23ff. seems beyond doubt (J. W. Wevers, "Proto-Septuagint Studies", 63, note 23. *The Seed of Wisdom. Fs. T. J. Meek*, Toronto 1964, 58–77). The information from Aristobulus (first half of the 2nd century BCE), transmitted by Eusebius, *Praeparatio Evang.* XIII, 12, 1–2, according to whom there were partial translations of the Law before the one described here, in which Pythagoras and Plato inspired the authors, belongs to the Jewish-Christian issue of plagiarism by Greek writers from Moses and thus has no historical credibility at all: see G. Dorival, "L'histoire de la Septante dans le judaïsme antique", 45–46.

[22] εἴς τε τὴν τοῦ νόμου καὶ τῶν προφητῶν καὶ τῶν ἄλλων πατρίων βιβλίων ἀνάγνωσιν ("for the reading of the Law, the prophets and other books of the ancestors"). Van Esbroeck has analysed the Georgian version of the *Letter of Aristeas* and in it he finds traces of a document, probably from Jerusalem, used with some changes by the translator and also by Epiphanius of Salamina in his treatise *De mensuris et ponderibus*, 3 and 6: see M. Van Esbroeck, "Une forme inédite de la lettre du roi Ptolémée".

d) *Date of Composition and Sources*

The date of the letter is an almost insoluble problem since the opinions of scholars range from the end of the 3rd century BCE until close to the 2nd century CE.[23] However, linguistic analysis allows further precision, as Bickermann has shown,[24] from the use of Ptolemaic titles, analysis of the documents and other formulaic expressions used as well as from the religious and political tendency of the work, as Meisner has pointed out.[25] Prominent are glorification of the Hellenistic ideal of a philanthropic king and the warning against the abuse of power; in the religious sphere the emphasis given to Jerusalem is paramount; the idealised description of the cult, the close links between the communities of Jerusalem and Alexandria, as well as the complete silence on the important cult of Leontopolis are notable.[26] All this shows that the author of the letter wishes to distance the Alexandrian community from the Jews of Onias so that the decade between 127 and 118 BCE seems the most suitable period for the origin of the letter.[27] And in any case it is earlier than Flavius Josephus, given that around 70 CE he rewrites the letter in *Antiquities* XII, 12–118.

The author has used several sources, some already identified, others more difficult to find due on the one hand to our preserving so little of the literary production of Hellenism and on the other to the pseudepigraphic nature of the writing which tends to disguise and change the material used. In §31 Hecateus of Adbera is mentioned; probably the work was used as a basis for the first part or the περὶ Ἰουδαίων cited by Josephus in *Contra Ap.* I, 183–205, falsely attributed to Hecateus of Abdera, together with other Greek reports of journeys to Palestine or pilgrims' guides.[28] For the symposium passage,

---

[23] See S. Jellicoe, *SMS*, 47–52 and G. Dorival, "L'histoire de la Septante dans le judaïsme antique" 41–42.

[24] E. Bickermann, "Zur Datierung des Pseudo-Aristeas", 121ff.: proposes *c.* 145–125 BCE as the most probable date. Momigliano instead opts for 110–100 BCE, see A. Momigliano, "Per la data e la caratteristica della Lettera di Aristea", *Aegyptus* 12 (1932) 161–72, p. 168.

[25] N. Meisner, "Untersuchungen zum Aristeasbrief", 204–17.

[26] A Jewish military colony near Memphis, founded by Onias, see V. A. Tcherikover and A. Fuks, CPJ I, Cambridge, Mass. 1957, 3ff. See A. F. J. Klijn, "The Letter of Aristeas and the Greek Translation of the Pentateuch in Egypt", *NTS* 11 (1964–65) 154–58, and S. Jellicoe, "The Occasion and Purpose of the Letter of Aristeas: A Reexamination", *NTS* 12 (1965–66) 144–50.

[27] N. Meisner, "Aristeasbrief", 43.

[28] N. Meisner, "Aristeasbrief", 39.

which covers more than a third of the whole letter, in most of the answers the line of thought of ancient Hellenistic treatises called περὶ βασιλείας can be followed. The sources of other sections cannot be traced, but they certainly belong to the topic of this kind of literature.[29] To the king's question of why no Greek historian or poet mentioned the Jewish Law, the answer is that the Jewish scriptures cannot be touched by the gentiles, illustrating this by mentioning two warning miracles (§§312–16). Also, interpretations are divided when clarifying the sources of this passage: for some the writing of Pseudo-Hecateus is latent here whereas Bayer suspects that underlying this narrative is the lost writing by Demetrius with the title περὶ ὀνείρων in which miraculous cures from Sarapis are described, stories which the author of the letter transfers to the God of the Jews.[30] The number of seventy-two translators who came from Jerusalem is to be ascribed to literary fiction, as is the picture it conveys of the philological work carried out in Alexandria. Analysis of the style and translation techniques of the Pentateuch indicate several translators or the work of a team supervisor but these could never number seventy-two. This number, 70/72, is made up by choosing two for each of the twelve tribes and probably evokes the seventy old men present at Sinai when Moses received the Law.[31] It is also the total of the members of Sanhedrin, as we shall see. As for the philological work, the author of the letter transposes to the event of translation inexact representations about what he thought of the work carried out in Alexandria: i.e. neglected texts were restored and transformed into genuine texts through discussion and comparison carried out by the philologists.[32]

---

[29] N. Meisner, "Aristeasbrief", 40, and P. Hadot, "Fürstenspiegel", *RAC* 8 (1972), 555–631, pp. 587–89.

[30] E. Bayer, *Demetrios Phalereus der Athener*, Stuttgart–Berlin 1942, 102ff.

[31] See Ex. 24:1 and G. Dorival, "La Bible des Septante: 70 ou 72 traducteurs?".

[32] See G. Zuntz, "Aristeas Studies II. Aristeas on the translation of the Torah", *JSS* 4 (1959), 109–26, and the disputed passage from the letter: τυγχάνει γὰρ Ἑβραϊκοῖς γράμμασι καὶ φωνῇ λεγόμενα, ἀμελέστερον δὲ καὶ οὐχ ὡς ὑπάρχει, σεσήμανται, καθὼς ὑπὸ τῶν εἰδότων προσαναφέρεται ("for these [works] are written in Hebrew characters and language. But they have been transcribed [lit. indicated] somewhat carelessly and not as they should be [lit. as is the case], according to the report of the experts" *Letter of Aristeas* §30). On the discussion of the meaning of σεσήμανται, see D. W. Gooding, "Aristeas and Septuagint Origins: A Review of Recent Studies", *VT* 13 (1963), 357–79. Gooding proves that σεσήμανται clearly means 'were written', not 'were translated' or 'were interpreted'. Dorival suggests translating it as 'ont été traduits oralement' (see G. Dorival, "L'histoire de la Septante dans le judaïsme antique", 54), although he admits the difficulty that this meaning

e) *Purpose of the* Letter

The purpose of the letter is definitely apologetic. It is more difficult to determine the main recipients that the author has in mind, the Jews themselves (and in this supposition either the Palestine community or the Alexandrian diaspora), the Greeks to let them know Israel's glorious past, or the court of the Ptolemies. This detail affects the debate about the origins of the LXX. Thus Kahle's theory, that the letter was the endorsement of the official unified version imposed by the Jewish authorities in the same period when the document was written, after a long period in which various Greek versions were in circulation, like the Targums, has to be rejected as unusual.[33] On the other hand, P. Lagarde and his successors, although accepting the legendary elements shown by the letter, maintain the reference to a single event, the translation of the Pentateuch in the 3rd century BCE, as a historical nucleus. Klijn has stated that is a propaganda writing in favour of the original LXX against a revision made *c.* 140 BCE in the Jewish colony of Leontopolis which was in competition with the one in Alexandria.[34] All the same, although more and more traces of the revision of the LXX continue to appear from a very early period, we know too little about the Jewish settlement at Leontopolis to be able to defend this hypothesis without excessive imagination. For Stricker the letter refers to a royal undertaking by Ptolemy which consisted of codifying Hellenistic poetry and all the religions practised in Egypt with the aim of placing them under official control; for this it was necessary to translate the Egyptian (Manetho), Babylonian (Berossus) and Jewish (LXX) religious texts.[35]

---

of the verb is not accepted in the dictionaries. In my view, however, a new meaning of the verb has been introduced from synagogal practice as known from translations into Aramaic. However, in the case of the LXX we have no witness to this practice and its translation techniques are very different from those used in the Targum. As Dorival himself admits (*ibid.* 51–52), ancient witnesses on the existence of partial translations of the Bible before the LXX cannot be accepted. On the work and techniques of the Alexandrian philologists in respect of classical texts, especially by Homer, see R. Pfeiffer, *History of Classical Scholarhsip. I: From the Beginnings to the End of the Hellenistic* Age, Oxford 1968. See also J. Trebolle Barrera, *The Jewish Bible and the Christian Bible*, translated from the Spanish by W. G. E. Watson, Leiden–New York–Köln 1998, 137–41.

[33] For a more detailed explanation of his theory see the following chapter.

[34] A. F. J. Klijn, "The Letter of Aristeas".

[35] B. H. Stricker, *De Brief van Aristeas. De hellenistische codificaties der praeheleense godsdiensten*, Amsterdam 1956. Rost again insists on the idea that the Greek translation

However, the success of the Greek Bible within Hellenistic Judaism is difficult to explain if the translation had been due to a coercive act based on the Hellenising politics of the Ptolemies.[36]

Howard, instead, maintains that the letter is not propaganda writing against Hellenism, nor is it trying to make one particular translation prevail over another, whether this is earlier than or contemporary with the letter. Instead, what it is trying to defend is the Judaism of the diaspora against the attacks of Palestinian Judaism. The Palestinian Jews accused their brothers in Alexandria of using an inaccurate translation of the Pentateuch and so were not fulfilling the Law.[37] However it cannot be ignored that although these differences between the Hebrew and Greek texts were very upsetting, there never was a real opposition between the theology of the diaspora and that of Palestine. This is what Hanhart states in setting the LXX translation in Alexandria at the same level as the production of apocalyptic material in Palestine, as the special tool which Judaism used to defend itself from Hellenism.[38]

f) *The* Letter *in Jewish Tradition*

The information and commentaries about the origin of the Greek translation of the Bible in Jewish sources are later than the Letter of pseudo-Aristeas, but they may preserve some nucleus of earlier tradition alluding to the historical circumstances surrounding the translation. K. Müller has examined these data in a monograph and published the results in a recent article.[39] The texts are taken from the treatises of the Talmud and Tosephta which include the same tradition with several variations. The information revolves around the following topics:

---

has its origin for reasons of public law and not because of the needs of Greek-speaking Jewish communities: see L. Rost, "Vermutungen über den Anlass zur griechischen Übersetzung der Tora", in H. J. Stoebe (ed.), *Wort–Gebot–Glaube.* ATANT 59, Zurich 1970, 39–44. The same idea is reflected in D. Barthélemy, "Pourquoi la Torah a-t-elle été traduit en grec?", *On Language, Culture, and Religion: In Honor of Eugene A. Nida*, The Hague 1974, 23–41, especially pp. 29ff.

[36] R. Hanhart, "Fragen um die Entstehung der LXX", *VT* 12 (1962) 139–63.

[37] G. E. Howard, "The Letter of Aristeas", 8–9.

[38] R. Hanhart, "Das Wesen der makedonisch-hellenistischen Zeit Israels", *Wort, Lied und Gottesspruch*, 49–58.

[39] K. Müller, "Die rabbinischen Nachrichten".

1. The number of translators.
2. The number of changes inserted by the translators.
3. The fact that the translation is incorrect and comprises a sort of profanation together with a with some political unrest against Ptolemy.

With respect to the number of translators, the sources fluctuate between five (*Abot of Rabi Natan*, 37; *Sôferîm* 1, 7), seventy (*Sefer Torâ* 1, 8) and seventy-two (*Sôferîm* 1, 8; *Maseket Sôferîm* 1, 8).

The rejection of the translation by the Jews is evident in two rabbinic statements:

1. The day the Law was translated was as hard for Israel as the day they made the golden calf; for the Torah could not be translated according to all its demands.[40]
2. On the 8th day of *Ṭebet*[41] the Law was written in Greek in the days of king Ptolemy. And for three days darkness came over the world.[42]

Also the number of changes made by the translators differs according to source: ten in *Tanhuma šemot* 22 and *Abot of Rabi Natan* 37; thirteen in *Sôferîm* 1, 8 and *Sefer Torâ* 1, 9; and eighteen in *Exodus Rabâ* 5, 5 and in the *Midraš hagadol* to Dt. 4:19. However, as happens in the case of the *Tiqqûnê Sôferîm* the attempts at an exact list are expressions of late reworkings of the tradition.[43] The kernel of truth which these rabbinic details reflect is that very soon differences were felt between the LXX and the Hebrew text. According to Müller,[44] of the changes quoted five are attested in the LXX and the other three show contact with it.[45] The other changes have to

---

[40] *Sôferîm* 1, 7–8; *Sefer Torâ* 1, 8–9.

[41] Corresponding to December–January; see E. Schürer, *The History of the Jewish People in the Age of Jesus Christ (175 BC–AD 135)*, revised and edited by G. Vermes and F. Millar, I, Edinburgh 1973, Appendix III, *The Jewish Calendar*, 587–601.

[42] Gaonic additions to *Megillat Ta'anit*, 13. However, as we have seen in the previous chapter, rabbinic tradition did not completely oppose the Greek translation. A remark included in the Jerusalem Talmud, *Meg.* 1, 9, considers how Greek is the only language into which the Law can be translated in the most suitable way.

[43] S. Lieberman, *Hellenism in Jewish Palestine*, New York 1962, 29, "Corrections of the Soferim".

[44] K. Müller, "Die rabbinischen Nachrichten", 73ff.

[45] Gen. 2:2 ἐν τῇ ἡμέρᾳ τῇ ἕκτῃ; Ex. 4:20a ἐπὶ ὑποζύγια; Ex. 12:40b καὶ ἐν γῇ χανααν; Num. 16:15b ἐπιθύμημα = 'object of value' instead of *ḥamor* = 'ass', as a tendency to distance this animal from important people; and Lev. 11:5a τὸν δασύποδα = 'hare' for *'arnebet* and not τὸν λαγών – as *Baraita Meg.* 9b of the Babylonian Talmud explains – so that they would not say that the Jews, in order to mock Ptolemy's wife (from the Lagides family), inserted her name among the unclean animals. The

be attributed to the contemporary context of ever-changing Jewish exegesis. The persistent memory of these changes made by king Ptolemy comprises the strongest support for the hypothesis that the translation of the LXX was due to a violent act based on the politics of Hellenisation by Ptolemy II, indicated in the *Letter of Aristeas*.[46] Some rejection and Jewish opposition to the LXX translation for fear of profaning the Torah is evident almost from the very start and, of course, before Christianity adopted it as the Bible of the Church. This is latent in the prologue to Sira,[47] in certain passages of Philo and even in the *Letter of Aristeas* (§§312–16). In this passage Demetrius replies to king Ptolemy that no Greek author has dared to cite the Jewish Law because it was sacred and untouchable, and he confirms it citing two warning miracles: Theopompus[48] spoke and Theodectes[49] remained blind in punishment for his daring (ὑπὸ τοῦ θεοῦ πληγέντες §313). Furthermore, Theopompus was told the reason for his punishment in a dream: it was an indiscretion to deliver divine things to the profane.[50] Probably the same reluctance and fear of profanation are latent in the paragraph of the letter which explains why the translators wash their hands every morning when saying the prayer, 'as witness that they are doing nothing wrong';[51] and in

---

changes mentioned which indicate contacts with the LXX are Gen. 1:1 (ἐν ἀρχῇ); 2:2a; 18:12b; and 49:6b. On this translation of the changes inserted by the translators, see G. Veltri, *Eine Tora für den König Talmai*, 22–112. Veltri concludes that most of the alterations are exegetical changes which presuppose the Masoretic text and not a different *Vorlage*, a sort of Proto-Septuagint, as E. Tov, "The Rabbinic Tradition", asserts.

[46] βουλομένων δ' ἡμῶν καὶ τούτοις χαρίζεσθαι καὶ πᾶσι τοῖς κατὰ τὴν οἰκουμένην Ἰουδαίοις καὶ τοῖς μετέπειτα, προῃρήμεθα τὸν νόμον ὑμῶν μεθερμηνευθῆναι γράμμασιν Ἑλληνικοῖς ἐκ τῶν παρ' ὑμῶν λεγομένων Ἑβραϊκῶν γραμμάτων, ἵν' ὑπάρχῃ καὶ ταῦτα παρ' ἡμῖν ἐν βιβλιοθήκῃ σὺν τοῖς ἄλλοις βασιλικοῖς βιβλίοις ("It is our wish to grant favours to them and to all the Jews throughout the world, including future generations. We have accordingly decided that your Law be translated into Greek letters from what you call the Hebrew letters, in order that they too should take their place with us in our library with the other royal books"). See *Letter of Aristeas* § 38.

[47] οὐ γὰρ ἰσοδυναμεῖ αὐτὰ ἐν ἑαυτοῖς Ἑβραϊστὶ λεγόμενα καὶ ὅταν μεταχθῇ εἰς ἑτέραν γλῶσσαν ("for these matters do not have the same force said in Hebrew as when they are translated into another language").

[48] A disciple of Isocrates, *c.* 378–300 BCE.

[49] Orator and tragic poet, *c.* 375–334 BCE. On this type of warning miracle in antiquity as a divine punishment, especially in the context of incubation, see N. Fernández Marcos, *Los Thaumata de Sofronio*, Madrid 1975, 180–92.

[50] τὰ θεῖα . . . εἰς κοινοὺς ἀνθρώπους ἐκφέρειν, (*Letter of Aristeas* § 313).

[51] *Letter of Aristeas* § 306.

Philo's *Vita Mosis* 2, 36, where the old men stretch their hands to heaven begging God not to let them fail completely.[52]

According to Müller,[53] the fluctuation in the number of translators (72/70/5) is best explained within the framework of rabbinic reflections on competence to make changes in a copy of the Torah. As a result of the rabbinic theories on the genesis and composition of the supreme court (*bêt dîn haggādôl*) only 72/70 or five members could be responsible for the divergences of the LXX, a common number in the commissions of the great Sanhedrin. It would thus be a projection into the past of the condition of the rabbinic period connected with the commissions responsible for making any change in the Torah. Others, however, think that the number five is due to giving that numerical value to the letter *h* of the article in *haz-z^eqēnîm* ('the ancients').

The author of the extra-canonical treatise *Sôpherîm* solved this difference of tradition as follows: two translations of the Law were made by king Ptolemy, the first completed by five ancients; and the day the Law was translated was as hard for Israel as the day they made the golden calf. The other translation made by seventy-two ancients with divine help was received with great success.[54]

g) *Later Legend concerning the Origin of the Septuagint*

The complex and ambiguous reception given to the Greek version in rabbinic tradition is in contrast with the enthusiasm that it roused, right from the start, in Hellenistic Judaism and in Christian tradition. In Greek-speaking Jewish circles and among Christians writers,

---

[52] ... αἰτούμενοι τὸν θεὸν μὴ διαμαρτεῖν τῆς προσθέσεως, *Vita Mosis* II, 36.

[53] K. Müller, "Die rabbinischen Nachrichten", 90ff.

[54] *Sôferîm* 1, 8. Veltri has again set out a critique of the rabbinic information connected with the origins of the LXX. The main conclusions of his monographs can be summarised in the following points: (1) in rabbinic tradition the LXX was never considered to be a Targum but a Writing by King Ptolemy; (2) there was no rejection of the LXX by rabbinic Judaism and Christianity did not influence the Jewish appraisal of that version. The shift from a positive to a negative appraisal did not occur until the Gaonic period; (3) basically, the translation with all its requirements was considered to be impossible. Hence some accounts consider it to be a failure and compare it with the golden calf; and (4) the changes made by King Ptolemy belong to rabbinic exegesis not to the actual text. These changes reflect the difficulties of the Masoretic text and do not refer to a different Hebrew text used by the translators.

the content of the letter was further developed such that legendary elements were progressively added until Jerome's verdict was reached on the assignment of the translators.

Still in the Alexandrian circle, Philo develops his inspiration theory about the translation, making it equivalent to the original Hebrew.[55] Several new elements are inserted which are added to those mentioned in the letter: Eleazar is high priest and *king* of Judea; Aristeas's request is attributed to *divine inspiration*. It is now the translators who choose the place to make the translation and the *Island of Pharos* is expressly mentioned, though it is not specified in the letter. Once enclosed there, the translators "as if inspired by the deity, prophesied not some one and others another but all the same names and words, as if an invisible prompter were whispering them to each".[56] And further on he insists that both the original and the translation are a single text and that the translators are prophets and hierophants like Moses.[57] Finally he tells us of an annual feast on the Island of Pharos which commemorated such an auspicious event.[58]

In the 2nd century CE, Justin confuses Eleazar with king Herod (37 BCE–4 CE!) and states that Ptolemy sent an embassy to Jerusalem to obtain the 'books of prophecies'.[59] In the *Dialogue with Tryphon* 78, 7 the translation is not only of the Pentateuch but extends to the whole Old Testament.

---

[55] For an account of his thoughts on the narrative in the *Letter of Aristeas*, see Philo, *Vita Mosis* II, 25–44, especially 36–37.

[56] καθάπερ ἐνθουσιῶντες προεφήτευον οὐκ ἄλλα ἄλλοι, τὰ δ' αὐτὰ πάντες ὀνόματα καὶ ῥήματα, ὥσπερ ὑποβολέως ἑκάστοις ἀοράτως ἐνηχοῦντος, *Vita Mosis* II, 37. Note the use of the verb ἐνθουσιάω = 'to be in ecstasy, inspired or possessed by a deity', a technical term in classical antiquity for inspiration, see Plato, *Ion* 535c–536b; *Phaedo* 253a, etc.; see, similarly L. Gil, *Los antiguos y la inspiración poética*, Madrid 1966. And for the concept of inspiration in Philo, see A. Piñero, *La 'Theopneustia' bíblica en los primeros siglos*. Doctoral diss. Madrid, Complutensian Univ., 1974. Note also that ὑποβολεύς = 'he who suggests, reminds', is used for the prompter in the theatre (Plutarch 2.813ff.), probably the image alluded to here.

[57] Philo, *Vita Mosis* II, 40: ἱεροφάντης = the one who initiates (someone) into the rites and introduces (him) into the worship of the mystery religions.

[58] Philo, *Vita Mosis* II, 41.

[59] ὅτε δὲ Πτολεμαῖος ὁ Αἰγυπτίων βασιλεύς, βιβλιοθήκην κατεσκεύαζε καὶ τὰ πάντων ἀνθρώπων συγγράμματα συνάγειν ἐπειράθη, πυθόμενος καὶ τῶν προφητειῶν τούτων, προσέπεμψε τῷ τῶν Ἰουδαίων τότε βασιλεύοντι Ἡρώδῃ ἀξιῶν διαπεμφθῆναι αὐτῷ τὰς βίβλους τῶν προφητειῶν ("and when Ptolemy, the king of the Egyptians, organised the library and proposed collecting together all the writings of all men, when he heard about these prophecies, sent an embassy to Herod, at that time king of the Jews, asking him to get them to send him the books of prophecies"), Justin, *Apologia* I, 31.

Irenaeus sets the event in the time of Ptolemy Lagos (305–285 BCE) and the request for exemplars of the Law is addressed to the people of Jerusalem.[60] After the translators were separated (without saying how), when the translations are compared in the king's presence they turn out to be identical, so that even the Gentiles who are present had to accept that the Scriptures had been translated by divine inspiration. Already there appears the apologetic motif of the superiority of the LXX, especially to the more recent Jewish versions of Aquila, Symmachus and Theodotion, some of which had been in circulation since the time of Irenaeus.

The anonymous author of the *Exhortation to the Greeks*[61] adds – as proof that his apologetic account which is intended for the Greeks is not a fable – that when he visited Alexandria and the Island of Pharos he himself could see the remains of the cells of the translators and that the natives told all this as the tradition of their ancestors.

Clement of Alexandria and Tertullian also refer to the *Letter of Aristeas* in terms not very unlike those used by Irenaeus.[62] And it is paradoxical that towards the end of the 2nd or at the beginning of the 3rd century CE, the *Letter of Aristeas*, a Jewish propaganda document which recommends the Greek translation of the Pentateuch, has become the principal witness for the defending the whole LXX, now adopted by Christianity as its official Bible.

The legend would continue to grow or the same topics would be repeated,[63] until Jerome, without rejecting the historicity of the *Letter of Aristeas*, was to ridicule the details of the later legend, setting the office and function of the translators in their true limits. In the prologue to his Vulgate translation of the Pentateuch he set out the

---

[60] Irenaeus, *Adv. Haereses* III, 21, 2. Fragments preserved in Eusebius, *Hist. Ecc.* V, 8, 11–15.

[61] *Cohortatio ad Graecos*, 13, a work attributed to Pseudo-Justin in the 3rd century CE, see *PG* 6, 241–326.

[62] Clement of Alexandria, *Stromata* I, 22, 148; Tertullian, *Apologeticum* 18, 5–9. The latter states that the Hebrew exemplars used for the translation could be seen in the Serapeum of Alexandria.

[63] According to Epiphanius (310–403), *De Mens. et Ponderibus*, III (*PG* 43, 242), the 72 old men were shut up in twos from morning to night (ζυγὴ ζυγὴ κατὰ οἰκίσκον) in 36 cells, and 36 canoes brought them each night to feast with the king. Augustine (354–430), in *De Civitate Dei*, XVIII, 42, and XV, 11–13 repeated the same well-known points. For later authors A. Pelletier, *Lettre d'Aristée à Philocrate*, 93–96, can be consulted. And for discussion of these ancient witnesses, see P. Wendland, "Zur ältesten Geschichte der Bibel in der Kirche", *ZNW* 1 (1900), 267–99.

following unambiguous details: "Et nescio quis primus auctor Sep-tuaginta cellulas Alexandriae mendacio suo extruxerit, quibus divisi eadem scriptitarint, cum Aristheus eiusdem Potolomei ὑπερασπιστής et multo post tempore Iossepphus nihil tale rettulerint, sed in una basilica congregatos contulisse scribant, non prophetasse. *Aliud est enim vatem, aliud esse interpretem.*[64] In this and in other prologues to the Vulgate he also specifies that the original version of the *Letter of Aristeas* refers only to the translation of the Pentateuch. In these pro-logues, an attempt can be seen to justify and recommend his new translation based on Hebrew as against the LXX held to be inspired even by his contemporary, Augustine. The prestige which the LXX enjoyed as the Bible of the Church required an explanation for the new Vulgate translation, a translation which very soon was to replace the Greek version in the West.

h) *The Completion of the Septuagint*

The *Letter of Aristeas* only refers to the translation of the Pentateuch into Greek in the 3rd century BCE. However, the process of the translation of Hebrew Bible into Greek continued in the 2nd and 1st centuries CE. That is to say, the translation into Greek of the Bible took four centuries, was the work of several translators and, as is obvious, throughout this period the translation techniques also varied. Not only that but, besides the translation of the Hebrew books, the Bible of Alexandria was enriched by including new books written in Greek such as Wisdom, Judith, Baruch, the Letter of Jeremiah or 1 and 2 Maccabees, and adds Greek supplements to other books such as Esther and Daniel.

It is not always easy to date these translations and new composi-tions. For this we have two basic criteria, one is external, from wit-nesses where these translations are already quoted, and the other is internal, from the analysis and characteristics of the translation. Recently, Dorival has set out the current position concerning the chronology and geography of these translations and we refer to him for further information.[65] However, this transformation of the Bible

---

[64] *Biblia Sacra iuxta Vulgatam Versionem*, ed. R. Weber, I, Stuttgart, 1969. On bib-lical prologues before Luther, see M. E. Schild, *Abendländische Bibelvorreden bis zur Lutherbibel*, Heidelberg 1970, pp. 24–42.

[65] G. Dorival, "L'achèvement de la Septante dans le judaïsme", M. Harl, *et al.*, *La Bible grecque des Septante*, 83–111.

through being translated into Greek does not end here. It affects the titles of the books, their grouping and sequence, the arrangement of the material, the different editions of certain books, and several other divergences of lesser importance but of great cultural and exegetical interest.[66] All this transforms the Bible of Alexandria, even though it is largely a translation, into a literary work that warrants being studied for its own sake.[67]

SELECT BIBLIOGRAPHY

Andrews, H. T., "The Letter of Aristeas". *Apocrypha and Pseudepigrapha of the Old Testament*, ed. R. H. Charles, Oxford 1913, 83–122.

Aptowitzer, V., "Die rabbinischen Berichte über die Entstehung der LXX". *Ha-Qedem* 2 (1909), 11–27, 102–22; 3 (1910), 4–17.

Beavis, M. A. L., "Anti-Egyptian Polemic in the Letter of Aristeas 130–65 (The High Priest's Discourse)". *JSJ* 18 (1987), 145–51.

Bickermann, E., "Zur Datierung des Pseudo-Aristeas". *ZNW* 29 (1930) = *Studies in Jewish and Christian History*, Leiden 1976, 109–37.

Boccaccini, G., "La sapienza dello Pseudo-Aristea". *Biblische und judaistische Studien. Festschrift für Paolo Sacchi*, ed. A. Vivian, Frankfurt–Bern–New York–Paris 1990, 143–76.

Cohen, N. G., "The Names of the Translators in the Letter of Aristeas: A Study on the Dynamics of Cultural Transition". *JSJ* 15 (1984), 32–64.

Delling, G. (ed.), *Bibliographie zur jüdisch-hellenistischen und intertestamentarischen Literatur 1900–1965*, Berlin 1969, 61–63, 2nd edn, Berlin 1976, 97–98.

Dorival, G., "L'histoire de la Septante dans le judaïsme antique". M. Harl *et al., La Bible grecque des Septante*, 1988, 31–83.

———, "La bible des Septante: 70 ou 72 traducteurs?". *Tradition of the Text*, 1991, 45–62.

Esbroeck, M. van, "Une forme inédite de la lettre du roi Ptolémée pour la traduction des LXX". *Bib* 57 (1976), 542–49.

Fernández Marcos, N., "El 'sentido profundo' de las prescripciones dietéticas judías (Carta de Aristeas 143–69)". *Salvación en la Palabra*, 1986, 553–62.

———, "Letter of Aristeas". *Apócrifos del Antiguo Testamento* II, ed. A. Díez Macho, Madrid 1983, 9–64.

Freudenthal, J., *Hellenistische Studien* I und II, Breslau 1875, 185ff.

Hadas, M., *Aristeas to Philocrates*, New York–London 1951.

Howard, G., "The Letter of Aristeas: A Re-evaluation". *BIOSCS* 4 (1971), 8–9.

Isserlin, B. S. J., "The Names of the 72 Translators of the Septuagint (Aristeas 47–50)". *Journal of the Ancient Near Eastern Society of Columbia University (The Gaster Festschrift)* 5 (1973), 95–106.

Jellicoe, S., *SMS*, 29–58.

Kahana, A., *Ha-sefarim Ha-ḥiṣonîm*, Tel-Aviv 1956, II, 1–71.

---

[66] See H. B. Swete, *An Introduction to the Old Testament in Greek*, 197–288, and Z. Frankel, *Über den Einfluss der palästinischen Exegese auf die alexandrinische Hermeneutik*, Leipzig 1851, and M. Harl, "Les divergences entre la Septante et le texte massorétique", M. Harl *et al., La Bible grecque des Septante*, 201–22.

[67] See M. Harl, *La langue de Japhet*, 33–42.

Kraus Reggiani, C., *La lettera di Aristea a Filocrate, introduzione, esame analitico, traduzione*, Rome 1979.

Meecham, H. G., "The Letter of Aristeas: A Linguistic Study". Diss. Manchester 1935.

Meisner, N., "Aristeasbrief". *JSHRZ* II–I, Gütersloh 1973, 35–85.

———, "Untersuchungen zum Aristeasbrief". Diss. Berlin 1973.

Mélèze Modrzejeeski, J., *Les Juifs d'Egypte. De Ramsès II à Hadrian*, Paris 1991.

Mendels, D., "On 'Kingship' in the 'Temple Scroll' and the Ideological Vorlage of the seven Banquets in the Letter of Aristeas to Philocrates". *Aegyptus* 59 (1979), 127–37.

Müller, K., "Die rabbinischen Nachrichten über die Anfänge der Septuaginta". *Wort, Lied und Gottesspruch*, 73–93.

Murray, O., "Aristeas and his Sources". *Studia Patristica* XII, Berlin 1975, 123–28.

Murray, O., "Aristeasbrief". *RAC* Sup I, (1986), 573–87.

Parente, F., "La 'Lettera di Aristea' come fonte per la storia del giudaismo alessandrino rante la prima metà del I secolo a.C.". *ASNP* 2 (1972), 177–237 and 517–67.

Pelletier, A., *Flavius Josèphe adaptateur de la lettre d'Aristée: une réaction atticisante contre la koiné*, Paris 1962.

———, "Josephus, the Letter of Aristeas, and the Septuagint". *Josephus*, 1989, 97–115.

———, *Lettre d'Aristée à Philocrate*. SC 89, Paris 1962.

Schürer, E., "Pseudo-Aristeas". *The History of the Jewish People*, III. 1, 1986, 677–87.

Shutt, R. J. H., "Letter of Aristeas". In J. H. Charlesworth (ed.), *The Old Testament Pseudepigrapha*, II, New York 1985, 7–34.

Swete, H. B., *An Introduction to the Old Testament in Greek*, Cambridge 1914, 10–28 and 531–606 (edition of the letter by H. St J. Thackeray).

Tcherikover, V., "The Ideology of the Letter of Aristeas". *HTR* 51(1958) 59–85.

Tov, E., "The Rabbinic Tradition concerning the Alterations Inserted into the Greek Pentateuch and their Relation to the Original Text of the LXX". *JSJ* 15 (1984), 65–89.

Tramontano, R., *La lettera di Aristea a Filocrate*, Naples 1931.

Troiani, L., "Il libro di Aristea ed i giudaismo ellenistico (Premesse per un'interpretazione)". *Studi Ellenistici* II, Pisa 1987, 31–61.

Veltri, G., *Eine Tora für den König Talmai. Untersuchungen zum Übersetzungsverständnis in der jüdisch-hellenistischen und rabbinischen Literatur*, Tübingen 1994.

Walter, N., "Jewish-Greek Literature of the Greek Period". *The Cambridge History of Judaism*, 1989, 385–408.

———, "Jüdisch-hellenistische Literatur vor Philon von Alexandrien (unter Ausschluss der Historiker)". *ANRW* II, 20, 1 (1987), 67–120.

Wendland, P., *Aristeae ad Philocratem epistula*, Leipzig 1900.

———, "Der Aristeasbrief". *Apokryphen und Pseudepigraphen des Alten Testaments*, ed. E. Kautzsch, Tübingen 1900, II, 1–31.

Willrich, H., "Urkundenfälschung in der hellenistisch-jüdischen Literatur". *FRLANT* nf 21 (1924), 86–91.

For more detailed studies on the various aspects and problems of the letter, see *CB* 45–47 and C. Dogniez, *BS* 15–21.

CHAPTER FOUR

MODERN INTERPRETATIONS OF THE ORIGINS OF THE SEPTUAGINT

Most recent studies on the *Letter of Aristeas* have been carried out in connection with the origins of the LXX and are stimulated by problems that have arisen from textual criticism of the Greek Bible. Each position adopted from the beginning of the century in this respect has repercussions on the interpretation of the *Letter*, since every theory about the origin and early history of the LXX uses it as a reference point. There is almost unanimous agreement that it is a propaganda document in favour of a Greek translation of the Pentateuch. The discrepancy revolves around the following questions: To which translation does it refer and when was it made? The diametrically opposed positions that mark out the frame of polemics are those of Lagarde and the Göttingen School on the one hand, who defend on principle the single origin of the LXX (although tempered by many nuances as more is known about the textual history of the various books), and the position of Kahle and his disciples on the other hand, who maintain a plural or multiple origin of the translation in the manner of a Greek Targum. These two theories have polarised the attention of specialists in the course of this century and continue to be latent as basic interrogatives in every attempt to restore the original LXX which is the goal of every critical edition. Besides these other hypotheses have arisen, which without expressly favouring any of the theories proposed have tried to incorporate the data from tradition within new coherent explanations, with greater or less success. Some of them already belong to the past and have no more than historical interest, but we shall consider them briefly so that the history of research can be better understood.

a) *The Septuagint as a Greek Targum (P. Kahle)*

Kahle set out his theory for the first time in 1915 and maintained it throughout his life, followed by his disciple A. Sperber.[1] According

---

[1] P. Kahle, "Untersuchungen"; Kahle, *The Cairo Geniza*; although he already

to Kahle, there never was an *Ur-Septuagint* or single original text. Instead from the beginning there were several translations that arose from liturgical necessity in the various synagogues, just like the Aramaic Targums. In the face of this pluralism, from time to time attempts were made at unification. However, a definitive and official text came not at the beginning but at the end of a long process of previous attempts. In this supposition, translations of greatly varying quality circulated in the Jewish communities. At a given moment the need was felt for approving a recognised and official translation. The *Letter of Aristeas* alludes to this version sanctioned by the Jewish authorities, a unified version made around 100 BCE, since in *c.* 132 BCE, in the prologue of Sira, the Law, the prophets and other writings are mentioned already as integral parts of the new translation. The *Letter of Aristeas* is thus a piece of propaganda writing recommending this approved version as against many others that continued to be used for some time; in spite of the letter these did not completely disappear. Remnants are preserved in biblical quotations of the New Testament, especially in the book of Acts and in the letter to the Hebrews which agree surprisingly with the text of the Samaritan Pentateuch; and the same applies to the quotations from the books of Jubilees.[2] Traces of these multiple versions are reflected in the actual tradition of the LXX for some books that have been transmitted in duplicate texts.[3] And not only this, but along the same lines he interprets a series of data from the documents recently discovered which at first surprised LXX critics, such as the variants of Papyrus Fouad 266 (1st century BCE), Papyrus Gr. 458 Manchester (2nd century BCE), which contain readings related to the Lucian recension; the Greek fragments from Qumran Cave 4, the Greek fragments of the Twelve prophets identified by Barthélemy, the Lucianic readings predating the recension of the historical Lucian known through Justin, Philo, Josephus and Old Latin, the anonymous versions *quinta*, *sexta* and *septima* used by Origen for compiling the Hexapla; the non-

---

applied it earlier to the Samaritan Targum. In 1954, ("Die im August 1952 entdeckte Lederrolle") in support of his theory, he interprets the Greek fragments of the Minor Prophets identified by D. Barthélemy, "Redécouvert d'un chaînon manquant de l'histoire de la Septante", *RB* 60 (1953), 18–29, a position restated in P. Kahle, "Problems of the Septuagint", *Studia Patristica*, ed. K. Aland and F. L. Cross, Berlin 1957, I (= TU 63) 328–38.
    [2] P. Kahle, "Untersuchungen", 400ff.
    [3] For example, Judges, Tobit, Daniel. See the next chapter.

Septuagintal quotations of Philo, the Theodotionic text of Daniel and the presence of Theodotionic quotations in the New Testament and the apostolic Fathers, the Hebraisms of the Coptic versions, etc.[4] Both Theodotion and Lucian revised other very ancient translations but not the LXX. This explains the presence of Theodotionic and Lucianic readings in documents that are chronologically earlier than the date usually given for Theodotion and Lucian.

The basic task, therefore, does not consist in discovering or reconstructing, by the procedures used in textual criticism, an imaginary primitive text, but in carefully comparing all that remains of these earlier translations, before the standardised text of the Greek Bible.[5] Kahle's hypothesis is taken up and developed further by his disciple A. Sperber. Combining the theory of Wutz – to which we shall refer later – with Kahle's, Sperber presupposes in the history of the LXX a transitional period in which Greek was used both for the transcription of Hebrew and for translation.[6] Next there arose sporadic translations according to the needs of the communities in the diaspora in which Hebrew was gradually disappearing as a spoken language. In the period before Christianity came on the scene, there were at least two Greek translations of the Old Testament which can be identified on the basis of quotations from the Old Testament in the New. Building on these suppositions, Sperber introduced the expression 'Bible of the apostles' as a common denominator for all those texts where the Old Testament is quoted in the New Testament and which diverge from the LXX we know.[7] In the Hexapla also he finds traces of more than one Greek translation. The obelised[8] section reflects a translation into Greek of a Hebrew Bible which at this period included the whole Old Testament, a direct Hebrew exemplar of which we have in the Samaritan Pentateuch.

However, although Kahle's theory is so rich in ideas, the textual links required to make it true, or at least likely, are missing. The

---

[4] P. Kahle, *The Cairo Geniza*, 191–261.

[5] "The task which the Septuagint presents to scholars is not the 'reconstruction' of an imaginary 'Urtext' nor the discovery of it, but a careful collection and investigation of all the remains and traces of earlier versions of the Greek Bible which differed from the Christian standard text," P. Kahle, *The Cairo Geniza*, 264.

[6] A. Sperber, "Das Alphabet der Septuaginta-Vorlage", *OLZ* 32 (1929), 533–40.

[7] A. Sperber, "New Testament and LXX" (in Hebrew). *Tarbiz* 6 (1934), 1–20; Sperber, "New Testament and Septuagint", *JBL* 59 (1940), 193–293.

[8] I.e. the one found in the LXX even though it does not correspond to the Masoretic text we know. See chapter 12.

LXX became the Christian Bible only for the purpose of canonising its different books in the 2nd century CE. In the period when Christianity appeared one should recognise, both for the books cited in the Qumran writings and in the quotations in the New Testament,[9] that it is incorrect to exaggerate the distinction between the Palestinian and Alexandrian canons as if the latter were the one that the Church would one day inherit. On the contrary, in both sets of writings – Qumran and New Testament – the same Old Testament books are mentioned; these quotations correspond therefore to a period of textual instability before it was fixed at the Synod of Yamnia (c. 100 CE). As for the quotations in the New Testament, the cornerstone of Kahle's theory, it presents much more complex problems than he had realised. Moreover, there are other hypotheses that can explain the many divergences from the Septuagintal text: quoting from memory, mixed quotations, adaptation of prophecy to context, the many revisions to which the original text was subject from very early on, etc. The Semitic tradition that seems to underlie Stephen's speech (Acts 7), which Kahle attributed to the existence of Greek texts related to the Samaritan Pentateuch, has an immediate antecedent in the Hebrew texts from Qumran and comprises an example of textual pluralism in Hebrew in the centuries prior to the Christian era.[10] The recently discovered papyri of the LXX in the pre-recensional period are not substantially different in form, in spite of the interpretation given them by Kahle, but at most are traces of very early revisions along the lines indicated by Barthélemy.[11] From analytical study of individual books, the school of LXX scholars in the USA and Canada has confirmed the basic soundness of Lagarde's approach although it has refined his initial position. P. Katz, Kahle's disciple, devotes at his request a monograph to the biblical text of Philo[12] and comes to conclusions that are opposed to his master's,

---

[9] For discussion of this point, see chapter 20.

[10] J. de Waard, *A Comparative Study of the Old Testament Text in the Dead Sea Scrolls and in the New Testament*, Leiden 1965, especially pp. 80–81, and F. M. Cross, "The History of the Biblical Text in the Light of Discoveries in the Judean Desert", *HTR* 57 (1964) 281–99. The bibliography on the history of the text in this period has greatly increased as a result of the publications of the documents from Qumran. See particularly N. Fernández Marcos, "La Biblia de los autores del Nuevo Testamento", *II Simposio Bíblico Español*, ed. V. Collado Bertomeu and V. Vilar-Hueso, Valencia–Córdoba 1987, 171–80.

[11] D. Barthélemy, *Les Devanciers d'Aquila*, Leiden 1963.

[12] P. Katz, *Philo's Bible: The Aberrant Text of Bible Quotations in some Philonic Writings and its Place in the Textual History of the Greek Bible*, Cambridge 1950.

results which he did not accept.[13] Internal arguments and the data we have for the historical nucleus preserved in the *Letter of Aristeas* are sufficient proof that in the case of the LXX a process like that of the Aramaic Targums did not occur.

b) *An Alexandrian Origin but in the Maccabean Period (c. 146 BCE)*

This is the hypothesis held by H. Graetz in a short article[14] towards the end of the last century. He starts from some texts which, in Graetz' opinion, already reflect the polemic between Pharisees and Sadducees (Lev. 23:11-16). Proving that translators resolve the dilemma along Pharisaic lines means that the version could not have been made before the Maccabean period when these differences started to manifest themselves. He also bases his theory on other peculiar features of the version, such as the translation of *'arnebet* by δασύπους (Lev. 11:5ff.) and not by λαγώς. Instead of the rabbinic explanation for this choice which we saw in the previous chapter, according to Graetz this synonym was not chosen to avoid offending the Lagides but because at that time δασύπους was the word more in use for 'hare' (*'arnebet*).

Similarly, in Ez. 8:12 the first half of the verse is missing from the LXX; Origen adds it with a preceding asterisk and the following note: "the words 'the king shall mourn' were perhaps omitted intentionally by the translators, to avoid suspicion that the king had occasion to suffer".[15] The translation of *melek* by ἄρχων instead of βασιλεύς (Dt. 17:14-19) would be explained in the same way. These details confirmed the thesis of Aristeas that an Alexandrian king promoted the translation; only that the king in question to which the letter refers would be Ptolemy VI Philometor (181–145 BCE), a benefactor of the Jews, patron of Onias IV and founder of the temple of Leontopolis.

---

[13] P. Katz, *Philo's Bible*, 95ff. and 114ff. Ninety-five percent of Philo's quotations are from the LXX; about 4% are of a different type in certain manuscripts, in others, the same as LXX. About 1% are of a different type in all the manuscripts. Philo's commentary is based on the text of the LXX. The quotations which differ in the lemma seem to have been changed and do not match the commentary. The non-Septuagintal texts in Philo are from Aquila. Later, Philo must have gone through Jewish hands in a period when Aquila's translation was obligatory.

[14] H. Graetz, "The Genesis of the So-called LXX".

[15] H. Graetz, "The Genesis of the So-called LXX", 151.

However, Swete's reply,[16] based on linguistic arguments, was enough to emphasise the weakness of Graetz' arguments, which were insufficient to make a change of such magnitude in the date of the letter.

c) *A Palestinian Origin*

This hypothesis was formulated by M. Gaster in the Schweich Lectures of 1923.[17] According to him, the Greek Pentateuch did not arise in Alexandria but in Palestine, since only the Palestinian origin of the version could count on enough prestige and support to be accepted among the Jews of the diaspora. The movement that produced the Greek Pentateuch represents only a further facet of the general resistance to Hellenisation of the peoples of Near East by means of affirming the antiquity and superiority of their own culture. By translating the scriptures into Greek the Jews took the war to the enemy camp. However, here an additional factor comes into play, the rivalry between Jews and Samaritans. The two groups presented themselves to king Ptolemy with their respective translations into Greek so that he could decide the dispute. The king of Egypt declared in favour of the Jewish version which in future became the official text, fixing in this way the superiority of the Jewish Pentateuch of Jerusalem over the Samaritan Pentateuch, an event reflected in the exchange of presents in the *Letter of Aristeas*. From the Jewish-Hellenistic historian's knowledge of the biblical traditions he dates the version towards the end of the 4th or the beginning of the 3rd century BCE, i.e. under Ptolemy I (323–285). In this hypothesis, the *Samariticon*[18] would in fact be the Samaritan Pentateuch, of the same date as the Jewish version of the LXX and responding to the same caste spirit. Both versions would represent the first step towards the Targums, and would have been made for the use of the people and not for liturgical service where the Hebrew would continue to be used in Palestine until the Aramaic liturgical Targums appeared.

The ferment of resistance to Hellenisation which is part of Gaster's theory has been made explicit recently by R. Hanhart.[19] However

---

[16] H. B. Swete, "Graetz's Theory of the LXX".

[17] M. Gaster, *The Samaritans*.

[18] See chapter 9.

[19] R. Hanhart, "Zum Wesen der makedonisch-hellenistischen Zeit Israels", *Wort, Lied und Gottesspruch* II, Würzburg 1972, 49–59.

the rest of the theory is not convincing since recent study of the language has more than proved the Alexandrian origin of the Pentateuch and of other books such as Isaiah, 1–4 Kings, Jeremiah, Job, Proverbs.[20]

d) *A Liturgical Origin*

This theory is connected with Thackeray, who developed it in the 1920 Schweich Lectures (published in 1923).[21] He attempted to give a valid and coherent explanation that could embrace all the books of the LXX. The origin of various parts of the LXX is conditioned by the liturgical requirements of the synagogue. As a result, the translation was made in four stages:

1. First, the Law or Pentateuch in the 3rd century BCE, as a unit and by a small team. The vocabulary and style indicate its Alexandrian origin. Apart from the last part of Exodus, there are very few divergences from the Hebrew text.[22]

2. In a second phase the latter prophets were translated: Isaiah, Jeremiah, Ezekiel and the twelve minor prophets, beginning with Isaiah, the book having a language and style most like the Pentateuch. The sequence was dictated by use in the synagogue, since these books provide the material for the second liturgical reading or *haftarah* after the reading from the Law.

3. At a further stage a partial, expurgated version of the former prophets was produced including 1 Samuel, 2 Samuel 1–11 (omitting the Uriah episode), 1 Kgs beginning with 2:12 (Solomon's accession to the throne) and continuing up to 21:43. Finally the work was re-edited by a single author who filled in the gaps of previous translators.[23] And these three parts comprise the Alexandrian version proper, divided into three volumes.

---

[20] See in general A. Deissmann's studies in the light of the papyri and for Isaiah, J. L. Seeligmann, *The Septuagint Version of Isaiah: A Discussion of its Problems*, Leiden 1948, 95–122, and J. Ziegler, *Untersuchungen zur LXX des Buches Isaias*. ATA XII, 3 Münster 1934, chap. VIII: 'Der alexandrinisch-ägyptische Hintergrund der Is-LXX'.

[21] See *Select Bibliography*. However he had already expressed it more clearly in 1915 in his article "Septuagint" in the *ISBE*.

[22] For this part of Exodus, see the monograph by D. W. Gooding, *The Account of the Tabernacle: Translations and Textual Problems of the Greek Exodus*, Cambridge 1959, and D. Fraenkel, "Die Quellen der asterisierten Zusätze im zweiten Tabernakelbericht Exodus 35–40", *Studien zur Septuaginta*, 140–86,

[23] See H. St J. Thackeray, *The Septuagint and Jewish Worship*, 16–28.

4. The Writings (*kᵉtûbîm*) have a special place. If we except the Psalter, where the translators took hardly any liberties, the rest of the translation was the product of free paraphrases and extracts which sometimes include legendary additions and are directed more to the general public than to the faithful of the synagogue. This explains the partial translation of Job (one-sixth shorter than the Hebrew *textus receptus*)[24] made by someone who had studied the Greek poets; and the fact that Proverbs contains sayings that do not occur in the Hebrew and that the translator composed fragments in iambs and hexameters. With the same liberties, 1 Ezra is composed of extracts from the Hebrew books of Chronicles–Ezra–Nehemiah, pasted together around a fable of non-Jewish origin, the legend of the three bodyguards of king Darius (Ezra 3–5). The same author of 1 Ezra edited the first version of Daniel (Dan.-LXX) incorporating extraneous elements missing from the Masoretic text such as the hymn of the three youths, the short story of Susannah and the episode of Bel and the Dragon. This liberty reached its peak in the translation of the book of Esther, where the Greek additions, missing from the Hebrew text, make up two-thirds of the total story.

At the time of being translated, these Writings, which later acquired official recognition, were not so binding as the Law and the Prophets, and allowed the translator a degree of creativity.

One of the weak points of Thackeray's theory is that he leaves out of this process the translation of Joshua and Judges, two books that raise problems due to the different recensions in which their text has been transmitted. Nonetheless, it is the most ambitious hypothesis to try to incorporate in a coherent way the whole process of decanting the Bible from Hebrew to Greek in its different stages. Of course some links do not have positive support from the data and others have been discarded owing to later research, such as the theory concerning the division of the books into two halves for its translation. Thackeray's studies were based on Swete's manual edition. Now it is known that phenomena that Thackeray attributed to the translators are due to later stages of the transmission of the text, as was proved once the material had been conveniently stratified in the critical editions. On the other hand, continuous reading of the

---

[24] See N. Fernández Marcos, "The Septuagint Reading of the Book of Job", *The Book of Job*, ed. W. A. M. Beuken, Leuven 1994, 251–66.

Law together with the *haftārôt* of the prophets is unlikely, as Perrot has recently confirmed, and thus there was no liturgical need for a complete translation of the Torah.[25]

e) *The Transcription Theory*

Although of no interest today as an explanation for the origins of the LXX, in its time it was the object of scholarly debate and unleashed a series of publications from the beginning of the 1920s until the end of the 1930s.[26] It had already been raised by the Danish scholar Tychsen in the 18th century,[27] but scholars paid almost no attention to it. The name that has been almost exclusively identified with this theory is F. X. Wutz (1883–1938). He defended it in a series of publications, from 1922 until his death, with a huge collection of material.[28] According to him, the translators of the LXX used a Hebrew text that had already been transliterated into Greek characters; with the result that he undertook the task of tracing that text by means of the remains of transliterations preserved in the LXX: proper names, difficult words that they did not understand, palaeographic mistakes, etc. By means of these isolated indications he tried to recover the consonantal Hebrew text that the translators used as a *Vorlage*, a text which of course would have the advantage of being much older than the Masoretic text as we have it in Hebrew manuscripts.[29] As well as the material transliterated in the LXX, he used transcriptions from the second column of the Hexapla by means of photographs of the Milan palimpsest discovered by G. Mercati, transcriptions of "the three", especially Theodotion, and for proper names the *Onomastica Sacra* by Eusebius and Jerome's transcriptions.

There is no doubt at all that the data handled by Wutz are well-founded. It is clear that the LXX preserves a large number of transcriptions, not only of proper and place names but even of other difficult terms, the meaning of which was not clear to the translators.

---

[25] C. Perrot, "La lecture de la Bible dans la diaspora hellénistique", *Études sur le judaïsme hellénistique*, ed. R. Kuntzmann and J. Schlosser, Paris 1984, 109–32.

[26] See *CB* 43, *Wutz's Theory*.

[27] O. G. Tychsen, *Tentamen de variis codicum hebraicorum VT MSS generibus*, Rostock 1772, 54–65.

[28] See *CB* 43–44.

[29] See F. W. Wutz, *Die Transkriptionen von der Septuaginta* I, 61ff.; 101ff.; II, *passim*.

It is even possible that parts of the Hebrew Bible used in the liturgy
were transcribed into Greek for the convenience of the faithful who
had lost contact with the original script of Hebrew when it became
a sacred language and disappeared as a spoken language. However,
from these scant and uncertain data Wutz sets out an elaborate and
subtle theory which violates the translation process, forcing it into a
precise chronology on the basis of transcriptions. The hypothesis of
a change to the Greek script continues to be a probable conjecture
until the transcriptions of the Hexaplaric *secunda* (*c.* 230 CE). Even
the origin and purpose of this *secunda* poses such problems[30] that it
cannot be used to support a global theory about the origins of the
LXX.

It is much more likely that the translators transliterated the proper
names as they were pronounced in their time; hence the importance
of the transcriptions for studying the pronunciation of pre-Masoretic
Hebrew, used with due caution, stratified chronologically and taking into account the corruptions due to transmission and the diachronic
evolution of the vocalic and consonantal systems of Greek and Hebrew.

Wutz's theory inserts an unnecessary stage into the translation
process. If the translator is able to handle a Hebrew text transliterated into Greek it can be assumed that he knows enough Hebrew
to translate directly from the original. Furthermore, there is absolutely
no decisive proof that the translators used transliterated texts. If they
had, it would have produced endless ambiguities, considering that
the four Hebrew phonemes comprising the sibilants (s, $ṣ$, $ś$, $š$) are
transcribed by a single phoneme in Greek, namely *sigma*; the same
difficulties must have applied in distinguishing the gutturals. On the
other hand there are indications of similar Hebrew letters being confused in translating, such as d/r and y/w, whose Greek equivalents
are not so alike as to be confused by copyists.

f) *Other Theories*

As we have seen, none of the theories set out explains in a satisfactory way the translation of the Pentateuch into Greek as it is
described in the *Letter of Aristeas*, and thus none of them has gained
general acceptance among specialists. Although scholars continue

---

[30] See chapter 12.

to argue the case between the needs of the Jewish community of Alexandria and the initiative of King Ptolemy as principal cause of the translation, the most recent publications tend to favour the official initiative, the cultural and legislative politics of the Ptolemaic court, as the main reason for the translation. Several indications support this supposition. First of all, the Alexandrian Jewish sources as well as the rabbinic sources refer to the translation as a royal initiative and are silent on the motive of the liturgical or cultural needs of the Jewish community. No privately instigated translation is known before the 2nd century BCE, and it would be of the Prophets as a continuation of the Torah. All the examples known of translations made in this period[31] are due to royal or official undertaking more or less in the direction indicated by the *Letter of Aristeas*. Accordingly, an historical nucleus has to be accepted in the traditions included in this letter.

Some scholars also insist on the importance of the codification of public law in the court of the Ptolemies, a codification which included the Law of the Jews. This hypothesis, defended in various forms by Bickermann, Stricker, Rost and Barthélemy,[32] has been developed by Mélèze Modrzejewski from the publication of Oxyrhynchus Papyrus 3285, which presents the ancient local law of the indigenous inhabitants of Egypt. According to him, around 275 BCE all the judicial apparatus of the Lagides was translated from Demotic into Greek. The same happened to the Torah of the Jews so that the royal officials could understand it. As a result, the translation of the Law into Greek received a sort of official sanction, thanks to its inclusion in the judicial system of Ptolemy II Philadelphus.[33] However thought provoking this hypothesis might be, there is no incontrovertible proof for the inclusion of the Law into the juridical system of the Lagides,

---

[31] Manetho wrote the history of the pharaohs at the request of Ptolemy II, Berossus dedicates the history of Babylonia to Antiochus I of Syria, Hermippus prepares a Greek commentary on Zoroaster, again on royal demand, the Greek edicts of Asoka around 250 BCE are due to the initiative of that Indian emperor; see G. Dorival, "Les origines de la Septante", 71, and E. Benvéniste, "Édits d'Asoka en traduction grecque", *Journal Asiatique* 252 (1964), 137–57.

[32] See E. Bickerman, *Studies in Jewish and Christian History* I, Leiden 1976, 137–66 and 167–200; B. H. Stricker, *De brief van Aristeas*, Amsterdam 1956; L. Rost, "Vermutungen über den Anlass zur griechischen Übersetzung der Tora"; D. Barthélemy, "Pourquoi la Torah a-t-elle été traduite en grec?", *Études d'histoire du texte de l'Ancien Testament*, Freiburg–Göttingen 1978, 322–40.

[33] See G. Dorival, "Les origines de la Septante", 73–76.

and it must be admitted that the Pentateuch is more than a law code. Ptolemy's cultural policy is attested, besides the evidence transmitted by the *Letter*, by the information about the classification of the works kept in the Library of Alexandria in the time of Callimachus (260–240). However, if there had been a copy of the Pentateuch in Greek in that library, it is difficult to think that there was no reference to the Greek Bible in Greek and Latin writers before the treatise *De Sublimitate* by Pseudo-Longinus (1st century CE) unless those writers were repelled by the strange contents of the LXX and the bad Greek of the translation compared with the literary usages of the time.[34] There is no doubt that the socio-religious and apologetic needs of the community of Alexandria were latent as is shown by the new literary genres in Greek that the Jews of the diaspora cultivated, but it is difficult to avoid the essence of the *Letter of Aristeas* according to which the initiative for the undertaking came from the court of King Ptolemy.

g) *The Proto-Septuagint*

The problem of the proto-Septuagint, which had leapt onto the scholarly stage after 1915 with the debate between Lagarde (single origin) and Kahle (multiple origin) of the version, came to the forefront again in the 1940s with the publication of the commentary on Daniel by Montgomery, on Greek Joshua by Margolis, the writings of A. Sperber, and the publication of the Chester Beatty, Rylands and Scheide papyri.[35] What for Lagarde was a working hypothesis with a good dose of intuition has been confirmed by the inductive analysis of several LXX books: by Rahlfs for Ruth, by Margolis for Joshua, by Montgomery for Daniel and Kings, by Moore for Judges, and by Ziegler for Prophets. To this must be added the works by Gehman on the secondary versions and the recent editions and studies by Wevers on the Greek Pentateuch and by Hanhart on 2 Maccabees,

---

[34] See G. Dorival, "La Bible des Septante chez les auteurs païens (jusqu'au pseudo-Longin)", *Cahiers de Biblia patristica* 1, Strasbourg 1987, 9–26; A. Momigliano, *Alien Wisdom*, Cambridge 1978, pp. 91–92: "The LXX remained an exclusive Jewish possession until the Christians took it over. We do not even know whether it was deposited in the great Ptolemaic foundation, the library of Alexandria," p. 92. See also G. Rinaldi, *Biblia Gentium*, Rome 1989.

[35] H. M. Orlinsky, "On the Present State of Proto-Septuagint Studies", 81ff.

Esther and 1 Ezra. Lagarde's principles, plausible *a priori*, have been shown as solid and consistent. The variants in the pre-recensional papyri indicate that the revisions of LXX have to be put back to a date closer to its composition. However the basic assumptions remain unchanged.

In 1949, P. Katz, Kahle's disciple, abandoned his teacher's theories precisely because of his studies on biblical quotations in Philo and Justin:[36] the idea that originally competing and simultaneous partial or complete translations once existed has no support in the facts when these are only arranged chronologically.[37] Years later Wevers, in an overall view of LXX studies within the perspective of origins, would again insist on the basic reorganisation of the Lagarde–Rahlfs position which shapes all the editorial work of the *Septuaginta-Unternehmen* of Göttingen: "The future of proto-Septuagint studies depends on the classical line, with some necessary modifications to be sure, rather than on the general lines of Kahle's approach."[38]

---

[36] P. Katz, "Das Problem des Urtextes der Septuaginta", and Katz, *Philo's Bible*.

[37] P. Katz, "Das Problen des Urtextes der Septuaginta", 17: "Die Vorstellung, als hätten konkurrierende Teil oder Vollübersetzungen ursprünglich nebeneinander bestanden hat also keine Stütze an den Tatsachen, wenn man diese nur geschichtlich einordnet." And on p. 18 he adds: "So bleibt nur die Analogie zu den palastin. Targumen. Tatsächlich finden sich an die Targume gemahnende Deutungen, aber so sporadisch, dass sie den Vergleich mit der starren Konsequenz der Targume nicht aushalten. Hier zeigt sich nur eben der Einfluss der Umwelt auf die Übersetzer, die dadurch noch lange nicht zu Targumisten werden. Beachtet man diese Einschränkung aber nicht und schliesst aus solch vereinzelten Analogien weiter auf eine ursprüngliche Vielheit von Übersetzungen, so ist das eine *petitio principii*. Denn bis heute ist keine einzige Stelle nachgewiesen, für die wir mehr als *eine* vorrezensionelle Übersetzung besässen, womoglich als Wiedergabe eines dem unsern überlegenen Hebräers. Solange dieser Nachweis aber fehlt, ist alle Rede von ursprünglichen Paralleltargumen blosse Vermutung auf Grund des aus vereinzelten Beobachtungen *a priori* erschlossenen Targumcharakter."

[38] J. W. Wevers, "Proto-Septuagint Studies", 77, with an extensive bibliography. And the information published by him periodically on current research in the field of the LXX in *Theologische Rundschau*. See also J. W. Wevers, "The Göttingen Septuagint", *BIOSCS* 8 (1975), 19–23, and R. Hanhart, J. W. Wevers, *Das Göttinger Septuaginta-Unternehmen*, Göttingen 1977. "So one may conclude that in the Kahle vs Lagarde–Rahlfs controversy Kahle was wrong and the Lagarde school was right" confirms J. W. Wevers, "Barthélemy and Proto-Septuagint Studies", 26, although in the very next line he insists on the complexity of the text history of the Septuagint in the various books and how the method proposed by Lagarde for restoring the LXX has to be revised and refined in many ways.

SELECT BIBLIOGRAPHY

Dorival, G., "Les origines de la Septante". M. Harl *et al.*, *La Bible grecque des Septante*, 1988, 66–78.

Gaster, M., *The Samaritans*, London 1925, especially pp. 112–30.

Graetz, H., "The Genesis of the So-called LXX, the First Greek Version of the Pentateuch". *JQR* 3 (1891), 150–56.

———, "The LXX: A Reply to Prof. Swete". *ET* 2 (1890), 277–78.

Hanhart, R., "Fragen um die Entstehung der LXX". *VT* 12 (1962), 139–62.

———, "Zum gegenwärtigen Stand der Septuagintaforschung". *De Septuaginta*, 1984, 3–18.

Jellicoe, S., *SMS*, 59–70.

Kahle, P., "Die im August 1952 entdeckte Lederrolle mit dem griechischen Text der kleinen Propheten und das Problem der LXX". *TLZ* 79 (1954), 81–94 (= *Opera minora* 113–28).

———, "Die Septuaginta. Prinzipielle Erwägungen". *Festschrift O. Eissfeldt*, Halle 1947, 161–180.

———, *The Cairo Geniza*, Oxford 1959, 191–304.

———, "Untersuchungen zur Geschichte des Pentateuchtextes". *TSK* 88 (1915), 399–439 (= *Opera Minora*, Leiden 1956, 3–37).

Katz, P., "Das Problem des Urtextes der Septuaginta". *TZ* 5 (1949), 1–24.

———, "The Recovery of the Original LXX: A Study in the History of Transmission and Textual Criticism". *Actes du Iᵉʳ Congrès de la fédération internationale des associations d'études classiques*, Paris 1951, 165–82.

Lagarde, P. A. de, *Anmerkungen zur griechischen Übersetzung der Proverbien*, Leipzig 1863.

———, *Librorum Veteris Testamenti canonicorum pars prior Graece*, Göttingen 1883.

Orlinsky, H. M., "Current Progress and Problems in Septuagint Research". *The Study of the Bible Today and Tomorrow*, ed. H. R. Willoughby, Chicago 1947, pp. 155–57.

———, "On the present State of Proto-Septuagint Studies". *JAOS* 61 (1941), 81–91.

Pietersma, A., "Septuagint Research: A Plea for a Return to Basic Issues". *VT* 35 (1985), 296–311.

Rost, L., "Vermutungen über den Anlass zur griechischen Übersetzung der Tora". *Wort, Gebot, Glaube*, Walter Eichrodt zum 80. Geburtstag, ed. H. J. Stoebe, ATANT 59, Zurich 1970, 39–44.

Skehan, P. W., "The Earliest LXX and Subsequent Revisions". *Jerome Biblical Commentary*, New York 1968, 570–72.

Swete, H. B., "Graetz's Theory of the LXX". *ET* 2 (1890). 209.

Thackeray, H. St J., "Septuagint", in *ISBE* IV 1915, 2722–32.

———, *Some Aspects of the Greek Old Testament*, London 1927, 21–31.

———, *The Septuagint and Jewish Worship: A Study in Origins*, London 1923.

Vattioni, F., "Storia del testo biblico: L'origine dei LXX". *AION* 40 (1980), 115–30.

Wevers, J. W., "An Apologia for Septuagint Studies". *BIOSCS* 18 (1985), 16–38.

———, "Barthélemy and Proto-Septuagint Studies". *BIOSCS* 21 (1988), 23–34.

———, "Proto-Septuagint Studies". *The Seed of Wisdom: Fs. T. J. Meek*, Toronto 1964, 58–77.

Wutz, F. X., *Die Transkriptionen von der LXX bis zu Hieronymus*. BWAT II, 9 *Lieferung* 1 (1925), 1–176; *Lief.* 3 (1933), 177–571.

———, *Onomastica Sacra. Untersuchungen zum Liber interpretationis nominum hebraicorum des hl. Hieronymus. I Quellen und System der Onomastica. II Texte und Register*. TU 41 (1915).

———, *Systematische Wege von der Septuaginta zum hebräischen Urtext*, Stuttgart 1937. Further bibliography on Wutz's theory in *CB* 43–44.

CHAPTER FIVE

THE SEPTUAGINT AND THE HEBREW TEXT

a) *Two Texts Face to Face*

Beyond the translation of the Torah or Pentateuch into Greek, to which the *Letter of Aristeas* refers, the process of translation or creation of the other books of the Greek Bible which we know today as the LXX, occurred in separate stages, that are difficult to determine, between the 2nd century BCE and the 1st century CE. This inadequately known process, as well as the geographical origin of the translation or creation of the various books, has been described by G. Dorival in a short compendium that summarises the present state of knowledge on the subject.[1]

The results of this process, however, are well known. A simple comparison between the Greek Bible and the Hebrew Bible shows a series of books in the LXX that are not included in the Hebrew canon: 1 Ezra, Wisdom of Solomon, Ecclesiasticus, Judith, Tobit, Baruch, Letter of Jeremiah and the four books of Maccabees. To these are added the Supplements to the book of Esther and the additions to the book of Daniel. And within the books included in the Hebrew canon the differences are no less important: different titles and arrangement of the various books, different sequence and contents,[2] cases in which the LXX represents a different textual tradition or a different edition from the Masoretic text.[3] Another kind of difference is only evident when we subject both texts to the meticulous examination of textual criticism; these differences are due to a different vocalisation of the consonantal Hebrew text, to the linguistic comprehension of the translators, and to their particular translation technique and the theological and modernising interpretations.[4]

---

[1] G. Dorival, "L'achèvement de la septante dans le judaïsme. De la faveur au rejet", in Harl, *et al.*, *La Bible Grecque des Septante*, 83–111.

[2] See H. B. Swete, *An Introduction to the Old Testament in Greek*, Cambridge 1914, 197–288.

[3] O. Munnich, "Écarts principaux entre la Septante et le texte massorétique (livre par livre)", M. Harl, *et al.*, *La Bible grecque des Septante*, 173–82.

[4] M. Harl, "Les divergences entre la Septante et le texte massorétique", M. Harl, *et al.*, *La Bible grecque des Septante*, 201–22.

As a consequence of this complex process, the Bible of Alexandria which the Greek-speaking Jew used cannot be considered a simple reproduction of the original Hebrew text but an autonomous literary work organised around a new constellation of meanings within the Greek system. And it can be said that the discrepancy between the original and its reproduction appeared right from the first moment of translation, as testified by the author of the prologue to the translation of Ecclesiasticus, towards the end of the 2nd century BCE.[5] An echo of this inappropriateness of the Greek translation is also preserved in the many rabbinic references to the changes which the seventy elders inserted into the translation for king Ptolemy.[6]

If these differences did not constitute a serious problem when the Hebrew text itself had not yet been standardised, they became a burning problem when the single consonantal text started to become normative and binding towards the end of the 1st century CE. As we saw when examining the reception of the *Letter of Aristeas*,[7] an attempt to reduce the unease aroused by these discrepancies between the Hebrew Bible and the Greek Bible of Alexandria within the Jewish community went in two directions. One part of Jewish tradition, with Philo at its head, though it was to find an echo in Augustine, chose to consider the LXX an inspired translation with the same authority as the Hebrew Bible. According to this inspirationist movement, God had revealed himself to the people of Israel through Moses in the Hebrew Bible and through the translators in the Greek Bible and both texts were inspired. However, there was also another philological tendency within Judaism that was apparent in a series of early revisions intended to correct the text of the LXX in order to adapt it to the Hebrew text in current use. This trend, which is already evident in the Hebraising corrections of some pre-Christian papyri, would become more obvious in the καίγε revision and culminated in the new Jewish translations by Aquila, Symmachus and Theodotion or in the new translation into Latin by Jerome.[8] Furthermore, these divergences would condition the history of the transmission of the biblical text, and emerge with force in the

---

[5] For the same things said in Hebrew do not have the same force when translated into another language", Ben Sira, Prologue 20.

[6] See chapter 3, pp. 44–47.

[7] See pp. 47–50.

[8] See *infra*, chapters 7–9.

critical moments of the scientific study of the Bible. Two examples are Origen's Hexapla, the first attempt at synchronic comparison of the different texts in circulation, and the Polyglot Bibles of the 16th and 17th centuries, synoptic editions of the various texts, each retaining its own autonomy.

Until the middle of this century, the differences between the LXX and the Hebrew text were usually explained by resorting to the idiosyncrasy and translation techniques of the translators, to editorial reworking of the text in favour of an actual theology or to other tendentious purposes. This is how H. S. Gehman, J. W. Wevers and the Scandinavian school argued, up to H. S. Nyberg.[9] That is to say, the same reasoning that P. de Lagarde had sketched out at the close of the 19th century for the reconstruction of the LXX was applied to the Hebrew text. In other words, at the beginning of textual transmission, around 130 CE, there was only one Hebrew text (the theory of the archetype) which was being reproduced with extreme precision, ensuring the uniformity of the consonantal text.[10] As a result, all the discordant readings to be found in the Samaritan Pentateuch or in medieval manuscripts are due to copyist errors or to tendentious changes to the original by the scribes of the dissident sects. The same criterion is usually used with the versions and their divergences from *hebraica veritas*. In the words of D. Barthélemy: "Scholars were more and more reluctant to admit that every variant of the LXX was based on a Hebrew *Vorlage* distinct from the MT."[11] However, there was no lack of scholars in this period who succeeded in discovering the high value of the LXX for the restoration of the Hebrew text in some books in which the Masoretic text was particularly corrupt. It is sufficient to mention names such as O. Thenius, J. Wellhausen and S. R. Driver for the books of Samuel, C. H. Cornill for Ezekiel, J. A. Montgomery for Kings and Daniel.[12]

---

[9] H. S. Nyberg, *Studien zum Hoseabuche*, Uppsala 1935; H. S. Gehman, "Exegetical Methods Employed by the Greek Translator of 1 Samuel", *JAOS* 70 (1950), 292–96, and J. W. Wevers, "A Study in the Exegetical Principles of the Translator of II Sam. XI:2–I Kings II:11", *CBQ* 15 (1953), 30–45.

[10] On the differences between the theory of "a single recension" and "a single archetype" which ultimately were considered as synonymous, see M. H. Goshen-Gottstein, "Hebrew Biblical Manuscripts: Their History and their Place in the HUBP Edition", *Bib* 48 (1967), 243–90, especially pp. 254–62.

[11] *Text, Hebrew*, in IDBS (1976), 878.

[12] O. Thenius, *Die Bücher Samuelis*, Dresden 1842; J. Wellhausen, *Der Text der Bücher Samuelis*, Göttingen 1871; S. R. Driver, *Notes on the Hebrew text and the Topography*

P. Kahle must be mentioned as the principal opponent of Lagarde's theory; he defended a plural origin of the LXX, just as happened with the Aramaic Targums.[13]

Parallel to this movement of textual re-evaluation of the LXX there arose another, with Z. Frankel as its main exponent; he interpreted the differences between the Masoretic text and the Greek Bible as the result of the influence of Jewish exegesis.[14] This tendency to highlight the periphrastic nature of the LXX culminated in the statement, attributed to R. Kittel, that the LXX is not a translation but a theological commentary on the Hebrew text.[15] Only H. M. Orlinsky dared to state, before 1950, that the Hebrew manuscripts used by the translators of the LXX in some books such as Job, Jeremiah or Esther differed *recensionally*, and not only in small details, from the Masoretic textual tradition, and then add that these traditions perished some time ago.[16]

b) *Qumran and the Septuagint*

It is difficult to overestimate the impact made by the finds from the Desert of Judah on the understanding of the history of the biblical text and more particularly on the early history of the LXX and its relationship to the Hebrew text. Evidence of the enormous activity expended in this field of research in recent years is provided by the number of publications in progress,[17] which will probably increase as the pace of the official editions of those documents increases. The importance of these finds lies not only in the Greek fragments found in Qumran and Naḥal Ḥever but especially in the Hebrew texts.

---

of the Books of Samuel, Oxford 1890; C. H. Cornill, *Das Buch des Propheten Ezechiel*, Leipzig 1886; J. A. Montgomery, *A Critical and Exegetical Commentary on the Books of Kings*, Edinburgh–New York 1951, and Montgomery, *A Critical and Exegetical Commentary on the Book of Daniel*, Edinburgh 1927.

[13] For a description of P. Kahle's theory on the origins of the LXX in the same way as the Targums, see pp. 53–57.

[14] Z. Frankel, *Vorstudien zu der Septuaginta*, Leipzig 1841, and Frankel, *Über den Einfluss des palästinischen Exegese auf die alexandrinische Hermeneutik*, Leipzig 1851.

[15] Cited by S. Jellicoe, *SMS*, 316.

[16] "But those text-traditions have long perished, driven out by the Hebrew text that was used by the Mishnah and Talmud, by Theodotion, Aquila, Symmachus, Origen, Jerome, from the first–second to the fifth centuries AD", H. M. Orlinsky, "On the Present State of Proto-Septuagint Studies", *JAOS* 61 (1941), 78–109, p. 85.

[17] Compare for example the one page devoted to the topic in the *CB* (1973) with the fifteen pages of the *BS* (1995).

And within these, those fragments that are compared with the LXX allow certain conclusions to be drawn on the state of the biblical text in the two centuries that preceded the standardisation of the consonantal text.

Beginning with the Greek texts, prior to Qumran we only knew two pre-Christian papyri, from Egypt, with fragments of Deuteronomy: Pap. Rylands 458 (Rahlfs 957) from the 2nd century BCE and Pap. Fouad 266 (Rahlfs 848) from the 1st century BCE. However, Qumran has come to increase this stock with new fragments from the books of Exodus, Leviticus, Numbers, Deuteronomy and the Letter of Jeremiah, from Caves 4 and 7.[18] In spite of the meagre amount of documents recovered, the repercussions of these finds for LXX studies and its origins are enormous. In fact, the Greek manuscripts from Qumran certainly support P. Lagarde's theory on the origins of this version. The emergence of Greek texts of the Pentateuch a century and a half or two centuries from the Alexandrian translation, and which fit in perfectly with the textual tradition represented by the great uncial codices, tips the balance, we think conclusively, in favour of Lagarde's theory rather than Kahle's. At the same time, they reveal to us a new facet of the early history of the LXX: the recensional activity did not begin with Origen, nor was it even motivated by Jewish-Christian polemics, but goes back to a period quite close to the origins of the translation itself, when the LXX was transmitted within the Jewish communities and had not yet cut the umbilical cord that tied it to the Hebrew text.

The other important group of Greek texts comes from a cave lying on the southern slope of Naḥal Ḥever, a few kilometres south of En-Gedi. They are important fragments of a parchment scroll, which Barthélemy presented in a pioneering article to the academic world in 1953.[19] Ten years later he published a transcription together with a study of its implications for the history of the LXX, possibly the most stimulating monograph of recent decades in the field of the Greek Bible.[20] As late as 1962, B. Lifshitz published other fragments

---

[18] See E. Ulrich, "The Greek Manuscripts of the Pentateuch from Qumrân, Including Newly-Identified Fragments of Deuteronomy (4QLXXDeut)", *De Septuaginta*, 1984, 71–82, and Ulrich, "The Septuagint Manuscripts from Qumran: A Reappraisal of their Value", P. W. Skehan, E. C. Ulrich, J. E. Sanderson, *Qumran Cave 4. IV: Palaeo-Hebrew and Greek Biblical Manuscripts*. DJD IX, Oxford, 1992.

[19] D. Barthélemy, "Redécouverte d'un chaînon manquant de l'histoire de la Septante", *RB* 60 (1953), 18–29.

[20] D. Barthélemy, *Les Devanciers d'Aquila*. VTS 10 (1963).

from the same cave which belonged to the same scroll of the Minor Prophets.[21] And finally in 1990, the official edition came out with all the fragments published previously plus other additional unidentified fragments, photographs, a palaeographic study and a reconstruction of the text based on detailed analysis of the translation techniques, the spelling and the condition of the preserved sections.[22] In the palaeographic study of these documents, P. J. Parsons opted for dating them towards the end of the 1st century BCE.[23]

With the obligatory refinements in matters of detail, Barthélemy's fundamental thesis, according to which these fragments belong to a consistent revision of the LXX to bring it close to a Hebrew text very similar to but not identical with the proto-Masoretic text, has been firmly accepted. Some of the particular features of this revision which Barthélemy noted,[24] and others identified in later studies, can be debated. It is also possible to discuss the length and identification of this revision in other books of the Bible as well as its uniformity since it seems instead that it forms part of a longer translation with its own characteristics in the other books. Or its relationship to rabbinic hermeneutics of the 1st century CE could be discussed. However, there is absolutely no doubt that these fragments belong to the LXX, which we knew through more reliable ancient witnesses, but it was revised to adapt it with greater literalism to the current Hebrew text. This proof also consolidates P. de Lagarde's hypothesis about the unity of the translation as against an original pluralism as postulated by P. Kahle.

The finds from Naḥal Ḥever, together with its general interpretation within the framework of the early history of the LXX provided by Barthélemy, became an obligatory reference point for all later studies. Displayed before us was a new image of the pre-Hexaplar LXX, a shadowy zone of which we knew scarcely anything were it not for the quotations in the NT, some pseudepigraphical writings, the Jewish-Hellenistic historians, Philo, Josephus and the writings of Justin. And it had important consequences, as we shall see, for the

---

[21] B. Lifshitz, "The Greek Documents from the Cave of Horror", *IEJ* 12 (1962), 201–207.

[22] E. Tov, with the collaboration of R. A. Kraft, and a contribution by P. J. Parsons, *The Greek Minor Prophets Scroll from Naḥal Ḥever(8ḤevXIIgr): The Seiyâl Collection*. DJD VIII, Oxford 1990.

[23] Tov, *The Greek Minor Prophets*, 26.

[24] Barthélemy, *Les Devanciers d'Aquila*, 48–78.

image we have of the three more recent Jewish translators, Aquila, Symmachus and Theodotion through the ancient sources.[25]

However, the documents from Qumran have revolutionised the textual history of the LXX due to the Greek fragments discussed and due to the Hebrew texts discovered there, related in one way or another with the *Vorlage* used by the Greek translators. In first place must be mentioned the recovery of new originals in Hebrew or Aramaic for books or parts of books which were unknown until now, such as the five manuscripts, four in Hebrew and one in Aramaic, of the book of Tobit found in Cave 4, or the appearance in Cave 11 (11QPs[a]) of two Hebrew compositions undoubtedly related with an ancestor from which the Greek translation of Psalm 151 came. No less important is the discovery of readings that are different from the *textus receptus* but that agree with LXX readings; before Qumran these were usually explained as the result of a different exegetical tradition and not as belonging to a different textual tradition. For example, 4QGen–Exod[a], from the Herodian period, agrees with the LXX that Jacob had seventy-five descendants instead of seventy as transmitted by the *textus receptus*. 4QDeut[d] contains the final verses of the Song of Moses (Deuteronomy 32) in a composite text which for the first time provides us with readings in Hebrew which underlie the forms these verses have in the LXX.[26] Even though these occasional agreements should not be exaggerated and one should not make hasty and more wide-ranging classifications about the various textual types, to some extent in connection with the LXX one can speak of a nemesis of Qumran in much the same way that E. G. Turner spoke of a "papyrological nemesis [which] awaits those who, without good reason, throw away explicit ancient testimonies".[27]

Among the Hebrew documents from Qumran, those that merit special attention are the ones that contribute fragments of a different text from the *textus receptus* not only in actual variants but also from the literary aspect. In Cave 4, fragments of Samuel and Jeremiah were found with a text very close to the one used as a *Vorlage* by

---

[25] See *infra* chapters 7, 8 and 9.

[26] P. W. Skehan, "A Fragment of the 'Song of Moses' (Deuteronomy 32) from Qumran", and Fernández Marcos, "La Septuaginta y los hallazgos del Desierto de Judá", 236–38.

[27] "It is clear that a papyrological nemesis awaits those who, without good reason, throw away explicit ancient testimonies," E. G. Turner, *Greek Papyri: An Introduction*, Oxford 1968, p. 100.

the translators of the LXX. From the beginning these facts provoked an avalanche of studies on the biblical text and a fierce debate, which is still open, in the hope that the complete publication of the documents from Qumran can throw some new light on the theories circulating today. The best known is the theory of local texts set out by F. M. Cross in 1953 and retained with a few refinements until his most recent publications.[28] It is the only theory claiming to explain in full the history of the biblical text. It postulates, at least for the Pentateuch, the existence of three textual families from three different places, which Cross identifies as Egypt (*Vorlage* of the LXX, from a full text, though not always, related at its oldest stage to the Palestinian text), Palestine (which is an expansionist text) and Babylonia (with a short text, where preserved). The lack of links that would allow us to reconstruct all the vicissitudes of the complex textual history, and its somewhat speculative nature, have caused this hypothesis of local texts, followed in general by Cross's disciples and the Harvard school, to be received cautiously by others and even to be rejected.[29] It has also to explain the fact that among the documents of Qumran, i.e. in the same geographical area, very different textual types are being discovered that are proto-Masoretic, proto-Samaritan, Septuagintal and of other types which for lack of better terminology are called "independent". However, in spite of the vulnerability of Cross' theory of local texts, today the coexistence of different textual types is accepted as fact at least during the two centuries before the standardisation of the consonantal text. Furthermore, specialists such as S. Talmon and E. Tov postulate greater pluralism or question the very concept of textual type.[30] Talmon focuses his attention on the

---

[28] F. M. Cross, "A New Biblical Fragment Related to the Original Hebrew Underlying the Septuagint"; Cross, "The History of the Biblical Text in the Light of Discoveries of the Judaean Desert"; Cross, "The Contribution of the Qumran Discoveries to the Study of the Biblical Text"; Cross, "The Evolution of a Theory of Local Texts", *Qumran and the History of the Biblical Text*, 306–321; Cross, "Some Notes on a Generation of Qumran Studies", *The Madrid Qumran Congress* I, 1992, 1–21.

[29] See R. Hanhart, "Zum gegenwärtigen Stand der Septuagintaforschung", *De Septuaginta*, 1984, 3–18, p. 10; G. Howard, "Frank Cross and Recensional Criticism"; S. Talmon, "The Old Testament Text I", *The Cambridge History of the Bible*, I, 193–99.

[30] See S. Talmon, "The Textual Study of the Bible: A New Outlook", S. Talmon, F. M. Cross, eds, *Qumran and The History of the Biblical Text*, 321–401; E. Tov, "Determining the Relationship between the Qumran Scrolls and the LXX: Some Methodological Issues", *The Hebrew and the Greek Text of Samuel*, 45–67; Tov, "A Modern Textual Outlook Based on the Qumran Scrolls".

sociological groups which conditioned the transmission of the text. According to him, of the various textual groups in existence only those survived which counted on the support of a religious community entrusted with transmitting them, the Samaritan community for the Samaritan Pentateuch, the pharisaic–rabbinic community for the pre-Masoretic text and the Christian community for the text of the LXX. In his analysis, instead, E. Tov highlights not only the agreements between the Qumran texts and some of the texts previously known, such as the Masoretic Text, the Samaritan Pentateuch or the LXX, but stresses the many disagreements or independent readings that prevent these texts from being included in a particular textual group. He picks out a series of Qumran texts which he calls non-aligned, either because they follow an inconsistent pattern of agreements and disagreements with the Masoretic, Samaritan or LXX text, or because they are texts in some sense independent of these three traditions. According to E. Tov, these texts include about 15% of the documents from Qumran.[31] B. Chiesa has joined in the debate, criticising the methodology of Tov's analysis from a tradition which is deeply rooted in textual criticism like the classical tradition and particularly the Italian school. For Chiesa the textual filiation of a document does not have to be defined by agreements or disagreements between each other or from unique or exceptional variants. The latter are useful only to set a text in its cultural and historical context, because they are ideological variants. In textual criticism, instead, what matters is the nature of the variants and especially the conjunctive or disjunctive mistakes that enable the textual filiation of the various witnesses to be determined. Based on this type of reading and in spite of the plurality of texts, for B. Chiesa it is possible to sketch out a *stemma* or at least make an attempt, of the biblical texts in order to reach the base text.[32] E. Ulrich opts for a more conciliatory stance. He emphasises on the one hand our need for a more precise terminology in the debate, and on the other the urgency of further studies which will specify to what extent the various theories are adapted to the new data appearing right now when publication of the documents has been considerably speeded

---

[31] E. Tov, "Some Notes on a Generation of Qumran Studies: A Replay", *The Madrid Qumran Congress I*, 1992, 15–21, p. 20.
[32] B. Chiesa, "Textual History and Textual Criticism of the Hebrew Old Testament", *The Madrid Qumran Congress I*, 1992, 257–72.

up.[33] And A. S. van der Woude, without concealing the textual pluralism that has become apparent in the documents from Qumran,
insists that we should not simply take for granted a similar pluralism in the priestly circles of Jerusalem and among the Temple scribes.
According to van der Woude, the events of 70 CE hastened the final
phase of the standardisation of the text, but this was not the result
of an historical accident or of a drastic recension by pharisaic Judaism.
Instead it had been gestating as a tendency since the beginning of
the 1st century CE in certain circles of Judaism, as can be perceived
from the corrections in the Twelve Prophets fragments from Naḥal
Ḥever towards a proto-Masoretic type of text.[34]

However, beyond the present debate concerning different textual
types, their terminology and the facts of the various theories, we
should not lose sight of the re-evaluation of the text of the LXX
due to many readings being confirmed in the Hebrew documents
from Qumran and the verification of Hebrew base texts which underlie the great changes evident in that translation as against the Masoretic
text in books such as Samuel and Jeremiah.[35] Its disagreements with
the *textus receptus* may in theory go back to a Hebrew *Vorlage* which is
earlier than the standardisation of the consonantal text. Furthermore,
in some books the Greek translation was made before the final redaction of the book had been completed in the form it has today in
the Masoretic text. This is why, as we shall see below, the LXX has
become the chief source of information that affects the literary criticism of the Old Testament.

c) *The Use of the Septuagint in Hebrew Textual Criticism*

The impact of the Qumran finds on the history of the biblical text
has also produced, in parallel fashion, a transformation in the use
of the Greek Bible in biblical text criticism. According to the latest

---

[33] E. Ulrich, "Pluriformity in the Biblical Text, Text Groups, and Questions of
Canon".
[34] A. S. van der Woude, "Pluriformity and Uniformity: Reflections on the
Transmission of the Text of the Old Testament".
[35] For the book of Jeremiah, see J. G. Janzen, *Studies in the Texts of Jeremiah*,
Cambridge, Mass. 1973, and E. Tov, "Some Aspects of the Textual and Literary
History of the Book of Jeremiah"; and P.-M. Bogaert, "De Baruch à Jéremie. Les
deux rédactions conservées du livre de Jéremie", *Le livre de Jérémie. Le prophète et son
milieu. Les oracles et leur transmission* ed. A.-M. Bogaert, Leuven 1981, 145–67 and
168–73 respectively.

studies on the history of the biblical text, there are two principles that should govern the use of the LXX for the edition of the Hebrew text: (1) the existence of textual pluralism in the period before the Common Era, and (2) the polymorphism of texts within the LXX itself, that is to say, the differences evident in the process of translation and transmission of the various books.

Thanks to the documents from Qumran, today we are aware of something that neither Origen nor Jerome could have suspected, in spite of realising that there were differences between the LXX and the Hebrew text of their time: the Greek Bible contains genuine, textual and literary variants from the Hebrew to the extent that we have to respect both traditions, without trying to reduce or adjust one to the other. As a result, in some books of the Old Testament, the Hebrew and the Greek transmit differing editions which, in the present state of our knowledge, cannot be reduced to a common original. In such cases the practice of resorting to the LXX for critical restoration of the Hebrew text is not only utopian but methodologically incorrect.[36] From the moment that the priority of one tradition over the other cannot be proved, one of them cannot be used to correct the other, because it is not always easy to distinguish between textual evolution and the literary evolution of the various traditions. In these cases, before attempting to restore the original it would be more prudent to reconstruct each of the different traditions in which a particular biblical book has come to us.[37] The sociological dimension of the text emphasised by S. Talmon also counsels respect for the various traditions that the different religious groups transmit,[38] a procedure which in their way the authors of the Polyglot Bibles used in editing synoptically the different texts that were circulating in the various ancient languages.

However, this allegiance of the LXX to its *Vorlage* in large discrepancies has helped to increase caution also in the case of the smaller variants. Even so, in these latter cases, before resorting to the hypothesis of a different Hebrew *Vorlage*, other possible explanations that are more plausible have to be eliminated as new critical editions of

---

[36] See D. Barthélemy, *Études d'histoire du texte de l'Ancien Testament*, Freiburg–Göttingen 1978, 368–69, and Barthélemy, *Critique textuelle de l'Ancien Testament. 1 Josué, Juges, Ruth, Samuel, Rois, Chroniques, Esdras, Néhémie, Esther*, Freiburg–Göttingen 1982, *107 and *111.

[37] D. Barthélemy, "Études d'histoire du texte", pp. 368–69, and Barthélemy, "L'enchevêtrement de l'histoire textuelle", pp. 38–40.

[38] S. Talmon, "The Textual Study of the Bible", p. 327.

the LXX continue to appear and improve our knowledge of the translation techniques of the various books and of Hebrew lexicography and Jewish exegesis.[39] That is to say, the use of the LXX in text criticism has become much more complex and refined after Qumran. And only by taking into account all the aspects mentioned will we avoid in future the criticisms deserved by its inappropriate use in earlier editions of the *Biblia Hebraica*.[40] In the minor discrepancies and variants we have to remember some of the principles set out by J. W. Wevers after long years of experience as editor of the Pentateuch in the *series major* of Göttingen: (1) Above all the nature and limitations of the target language for reproducing the source language have to be understood. We need to be aware that grammatical elements cannot be translated. And before searching for a possible different *Vorlage* or for a theological background of the translator, the first question to be resolved must be to what extent the discrepancies between the LXX and the Hebrew text are conditioned by the linguistic possibilities of Greek to express the linguistic structure and peculiar features of the source language.[41] (2) Before quoting evidence from the Septuagint there must be some certainty that the reading in question is authentic LXX and not the result of internal corruption in the Greek or a copyist's error. And (3) before using the LXX properly in Hebrew text criticism, the distinctive points of view and procedures used by the particular translator in his translation have to be known.

To summarise, the LXX contains, in Tov's words, "more *significant* variants than all other textual witnesses together. Furthermore, apart from a few scrolls from Qumran, the LXX is the only source that contains a relatively large number of variants which bear on the *literary* criticism of the OT".[42] In these last cases and with the infor-

---

[39] See J. Barr, "The Use of Evidence from the Versions", *Comparative Philology and the Text of the Old Testament*, Oxford 1968, 238–72; E. Tov, *The Text-Critical Use of the Septuagint in Biblical Research*, Jerusalem 1981, and A. Aejmelaeus, "What can We Know about the Hebrew *Vorlage* of the Septuagint?", *On the Trial of Septuagint Translators. Collected Essays by A. Aejmelaeus*, Kampen 1993, 77–115.

[40] For an account of these criticisms, see Fernández Marcos, "The Use of the Septuagint in the Criticism of the Hebrew Bible", 63–66.

[41] See J. W. Wevers, "The Use of Versions for Text Criticism: The Septuagint", and the clear-sighted article by J. Heller, "Grenzen sprachlicher Entsprechung der LXX. Ein Beitrag zur Übersetzungstechnik der LXX auf dem Gebiet der Flexionskategorien", *MIOF* 15 (1969), 234–48.

[42] E. Tov, *The Text-Critical Use of the Septuagint*, p. 272.

mation we now have, we should respect the autonomy and special nature of the translation as witness of a different literary tradition from the *textus receptus*. As is evident, in such cases it does not seem reasonable to use it as a source for restoring the authentic Hebrew text.[43] However, in spite of all these reservations, in most of the books, the LXX variants, when used intelligently and with due caution, with the premises set out above, can become an important aid for biblical text criticism and for editing the Hebrew text.

Nor should there be any need to say that this subsidiary use of the LXX to explain difficult Hebrew passages is little more than an insignificant part of the correct use of this version, since it is not possible to ignore other dimensions that only recently have come to the fore: its repercussions on the literary criticism of the Old Testament, and interest in it as an autonomous literary work within the Greek linguistic system.[44]

d) *Textual Criticism and Literary Criticism*

Reflection over recent years on the history of the biblical text and the various text traditions has unleashed a series of studies on the effect of textual criticism on the literary criticism of the Bible.[45] Textual criticism is concerned with the transmission of the text once it has been fixed. Literary criticism, instead, studies the period of the literary formation of a book or set of books until the final edit. The problem arises when parts of a biblical book or early editions of complete books have been put into writing and circulated before the literary editing was complete. This is the case for the LXX translation: the translation was completed at a particular time in history and later the Hebrew texts of some of the books were re-edited with

---

[43] See D. Barthélemy, *Critique textuelle de l'Ancien Testament*, p. *111: "Mais le Comité a senti de plus en plus clairement la nécessité de ne pas déflorer la Septante pour retoucher le Texte Massorétique. Aucune de ces formes traditionnelles ne doit être traitée comme une carrière d'où l'on tirerait les bonnes leçons avec lesquelles on reconstruirait un texte original."

[44] Emphasised particularly by M. Harl and her team in the French translation of the Septuagint, *La Bible d'Alexandrie 1–5*, Paris 1986–95.

[45] See E. Tov, *The Text-Critical Use of the Septuagint*, 293–306; Tov, *Textual Criticism of the Hebrew Bible*, 313–49, with an extensive bibliography, and J. Trebolle Barrera, *The Jewish Bible and the Christian Bible*, translated from the Spanish by W. G. E. Watson, Leiden–New York–Köln 1998, pp. 389–97.

expansions, revisions or alterations of a different kind. Editions were put into circulation that were later replaced by new revised editions of the same book, revised editions which became official in the canonisation process of the Hebrew text. As a result, the first editions have only been preserved for posterity either by chance, as in the case of the texts found in Qumran, or else because they were transmitted by non-Jewish communities, such as the Christian community in the case of the LXX.

This problem should not be confused with the problem posed by the existence of double texts within the Septuagintal tradition, discussed in the next chapter. In fact the double texts of Judges, Daniel, Esther or Tobit belong to the text tradition of the LXX, most of them have a textual connection with that translation and only indirectly can they affect the literary criticism of those books. Other cases such as Job, Proverbs or Ben Sira display problems that are much too complex to be included in this section, since it is not easy to prove that the differences between the Masoretic text and the Greek translation of these books go back to editions that are different from the Hebrew. With respect to Job, at least, my view is that these differences are due to the translation techniques used.[46] Consequently, there are differences in extent, which are now considered to belong only to literary layers that are earlier than or parallel to what is found in the editions of the Masoretic text, whether they are chapters, sections or complete books.

Of course, in describing these phenomena no decision is being made about the literary priority of either text. In fact, there is a subjective dimension in this description which is apparent when one notices that their number and contents fluctuate, depending on the scholar. The problem worsens because the discussion combines data from the LXX (often supported by the Old Latin) and Qumran on the one hand and data from the Masoretic Text, the Targum, Peshitta and Vulgate on the other. As the problem has been posed only recently, it is not surprising that this section is still germinating and requires further screening which will only happen as new studies continue to make clear the borders of these vast regions where text criticism and literary criticism overlap. In fact, only in the light of all the published witnesses and a comparative study of them will it be possible to speak of different editions, different *Vorlage*, or to estab-

---

[46] See N. Fernández Marcos, "The Septuagint Reading of the Book of Job", *The Book of Job*, ed., W. A. M. Beuken, Leuven 1994, 251–66.

lish connections which lead to a genetic dependence among the different texts. Accordingly, in what follows I refer briefly only to those cases on which there is most agreement.

The book of Jeremiah

As is well known, the Greek text of Jeremiah is one-sixth shorter than the Masoretic text, i.e. about 2,700 words of the *textus receptus* are missing from the Greek version. In addition, the sequence of chapters and verses is often different in the Hebrew from the Greek version. The dilemma facing biblical criticism is whether these differences are due to the Greek translator or whether he translated a Hebrew text that is not the same as the one we have. When the fragments 4QJer[b] and 4QJer[d], which replicate these two main features of the LXX text, became known, it seemed clear, as is evident from the studies by J. G. Janzen and E. Tov, that the LXX translated a Hebrew text that was close to the one found in Qumran Cave 4.[47] Indeed, 4QJer[b] contains readings from Jer. 9:22–10:18 which are fragmentary but by good luck they confirm the sequence and peculiar arrangement of the LXX in 10:5-10 against the Masoretic text. Just like the LXX, Qumran transposes v. 5 after v. 9 and omits vv. 6-8 and 10. E. Tov and P.-M. Bogaert interpret these facts in the same way as J. G. Janzen, emphasising their repercussions for the literary criticism of the book of Jeremiah. The translator of Jeremiah did not shorten the Hebrew text as many exegetes had thought but instead, to judge from the comparative study of these two texts, it was the redactor of the Masoretic text who edited an expanded form of a text similar to the *Vorlage* of the LXX. Accordingly, Jeremiah-LXX reflects a first, shorter edition of Jeremiah, which is earlier than the second enlarged edition transmitted by the Masoretic text.[48]

---

[47] See J. G. Janzen, *Studies in the Texts of Jeremiah*, Cambridge, Mass. 1973, and E. Tov, "Some Aspects of the Textual History of the Book of Jeremiah", 145–67. Sonderlund has recently opposed it in a recent study of Janzen's thesis (see S. Sonderlund, *The Greek Text of Jeremiah: A Revised Hypothesis*, Sheffield 1985, 193–248), and opts for an intermediate position, i.e. a translator who follows a shorter Hebrew *Vorlage* who also abbreviates. However, Janzen has replied, refuting Sonderlund's thesis, see J. G. Janzen, "A Critique of Sven Sonderlund's *The Greek Text of Jeremiah: A Revised Hypothesis*", *BIOSCS* 22 (1989), 16–47.

[48] See E. Tov, *Textual Criticism of the Hebrew Bible*, 319–27, and P.-M. Bogaert, "De Baruch à Jérémie. Les deux rédactions conservées du livre de Jérémie", *Le Livre de Jérémie. Le prophète et son milieu, les oracles et leur transmission*, ed. P.-M. Bogaert, Leuven 1981, 168–73, and Bogaert, "*Urtext*, texte court et relecture: Jérémie XXXIII 14–26 TM et ses préparations", *Congress Volume Leuven 1989*, ed. J. A. Emerton, Leiden 1991, 236–47.

Other literary units or sections of books
Besides the book of Jeremiah, other sections of books have been noticed in which the text of the LXX may affect their literary development: Exodus 35–40 (LXX), a parallel account of the building of the tabernacle which is considerably different from the Masoretic text, unlike Exodus 25–31 (LXX) where it follows it very closely;[49] the transition of the book of Joshua to Judges, where Josh. 24:33 (LXX) adds a section that may reflect an earlier stage in the development of the Masoretic text;[50] the different redactions of the David and Goliath story (1 Sam. 16–18), which is very much shorter in the ancient LXX than in the Masoretic text, although the interpretation of these facts has not yet been agreed among biblical scholars;[51] the differing chronologies reflected in the Greek and Hebrew texts of 1–2 Kings;[52] Ez. 36:23c-38, which is missing from Papyrus 967 of the LXX and the *Wirceburgensis* codex of the Old Latin, and the same applies to chapters 36–39 which are set out in different ways in this papyrus and in the Masoretic text,[53] although some scholars prefer to explain the omission in Papyrus 967 as a problem of internal transmission in Greek.

If these phenomena, or some of them, occurred in the period of literary growth of the biblical book before its final edition was concluded, they have to be analysed by using the methods of literary criticism but not the criteria of text criticism. However, since they came to light from comparing the different traditions of the biblical text, it is necessary to combine the information obtained from both types of criticism to reach a suitable solution to the problem. Text criticism and literary criticism each have their methods which must

---

[49] See A. Aejmelaeus, "Septuagintal Translation Techniques: A Solution to the Problem of the Tabernacle Account", *Septuagint, Scrolls and Cognate Writings*, 1992, 381–402. Aejmelaeus opts for a middle solution in which the use of a different *Vorlage* and various free translation techniques are not mutually exclusive.

[50] See A. Rofé, "The End of the Book of Joshua according to the Septuagint", *Henoch* 4 (1982), 17–36.

[51] See D. Barthélemy, D. Gooding, J. Lust, E. Tov, *The Story of David and Goliath, Textual and Literary Criticism*, Freiburg–Göttingen 1986.

[52] J. D. Shenkel, *Chronology and Recensional Development in the Greek Text of Kings*, Cambridge, Mass. 1968.

[53] See P.-M. Bogaert, "Le témoignage de la Vetus Latina dans l'étude de la tradition des Septante-Ézéchiel et Daniel dans le Papyrus 967", *Bib* 59 (1978), 384–95, and E. Tov, "Recensional Differences between the MT and the LXX of Ezekiel", *ETL* 62 (1986), 89–101.

not intrude on each other's analysis. In any event, they bring us to a frontier zone of the history of the biblical text, the study of which has been outlined barely, that demands the collaboration of different disciplines and the application of much energy before more satisfactory and convincing results are obtained.

Select Bibliography

Aejmelaeus, A., "What can We Know about the Hebrew *Vorlage* of the Septuagint?". *ZAW* 99 (1987), 58–89.

Albright, W. F., "New Light on Early Recensions of the Hebrew Bible". *BASOR* 137 (1955), 27–34.

Barthélemy, D., "L'enchevêtrement de l'histoire textuelle et de l'histoire littéraire dans les relations existant entre la Septante et le Texte Massorétique". *De Septuaginta*, 1984, 21–40.

Chiesa, B., "Textual History and Textual Criticism of the Old Testament". *The Madrid Qumran Congress I*, 1992, 257–72.

Cross, F. M., "A New Qumran Biblical Fragment Related to the Original Hebrew Underlying the LXX". *BASOR* 132 (1953), 15–26.

———., "The Contribution of the Qumran Discoveries to the Study of the Biblical Text". *IEJ* 16 (1966), 81–95.

———, "The History of the Biblical Text in the Light of Discoveries in the Judean Desert". *HTR* 57 (1964), 281–99.

Cross, F. M., and S. Talmon (eds), *Qumran and the History of the Biblical Text*, Cambridge, Mass.–London 1975.

Fernández Marcos, N., "La Septuaginta y los hallazgos del Desierto de Judá". *Simposio Bíblico Español*, 1984, 229–45.

———, "The Use of the Septuagint in the Criticism of the Hebrew Bible". *Sefarad* 47 (1987), 59–72.

Goshen-Gottstein, M. H., "Theory and Practice of Textual Criticism: The Text-critical Use of the Septuagint". *Textus* 3 (1963), 130–58.

Howard, G., "Frank Cross and Recensional Criticism". *VT* 21 (1971), 440–50.

Margolis, M. L., "Complete Induction for the Identification of the Vocabulary in the Greek Versions of the Old Testament with its Semitic Equivalents: Its Necessity and the Means of Obtaining it". *JAOS* 30 (1910), 301–12.

Olmstead, A. T., "Source Study and the Biblical Text". *AJSL* 31 (1913/14), 1–35.

Rabin, C., "The Dead Sea Scrolls and the History of the OT Text". *JTS* ns 6 (1955), 174–82.

Seeligmann, I. L., "Indications of Editorial Alteration and Adaptation in the Masoretic Text and in the Septuagint". *VT* 11 (1961), 201–21.

Skehan, P. W., "A Fragment of the 'Song of Moses' (Dt 32) from Qumran". *BASOR* 136 (1954), 12–15.

Talmon, S., "Aspects of the Textual Transmission of the Bible in the Light of Qumran Manuscripts". *Textus* 4 (1964), 95–132.

Tov, E., "A Modern Textual Outlook Based on the Qumran Scrolls". *HUCA* 53 (1982), 11–27.

———, "Some Reflections on the Hebrew Texts from which the Septuagint Was Translated". *JNSL* 19 (1993), 107–22.

———, *Textual Criticism of the Hebrew Bible*, Minneapolis–Assen–Maastricht 1992.

———, "The Contribution of the Qumran Scrolls to the Understanding of the LXX". *Septuagint, Scrolls and Cognate Writings*, 1992, 11–47.

———— (ed.), *The Hebrew and Greek Texts of Samuel*, Jerusalem 1980.
————, "The Nature of the Hebrew Text Underlying the LXX: A Survey of the Problems". *JSOT* 7 (1978), 53–68.
————, *The Text-Critical Use of the Septuagint in Biblical Research*, Jerusalem 1997.
Ulrich, E. C., "Horizons of Old Testament Textual Research at the Thirtieth Anniversary of Qumran Cave 4". *CBQ* 46 (1984), 613–36.
————, "Pluriformity in the Biblical Text, Text Groups, and Questions of Canon". *The Madrid Qumran Congress I*, 1992, 23–41.
————, "The Septuagint Manuscripts from Qumran: A Reappraisal of their Value". *Septuagint, Scrolls and Cognate Writings*, 1992, 49–80.
Wevers, J. W., "The Use of Versions for Text Criticism: the Septuagint". *La Septuaginta* 1985, 15–24.
Woude, A. S. van der, "Pluriformity and Uniformity. Reflections on the Transmission of the Text of the Old Testament". *Sacred History and Sacred Texts in Early Judaism*, J. N. Bremmer and F. García Martínez, eds, Kampen 1992, 151–69.

This can be supplemented by the extensive recent bibliography on the topic compiled by C. Dogniez, *BS* 52–70.

CHAPTER SIX

THE DOUBLE TEXTS OF THE GREEK BIBLE AND TARGUMISM

a) *Introduction*

In the preceding chapter we considered Kahle's position which he defended throughout his life – the targumic and plural origin of the LXX. His thesis is based on quotations from the Old Testament in the New, and on the biblical text of Philo and Josephus. He uses only indirectly the argument of double texts that Septuagintal tradition has transmitted to us for some books. And, according to Kahle, Acts 7:4-32 follows a popular text very close to the Samaritan Pentateuch; the Hebrew text presupposed by the book of Jubilees agrees at times with the Samaritan Pentateuch and sometimes with the text of the LXX, but it rarely goes with the Hebrew *textus receptus*. He comes to the same conclusions in the book of Enoch, the Assumption of Moses and 4 Ezra, especially with respect to the numbers and chronologies used. Targum Onqelos and Targum Jonathan are only revisions based on a biblical text of earlier Targums that were in circulation at least for private use.[1] And, according to Kahle, the same happened with the LXX. Various Greek translations were circulating. However, at a given moment, to which the *Letter of Aristeas* refers, an official revision of them was commissioned and this is

---

[1] On the existence of these earlier Targums, see A. Díez Macho, "Targum", *EncBibl* VI (1965), 865–81, p. 867. Remains of some of them have been found in Qumran, such as the Targum of Job from Cave 11, written in the time of Gamaliel the Elder, Paul's teacher.

The quotations and allusions in the pseudepigrapha comprise a topic that has scarcely been studied and is, no doubt, promising. The entry is missing from the *CB* by Brock–Fritsch–Jellicoe and in the *BS* by C. Dogniez, indicating how little it is discussed; and it is missing from the *SMS* by Jellicoe and in Swete's manual, *An Introduction to the Old Testament in Greek*, Cambridge 1914. Even though Swete devotes a whole chapter (pp. 369ff.) to the use made of the LXX by Hellenistic authors (Greeks and Jews) where he extends his analysis to the fragments of Jewish-Hellenistic historians, Wisdom, Sira, 2 and 4 Maccabees, and the Jewish sections of the Sibylline Oracles. On the use of the LXX in the *Letter of Pseudo-Aristeas*, see chapter 3, n. 21, above.

basically what we call the LXX. Nevertheless, remains of the translations earlier than the official revision have been preserved in LXX manuscripts, in the biblical quotations in the New Testament and in Philo, Josephus and the intertestamental pseudepigrapha.[2] Fewer variants were transmitted in the Pentateuch, as the official revision had been imposed more rigorously. However, in the rest of the LXX many traces of this textual pluralism persist as these writings were less binding for the Jews. Hence we have as proof the double text of Judges or the Theodotionic text of Daniel.

As we have just seen, although Kahle mentions the double texts, he puts no emphasis on them when developing his theory. He only mentions the books of Judges and Daniel, ignoring others that might have favoured his hypothesis by supporting it with new data, such as the double texts of Tobit and Habakkuk 3. Thus it seems appropriate to examine systematically the double texts of the LXX in the light of more recent studies both of the LXX and of targumism, which since Kahle, has been the subject of new and brilliant studies by A. Díez Macho and his school.

On the other hand, the name Targum, which is used for the LXX in recent publications,[3] requires a clarification of the specific translation techniques of the Greek Bible in relation to targumism. In the perspective of the Greek double texts of the LXX, this examination has not been carried out systematically, not even in Kahle's time. The same applies to later studies. If we survey the few articles on the Targum and the LXX we realise that they are limited to the study of a few occasional parallels, for example the articles by

---

[2] P. Kahle, "Untersuchungen zur Geschichte" (= *Opera Minora*), 36: "Die Geschichte der griechischen Pentateuchübersetzung ist gleichbedeutend mit einer allmählichen Angleichung von Übersetzungen, die dem alten Vulgärtext nahestanden – von dem sich eine Gestalt bei den Samaritanern erhielt – an den *textus receptus* der Juden. Die älteste Form dieser Übersetzung rekonstruiren zu wollen, ist eine Utopie. Man wird im besten Fall eine oder die andere Revision dieser Übersetzung mit einiger Sicherheit bestimmen können. Die weitere Verbreitung einer Textgestalt ist zumeist erst die Folge von Überarbeitungen und steht am Abschlusse einer gewissen Entwicklung."

[3] Díez Macho, *El Targum*, 8. The Targums are "translations from the Hebrew Bible into Aramaic for liturgical use in the synagogue. As they do not fulfil all these conditions, some versions such as the LXX and Peshitta are not called Targumim, even though the first has some Targum characteristics, except that is not an Aramaic translation" (*ibid.*, p. 112). "Usually the Targumim, including the literal ones, such as the *Targum of Job* from Qumran Cave 11, have some degree of paraphrase. In this respect the LXX has every right to be classed as a Targum" (*ibid.*, p. 113).

Brockington and Delekat on Isaiah, by Churgin on the Pentateuch or by Kaminka on the book of Proverbs.

Brockington analyses passages in which Isaiah-LXX inserts the idea of salvation that is not explicit in the Hebrew text. The Aramaic Targum of Isaiah also puts the same emphasis on salvation. Accordingly, both translations show the same trait of soteriological interpretation, though they do not include the element of salvation in the same passages. The similarity and the many parallels persist but there is no clear proof of borrowing or influence between the two versions. At most, the Targum of Isaiah and LXX depend on the same tradition, which to a large extent must have been oral and reflected a common source of traditional exegesis.[4] A few years later, when Delekat established the many agreements of interpretation between Isaiah-LXX and the Targum, he wondered whether the Greek translation of Isaiah might not be a revision of an Egyptian Aramaic Targum, with no need to resort to the Hebrew text.[5]

In the Pentateuch, Churgin found a few parallels such as the distinction made by the translators between θυσιαστήριον for 'altar of the religion of Israel' and βωμός for 'idolatrous altar',[6] a distinction retained by Targum Onqelos, Targum Jonathan and Targum Pseudo-Jonathan, since they translate the first term by *madbeha'* and the second by *'egora'*. However, it has to be accepted that the parallels collected and agreements in exegetical interpretation in the Pentateuch are somewhat meagre.[7]

For Proverbs, Kaminka provides a series of parallels between the LXX and the Targum, based on translation errors due to the confusion of certain consonants, to a different vocalisation of the Hebrew text or due to having induced a similar basic interpretation in both versions; and he adds a few passages in which the influence of the Aramaic Targum in the LXX can be suspected, also insinuating that the Targum is older and used unevenly in the Greek version.[8] It is

---

[4] See L. H. Brockington, "LXX and Targum", 85–86.

[5] L. Delekat, "Ein Septuagintatargum", 244: "Diese Erscheinungen zwingen die Frage zu stellen, ob nicht vielleicht Jes.-Gr. nur eine Supervision eines ägyptisch-aramäischen Targums ist, die möglicherweise ohne Zuziehung des hebräischen Textes aufgefertig wurde."

[6] See S. Daniel, *Recherches sur le vocabulaire du culte dans la Septante*, Paris 1966, 15–51.

[7] Churgin, "Targum and LXX".

[8] A. Kaminka, "LXX und Targum zu Proverbia", 174.

also important to note that the Aramaic translation of Proverbs diverges from the Hebrew text more than in any other book in a large number of passages which agree with LXX.[9] However, as a counter-argument to this approach, Gerleman's monograph[10] should not be forgotten. According to it, in LXX-Prov the Hellenising tendencies of the translator are evident as are the reminiscences of Homer and Plato which are evident particularly in the vocabulary, the reshaping of many phrases and even the insertion of Greek sayings and proverbs.

As we shall see at the end of the chapter, there has been a change of approach in this respect in more recent publications, which concentrates either on phenomena of a midrashic type in certain books of the LXX (Gooding) or on their translation techniques (Rabin, Talmon, Goshen–Gottstein).

Before moving on to examine the texts that have been transmitted in a double parallel tradition (either whole books or only a few chapters), two prior considerations need to be taken into account:

1. The first affects the distribution of these texts in the manuscripts. For example, the Vatican ms., both in Judges and in Tobit and Daniel is the one transmitting the shortest recension. This tendency to shorten the Vatican (which also lacks the two books of Maccabees) has already found a response in other publications.[11] Apart from Judges, which presents more complex problems, this short revision is followed by most of the minuscule mss.

2. The books of Daniel and Ezra–Nehemiah are the only two in the whole Bible of which we have no Targums, and are precisely the two books with part of the canonical text in Aramaic.

b) *Double Texts in the Septuagint*

The book of Daniel (LXX and Theodotion)
Until a few years ago the two parallel texts of the book of Daniel were not a problem in terms of the origin of the LXX; the text called θ' belonged – so it was thought – to Theodotion and at a certain moment (between the 3rd and 4th century CE, since *Pap* 967

---

[9] A. Kaminka, "LXX und Targum zu Proverbia", 171.
[10] G. Gerleman, *Studies in the Septuagint III: Proverbs*, Lund 1956.
[11] S. Jellicoe, "The Hesychian Recension Reconsidered", *JBL* 82 (1963), 409–18.

still contains the Septuagintal translation) it replaced the original translation. However, in 1966, A. Schmitt, one of Ziegler's disciples, published a monograph that upset this traditional image of the Theodotion of Daniel.[12] The germ of this work, carried out at Ziegler's request and directed by him, was already present in the edition of Daniel that he published for the Göttingen series.[13] Ziegler's intuition was confirmed by Schmitt's analysis. In text θ' of Daniel many words can be noticed which do not occur (or occur only rarely) in the LXX whereas they are attested in Symmachus. Many other indications point in this direction although they are not completely decisive, given our scant knowledge of Symmachus and his translation techniques. The deuterocanonical parts of the book (Susannah, Hymn of the Three Youths, Bel and the Dragon) indicate special contact with this translator. However, undoubtedly the most sensational conclusion is the denial of Theodotion's literary paternity for this text.[14] In spite of that, the relationship between the two parallel texts of Daniel remains unexplained, although it is not likely that they go back to a Targumic original. Instead, the various Greek texts of Daniel need to be analysed in the light of new texts of the book of Daniel which have been found in Qumran Cave 4, though their textual stratification has yet to be established.[15]

Schmitt's thesis opens the way for a solution to the problem of proto-Theodotion, due to the presence of Theodotionic readings in the New Testament and the Apostolic Fathers, i.e. prior to the historical Theodotion.[16] Since, as we shall see in the following chapters, successive revisions of the LXX increasingly complicate this

---

[12] Schmitt, *Stammt der sogenannte "θ'"-Text*.

[13] J. Ziegler, *Susanna-Daniel-Bel et Draco. Septuaginta XVI*, 2, Göttingen 1954, 28, n. 1.

[14] A. Schmitt, *Stammt der sogenannte "θ'"-Text*, 110–12: "Schon allein die Wortuntersuchung im 3. Kapitel (s. 102–107) zeigt eindeutig, dass auch dieser Teil des θ'-Textes nichts mit Theodotion zu tun hat" (p. 112). On the reservations expressed by D. Barthélemy regarding these conclusions by Schmitt, see chapter 9, n. 35. Busto Saiz has also reacted against Schmitt's thesis ("El texto teodociónico de Daniel y la traducción de Símaco") and rejects his suggestion that this text is related to Symmachus. However, Schmitt reaffirms his position in a recent article: see A. Schmitt, "Die griechische Danieltexte ("θ" und o') und das Theodotionproblem", *BZ* 36 (1992), 1–29.

[15] See E. Ulrich, "Daniel Manuscripts from Qumran. Part 1: A Preliminary Edition of 4QDan^a", *BASOR* 268 (1987), 17–37, and Ulrich, "Part 2: Preliminary Editions of 4QDan^b and 4QDan^c", *BASOR* 274 (1989), 3–26.

[16] See chapter 8.

stage of transmission, the only firm gain in this territory seems to be the moment of the fluctuation of the traditional image of the three Jewish translators as transmitted by the ancient sources. In the case of Daniel, the translation of the LXX was inadequate enough to be revised and replaced by θ'. Even so, Montgomery places the reviser of θ' on a par with Onqelos (he calls him the Hellenistic Onqelos). This revision was to be preceded by the oral Targums and does not exclude the possibility that there were literary predecessors of the historical Theodotion.[17]

Recent studies by Hamm, Schüpphaus, Koch and Grelot[18] have not substantially altered the approaches of Montgomery. Papyrus 967, edited by Hamm in its Daniel section, provides the pre-Hexaplaric text of LXX with scarcely any gaps; however, sometimes it follows the Hebrew text and text θ' against LXX. Should we postulate a common *Vorlage* for the LXX and text θ' in Daniel?

Schüpphaus limits his study to the deuterocanonical sections; according to text θ' this would suppose a reshaping of content and style of the Septuagintal version. Koch notes how text θ' brings proper names up to date; the author of this text would come from Syria rather than from Egypt. More specifically, his location would probably be one of the Hellenised cities of the Syro-Mesopotamian region in the transition period between Seleucid and Roman control. However, Koch accepts that more extensive research is required to resolve the problem.

For Grelot, Dan 4-LXX was translated from Hebrew due to the revival of that language because of the Maccabean revolt and the Qumran movement. Another Greek translator earlier than the New Testament took as the basis of his translation the main text in Hebrew–Aramaic which the synod of Yamnia was later to canonise; this was the origin of text θ' of Daniel.

---

[17] J. A. Montgomery, *Daniel*, 35ff., possibly the best study so far on the Greek texts of Daniel. On the problem of Proto-Theodotion he concludes (p. 50): "That there existed some such body of received translation before the Christian age lies beyond doubt; but we must not too quickly assume a written version. Very much can be explained by the hypothesis of a Hellenistic oral Targum, necessary in the first place for correction of faulty renderings, and specially of lacunae in G. (It is found that early 'Theodotionic' readings generally appear in such cases). And then we may link up this oral tradition of the early part of the 2d. Christian cent. He is the Hellenistic Onkelos, whose work was facilitated by the presence of the Scriptures, possessed by him *memoriter*. Of course such a theory does not exclude the possibility of literary predecessors of the historical Theodotion."

[18] See Select Bibliography.

It would seem that all the studies mentioned ignore or do not accept as convincing Barthélemy's conclusions in his important monograph on 'the forerunners of Aquila':[19] Theodotion is party leader of the καιγέ recension, Jonathan ben 'Uzziel, the only representative of the school of that name. His work belongs to the wider framework of the revision of the early LXX to fit it to the Hebrew text current in Palestine in the 1st century CE. By putting back the period of this revision by more than a century, a plausible explanation is found for the presence of Theodotionic readings in the New Testament and in 2nd century Christian writers. M. Delcor uses Barthélemy's explanation in his commentary on the book of Daniel.[20]

However, on this argument there remains an impasse which has not been satisfactorily resolved, nor will it until all the material attributed to Theodotion has undergone careful examination.[21] If Schmitt's thesis is confirmed, that text θ' of Daniel does not belong to Theodotion, it will not belong to the καίγε revision either. It would be *petitio principii* inasmuch as its belonging to this recension has been obtained by comparison with the Theodotionic material we have from which precisely the longest text, text θ' of Daniel, would have to be excluded. At present the most obvious solution is to look for it along the lines of greater flexibility in respect of attributions to the Hexapla and in respect of the actual structure of these revisions. Later revisions of the same book or even different editions of it cannot be excluded.[22] However, all that this tells us is that we are still far from finding a solution for the two parallel texts of Daniel. If, as Schmitt claims against traditional opinion, text θ' is not from Theodotion, at a later stage research must be carried out as to which translation school its author belongs or to which textual tradition its reviser is closest. When editing the book of Esther, Hanhart radicalised the problem even more by insisting on the need for specific research to establish on more solid criteria the priority of the

---

[19] The chapter on Aquila in D. Barthélemy, *Les Devanciers d'Aquila*. VTS 10 (1963).

[20] M. Delcor, *Le libre de Daniel*, Paris 1971.

[21] For a survey of the most important fragments attributed to Theodotion, see A. Schmitt, *Stammt der sogenannte "θ"-Text*, 112: *Anhang*. In his review of D. Barthélemy, *Les Devanciers d'Aquila*, Wevers expresses reservations about text-θ' of Daniel belonging to the καίγε recension; J. W. Wevers, *Septuaginta Forschungen seit 1954*. TR NF 33 (1968), 71: "Nicht so eindeutig ist der Beweis bei einigen Mss für Chron, bei Cant und dem Theod. Text von Daniel" (i.e. the proof that it also belongs to the καίγε recension).

[22] See D. Barthélemy, *Les Devanciers d'Aquila*, 156–57.

Septuagintal text of Daniel: "The obvious similarity between the translation style of 'text L' of Esther and of 'text-o' of Daniel requires a special examination, particularly in respect of the problem of whether the stated priority of 'text-o' as against 'text-θ' in Daniel rests on the same certain criteria as the priority of 'text-o' against 'text-L' of Esther."[23]

From the point of view that interests us here, i.e. the Greek double texts and targumism, it is appropriate to emphasise the results of two recent studies, although the whole problem of the history of the text in the book of Daniel is still far from being satisfactorily resolved. After a study of the Greek texts of Daniel and especially of Papyrus 967, Bogaert concludes that Theodotion's work is sometimes evident as a new translation and sometimes as a careful revision of his Septuagintal forerunner.[24] As for Jeansonne, he insists that the primitive LXX of Daniel 7–12 makes every effort to translate the underlying Semitic text with rigorous precision and it does not necessarily have to coincide with the actual Masoretic text. At all events, however, in the translation techniques there is no indication of any kind of theological bias corresponding to what can be found in the Targumim.[25]

The double text of Tobit

The book of Tobit has reached us in three text forms, two of them complete (G_I and G_{II}) and one incomplete (G_{III}). The first has been transmitted in most of the Greek manuscripts, followed by the Coptic–Sahidic, Ethiopic, Armenian and Syro-Hexaplaric versions; the second form has been transmitted by Codex Sinaiticus and the Old Latin, which is closely related to Sinaiticus. Finally, the third

---

[23] R. Hanhart, *Esther. Septuaginta* VIII, 3, Göttingen 1966, 91 n. 3: "Die offensichtliche Ähnlichkeit des Übersetzungscharakter im 'L-Text' von Est und im "'o'-Text" von Dan bedürfte einer besonderen Untersuchung, vor allem hinsichtlich der Frage, ob die behauptete Priorität des "o'-Textes" gegenüber dem "θ'-Text" in Dan auf ebenso sicheren Kriterien beruht wie die Priorität des "o'-Textes" gegenüber dem "L-Text" in Est (vgl s. 88f.)". A similar opinion is expressed by J. W. Wevers, in "Septuaginta Forschungen seit 1954", *TR NF* 33 (1968), 32: "Der doppelte Daniel-text mit verschiedener Hexaplatradition zeigt die dringende Notwendigkeit, sich mit diesem Problem zu beschäftigen."

[24] "Comparée à la première traduction de Daniel (967) l'oeuvre de 'Theodotion' apparaît tantôt comme une nouvelle traduction, tantôt comme une révision attentive de l'oeuvre de son prédécesseur," P.-M. Bogaert, "Relecture et refonte historicisante", 202–203.

[25] See S. P. Jeansonne, *The Old Greek Translation of Daniel 7–12*, 131–33.

form, which is closer to the second than to the first, transmits part of it in a few minuscule manuscripts.[26] The relationship among the three text forms has been established by Hanhart in connection with his critical edition of the book as follows: their agreements are so important that mutual interdependence has to be assumed; however, on the other hand their differences are so serious that their interrelationship cannot be defined as a recension but instead they are autonomous textual forms.[27]

Brooke – McLean – Thackeray, instead, printed both texts separately plus the text of the Old Latin.[28] Recently, J. R. Busto devoted a monograph to the question of the priority of the two texts. Against the widespread idea in biblical textual criticism since de Lagarde that the short text has priority as a text tends to expand in the course of transmission, Bust has reached the conclusion that the short text of the Vatican–Alexandrian is the result of a conscious revision of the Alexandrian text, a revision which tends to improve that popular translation stylistically, making it more readable to a Greek public.[29] This means that for the moment there are no data for supposing a targumic origin of the book[30] whereas on the other hand many other indications indicate the textual dependence of the three forms. The problem of critical restoration becomes more difficult because the transmission is not uniform (part is in Greek and part is in Latin) and because the transitional links that would allow us to go back to

---

[26] See. R. Hanhart, *Septuaginta VIII, 5. Tobit*, Göttingen 1983, 31–36.

[27] "Der griechische Text ist in zwei, zum Teil in drei Textformen überliefert, deren teilweise Übereinstimmungen zwar dermassen eindeutig sind, dass gegenseitige Abhängigkeit mit Sicherheit angenommen werden muss, deren Uhterschiede aber so tiefgreifend sind, dass ihr Verhältnis zueinander nicht als Rezension sondern als selbständige Textform bestimmt werden muss." See R. Hanhart, *Text und Textgeschichte des Buches Tobit*, 11.

[28] A. E. Brooke, N. McLean and H. St J. Thackeray, *The Old Testament in Greek: VIII–I Esther, Judit, Tobit*, Cambridge 1940.

[29] See J. R. Busto Saiz, *El doble texto griego de Tobit*. Analysing a particular passage, Rosso has reached the conclusion that the reading transmitted by S in Tobit 7:9 is original; see L. Rosso, "Un'antica variante del libro di Tobit (Tob VII, 9)", *Rivista degli Studi Orientali* 50 (1976), 73–89. Busto Saiz also analyses a series of readings from the Old Latin which can help in recovering the authentic text of Tobit, J. R. Busto Saiz, "Algunas aportaciones de la Vetus Latina para una nueva edición crítica del libro de Tobit", *Sefarad* 38 (1978), 53–69. However, against these suggestions, R. Hanhart, the editor of the book, who utterly gives up reconstructing the original text of Tobit, transfers the problem to the level of textual history and commentary on the book.

[30] As insinuated by A. Díez Macho, "Targum y Nuevo testamento", *Mélanges Eugène – Tisserant*. ST 231, Rome 1964, 153–85.

the original text are missing.[31] On the other hand, it must not be forgotten that the Targums of the Hagiographers never enjoyed official recognition. With the exception of Esther, they were not used in the liturgical service of the synagogue, a fact which makes difficult the hypothesis of those who consider the second form of the text as a homiletic expansion of the first; and lastly, they were not produced until a very late period.[32] Naturally these results have to be open to the new data from the recently published Hebrew and Aramaic fragments from Qumran as well as to any other new source of knowledge.

The book of Judges

Lagarde inaugurated the plan of printing the texts of A and B separately,[33] but for reasons of space he only did this in chapters 1–5.[34] In this double text Kahle sees the confirmation of his theory on the targumic origin of the LXX.[35] For Moore also they are two different traditions: the more recent B tradition could have made use of the A tradition, but it is a new tradition used by Cyril of Alexandria in the 4th century CE against the rest of the Egyptian Fathers before him who cite the text of A.[36] Even so, Pretzl, Soisalon-Soininen and others insist that the similarities between the two texts is so great that they cannot be different translations but separate 'recensions' of the same translation.[37] Lagarde, Kahle and Moore focused their attention on the differences, which are chiefly evident in difficult passages, but ignored the many similarities in language and construction between both texts. These similarities indicate a common archetype which through its successors and, apparently, independent stages of revision, has ended up producing the texts of A and B that we have. Furthermore, methodologically, today families of manuscripts rather

---

[31] See R. Hanhart, *Text und Textgeschichte des Buches Tobit*, 11–20.

[32] See *Bible Translations* in "Encyclopaedia Judaica". Although, some of these, such as the Targum of Job from Qumran Cave 4, are very old and often included ancient traditions of Palestinian origin.

[33] *Qumran Cave 4. XIV: Parabiblical Texts, Part 2*. DJD XIX, ed. M. Broshi, E. Eshel, J. Fitzmyer *et al.*, Oxford 1995, 1–76.

[34] P. de Lagarde, *Septuaginta-Studien I*, 1891, Göttingen.

[35] P. Kahle, *The Cairo Geniza*, 235: "Whoever is acquainted with conditions prevailing in older Targums at a time before an authoritative text was fixed will recognize in these two Greek texts typical examples of two forms of an old Targum."

[36] G. F. Moore, *Judges*, XLVI.

[37] See Select Bibliography and E. Jenni, "Zwei Jahrzehnte Forschung an den Büchern Josua bis Könige", *TR NF* 27 (1961), 20–32, especially pp. 24ff.

than isolated manuscripts are compared, so that the original single tradition which underwent various forms of revision is even more obvious. The articles by Schreiner and Sáenz-Badillos point in this direction.[38] Bodine's monograph, the most recent overall study of the topic, has resolved most of the difficulty by concluding that the Greek text of the family of manuscripts represented by B corresponds to the Theodotionic or καίγε recension of the original LXX made at the turn of the era in order to make it agree with the Hebrew text current at the time. Nor does family A represent the LXX; instead it is a late revision which is very close to the Hexaplaric recension. The original LXX has survived chiefly in the group of Lucianic manuscripts and in the Old Latin, and in a special way in those passages where the two traditions coincide.[39]

Habakkuk 3 in the LXX and in Codex Barberini
The parallel text to the LXX that six manuscripts provide for Habakkuk 3 has been a veritable puzzle for Septuagintalists since the time of Montfaucon, who attributed it to the *septima* mentioned by Origen in the Hexapla.[40] It is strange that Kahle did not pay attention to it, since at first glance it seems a suitable piece for the shaping of his theory. I have discussed this text, traditionally called Barberini because of the main manuscripts that transmit it, in another monograph.[41] After proving that it is a different translation from the LXX – not merely a revision – and that it does not translate an Aramaic Targum, he concluded that this discordant text belongs to the translation school of Symmachus. Its lexicon and the translation techniques used confirm this. Many other indications make this result likely, such as the contacts it shows with the Lucianic recension, with the Coptic versions and *Codex Washingonianus* (W) and with the Vulgate. However, that text cannot be the same as the version by Symmachus

---

[38] See Select Bibliography. It was not possible to consult the doctoral thesis by J. H. Ludlum, "The Dual Greek Text".

[39] See W. R. Bodine, *The Greek Text of Judges*, 134–36 and 185–86.

[40] The manuscripts in question are uncials, the *Codex Venetus* (V) of the 13th century and five minuscules: mss 62, 86, 147 and 107 (see J. Ziegler, *Duodecim Prophetae. Septuaginta*. XIII, Göttingen 1967, 273ff.), and the ms. *Fondo San Salvatore* 118 of the University Library of Messina; see W. Baars, "A New Witness to the Text of the Barberini Greek Version of Habakkuk III", *VT* 15 (1965), 381–82. It is called 'text Barberini' as it appears in ms. 86 = *Barberinus graecus* 549 (9th–10th cents) of the Vatican Library in Rome.

[41] N. Fernández Marcos, "El texto Barberini de Habacuc III reconsiderado".

as we know it from the Hexaplaric fragments preserved in Habakkuk 3. This poses new questions about the existence of a school of Symmachus or perhaps even 'predecessors' of that translator, just as recently they have been discovered for Aquila and Theodotion. By setting the Barberini text of Habakkuk 3 within the circles of influence of the translator Symmachus, the existence of two competing translations at the level of the origins of the LXX is discarded. This Barberini text is later than that of the LXX; its vocabulary is close to that of Symmachus and in any case to that of later books of the LXX. As a result it does not affect the problem of the targumic origins of the Greek version.[42]

Duplicates in the books of Kings
The problems posed by the text of the LXX in these books are old and still await a solution that will be facilitated by the full publication of a Hebrew text found in Qumran (4QSam^{a-c}).[43] All the duplicates belong to the γγ section (= 3 Kgs 2:12–21:43) in Thackeray's classification.[44] Gooding has written several articles on the books of LXX-Kings and in particular on one of these duplicates.[45] Apparently, the multiple rearrangements of material in 3 Kings correspond to an intentional pattern of reorganising the whole book, a pattern which goes far beyond this particular book. This reinterpretation and redistribution of material penetrated the Greek text as a result of a later revision and not at the time of its original translation. The reason for the first two duplicates lies in the chronological differences between the LXX and the Hebrew text. The LXX, which follows

---

[42] An extensive bibliography on the topic is to be found in N. Fernández Marcos, "El texto Barberini de Habacuc III reconsiderado".

[43] Under the direction of Professor Frank Cross in the series "Discoveries in the Judaean Desert". E. C. Ulrich has studied these texts and has provided a foretaste of his results in "4QSam^{a} and Septuagintal Research", *BIOSCS* 8 (1975), 24–39. See also E. C. Ulrich, *The Qumran Text of Samuel and Josephus*, Missoula, Mont. 1978, and E. Tov (ed.), *The Hebrew and Greek Texts of Samuel*, Jerusalem 1980.

[44] See H. St J. Thackeray, *The Septuagint and Jewish Worship*, London 1923, 114:
α = 1 Kgs
ββ = 2 Kgs 1:1–9:1
βγ = 2 Kgs 11:2–3 Kgs 2:11
γγ = 3 Kgs 2:12–21:43
γδ = 3 Kgs 22–4 Kgs. According to Thackeray's theory, in the first Alexandrian translation of these books the third and fifth parts were omitted as unedifying. A later translator, probably Theodotion, filled in these gaps. See also J. A. Montgomery and H. Gehman, *Kings*, ICC, 20.

[45] See *CB* 107–108, and D. W. Gooding, "Problems of Text and Midrash".

its own chronological system, has a translation of the summary of Josaphat's reign in 16:28a-h and a different translation of the same summary according to the Masoretic text in 22:41-51. Similarly, the LXX, following its own chronology, places a translation of the introduction to the reign of Joram in 4 Kgs 1:18a-d and following the Masoretic text inserts another different translation of the same introduction in 4 Kgs 3:1-3.

In both cases they are different translations from different hands: the original LXX, which corresponds to a non-Masoretic Hebrew *Vorlage*, and a second translation, which is closer to the Masoretic text and has all the signs of being more recent.

Another type of duplicate is due to midrashic exegesis and tends to develop the *Leitmotiv* of Solomon's wisdom. For example, the duplicate of 3 Kgs 12:24a-z is inserted in order to vilify Jeroboam.

The peculiar interpretations of this part of 3 Kings fit well into the spirit of haggadic midrash which at times allows itself the freedom to invent, leaving some margin to the imagination of the homilist. This version has a certain similarity with that of the author of Chronicles compared with that of Samuel–Kings. Chronicles is not a commentary on Samuel–Kings, whereas LXX-3 Kgs is precisely a commentary on LXX-1 Kgs. Chronicles never allows a favourable narrative to come after an unfavourable one about the same person. This is typical of midrash which already presupposes an official biblical text. Therefore 3 Kings and its Hebrew *Vorlage* in the present state of our knowledge can best be described as hybrid texts: partly biblical text and partly haggadic midrash. To this mix has to be added the element of targumic interpretation which inevitably accompanies every translation of a biblical text and which in 3 Kings has been inserted in two stages:

1. at the first level of the original translation,
2. on the occasion of duplicate translations and their inclusion in the text.[46]

---

[46] D. W. Gooding, "Problems of Text and Midrash". Recently, T. Muraoka has formulated the hypothesis of a double translator for the books of Kings, though it differs from Thackeray's. In fact, Thackeray suggested different translations for the majority text of the other sections of the books. Muraoka, instead, after admitting the recensional nature of the majority text in these two sections, proposes different translators for the minority text (boc$_2$ e$_2$) of βγ, γδ and for the majority text of the other sections of the books. However, D. Barthélemy rejects Muraoka's new hypothesis in "Prise de position sur les autres communications du colloque de Los Angeles", *Études d'histoire du texte de l'ancien Testament*, Fribourg–Göttingen 1978, 255–66.

However, this midrashic or targumic interpretation of the duplicates of Kings has been vigorously opposed by Trebolle in a series of studies on these books which combine the results of textual criticism with the progress made by literary criticism. The LXX of 1 Kings, with its duplicates and different chronology, reflects a textual type which is different from those transmitted by the Masoretic text. These results agree better with the image of textual pluralism which the Qumran documents have disclosed for some biblical books such as Samuel or Jeremiah. In this hypothesis, the textual pluralism which Kahle postulated for the origins of the LXX would have to be transferred to the stage and fluctuation of the Hebrew text at the moment when the translation was being made, a translation which shows itself to be faithful to its *Vorlage* as new texts gradually emerge from the Dead Sea Scrolls.[47]

With the parallel texts analysed so far, the problem of double texts in the LXX is not exhausted. In several deuterocanonical books such as Daniel, Esther, Baruch, there are several Greek supplements to the parts translated from Hebrew. However, none of these additions has its Hebrew equivalent in the original. An exception is LXX-1 Ezra which is a different edition from Hebrew Chronicles–Ezra–Nehemiah. Most of it is a faithful translation, but with additions, deletions and a new arrangement of material. Only 1 Ezra 3:1–5:6, the story of the three bodyguards of king Darius, has no equivalent in Hebrew.[48] The problem posed by LXX-1 Ezra and its relationship to LXX-2 Ezra has no easy solution. For Howorth, 1 Ezra would be the original LXX translation, whereas 2 Ezra would be the translation by Theodotion which replaced the LXX in one stage of transmission.[49] Since no LXX translator took so many liberties as those

---

[47] See J. Trebolle, *Salomón y Jeroboán. Historia de la recensión y redacción de 1 Reyes 2–12, 14*, Salamanca–Jerusalem 1980. For other publications by the same author which use the same line of research, see C. Dogniez, *BS*, 168–69. For the story of David and Goliath there is also general agreement on the literal character of the Greek version and the shortened form of its *Vorlage*: see D. Barthélemy, D. W. Gooding, J. Lust and E. Tov, *The Story of David and Goliath: Textual and Literary Criticism. Papers of a Joint Venture*, Fribourg–Göttingen 1986, 156.

[48] For the equivalents between Greek and Hebrew, see H. B. Swete, *An Introduction to the Old Testament in Greek*, 265ff., and R. Hanhart, *Esdrae Liber I. Septuaginta VIII, 1*, Göttingen 1974, 54.

[49] See H. H. Howorth, "The Apocryphal Book Esdras A and the LXX", *PSBA* 23 (1901), 147–59.

we note in 1 Ezra in relation to the original, it must be supposed that two editions of the book in Hebrew circulated and the one finally accepted in the Hebrew canon was the longer. Other theories about the relation between 1 and 2 Ezra on the one hand and the Hebrew books Chronicles–Ezra–Nehemiah on the other, can be seen in Pfeiffer[50] and Jellicoe.[51] This involved problem has no acceptable solution, as has been shown by the sober conclusions reached by Hanhart, editor of the book of 1 Ezra in the *editio maior* of Göttingen:[52] the comparison between 1 and 2 Ezra cannot show with certainty a literary dependence between the two texts.

At those points where a weak contact between the two is noticeable, the text of 2 Ezra can be clearly defined as secondary to the text of 1 Ezra. However, in principle the independence of both texts has to be preserved as the basis for restoring the original text of 1 Ezra, common textual forms being attributed to the influence of 2 Ezra precisely because it is a more faithful translation than the older one of Ezra.

The whole book of Esther has been published by R. Hanhart in double text form, known as text o' and text L. According to Hanhart, who has studied the whole manuscript translation of the book, text L is not a recension of text o' but a reworking of the Greek translation of Esther based largely on text o'. It is not the only reworking of the text as soon others were to emerge: one of them corresponds to the *Vorlage* of the Old Latin and traces of a third are to be found in the text known by Josephus. Since none of these text forms is explained independently of text o', they all go back to a single underlying text of the book of Esther.[53]

Exodus 35–40 matches the sequence of Exodus 25–31, where instructions are given for the building of the tabernacle. However, whereas in Exodus 25–31 the LXX generally follows the sequence

---

[50] R. H. Pfeiffer, *History of New Testament Times with an Introduction to the Apocrypha*, New York 1949, 246–50.

[51] *SMS* 291ff.; *CB* 110–12, and C. Dogniez, *BS* 171–74.

[52] R. Hanhart, *Text und Textgeschichte des 1 Esrabuches*, 17–18.

[53] See R. Hanhart, *Septuaginta. VIII/3 Esther*, Göttingen 1966, 87–99, p. 99: "Die aus dem "L-Text", der altlat. Überlieferung und Iosephus bruchstückhaft erkennbare Existenz weiterer griechischer Textformen neben dem o'-Text ist aber – da keine dieser Textformen unabhängig vom o'-Text erklärbart ist -trotz ihrer Mannigfältigkeit ein Beweis nicht gegen, sondern für die Existenz eines einheitlichen, allgemein anerkannten und verbreiteten griechischen Grundtextes des Est-Buches". For studies after Hanhart's critical edition, see C. Dogniez *BS* 174–77.

of the Masoretic text, in Exodus 35–40 there are significant changes which do not correspond to the translation techniques used by the translators of the Pentateuch. A summary of the main theories explaining this phenomenon can be found in the introduction to the translation of this book in the *Bible in Alexandria*:[54] the intervention of two translators from different periods as responsible for the present text of the Greek version (J. Popper); a single translator for both sections, who was responsible for the main divergences from the Masoretic text (A. H. Finn); a single translator who, however, included a very early rearrangement of the original Greek text (D. W. Gooding).[55] The problem cannot be considered as resolved, and perhaps we have to wait for new data or for the light that can be thrown on this part of Exodus by the textual tradition of the Old Latin to acquire more accurate results. Wevers does not consider it necessary to postulate a different *Vorlage* for the consonantal text from the one we have, as the origin of the version of Exodus 35–40. He even dares to suggest that this Greek text was created by a different translator and was later than the translation of Exodus 25–31.[56] And Aejmelaeus thinks that the hypothesis of a different *Vorlage* and the hypothesis of different translation techniques are not necessarily mutually exclusive. It is possible that both phenomena were operative in the same text: a different *Vorlage* and a freer translation technique.[57]

Yet, in the 'Greek text II' of Sira (represented by the Complutensian which follows ms. 248) some have seen traces of a new Greek translation of the book of Ben Sira (Ecclesiasticus).[58] But, it seems, these conclusions were false due to using defective editions. For Ziegler, editor of the book in the *series major* of Göttingen, this text is not a new independent translation. Its author used the text of Greek I and translated afresh where he thought necessary. However, Ziegler assumes that several translations were in circulation at least for the first part of the book – when they began to show that the first part

---

[54] *La Bible d'Alexandrie. 2 L'Exode*, ed. A. Le Boulluec and P. Sandevoir, Paris 1989, 61–67.

[55] See D. W. Gooding, *The Account of the Tabernacle: Translations and Textual Problems of the Greek Exodus*, Cambridge 1959, 99–101.

[56] J. W. Wevers, "The Building of the Tabernacle", *JNSL* 19 (1993), 123–31.

[57] A. Aejmelaeus, "Septuagintal Translation Techniques", 398: "It is possible to have both free translation and different Vorlage in the same text. And this is the case in the tabernacle account."

[58] J. Ziegler, *Sapientia Iesu Filii Sirach. Septuaginta XII, 2*, Göttingen 1965, 73.

does not correspond to the Hebrew – translations which have left
their mark in the recensions of Lucian and Origen and especially in
the Old Latin.[59] Furthermore, Thiele suspects that the *Vorlage* of the
Old Latin of Sira was a particular Greek text that is no longer preserved except in fragments through Greek text II, because it was
displaced by the success of the more popular Greek text.[60]

c) *Targumism*

An extensive bibliography on targumism has been produced due, in
part, to the discovery in 1956 of the Palestine Targum Neophyti I
by professor A. Díez Macho.[61] However, perhaps the best description of targumism as a general exegetical movement is to be found
in the work by Le Déaut.[62] This type of hermeneutics tends to make
the biblical text more comprehensible to a particular audience; hence
the addition of a subject, a complement, a pronoun or even a change
of person in a verb in order to make the narrative more lively. This
tendency also gives rise to a penchant for glosses. These explanations
are often made with the help of parallel passages. This associative
exegesis alone explains a sufficient number of variants in the LXX.[63]

---

[59] J. Ziegler, *Sapientia Iesu Filii Sirach*, 74: "So ist es auch nicht richtig, von nur
einer zweiten griech. Übersetzung zu sprechen, sondern es ist anzunehmen, dass
mehrere griech. Übersetzungen im Umlauf waren, von denen uns namentlich im
ersten Teil des Buches ziemlich umfangreiche Überreste in der OL-Rezension und
vor allem in La überliefert sind." On the fluctuation of the text of Sira in the first
centuries of its history, see J. W. Wevers, "Septuaginta Forschungen seit 1954", *TR
NF* 33 (1968), 41ff. Wevers notes that Greek text II must be prior to the New
Testament since Sir 48, 10[c] is cited by Lk. 1:17: "In der Tat ist Gr II sicher älter
als das NT und könnte gut aus der Zeit v. Chr. sein," *ibid.* 42. Parallel texts can
also be found in pseudepigraphical books such as the "Testament of Abraham",
preserved in two recensions (see M. R. James, *The Testament of Abraham*, Cambridge
1892, and M. Delcor, *Le Testament d'Abraham*, Leiden 1973), or the "Testament of
the Twelve Patriarchs" (see R. H. Charles, *The Apocrypha and Pseudepigrapha of the Old
Testament*, II, Oxford 1913, 288ff., and M. de Jonge, *Testamenta XII Patriarcharum
edited according to Cambridge University Library Ms Ff 1.24 fol. 203a–262b*, Leiden 1970).

[60] W. Thiele, "Sirach (Ecclesiasticus)", *Arbeitsbericht der Stiftung* 39 (1995), 26–29.

[61] See Select Bibliography and the introductions to the edition of ms. Neophyti
1 by A. Díez Macho. In addition, B. Grossfeld, *A Bibliography of Targum Literature*,
vol. I, New York 1972, can be consulted, if properly used and corrected from the
criticisms published by W. Baars in his review in *VT* 25,1 (1975), 124–28; vol. II,
1977 and vol. III, 1990.

[62] Le Déaut, "Un phénomène spontané de l'herméneutique juive ancienne", and
in A. Díez Macho, *El Targum*, 23ff.

[63] See I. L. Seeligmann, "Indications of Editorial Alterations and Adaptation in
the Masoretic Text and the Septuagint", *VT* 11 (1961), 201–21.

There is a tendency to bring the proper names of places and people up to date, even identifying anonymous or little-known persons
with famous figures from biblical history. As an indication of a popular mentality it increases the miraculous element in the narratives.
The liturgical context explains the mutual influence between passages from the Torah and the Prophets which were read on the
same day. Le Déaut ends by defining targumism in this sense as
"the combination of spontaneous and unconscious phenomena which
arise from the first contact of the old translator with the biblical text
when it is a liturgical version". It is midrash, but at the level of first
contact with the text.[64]

As is evident, in this wide sense one can speak of the LXX as a
Targum and even as the first Targum. And the influence of Jewish
hermeneutics on the Septuagintal version has been emphasised especially by certain Jewish scholars since Frankel, Prijs and Seeligmann,[65]
until the more recent studies by Goshen-Gottstein and Rabin in connection with the biblical project of the Hebrew University of Jerusalem,[66] and from a different perspective by D. Gooding.

This inclusion of targumic elements in the LXX happens in a
very sober and moderate way to the point that in some books it is
barely noticeable especially if we compare them with the procedure
and translation techniques used in Aramaic Targums. On the other
hand, from the analysis of double texts that we have sketched out
in the present state of research, no proof is forthcoming about the
targumic origin of the LXX as Kahle understood it. The translation
of the Pentateuch, if we except the last chapters of Exodus,[67] shows
a fundamental unity even in a period when textual pluralism was
not yet a major problem.

Of all the parallel texts discussed, in very few cases can one speak
of different translations (Exodus 35–40?, Habakkuk 3, Daniel?). And
even in these it can be shown that a chronologically different translation is later than another, i.e. that they were not in competition

---

[64] R. Bloch, *Midrash* in DBS V, 1957, 1263–81.

[65] Z. Frankel, *Vorstudien zu der LXX*, Leipzig 1941; Frankel, *Über den Einfluss der palästinischen Exegese auf die alexandrinische Hermeneutik*, Leipzig 1851; L. Prijs, *Jüdische Tradition in der LXX*, Leiden 1948, and I. L. Seeligmann (see note 62 above).

[66] M. H. Goshen-Gottstein, "Theory and Practice of Textual Criticism: The Text-critical Use of Septuagint", *Textus* 3 (1963), 130–59; Ch. Rabin, "The Translation Process and the Character of the LXX", *Textus* 6 (1968), 1–27.

[67] D. W. Gooding, "Problems of Text and Midrash".

from the beginning as different options. In the rest of the double texts, one of them is clearly a revision of the other, or both are revisions of a common text now lost, in view of the number of similarities between them. Almost always a single basic text is the best explanation for the later development of the history of the text.

Duplicates originated and were transmitted for various reasons depending on the books and do not correspond to a single cause. However, the underlying unity of the LXX tradition prevents projecting the problem of double texts back to the very origins of the LXX. Only in the case of Samuel–Kings is there particular complexity since textual pluralism, as the texts from Qumran have shown, affects even the Hebrew *Vorlage*.[68]

For the same reason, no duplicates of the LXX can be proposed as witness for dating the Aramaic Targums. Furthermore, even the targumisms and other midrashic phenomena present in the LXX as a translation have to be used with extreme caution when dating targumic traditions, for it is very difficult to determine whether they come from the translator's first meeting with the text or are the product of later revisions or reworkings.[69]

Select Bibliography

Bodine, W. R., *The Greek Text of Judges: Recensional Developments*, Chico, Calif. 1980.

Bogaert, P.-M., "Relecture et refonte historicisante du livre de Daniel attestées par la première version grecque (Papyrus 967)". *Études sur le judaïsme hellénistique*, ed. R. Kuntzmann and J. Schlosser, Paris 1984, 197–224.

Brockington, L. H., "LXX and Targum". *ZAW* 66 (1954), 80–86.

Bruce, F. F., "The Oldest Greek Version of Daniel". *OTS* 20 (1977), 22–40.

Busto Saiz, J. R., *El doble texto griego de Tobit y su inserción en la historia de LXX*. Memoria de Licenciatura, Madrid, Complutensian Univ. 1975.

———, "El texto teodociónico de Daniel y la traducción de Símaco". *Sefarad* 40 (1980), 41–55.

Churgin, P., "Targum and LXX". *AJSL* 50 (1933–34), 41–65.

Delcor, M., "Un cas de traduction targumique de la Septante à propos de la statue en or de Dan III". *Textus* 7 (1969), 30–35.

Delekat, L., "Ein Septuagintatargum". *VT* 8 (1958), 225–52.

Engel, H., *Die Susanna-Erzählung. Einleitung, Übersetzung und Kommentar zum Septuaginta-Text und zur Theodotion-Bearbeitung*, Fribourg–Göttingen 1985.

---

[68] F. M. Cross, "The History of the Biblical Text in the Light of Discoveries in the Judean Desert", *HTR* 57 (1964), 281–99, and C. Dogniez, *BS* 154–56.

[69] D. W. Gooding, "On the Use of the LXX for Dating Midrashic Elements in the Targums", *JTS* 25 (1974), 1–11. Of the three examples from Exodus studied by Gooding, only the second probably derives from the translators; the other two are the result of later revisions.

Fernández Marcos, N., "El texto Barberini de Habacuc III reconsiderado". *Sefarad* 36 (1976), 3–36.

Good, E. M., "The Barberini Greek Version of Habbakuk III". *VT* 9 (1959), 11–30.

Gooding, D. W., "On the Use of the LXX for Dating Midrashic Elements in the Targums". *JTS* 25 (1974), 1–11.

———, "Problems of Text and Midrash in the Third Book of Reigns". *Textus* 7 (1969), 1–29.

———, "Two Possible Examples of Midrashic Interpretation in the Septuagint Exodus". *Wort, Lied und Gottesspruch* I, 39–49.

Gordon, R. P., "The Second Septuagint Account of Jeroboam: History or Midrash?". *VT* 25 (1975), 368–94.

Gray, J., "The Masoretic Text of the Book of Job, the Targum and the Septuagint Version in the Light of the Qumran Targum (11QtargJob)". *ZAW* 86 (1974), 331–50.

Grelot, P., "La Septante de Daniel IV et son substrat sémitique". *RB* 81 (1974), 5–25.

Hamm, W., *Der Septuaginta-Text des Buches Daniel Kap. 1–2 nach dem Kölner Teil des Papyrus 967*, Bonn 1969.

———, *Der Septuaginta-Text des Buches Daniel Kap. 3–4 nach dem Kölner Teil des Papyrus 967*, Bonn 1977.

Hanhart, R., *Text und Textgeschichte des 1 Esrabuches*. MSU XII, Göttingen 1974, 17ff.

———, *Text und Textgeschichte des Buches Tobit*. MSU XVII, Göttingen 1984.

Holmes, S., *Joshua: The Hebrew and Greek Texts*, Cambridge 1914.

Jeansonne, S. P., *The Old Greek Translation of Daniel 7–12*, Washington, D.C. 1988.

Kahle, P., *The Cairo Geniza*, Oxford 1959.

———, "Untersuchungen zur Geschichte des Pentateuchtextes". *TSK* 88 (1915), 399–439 (= *Opera Minora*, Leiden 1956, 3–37).

Kaminka, A., "LXX und Targum zu Proverbia". *HUCA* 8–9 (1931–32), 169–91.

Katz, P., "Notes on the Septuagint III: Coincidences between LXX and Tg° in Genesis XV". *JTS* 47 (1946), 166–68.

Koch, K., "Die Herkunft der proto-Theodotion-Übersetzung des Danielbuches". *VT* 23 (1973), 262–65.

Ludlum, J. H., "The Dual Greek Text of Judges in Codices A and B". Diss. Yale 1957.

Montgomery, J. A., *Daniel*, ICC 1950.

Moore, G. F., *Judges* in ICC 1949.

Pretzl, O., "LXX-Probleme im Buch der Richter". *Bib* 7 (1926), 233–69 and 353–83.

Rabin, Ch., "Cultural Aspects of Bible Translation". *Armenian and Biblical Studies*, ed. M. Stone, Jerusalem 1976, 35–49.

Saenz-Badillos, A., "Tradición griega y texto hebreo del Canto de Débora". *Sefarad* 33 (1973), 245–59.

Schmitt, A., *Stammt der sogenannte "θ'"-Text bei Daniel wirklich von Theodotion?*, MSU IX, Göttingen 1966.

Schreiner, J., "Textformen und Urtext des Deboraliedes in der LXX". *Bib* 42 (1961), 173–200.

———, "Zum B-Text des griechischen Canticum deborae". *Bib* 42 (1961), 333–58.

Schüpphaus, J., "Das Verhältnis von LXX- und Theodotion-Text in den apokryphen Zusätzen zum Danielbuch". *ZAW* 83 (1971), 49–72.

Soisalon-Soininen, I., *Die Textformen der Septuaginta-Übersetzung des Richterbuches*, Helsinki 1951.

Weissert, D., "Alexandrinian Analogical Word-Analysis and Septuagint Translation Techniques". *Textus* 8 (1973), 31–44.

Wright, B. G., *No Small Difference: Sirach's Relationship to its Hebrew Parent Text*, Atlanta, Ga. 1989.

Targumism

Aejmelaeus, A., "Septuagintal Translation Techniques: A Solution to the Problem of the Tabernacle Account". *Septuagint, Scrolls and Cognate Writings*, 1992, 381–402.

Barc, B., "Du temple à la synagogue. Essai d'interprétation des premiers targumismes de la Septante". *Selon les Septante*, 1995, 11–26.

Bowker, J., *The Targums and Rabbinic Literature*, Cambridge 1969.

Brown, J. P., "The Septuagint as a Source of the Greek-Loan-Words in the Targums". *Bib* 70 (1989), 194–216.

Díez Macho, A., *El Targum. Introducción a las traducciones aramaicas de la Biblia*, Barcelona 1972. Reprints in Madrid, CSIC 1979 and 1982.

Le Déaut, R., *Introduction à la litterature Targumique*, Rome 1966.

———, "La Septante: un Targum?". *Études sur le judaïsme hellénistique*, ed. R. Kutzmann and J. Schlosser, Paris 1984, 147–95.

———, "Un phénomène spontané de l'herméneutique juive ancienne, le targumisme". *Bib* 52 (1971), 505–25.

PART THREE

THE SEPTUAGINT IN JEWISH TRADITION

CHAPTER SEVEN

AQUILA AND HIS PREDECESSORS

In current research on the LXX, a dividing line cannot be drawn between the new translations into Greek of the Bible exactly as they are described in the ancient sources and successive revisions that the Septuagintal text very soon underwent.[1] The reason for the new translations by Aquila, Symmachus and Theodotion is generally accepted as being the adoption of the LXX by Christians and its consequent rejection by the Jews. This appropriation would explain the need for translations that would reflect the original Hebrew more faithfully, a need sharpened by Jewish–Christian polemic concerning the correct interpretation of the Scripture as is reflected, for example in Justin's *Dialogue with Tryphon*.[2] It would also contribute to the gradual abandonment of the LXX by the Jews, the fixing of the Hebrew canon and the Synod of Yamnia (*c.* 100 CE) which obviously excluded several biblical books written in Greek and transmitted by the Alexandrian Bible.

However, this explanation is no longer satisfactory since, on the one hand, there are indications of the rejection of the LXX by the Jews prior to the 2nd century CE, as we saw at the close of chapter 3.[3] Furthermore, there are manuscript witnesses that come from the Jews and are earlier than Christianity, the most surprising of which is the Twelve Prophets scroll from Naḥal Ḥever, which exhibits clear signs of correction of the Greek text to fit it to the Hebrew text then current. Accordingly, the aim of conforming more to the Hebrew text in these early revisions of the LXX which later would lead to the calque-translation of Aquila, was earlier than Jewish–Christian polemic. Equally unsatisfactory is the explanation of Aquila's literalism as the result of applying halakhic exegesis of the Palestine

---

[1] See chapter 16 and E. Tov's review of S. Jellicoe, *SMS*, in *RB* 77 (1970), 84–91.

[2] For example, Aquila removes the word Χριστός from his translation, replacing it with ἠλειμμένος, as can be seen in 1 Sam. 2:35; 2 Sam. 1:21; Ps. 2:2; 38:8; Is. 45:1 and Dan. 9:26. See D. Barthélemy, "L'Ancien Testament a mûri à Alexandrie", *TZ* 21 (1965), 358–70, p. 362 n. 11.

[3] See p. 46. As is made clear in the prologue to Sira, the warning miracles for having approached the sacred text (*Letter of Aristeas*, §§314–16) and account of the changes brought in by King Ptolemy.

rabbis to the Greek Bible. Some scholars think that this tendency had pedagogic roots and was directed to Greek-speaking Jews with a rudimentary knowledge of Hebrew so that they would be able to understand the text of the Old Testament.[4] The more common opinion propagated by Barthélemy, according to which Aquila made his translation following strictly the hermeneutical principles of Rabbi Aqiba, was never fully accepted and has recently been questioned by Grabbe. A literal translation cannot depend on a particular form of hermeneutics. Grabbe holds that more research is necessary concerning the reliability of the translations attributed to Aqiba and that he was not the only rabbi to use the exegetical techniques attributed to him. Furthermore, the preposition 'et is only translated as σύν when it is followed by the article, since in no rabbinic source is it stated that Akibah gave 'et an inclusive meaning only when it was followed by the article. All in all, Aquila's translation techniques are closer to modern literal translators than to the rabbinic exegetes of antiquity.[5] The same line of thought is followed by A. Paul, for whom Aquila's literalness serves the ideology and polemic of a school. It formed part of a wider programme of the restoration of Judaism and of the sacred tongue precisely when Hadrian was changing Jerusalem into *Aelia Capitolina*. The answer to this desire for restoring the sacred tongue and the frontiers of Judaism was Aquila's translation, a translation which takes apart the language of the LXX and restores the meanings of the original, creating a kind of rabbinic Bible in Greek, replacing the LXX already inherited by the Christians.[6]

From these preliminary observations I will now go on to consider each of the Jewish translators who have transmitted the ancient tradition to us, primarily for methodological reasons. Besides, although their historical personality has to some extent been blurred by recent discoveries, the figures of Aquila and Symmachus are clearly defined as independent translators, not mere revisers.[7]

---

[4] This is the opinion of G. Vermes in his review of *Les Devanciers d'Aquila* published in *JSS* 11 (1966), 264. In the time of Origen it was used by Jews who did not understand Hebrew: φιλοτιμότερον πεπιστευμένος παρὰ Ἰουδαίοις ... ᾧ μάλιστα εἰώθασιν οἱ ἀγνοοῦντες τὴν Ἐβραίων διάλεκτον χρῆσθαι, ὡς πάντων μᾶλλον ἐπιτετευγμένῳ ('[Aquila], the most reliable and the one with the highest esteem among the Jews, the one those who do not know Hebrew tend to use as the best constructed of all'), *Ep. ad Afr.*, 2.

[5] L. L. Grabbe, "Aquila's Translation and Rabbinic Exegesis", 527–36.

[6] A. Paul, "La Bible grecque d'Aquila et l'idéologie du judaïsme ancien", 227 and 244–45.

[7] See L. L. Grabbe, "The Translation Technique of the Greek Minor Versions", 505–56, pp. 516–17.

a) *Ancient Witnesses*

Aquila's name must have been common in antiquity since it is attested in the apostolic age.[8] This translator was a gentile by birth and came from Sinope, a Roman colony in Pontus. Epiphanius provides more details about his life.[9] He lived during the reign of the emperor Hadrian (117–338) to whom he was related (he was probably his brother-in-law: πενθερίδης, *The Dialogue of Timothy and Aquila*, 117; πενθερός according to Pseudo-Athanasius in the *Chronicon Pascale*).[10] Hadrian commissioned him to supervise the building of *Aelia Capitolina* on the esplanade of Jerusalem and there he was converted to Christianity under the influence of those returning from Pella. However, he was excommunicated since he refused to give up astrology. Out of resentment he underwent circumcision, devoting himself to learning Hebrew in order to translate the Bible into Greek with the aim of displacing the LXX which at the time represented Christian interpretation.

Basically the same story is repeated in the *Synopsis Sacrae Scripturae*, 77, by Pseudo-Athanasius and in the *Dialogue of Timothy and Aquila* by Epiphanius. In spite of the latter's polemical and partisan nature, more than one detail of the story is suspect. Jerome and Origen on the other hand give us a much more positive judgement of the translator Aquila, recognising his mastery as a translator and his faithfulness to the Hebrew text.[11]

As for rabbinic tradition, it agrees with Christian tradition in describing Aquila as a proselyte, *ha-gēr*.[12] After his conversion to Judaism they add that he was a disciple of Rabbi Eliezer and Rabbi

---

[8] Acts 18:2 Ἰουδαῖον ὀνόματι Ἀκύλαν, Ποντικὸν τῷ γένει ("a Jew called Aquila, a native of Pontus").

[9] Epiphanius, *De Mens. et Ponderibus*, 14ff.

[10] This may be explained by a passage by Theodoret of Cyrus, in the fourth question on the book of Judges: πενθερὸν δὲ αὐτὸν κέκληκεν ὡς τῆς γαμετῆς ἀδελφόν. καὶ γὰρ νῦν πολλοὶ τοὺς τοιούτους πενθερίδας καλοῦσι ("However he is called brother-in-law as the bride's brother and now many call those or such people *pentheridas*"); see N. Fernández Marcos and A. Sáenz-Badillos, *Theodoreti Cyrensis Quaestiones in Octateuchum. Editio Critica*, Madrid 1979, 290, 16–18.

[11] See Origen, *Ep. ad Afr.* 3; Jerome, *Praef. in Job*, and especially in *Ep. ad Marcellam*, where he states: "et -ut amicae menti fatear- quae ad nostram fidem roborandam plura reperio". And in the Commentary on Isaiah 49:5 he calls him "eruditissimus linguae graecae". In fact, in Aquila's translations that special anti-Christian κακουργία with which Theodoretus branded him is not noticeable, but these versions are due to a peculiar translation technique as has been shown by F. Field, *Origenis Hexaplorum quae supersunt*, XIX–XX, analysing seven examples of debated conflicting passages.

[12] *Jerusalem Talmud, Meg.* 1,11; *Kiddush.* 1,1.

Joshua, or according to other witnesses, of Rabbi Akiba. The similarity of his name with the name of the author of Targum Onqelos,
who translated the Pentateuch into Aramaic, has caused considerable confusion. In the Babylonian Talmud and in the Tosephta, the
same or similar incidents are ascribed to Onqelos as are attributed
to Aquila in the Jerusalem Talmud and the Palestinian *midrashim*.
Today, the tendency is to ascribe the Talmud passages to Aquila,
concluding that when his name was changed to Onqelos in the
Babylonian sources, the anonymous Aramaic translation of the
Pentateuch was attributed to Onqelos the proselyte.[13]

The information from Epiphanius, who put his zenith in the twelfth
year of Hadrian (= 129/30),[14] is in agreement with his being a disciple of Akiba who taught from 95 to 135. Taking into account his
learning of Hebrew as an adult and the necessary familiarity with
methods of rabbinic exegesis, it is unlikely that he finished his work
before 140. This date also fits the remark by Irenaeus who wrote
his book *Adv. Haereses c.* 190, where he describes Aquila's translation
as comparatively recent.[15]

The Jerusalem Talmud informs us of the enthusiastic welcome
that the Jews gave his translation.[16] His teachers congratulated him
with the words of Ps. 45:3: *yafyafita mibenê 'adām* = "You are the most
handsome of all men." Preference for Aquila's translation continued
in Jewish circles over the centuries that followed.[17] And even in the
time of Justinian, use of this version was permitted in synagogues,
as well as the *Septuaginta*.[18]

This is an indication that its destiny was linked with that of the
Greek language in the East and that it only became irrelevant as a

---

[13] L. J. Rabinowitz, "Onkelos and Aquila", 1405

[14] Epiphanius, *De Mens. et Ponderibus*, 13: . . . ἕως ᾿Ακύλα τοῦ ἑρμενευτοῦ, ἤγουν
ἕως δωδεκάτου ἔτους ᾿Αδριανοῦ ("until the translator Aquila, i.e, until the twelfth
year of Hadrian").

[15] Irenaeus, *Adv. Haereses* III, 21,1: οὐχ ὡς ἔνιοί φασιν τῶν νῦν μεθερμηνεύειν
τολμώντων τὴν γραφήν . . . ὡς Θεοδοτίων . . . ὁ Ἐφέσιος καὶ ᾿Ακύλας ὁ Ποντικός,
ἀμφότεροι ᾿Ιουδαῖοι προσήλυτοι ("Not as some of those who have dared to translate Scripture now state . . . for example Theodotion of Ephesus and Aquila from
Pontus, both Jewish proselytes").

[16] *Meg.* 1,9.

[17] See Jerome, in his Commentary on Ez. 3:5, and Augustine, *De Civitate Dei* 15,
23.

[18] Justinian, *Novella* 146: "at vero ii qui Graeca lingua legunt LXX interpretum
utentur translatione . . . verum . . . licentiam concedimus atiam Aquilae versione
utendi". The whole document is translated by P. Kahle in *The Cairo Geniza*, Oxford
1959, 315–17.

result of the Arab invasion and the disappearance of Greek as *lingua franca* in the Near East.

b) *The Sources of this Version*

The complete translation by Aquila was lost, and until 1897 all that was known of his text were a few quotations preserved in the commentaries by the Fathers, more rarely in Talmudic literature and some readings from the Hexapla, usually copied in the margins of manuscripts which transmitted the LXX. These fragments are collected in the work by Field.[19]

However, already in 1896 Klostermann announced the discovery by Cardinal Mercati of a palimpsest, O.39 of the Ambrosian Library of Milan, which contains large fragments of a Hexapla of Psalms, and published a specimen of it.[20]

In 1897, Burkitt published manuscript fragments of the actual translation by Aquila which he discovered among the heaps of material from the Cairo Genizah.[21] They belonged to a badly preserved copy of a version by Aquila of readings in the synagogue. It contains 1 Kgs 20:7-17 and 2 Kgs 23:11-27 (Hebrew numbering). The fragments come from Jewish circles between 4th and 6th centuries CE, and were still in the possession of Jews in the 11th century when they were made into a palimpsest. As they are continuous fragments they help to improve our knowledge of Aquila's syntax. The *Tetragrammaton* is written in palaeo-Hebrew, which confirms Origen's statement in his commentary on Ps. 2:2: καὶ ἐν τοῖς ἀκριβεστέροις δὲ τῶν ἀντιγράφων ἑβραίοις χαρακτῆρτι κεῖται τὸ ὄνομα, ἑβραϊκοῖς δὲ οὐ τοῖς νῦν ἀλλὰ τοῖς ἀρχαιοτάτοις ("and in the most faithful manuscripts, the name is in Hebrew characters, not those of today but very ancient characters").[22]

In 1900, among the chests of the Cairo Genizah, C. Taylor found fragments of Pss 90:17 to 103:17 (Hebrew numbering) and a Hexaplaric fragment of Ps. 22 with only the columns of Aquila, Symmachus and the LXX preserved.[23] That same year, Grenfell and Hunt

---

[19] F. Field, *Origenis Hexaplorum quae supersunt*. And later in the critical apparatus of the Cambridge and Göttingen editions.

[20] E. Klostermann, "Die Mailänder Fragmente der Hexapla", *ZAW* 16 (1896), 334–37.

[21] F. C. Burkitt, *Fragments of the Books of Kings*.

[22] F. C. Burkitt, *Fragments of the Books of Kings*. Foreword by C. Taylor, V–VII.

[23] C. Taylor, *Hebrew–Greek Cairo Genizah Palimpsests*, Cambridge 1900.

published a papyrus from the second half of the 3rd century which contains a letter from an Egyptian Christian from Rome to his fellow countrymen in Egypt.[24] In this document J. R. Harris identified a fragment of Aquila containing Gen. 1:1-5.

In 1915, Lütkemann and Rahlfs increased the known material from Aquila for Isaiah 1–6 by publishing the Hexaplaric notes of ms. 710.[25] If the edition of the commentary on Isaiah by Theodoret of Cyr contributed little new Hexaplaric material,[26] the same did not apply to the commentary on Isaiah by Eusebius of Caesarea discovered by Möhle in 1930, which increased the Hexaplaric material of that prophet by about 20%.[27]

In 1946, P. Katz reclaimed for Aquila a quotation of Gen. 17:1 which occurs in a discordant text of Philo (*De Gigantibus*, 63).[28] Finally, in 1958 the fragments of Psalms 17–18 discovered by Mercati were published for the first time, followed in 1965, by the volume of Observations.[29] The other manuscripts with indirectly transmitted Hexaplaric readings, *Canon. graecus* 62 and *Vat. Gr.* 752, have been edited and studied by A. Schenker,[30] who promises to publish soon the readings from *Ott. Gr.* 398.[31]

In *ms. Hab e 43 f. 51* of the Bodleian in Oxford, which contains the Hebrew text of Prov. 17:16–19:3, Rüger discovered interlinear

---

[24] B. P. Grenfell and A. S. Hunt, *The Amherst Papyri I*, London 1900. New reading, translation and commentary in A. Deissmann, *Licht vom Osten*, Tübingen 1923, 172–79.

[25] L. Lütkemann and A. Rahlfs, *Hexaplarische Randnoten zu Isaias 1–16 aus einer Sinai-Handschrift herausgegeben.* MSU VI, Berlin 1915 [*Sinai Cod. Gr 5 (Rahlfs 710) 10th cent*].

[26] A. Möhle, *Theodoret von Kyros Kommentar zu Jesaia.* MSU V, Berlin 1932.

[27] A. Möhle, *Ein neuer Fund zahlreicher Stücke aus Jesaia-Übersetzungen des Akylas, Symmachos und Theodotion.* The material from these commentaries is already included in the hexaplar apparatus of the critical edition of Isaiah by J. Ziegler, Göttingen 1939. The manuscript discovered by Möhle with the Commentary on Isaiah is in the possession of the *Septuaginta-Unternehmen* of Göttingen and the critical edition is also by Ziegler, *Eusebius Werke IX. Der Jesajakommentar*, Berlin 1975.

[28] P. Katz, "A Fresh Fragment Recovered from Philo", *JTS* 47 (1946), 31–33. The text in question is: περιπάτει εἰς πρόσωπόν μου καὶ γίνου τέλειος. According to Katz, because of the lexicon and the translation techniques, it belongs to Aquila and should be included in the Hexaplar apparatus. As is known, Philo's 'anomalous' is strongly influenced by Aquila, see P. Katz, *Philo's Bible*, Cambridge 1950, 116ff.

[29] G. Mercati, *Psalterii Hexapli reliquiae* II, Rome 1958; I *Osservazioni*, Rome 1965.

[30] A. Schenker, *Hexaplarische Psalmenbruchstücke. Die hexaplarischen Psalmenfragmente der Handschriften Vaticanus graecus 752 und Canonicianus graecus 62*, Fribourg–Göttingen 1975.

[31] A. Schenker, *Hexaplarische Psalmenbruchstücke*, VIII.

Greek glosses to the Hebrew text, in majuscule, which probably came from a reader who knew the Greek according to Aquila's translation. As an integral part of the finds from the Cairo Genizah, these glosses must be placed alongside the fragments of Aquila published by Burkitt and Taylor.[32] And into Aquila's translation have to be inserted at least several glosses on Malachi and Job from a fragment from the Cairo Genizah and published by de Lange.[33]

The Syro-Hexaplaric version, with its frequent glosses by "the three", has been another source used by Field in collecting Hexaplaric readings besides those from the margins of Greek mss and the quotations in the Fathers. And now, W. Baars, by publishing in 1968 new fragments of the Syro-Hexapla, has provided us with a list of Hexaplaric, readings some of which are completely new.[34] The recovery of new material from direct or indirect sources is not exhausted as shown by the new Hexaplaric readings from a catenary manuscript of Psalm 118.[35]

c) *Characteristics*

Aquila's translation techniques, his fidelity to the Hebrew text, and his Semitised syntax that is peculiar to a calque language, which we know of from ancient sources, have been confirmed as more and more continuous texts of that translator have been discovered. Study of them was taken up by Field[36] and especially by Reider,[37] and more recently by Barthélemy in connection with the exegetical methods of Palestinian rabbis, and by K. Hyvärinen.[38] Let us look at some of his most significant characteristics:

---

[32] See H. P. Rüger, "Vier Aquila-Glossen in einem hebräischen Proverbien-Fragment aus der Kairo-Geniza", *ZNW* 50, 3–4 (1959), 275–77.

[33] N. R. M. de Lange, "Some New Fragments of Aquila on Malachi and Job?", *VT* 30 (1980), 291–95.

[34] W. Baars, *New Syro-Hexaplaric Texts: Edited Commented upon Compared with the Septuagint*, Leiden 1968, especially pp. 144–45.

[35] G. Dorival, "L'apport des chaînes exégétiques grecques à une réédition des Hexaples d'Origène (A propos du psaume 118)", *RHT* 4 (1974), 45–74 especially pp. 70–74.

[36] F. Field, *Origenis Hexaplorum quae supersunt*, XXI–XXIV.

[37] J. Reider, *Prolegomena to a Greek–Hebrew*.

[38] D. Barthélemy, *Les Devanciers d'Aquila*, especially pp. 81–87, and K. Hyvärinen, *Die Übersetzung von Aquila*, Uppsala 1977.

1. Aquila expresses the same Hebrew words with the same Greek words and in the same order, even though the meaning in the target language is obscured: Gen. 18:12 Sarah laughed *bᵉqirbāh*, LXX ἐν ἑαυτῇ, α' ἐν ἐγκάτῳ αὐτῆς. 1 Samuel 13:21 *ha-pᵉṣirâ pîm*, ἡ προσβόλησις στόματα (*sic!*). However, it should be specified that several times Aquila did not follow a consistent system of stereotyped translation.[39]

2. He translates Hebrew words with an eye on etymology, even though this procedure produces semantic shifts in Greek that are difficult to fit into the context: Ps. 22:13 *kittᵉrûnî*, α' διεδηματίσαντό με. He coins this neologism from διάδημα, a translation of *keter* = "crown". The LXX instead translates περιέσχον με.

3. He aims to be faithful to the syllables and even to the letters of the original. He reproduces the Hebrew locative *-â* by -δε and the particle *'et* (which marks the accusative) by σύν: Gen. 12:9 *ha-negᵉbbâ*, α' νοτόνδε; Ex. 28:26 *baitah*, α' οἰκόνδε; Gen. 1:1 *'ēt ha-šāmayîm wᵉ'ēt hā-'āreṣ* α' σὺν τὸν οὐρανὸν καὶ σὺν τὴν γῆν. Similarly, he translates the Hebrew personal pronoun *'ānoki* by ἐγώ: *wᵉ'anokî bᵉaltî*, α' καὶ ἐγώ εἰμι ἐκυρίευσα, Jer. 38(31):32.

4. Sometimes he resorts to a kind of mannerism attested in rabbinic hermeneutics which consists in breaking up a Hebrew root comprising several letters and translating it with two Greek words: Ex. 32:25 *lᵉšimṣâ* = 'into an object of malignant joy' (LXX ἐπίχαρμα), α' εἰς ὄνομα ῥύπου (i.e. he reads *lᵉšem sᵉ'â*). This is possible because Aquila shares the ancient view about Hebrew roots which is ignorant of the principle of triliteralism, accepted for the first time by the Hebrew grammarian J. Hayyug in the 11th century CE. As a result, in translation he frequently confuses two similar roots.

5. He also resorts to the device of inserting Hebrew words with Greek colouring, making use of the homophony. In Dt. 11:30, Aquila translates *'ēlôn* = 'holm oak' as αὐλών, which in Greek really means 'hollow, ditch, gully'. The result is that in Aquila, Greek words sometimes acquire completely different meanings to those in general use and the dictionaries are used as mere *indicators* of the Hebrew word to those trying to translate.[40]

6. Compound particles are reproduced just as they are, so that no Hebrew element is lost in Greek. For example, Gen. 2:18 *kᵉnegdô*, α' ὡς κατέναντι αὐτοῦ (against LXX κατ' αὐτόν).

---

[39] See J. Barr, *The Typology of Literalism*, 312.
[40] As noted by J. Barr in his review of *Index to Aquila*, *JSS* 12 (1967), 303.

7. In continuous fragments that have been preserved, the *Tetra-grammaton* is written in palaeo-Hebrew characters. Moving from the square script, the *waw* and the *yod* were drawn almost in the same way (יהוה). This similarity gave rise to the curious transcription ΠΙΠΙ in Greek by copyists who no longer understood what it meant.[41] However, within the Greek text it was pronounced κύριος. Similarly, Aquila uses special translations for the divine names, with ἱκανός for *šadday* and ἰσχυρός for *'El*, following the procedure of translating according to etymology.[42]

8. For the verbs he often used formations in -ίζειν and -οῦν, and for nouns the suffixes -μός, -της, -σις and -μα.

9. He is more consistent than the LXX in retaining the aspects and functions of the various Hebrew conjugations. The *piel* and *hiphil* are chiefly expressed by verbs in -οῦν, -άζειν, -ίζειν. When the Hebrew verb is intransitive, it is usually translated by the Greek verb in the passive, thus *'or* for φωτίζεσθαι. In this case the *piel* and *hiphil* of the same verb are translated by the Greek active; for example *hē'îr* for φωτίζειν. As is evident he is more demanding than the LXX in the nuances of Hebrew voices.

10. In exegesis his literalist tendency set up a barrier to the allegorical methods of interpretation that had culminated in Philo and the Alexandrian School. The literalism is particularly evident in the lexicon, although it should be stressed that Aquila is a master in his choice of words and has full command of Greek. However, in syntax Aquila's supposed literalism needs to be more nuanced since he allowed himself a degree of freedom in adapting the Greek language system reasonably well.[43]

11. To a very large extent the Hebrew text used by the translator is proved to be the same as the *textus receptus*, at least in respect of the consonantal text. However, there are passages where the translation must suppose a different *Vorlage* from the Masoretic text as an indication that the standardisation of the Hebrew text supposed by the Synod of Yamnia (*c.* 100 CE) did not take effect immediately or in a radical way,[44] but instead was more the expression of an ideal to be aimed for.

An index of Aquila has for years been one of the most pressing

---

[41] See, for example, Ps. 21(22):20-28.
[42] See K. Hyvärinen, *Die Übersetzung von Aquila*, 36–38.
[43] See K. Hyvärinen, *Die Übersetzung von Aquila*, 43–86 and 111–12.
[44] J. Reider, *Prolegomena to a Greek–Hebrew*, 292ff.

projects for students of the LXX. Back in 1913, Reider announced that in Dropsie College they were working on indexes of the three Jewish translators which were to appear as a supplementary volume to the concordance of Hatch – Redpath.[45] In the same place he put forward some methodological proposals that had to be taken into account in compiling them, such as the separation of words exclusive to each of "the three" from words they had in common; separating witnesses from Greek sources from those obtained by the retranslation of secondary versions, etc.[46] In a joint publication, Katz and Ziegler were to repeat their wishes for the compilation of indexes to Aquila, Symmachus and Theodotion as soon as possible, and they also specify a series of preliminary criteria to be followed.[47] Finally, in 1966, we had the satisfaction of seeing the appearance of the first of them, Aquila, on which Reider worked, now completed and revised by N. Turner.[48] Unfortunately, he only carried out part of his task, for there are so many limitations which reviews of the book have pointed out that it cannot be used without a rigorous check on the data in the actual sources.[49] Another defect of this work, which requires revision and correction, is that it was only possible to be exhaustive in those books in which the critical edition with a sound Hexaplaric apparatus have appeared in the *editio magna* of Göttingen. From this point of view, the publication of the Index could be conceived as premature except that it is necessary to combine the study of lexicon and grammar with the publication of editions, given the extremely slow progress of this type of undertaking.

---

[45] J. Reider, *Prolegomena to a Greek–Hebrew*, 321 in a footnote

[46] J. Reider, *Prolegomena to a Greek–Hebrew*, 307ff.

[47] P. Katz and J. Ziegler, "Ein Aquila-Index in Vorbereitung".

[48] J. Reider and N. Turner, *An Index to Aquila Greek–Hebrew, Hebrew–Greek, Latin–Hebrew with the Syriac and Armenian Evidence*, VTS 12 (1966).

[49] J. Barr describes the Latin–Hebrew Index as "a source of endless confusion" in *JSS* 12 (1967), 296–304, p. 302. See also, E. Tov in "Some Corrections to Reider – Turner's Index to Aquila", and especially R. Hanhart, who in *TRev* 64 (1968), 394, undoubtedly makes the harshest judgement against the *Index*. After suggesting a new revision to correct all the mistakes, checking the passages of the book in Field, Hatch – Redpath and the other Hexaplaric material which appeared later than these publications, he closes with the following words: "Und hier muss man, damit nicht die kommenden Beiträge zur Septuaginta-Forschung mit einer Fülle an falschen oder ungenauen Zitaten überschwemmt werden, jeden Septuaginta-Forscher davor warnen, dieses Buch zu benutzen, ohne eine jede seiner Angaben an den ihm zugrunde liegenden Quellen nachgeprüft zu haben." Ziegler followed Hanhart's advice in his edition of the book of Job and discovers 114 false attributions to Aquila in Turner's Index for the book of Job alone, see J. Ziegler, *Beiträge zum griechischen Iob*, 53–66.

d) *Current Research and Future Prospects*

Undoubtedly the most important contribution to the the study of "the three" in the last few years is the work by Barthélemy mentioned above.[50] From the fragments of the Twelve Prophets discovered in Naḥal Ḥever he succeeded in identifying a recension of the LXX that brings the original Greek text close to the Hebrew text at that time and puts into practice the exegetical techniques of Palestinian rabbis. Barthélemy calls this recension "R" or καίγε, and finds traces of it in various books of the LXX into which it had penetrated in an uneven fashion at one of the stages of the manuscript transmission. Within this movement the work of Aquila does not yet appear as completely new and original in the 2nd century but as the perfecting and culmination of this process begun by the καίγε group in the 1st century CE in the circles of Rabbi Hillel. Barthélemy notes a series of translation techniques of the καίγε group perfected by Aquila.[51] The latter, under the aegis of Rabbi Akiba, improved the work of the καίγε group in such a way that it succeeded in eclipsing its predecessors in the Jewish world.

Within this new perspective, opened up by Barthélemy's monograph, it remains for the future to clarify how in this process of the revision of the LXX which culminated in the version by Aquila, ancient information and the testimony of manuscripts about a double edition of this version are to be reinterpreted.[52] Can they be understood as the two different stages revealed in this process, the stages of the καίγε and of the definitive translation by Aquila? In agreement with the characteristics set out above are Field's words about the style of these two editions: "primam liberiorem in qua sensum potius quam singulas voces apte reddere studebat; alteram vero quae κατ' ἀκρίβειαν nominabatur".[53] Something similar was to happen with Aquila, who perfected the method of the καίγε group, taking its literalism to the extreme. However, to explain this point and to prove that they are not simply marginal corrections to the single edition, it will be necessary first to re-examine the reliability of those attributions and the guarantee of the witnesses. It is surprising that the passages where Jerome mentions two editions of

---

[50] D. Barthélemy, *Les Devanciers d'Aquila*.
[51] D. Barthélemy, *Les Devanciers d'Aquila*, 81–88.
[52] F. Field, *Origenis Hexaplorum quae supersunt*, XXV–XXVII.
[53] F. Field, *Origenis Hexaplorum quae supersunt*, XXXV, following Jerome.

Aquila are all from Jeremiah, Ezekiel and a quotation from Daniel. However, neither in his commentaries on Isaiah, the Twelve Prophets or Psalms nor in his many letters in which he alludes to Aquila, does he again mention this double edition. Even so, the list – fairly lengthy – of double readings compiled by Field is more reliable; some are attested by more than one route, two manuscripts or a Greek manuscript and the Syro-Hexapla and occur in a greater number of books.[54] Within this process, the attribution to Aquila of the text of Qoheleth printed in current editions as from the LXX still needs to be clarified, and likewise the affiliation to the καίγε group of the Septuagintal text of Song, Lamentations and Ruth.[55] And should this hypothesis be confirmed, it must be explained how the fragments attributed to Aquila in these books were inserted within the revisions.

Since each book of the LXX presents its own problems, the possibility cannot be ruled out that the tendency to a greater literalness may have influenced the Alexandrian version of some hagiographers.

The improvements to the index to Aquila suggested by the reviews cited above are as follows:

1. A revision is urgently needed of the published index to correct the large number of mistakes that have slipped in at various stages of the work.

2. It is necessary to complete this in the light of the new material that is gradually being published, much of it already included in the critical editions of Göttingen.

In the field of Aquila's translation techniques and syntax, a new monograph is required that takes recent material (especially those

---

[54] F. Field, *Origenis Hexaplorum quae supersunt*, XXVI–XXVII. The books included are Ex., Lev., Num., Kgs, Pss, Is., Jer., Ez., Jon., and Mic.

[55] D. Barthélemy, *Les Devanciers d'Aquila*, 32–34. Recently for the LXX of Qoheleth, Hyvärinen has reached the conclusion that it is neither the ancient LXX nor Aquila's version, but instead a mixed text, "eine von den rabbinen angeregten Rezensionen ist, die auch die merkwürdige Übersetzung der *nota accusativi* aufweist, ohne dass sie deswegen als eine Aquila-Version betrachtet werden konnte. Sie ist unter Leitung von r. Akiba, möglicherwerse in der 70er Jahren übersetzt und später vielleicht von Aquila revidiert worden," see K. Hyvärinen, *Die Übersetzung von Aquila*, 88–99, p. 99. According to Jarick there is no basis for denying Aquila as the author of the readings that the manuscripts attribute to him in Qoheleth, whereas there are good reasons in support of those attributions? In connection with the problem of a double edition of Aquila in Qoheleth, it cannot be decided for certain whether Qoheleth-LXX is the first edition of Aquila and Qoheleth-Aquila the second, see J. Jarick, "Aquila's *Qohelet*", p. 139.

fragments that preserve a continuous text such as the ones discovered by Mercati for the Psalms) into account. Above all, there is a need for a systematic study of all the minor versions, in the light of the various types of ancient Jewish hermeneutics, that avoids linking a particular translation to a specific character of ancient Jewish literature for no reason.[56]

And finally, there is a need to study Aquila's influence on Jewish versions into Mediaeval and Modern Greek, especially the *Graeco-Venetus* and the interlinear version of the book of Jonah, which took literalism to the extreme of making the Greek words keep the same gender they had in the original Hebrew. However, we shall discuss this in more detail in chapter 11.

With the Arabic invasion, use of Aquila by the Jews in the East is no longer attested, when Greek ceased to be *lingua franca* in the whole Near East. However, it always remained as an achievement and an ideal in Jewish thought because of its faithful reproduction of the sacred language; it survived in the Greek loanwords in post-biblical Hebrew and in new attempts at Jewish translations into Byzantine Greek and Modern Greek in the mediaeval and modern diaspora.

SELECT BIBLIOGRAPHY

Barr, J., *The Typology of Literalism in Ancient Biblical Translations*. MSU XV, Göttingen 1979.
Barthélemy, D., *Les Devanciers d'Aquila*, VTS 10 (1963).
Burkitt, F. C., *Fragments of the Books of Kings According to the Translation of Aquila*, Cambridge 1897 = New York 1969, XVIII–XXII.
Busto Saiz, J. R., "El léxico peculiar del traductor Aquila". *Emerita* 48 (1980), 31–41.
Daniel, S., "Minor Greek Versions". *Encyclopaedia Judaica* 4, Jerusalem 1971, 955–56.
Declerck, J., "Le Διάλογος πρὸς 'Ιουδαίους du *codex Athonensis Vatopedinus*". *Byz* 82 (1989), 118–121.
Field, F., *Origenis Hexaplorum quae supersunt*, Oxford 1875, *Prolegomena*, XVI–XXXVII.
Gil Ulecia, A., "Aquila". *EncBibl* I (1963), 621–24.
Grabbe, L. L., "Aquila's Translation and Rabbinic Exegesis". *JJS* 33 (1982), 527–36.
———, "The Translation Technique of the Greek Minor Versions: Translations or Revisions?". *Septuagint, Scrolls and Cognate Writings*, 1992, 505–56.
Greenspoon, L., "Aquila's Version". *ABD* 6 (1992), 320–21.
Hyvärinen, K., *Die Übersetzung von Aquila*, Uppsala 1977.
Jarick, J., "Aquila's *Koheleth*". *Textus* 15 (1990), 131–39.
Jellicoe, S., "Aquila and his Version". *JQR* 59 (1968–69), 326–32.
———, *SMS*, 76–83.
Katz, P., and J. Ziegler, "Ein Aquila-Index in Vorbereitung". *VT* 8 (1958), 264–85.

---

[56] See L. L. Grabbe, "Aquila's Translation and Rabbinic Exegesis", p. 536.

Kipper, J. B., "Ein übersehenes Fragment Aquila's in Jr 38 (31), 22b?". *Bib* 66 (1985), 580–81.

Lange N. R. M. de, "Some New Fragments of Aquila on Malachi and Job?". *VT* 30 (1980), 291–94.

Liebreich, L. J., "Silverstone's Aquila and Onkelos". *JQR* ns 27 (1936–37), 287–91.

Möhle, A., "Ein neuer Fund zahlreicher Stücke aus Jesaia-Übersetzungen des Akylas, Symmachos und Theodotion". Probe eines neuen "Field". *ZAW* NF 11 (1934), 176–83.

Paul, A., "La Bible grecque d'Aquila et l'idéologie du judaïsme ancien". *ANRW* II, 20, 1 (1987), 221–85.

Rabinowitz, L. J., "Onkelos and Aquila". *Encyclopaedia Judaica* 12, Jerusalem 1971, 1405–406.

Rahlfs, A., "Über Theodotion-Lesarten im Neuen Testament und Aquila-Lesarten bei Justin". *ZNW* 20 (1921), 182–99.

Reider, J., *Prolegomena to a Greek–Hebrew and Hebrew–Greek Index to Aquila*, Philadelphia 1916 = *JQR* ns (1913), 321–56, 577–620; 7 (1916), 287–366.

———, and N. Turner, *An Index to Aquila Greek–Hebrew, Hebrew–Greek, Latin–Hebrew with the Syriac and Armenian Evidence*, VTS 12 (1966), (and the review of this work by J. Barr in *JSS* 12 [1967], 303, and by R. Hanhart in *TRev* 64, 65 [1968], 391–94).

Silverstone, A. E., *Aquila and Onkelos*, Manchester 1931.

Soisalon-Soininen, I., "Einige Merkmale der Übersetzungsweise von Aquila". *Wort, Lied und Gottesspruch*, 1972, I, 177–84.

Swete, H. B., *An Introduction to the Old Testament in Greek*, Cambridge 1914.

Tov, E., "Some Corrections to Reider – Turner's Index to Aquila". *Textus* 8 (1973), 164–74.

Ziegler, J., *Beiträge zum griechischen Iob*, Göttingen 1985, 53–66 and 110–12.

CHAPTER EIGHT

SYMMACHUS THE TRANSLATOR

a) *Ancient Witnesses*

As is the case for so many persons in antiquity, we know very little with certainty about Symmachus and the circumstances and characteristics of his work. Unlike Aquila and Theodotion, no specialist has identified him as the author of an Aramaic Targum. All the same, in 1862 Geiger had already connected him with Sumkos ben Yosef of the Talmud, a disciple of Rabbi Meir, who flourished towards the end of the 2nd century CE and apparently knew Greek.[1] Recently, D. Barthélemy again defended this identification, based upon agreements between the *haggadâ* by Rabbi Meir and the one by Symmachus.[2]

From his silence it has been deduced that Irenaeus possibly did not know him. In that case, he seems to have flourished after 200 CE. However, Origen's first commentaries of *c.* 230 CE already mention him. In any event, it is extremely difficult to determine the chronology of this translator, as is shown by Mercati's words at the close of his massive study on the topic.[3] This is compounded by the new problem raised by possible Symmachian readings before the Common Era discovered recently[4] and the early revisions of the LXX to be analysed at the end of this chapter.

---

[1] A. Geiger, "Symmachus der Übersetzer der Bibel".

[2] D. Barthélemy, "Qui est Symmache?", 460ff. Barthélemy discovers five traits common to the Greek translator and to Sumkos ben Yosef: (1) a lively and original intellect; (2) a close relationship with Rabbi Meir; (3) a desire to be free as against literalist exegesis; (4) a very muted acceptance by contemporary Judaism; (5) ill repute concerning his Jewish and possibly Samaritan origin.

[3] G. Mercati, *L'età di Simmaco l'interprete.*

[4] S. Jellicoe, *SMS* 96: "The older view, as expressed by Swete, which would place the *terminus ad quem* prior to *c.* AD 230 on the ground that Origen's earliest commentaries which were written about that time reflect a knowledge of Symmachus' version, is no longer valid, since recent discoveries have shown that 'Symmachian' readings antedate the Christian era." And on pp. 94–95: "Like Aquila and Theodotion he presents the modern student of the LXX with the problem which has already received mention, the appearance of characteristic readings before his time." We would all like to know to which discoveries Jellicoe is referring, especially as it is

Symmachus is mentioned in Christian tradition by Epiphanius, Eusebius, Jerome and Palladius. Of course, the information given by these authors does not always agree, the versions by Epiphanius and Eusebius being the most contradictory. According to Epiphanius he is a Samaritan despised by his people, who undergoes circumcision again; he lived in the time of the emperor Severus.[5] However, for Eusebius and Jerome he is an Ebionite whose memories circulated in their lifetimes. And Eusebius added that Origen received them together with interpretations of Scripture by Symmachus from a certain Juliana who in turn had received them from Symmachus himself.[6] Finally, Palladius remembers the two years that Origen remained

---

a matter of such importance. At the close of the chapter we will see what indications actually exist of these Symmachian readings prior to the historical Symmachus.

[5] Epiphanius, *De Mens. et Ponderibus*, 16: ἐν τοῖς τοῦ Σευήρου χρόνοις Σύμμαχός τις Σαμαρείτης, τῶν παρ᾽ αὐτοῖς σοφῶν μὴ τιμηθεὶς ὑπὸ τοῦ οἰκείου ἔθνους... προσηλυτεύει καὶ περιτέμνεται δευτέραν περιτομήν... Οὗτος τοίνυν ὁ Σύμμαχος πρὸς διαστροφὴν τῶν παρὰ Σαμαρείταις ἑρμηνειῶν ἑρμηνεύσας τὴν τρίτην ἐξέδωκεν ἑρμηνείαν ("In the time of Severus, a certain Symmachus, a Samaritan and one of their wise men, disgraced by his own people... becomes a proselyte and is circumcised with a second circumcision... So this Symmachus, distorting the Scriptures of the Samaritans by translating them, produced the third translation").

[6] Eusebius, *Hist. Ecc.* VI, 17: τῶν γε μὴν ἑρμηνευτῶν αὐτῶν δὴ τούτων ἰστέον Ἐβιωναῖον τὸν Σύμμαχον γεγονέναι... καὶ ὑπομνήματα δὲ τοῦ Συμμάχου εἰς ἔτι νῦν φέρεται, ἐν οἷς δοκεῖ πρὸς τὸ κατὰ Ματθαῖον ἀποτεινόμενος εὐαγγέλιον, τὴν δεδηλωμένην αἵρεσιν κρατύνειν. ταῦτα δὲ ὁ Ὠριγένης μετὰ καὶ ἄλλων εἰς τὰς γραφὰς ἑρμηνειῶν τοῦ Συμμάχου σημαίνει παρὰ Ἰουλιανῆς τινος εἰληφέναι, ἣν καί φησιν παρ᾽ αὐτοῦ Συμμάχου τὰς βίβλους διαδέξασθαι ("And from these same interpreters it is important to know that Symmachus was an Ebionite and up to now some reports about Symmachus are circulating in which, it seems, by arguing against the gospel of Matthew he strengthens the heresy mentioned. And Origen explains that he received these reports together with other Symmachian interpretations of Scripture from a certain Juliana, who – she says – received the books from Symmachus himself"). And Jerome, *De vir. ill.*, 54: "Theodotionis Hebionaei et Symmachi eiusdem dogmatis." The passage from Eusebius, particularly the clause ἐν οἷς δοκεῖ πρὸς τὸ κατὰ Ματθαῖον ἀποτεινόμενος εὐαγγέλιον, has occasioned some debate depending on whether ἀποτείνεσθαι πρός τινα is understood to mean "to dedicate oneself to" or with the nuance of opposition, "to start hurling insults against". It seem that Jerome did not understand the expression when he translates, "qui in evangelium quoque κατὰ Ματθαῖον scripsit commentarios" (*De vir. ill.*, 54). For Harnack instead, the translation of this passage runs as follows: "Er befestigt die Häresie der Ebioniten, indem er sich an das Matth.-Ev. wendet (d. h. es polemisch herbeizieht)", see A. von Harnack, *Geschichte der altchristlichen Literatur bis Eusebius* I, 1 Berlin 1893, 210, stating that Symmachus wrote an Ebionite commentary on the gospel of Matthew. The same opinion is held by H. J. Schoeps, *Theologie und Geschichte des Judenchristentums*, 34: "Sie dürfte identisch sein mit dem ebionitischen Matthäuskommentar, den uns Euseb VI, 17 bezeugt hat." Schoeps translates like Harnack and according to him there are two interpretations: a) "dass er das Mt.Ev. polemisch bei seiner Verteidigung des Ebionitismus heranzieht, oder b) eine von Standpunkt des Ebioniten Evangelium gegen den kanonischen Mt. gerichtete Schrift

with Juliana who sheltered him, probably during the persecution of the emperor Caracalla, *c.* 216.[7] Ambrosiaster (*Proleg. in comm. in Gal.*) and Augustine (*contra Faust.* XIX, 4, c; *contra Crescon.* 1,36) mention the sect of Symmachians who probably took their name from our translator.[8]

J. Gwynn noted that Epiphanius dates Symmachus before Theodotion, probably in the reign of Marcus Aurelius (161–80).[9] Taking into account the dates of Palladius to which we referred earlier, the literary activity of Symmachus has to be set very early, in the last years of this emperor, and Swete wonders whether Epiphanius may not have reversed the sequence of the two translators, so that Theodotion would have to be put under Marcus Aurelius and Symmachus under Commodus (180–92).[10] However, according to Busto Saiz there is no need to assume this inversion if we accept that Origen met Juliana in about 216.[11]

In recent years the debate on the identity of Symmachus, his origin and the date of his translation has been taken up again. As a

verfast hat" (*ibid.*, 369). G. Zahn, *Herkunft und Lehrrichtung* also claims to defend the Ebionite association of this translator. D. Barthélemy, instead, who prefers the information given by Epiphanius as a more secure foundation about Symmachus, has found seven other passages from the work by Eusebius in which that expression occurs and concludes that it always means "to argue against" and never "to lean on" (D. Barthélemy, *Qui est Symmache?*, 456ff.). Against Schoeps he claims categorically that he was not an Ebionite, at least in the meaning given to that sect in the *Kerygmata Petri*. This last interpretation is the one defended by O. Bardenhewer in *Geschichte der altkirchlichen Literatur* I, Freiburg in Br. 1913 (= Darmstadt 1962), 379.

[7] Palladius, *Historia Lausiaca* LXIV (ed. C. Butler, *The Lausiac History of Palladius*, Cambridge 1898): Ἰουλιανή τις πάλιν παρθένος ἐν Καισαρείᾳ τῆς Καππαδοκίας λογιωτάτη ἐλέγετο καὶ πιστοτάτη ἥτις Ὠριγένην τὸν συγγραφέα φεύγοντα τὴν ἐπανάστασιν τῶν Ἑλλήνων ἐδέξατο ἐπὶ δύο ἔτη ἰδίοις ἀναλώμασι καὶ ὑπηρεσίᾳ ἀναπαύσασα τὸν ἄνδρα. Εὗρον δὲ ταῦτα ἐγὼ γεγραμμένα ἐν παλαιοτάτῳ βιβλίῳ στιχερῷ, ἐν ᾧ ἐγέγραπτο χειρὶ Ὠριγένους· Τοῦτο τὸ βιβλίον εὗρον ἐγὼ παρὰ Ἰουλιανῇ τῇ παρθένῳ ἐν Καισαρείᾳ, κρυπτόμενος παρ᾽ αὐτῇ· ἥτις ἔλεγε παρ᾽ αὐτοῦ Συμμάχου τοῦ ἑρμηνέως τῶν Ἰουδαίων αὐτὸ εἰληφέναι. ("And of a certain Juliana, a virgin in Caesarea of Cappadocia, it was said that she was very learned and virtuous. For two years she took Origen in, the writer who was fleeing from the uprising of the pagans, and attended to him with her own goods and services. And I found that written in an old book, in verse, in which was written in Origen's hand: 'I found this book in the house of Juliana, the virgin of Caesarea; it was hidden in her house. And she said that she had received it from Symmachus himself, the translator of the Jews'").

[8] A. von Harnack, *Geschichte der altchristlichen Literatur* I,1, 209ff.

[9] J. Gwynn, "Symmachus", *DCB* 4, 748–49. In this hypothesis the Σευήρου of the *De Mens. et Ponderibus*, 15, would be a corruption of Οὐήρου, the surname of Marcus Aurelius.

[10] H. B. Swete, *An Introduction to the Old Testament in Greek*, 50.

[11] J. R. Busto Saiz, *La traducción de Símaco en el libro de los Salmos*, 319.

result of these recent studies, today the thesis of the Jewish origin of Symmachus tends to predominate, proving Epiphanius to be right. This is against him belonging to the Christian sect of the Ebionites, as Eusebius and Jerome maintain, followed by modern scholars such as H. J. Schoeps, for whom the translation by Symmachus would be the Old Testament of that sect.

However, the English edition of the new Schürer, published in 1986, continues to exclude Symmachus from the chapter on Jewish translators of the Bible, under the pretext that, although he was familiar with the early Jewish recensions, he himself was not a Jew.[12] Most specialists, however, including myself, agree that the probable source of Epiphanius is Origen and therefore the information is more trustworthy. On the other hand, as Barthélemy, Van der Kooij and Salvesen have noted, the mistake by Eusebius comes from a quotation by Irenaeus (*Adversus Haer.* III, 21.1) in his *Historia Eccles.* V, 8: there, Irenaeus, who does not know Symmachus, says that the Ebionites followed Aquila and Theodotion in the translation of ʿalmâ in Is. 7:14 as νεᾶνις. As this translation also occurs in Symmachus, Eusebius concluded, from the commentaries by Irenaeus, that Symmachus was an Ebionite.[13] On the other hand, in the exegesis of Symmachus there is no trace of Ebionism,[14] whereas there is sufficient evidence that he was well acquainted with the rabbinic exegesis of his time and the *targumîm*.[15] As for his origin and the date of his translation, there are considerable indications to locate him in Galilee and possibly in Caesarea Maritima, around 200 CE, and it is even probable that he was Sumkos ben Yosef.[16]

---

[12] I.e. its author continues to prefer the testimony of Eusebius, E. Schürer, *The History of the Jewish People in the Age of Jesus Christ.* Vol III. 1, revised and edited by G. Vermes, F. Millar and M. Goodman, Edinburgh 1986, p. 493: "Because Symmachus, although he was acquainted with earlier Jewish recensions, including that represented in the Leather Scroll of the Minor Prophets found at Qumran, and was capable of using the Hebrew text independently, was not himself Jewish."

[13] D. Barthélemy, "Qui est Symmache?", p. 460; A. van der Kooij, "Symmachus, 'de vertaler der Joden'", p. 7, and A. Salvesen, *Symmachus in the Pentateuch,* 289–90.

[14] See A. Salvesen, *Symmachus in the Pentateuch,* 290–94 and 297: "There are no traces of any Ebionite belief in his Pentateuch translation."

[15] See J. González Luis, "La versión de Símaco a los Profetas Mayores", 288–354, and González Luis, "Los 'targumim' y la versión de Símaco"; J. R. Busto Saiz, *La traducción de Símaco en el libro de los Salmos,* 311–23; A. van der Kooij, "Symmachos, 'de vertaler de Joden'", 13–17, and A. Salvesen, *Symmachus in the Pentateuch,* 178 and 297.

[16] See A. van der Kooij, "Symmachos, 'de vertaler der Joden'", 18–20, and A. Salvesen, *Symmachus in the Pentateuch,* 294 and 297: "The translation combined the best Biblical Greek style, remarkable clarity, a high degree of accuracy regarding the Hebrew text, and the rabbinic exegesis of his day: it might be described as a Greek Targum, or Tannaitic Septuagint."

b) *Sources for Symmachus*

As in the case of Aquila towards the close of the 19th century, we knew of no other texts of Symmachus except those transmitted by quotations in the Fathers and marginal glosses to a few biblical manuscripts. There are many readings from "the three" in the commentaries of Eusebius, Procopius, Theodoret, Jerome and others. Likewise, some manuscripts of the LXX such as *Athos Pantocrator 24* (= v of Brooke–McLean) or the *Vaticanus Graecus 747* (= *j* of Brooke–McLean) for the Pentateuch, or even the *Codex Marchilianus* (Q) and mss 86 and 710 for the prophets, were particularly rich in this type of marginal reading. Their readings occur in other catenary manuscripts[17] and especially the Syro-Hexaplaric version. The channel through which these readings were transmitted was the Hexapla, for we know that Symmachus filled the fourth column of this great synoptic work. The Hexaplaric fragments are collected in the work by Field.[18] As we saw in the previous chapter, in 1896 the discovery by Mercati of the Hexaplaric Psalter in a Milan palimpsest was announced, a text that was published in 1958. It is difficult to overestimate the importance of this edition, since in fact for Symmachus it provides for the first time a set of continuous texts long enough to enable study of his style and translation techniques.

To this highly important material have to be added other more fragmentary publications: in Taylor's publication in 1900 there are fragments of Hexaplaric Psalm 22 and consequently fragments of Symmachus[19] from the Cairo Genizah material. In 1910, C. Wessely published a new fragment which contained Psalms 68:13-14, 30-33 and 80:11-14, fragments which he attributed hastily and incorrectly to Aquila but which Nestle, Mercati and Capelle claimed almost simultaneously for Symmachus.[20] They are parchment fragments of the 3rd/4th centuries CE from El Fayum and now form part of the

---

[17] See chapter 18.

[18] F. Field, *Origenis Hexaplorum quae supersunt*.

[19] C. Taylor, *Hebrew–Greek Cairo Genizah Palimpsests Including a Fragment of the 22ᵈ Psalm According to Origen's Hexapla*, Cambridge 1900. It contains the text of Symmachus for Ps. 22:15-18. See *ibid.* pp. 39–41.

[20] C. Wessely, "Un nouveau fragment"; E. Nestle, "Symmachus, not Aquila"; G. Mercati, "Frammenti di Aquila o di Simmaco?"; P. Capelle, "Fragments du Psautier d'Aquila?". Capelle excludes Aquila as the author of these fragments. They seem to be by Symmachus, he says, but does not actually state this categorically. The lack of documentation for Theodotion, the *quinta* and the *sexta* for this passage precludes anything more explicit.

Rainer collection in Vienna. A mere glance at the fragments collected by Field alongside the texts of Wessely shows that they are by Symmachus. Wessely was probably mistaken because they preserve the *Tetragrammaton* written in palaeo-Hebrew characters. However, this is precisely why the fragments are even more interesting, since besides being the oldest witness we have of the version by Symmachus – an indication that in the 3rd/4th centuries it was still being copied in Egypt – they prove that the *Tetragrammaton* was preserved in palaeo-Hebraic not only in the version by Aquila but also in that by Symmachus and perhaps the one by Theodotion.

The discovery of Eusebius' commentary on Isaiah, published recently, considerably increased the material from Symmachus for this book.[21] However, both this material and the material mentioned earlier is already incorporated in the critical editions of Göttingen and Cambridge, with the exception of the book of Psalms as this edition of the Göttingen series (1931; 2nd edn 1967) has no Hexaplaric apparatus.

These are the remains we have of the translator Symmachus. However, the possibility that the future will provide us with even more interesting discoveries in this respect is not to be excluded. If we can trust the report of a Greek between 1565 and 1575, in the library of a certain Konstantinos Barenos there was a Symmachian translation of the whole Psalter and other portions of the Old Testament. This has probably been lost in the meantime or it lies in an undiscovered library of the Eastern Mediterranean.[22]

c) *Characteristics*

Until about twenty years ago, in order to study the translation techniques, syntax and style of Symmachus, we could only refer to a

---

[21] A. Möhle, "Ein neuer Fund zahlreicher Stücke aus der Jesaja-Uebersetzung des Akylas, Symmachus und Theodotion". Probe eines neuen "Field" *ZAW* NF 11 (1934), 176–83, and J. Ziegler, *Eusebius Werke IX. Der Jesaja-Kommentar*, Berlin 1975.

[22] R. Forster, *De antiquitatibus et libris mss. Constantinopolitanus*, Rostock 1877. In connection with a copy of a translation of the psalms which was found in the bishop's residence in Rodosto, Bratke was able to show, after considerable effort (see "Das Schicksal der Handschriften in Rodosto bei Konstantinopel", *TLZ* [1894], 6) that it was destroyed in a fire in 1838 together with the irreplaceable original of the ὑπομνήματα by Hegesippus, see H. J. Schoeps, *Theologie und Geschichte des Judenchristentums*, 35, n. 2. On the possibility that manuscripts of Symmachus can be found in some libraries in Greece, see H. Hody, *De Bibliorum Textibus Originalibus, Versionibus Graecis et Latina Vulgata*, Oxford 1705, 588.

monograph from the mid-18th century by C. A. Thieme[23] and some random remarks from the articles by Schoeps which, as will be seen, were not written for a philological purpose. However, thanks to studies by J. R. Busto Saiz on the book of Psalms and by J. González Luis and A. Salvesen on the Pentateuch, today we have more reliable criteria for the style and translation techniques used by Symmachus.[24] In fact, for the books mentioned, these scholars have analysed the way in which Symmachus translates nouns and pronouns, Hebrew verb forms, particles and particles of speech. In general they prove that the translation by Symmachus was literal, less so than Aquila but more than the LXX. But he also reproduces the meaning of the original Hebrew clearly and fluently. His Greek, although obviously translation Greek, is very like the language of contemporary Greek writers and was probably intended for middle-class Hellenised Jews. And it is possible that Symmachus was trying to avoid the feeling of absurdity that Aquila's translation could evoke in readers unfamiliar with Hebrew, showing by his translation that it was possible to translate the Bible into Greek with an acceptable style.[25]

Studies of the language of Symmachus have been excessively one-sided by defining it in contrast to the translation by Aquila. The emphasis has been placed on Symmachus as transmitting the sense of the phrase as against Aquila's literalism, the latter constantly violating the syntax and hyperbaton of classical Greek.[26] To this have contributed Jerome's words according to whom Aquila tried "verbum de verbo exprimere" whereas Symmachus "sensum potius sequi".[27] Barthélemy even asserts that Symmachus' language is close to that of his contemporaries Lucian and Galen.[28]

However, this is true only in part, since on the one hand, Symmachus' literalism in respect of the Hebrew text is comparable to that

---

[23] C. A. Thieme, *Pro puritate Symmachi dissertatio.*

[24] See Select Bibliography. The study of the psalms by Busto Saiz is important as the book includes more continuous passages that have emerged recently but have not been taken into account by the few previous studies. The studies by González Luis and Salvesen have the advantage of tackling a corpus of writings – the Major Prophets and the Pentateuch – for which there are already critical editions and in which, therefore, the Hexaplar material is more correct.

[25] See J. R. Busto Saiz, *La traducción de Símaco en el libro de los Salmos*, 278–86, and A. Salvesen, *Symmachus in the Pentateuch*, 198–264.

[26] H. B. Swete, *An Introduction to the Old Testament in Greek*, 51.

[27] Jerome, *Praef. in Chron. Eus.* and *Praef. in Job.*

[28] D. Barthélemy, "Qui est Symmache?", 463.

of Aquila, apart from his real concern for conveying the sense. On the other hand, comparison with contemporary Greek writers can throw light on some aspects of the lexicon, but these should not be exaggerated since Symmachus' Greek continues to be translation Greek, which places it on a different level from writers such as Lucian, Plutarch or Galen.[29]

With these provisos we can move on to examine some of the techniques he uses to improve a translation such as Aquila's, which could not be read by a Greek-speaking public who did not know Hebrew.

1. Symmachus tends to change paratactic Hebrew constructions joined by καί in the LXX into syntagms of a participle plus a finite verb. He also replaces Hebrew constructions with b^e plus infinitive with genitive absolutes. Let us look at these features, comparing them with the LXX construction:

Ps. 26:2 LXX: ἠσθένησαν καὶ ἔπεσαν
                σ' σφαλέντες ἔπεσον
Ps. 9:4 LXX: ἐν τῷ ἀποστραφῆναι τὸν ἐχθρόν μου
                σ' ἀναστραφέντων τῶν ἐχθρῶν μου

2. In Greek he usually smoothes over the sequence of two consecutive verbs, which reflects a known Hebraism, by using an adverb or adjective in apposition:

Gen. 4:2 LXX: προσέθηκεν τεκεῖν
                σ' πάλιν ἔτεκεν

In other words, he adapts Hebrew idioms to Greek usage as can be seen in the following translations where the LXX retains the Hebraism:

2 Sam. 12:5 LXX: υἱὸς θανάτου
                   σ' ἄξιος θανάτου
1 Sam. 9:20 LXX: μὴ θῆς τὴν καρδίαν σου
                   σ' μὴ μεριμνήσῃς
1 Sam. 30:21 LXX: ἠρώτησαν αὐτὸν τὰ εἰς εἰρήνην
                   σ' ἠσπάσαντο αὐτούς
Ex. 5:7 LXX: καθάπερ ἐχθὲς καὶ τρίτην ἡμέραν
                   σ' καθάπερ καὶ πρότερον

---

[29] See J. R. Busto Saiz, *La traducción de Símaco en el libro de los Salmos*, 284–85. Busto notes how the word order and sparing use of illative particles show that there is a wide gulf between the translation by Symmachus and texts originally composed in Greek.

3. He elegantly translates concepts expressed in Hebrew by more than one word using a sufficiently expressive Greek word:

Is. 52:8 LXX: ὀφθαλμοὶ πρὸς ὀφθαλμούς
σ᾽ ὀφθαλμοφανῶς

4. Unlike Aquila, he does not restrict a particular Greek word to the same Hebrew term but, especially in translating the particles, he uses greater variety. However, this variety should not be exaggerated. As Salvesen has noted, Symmachus tends to standardise the vocabulary,[30] and Busto insists on how literal Symmachus is and how rarely he uses illative particles.[31] The only thing that stands out is the frequent use of ἆρα, quite rare in the other biblical translators, to translate the Hebrew particle that introduces a direct question.[32]

5. He tones down anthropomorphisms and other expressions in connection with the deity. He avoids comparisons between man and God. He does not accept the existence of other gods so that the expression "other gods" in Dt. 31:20 is translated "false gods". Similarly, he tends to eliminate the presence of angels: in Gen. 6:2 neither "the sons of God" nor "angels" couple with the daughters of men but the "powerful ones" (υἱοὶ τῶν δυναστευόντων).[33] Here are some other classical examples of this trait of his translation:

Ps. 43:24 LXX: ἱνατί ὑπνοῖς, κύριε
σ᾽ ἱνατί ὡς ὑπνῶν εἶ, δέσποτα
Gen. 1:27 LXX: καὶ ἐποίησεν ὁ θεὸς τὸν ἄνθρωπον, κατ᾽ εἰκόνα
θεοῦ ἐποίησεν αὐτόν
σ᾽ καὶ ἔκτισεν ὁ θεὸς τὸν ἄνθρωπον ἐν εἰκόνι
διαφόρῳ, ὄρθιον ὁ θεὸς ἔκτισεν αὐτόν.[34]

---

[30] A. Salvesen, *Symmachus in the Pentateuch*, 242–49.
[31] J. R. Busto Saiz, *La traducción de Símaco en el libro de los Salmos*, 278 and 285.
[32] J. R. Busto Saiz, *La traducción de Símaco en el libro de los Salmos*, 271.
[33] A. Salvesen, *Symmachus in the Pentateuch*, 192.
[34] The free nature of the translation by Symmachus in a book such as Genesis, which is well documented by the manuscripts (see J. W. Wevers, *Septuaginta. Vetus Testamentum Graecum. I Genesis*, Göttingen 1974), has caused some puzzlement among scholars. For Schoeps the translator did so because he tended to avoid anthropomorphisms (the reason would be "die für σ᾽ typische Scheu vor Anthropomorphismen", see H. J. Schoeps, *Symmachus und der Midrash*, 49ff.). It is true that a few verses earlier, in Gen. 1:26 according to the witness of Philoponus, Symmachus applies a technique that he often uses, the insertion of ὡς for nuance: καὶ εἶπεν ὁ Θεός· ποιήσωμεν ἄνθρωπον ὡς εἰκόνα ἡμῶν καθ᾽ ὁμοίωσιν ἡμῶν. However that may be, this is one of his well-known techniques, whereas the passage we are discussing goes beyond refining the anthropomorphism and inserts a different exegesis of the creation of man. The idea of man as *imago Dei* was repugnant to Josephus for

Other characteristics noted by Thieme in the work mentioned, such as frequent use of paraphrase even when no dogmatic reasons are involved, or the reduction of transcriptions from Hebrew as much as possible, are much more subject to revision. The conclusions drawn by Schoeps about Symmachus belonging to the Ebionite sect from the translation of *'ebyon* by πένης and *'anî* by πτωχός are to be rejected. In fact, no traces of Ebionism have been found, at least in his translation of the Pentateuch.[35] More convincing for me, instead, are Schoeps' remarks on this translator's knowledge of Greek mythology. In fact the systematic translation of *r^efā'îm* by θεομάχοι (Job 26:5; Prov. 9:18; 21:16) can only be understood from the association of these characters with the giants of Greek sagas. The same applies to the translation of Λάμια for *lîlît* in Is. 34:14 (LXX translates ὀνοκένταυροι), 'night demon', the feminine equivalent of Satan in Jewish demonology, which in the Greek version by Symmachus evokes the fabulous monster who feeds on human flesh.[36]

This translation often reproduces the late meaning of Hebrew roots, as Geiger has illustrated[37] and Schoeps has noticed in it contacts with Midrash and rabbinic hermeneutics.[38] González Luis insists that most of the hermeneutical techniques used by the Targum are to be found in Symmachus although in a more concise and sober

philosophical reasons, and also in connection with the biblical ban on making images of the deity (see J. Jervell, "Imagenes und Imago Dei. Aus der Genesis-Exegese des Josephus" *Josephus-Studien. Untersuchungen zu Josephus, dem antiken Judentum und dem Neuen Testament. Festschrift für Otto Michel*, Göttingen 1974, 197–204, and M. Smith, *The Image of God. BJRL* 40 [1958], 473–512). According to Schoeps, this translation of Symmachus was inspired by the Midraš Rabba on Qoh. 7:29 which interprets Hebrew *yāšār* as 'upright, erect', not as 'just', in contrast to animals. However, as noted by A. Salvesen (*Symmachus in the Pentateuch*, 6–7), the context of the Midraš shows that *yāšār* is taken in the moral sense, whereas the translation by Symmachus clearly suggests a physical meaning. In fact, the clearest parallels to this translation by Symmachus are to be found in Christian writers: the interpretation of the creation of man as erect in contrast to the creation of animals is one of the most widespread *topoi* in the anthropological reflections of antiquity, see Justin, *Apologia*, 55, 3; Lactantius, *inst.* 2, 1, 14; *opif. Dei* 10, 16; Augustine, *De civ. Dei* 19, 4; Athanasius in PG 25, 64B. And on the etymology of ἄνθρωπος, see I. Opelt, "Christianisierung heidnischer Etymologien", *JAC* 2 (1959), 70–86, p. 82.

[35] H. J. Schoeps, "Ebionitisches bei Symmachus". In the nine fragments of Psalms published by Mercati, Symmachus translates *'anî* in Ps. 17(18):28 by πρᾶον, not πτωχός. See also A. Salvesen, *Symmachus in the Pentateuch*, 290–94.

[36] See H. J. Schoeps, "Mythologisches bei Symmachus".

[37] A. Geiger, "Symmachus der Übersetzer der Bibel", and L. J. Liebreich, "Notes on the Greek Version of Symmachus".

[38] H. J. Schoeps, "Symmachus und der Midrash".

form.[39] Here he is in agreement with Salvesen, for whom the *haggadâ* of Symmachus compared with that of Onqelos is more concise in form.[40] Salvesen also insists on the analogies between Symmachus and the exegesis of the Targumim, especially the Palestinian, and shows that some of his translations seem to have been made through Aramaic.[41] From the studies by Ziegler and Cannon and more recently by González Luis and Salvesen we know to what extent Jerome incorporates in the Vulgate quite a number of his readings: in this undertaking he follows Symmachus more than any other translator.[42]

d) *Current Research and Future Prospects*

In contrast to Aquila and Theodotion, no specialist has identified Symmachus as the author of an Aramaic Targum, although on occasion his translation does reflect some semantic Aramaisms. Instead these translators are connected by the fact that Symmachian readings have been identified which are earlier than the historical Symmachus as he is described in the ancient sources. It is surprising, however, that while much has been said about *Ur*-Theodotion and more recently of the predecessors of Aquila, no-one has alluded, at least explicitly, to the traces of Symmachian readings prior to the historical Symmachus. Nevertheless, it must be accepted that this problem is posed with less force than in the other two cases and has thus scarcely been hinted at in the past.

Even so, a few sporadic indications collected and treated systematically could help us to reflect by introducing one more discordant element into the already crowded field of revisions of the LXX. In any event I will try to clarify the real background to the Symmachian translation.

As early as 1889, E. Hatch noted how a series of words in the

---

[39] J. González Luis, "Los 'targumim' y la versión de Símaco".
[40] A. Salvesen, *Symmachus in the Pentateuch*, 263.
[41] A. Salvesen, *Symmachus in the Pentateuch*, 177–94.
[42] J. Ziegler, *Die jüngeren griechischen Übersetzungen als Vorlagen*, 6 and 76ff.: "die vorliegende Schrift wird zeigen, dass wir sehr oft in unserer Vulgata Aquila und Theodotion, namentlich aber Symmachus in lateinischer Verkleidung begegnen" (p. 6). W. W. Cannon, "Jerome and Symmachus: Some Points in the Vulgata Translation of Koheleth", *ZAW* NF 4 (1927), 191–99, and F. Field, *Origenis Hexaplorum quae supersunt. Prolegomena* XXXIVff. See also J. González Luis, "La traducción Vulgata y Símaco", and A. Salvesen, *Symmachus in the Pentateuch*, 265–79, p. 279: "It is evident from a comparison of the versions that Jerome especially favoured Sym.'s version."

New Testament that do not occur anywhere else in the Greek Bible are attested in "the three", especially in Symmachus.[43] These agreements by themselves do not argue dependence, since the factor of greater chronological proximity between the New Testament writers and the translations by "the three" would be enough to explain these linguistic preferences which are lacking from the LXX.

However, the situation becomes complex when we detect not only the closeness of Symmachus to the lexicon of the New Testament writers, but his close relationship with the lexicon of the book of Wisdom, as Fichtner has noted,[44] with Proverbs, 1–4 Maccabees and especially with the book of Sira (translated in 132 BCE, as indicated in the prologue), to the point that Ziegler even states that Symmachus and the Greek translator of Sira belong to the same school of translation.[45] To explain these surprising agreements, Ziegler does not use the hypothesis of the existence of proto-Symmachian texts, although he admits that similar texts were in circulation, as has been confirmed by the Twelve Prophets scroll from Qumran.[46] However, he prefers to resolve the *aporia* along the lines that these terms which also occur in Symmachus were common currency at the time, in the 2nd and 1st centuries BCE.[47] Even so, Ziegler's argument cannot satisfy us as it is inconsistent. On the one hand, he admits that the translator of Sira (2nd century BCE) and Symmachus belong to the same trans-

---

[43] E. Hatch, *Essays in Biblical Greek*, Oxford 1889, 25–26. Some of these are: ἐγκακεῖν, σ' in Gen. 27:46 and in Lk. 18:1 etc.; ἐμβριμᾶσθαι· σ' in Ps. 75:7 and Is. 17:13 and in Mt. 9:30 etc.; ἐνθύμησις, σ' in Job 21:27 and in Mt. 9:4 etc.; ἐπίβλημα, σ' in Josh. 9:11 and in Mt. 9:16, etc.; θεομάχος, only in σ' for Job 26:5; Prov. 9:18 and 21:16 and in Acts 5:39; ὁροθεσία, σ' in Ex. 19:12 and Acts 17:26; σπλαγχνίζεσθαι, σ' in 1 Sam. 23:21 and in the NT *passim*; ἀναστατοῦν σ' (five times as against once in LXX and once in Aquila) and twelve times in the synoptics. See also H. B. Swete, *An Introduction to the Old Testament in Greek*, 460.

[44] J. Fichtner, "Der AT-Text der Sapientia Salomonis", *ZAW* 57 (1939), 155–92. The kinship in the lexicon and the agreement with Symmachus against the LXX in OT quotations leads Fichtner to conclude that the author of Wisdom used biblical texts translated by a predecessor of Symmachus (pp. 168 and 191ff.).

[45] J. Ziegler, "Zum Wortschatz des griechischen Sirach", *Festschrift O. Eissfeldt*, BZAW 77, 1958, 284: "Beide (Sirach und Symmachus) gehören einer gemeinsamen Übersetzerschule an, die eine einheitliche Tradition weitergeben."

[46] According to Barthélemy, although each book requires separate discussion, for the Twelve Prophets it has been shown that Symmachus knows and uses both the *kaige* recension and the Hebrew text in his translation, whereas he does not seem to know the unrevised LXX or Aquila's version, see D. Barthélemy, *Les Devanciers d'Aquila*, 261–65.

[47] J. Ziegler, "Zum Wortschatz", 287: "es ist eben so, dass die mit Symmachus übereinstimmenden Vokabeln damals (im 2. und 1. Jh. v. Chr.) 'gängig' waren".

lation school; on the other, he refuses to accept predecessors of Symmachus – proto-Symmachian texts – resorting to the argument that these lexical agreements have to be considered as words that belonged to the language current at that time. This explanation may be valid for the agreements in vocabulary with the New Testament, due to its greater closeness in time with the historical Symmachus compared with the LXX. However, for the agreements with Sira, can one speak of 'words current at that time' ("die . . . damals 'gängig' waren") when four centuries lie between Sira and the translation by Symmachus? Why should Sira agree precisely with Symmachus and not agree in the same way with Aquila and Theodotion, if those words were common currency then? It seems clear that Ziegler's reply evades the issue, and, lacking any better explanation, consideration must again be given to other explanations that fit the facts better and throw light on the possible base texts used by Symmachus in his translation. These aspects seem all the more interesting since other witnesses of Symmachian readings prior to Symmachus have emerged. Here are some of them:

Swete drew attention to the lexical agreements with Symmachus of the gospel of Peter, which is not later than 170 CE:[48] in particular, the use of the verb ὑπορθόω (10:39), a word exclusive to Symmachus in Pss 43:19 and 72:2.[49] And Thackeray noted in respect of Josephus that the closest allied biblical text to Josephus in Samuel–Kings was Symmachus – together with the proto-Lucianic – and mentions a series of interesting parallels.[50] In the book of the Twelve Prophets, Swete was surprised to find in Justin more than one reading attributed

---

[48] H. B. Swete, *An Introduction to the Old Testament in Greek*, 50, n. 4, and Ph. Vielhauer, *Geschichte der urchristlichen Literatur*, New York 1975, 643. For the gospel of Peter, see the edition by E. Klostermann in *Apocrypha* I, KT 3, Berlin 1933.

[49] It does not occur elsewhere in Greek literature, until the 4th century CE, in Dositheus. However, although the agreement is surprising it is not decisive nor can it be concluded that this apocryphon knows and cites Symmachus. Since the quotation of Ps. 21:2 in 4:19 agrees with no known Greek version i.e.: ἡ δύναμίς μου, ἡ δύναμίς μου κατέλιψάς με. Whereas known biblical texts for this passage are
LXX: ὁ θεὸς ὁ θεός μου ἱνατί ἐγκατέλιπές με;
α' ἰσχυρέ μου, ἰσχυρέ μου, ἱνατί ἐγκατέλιπές με
σ' θ' ὁ θεός μου, ὁ θεός μου (the rest is missing).
Nor do the other free quotations by this gospel of Dt. 21:22ff. (in 2:5 and 5:15) or Is. 8:29/10:27 allow any conclusions to be drawn in this respect.

[50] H. St J. Thackeray, *Josephus: The Man and the Historian*, New York 1929, 75–99, especially p. 86, n. 33. For 1 Sam. we have contacts with Symmachus in the following passages: 13:20 (ὕνιν); 15:23 (ἀπειθεῖν), 30 (τιμῆσαι); 61:21 and 31:4 (ὁπλοφόρος); 17:39 (+ ἀγύμναστος γάρ εἰμι).

to Symmachus, which led him to conclude that these variants belong to an older version or recension from which both Symmachus and Justin took them.[51] Today, though, with the data from the Greek fragments of Naḥal Ḥever, we would have to resolve these agreements in the best way possible on the basis of the καίγε recension used in that book by both Symmachus and Justin.[52] However, once the length of this recension has been established, it is necessary to study in more detail the link between Symmachus and the καίγε recension in the other books in order to stratify the textual shape of the Greek Bible precisely for the Christian period.

Along the same lines, the perplexing field of New Testament quotations remains to be studied.[53] In respect of these quotations of the Old Testament in the Apocalypse of John, Trudinger cites the study by Smits, which provides information according to which the Greek version of Symmachus seems to underlie the wording of the Old Testament material cited in the Apocalypse.[54] And Tabachowitz connects the ἴστε γινώσκοντες of Eph. 5:5 – as a formula which corresponds to the Symmachian technique of translation – with the ἴστε γιγνώσκοντες of Jer. 49(42):22 as an asterisked addition of Symmachus for the Hebrew expression yādoaʿ tēdʿeʿû, the same syntagm that LXX translates at the end of v. 19 by γνόντες γνώσεσθε. It is an interesting coincidence on which Tabachowitz comments as follows: "Aus der Übereinstimmung mit der besprochenen Stelle des Epheserbriefes ist zu schliessen, dass solch eine *Übersetzungsvariante* schon zur Zeit des Paulus gebräuchlich war und ihn zur Wahl des Ausdrucks angeregt hat."[55]

Elsewhere we have shown how text Barberini of Hab. 3 belongs to the translation school of Symmachus both for its lexicon and the translation techniques used, but it could not be identified with the

---

[51] H. B. Swete, *An Introduction to the Old Testament in Greek*, 422: "In the Minor Prophets it is startling to find in Justin more than one rendering which is attributed to Symmachus; and as it is in the highest degree improbable that his text has been altered from the text of Symmachus... we are led to the conclusion that these readings belong to an older version or recension from which both Justin and Symmachus drew."

[52] D. Barthélemy, *Les Devanciers d'Aquila*, 203ff. and 261ff.

[53] See chapter 21 for an extensive survey of current research and the most important questions to be resolved.

[54] L. P. Trudinger, "Some Observations Concerning the Text of the Old Testament in the Book of Revelation", *JTS* NS 17 (1966), 82–88, and C. Smits, *Oud-Testamentische Citaten in het Nieuwe Testament*, 2 vols, The Hague 1952–55.

[55] D. Tabachovitz, *Die Septuaginta und das Neue Testament*, Lund 1956, 92.

final edition of Symmachus as we know it from the Hexaplaric fragments preserved for this chapter. In dating this translation before the end of the 1st century CE, we use as an explanation either a school of Symmachus with certain translation techniques, or at least the existence of a non-uniform text of Symmachus which has to include also some predecessors before the final edition.[56]

From analysis and study of the Theodotionic text of Daniel, Schmitt deduces that this text, traditonally attributed to Theodotion, is more likely to belong to Symmachus, specifically and above all the deuterocanonical sections or Greek supplements to the book, due to the strong contacts they have with that translator.[57] However, the data provided by Schmitt have convinced neither Barthélemy nor Busto Saiz,[58] although Schmitt continues to maintain his thesis that the Theodotionic text of Daniel is not the same as the Theodotion transmitted by the Hexapla and it cannot be proved that the reviser of the canonical sections of Daniel was the same as the reviser of the deuterocanonical sections.[59]

A new discovery among the Hexaplaric readings rescued by W. Baars in his publication of new fragments of the Syro-Hexaplaric version has increased the number of Symmachian readings before the historical Symmachus. It is no longer only a question of identical

---

[56] Translations that might justify what Jerome says about two editions of Symmachus and the ascriptions to him by some manuscripts and ancient writers of two readings for the same passage. See N. Fernández Marcos, "El texto Barberini de Habacuc III reconsiderado".

[57] A. Schmitt, *Stammt der sogenannte "θ'"-Text bei Daniel wirklich von Theodotion?*, MSU IX, Göttingen 1966, 111: "Es sind auffallende Berührungen mit σ' vorhanden, jedoch reichen diese noch nicht zum Beweis aus, dass die deuterokanonische Stücke des "θ'"-Textes wirklich von σ' stammen. Hierzu müsste vor allem die Syntax von σ' noch genau erforscht werden, um auf diese Frage eine Antwort geben zu können."

[58] D. Barthélemy, *Critique textuelle de l'Ancien Testament 3*, Fribourg–Göttingen 1992, p. CLXXVIII: "Mais ici il ne faut pas oublier que le 'Theodotion' de Daniel est de tous les prétendus θ' *celui qui présente les meilleurs titres d'identité* puisque, pour l'identifier, ce n'est pas de la structure des hexaples que nous dépendons, mais que nous disposons ici des témoignages formels d'Origène et de Jérôme. Mieux vaudrait donc mettre en doute toutes les autres attributions de textes à Théodotion que celle-ci qui doit demeurer pour nous *la pierre de touche de l'authenticité théodotionienne.*" Busto Saiz also concludes, against Schmitt's suggestion, that the Theodotionic text of Daniel in the deuterocanonical sections definitely does not belong to Symmachus, see J. R. Busto Saiz, "El texto teodociónico de Daniel y la traducción de Símaco", 54–55.

[59] A. Schmitt, "Die griechischen Danieltexte (θ' und o') und das Theodotionproblem", *BZ* 36 (1992), 1–29, p. 29.

vocabulary due to greater closeness in time but a complete identical clause. The new reading of Symmachus recovered for Dt. 32:35, ἐμοὶ ἐκδικήσεις καὶ ἀνταποδώσω[60] is probably the source of this curious quotation in Rom. 12:19 and Heb. 10:30.

Lastly, M. Philonenko has noticed a series of agreements between the translation by Symmachus and the *Paralipomena Jeremiae*. These agreements have led him to conclude that the author of this pseudepigraphical text used the translation by Symmachus, which means that the final redaction of that work has to be dated back to the end of the 2nd century CE.[61] As explained elsewhere, these agreements have to be set in the context of Symmachian witnesses before the historical Symmachus. To some extent these indications tell us that not only Aquila but also Symmachus had his predecessors.[62] Symmachus certainly knew Aquila when making his translation; sometimes he accepts elements from that version and others he expressly rejects. He probably also knew and used Theodotion and the καιγέ revision. And although it cannot be stated with certainty, he probably also knew the ancient LXX.[63] It is not surprising then that these Symmachian readings detected before the historical Symmachus belong to some of those *Vorlage* that he knows and with which in part he identifies.

As yet we have only incomplete knowledge of the phases of the Greek Bible before the period of the great recensions. However there are enough indications that quite early on revisions were in circulation that were used not only by Symmachus but also by Aquila, at least, to complete their editions. In the words of L. Gil,[64] "the originality and independence of our author would be less if one had to think that he used the long tradition of revisions of the Greek Bible"; but the process would be much more consistent and above all it would fit the facts better as they are being revealed through recent finds and specialist studies. Even so, this dependence on earlier revisions should not be exaggerated, and Symmachus should continue to remain as a new, independent translation.[65] In future it is

[60] W. Baars, *New Syrohexaplaric Texts*, Leiden 1968, 148.

[61] M. Philonenko, "Les *Paralipomènes de Jérémie* et la traduction de Symmaque", p. 145.

[62] See N. Fernández Marcos, "Símmaco y sus predecesores judíos", pp. 197–98.

[63] See A. Salvesen, *Symmachus in the Pentateuch*, 262.

[64] L. Gil, "Símmaco", 702.

[65] See L. L. Grabbe, "The Translation Technique of the Greek Minor Versions: Translations or Revisions?", *Septuagint, Scrolls and Cognate Writings*, 1992, 505–56,

imperative to complete monographs on the lexicon and translation techniques of Symmachus in order to sift critically what is attributed to him and to gain a better knowledge of this author's language. Indirectly it would make it possible to interpret better those readings found in documents that are earlier than him.

Among the manuscripts of unpublished theses in the possession of Dropsie College is one by L. J. Liebreich with the title "Prolegomena to a Greek–Hebrew and Hebrew–Greek Index to Symmachus. Letter Alpha".[66] Nothing more is known about it, even though the author published some notes on Symmachus in 1944.[67] Katz and Ziegler suggested that as soon as possible scholars of the Greek Bible should compile indexes to Symmachus and Theodotion, like the one for Aquila,[68] and they put forward some methodological remarks to that effect. However, so far we do not have such essential reference works.[69] Similarly, in the area of translation techniques and syntax, only the last monographs discussed have helped to remove outdated topics that are persistently repeated.[70]

---

p. 517: "Symmachus is so often different from the *kaige* – as well as from the LXX and Aquila – as to make the question of a revision difficult. It seems to be an independent translation, though one could argue that the LXX, *kaige*, and Aquila all had their influence on it."

[66] In *JQR* NS 24 (1933), 102.

[67] L. J. Liebreich, "Notes on the Greek Version of Symmachus".

[68] P. Katz and J. Ziegler, "Ein Aquila-Index in Vorbereitung. Prolegomena und Specimina" II. *VT* 8 (1958), 274. And also J. Ziegler, *Die Septuaginta. Erbe und Auftrag.* Würzburg 1962, 17: "Ihre Vokabeln (of Aquila, Symmachus and Theodotion) sind nur fehler- und lückenhaft in der Konkordanz von Hatch–Redpath verzeichnet. Es ist unerlässlich, dass baldmöglichst griechisch-hebräische und hebräisch–griechische Indizes dieser drei wichtigen Übersetzungen (des Aquila, Symmachus und Theodotion) erarbeitet werden."

[69] To some extent, J. R. Busto Saiz has done this for the book of Psalms in the third part of *La traducción de Símaco en el libro de los Salmos*, pp. 443–756.

[70] One example of transliteration is enough. Does Symmachus transliterate Hebrew as little as possible, as has been said repeatedly up to now? A few partial soundings indicate that this is not always the case. For example, in the book of Isaiah, Symmachus transliterates words that Aquila translates, some of them well known: σουρ in Is. 10:26; ωιμ in 13:21; αμιρ in 17:9; ἀμών (ἀμαύν) in 33:3. On this last transliteration, see H. J. Schoeps, "Ein neuer Engelname in der Bibel? (Zur Übersetzung des Symmachus Jes 33,3)", in *Zeitschrift für Religions- und Geistesgeschichte* I (1948), 86–87.

Select Bibliography

Barthélemy, D., "Qui est Symmache?". *P. W. Skehan Festschrift. CBQ* 36 (1974), 451–65.

Busto Saiz, J. R., "El texto teodociónico de Daniel y la traducción de Símaco". *Sefarad* 40 (1980), 41–55.

———, *La traducción de Símaco en el libro de los Salmos*, Madrid 1978 (reprint 1985).

Capelle, P., "Fragments du Psautier d'Aquila?" *RBén* 28 (1911), 64–68.

Fernández Marcos, N., "El texto Barberini de Habacuc III reconsiderado". *Sefarad* 36 (1976), 3–36.

———, "Símaco y sus predecesores judíos". *Biblische und judaistische Studien. Festschrift für Paolo Sacchi*, ed. A. Vivian, Frankfurt–Bern–NewYork–Paris 1990, 193–202.

Field, F., *Origenis Hexaplorum quae supersunt*, Oxford 1875.

Geiger, A., "Symmachus der Übersetzer der Bibel". *Jüdische Zeitschrift für Wissenschaft und Leben* I (1862), 39–64.

Gil, L., "Símmaco". *EncBibl* 6 (1965), 701–702.

Gonzalez Luis, J., "La traducción Vulgata y Símaco". *Tabona* 4 (1983), 267–80.

———, "La versión de Símaco a los Profetas Mayores", Madrid, Diss. Complutensian Univ. 1981.

———, "Los 'targumim' y la versión de Símaco". *Simposio Bíblico Español*, 1984, 255–68.

Graetz, M. J., "Symmachus ben Joseph". *Encyclopaedia Judaica* 15 (1971), 578–79.

Greenspoon, L., "Symmachus's Version". *ABD* 6, 1992, 251.

Jellicoe, S., *SMS*, 94–99.

Klijn, A. F. J., "The Study of Jewish Christianity". *NTS* 20 (1973–74), 419–31.

Labate, A., "L'apporto della catena Hauniense sull'Ecclesiaste per il testo delle versioni greche di Simmaco e della LXX". *RivB* 35 (1987), 57–61.

Liebreich, L. J., "Notes on the Greek Version of Symmachus". *JBL* 63 (1944), 397–403.

Mercati, G., "Frammenti di Aquila o di Simmaco?" *RB* 8 (1911), 266–72.

———, *L'età di Simmaco l'interprete e S. Epifanio ossia se Simmaco tradusse in greco la Bibbia sotto M. Aurelio il filosofo*, Modena 1892 = *ST* 76 (1937), 20–92.

Nestle, E., "Symmachus, not Aquila". *ET* 22 (1910), 377.

O'Connell, K. G., "Greek Versions (Minor)". *IDBS* (1976), 377–81.

Perles, F., "Symmachus". *JE* 11 (1905), 619.

Philonenko, M., "Les *Paralipomènes de Jérémie* et la traduction de Symmaque". *RHPhR* 34 (1984), 143–45.

Salvesen, A., *Symmachus in the Pentateuch*, Manchester 1991.

Schoeps, H. J., *Ebionitisches bei Symmachus*. Coniectanea Neotestamentica 6, Uppsala 1942 (= *Symmachusstudien* I), 62–93.

———, "Mythologisches bei Symmachus". *Bib* 26 (1945), 100–111 (= *Symmachusstudien* II).

———, "Symmachus und der Midrash". *Bib* 29 (1947), 31–51 (= *Symmachusstudien* III).

———, *Theologie und Geschichte des Judenchristentums*, Tübingen 1949, especially pp. 33–37 and 350–80.

Swete, H. B., *An Introduction to the Old Testament in Greek*, Cambridge 1914, 49–53.

Thieme, C. A., *Pro puritate Symmachi dissertatio*, Leipzig 1755.

van der Kooij, A., "Symmachus, 'de vertaler der Joden'". *Nederlands Theologisch Tijdschrift* 42 (1988), 1–20.

Wessely, C., "Un nouveau fragment de la version grecque du Vieux Testament par Aquila" [in fact Lymmachus]. *Mélanges offerts à M. E. Châtelain*, Paris 1910, 224–429.

Zahn, G., "Herkunft und Lehrrichtung des Bibelübersetzers Symmachus". *NKZ* 34 (1923), 197–209.

Ziegler, J., "Die jüngeren griechischen Übersetzungen als Vorlagen der Vulgata in den prophetischen Schriften". *Beilage zum Personal- und Vorlesungsverzeichnis d. Staatl. Akademie zu Braunsberg-Ostpr.* WS 1943–44, 1–92 (= *Joseph Ziegler Sylloge* 139–229).

———, "Textkritische Notizen zu den jüngeren griechischen Übersetzungen des Buches Isaias". *Nachr. d. Ak. d. Wiss. zu Göttingen, Philolog.-Hist. Klasse* 1939, 75–102. (= *Joseph Ziegler Sylloge*, Göttingen 1971, 71–139).

CHAPTER NINE

THEODOTION AND THE ΚΑΙΓΕ REVISION

It is now three decades since S. Jellicoe, after much effort in analysis and systematisation, ended by admitting that "Paradoxical though it may seem, less is known today of Theodotion than ever before."[1] Today matters are slightly clearer, and in one way or another definitive conclusions have been reached concerning all the points debated. Accordingly we shall take the course followed in previous chapters, aware of the increasing discrepancy between ancient information about the historical Theodotion and the unexpected results of modern research, filled as they are with question marks. To remedy this discrepancy and in the hope that more exhaustive studies will be extended in a systematic way to all the Theodotionic material we have, we shall insist on complete rigour on the last point about current research, leaving the specialised reader to form his own judgement or adopt a position in respect of the many points now subject to revision.

a) *Ancient Witnesses*

The scant information we have about Theodotion (θ') from Irenaeus, Epiphanius and Jerome leaves us somewhat perplexed. Apparently the most reliable information is from Irenaeus, who describes him as a Jewish proselyte from Ephesus.[2] The account by Epiphanius[3] seems to be too much like the one about Aquila for it to be trustworthy, even though it conditioned all later interpretations concerning Theodotion. Barthélemy has stressed its chronological contradictions.[4] He accepts instead the testimony of Irenaeus and identifies Theodotion

---

[1] S. Jellicoe, *SMS*, 94. He makes this statement after devoting more than twelve pages to Theodotion, more than to Aquila and Symmachus combined.
[2] *Adversus Haer.* III, 21.1: Θεοδοτίων ἡρμήνευσεν ὁ Ἐφέσιος καὶ Ἀκύλας... ἀμφότεροι Ἰουδαῖοι προσήλυτοι ("They translated Theodotion of Ephesus and Aquila... the two Jewish proselytes").
[3] Who makes him a native of Pontus and a disciple of Marcion of Sinope, see *De Mens. et Ponderibus*, 17.
[4] D. Barthélemy, *Les Devanciers d'Aquila*, 144ff.

as Jonathan ben 'Uziel, the author of the Targum bearing his name.[5] According to Jerome he was an Ebionite.[6]

Nothing certain can be said concerning the date that he made his translation. The sequence Aquila–Symmachus–Theodotion in which they are normally cited in ancient sources is probably due to the way their respective versions were arranged in the columns of the Hexapla; Aquila came first as it was the closest to the Hebrew text, and Theodotion was next to the LXX as he coincided most with the Alexandrian version. Furthermore, if we trust the statements of Epiphanius and Jerome, Theodotion edited a revision of the LXX on the basis of the standardised Hebrew text before a new independent translation.[7] Proof that he made his revision on the basis of the Hebrew *textus receptus* is the fact that in the book of Job he filled in the missing sections of the LXX version so that it is one-sixth longer than the original LXX.[8]

There are two further problems in connection with Theodotion which *since ancient times* have puzzled students of the Greek Bible. (1) On the one hand, the existence of a "double text" in the book of Daniel, already noted by Jerome: a Septuagintal text and another attributed to Theodotion,[9] with the peculiarity that the various churches accepted the one by Theodotion which ultimately displaced

---

[5] He lived in the first half of the 1st century CE (sees D. Barthélemy, *Les Devanciers d'Aquila*, 148ff.). This identification within the overall theory set out by Barthélemy requires an end to the traditional image of a 2nd century CE Theodotion and explains why it has not been accepted unreservedly by LXX specialists; see the last section of this chapter.

[6] "Editiones . . . Aquilae . . . Pontici proselyti et Theodotionis Hebionaei" (Jerome, *De vir. illustribus*, 54).

[7] Epiphanius, *De Mens. et Ponderibus*, 17: τὰ πλεῖστα τοῖς οβ' συναδόντως ἐξέδωκεν ("he edited a text which largely agreed with the LXX"); Jerome, *In Eccl.* 2: "Septuaginta et Theodotio . . . in plurimis locis concordant"; Jerome, *Praef. in Psalmos*: "simplicitate sermonis a LXX interpretibus non discordat".

[8] See Origen, *Ep. ad Afr.*, 3ff.; Jerome, *Praef. ad Job* in his Vulgate translation. Even though it belongs to the group of "Writings" it is difficult to accept such liberties with the translation of this book into Greek. Hence, some scholars have resorted to the hypothesis of a Hebrew *Vorlage* that is different from the Masoretic text and shorter, see E. Hatch, "On Origen's Revision of the LXX: Text of Job", *Essays in Biblical Greek*, Oxford 1889 (= Amsterdam 1970), 215–45. Even so, my view is that the short text of the LXX translation of Job is due to the translator himself and the translation techniques he used, see N. Fernández Marcos, "The Septuagint Reading of the Book of Job", *The Book of Job*, ed. W. A. M. Beuken, Leuven 1994, 251–66.

[9] Jerome, *Praef. in Danielem*: "Danielem prophetam iuxta LXX. interpretes ecclesiae non legunt, utentes Theodotionis editione"; and de Dan-LXX dice in *c. Rufinum* II, 33: "hoc unum affirmare possum quod multum a veritate discordet et recto iudicio repudiata sit".

the LXX completely. Since in the Vatican ms. (4th century CE) for
Daniel, the Theodotionic text occurs instead of the LXX, whereas
Pap. 967 (2nd century CE) still contains the Septuagintal text, the
supplanting might have occurred in the second half of the 3rd century CE.[10] And (2) on the other hand, there are Theodotionic readings in documents that are much earlier than the historical Theodotion
as described by the sources.

It seems that Origen quotes the Theodotionic text of Daniel in
his writings out of respect for Church tradition and the same applies
to biblical quotations by Clement of Alexandria.[11] However Theodotionic readings occur not only in these writers but also in much
earlier writers such as Justin, Clement of Rome, Shepherd of Hermas,
Letter of Barnabas, Epistle to the Hebrews, Apocalypse of John
and the synoptic gospels.[12] Now, as nearly all of these quotations are
limited to the book of Daniel, the problem of Proto-Theodotion
depends on the one hand upon the Theodotionic authenticity of this
recently disputed text[13] and on the other upon the extent to which
Barthélemy's theory is accepted when he identifies Theodotion as
the party head of the καίγε recension and so earlier than Aquila by
at least half a century.[14] Only when these two presuppositions are
clarified can the problems that arise from these readings be interpreted correctly.

---

[10] W. Hamm, *Der Septuaginta-Text des Buches Daniel Kap. 1–2 nach dem Kölner Teil
des Papyrus 967*. Papyrologische Texte und Abhandlungen 10, Bonn 1969; W. Hamm,
Der Septuaginta-Text des Buches Daniel. Kap. 3–4 nach dem Kölner Teil des Papyrus 967.
Papyrologische Texte und Abhandlungen 21, Bonn 1977; A. Geissen, *Der Septuaginta-
Text des Buches Daniel Kap. 5–12, zusammen mit Susanna, Bel et Draco, sowie Esther kap.
1,1a–2,15*. Papyrologische Texte und Abhandlungen 5, Bonn 1968. The LXX text
of Daniel was only known up to then from ms. 88 and the Syro-Hexaplaric version. Publication of this papyrus also had the advantage of providing the only *pre-
Hexaplaric* known for Dan-LXX.

[11] Clement of Alexandria, *Paed.* II, 8; III, 3; *Strom.* I, 4, 21.

[12] Some of these are: Mk. 14:62 = Dan. 7:13; Heb. 10:33 = Dan. 6:23; I Clem.
34:6 = Dan. 7:10; Hermas, *Vis.* IV, II.4 = Dan. 6:26; Justin, *Dialogue with Tryphon*
31,2–7 = Dan. 7; and it seems that in the Apocalypse of John there are more quotations from Dan-θ' than from Dan-LXX, see P. Grelot, "Les versions grecques de
Daniel", *Bib* 47 (1966), 381–402.

[13] A. Schmitt, *Stammt der sogenannte "θ'"-Text*, especially pp. 110–12.

[14] See the last section of this chapter on the καίγε revision and its relationship
to the historical Theodotion.

b) *Sources*

At present it is quite difficult to identify the Theodotionic material, and a new systematic analysis of all the sources is required in order to verify these attributions. Traditionally, text -θ' of Daniel has been used as it is the longest fragment that we have and to a large extent the characteristics of this writer have been determined from this text. However, A. Schmitt concludes his monograph with the emphatic statement that θ' of Daniel has no connection with Theodotion.[15] On the other hand, enough indications have been found to cause us to mistrust the attribution of the sixth Hexaplaric column to Theodotion. For the book of Psalms, Mercati has shown that it is not the sixth column that represents Theodotion but the *fifth*. Apparently, abridged copies of the Hexapla were in circulation which omitted one of the columns or wrote it only in the form of marginal notes alongside another column.[16] And in *Dodekapropheton*, if we accept the rather disputed hypothesis of Barthélemy, readings preceded by the siglum θ' do not reflect authentic Theodotion either, but a late and eclectic recension.[17] Thus is seems clear that in the βγ section of Kings in Thackeray' s terminology (= 2 Sam. 11:2-1 Kgs 2:11),[18] the copyists of some manuscripts such as M, *j* and z of Brooke–McLean, confused the siglum θ' of Theodotion with the one for Theodoret, attributing to him a series of proto-Lucianic readings which are easily identifiable as they agree with readings of mss boc₂e₂, representatives of the Lucianic recension in this section of Kings.[19] For all these views, the material that certainly comes from Theodotion has been considerably reduced as a result of the discoveries and studies of recent years.

---

[15] A. Schmitt, *Stammt der sogenannte "θ'"-Text*, p. 112: "Der sogenannte θ'-Text hat nichts mit dem Übersetzer zu tun, der uns durch seine griechische Übersetzung anderer alttestamentlicher Bücher unter der Sigel "θ'" bekannt ist." However, we can note Barthélemy's strong reaction to Schmitt's thesis: "Je considère au contraire le "Théodotion" de Daniel comme l'élément du groupe καίγε qui a les plus des titres à être attribué au Théodotion historique," see D. Barthélemy, "Prise de position sur les autres communications du colloque de Los Angeles", in D. Barthélemy, *Études d'histoire du texte de l'Ancien Testament*, Fribourg–Göttingen 1978, 255–89, p. 267.

[16] G. Mercati, *Psalterii Hexapli Reliquiae*, II Rome 1958, XIXff.

[17] Here the *quinta* also represents the real Theodotion, head of the group of the καίγε recension: "Concluons seulement que la *quinta* du Dodékaprophéton a plus de titres à être une oeuvre originale de Théodotion que n'en possède la recension attribuée à cet auteur par les Hexaples," see D. Barthélemy, *Les Devanciers d'Aquila*, 260.

[18] See chapter 4, pp. 59–61.

[19] D. Barthélemy, *Les Devanciers d'Aquila*, 91–139.

For the other books – and retaining the preceding nuances – we continue to preserve him in patristic quotations and the marginal glosses to the LXX. The largest fragments occur in Septuagintal manuscripts, already incorporated with an asterisk into the LXX from the time of Origen. The books preserving the longest Theodotionic text are Job, Proverbs, Isaiah, Jeremiah and Ezekiel.[20] The *Codex Marchialanus* (Q) transmits in the margin long quotations from Theodotion for Jeremiah (Jer. 40[33]:14-26; 46[39]:4-13) lacking the LXX text. This Theodotionic material of Jeremiah and of the book of Job, incorporated in the LXX with an asterisk, seems to combine the main characteristics of the καίγε recension.

c) *Characteristics*

We know little about his style except for its most significant feature, which was to leave difficult Hebrew words transcribed (ἀνερμηνεύστους). Field lists about ninety of them, relating chiefly to names of animals, trees and plants, clothes, cloths and other things connected with the cult;[21] the books Isaiah, Ezekiel, Leviticus and Judges stand out. However, difficulty is not always the reason for transcription, as

---

[20] A. Schmitt, *Stammt der sogenannte "θ'"-Text*, p. 112, quotes the longest Theodotionic fragments preserved. It is copied here for the use of readers and to assist further research:

Prov. 11:3; 14:4; 20:14-19; 21:5.

Job 12:9; 14:18-19; 15.10:26-27; 18:15-16; 20:3-4.20-23; 21:28-33; 22:29-30; 24:14-18; 26:5-11; 29:19-20; 31:1-4; 33:28-29; 34:3-4, 28-33; 35:7-10; 36:5-9, 29-33; 37:1-5, 11-12; 39:13-18.

Is. 5:1; 7:11, 13, 15; 8:18; 9:6; 11:7; 22:10-11; 24:19-20; 25:5; 27:1, 8; 30:27; 33:7; 44:9-11; 45:9, 14; 51:9-10; 54:9-10; 59:18.

Jer. 2:1; 7:2; 10:5; 11:7; 16:5; 17:1-5; 23:36; 26(46):26; 28(51):45; 31(48):45; 34(27):5.15; 36(29):14; 37(30):9; 40(33):14; 45(38):12; 46(39):4; 47(40):4; 51(44):11; 52:2.

Ez. 1:24; 7:14, 19; 10:14; 11:12; 13:5; 17:20; 26:17; 27:31; 32:19, 23; 33:27; 35:6, 11-15; 38:4.

This material has to be completed by the material belonging to the καίγε revision studied by D. Barthélemy, *Les Devanciers d'Aquila*, especially the material that has found greater acceptance among scholars: the fragments of the *Dodekapropheton* from Naḥal Ḥever, sections βγ and γδ of Samuel–Kings, the sixth column of the Hexapla when it really does transmit Theodotion and the *quinta* of the Psalter. It is also very likely that Lamentations, Song and Ruth were *translated*, not revised, by members of the καίγε group.

[21] F. Field, *Origenis Hexaplorum quae supersunt*, XL–XLI. Although perhaps this list has to be shortened, taking into account that some of these readings are shared

shown by the spelling of God's name, ἤλ ('El) , in Mal. 2:11, although it is inexplicable that the translator would not know it. In addition, in Gen. 2:7 and 3:17 he places the transcription αδαμα after the translation γῆ, which suggests scrupulous faithfulness to the text rather than ignorance of the words. Since most of the *realia* on which the transcriptions concentrate have no equivalent in Greek, it is possible that the reason for the transcription is to be found in Theodotion's disapproval of the choices made in the LXX translation.

It is usually said that his style takes a middle course between the literalism of Aquila and the good sense of Symmachus, these being the three translators closest to the LXX.[22] No trace of a double edition of Theodotion can be found, except for a suspect reading in Ez. 1:4 and a corrupt section of Jerome in respect of the Hexapla to Jer. 29:17. If the equation θ' = καίγε revision,[23] is confirmed – to the extent that this occurs in the various books of the Greek Bible – here need to be added the main characteristics noted by Barthélemy for this recension[24] and those which later are to be discovered in

---

with Aquila, Symmachus or even the LXX and others are anonymous. This feature of the transcriptions should not be exaggerated as is shown by the fact that in other passages, especially in Kings, where the LXX leaves the Hebrew term transliterated, Theodotion translates it (see *ibid.* XLII). Tov thinks that the judgement on Theodotion based on Field is valid with respect to the transcriptions, but it needs to be recast on the basis of new data, see E. Tov, "Transliterations of Hebrew Words in the Greek Versions of the Old Testament", *Textus* 8 (1973), 78–92.

[22] An example is Gen. 1:23:
    ο' ἄρχετε τῶν ἰχθύων
    α' ἐπικρατεῖτε ἐν ἰχθύϊ
    σ' χειροῦσθε τοὺς ἰχθύας
    θ' παιδεύετε ἐν τοῖς ἰχθύσι

[23] O'Connell has shown that the θ'-material of Exodus belongs to the καίγε revision, see K. G. O'Connell, *The Theodotionic Revision of the Book of Exodus*, pp. 292–93. This has also been confirmed for the Theodotionic material of Joshua by L. Greenspoon, *Textual Studies in the Book of Joshua*, 379–81. Bodine identifies the καίγε revision in the text transmitted by the family of the Vatican Codex (B) for the book of Judges, whereas the sixth column of the Hexapla in that book contains a Hebraising revision which he proposes to attribute to the traditional Theodotion of the 2nd century CE, see W. R. Bodine, *The Greek Text of Judges: Recensional Developments*, 185–86.

[24] D. Barthélemy, *Les Devanciers d'Aquila*, 48ff. The chief ones are: (1) the removal of ἕκαστος, a masculine distributive, replacing it with ἀνήρ, a calque translation of Hebrew *'iš*; (2) the use of ἐπάνωθεν plus genitive to translate *mē'al*; (3) the etymological translation of *nāṣab/yāṣab* by forms of the verb στηλόω instead of ἵστημι; (4) the specific distinction between κερατίνη for *šōfār* = 'horn' and σάλπιγξ for *ḥaṣoṣrā* = 'trumpet'; (5) the removal of the historical present; (6) the atemporal use of the Hebrew negation of existence *'ên* = οὐκ ἔστιν; (7) the translation of *'ānokî* by ἐγώ εἰμι and of *'^anî* by ἐγώ; (8) the translation of *liqra't* by εἰς συνάτησιν instead of εἰς ἀπάντησιν, etc.

other books studied, which in any case indicate that the καίγε revision was not the work of a single author. Instead it was a project or tradition of non-uniform revisions made by a group of authors which was to include a slight Hebraising revision in favour of the proto-Masoretic text – without attaining the consistency apparent in Aquila – and a desire to standardise and extend to various books of the LXX certain translation choices already used by some translators such as the translator of Psalms. Hence the καίγε revision has certain peculiar characteristics in particular books. Barthélemy himself has accepted the criticism of some of the characteristics he describes, such as the elimination of the historical present, and faced with the proliferation of new characteristics in more recent studies, has chosen to reduce the marks of this revision to four:

(1) translation of καίγε by the Hebrew particle *gam*; (2) translation of ἐγώ εἰμι by *'ānokî* before a verb in the first person; (3) general use of ἀνήρ for all the occurrences of *'iš*; (4) translation of *'ên* by οὐκ ἔστι, without taking into account the agreement of tenses.[25]

Lastly, we note that there are still too many unknowns in connection with Theodotionic attributions in the sources and too few systematic studies on the material of this version for any more detail on the characteristics of this translator, whose identity still continues to be in the forefront of discussion.

d) *Current Research and Future Prospects*

One of the problems that has most polarised research on this translator has been the proto-Theodotionic problem, i.e. the proof of Theodotionic readings earlier than the historical Theodotion. At the close of the last century, G. Salmon had the intuition to foresee problems which only recent work has proved true: "the question with which we are really concerned is whether he (Theodotion) did more than revise a previous translation different from the Chigi Septuagint".[26] He postulates the existence of an older translation, the source not only of the Theodotionic quotations in the New Testament and the Apostolic Fathers, but even the basis for the revision known

---

[25] D. Barthélemy, "Prise de position sur les autres communications du colloque de Los Angeles", in D. Barthélemy, *Études d'histoire du texte de l'Ancien Testament*, 267–69.

[26] G. Salmon, *A Historical Introduction*, 599.

as Dan-θ'. He compares 1 Ezra with Dan-LXX and concludes that they are the work of the same author. As for the agreements of Bar. 1:15-18 with Dan-θ' 9:7-10 on the one hand and of Bar. 3:11-16 with Dan-θ' 9:15-18 on the other – when most critics date the book of Baruch in the pre-Christian period[27] – he tends to think that there was a version of Daniel that is closer to the θ' text than to the LXX in the 1st century CE and probably earlier.

A. Rahlfs, instead, tries to show that the two main readings mentioned in support of the theory of an *Ur*-Theodotion (Is. 25:8, cited in 1 Cor. 15:54, and Zac. 12:10, cited in Jn 19:37) do not prove that Paul and John depended on the text of Theodotion. Instead, they can be explained in other ways.[28]

However, as a result of Barthélemy's interpretation of the Greek fragments of Naḥal Ḥever as belonging to the καίγε revision, the problem of proto-Theodotion has become involved in a new process which resolves most of these unknowns. This new interpretation resolves the chronological contradictions that have led to a cul-de-sac in studies in the first half of this century. One thing seems clear today: the proto-Theodotion problem cannot be understood separately from the καίγε revision. Barthélemy goes further, and by elevating him to the head of that recension, leaves no room for a historical Theodotion. He holds that Theodotion is earlier than Aquila (in line with the sequence established by Irenaeus) and thus dates

---

[27] E. Tov, *The Book of Baruch: Edited, Reconstructed and Translated*, Missoula, Mont. 1975, and C. A. Moore, "Toward the Dating of the Book of Baruch", *CBQ* 36 (1974), 312–20. Recently, E. Tov has analysed the passages from Baruch and Daniel-θ' with the same readings and concludes that "the resemblances between Dan-Th and Bar are merely superficial and have no bearing upon the proto-Theodotionic problem", see "The Relation between the Greek Versions of Baruch and Daniel", *Armenian and Biblical Studies*, ed. M. E. Stone, Jerusalem 1976, 27–34, p. 34.

[28] A. Rahlfs, "Über Theodotion-Lesarten im Neue Testament und Aquila-Lesarten bei Justin". According to Rahlfs, the quotation in Jn 19:37 ὄψονται εἰς ὃν ἐξεκέντησαν = Zac. 12:10 Theodotion, as against ἐπιβλέψονται πρός με ἀνθ' ὧν κατωρχήσαντο, is not enough to show dependence, since that translation could have come from the reading *dāqārû* = 'they crossed' in the Hebrew text, instead of *rāqādû* = 'they danced', as read in the LXX, due to the frequent metathesis of *d/r*. And in the case of Is. 25:8 κατεπόθη ὁ θάνατος εἰς νῖκος = 1 Cor. 15:54 as against κατέπιεν ὁ θάνατος ἰσχύσας, it proves that the reading κατεπόθη in *Marchalianus* is incorrect and that the Syro-Hexaplaric version reads κατέπιεν. However, his argument is not convincing, nor has it been accepted by Ziegler in the critical edition of Isaiah, see J. Ziegler, *Isaias. Septuaginta. Vetus Testamentum Graecum* XIV, Göttingen 1939. Rahlfs is also against accepting an *Ur-Aquila*. It was the safest thing for a loyal follower of de Lagarde to do before the hypothesis of the predecessors of Aquila was known.

him to the first half of the 1st century CE.[29] The reverse sequence maintained in the other ancient sources and accepted by tradition was mistakenly imposed due to the positions of the three recent translators in the Hexapla. In his review of O'Connell's book, Barthélemy again confirms his conclusions, and completely rejects the proto-Theodotion problem as well as the information from Epiphanius on the 2nd century CE Theodotion. For Barthélemy there is only the Theodotion we know from Irenaeus who in future has to be identified with the καίγε revision and dated in the 1st century CE.[30]

However, following Jellicoe, it can be asked whether it might not be more prudent to accept the καίγε recension as a first stage in the Theodotionic revision (= proto-Theodotion) without removing from the scene the later revision attributed to the historical Theodotion. Like Lucian of Antioch, the traditional Theodotion is too well documented in ancient sources to allow him to disappear so quickly from history.[31] This applies especially when a new examination is being demanded of all the sigla used in the margins of the manuscripts in order to resolve the problems of authorship, once it has been proved that Origen did not exclusively reserve the sixth column of Hexapla for the revision known as Theodotion. It is true that the extent and later features that must be attributed to Theodotion of the 2nd century CE as against those of the καίγε revision are not clear. However, Theodotion's existence and activity are too well documented by tradition for him to be eliminated *tout court*.[32]

In any event, A. Schmitt's thesis has not made it easy for us in this complicated investigation to clarify the process that led to the formation of the θ'-text of Daniel and its attribution to Theodotion.[33] If the θ'-text of Daniel cannot be attributed to Theodotion by comparison with other material from the Greek Old Testament that is prefixed with the siglum θ', is all this material homogeneous and is it all from Theodotion?

We have already seen how some of these sigla are not to be trusted, for example those in section βγ of Kings, where it would

---

[29] D. Barthélemy, *Les Devanciers d'Aquila*, 144ff.

[30] D. Barthélemy in his review of the book by K. G. O'Connell, see Select Bibliography.

[31] S. Jellicoe, "Some Reflections on the καίγε Recension", *VT* 23, 1 (1973), 15–25, p. 24.

[32] See L. Greenspoon, "Theodotion", p. 448.

[33] A. Schmitt, *Stammt der sogenannte "θ'"-Text*, 110–12.

seem that the glossator of ms. *j* understood the siglum θ' as an abbreviation of Theodotion and completed or retouched the readings attributed to him with the help of the biblical text of Theodoret, or of an Antiochene or Lucianic text.

In the Twelve Prophets, according to Barthélemy, the supposed Theodotion (θ') in spite of his relish for transcribing divine names, plunders the other Hexaplaric versions, that is, depends upon them and spurns the literalism already present in the καίγε recension.[34] Do we not run the risk of selecting as authentic the Theodotion material preceded by the siglum θ' which fits our own theories? What do we know of Theodotion's literalism and translation techniques, based only yesterday on the θ'-text of Daniel which we now know is *not* from Theodotion?

If Dan-θ' does not belong to Theodotion, taking into account that his quotations are extant in the New Testament and the Apostolic Fathers, the question remains as to which process of revision, of those known so far, does this text belong. For it is certain that already in the 1st century CE, alongside Dan-LXX, another Greek text was in circulation that was closely related to it, later called θ', and attributed to Theodotion by the whole of Christian tradition. However, it is also certain that, if Theodotion revised it, that revision was not very thorough, since he did not complete, as he did in Job and Jeremiah, the sections missing from the LXX but found in the Hebrew *textus receptus*, and it is difficult to assume that these sections were missing from the Hebrew *Vorlage* in his time. As a result, we are not so distant as might seem from Montgomery's position in respect of the problems raised by the double text of Daniel and proto-Theodotion.[35]

---

[34] D. Barthélemy, *Les Devanciers d'Aquila*, 253ff.

[35] J. A. Montgomery, *Daniel*, ICC, 50: "Theodotion is the Hellenistic Onkelos whose work was facilitated by the presence of a large amount of customary oral translation of the Scriptures, possessed by him *memoriter*. Of course such a theory does not exclude the possibility of literary predecessors of the historical Theodotion."
The provisional nature of the results gained up to now on the true identity of Theodotion are clear from Barthélemy's harsh critique of Schmitt's thesis. After going through each of Schmitt's arguments against the authenticity of Daniel-θ', Barthélemy concludes that Daniel-θ' exhibits characteristics that place it within the καίγε group and that its vocabulary gives it the air of belonging to the family of other witnesses in this group. Also, of all the revisers of the καίγε group he is the author with the most right to be identified as the historical Theodotion. See D. Barthélemy, "Notes critiques sur quelques points d'histoire du texte", in D. Barthélemy, *Études d'histoire du texte de l'ancien testament*, Fribourg–Göttingen 1978, 289–303, p. 301. If the author of Daniel-θ' and the other books of the Old Testament cannot be

It is also necessary to remove the debate over Theodotion and the καίγε revision from the book of Daniel in which it has become polarised to excess. O. Munnich's work has emphasised the close connection of the καίγε group with the Septuagintal version of the Psalms.[36] Barthélemy had already noted the relationship between these two choices of translation.[37] For Munnich, the Greek Psalter had exercised special influence on the καίγε group before the Common Era, comparable to the influence of the translation of the Pentateuch on later translations of other books in the LXX. This influence is evident in the translation choices made by the revisers of the καίγε group, choices which were conditioned by literary and stylistic concerns rather by particular theological or exegetical principles. Thus Munnich keeps the καίγε revision free from the geographical and exegetical situation in which Barthélemy had set it, i.e. 1st century CE Palestine and the Hillelite rabbinate.[38] And it cannot be forgotten that the latest paleographic analysis of the scroll of the Twelve Prophets from Naḥal Ḥever dates it to the 1st century BCE, i.e. before Hillel appeared.[39]

To summarise, the latest research on the antecedents of the καίγε revision has helped to refine some of Barthélemy's conclusions. As a result, the καίγε revision is described as a non-uniform group of a Hebraising revision, or as a project marked by the desire to extend to the various books of the LXX certain translation choices already present in the translators of some books of the LXX such as Psalms. As a result, it does not seem to be so tied to the exegetical rules of the Palestinian rabbinate as Barthélemy claimed, and in terms of dating, it can already be detected towards the close of the 1st century BCE. As they depended more on literary influences than on doc-

---

the same person, the name Theodotion has to be reserved for the author of Daniel and removed from the rest of the Old Testament, since for most of the books of the Old Testament the siglum θ' only means that it has been taken from the sixth column of the Hexapla. However, as has been shown, this column does not always contain Theodotion (*ibid.* p. 395).

[36] O. Munnich, "La Septante des Psaumes et le groupe kaige", *VT* 33 (1983), 75–89, and Munnich, "Contribution à l'étude de la première révision de la Septante".

[37] "Il me semble difficile d'étudier de près le groupe καίγε sans noter les liens étroits qui le rattachent à la 'Septante' des Psaumes dont il prolonge très souvent les options dans le domains des correspondences hébreo-grecques, see D. Barthélemy, "Prise de position sur les autres communications du colloque de Los Angeles", p. 269.

[38] O. Munnich, "Contribution à l'étude de la première révision de la Septante", pp. 217–18.

[39] See L. Greenspoon, "Recensions, Revision, Rabbinics", p. 164.

trinal principles, the members of the group did not treat the text in a systematic way. This explains the different criteria among the texts attributed to Theodotion. And finally, the extent of the intervention by the historical Theodotion on the material already revised by the καίγε group continues to be an enigma. Perhaps the historical Theodotion finished the light Hebraising revision of the καίγε group following the proto-Masoretic text, exactly as is evident from the asterisked additions, which come from Theodotion, in books such as Job, Proverbs, Isaiah, Jeremiah, Ezekiel and the sixth Hexaplaric column of the book of Judges.[40]

SELECT BIBLIOGRAPHY

Baars, W., "An Ancient Greek Fragment of Daniel 3, 51b-52 (With One plate)". *Textus* 6 (1968), 132–34.

Barthélemy, D., *Les Devanciers d'Aquila*. VTS 10 (1963), especially pp. 144–56 and 253–60.

Biberstein, K., *Lukian und Theodotion im Josuabuch. Mit einem Beitrag zu Josuarollen von Hirbet Qumran*, Munich 1994.

Bodine, W. R., "Kaige and Other Recensional Developments in the Greek Text of Judges". *BIOSCS* 13 (1980), 45–57.

———, *The Greek Text of Judges: Recensional Development*, Chico, Calif. 1980.

Busto Saiz, J. R., "El texto teodociónico de Daniel y la traducción de Símaco". *Sefarad* 40 (1980), 41–55.

Cooper, C. M., "Theodotion's Influence on the Alexandrian Text of Judges". *JBL* 67 (1948), 63–68.

Cox, C. E., "(Job 32 . . .) Origen's Use of Theodotion in the Elihu Speeches". *The Second Century, A Journal of Early Christian Studies* 3 (1983), 89–98.

Engel, H., *Die Susanna-Erzählung. Einleitung, Übersetzung und Kommentar zum Septuaginta-Text und zur Theodotion-Bearbeitung*, Fribourg–Göttingen 1985.

Field, F., *Origenis Hexaplorum quae supersunt*, Oxford 1875. *Prolegomena* XXXVIII–XLII.

Gil, L., "Theodotion". *EncBibl* 6 (1965), 934–35.

Greenspoon, L., "Recensions, Revisions, Rabbinics: Dominique Barthélemy and Early Developments in the Greek Traditions". *Textus* 15 (1990), 153–67.

———, "Theodotion's Version". *ABD* 6 (1992), 447–48.

Gwynn, J., "Theodotion". *DCB*, 4, 970–79.

Jellicoe, S., *SMS*, 83–94.

———, "Some Reflections on the 'kaige' Recension". *VT* 23 (1973), 15–25.

Montgomery, J. A., *Daniel*, ICC 1950.

Munnich, O., "Contribution à l'étude de la première révision de la Septante". *ANRW* II, 20, 1 (1987), 190–220.

———, "La Septante des Psaumes et le groupe kaige". *VT* 33 (1983), 75–89.

O'Connell, K. G., *The Theodotionic Revision of the Book of Exodus*, Harvard 1972 [Review

---

[40] "In particular, if the attribution of the greater part of the revision in evidence in the Judges sixth column to second-century Theodotion is valid, then his own work must be differentiated from prior revisional efforts and analyzed in its distinctiveness", see W. R. Bodine, *The Greek Text of Judges*, p. 196.

by D. Barthélemy in *Bib* 55 (1974), 91–93, and by E. Tov in *JBL* 93 (1974), 114–15].

Pazzini, M., "La trascrizione dell'ebraico nella versione di Teodozione". *SBFLA* 41 (1991), 201–22.

Rahlfs, A., "Über Theodotion-Lesarten im Neuen Testament und Aquila-Lesarten bei Justin". *ZNW* 19–20 (1919–20), 182–99.

Sáenz-Badillos, A., "El hebreo del s. II d.C. a la luz de las transcripciones griegas de Aquila, Símmaco y Teodoción". *Sefarad* 35 (1975), 107–30.

Salmon, G., *A Historical Introduction to the Study of the Books of the NT*, London 1889, 594–606.

Schmitt, A., *Stammt der sogenannte "θ"-Text bei Daniel wirklich von Theodotion?* MSU IX, Göttingen 1966.

Schüpphaus, J., "Das Verhältnis von LXX- und Theodotion-Text in den apokryphen Zusätzen zum Danielbuch". *ZAW* 83 (1971), 49–72.

Swete, H. B., *An Introduction to the Old Testament in Greek*, Cambridge 1914, 42–49.

Tov, E., "Die griechische Bibelübersetzungen". *ANRW* II, 20, 1 (1987), 121–189, especially pp. 175–79.

Tov, E., "Transliterations of Hebrew Words in the Greek Versions of the Old Testament: A Further Characteristic of the *kaige-* Th. Revision?". *Textus* 8 (1973), 78–92.

CHAPTER TEN

OTHER ANCIENT VERSIONS

Of the remaining versions we know from the Hexaplaric fragments and some information from the Fathers, some are anonymous (*quinta, sexta, septima,* ὁ ἑβραῖος, ὁ σύρος, τὸ σαμαρειτικόν), others are attributed to particular people (Josephus, Ben La'anah Ben Tilgah) but only known through a mosaic of readings which makes difficult any attempt to insert them into the history of the LXX. Jellicoe deals with the *quinta, sexta* and *septima* in the chapter on the Hexapla,[1] as it is the main channel through which its readings have been transmitted. However, with Field and Swete, we prefer to set it in the context of other versions different from the LXX as being the most suitable, since Aquila, Symmachus and Theodotion are also known to us almost exclusively through the Hexapla.

As the fragments preserved are very sparse and so difficult to identify, further questions on whether they are true versions or only revisions of the LXX are even more difficult; whether they cover the whole Greek Bible or only some of its books; whether they come from Jewish circles or instead already originated among Christians. In spite of that, they comprise valuable documents which reflect moments of intense philological activity around the Greek Bible, and it cannot be excluded that one day a possible find will unexpectedly reveal its true being. In the meantime, let is look at the data we have on each.

a) *The* Quinta *(E')*

In his *Historia Ecclesiastica* VI, 16, Eusebius provides the following information:

> So meticulous was Origen's research on the divine Scriptures that he even learned Hebrew and made his own the original Scriptures which the Jews present with their own signs of the Hebrews and studied the

---

[1] S. Jellicoe, *SMS*, 118–24.

editions of other translators of the sacred Scriptures as well as the
LXX; and he found others still which differed, apart from the well-
known translations of Aquila, Symmachus and Theodotion; he published them tracking them down in I know not which hiding-places,
for they had been hidden since ancient times. Since he did not know
whose they were as they were hidden, he only noted that he had found
one in Nicopolis of Actium and the second in a similar place. In the
Hexapla of the psalms, after the four known editions, after placing to
the side not only the *quinta* but also the versions *sexta* and *septima*, of
one it is also indicated that it was found in Jericho in a jar in the
time of Antoninus, son of Severus[2]

Against this description by Eusebius, Epiphanius inverts the sequence,
stating that the *quinta* was found in Jericho *c.* 217 CE and the *sexta*
in Nicopolis under Severus Alexander (222–35 CE),[3] and adds that
the *sexta* was also found in a jar. Jerome mentions these three editions but does not add the details of their discovery.[4]

Even though these reports read like fiction – resorting to the discovery of a book hidden for a long time to endow it with more
authority – the account by Eusebius gives all the signs of having a
historical core. Origen was in Palestine in 217 CE and in Greece in
231; thus it is possible to connect these stays with the events reported.
As Mercati accepts, the witnesses favour the text of Eusebius since
it is found in all the manuscripts and is cited by many Fathers.[5]
Furthermore, this report occurs in a manuscript containing a *catena*

---

[2] Eusebius, *Kirchengeschichte*, VI, 16, 1–3 (ed. Schwartz): Τοσαύτη δὲ εἰσήγετο τῷ
Ὠριγένει τῶν θείων λόγων ἀπηκριβωμένη ἐξέτασις, ὡς καὶ τὴν Ἑβραΐδα γλῶτταν
ἐκμαθεῖν τάς τε παρὰ τοῖς Ἰουδαίοις φερομένας πρωτοτύπους αὐτοῖς Ἑβραίων
στοιχείοις γραφὰς κτῆμα ἴδιον ποιήσασθαι ἀνιχνεῦσαί τε τὰς τῶν ἑτέρων παρὰ
τοὺς ἑβδομήκοντα τὰς ἱερὰς γραφὰς ἑρμηνευκότων ἐκδόσεις καί τινας ἑτέρας παρὰ
τὰς κατημαξευμένας ἑρμηνείας ἐναλλαττούσας, τὴν Ἀκύλου καὶ Συμμάχου καὶ
Θεοδοτίωνος, ἐφευρεῖν, ἃς οὐκ οἶδ᾿ ὅθεν ἔκ τινων μυχῶν τὸν πάλαι λανθανούσας
χρόνον ἀνιχνεύσας προήγαγεν εἰς φῶς· ἐφ᾿ ὧν διὰ τὴν ἀδηλότητα, τίνος ἄρ᾿ εἶεν
οὐκ εἰδώς, αὐτὸ τοῦτο μόνον ἐπεσημήνατο ὡς ἄρα τὴν μὲν εὕροι ἐν τῇ πρὸς Ἀκτίοις
Νικοπόλει, τὴν δὲ ἐν ἑτέρῳ τοιῷδε τόπῳ· ἔν γε μὴν τοῖς Ἑξαπλοῖς τῶν Ψαλμῶν
μετὰ τὰς ἐπισήμους τέσσαρας ἐκδόσεις οὐ μόνον πέμπτην, ἀλλὰ καὶ ἕκτην καὶ
ἑβδόμην παραθεὶς ἑρμηνείαν, ἐπὶ μιᾶς αὖθις σεσημείωται ὡς ἐν Ἰεριχοῖ εὑρημένης
ἐν πίθῳ κατὰ τοὺς χρόνους Ἀντωνίνου τοῦ υἱοῦ Σευήρου. The translation of this
passage is mine.
[3] Epiphanius, *De Mens. et Ponderibus*, 18. The information provided by Pseudo-
Athanasius, *Synopsis Script. Sacrae*, 77, seems to derive from Epiphanius since he has
the same sequence and attribution of these versions.
[4] Jerome, *De vir. illustribus*, 54: "quintam et sextam et septimam editionem, quas
etiam nos de eius bibliotheca habemus, miro labore repperit et cum ceteris editionibus comparavit"; see also *In ep. ad Titum* and *In Hab.* II, 2; III, 13.
[5] G. Mercati, "Sul testo e sul senso di Eusebio H.E. VI, 16".

of psalms and preserves Hexaplaric fragments. It is possible that it goes back to Origen himself and from him passed to Eusebius.[6]

We do not know how long these versions were; nor is there proof that any of them covered the whole Old Testament. However, readings from the *quinta* have been found in the books of Kings,[7] Job, Psalms, Song and the Twelve Prophets. In the Pentateuch no commentary mentions it. Field notes some remnants of the *quinta* in Gen. 6:3; 34:15 and 35:19.[8] However, they are scattered in the recent critical edition by Wevers which attributes the reading of ms. 64 in Gen. 34:15 (εὐνοήσομεν) to Symmachus and the other two are rejected as glosses.[9] The longest fragments preserved for the *quinta* come from the book of Psalms, once the last column of the Milan palimpsest was identified as belonging to this version. H.-J. Venetz has recently published a monograph on the *quinta* of the Psalms which will require traditional views on this version to be modified. It is to be included in the καίγε group as the characteristics of that recension define it best. Field's opinion of its style as "omnium elegantissimus . . . et cum optimis Graecis suae aetatis scriptoribus comparandus" can be considered today as no more than a brilliant generalisation.[10]

In the Twelve Prophets also, Barthélemy equates the *quinta* with the καίγε recension.[11] However, this equation is only valid for the authentic *quinta* which in Barthélemy's opinion occurs exclusively in Jerome's quotations. The thirty-five readings transmitted by *Barberinus graec.* 549 (= Rahlfs' 86) do not represent the *quinta* but an edition according to the Hebrews, which Cyril of Alexandria cites in his commentary on the Twelve Prophets. The confusion in ms. 86 is

---

[6] G. Mercati, "D'alcuni frammenti esaplari", 29. The text in question runs as follows: ε' ἔκδοσις ἣν εὗρον ἐν Νικοπόλει τῇ πρὸς Ἀκτίοις· τὰ δὲ παρακείμενα αὐτῇ ἐστιν ὅσα ἐναλλάσσει παρ' αὐτήν· ς' ἔκδοσις εὑρεθεῖσα μετὰ καὶ ἄλλων βιβλίων Ἑβραϊκῶν καὶ Ἑλληνικῶν ἔν τινι πίθῳ περὶ τὴν Ἱεριχὼ ἐν χρόνοις τῆς βασιλείας Ἀντωνίνου τοῦ υἱοῦ Σευήρου ("the *quinta* edition which I found in Nicopolis which is next to Actium. Alongside it is everything which differs from it. The *sexta* edition found together with other Hebrew and Greek books in a jar in the vicinity of Jericho, in period of the reign of Antoninus, son of Severus"). This text is transmitted by the forewords to *catenae* XV, XVI, XVIIa and XVIIb of the Karo–Lietzmann families for the Psalms, see R. Devreesse, *Introduction à l'étude des manuscrits grecs*, Paris 1954, 107–108.

[7] F. C. Burkitt, "The So-called Quinta of 4 Kings".

[8] F. Field, *Origenis Hexaplorum quae supersunt*, XLIII.

[9] J. W. Wevers, *Septuaginta I Genesis*, Göttingen 1974, *ad loc.*

[10] F. Field, *Origenis Hexaplorum quae supersunt*, and for the *quinta* of the Psalms, H. J. Venetz, *Die Quinta des Psalteriums*, 51–72 and 194.

[11] D. Barthélemy, *Les Devanciers d'Aquila*. VTS 10, 1963, 213ff. and 260.

due to the fact that the siglum ε' of the *quinta* is also the abbreviation for the ἔ(κδοσις) κατὰ τοὺς Ἑβραίους mentioned by Cyril.[12]

If, then, this edition had been as widespread as Barthélemy would wish (= καίγε recension) it would not have been necessary to note, as Origen does, that he found it in Nicopolis of Actium. Furthermore, if we remove as spurious the thirty-five readings of ms. 86 from the *quinta* of Twelve Prophets, what do we have left of the *quinta* in this book to compare with that recension? Thirty-seven Greek words from Jerome's commentary, many of them re-translated, which do not always match the passages in which we have remnants of the καίγε. This and other objections have been raised recently by Howard against Barthélemy,[13] concluding that the *quinta* and the καίγε recension in the Twelve Prophets are not the same but are at most related to the same extent that καίγε, Justin, *Codex Washingtonianus*, the Coptic versions and Aquila also have readings in common.

Burkitt had a similar problem, due to the scarcity of fragments, in trying to identify the *quinta* in 2 Kings. It is known only from a collection of readings discovered in the margin of the Syro-Hexapla preceded by the siglum ω. Taylor hazarded the conjecture that it was a collection of variants placed in the margin of the Hexapla, a collection also containing some significant readings from the authentic LXX. Origen had rejected these readings in favour of the corresponding translations by Aquila and Theodotion; their inclusion in the right-hand margin of the Hexapla supposed an intermediate stage between their presence in the text and their complete disappearance.[14] However, in a recent examination of the material from Kings, Deboys concludes that the *quinta* of 2 Kings is a pre-Hexaplaric revision in favour of the proto-Masoretic text, and contrary to Barthélemy, he holds that in some way it can be identified with the Antiochene text of the ancient LXX.[15]

At present, until a systematic study of all the known fragments of the *quinta* is made, in the book of Psalms, it seems to belong to the καίγε recension and is therefore *a recension of the LXX* but with its own personality, so that it cannot simply be defined as one of Aquila's predecessors.[16]

---

[12] D. Barthélemy, "Quinta ou version selon les Hébreux".
[13] G. Howard, "The Quinta of the Minor Prophets".
[14] F. C. Burkitt, "The So-called Quinta of 4 Kings", 30.
[15] D. G. Deboys, "The Greek Text of 2 Kings", doctoral diss., Oxford 1981, p. 181, and Deboys, "Quinta/E' in Four Reigns".
[16] Venetz defines concisely the relationship between the *quinta* and Aquila by say-

b) *The* Sexta (Z')

The ancient sources cited above are also valid for the *sexta*. Its history is closely linked to that of the *quinta*, as the passage from Eusebius of Caesarea proves. Jerome speaks of the Jewish authors of versions *quinta* and *sexta*.[17] Some have already suspected the Christian origin of the *sexta* from Hab. 3:13 where it translates ἐξῆλθες τοῦ σῶσαι τὸν λαόν σου διὰ Ἰησοῦν τὸν χριστόν σου ('you went out to save your people by means of Jesus, your Christ').[18] Undoubtedly there is an unmistakable intention to translate the Hebrew preposition *lᵉ* by διά. However, as for the use of the singular instead of τοὺς χριστούς σου of the LXX, it is only being adjusted to the Hebrew text like the readings of Aquila, Symmachus and Theodotion in this same passage.

We have fragments of the *sexta* in Psalms, Song, Ex. 7:9 and Job 5:7; 30:16. Jerome mentions it in Hab. 2:11 and 3:13.[19]

We can say little about its style given the scant data available. Field notes the strange reading νεανικότης of the *sexta* in Pss 9:1 and 109:3.[20] However, given that this word is a *hapax* in the dictionaries, it must be considered an error for νεανιότης, which is well attested in Lampe's lexicon of Patristic Greek.

The note in the prologue to some *catenae* of the psalms which we mentioned above[21] added in speaking of the *quinta*: τὰ δὲ παρακείμενα αὐτῆς ἐστιν ὅσα ἐναλλάσει παρ' αὐτήν ('what is placed at its side is everything that differs from it'). Fresh light has been thrown on this ambiguous *scholion* with the publication of Hexaplaric fragments by Mercati. In fact, in smaller letters there is a series of readings written

ing that both shared a common homeland (Palestine) but different mentalities: "Die Quinta des Psalteriums wird nur dann genügend gewürdigt, wenn in ihr eine eigenständige Rezension des o'-Textes gesehen wird. Bei aller Betonung der auffallenden Übereinstimmungen und der gemeinsamen Heimat der beiden Texte (ε' und α') darf doch ihre jeweilige grundsätzliche Andersartigkeit nicht ausser acht gelassen werden," see H. J. Venetz, *Die Quinta des Psalteriums*, 193. On p. 1 Venetz also holds that the *quinta* of each book requires a separate study to be identified. Since Field considers it to be a unit, he describes it with the characteristics of the *quinta* of Hosea transmitted by ms. 86 but which, as we have seen, is not authentic. Accordingly his description is worthless.

[17] *Adv. Rufinum*, II, 34.

[18] J. Ziegler, *Septuaginta XIII Duodecim prophetae*, Göttingen 1967, 271.

[19] "Reperi, exceptis quinque editionibus, id est, Aquilae, Symmachi, Septuaginta, Theodotionis et quinta, in duodecim prophetis et duas alias editiones," *PL* 25, 1296. Undoubtedly this refers to the *sexta* and the *septima*.

[20] F. Field, *Origenis Hexaplorum quae supersunt*, XLV.

[21] See note 6.

next to or beneath the last column of the palimpsest. Mercati's conclusions concerning these readings are as follows:[22]

1. the readings written alongside or underneath those in the last
   column belong to the *sexta*;
2. these readings mark its differences from the *quinta*, not from
   the LXX;
3. as a result, in reconstructing the *sexta*, missing words must be
   supplied on the basis of the *quinta*, not the LXX.

What is surprising is how similar these variants, attributed by
Mercati to the *sexta*, are to readings from the LXX column, although
not always. Wevers provided evidence of this fact, expressing strong
reservations towards the identification proposed by Mercati and insisting that many of these readings are really to be attributed to the
LXX and not the *sexta*.[23] In the monograph mentioned, Venetz only
arrived at negative conclusions, defining the *sexta* as an unknown
among the Greek translations and recensions;[24] in all likelihood it
does not represent the καίγε group. Against Wevers, he holds instead
that there is no convincing proof for doubting that these marginal
readings from the Milan palimpsest do not belong to the *sexta*.

c) *The* Septima

According to Jerome, the *septima* existed especially in the books composed in verse: Job, Psalms, Lamentations and Song of Songs.[25]

---

[22] G. Mercati, *Psalterii Hexapli Reliquiae*, II, Rome 1958, XXXIIIff.

[23] J. W. Wevers, "Septuaginta-Forschungen seit 1954", *TR* nf 33 (1968), 65.
According to Wevers most of the marginal readings belong to the text of the fifth
column (= LXX), even where it is not a good translation from Hebrew: "Nur
scheinbar hilft die Annahme weiter, dass die *Sexta* nur eine geringfügige Revision
war, da alle Revisionen die Absicht hatten, die herrschende Textüberlieferung zu
verbessern. Viele von den Randlesarten der Kol 5, die der LXX entsprechen (das
gilt für 70 Lesarten bei insgesamt 95), beruhen entweder auf einem andern Text,
oder sind freie Übersetzungen, oder gehen auf Textmissverständnisse zurück. Ich
habe einige besonders auffallende Beispiele ausgewählt, die mich davon überzeu-
gen, dass der Ursprung zumindest vieler Lesarten LXX ist." And a little further on (p. 66): "In der Tat ergibt sich aus 30,1 und 3 der Beweis dass die Varianten
überhaupt nichts mit der *Sexta* zu tun haben." To these reservations it should be
added that the siglum for the *sexta* (ς') can be confused in the manuscripts with the
abbreviation for the conjunction καί.

[24] H. J. Venetz, *Die Quinta des Psalteriums*, 107–19, 118, 128 and the conclusion
on p. 194: "Die *Sexta* des Psalteriums konnte nur negativ charakterisiert werden
und bleibt daher weiterhin eine grosse Unbekannte innerhalb der verschiedenen
Übersetzungen und Rezensionen."

[25] Jerome, *In ep. ad Titum*: "nonnulli vero libri, et maxime hi qui apud Hebraeos

However, neither he nor any other ancient commentator ever cites a reading from the *septima*. Moreover, sometimes there is a reference to eight columns in some books in the Hexapla (ὀκτασελίδες), but nine columns are never mentioned.[26]

Finally, in several manuscripts that contain the Greek Old Testament, a note about the *septima* is usually inserted before *Dodekapropheton*, but sometimes also before the Psalter, after Chronicles and elsewhere, where it is identified with the edition by Lucian: ἑβδόμη τε ἔκδοσις ἡ τοῦ ἁγίου Λουκιανοῦ τοῦ μεγάλου ἀσκητοῦ καὶ μάρτυρος ('seventh edition, the one of the great Lucian, ascetic and martyr').[27] Faced with the lack of data and the confusion with Lucian's text, Mercati considers the possibility that the supposed *septima* in the Psalter was nothing else but the Septuagintal column transmitted separately, that is, the current ecclesiastical text corrected only from exemplars judged to be good.[28]

d) *The Hebrew*

Some 4th and 5th century Fathers attribute a certain number of non-Septuagintal readings to ὁ ἑβραῖος/τὸ ἑβραϊκόν. This title seems to denote three different contents in the Hexapla and *scholia*:

1. The second column of the Hexapla consisting of the transliteration of the Hebrew text into Greek letters (τὸ ἑβραϊκὸν Ἑλληνικοῖς γράμμασι). From among many examples that are preserved of these transliterations in Hexaplaric contexts, Field derives certain general rules on the transliteration of Hebrew consonants and vowels into Greek.[29] The interest and problems that arise in connection with the pronunciation of Hebrew as reflected in these readings will be

---

versu compositi sunt, tres alias editiones additas habent quam 'quintam' et 'sextam' et 'septimam' translationem vocant, auctoritatem sine nominibus interpretum consecutam".

[26] See chapter 13 on the composition and structure of the Hexapla.

[27] This belongs to a sort of rather general prologue which includes the successive deportations of the people of Israel throughout history, a work on the divine names and a review of the seven editions of the Bible, see R. Devreesse, *Introduction à l'étude des manuscrits grecs*, 118ff. See also, chapter 14, below, on the Lucianic recension. The identification of the *septima* as Lucian's edition is to be found in Pseudo-Athanasius, *Synopsis Scripturae Sacrae*, 77, in *PG* 28,436: ἑβδόμη πάλιν καί τελευταία ἑρμηνεία ἡ τοῦ ἁγίου Λουκιανοῦ ("finally, the seventh and last translation, by St Lucian").

[28] G. Mercati, *Psalterii Hexapli reliquiae*, XXXV.

[29] F. Field, *Origenis Hexaplorum quae supersunt*, LXXIff.

considered in more detail when discussing the Hexaplaric *secunda*.[30]

2. In other contexts it refers to the basic Hebrew text, that is to the first Hexaplaric column, especially in the expressions of Eusebius ἡ ἑβραϊκὴ λέξις/ἡ ἑβραϊκὴ ἀνάγνωσις. In spite of the ambiguity of these formulae, there are *scholia* that certainly refer to the Hebrew text.[31] Similarly, the expressions "in Hebraeo", "juxta Hebraeos" of Jerome's commentaries always refer to the Hebrew text, the *hebraica veritas*.

3. Lastly, another series of allusions refers unmistakably to a new interpreter. His readings appear in the margins of manuscripts like the other Hexaplaric variants, and the Fathers who cite him include Eusebius of Emessa, Diodorus, Acacius, Didymus, Polychron, Olimpiodorus, Chrysostom and Theodoret. Most of the fragments occur in Genesis, Job and Ezekiel; but also in Exodus, Jeremiah, Isaiah and Daniel. Very often he is cited together with another anonymous translator, the Syrian, who also remains in the shade.[32]

Many hypotheses have been proposed on this translator, none of them convincing.[33] It cannot refer to Aquila since there is a large number of translations that depart from the Hebrew *textus receptus*, and also in those passages where we have readings from Aquila and from the Hebrew they do not agree. One could think perhaps of those Hebrew teachers who served some Fathers of the Church, especially Origen and Jerome, to explain difficult passages of Scripture.[34] However, in G. Bardy's opinion, Jerome attributed information taken from other sources – especially from Origen whom he tacitly copied – and even his own hypotheses, to "a Hebrew".[35] Apart from that, he is mentioned in the Hexapla as an actual writer, ὁ ἑβραῖος. There

---

[30] See chapter 13.

[31] For example, in the gloss to Psalms 69, 70, 143 and 144 which runs: οὔτε παρὰ τῷ ἑβραίῳ, οὔτε παρὰ τοῖς ἄλλοις εὑρίσκεται ("It is found neither in the Hebrew nor in the others").

[32] J. W. Wevers, *Septuaginta ... I–V, Genesis–Deuteronomium*, Göttingen 1974–91, in the Hexaplaric apparatus, *passim*, and J. Ziegler, *Septuaginta XVI Ezechiel*, Göttingen 1952, 65ff.

[33] F. Field, *Origenis Hexaplorum quae supersunt*, LXXVI.

[34] Jerome, *Ad Am.* 3,2; Jerome, *Nah.* 3,8: "Referebat mihi Hebraeus; audivi ab Hebraeo; Hebraeus qui me in S. Scripturis erudivit," etc.

[35] G. Bardy, "Saint Jérôme et ses maîtres hébreux", 164: "Les formules *Memini et Dicebat Hebraeus* ne doivent donc pas nous faire illusion; une fois de plus, il faut les interpréter avec une certaine latitude ... nous voulions simplement montrer qu'il ne fallait pas toujours faire une entière confiance à Saint Jérôme lorsqu'il dit avoir reçu telle ou telle leçon de ses maîtres hébreux."

is no other solution than to accept him as a new translator who translated at least some books of the Old Testament (Genesis, Job, Ezekiel) into Greek and perhaps annotated others (there is some evidence in Exodus and Deuteronomy;)[36] a translator whose origin still remains unknown and whose translation techniques seem more like those of Symmachus than of Aquila.

The new critical editions of the LXX not only reduce such attributions, but they also recover new readings. Thus, against the fourteen variants attributed by Field to the Hebrew for the book of Genesis, no more than thirty-one can be read in the new edition by Wevers,[37] and some of these include complete verses. The same applies to the book of Job.[38] A provisional *sondage* of the new readings in Genesis allows the following results:

1. the considerable increase in witnesses has helped to clarify the identity of this translator more and more;
2. his readings are transmitted especially by the catenary mss and Procopius, an author connected with the origin of the *catenae*;
3. in most cases he is accompanied by the Syrian and has the same reading;
4. both these translators know Hebrew well and Greek especially, since in Gen. 38:29, for example, they reproduce the play on words of the original.[39]

In the opinion of Wevers, the Hebrew and the Syrian as well as the *Samariticon* refer to other translations; however to a large extent their origin continues to be an enigma.[40]

---

[36] On the possible palaeographic confusion in the manuscripts of the Syro-Hexaplaric version between the siglum ʿain to denote ὁ ἑβραῖος and the siglum *gamma* (= οἱ γʹ) which denotes the three more recent translators, due to the similarity of both letters in the Estrangelo script; see J. W. Wevers, *Septuaginta... II, 1 Exodus*, Göttingen 1991, 46.

[37] J. W. Wevers, *Septuaginta I Genesis*, in the Hexaplaric apparatus.

[38] See J. Ziegler, *Septuaginta XI, 4 Iob*, Göttingen 1982, p. 212 in the Hexaplaric apparatus and *passim*.

[39] Gen. 38:29: ὁ συρʹ ὁ ἑβρʹ τί διεκόπη ἐπὶ σὲ διακοπή for the *figura etymologica* in Hebrew, *mâ pāraṣtā ʿālêkā pāreṣ*. On the translation of the *figura etymologica* in the LXX, see N. Fernández Marcos, *Nombres propios y etimologías populares en la Septuaginta*. Sefarad 37 (1977), 239–61, especially pp. 251ff. How well 'The Hebrew' knew Greek is shown by the use of ἀναθυμίασις (Gen. 19:28) and τὸ μετάφρενον (Gen. 49:8).

[40] "Diese beziehen sich offensichtlich auf andere Übersetzungen, doch ist deren Herkunft grösstenteils noch ungeklärt," see J. W. Wevers, *Septuaginta I Genesis*, Göttingen 1974, 59.

e) *The Syrian*

Readings attributed to the Syrian (often in common with the Hebrew) are mentioned by Melito (according to a *catena* on Gen. 22:13), Didymus, Diodorus, Eusebius of Emessa, Policronio, Apollinar (for the book of Daniel), Chrysostom (three times, twice apparently attributed incorrectly), Theodoret (for Jeremiah and Ezekiel), Procopius and others.

Quotations from the Syrian occur in Genesis (some thirty times), Exodus, 1 Kings, Psalms, Lamentations and the later prophetic writings. For Jeremiah about thirty readings are known;[41] for Ezekiel approximately fourteen;[42] for Twelve Prophets six[43] and for Isaiah only three.[44] We have no evidence from the remaining books.

The identity of the translator continues to remain unknown. In his commentary on the Twelve Prophets, Theodore of Mopsuestia accepts that he does not know who he is: οὐδὲ γὰρ ἔγνωσται μέχρι τῆς τήμερον, ὅστις ποτὲ οὗτός ἐστιν ('since until today who he might be continues to be unknown').[45] Field surveys a series of passages where his reading agrees with the Peshitta; however, they are variants that do not prove any type of identification in the light of so many differences.[46] The following have been suggested as hypotheses:

1. It reproduces the readings of the Peshitta transmitted orally (J. Perles).
2. He is a certain Sophronius, the Greek translator of some works by Jerome and was to be known to posterity as 'The Syrian', either because its author Jerome lived a long time in the solitude of the borders of Syria or because the version by Sophronius was greatly appreciated by the Syrians (Semler, Döderlein and Eichhorn).[47]

---

[41] J. Ziegler, *Septuaginta XV Ieremias*, 106.

[42] J. Ziegler, *Septuaginta XVI Ezechiel*, 65–66.

[43] J. Ziegler, *Septuaginta XIII Duodecim Prophetae*, 108.

[44] J. Ziegler, *Septuaginta XIV Isaias*, 113, n. 3.

[45] *In Soph.* 1, 6; see H. N. Sprenger, *Theodori Mopsuesteni Commentarius in XII Prophetas*, Wiesbaden 1977, 283.

[46] F. Field, *Origenis Hexaplorum quae supersunt*, LXXIX: "Ex his exemplis, ni fallimur, certissime evincitur, Syrum nostrum anonymum cum versione Peschito (quae dicitur) nihil commune habere."

[47] Jerome, *De vir. illustribus*, 134: "Sophronius vir apprime eruditus ... de Virginitate quoque ad Eustochium, et vitam Hilarionis monachi, opuscula mea in graecum eleganti sermone transtulit; Psalterium quoque et prophetas quos nos de Hebraeo in Latinum vertimus."

However, against these hypotheses, two points can be raised. *Contra* Perles, it is difficult to believe that the discrepancies with the Peshitta were produced by corruption through oral transmission. As for identifying him as Sophronius, there is no mention in the quotation from Jerome that this translator translated the book of Genesis, so that we have about thirty readings of the Syrian. Although many passages are very close to Jerome's Vulgate,[48] it is easier to explain these affinities if Jerome used that translation during his stay in Syria than the other way round. Furthermore, in another set of quotations, there are clear disagreements between Jerome and the Syrian.[49]

Accordingly, all the indications are in agreement that he was a native Syrian, of unknown name, who made a new translation from Hebrew into Greek. This is Field's hypothesis, confirmed by Rahlfs[50] and followed by J. Ziegler. In fact, in Ez. 8:16 he translates *'ûlām* as κιγκλίς when the usual Greek word is κάγκελλον; so that these two synonyms are only different in Greek. And in Gen. 39:2, according to the testimony of Diodorus, he translates *maṣlîaḥ* as κατευοδούμενος, a synonym of ἐπιτυγχάνων of the LXX, a synonym only differentiated in Greek. If Diodorus had taken this reading from the Syriac, he could have said this, since the two Greek words have only one equivalent in Syriac. Finally, in Jer. 31(48):33 οὐκέτι οἱ ληνοβατοῦντες κελεύσουσι λέγοντες ἰά, ἰά ("those treading the grapes shall no longer intone this toast, saying: 'Ya! Ya!'") proclaims a Greek rather than a Syriac origin of this translation.[51]

Rahlfs, from a commentary by Theodoret of Cyr on Jgs. 12:6 in which the Ephraimites have to pronounce the word *šibbolet*, on seeing how the LXX and the Syrian reproduce it, concludes that the Syrian was forced to write in Greek. The text by Theodoret runs as follows: ὡς γὰρ ὁ σύρος φησί, τῶν ἄλλων τὸν ἄσταχυν σεμβλὰ καλούντων, οἱ τοῦ Ἐφραὶμ ἔκ τινος συνηθείας σεμβελὼ ἔλεγον, τοῦτο γινώσκων ὁ Ἰεφθάε λέγειν ἐκέλευσε, καὶ διελεγχομένους ἀνῄρει ('for as the Syrian says, whereas the others called ear of corn σεμβλά, those

---

[48] J. Ziegler, *Septuaginta XVI Ezechiel*, 66.

[49] Although the version into Greek by Sophronius of some of Jerome's works seems to have been lost, traces of it are perhaps to be found in some of the Hexaplaric *scholia* preceded by the siglum ὁ Λατῖνος, such as the one in Dt. 34:7, see J. W. Wevers, *Septuaginta III, 2 Deuteronomium*, Göttingen 1977, p. 375.

[50] A. Rahlfs, "Quis sit ὁ Σύρος?"

[51] Since κελεύειν as 'to propose a toast' and κέλευσμα as 'song of those treading the grapes' belong to refined Greek, see F. Field, *Origenis Hexaplorum quae supersunt*, LXXXII.

from Ephraim said σεμβελώ by a particular custom. Aware of this, Jephthah ordered them to say it and killed the condemned').[52]

Nor was it possible to reproduce the difference between σεμβλά and σεμβελώ in Syriac (since both words are written *šbbl*). It was difficult to be able to reproduce the difference between the Hebrew sibilants *š* and *s* in Greek. Accordingly, instead of a free translation as in the LXX, the Syrian uses a different vocalisation from Syriac which can be expressed in the transliteration into Greek.[53]

However, Sprenger criticises Rahlf's argument since the difference in sibilants would not have been noticed in Greek whether it translates from the Peshitta or whether directly from the Hebrew. Sprenger suspects that the difference in Greek pronunciation had been established by Theodoret himself, and as a result the problem of the Syrian cannot be resolved with strictly philological arguments. From the commentary by Theodore of Mopsuestia he concludes that he was an unknown Syrian who translated the Hebrew text into Syriac and whose translation was later displaced by the Peshitta.[54]

Mercati has helped to fix the date and the place from which this author came. With good reason he criticises the attribution to Melito of Sardis (d. 190) of the passage that mentions the Syrian in Genesis, and reclaims it for Eusebius of Emessa, later than Melito by almost a century and a half.[55] If Melito had known it, it is very strange that Origen does not cite him either in the Hexapla or in his other works. Mercati has shown that for the paragraph of the *catena* of Karo and Lietzmann's type II – the only fragment on which that attribution depends – the correct lemma is Εὐσεβίου ἐπισκόπου Ἐμίσης. With this correction the result is that one of the authors who cite it wrote before Constantine, making that emperor the *terminus a quo* for this new translation.

Since all the authors who cite him come from Syria or neighbouring countries, Didymus of Alexandria could not be a witness to

---

[52] See N. Fernández Marcos and A. Sáenz-Badillos, *Theodoreti Cyrensis Quaestiones in Octateuchum. Editio Critica*, Madrid 1979, p. 303.

[53] A. Rahlfs, "Quis sit ὁ Σύρος?", 408–11. The difference between Eastern Syriac, which preserves ancient Semitic *a*, and Western Syriac, where that vowel becomes *o*, is known.

[54] H. N. Sprenger, "Das Problem des ΣΥΡΟΣ".

[55] In 1882 A. von Harnack had already suspected the incorrect attribution of this fragment and declared himself in favour of Eusebius of Emessa (see *Geschichte der altchristlichen Literatur bis Eusebius*, Leipzig, 1958², I,1, 249).

the Syrian, since his name would have been inserted in the *catenae* due to confusion with the abbreviation for Diodorus.[56]

Finally, in a recent study Guinot maintains against Field and Rahlfs that in Theodoret's commentaries the Syrian is alluding to the Peshitta or at least a Syriac version very close to the Peshitta.[57]

f) *The* Samariticon

In the rich channel of transmission that is the Hexapla, sometimes *scholia* are found that allude to readings taken from the Samaritan Pentateuch.[58] Some of these variants are found in the margins of mss 85 and 130. Perhaps Origen included these Samaritan Hebrew readings in the Hexapla, translating them into Greek. Possibly, the *scholion* about two manuscripts for Num. 13:1, which alludes to that work, goes back to Origen.[59]

However, as well as these readings we find throughout the Pentateuch others preceded by the title τὸ σαμαρ(ε)ιτικόν/τὸ σαμ'. According to Field, there are forty-three such readings and four that are anonymous that belong to the same translator.[60] Kohn surveys up to forty-six.[61] Nearly all the readings agree with the Samaritan Targum as we know it through the defective editions we have.[62] This is explained either because both translate the same Hebrew text, i.e. the Samaritan Pentateuch, or because they reflect the same exegetical tradition or theological viewpoint.

Kohn goes further than Field and concludes that the *Samariticon*

---

[56] G. Mercati, "A quale tempo risale 'il Siro'?". A. Vööbus sees 'the Syrian' as an earlier stage of the Peshitta, see A. Vööbus, "Neus Licht auf das Problem des ὁ Σύρος", 110–11.

[57] J.-N. Guinot, "Qui est 'le syrien'?", 68.

[58] On this text, see A. F. von Gall, *Der hebräische Pentateuch der Samaritaner*, Giessen 1918; F. Pérez Castro, *Sefer Abisa'*, Madrid 1959, and L. Girón Blanc, *Pentateuco Hebreo-Samaritano. Génesis*, Madrid 1976.

[59] The *scholion* runs as follows: καὶ τούτων μνημονεύει Μωϋσῆς ἐν τοῖς πρώτοις τοῦ Δευτερονομίου ἃ καὶ αὐτὰ ἐκ τοῦ τῶν Σαμαρειτῶν Ἑβραϊκοῦ μετεβάλομεν καταλλήλως τῇ τῶν ο' ἑρμηνείᾳ τῇ ἐν τῷ Δευτερονομίῳ φερομένῃ ("and Moses mentions this in the first chapters of Deuteronomy; a thing which we have translated from the Hebrew of the Samaritans, quoting in corresponding order the LXX version of Deuteronomy"); see A. E. Brooke and N. McLean, *The Old Testament in Greek. Volume I. Part III: Numbers and Deuteronomy*, Cambridge 1911, p. 454.

[60] F. Field, *Origenis Hexaplorum quae supersunt*, LXXXIII.

[61] S. Kohn, "Samareiticon und Septuaginta".

[62] See J. R. Díaz, *Targum Samaritano*. EncBibl VI (1965), 881–84.

was a complete translation – like the one by Aquila, Symmachus or Theodotion – of the Samaritan biblical text, not made directly from the Hebrew but through the Targum.[63] Wevers reaches the same conclusion for most of the readings in Leviticus under this siglum transmitted by the catenary manuscripts and ms. M: they are translations of the Samaritan Targum.[64]

From the discovery of Pap. Giessen 13,19.22.26 – which contains several fragments of this Greek translation – it has been proved that the *Samariticon* was a complete translation of the Pentateuch and not simply a series of glosses on the Samaritan Targum. These fragments have been published by P. Glaue and A. Rahlfs and contain Gen. 37:3-4, 8-9 and Deuteronomy 24–29 with many lacunae.[65] The reading *garîzîm* instead of *'ebāl* (Dt. 27:4) was the key to detecting its Samaritan origin. The fragments show the same close relationship with the Samaritan Targum as the readings of the *Samariticon* and undoubtedly belong to a complete translation of the Samaritan Pentateuch. Thus it can be concluded – even though not one of the passages from Deuteronomy contained in Pap. Giessen is preserved in the *Samariticon* – that these Hexaplaric readings from the *Samariticon* and this papyrus belong to the same translation. Rahlfs instead considers Kohn's hypothesis that this translation was made from the Samaritan Targum to be much more dubious.[66] Both the Samaritan Targum and the *Samariticon* translate the Hebrew Pentateuch of the Samaritans. And the frequent contacts between them have to be explained either because one of the two has the other translation in front of him, as well as the original, or else because both follow the same exegetical tradition.

Apart from these fragments, in a Samaritan synagogue in Thessalonica an inscription was found, partly in Hebrew with Samaritan characters, which also contained the biblical text in Greek of Num. 6:22-27, the priestly blessing. The text of the inscription differs notice-

---

[63] S. Kohn, *Samareiticon und LXX*, 67. His other conclusions – to explain the agreements between the LXX and the biblical text of the Samaritans as interpolations from the *Samariticon*, and to attempt to see many other readings of the *Samariticon* incorporated in the Septuagintal tradition – require much further revision in the light of the new Hebrew texts that have been found in Qumran, some of which are clearly proto-Samaritan.

[64] J. W. Wevers, *Septuaginta II, 2 Leviticus*, Göttingen 1986, p. 31.

[65] P. Glaue and A. Rahlfs, "Fragmente einer griechischen Übersetzung", 31–64.

[66] P. Glaue and A. Rahlfs, "Fragmente einer griechischen Übersetzung", 56 and 62.

ably from the LXX and is faithful to the Samaritan Pentateuch, which in this case is different from the Hebrew *textus receptus*. It is thus one more link with the translation into Greek of the Samaritan Pentateuch or *Samariticon*.[67] E. Tov has again examined the fragments of Pap. Giessen and the inscription from Thessalonica and concludes that they do not belong to the *Samariticon*. Instead, in both cases these texts belong to the various revisions that the LXX translation underwent – revisions which tended to reproduce the Hebrew text more accurately – as it is closer typologically to Symmachus than to Aquila.[68] Even so, faced with the evidence of the variant αργαρ(ι)ζιμ in Dt. 27:4 he resorts to the hypothesis that the Papyrus (and correspondingly the inscription) form part of the Samaritan revision of the LXX carried out for the needs of the community.

Certainly it is not easy to decide whether Papyrus Giessen and the inscription from Thessalonica belong to a new translation of the Samaritan Pentateuch or they are simply a revision of the LXX made by the Samaritan community.[69] Nevertheless, these texts point to a Samaritan textual tradition that is also transmitted in Greek and has to be connected with ancient information concerning that tradition and with the Hexaplaric readings attributed to the *Samariticon*.

g) *Josephus the Translator*

This Josephus is only known from information published by J. Phelipeau when discussing different Hexaplaric sigla in connection with the Greek versions. He appears to be Theodoret of Cyr, although there are no printed editions of his works.[70] After the exegesis under the siglum for Lucian (λ), the following editorial note is inserted: ὅπου δὲ τὸ ϊ μετὰ τοῦ ω, Ἰωάννου Ἰωσήπου ("where you find the *yod* with the *omega* it is by John Joseph").

In spite of the brevity of the note, this remark brings to mind the

---

[67] B. Lifshitz and J. Schiby, "Une synagogue samaritaine à Thessalonique", where these fragments are published and analysed for the first time.

[68] E. Tov, "Pap. Giessen 13,19.22.26: A Revision of the LXX?", especially p. 382, and Tov, "Une inscription grecque d'origine samaritaine".

[69] See B. Lifshitz, "Prolegomenon", 74–75.

[70] The title of the book is: *Oseas primus inter prophetas. Commentarius illustratus, auctore Joanne Phelippaeo Societatis Jesu*, Paris 1636. The information was probably taken from one of the codices that Cardinal Rochefoucauld gave him, see J. B. Kipper, "Josipo (ou Josepo), tradutor grego", p. 300, n. 4.

one-hundred marginal readings preceded by the siglum Ιω' transmitted by ms. *Barberinus* 549 for Jeremiah.[71] They are all preceded by this abbreviation except for Jer. 38(31):22, where the reading is accompanied by the following note:[72] ὡς ἐπὶ ἀληθείας οὕτως εὗρον αὐτὸ κείμενον ἐν τῇ Ἰωσίππου ἐκδόσει ("in fact, this is how I found it written in the edition by Josephus").

There is no doubt, therefore, that he is a new translator called Josephus, and it is not a mere revision, since his text is completely unlike the LXX. As we only have his readings for the book of Jeremiah, we do not know whether his translation was limited to that book or covered the whole Old Testament. Theodoret of Cyr mentions him twice together with Aquila and Symmachus, attributing to each readings in the book of Joshua. Apparently, in these two cases he is referring to our translator and not to the Jewish historian with the same name, Flavius Josephus.[73] According to Devreesse he is also named several times in 1 Kings and the Psalms.[74] In three passages from Jeremiah (32:9, 24 and 45:14) he appears in the company of Aquila, Symmachus and Theodotion.

His translation techniques are rather free and periphrastic, and given the agreement of his readings with the Vulgate, it is possible that he knew Jerome.

The only overall study devoted to the translator Josephus is by the Brazilian J. B. Kipper.[75] This author records a complete list of *scholia* attributed to Josephus as well as the number of words and proper names contained in each of them. Some, like those of Jer. 15:15-16 or 44:11-12 even cover two verses, with 26 and 28 words

---

[71] = 86 de Rahlfs, see J. Ziegler, *Septuaginta . . . XV Ieremias*, 106.

[72] It reads as follows: ὅτι ἤδη εἰργάσατο κύριος παράδοξον ἐπὶ τῆς γῆς· παρθ(ένος) κυοφορήσει γὰρ ἄνθρωπον ("because the Lord already worked a marvel on the earth; for a virgin would give birth to a man").

[73] See N. Fernández Marcos and A. Sáenz-Badillos, *Quaestiones in Octateuchum*, 278, 16–18: τὴν δὲ ψιλὴν ὁ Ἀκύλας στολὴν ἡρμήνευσεν· ὁ δὲ Ἰώσηπος χλανίδα· τὴν δὲ γλῶσσαν, μάζαν χρυσῆν ("And Aquila translated the 'light armour' as 'clothing', but Josephus as 'woollen clothing' and the language as 'amalgam of gold'"); and on p. 279,7–8: τὸ μέντοι γαῖσον ᾧ τοὺς λοχῶντας διήγειρεν Ἰησούς, ἀσπίδα ἡρμήνευσεν ὁ Ἰώσηπος, ὡσαύτως δὲ καὶ ὁ Σύμμαχος ("However, Josephus translated as 'shield' the *gaison* with which Joshua aroused those who were ambushed, as does Symmachus").

[74] R. Devreesse, *Introduction à l'étude des manuscrits grecs*, 130, n. 4: see 1 Kgs 12:10: Σύρος καὶ Ἰώσηπος; and in mss *Vat.* 525 and 1223 on Ps. 48:1: ο' θ' σ' ι' πλούσιος καὶ πένης. ἄλλος ὁμοῦ. Devreesse identifies the 'Jewish edition' to which Cyril of Alexandria refers (see sub *quinta* ἔκδοσις κατὰ τῶν ἑβραίων), as this edition by Josephus, *ibid.* 130.

[75] J. B. Kipper, "Josipo (ou Josefo), tradutor grego".

respectively. About ten fragments cover a complete verse and in total there are thirty-four proper names, twenty personal names and fourteen toponyms. The translation is outstanding for its freedom, its variety of expressions, and its fondness for composite words, superlatives, paraphrase, etc.[76] It presupposes the Hebrew *textus receptus* as the basis for the translation, sometimes against the LXX. However, it also exhibits slight differences and some puzzling passages, an indication that the translator did not fully understand the original. There are so many disagreements with the LXX that cannot be satisfactorily explained as a revision of that version, but are surely a completely distinct translation from Hebrew. His vocabulary is riddled with rare terms that at best agree with those used in the later books of the LXX and especially with Symmachus. The few fragments, short as they are, contain a surprising number of *hapax legomena* as against the LXX and the three more recent translators,[77] leading to the suspicion that the criterion for preserving these fragments may have been precisely the fact that they were rare and unusual.

The remarkable agreements with the Vulgate readings suggest the possible influence that Jerome may have had on Josephus, through Sophronius, the Greek translator of some of his works,[78] since Jerome never mentions Josephus. However, there are so many differences from the Vulgate (twenty-four, as against twelve agreements) that it must be concluded either that Josephus and the Vulgate depend on a common third source or else that, like Jerome, in his translation Josephus felt the influence of Hebrew teachers or Jewish exegesis.

It is possible to think, as did Devreesse,[79] of a possible connection between Josephus and the ἔκδοσις κατὰ τῶν ἑβραίων that Cyril of Alexandria speaks about, the text of which has the same strange similarity with the Vulgate. However, it seems that this similarity has to be explained by Cyril's dependence, otherwise well attested, on Jerome.[80]

Since Jerome does not cite Josephus, although he is known to Theodoret of Cyr (d. 458), Kipper is inclined to date him to the 5th century and locate him most probably in Syria. However, I do not

---

[76] J. B. Kipper, "Josipo (ou Josefo), tradutor grego", 303ff.

[77] J. B. Kipper, "Josipo (ou Josefo), tradutor grego", 393–94.

[78] F. Field, *Origenis Hexaplorum quae supersunt*, XCIV, and J. B. Kipper, "Josipo (ou Josefo), tradutor grego", 448.

[79] See note 73.

[80] J. B. Kipper, "Josipo (ou Josefo), tradutor grego", 451–52, and H. Kerrigan, *St. Cyril of Alexandria Interpreter of the Old Testament*, Rome 1952, 254–67.

know whether it can be concluded from Jerome's silence that he did not know him. Perhaps he saw him as a competitor of his own time or somewhat earlier, and ignored him intentionally. The contacts with the Vulgate, the relationship of Josephus' vocabulary with the lexicon of Symmachus and of the late books of the LXX with the lexicon of the Fathers of that region and with Theodoret's quotations argue in favour of Syria as the homeland of this translator.[81]

Finally, S. Krauss wishes to see Ben La'anah and Ben Tilgah as two new translators of the Bible into Greek. He quotes them together in many midrashic passages and in one passage from the Jerusalem Talmud. Unfortunately, however, Krauss can only cite two readings in support of his hypothesis.[82]

SELECT BIBLIOGRAPHY

Quinta, Sexta *and* Septima

Barthélemy, D., "Quinta ou version selon les Hébreux". *TZ* 16 (1960), 342–53.
Burkitt, F. C., "The So-called Quinta of 4 Kings". *PSBA* 24 (1902), 216–19.
Deboys, D. G., "Quinta/E' in Four Reigns". *Tyndale Bulletin* 36 (1985), 163–78.
Field, F., *Origenis Hexaplorum quae supersunt*, Oxford 1875, XLII–XLVI.
Howard, G. E., "The Quinta of the Minor Prophets: A First Century Septuagint Text?". *Bib* 55 (1974), 15–21.
Jellicoe, S., *SMS*, 118–24.
Mercati, G., "D'alcuni frammenti esaplari sulla Va e VIa edizione greca della Bibbia". *ST* 5 (1901), 28–46.
———, "Sul testo e sul senso di Eusebio H.E. VI, 16". *ST* 5 (1901), 47–60.
Nestle, E., "Zu dem Bericht des Origenes über seine 5. und 6. Bibelübersetzung". *ZAW* 26 (1906), 168.
Venetz, H. J., *Die Quinta des Psalteriums. Ein Beitrag zur Septuaginta und Hexaplaforschung*, Hildesheim 1974.

Hebrew, Syriac and the Samariticon

Bardy, G., "Saint Jérôme et ses maîtres hébreux". *RBén* 46 (1934), 145–64.
Bloch, J., "ὁ Σύρος and the Peshitta". *Jewish Studies in Memory of J. Abrahams*, New York 1927, 66–73.

---

[81] J. B. Kipper, "Josipo (ou Josefo), tradutor grego", 393 and 454. The *scholion* on Jer. 38(31): 22 (given in note 72: παρθένος κυοφορήσει γὰρ ἄνθρωπον) has led to the belief that Josephus was a Christian, witness to an exegetical tradition that saw Christ's virgin birth prefigured in the text of Jeremiah. However, as Kipper notes (*ibid.*, 453), we do not know whether in this case Josephus is dependent on Jerome or whether both go back to the Jewish exegetical tradition which in the 3rd–2nd centuries BCE already interpreted the *'almâ* of Is. 7:14 as παρθένος. This means that it cannot be decided from the *scholion* whether Josephus was a Christian or a Jew.

[82] S. Krauss, "Two Hitherto Unknown Bible Versions in Greek".

Field, F., *Origenis Hexaplorum quae supersunt*, Oxford 1875, LXXI–LXXXIV.

Glaue, P., and A. Rahlfs, "Fragmente einer griechischen Übersetzung des samaritanischen Pentateuchs". MSU I, 2 = NGWGött (1911), 2, 167–200.

Guinot, J. N., *L'exégèse de Théodoret de Cyr*, Paris 1995, 186–90.

———, "Qui est 'le Syrien' dans les commentaires de Théodoret de Cyr?". *Studia Patristica* 25, ed. E. A. Livingstone, Leuven 1993, 60–71.

Kohn, S., "Samareitikon und LXX". *MGWJ* 38 (1894), 1–7; 49–67.

Lehmann, H. J., "Evidence of the Syriac Bible Translation in Greek Fathers of the 4th and 5th Centuries". *Studia Patristica* 19, ed. E. A. Livingstone, Leuven 1989, 366–71.

Lifshitz, B., "Prolegomenon". *Corpus Inscriptionum Judaicarum. Volume I*, ed. J.-B. Frey, New York 1975, 70–75.

Lifshitz, B., and J. Schiby, "Une synagogue samaritaine à Thessalonique". *RB* 75 (1968), 368–78.

Mercati, G., "A quale tempo risale il 'Siro'?. Nota". *Bib* 26 (1945), 1–11.

Perles, J., "De Syro in Hexaplis commemoratione". *Melemata Peschittoniana*, Vratislava 1859, 49–51.

Pummer, R., "The Present State of Samaritan Studies". *JSS* 22 (1977), 27–48.

Rahlfs, A., "Nachtrag. Ein weiteres Fragment der griechischen Übersetzung des samaritanischen Pentateuchs". MSU I, 2 = NGWGött (1911), 263–66.

———, "Quis sit ὁ Σύρος?". MSU I, 404–12 = NGWGött (1915), 420–28.

Romeny, B. T. H., "'Quis sit ὁ Σύρος' Revisited". *Origen's Hexapla and Fragments*, ed. A. Salvesen, Tübingen 1998, 360–98.

Sprenger, H. N., "Das Problem des ΣΥΡΟΣ". *Theodori Mopsuesteni Commentarius in XII Prophetas*, ed. H.-N. Sprenger, Wiesbaden 1977, 79–83.

Tov, E., "Pap. Giessen 13,19.22.26: A Revision of the LXX?". *RB* (1971), 355–84.

———, "Une inscription grecque d'origine samaritaine trouvée à Thessalonique". *RB* 88 (1974), 394–99.

Vööbus, A., "Neues Licht auf das Problem des ὁ Σύρος". *Peschitta und Targumim des Pentateuchs*, Stockholm 1958, 110–11.

Josephus, Ben La'anah, Ben Tilgah

Field, F., *Origenis Hexaplorum quae supersunt*, Oxford 1875, XCIII–XCIV.

Kipper, J. B., "Josippus". *Paulys Realencyclopädie der classischen Altertumswissenschaft*. Supp. 15, Munich 1978, 116–24.

———, "Josipo (ou Josefo), tradutor grego quase desconhecido". *Revista di Cultura Biblica* 5 (1961), 298–307; 387–95; 446–56.

Krauss, S., "Two Hitherto Unknown Bible Versions in Greek". *BJRL* 27 (1943), 97–105.

Ziegler, J., *Septuaginta XV. Ieremias–Baruch–Threni–Epistula Ieremiae*, Göttingen 1957, 106–108.

CHAPTER ELEVEN

JEWISH VERSIONS INTO MEDIAEVAL AND MODERN GREEK

The influence of Greek on Jewish literature has been noted for a long time through many linguistic loans that have been discovered in the Targums (even the oldest such as Neophyti), in the Jerusalem Talmud and in various Midrashim.[1]

Perles emphasises the influence of Byzantium in every sphere of Jewish life, on the technical terms of medicine, administration, law and even the liturgy through a series of lexical items that emerge in rabbinic writings.[2] And Neubauer surveys a range of information about Greek–Hebrew glossaries for the use of Caraites in the Middle Ages. These glossaries show that Jews in Greek-speaking countries, and perhaps in Rome, knew and used Greek during the Byzantine period.[3] The Caraite writers, and especially Judah Hadassi from Edessa in his *'eškol ha-kofer* (1148) continually use Greek words and phrases.[4] On the other hand, in several manuscripts in the Bodleian Library at Oxford there are hymns in Greek written in Hebrew characters.[5] Neubauer ends his survey by referring to the need for a complete Jewish–Greek lexicon from the earliest period of the Mishnah, which would be very useful not only for the study of Greek dialects (since being conservative by inclination the Jews would have

---

[1] S. Krauss, *Griechische und Lateinische Lehnwörter*, especially I, 221–37: *Die rabbinische Gräcität*; and for Neophyti, see A. Díez Macho, *Ms Neophyti 1, I–V Genesis–Deuteronomium*, Madrid–Barcelona 1968–78.

[2] J. Perles, "Jüdisch-byzantinische Beziehungen", 572 and 580ff.

[3] A. Neubauer, "On Non-Hebrew Languages Used by Jews", 17ff. One of these glossaries has been edited and studied by A. Papadopoulos-Kerameus (see Select Bibliography). Palaeographically it can be dated to between the 6th and 7th centuries CE.

[4] A. Neubauer, "On Non-Hebrew Languages Used by Jews", 20ff., and J. Perles, "Jüdisch-byzantinische Beziehungen", 575ff.

[5] I.e., written in Hebrew characters. See Numbers 2.501, 2.503, 2.504 and others from A. Neubauer, *Catalogue of the Hebrew Manuscripts in the Bodleian Library and in the College Libraries of Oxford*, Oxford 1886–1906. Some hymns used in Corfu have been published by Sp. Papageorgios in *Abhandlungen des 5ten internationalen Orientalisten Congresses*, Berlin 1882, 225ff.

preserved ancient forms) but also for study of the LXX and the New Testament, both works written or influenced by Jews.

In examining here the Jewish versions into medieval Greek and modern Greek, I wish above all to fulfil one aim: to establish the connection between the ancient versions of the Bible on the one hand and to follow the path of tradition which acted as a bridge until the production of the Constantinople Pentateuch on the other.

However, there are still two additional matters of interest, which I only mention in the hope that other more qualified specialists will discuss them:

1. the relationship of these versions with rabbinic Greek and the influence they could have had on it;[6]
2. the definition of relevant parallels with other calque languages such as Jewish-Spanish.[7]

a) *Witnesses*

In the margins of manuscript S. P. 51 (previously A. 147 *Inf.*) from the Ambrosian Library in Milan, a fragmentary Octateuch from the 5th century, there is a series of notes in cursive made by a corrector (F[b] in the edition by Brooke–McLean and Wevers) who was conversant with Jewish tradition. The text runs from Gen. 31:15 to Josh. 12:12;[8] marginal readings continue throughout these passages. These readings merit systematic examination. A first *sondage* allows us to

---

[6] See H. B. Rosén, "Palestinian κοινή in Rabbinic Illustration", *JSS* 8 (1963), 56–72; S. Sznol, "Ejemplos del griego rabínico a la luz del tesoro lexicográfico del DGE", *Emerita* 57 (1989), 329–43; Sznol, "Addenda a Sifre-Números", *Emerita* 63 (1995), 117–28; Sznol, "*Sefer ha Razim.* El libro de los secretos. Introducción y comentario al vocabulario griego", *Erytheia. Revista de estudios bizantinos y neogriegos*, 10 (1989), 265–88.

[7] See the publications by H. V. Sephiha and C. Sirat in the Select Bibliography, and the following studies by M. Morreale on Romanced Bibles: M. Morreale, "Apuntes bibliográficos para la iniciación al estudio de las traducciones bíblicas medievales en castellano", *Sefarad* 20 (1960), 66–109, and Morreale, "Vernacular Scriptures in Spain", *The Cambridge History of the Bible* 2, Cambridge 1969, 465–92.

[8] For a description of this important uncial, see H. B. Swete, *An Introduction to the Old Testament in Greek*, Cambridge 1914, 135–36; S. Jellicoe, *SMS*, 192–93; A. Rahlfs, *Verzeichnis der griechischen Handschriften des Alten Testaments*, Berlin 1914, p. 125; and J. W. Wevers, *Septuaginta ... I Genesis*, Göttingen 1974, 12; Wevers, *Septuaginta ... II, 1 Exodus*, 1991, 7–8; Wevers, *Septuaginta ... II, 2 Leviticus*, 1986, 7–8; Wevers, *Septuaginta ... III, 1 Numeri*, 1982, 7–8; Wevers, *Septuaginta ... III, 2 Deuteronomium*, 1977, 7–8.

conclude that the author of these corrections, written in minuscule script, is definitely working within the tradition of the Jewish versions, and there is remarkable agreement with the vocabulary of the Greek text of the Constantinople Pentateuch, even though it reflects a less developed stage of the language. Although the glosses remain anonymous, in a passage from Genesis, F[b] identifies its author as τὸ ἰουδαϊκόν.[9] Also, ms. i (= 56 of Rahlfs), which has several Hexaplaric readings, many of them agreeing with F[b], on two occasions identifies him by this title.[10]

Kahle claimed that these remnants of Hexaplaric material were taken from ancient translators of Jewish origin from the pre-Christian period or from the 1st century CE.[11] This is untenable since the readings themselves, although very uneven, indicate their late origin. In my view they are post-Hexaplaric and come from Jewish translations that circulated in the Byzantine period leaving traces in the margins of some manuscripts such as M, F, i.

As has been confirmed by recent editions and studies of Exodus, this material is an indication that in the post-Hexaplaric period the activity of translation into Greek continued, and that most of these translations are Jewish in origin. Most of these anonymous readings belong within the Jewish tradition of translation and, what is more interesting, they have surprising agreements with the translation into modern Greek of the Constantinople Pentateuch, although they obviously represent an older stage of the language: of the 488 readings that F[b] preserves in the book of Exodus, it shares 100 with the Constantinople Pentateuch.[12] Another later corrector of the same manuscript made a new Hebraising translation of Ex. 36:3–39:19 (= F[h]), closely connected with the text of the Complutensian. According to Wevers, one of the sources of the Complutensian had to share

[9] J. W. Wevers, *Septuaginta . . . I Genesis*, Göttingen 1974 in the second critical apparatus on Gen. 47:31 τὸ ιουδ' ἐπὶ προσκεφά(λαιον τῆς) κλίνης αὐτοῦ F[b]. Other approximations to the Hebrew can be seen in Ex. 6:3: ἐν ἰσχυρῷ ἱκανῷ to translate Hebrew *b[e]ēl šadday*; Ex. 15:1, 11, etc., see J. W. Wevers, *Septuaginta . . . II, 1 Exodus*, Göttingen 1991, in the Hexaplaric apparatus.

[10] See the editions by Wevers quoted above in Gen. 40:9: τὸ ιουδ' ἦν κλημ εναν[τ] 56; Gen. 43:11: τὸ ιουδ' ἀμύγδαλα 56. It is still mentioned in Ex. 16:31 in the corrections in cursive in the same manuscript F: τὸ ιουδ' . . . κοριανδροκόκκου F[b].

[11] P. Kahle, *The Cairo Geniza*, Oxford 1959, 245, n. 1. (For Gen. 43:2 there read Gen. 43:11).

[12] See J. W. Wevers, *Septuaginta . . . II, 1 Exodus*, 43–44, and Wevers, "A Secondary Text in Codex Ambrosianus of the Greek Exodus".

in the *stemma* a text on which F[h] also depended.[13] D. Fränkel reaches
the same conclusion in a well-documented article.[14]

In 1924 Blondheim published, in Greek transliteration, some fragments containing Qoh. 2:13-23 written in Hebrew characters. They
come from file H.1 of the Taylor–Schechter collection in the Cambridge University Library.[15] At the beginning of each verse one word
or the first two words of the Hebrew text are inserted, followed by
the Greek translation as a pedagogical aid to following the text in
both languages. Blondheim does not give these fragments a precise
date, although from the chronological order in which he arranges
them he indicates that they are later than the 12th century.[16] However,
judging from the stage of language they reflect, I would put them
between 600 and 1100.[17]

The interlinear translation into modern Greek with Hebrew characters of the book of Jonah was published by Hesseling in 1901.[18]
It is found in two manuscripts, one from the Bodleian of Oxford

[13] J. W. Wevers, "A Secondary Text in Codex Ambrosianus of the Greek Genesis",
p. 48: "This must mean that one of the sources of Compl must have shared in its
stemmata a parent text which also lay in the textual ancestry of F[h]. That source
is not one of the extant identified sources of Compl for the Pentateuch, viz. ms
108 and some of the *f* mss, but one no longer extant".

[14] D. Fränkel, "Die Quellen der asterisierten Zusätze im zweiten Tabernakelbericht
Exodus 35–40", especially 174–86, p. 176: "Weil nicht völlig ausgeschlossen werden
kann, dass die Bearbeiter der Complutensis sei es den Codex selbst, sei es die
wahrscheinlich jüdische Tradition, auf die sich der Text von F[b/h] gründet, kannten."

[15] D. S. Blondheim, "Échos du judéo-hellénisme", 3 and 14. See now N. R. M.
de Lange, "Two Genizah Fragments in Hebrew and Greek", pp. 64–75. De Lange
re-edits, transcribes and comments on this text of Qoheleth.

[16] Following the one by Arouk completed in 1101, see D. S. Blondheim, "Échos
du judéo-hellénisme", 2.

[17] With the greatest reserve and in spite of the difficulty of any transcribed text
as reflecting the corresponding phonetics. On the other hand the fragments are
very small and we know very little about the language spoken in this period, see
R. Browning, *Medieval and Modern Greek*, 59–72, especially p. 70. Not all the prepositions are constructed with the accusative, a move that would take place in the
following period (Browning, *Medieval and Modern Greek*, 86), but only σύν (a construction inherited from Aquila) and ἐν. However we do have ὑπὸ σοφίας (2:21),
ἀπουκάτω τοῦ ἡλίου (2:17, 18, 19, 20), ὄπιλθέν μου (2:18) etc. In addition note,
as Psaltes remarks, that "die Anfänge der ngr. Sprache nicht um 1000 n. Ch., wie
Psicari meinte, sondern, wie Hatzidakis und nach ihm K. Dieterich gezeigt haben,
schon im Anfang des Mittelalters (500 n. Ch.) und, wie die Papyri zeigen, noch
früher zu suchen sind", see St. B. Psaltes, *Grammatik der Byzantinischen Chroniken*,
Göttingen 1913, 1974 reprint, VIII.

[18] D. C. Hesseling, "Le livre de Jonas", 213–17.

and the other from Bologna. It is so incredibly literal that the translator even uses the same gender as the Hebrew noun although it is
different in Greek (e.g. ἄνεμος μεγάλη in 1:4 because the Hebrew
word *rûaḥ* is feminine). Hesseling dates it to the 13th century[19] and
Neubauer to the 12th.[20] Perhaps the date has to be set back even
further if we take into account the linguistic phenomena reflected,
even though the difficulty of reproducing the phonemes peculiar to
any text written with the characters of another language is compounded by the linguistic inconsistencies and the conservatism of a
literary text that already had a history in Greek. As is also the case
in the Constantinople Pentateuch, it cannot be reduced to a uniform linguistic system; instead, different phenomena coexist.[21] Sporadic
contacts with one of "the three" (Aquila, Symmachus and Theodotion)
are explained as it is a word-for-word translation from Hebrew.
Instead the agreements with the LXX in the lexicon and in some
constructions – sometimes against "the three" – are so striking, that
it is necessary to modify Hesseling's statement, that it is a completely
different version from the LXX.[22]

   To this material must be added other Greek fragments from the
deposits in the Cairo Genizah: biblical glosses in Greek, fragments
from Judges with glosses in Greek, fragments of a commentary on
Ezekiel with Greek glosses, etc.[23]

Graecus Venetus: Better known is the version of the Pentateuch together
with the books of Ruth, Proverbs, Song, Qoheleth and Lamentations

---

[19] D. C. Hesseling, "Le livre de Jonas", 210.

[20] A. Neubauer, "On Non-Hebrew Languages Used by Jews", 17. According to
Neubauer it is written in the dialect of the Island of Corfu and the text was read
in the synagogue as the *Ḥaftarâ* of *yôm Kippûr*.

[21] In spite of these qualifications, note that πᾶς has not yet been completely
replaced by ὅλος (Jon. 2:4); that not all the prepositions are constructed with the
accusative; that not every final -ν has been dropped, etc. Do these facts reflect the
stage of the language in which it was translated or are they linguistic archaisms
which belong naturally to a conservative sacred language?

[22] D. C. Hesseling, "Le livre de Jonas", 211: "On constatera que cette version
est absolument indépendante de celle des Septante." As I understand it, the translator had the LXX in front of him not only from the wording which is very close
to it but above all from the translation of "land/earth" as ξερά (1:9 and 2:11) in
agreement with Hebrew *yabbāšâ* and the use of κολοκύνθη (4:6) – the same word
as in the LXX – as against κικεών of Aquila–Theodotion or κισσός of Symmachus.

[23] See N. R. M. de Lange, "Greek and Byzantine Fragments in the Cairo
Genizah", and de Lange, Hebrew–Greek Genizah Fragments and their Bearing on
the Culture of Byzantine Jewry".

transmitted by *Cod. Gr.* VII of the Markan library of Venice (14th
century). It was published twice in the 18th century,[24] but the most
recent edition is by O. Gebhardt, published in Leipzig (1875), together
with a long introduction.[25] The translation was made directly from
the Masoretic text but with the occasional help of other Greek versions: LXX, Aquila, Symmachus and Theodotion. All the same, the
chief instigator of this translation was D. Kimhi, who flourished at
the beginning of the 13th century. Almost all the peculiar interpretations of the *Graecus Venetus* originate in Kimhi's *sefer ha-šorašim*. The
author's faithfulness to the original is evident in his efforts to translate it into Attic Greek, keeping the Doric dialect for the passages
of the book of Daniel composed in Aramaic. According to Delitzsch,
the author was a Jew, given that in Ex. 23:20 *ha-māqôm* (a circum-
locution to avoid God's name in late Judaism) is used to translate
τὸν ὀντωτήν, i.e. Yahweh.[26] Mercati instead thinks that this version
formed part of an Old Testament in two languages (or possibly
three): Hebrew, Greek (and Latin). The peculiar nature of the manuscript – its unusual format of 28 × 10 cm, the Semitic sequence
of the folios and the lines of unequal length (some very full and others extremely short) – led him to conclude that this version must
have been published in parallel with the Hebrew text. In fact, there
is now positive evidence of an attempt of this nature in the second
half of the 14th century: a Hebrew–Greek–Latin Bible with a new
version of the New Testament in Hebrew was composed in part by
a Basilian monk from the monastery of the Stoudios in Constantinople,
a bishop in southern Italy and later in Greece, a papal legate in the
East for the unification of the churches, called Simon Atumanos.[27]

The characteristics of the introduction have been carefully analysed
by Delitzsch in the introduction to the Gebhardt edition.[28] However,
we cannot use it as an example of a particular stage in the history
of the Greek language since it tries to restore classical forms artificially,
including the optative.

---

[24] See H. B. Swete, *An Introduction to the Old Testament in Greek*, 56–58, where some
fragments of this version are reproduced.

[25] The complete title is: *Graecus-Venetus. Pentateuchi Proverbiorum Ruth Cantici Ecclesiasticae
Threnorum Danielis versio graeca ex unico bibliothecae S. Marci Venetae codice nunc primum uno
volumine comprehensam atque apparatu critico et philologico instructam edidit O. G. Praefatus est
Fr. Delitzsch*, Leipzig 1875.

[26] See H. B. Swete, *An Introduction to the Old Testament in Greek*, 57.

[27] See G. Mercati, "Chi sia l'autore della nuova versione", 516.

[28] *Graecus-Venetus. Pentateuchi Proverbiorum Ruth*, pp. XLVIff.

The manuscript *Vat. Graecus* 343 contains a translation of the Psalter with the odes (*des.* at the end of the ninth ode) which for comparative linguistics has the advantage of being dated. At the end it bears the date 22 April 1450.[29] The language it reproduces lies at a stage halfway between the interlinear translation of Jonah and the Constantinople Pentateuch. It is possible that it was translated into modern Greek from the LXX, for it includes odes such as 7, 8 and 9 which have no Hebrew *Vorlage*. Also, this last ode follows the LXX completely, except for constructions no longer in use as they were archaic in the 15th century. Final -ν has not yet disappeared completely, but the dative is always replaced by another case, the pronouns have initial apheresis and ὅλος has completely displaced πᾶς.[30] However, as happens in most such cases where the authors are well educated, they do not consistently reproduce all the linguistic phenomena of the period in question, but include archaisms and learned words from biblical tradition.

Undoubtedly, though, the most typical translation into modern Greek written in Hebrew characters is the Constantinople Pentateuch, published in that city in 1547, the first printed work in Greek in a Greek-speaking country.[31] Several scholars, such as J. C. Wolff, M. Emile Legrand and L. Belléli himself,[32] have tried to transcribe the first chapters of Genesis of this version. The complete transcription of the work in Greek, edited together with a long linguistic introduction and provided with a glossary, was by Hesseling.[33]

Besides the enormous interest that it holds for the history of exegesis, from the linguistic point of view it is a precious document in vulgar Greek at a strategic point in its history; a few years later vulgar Greek would start to be contaminated and ultimately replaced

---

[29] This manuscript is described in R. Devreesse, *Bibliothecae Apostolicae Vaticanae Codices Vaticani Graeci. Tomus II: Codices 330–603*, Vatican City 1937, p. 18.

[30] See R. Browning, *Medieval and Modern Greek*, 73ff.

[31] It is a polyglot Pentateuch in Hebrew, Greek in Hebrew characters and Jewish-Spanish or Ladino, also in Hebrew characters. The version in Jewish-Spanish is the work of Sephardic Jews expelled from Spain in 1492 to become refugees in Turkey. The book of Deuteronomy has been edited recently by H. V. Sephiha (see Select Bibliography). Before this Pentateuch, the version into Modern Greek of the book of Psalms had already been made by Agapius, a monk on the island of Crete, based on the LXX. It was printed in Venice in 1543. See A. G. Masch, *Bibliotheca Sacra II, vol. II, sect. II* and R. Gottheil, "Bible Translations", in *JE* III, 188.

[32] See the two articles by L. Belléli listed in the Select Bibliography.

[33] D. C. Hesseling, *Les cinq livres de la Loi.*

by Turkish, the language with which it was in contact. This Greek has scarcely any foreign influences apart from Latin. Some of its most important characteristics as described by Hesseling are as follows.[34]

1. The relative pronoun ὅς is indeclinable, either from the influence of Hebrew 'ašer or due to the language itself evolving (Gen. 1:7 τὰ νερὰ ὃς ἀποπάνου).

2. The Hebrew infinitive construct is expressed by means of verbal nouns in -ος (Ex. 19:5 ἀκουσμὸ νὰ ἀκούσετε).

3. Proper names are not Hellenised, as frequently happens in the LXX, but transliterated.

4. The author also transliterates a series of common names of trees, dishes, animals, precious stones and others that could easily have been translated into Greek.

5. The lexicographical part is of the greatest interest because it contains ways of renewing the language by resorting to ingenious translation techniques: for example, to translate two Hebrew synonyms or two different meanings of the same word, it attributes very different meanings to two Greek words of dissimilar form but almost identical meaning: γεμίζω = "to fill"; γεμώνω = "to fill the hands", "to consecrate as priest", according to the meaning of the same Hebrew root in the *piel*; δαγκάνω = "to bite" (Num. 21:6.8-9); δαγκώνω = "to lend on interest" (Dt. 23:20), one of the meanings derived from same Hebrew verb *našak*.

6. Some terms are Slavonic in origin, others are Rumanian and many are Latin, such as κάγκελλον, καρροῦχα, κάστρον, πόρτα, σπίτι, στράτα.

Phonetics, as far as they can be reconstructed from being imperfectly reflected in the Hebrew characters, show the prothetic use of α as in ἀμοναχός (Gen. 2:18); proleptic assimilation of ε instead of α/ω (ἐδερφός, ἐνέπιον) and the replacement of ε with ι in an atonic syllable (ἰπί).[35] Also, epenthesis of ι as in ποίμινιο (Gen. 4:2) and the dropping of interconsonantal *yodh*. The vowels ε and ι become *yodh* before vowels as ἔννεα (Gen. 5:27) except in combinations that form a diphthong. Some cases of metathesis – common in modern Greek – such as πειάτε instead of εἴπατε. The *yodh* is dropped in most cases

---

[34] D. C. Hesseling, *Les cinq livres de la Loi*, VIIff., and N. Fernández Marcos, "El Pentateuco griego de Constantinopla", 193–97.
[35] This is already to be found in the translation of the book of Jonah at least three centuries earlier and is probably Cretan in origin.

after κ, χ and very often after λ, ν, γ. Final -ν is only preserved in the third persons singular and plural ending in -εν, -αν, -ην, -ον, -ουν, and in the genitive plural of the article and the noun. However, it is never dropped in πᾶν and in the pronominal forms ἐμέν, ἐσέν, αὐτόν. In the other cases complete irregularity prevails: the same word occurs with and without -ν, and at other times there is an -ν for no linguistic reason.[36]

The article is connected to the main word, creating forms such as ἡγῆς, ναιῶνας. The noun is reduced or regularised into a single declension, the same as for the article. There are very many indeclinable nouns such as ἀνήρ, πᾶν, πᾶσα and many neuter forms in -μα.

To summarise, the linguistic phenomena presented by the Constantinople Pentateuch cannot be reduced to a single system nor is it easy to describe the stage of language it reproduces. It is a monument to common language at the close of the Middle Ages, but is much closer to the southern dialects than to the northern.[37]

Hesseling's edition was harshly criticised by Belléli, especially for the scarcely uniform system of transcription and the mistakes in punctuation.[38] Other criticisms are more debatable and Hesseling defends himself against them. I am inclined to think that expressions such as φωνὴ αἵματα are due to the influence of Hebrew and do not mean that the genitive plural of nouns fell into disuse in the mid-16th century. Similar cases of a breakdown of Greek morphology due to excessive literalism can be found in Aquila.

Finally, to facilitate the teaching of Hebrew, in 1756 Moses ben Eliyah Fabian published a Greek version of Job in Constantinople.[39] The edition of a version into modern Greek written in Hebrew characters of the Aramaic sections of the Bible is due to A. Danon in 1914.[40] He presented this version to Byzantine scholars as a further stage in the development of modern Greek. It had been made by

---

[36] R. Browning, *Medieval and Modern Greek*, 79.

[37] For a summary of the elements marking the shift to Modern Greek, see St. B. Psaltes, *Grammatik der Byzantinischen Chroniken*, VIII, n. 1, and R. Browning, *Medieval and Modern Greek*, 73ff.

[38] See L. Belléli's review of D. C. Hesseling, *Les cinq livres de la Loi*, in *REJ* 35 (1897), 135–55, and Hesseling's reply in the same number, pp. 314–18. Apparently in the edition of this text Hesseling anticipated the same text that Belléli was preparing.

[39] L. Belléli, "Deux versions peu connues du Pentateuque", 250.

[40] The two works by A. Danon, cited in the Select Bibliography.

the Caraite Elias Afeda Beghi in 1627, who added a Hebrew–Greek glossary for the more difficult expressions of the Bible.

b) *Relationship to Earlier Jewish Versions*

In the introduction to his edition of the Greek Pentateuch of Constantinople – accepting Belléli's opinion in *REJ* 22 (1891), 250–63 – Hesseling insists on the literal nature of this version "qui est tout à fait indépendante de la traduction des Septante".[41] In a note he adds "Je n'ai pas non plus trouvé de traits de parenté entre notre version et celles dont les fragments nous sommes conservés dans les Hexapla d'Origène."[42] In his review of O. Gebhardt's edition of the *Graecus-Venetus*,[43] P. F. Frankl expresses a similar opinion against Delitzsch, Gebhardt and Freudenthal, who saw the *Graecus-Venetus* as the last link of Jewish Hellenism.[44]

Instead, by 1924 Blondheim had already found proof of influence by the LXX and especially by Aquila on the versions into medieval and modern Greek.[45] The data set out there confirm the continuity of Jewish tradition through the various links of the translations to medieval Greek. To that data can be added the relationship between the translator included in manuscript F[b] and the translator of the Constantinople Pentateuch. A systematic collation of the fragments of F[b] preserved in the Hexaplaric apparatus of Brooke–McLean with the LXX, "the three" and the Greek text of the Constantinople Pentateuch has given us the following results: the translator of F[b] belongs to the line of previous Jewish translations in adapting literally to the Masoretic text. And he represents an intermediate link within the tradition that leads to the Constantinople Pentateuch, i.e. the agreements in lexicon and idioms between both texts *cannot be explained only* by the fact that both faithfully translate the same Hebrew text. It can be proved from F[b] and the Constantinople Pentateuch using the same translation for words which have quite different synonyms in Greek.

---

[41] D. C. Hesseling, *Les cinq livres de la Loi*, II.
[42] D. C. Hesseling, *Les cinq livres de la Loi*, n. 5.
[43] Published in *MGWJ* 24 (1875), 513–19.
[44] P. F. Frankl, in *MGWJ* 24 (1875), 516: "Zwischen der jüdischhellenistischen Literatur und dem Werke eines griechischen Juden des 14. oder 15. Jahrhunderts lässt sich gar keine Continuität erkennen oder auch nur voraussetzen." And for Freudenthal's opinion, see J. Freudenthal, *Hellenistische Studien*, Breslau 1875, p. 129n.
[45] D. S. Blondheim, "Échos du judéo-hellénisme", 5ff.

If it is difficult to postulate direct dependence on F^b of the Greek translator of the Constantinople Pentateuch, it seems certain that both translators belong to the same tradition or even use the same *Vorlage*, although F^b obviously represents an older stage of the language than the Constantinople Pentateuch.[46] This hypothesis is supported by the fact that using the same general translation technique – fidelity to the Hebrew text – Aquila, Symmachus and Theodotion do not agree with F^b or with the Constantinople Pentateuch in the same proportion as these last two witnesses agree between themselves. This new fact, therefore confirms the hypothesis that the Constantinople Pentateuch depends on earlier Jewish translations into Greek which produced the translations of Aquila, Symmachus and Theodotion, as well as the translation into modern Greek of the Constantinople Pentateuch. This last document is an excellent witness of the modern Greek spoken before the influence of Turkish began to spread.

No less surprising are the agreements of the new Hebraising translation of Ex. 36:3–39:13 to be found in the same manuscript in cursive script (= F^h) with the text of the Complutensian, agreements which led Wevers to conclude that one of the sources of the Complutensian must have been related to one of the textual ancestors of F^{h}.[47]

In spite of the inherent difficulty in the exact phonetic reproduction of a Greek text in Hebrew script, the Constantinople Pentateuch retains great linguistic importance, given the scarcity of witnesses for this period, as an example of common colloquial language. The area of the Epiros must have been particularly productive in this class of translations since at least the *quinta*, according to the testimony of Eusebius of Caesarea,[48] was found in Nicopolis near Actium and the interlinear translation of the book of Jonah is written in the dialect of Corfu. The conservatism of the Jews in the Epiros region is evident in Belléli's remark as recorded by Blondheim that even now

---

[46] See J. W. Wevers, *Septuaginta... II, 1 Exodus*, Göttingen 1991, p. 44. In mentioning the Greek text of this Pentateuch, Perles was thinking of a possible oral translation that would have influenced this translation: "Sie lehnt sich wahrscheinlich an eine mündlich kursierende ältere Übersetzung und ist für den Wortschatz und die Aussprache des Mittelgriechischen von Wichtigkeit," see J. Perles, "Jüdischbyzantinische Beziehungen", 575, n. 1.

[47] See note 13 in this chapter. See also J. W. Wevers, *Septuaginta... II, 1 Exodus*, Göttingen 1991, 7–8, and D. Fränkel, "Die Quellen der asterisierten Zusätze im zweiten Tabernakelbericht Exodus 35–40".

[48] See chapter 10 on the *quinta*, p. 156.

Hebrew teachers translate the Pentateuch correctly with the words of the 1547 version, although it contains expressions that today are strange and obsolete.[49]

Accordingly we preserve sufficiently eloquent links of a Jewish-Greek or Greek-calque parallel to other calque languages that the Jews produced in similar cases of bilingualism,[50] especially in the versions in the Romance languages of the Middle Ages and perhaps in the Old Latin.[51]

This chain of Jewish translations into Greek, which culminates in the Constantinople Pentateuch, to some extent answers the question as to what happened to the brilliant culture of Hellenistic Judaism after the rebellion in the time of the emperor Trajan (115–16).[52] In some way it survived, as we can show through these stuttering fragments of Jewish-Greek and Byzantine culture provided by the biblical glosses in Greek and the Greek texts in Hebrew script that we have just outlined. The extent of this survival can only be determined when a systematic study of all these sources has been carried out. However, I do not wish to close this chapter without a final reflection. There are parallels that we cannot ignore between the first translation of the Jewish Law into Greek in 3rd century BCE Ptolemaic Alexandria and the version into modern Greek of the Constantinople Pentateuch. Both versions were made by Jews of the diaspora with the same liturgical and pedagogical aim. The LXX was also the legal framework for Jews living in the empire of the Lagides. In the inception of the Constantinople Pentateuch there are also indications of a politic of unifying the various Jewish communities of the capital which had become a melting pot of an immigrant population with very different origins. However, the differences cannot be ignored. The LXX very soon became an independent version that probably replaced the Hebrew Bible in the synagogue

---

[49] D. S. Blondheim, "Échos du judéo-hellénisme", p. 6, quoting L. Belléli in *REJ* 22 (1891), 251–52.

[50] See H. V. Sephiha, *Le ladino, judéo-espagnol calque*, and Sephiha, "Problématique du judéo-espagnol".

[51] D. S. Blondheim, *Les parlers judéo-romans et la "Vetus Latina"*, Paris 1925, 79, and U. Cassuto, "Jewish Translation of the Bible into Latin and its Importance for the Study of the Greek and Aramaic Versions", *Commentationes Judaico-Hellenisticae in memoriam Johannis Lewy*, Jerusalem, 1949, 161–72 = *Biblical and Oriental Studies*, Jerusalem 1973, 285–98.

[52] "What happened to this culture is one of the great unsolved questions of Jewish cultural history," see N. R. M. de Lange, "Hebrew–Greek Genizah Fragments", p. 46.

liturgy. The Constantinople version, instead, never became independent of the Hebrew text. In fact, the use of Hebrew characters made it impossible for non-Jews to read and so excluded any proselytising intention. However, it was the first translation into a colloquial language of part of Scripture to have the distinction of being printed; it continues to be a monument to the spoken Greek of 16th century Constantinople and will remain as an example and culmination of the chain of Jewish translations into Greek that inevitably accompanied the peculiar historical circumstances of Jewish life in the diaspora.[53]

Select Bibliography

Amigo, L., "Una aproximación al Pentateuco de Constantinopla (1547)". *Estudios Bíblicos* 48 (1990), 81–111.

———, *El Pentateuco de Constantinopla y la biblia medieval romanceada judeoespañola. Criterios y fuentes de traducción*, Salamanca 1983.

Belléli, L., "Deux versions peu connues du Pentateuque". *REJ* 22 (1891), 250–63.

———, "Une version grecque du Pentateuque du sixième siècle". *REG* 3 (1890), 288–308.

Blondheim, D. S., "Échos du judéo-hellénisme. Étude sur l'influence de la Septante et d'Aquila sur les versions néo-grecques des Juifs". *REJ* 78–79 (1924), 1–14.

Browning, R., *Medieval and Modern Greek*, London 1969.

Chaze, M., "Remarques et notes sur les versions grecque et ladino du Pentateuche de Constantinople, 1547". *Hommage à Georges Vajda. Études d'histoire et de pensée juives*, ed. G. Nahon, C. Touati, Leuven 1980, 323–32.

Danon, A., "Meirath 'enaim. Version en néogrec et en caractères hébraïques de Jérémie X,11; Dan. 2,5–7,28; et d'Esdras IV,7–VI,26 du Caraïte Elie Aféda Béghi (1627)". *JAs* 4 (1914), 5–65.

———, "Notice sur la littérature gréco-caraïte". *REJ* 63 (1912), 147–51.

Fedalto, G., "Per una biografia di Simone Atumano". *Aevum* 40 (1966), 445–67.

Fernández Marcos, N., "El Pentateuco griego de Constantinopla". *Erytheia. Revista de estudios bizantinos y neogriegos* 6 (1985), 185–203.

———, "Some Thoughts on the Later Judaeo-Greek Biblical Tradition". *BJGS* 2 (1988), 14–15.

Fränkel, D., "Die Quellen der asterisierten Zusätze im zweiten Tabernakelbericht Exodus 35–40". *Studien zur Septuaginta*, Göttingen 1990, 140–86.

Fürst, J., *Glossarium Graeco-Hebraeum oder der griechische Wörterschatz der jüdischen Midraschwerke*, Strasbourg 1890.

Gebhardt, O. von, *Graecus-Venetus. Pentateuchi Proverbiorum Ruth Cantici Ecclesiasticae Threnorum Danielis versio graeca ex unico bibliothecae S. Marci Venetae codice*, Leipzig 1875.

Hesseling, D. C., "Le livre de Jonas". *ByZ* 10 (1901), 208–17.

———, *Les cinq livres de la Loi (Le Pentateuque)*, Leiden–Leipzig 1897.

Kalitsunakis, J., *Grammatik der neugriechischen Volkssprache*, Berlin 1963.

---

[53] See N. Fernández Marcos, "El Pentateuco griego de Constantinopla", pp. 200–203.

Krauss, S., "Zur griechischen und lateinischen Lexikographie aus jüdischen Quellen". *ByZ* 2 (1893), 493–548.

———, *Griechische und Lateinische Lehnwörter im Talmud, Midrasch und Targum*, Berlin I, 1898, II, 1899 = Hildesheim 1964.

Lange, N. R. M. de, "Greek and Byzantine Fragments in the Cairo Genizah". *BJGS* 5 (1989), 13–17.

———, "Hebrew/Greek Manuscripts: Some Notes". *JJS* 46 (1995), 262–70.

———, "Hebrew–Greek Genizah Fragments and their Bearing on the Culture of Byzantine Jewry". *Proceedings of the Ninth Congress of Jewish Studies*, Jerusalem 1986, 39–46.

———, "Judaeo-Greek Studies: Achievements and Prospects". *BJGS* 17 (1995), 27–34.

———, "The Jews of Byzantium and the Greek Bible: Outline of the Problems and Suggestions for Future Research". *Rashi 1040–1990. Hommage à Ephraïm E. Urbach*, ed. G. Sed-Rajna, Paris 1993, 203–10.

———, "Two Genizah Fragments in Hebrew and Greek". *Interpreting the Hebrew Bible: Essays in honour of E. I. J. Rosenthal*, ed. J. A. Emerton and S. C. Reif, Cambridge 1982, 64–83 (1 Kgs 6:20–8:37 and Qoh. 2:13-23).

———, *Greek Jewish Texts from the Cairo Genizah*, Tübingen 1996.

Mercati, G., "Chi sia l'autore della nuova versione dall'ebraico del codice veneto greco VII". *RB* ns 13 (1916), 510–26.

Mirambel, A., *La langue grecque moderne. Description et analyse*, Paris 1959.

Neubauer, A., "On Non-Hebrew Languages Used by Jews". *JQR* 4 (1891–92), 9–19.

Papadopoulos-Kerameus, A., "Γλωσσάριον ἑβραϊκοελληνικόν". *Festschrift Dr. A. Karkavy*, St Petersburg 1908, I, 68–91.

Perles, J., "Jüdisch-byzantinische Beziehungen". *ByZ* 2 (1893), 569–84.

Sephiha, H. V., "Ladino (judéo-espagnol calque) et commentateurs". *RHR* 188 (1975), 116–28.

———, "Problématique du judéo-espagnol". *Bulletin de la Société de Linguistique de Paris* 69 (1974), 159–89.

———, *Le ladino, judéo-espagnol calque. Deutéronome. Versions de Constantinople (1547) et de Ferrara (1553). Édition, étude linguistique et lexique*, Paris 1973.

Sirat, C., "Un vocabulaire de mots d'emprunt gréco-latins dans un manuscrit hébreu du XIIIᵉ siècle". *BIRHT* 12 (1963), 103–13.

Sperber, D., *A Dictionary of Greek and Latin Legal Terms in Rabbinic Literature*, Bar-Ilan 1984.

Wevers, J. W., "A Secondary Text in Codex Ambrosianus of the Greek Exodus". *Philologia Sacra. Biblische und patristische Studien für Hermann J. Frede und Walter Thiele zu ihrem siebzigsten Geburtstag*, ed. R. Gryson, Freiburg 1993, 36–48.

Wevers, J. W., *Septuaginta . . . II, 1 Exodus*, Göttingen 1991, pp. 43–44.

PART FOUR

THE SEPTUAGINT IN CHRISTIAN TRADITION

CHAPTER TWELVE

TRANSMISSION AND TEXTUAL HISTORY

a) *Introduction*

Apart from some exceptions to which we shall refer later, and by contrast with the different reactions of the Jewish means before the translation of the LXX of which we spoke in the preceding section, it can be stated that the transmission and textual history of the Greek Bible took place mainly in Christian circles. This fact is important when describing both the internal history of transmission (palaeographic mistakes, typology of variants, etc.) and its external history (the avatars of the various manuscripts, their prologues, colophons and other annotations with which they are provided).[1]

From among the most significant exceptions must be noted *Pap. Gr.* 458 of the John Rylands Library (= Rahlfs 957), from the 2nd century BCE, the oldest known fragment of the LXX: it contains fragments of Dt. 23–28.[2] Papyrus *Fouad Inv Nr* 266 (= Rahlfs 848), dated around 50 BCE and with the *Tetragrammaton* written in square Hebrew letters: it contains fragments from Deuteronomy 17–33.[3] The Septuagintal manuscripts of the Pentateuch identified in Caves 4 and 7 in Qumran are pap7QLXXEx (= Rahlfs 805); 4QLXXLev^a (= Rahlfs 801); pap4QLXXLev^b (= Rahlfs 802); 4QLXXNum (= Rahlfs 803) and 4QLXXDeut (= Rahlfs 819). The fragments of Leviticus 2–5 found in 4QLXXLev^b, from the 1st century BCE are written in a script related to the script of papyrus *Fouad* 266, with the *Tetragrammaton* written in Greek (ἰάω) instead of a simple transcription or the translation κύριος.[4] Outside the Pentateuch, two other manuscripts of the LXX were found, i.e. fragments of the Letter of

---

[1] For the other aspect worth considering, the impact of the transmission of Christianity on the Scriptures inherited from the Jews, see the discerning approach of R. A. Kraft, "Christian Transmission of Greek Jewish Scriptures".

[2] K. Aland, *Repertorium der griechischen christlichen Papyri*, 96.

[3] K. Aland, *Repertorium der griechischen christlichen Papyri*, 95, and A. Leone, *L'evoluzione della Scrittura*, 47–48.

[4] K. Aland, *Repertorium der griechischen christlichen Papyri*, 90, and P. W. Skehan, "The Qumran Manuscripts and Textual Criticism", *VTS* 4 (1975), 155–59.

Jeremiah 43–44 in 7Q2 (= Rahlfs 804), both dated around 50 BCE,[5] and the scroll of the Twelve Minor Prophets (8ḤevXIIgr = Rahlfs 943), which D. Barthélemy identified and studied, and which was recently edited by E. Tov in the series *Discoveries in the Judaean Desert*. According to experts in papyrology, it is to be dated between 50 BCE and 50 CE, more probably towards the end of the 1st century BCE.[6]

Besides these documents which from their age could not come from Christian communities, the possibility has to be reckoned with that some other papyrus or fragment up to the 3rd century CE also comes from Jewish circles, although it is not always easy to decide this. This possibility almost becomes reality as new documents appear and when one considers the approximately forty pre-Hexaplaric papyri, i.e. earlier than the middle of the 3rd century CE, which O'Callaghan includes in his list of LXX papyri.[7]

The period of acclimatisation of the Greek Old Testament to the Christian Church extends from 70 to 135 CE and includes at least three phenomena that affect the transmission process of the Greek Bible:

1. The displacement of the scroll by the codex, a much discussed problem in respect of chronology, but generally accepted as a fact that determined the history of transmission in Jewish and Christian circles. In the synagogue the scroll continued to be used, which

---

[5] K. Aland, *Repertorium der griechischen christlichen Papyri*, 86 and 204. A. Leone, *L'evoluzione della Scrittura*, 48, n. 5. Probably some of the Greek fragments from Cave 7 that O'Callaghan has recently tried to identify as texts from the New Testament [J. O'Callaghan, "¿Papiros neotestamentarios en la cueva 7 de Qumran?", *Bib* 53 (1972), 91–100; O'Callaghan, "¿1 Tim 3,16; 4,1.3 en 7Q4?", *Bib* 53 (1972), 362–67; O'Callaghan, *Los primeros testimonios del Nuevo Testamento*, Cordoba 1995, 95–145] in fact come from the LXX or the Greek Pseudepigrapha like 1 Henoch, as has been suggested by some scholars opposed to his identification. Cf. especially V. Spottorno, "Nota sobre los papiros de la cueva 7 de Qumran", *Estudios Clásicos* XV, 63 (1971), 261–63, and C. H. Roberts, "On some Presumed Papyrus Fragments of the New Testament from Qumran", *JTS* 33 (1972), 446–47. This is not the place to enter fully into the debate that has arisen in connection with the identification of the fragments which has not generally been accepted by specialists. For the current state of affairs cf. J. A. Fitzmyer, "The Dead Sea Scrolls and Early Christianity", *Theology Digest* 42 (1995), 303–19 and V. Spottorno, "Can Methodological Limits be Set in the Debate on the Identification of 7Q5?", *DSD* 6 (1999), 66–77.

[6] D. Barthélemy, *Les Devanciers d'Aquila*. VTS 10 (1963), and E. Tov, *The Greek Minor Prophets Scroll from Naḥal Ḥever (8 ḤevXIIgr). The Seiyâl Collection I.* with the collaboration of R. A. Kraft and a contribution by P. J. Parsons, DJD VIII, Oxford 1990, p. 26.

[7] J. O'Callaghan, "Lista de los papiros de los LXX".

means that every scroll had its own textual history. The Church, instead, opted for the codex in the 2nd century, which is able to include the whole Bible, as can be seen in the great uncials. Even Pap. 967, from the 2nd/3rd century CE, included at least three scrolls or *megillôt*, i.e. Ezekiel, Daniel and Esther.[8] This substitution, which began in the 2nd century CE,[9] was gradual. Only after the 4th/5th century did the production of the codex exceed that of the scroll, until by the 6th/7th century the scroll finally disappeared.[10]

2. The general use of κύριος for the *Tetragrammaton* in manuscript transmission, even though in the *scriptoria* in which the Hexapla was transmitted it was obviously preserved, and being written in Greek, gave rise to a series of deformations collected in the lists of names of God reproduced by some Fathers of the Church.[11] In all likelihood the authors of the Pentateuch already used κύριος to translate the *Tetragrammaton*, perhaps even very early on. Certainly in the 1st century BCE, in Palestinian Judaism there was an archaising process of correcting the sacred name, writing it in Hebrew in the square or palaeo-Hebrew script, or transliterated into Greek,[12] whereas in Christian circles the use of κύριος again became general.

3. Finally, the introduction or at least the general use due to Christian influence of the abbreviations in the most frequent *nomina sacra*: θεός, κύριος, υἱός, Χριστός, Ἰησοῦς, πνεῦμα (abbreviated as θς, κς, υς, Χς, Ις, πνα), which also happened with a certain chronological fluctuation and frequent variations of one name for another.[13] In spite of the new documentation which has appeared in pre-Christian Egyptian papyri and in Hebrew and Greek texts from

---

[8] A. Leone, *L'evoluzione della Scrittura*, 18–20.

[9] Very probably it was a Christian adoption *c*. 100 CE or perhaps prior to this date, given the good number of Christian codices in papyrus during the 2nd century CE, see C. H. Roberts and T. C. Skeat, *The Birth of the Codex*, 54–62.

[10] R. Devreesse, *Introduction à l'étude des manuscrits grecs*, 9–11.

[11] See N. Fernández Marcos, "ἰαίε, ἐσερεέ, αἰά y otros nombres de Dios entre los hebreos", *Sefarad* 35 (1975), 91–106.

[12] See A. Pietersma, "Kyrios or Tetragramm", 99–101.

[13] See A. H. R. E. Paap, *Nomina Sacra in the Greek Papyri of the First Five Centuries A. D.: The Sources and some Deductions*, Leiden 1959, 124–25; J. O'Callaghan, *"Nomina Sacra" in papyris Graecis saeculi III neotestamentariis*, Rome 1970, 21 and 71–81, and S. Brown, "Concerning the Origin of the Nomina Sacra", *Studia Papyrologica* 9 (1970), 7–19.

Palestine found in Qumran, we have no proof that the abbreviations for the *nomina sacra* were used before the period of Christian transmission.[14]

Certain other changes in connection which those noted here can be suspected due to the LXX coming into Christian hands, but they cannot be proved.

After the 2nd century CE, the Atticist movement made itself felt also in the textual history of the LXX, as A. Rahlfs, J. Ziegler and others have shown. However, the Atticist corrections were not the only stylistic changes to the Greek Bible. Traces of at least two other types of revision can be detected in this stage of transmission:

1. the elimination of Semitisms which are replaced by a more literary *koiné* Greek, probably before the 2nd century CE;
2. the correction of the Greek text to accommodate it to the Hebrew text of the time, a process reflected in some pre-Hexaplaric papyri and in the καίγε recension which was to culminate in the recensional undertaking by Origen.[15]

b) *External Transmission*

The external transmission of the LXX is linked on the one hand with the history of the book and of writing in antiquity, a history to be found in manuals of Greek palaeography. On the other hand, it is subject to particular vicissitudes which the Greek Old Testament experienced at the hands of successive recensionists. For the history of books, material used, development of the uncial, semi-uncial and minuscule scripts,[16] the various systems of abbreviation and shorthand, colophons and other *scholia* of manuscripts, palimpsests, etc., we refer to the first part of the book by Devreesse on Greek manuscripts and the book by Metzger.[17] In particular, the two recent

---

[14] See C. H. Roberts, *Manuscript, Society and Belief in Early Christian Egypt*, London 1979, 28–31, and B. M. Metzger, *Manuscripts of the Greek Bible*, 36–37.

[15] G. D. Kilpatrick, *The Cairo Papyrus of Genesis*, 222ff.

[16] A minuscule which in turn is divided into ancient (9th–10th centuries), middle (10th–12th century) and recent (13th–14th centuries).

[17] R. Devreesse, *Introduction à l'étude des manuscrits grecs*; B. M. Metzger, *Manuscripts of the Greek Bible*, and C. Wendel, *Die griechisch-römische Buchbesschreibung verglichen mit der des Vorderen Orients*, Halle 1949.

monographs by Cavallo and Leone[18] can be used as a guide to the
biblical majuscules. The many studies on papyri and on particular
biblical manuscripts can be consulted in the specialised bibliography
of the LXX.[19] An idea of the importance of the biblical manuscripts
can be gained from the fact that in a list of uncials from the 4th
to 6th centuries there is an overwhelming proportion of biblical manuscripts (twenty) as against only four of a secular nature.

The collection of the Greek Old Testament comprises a unit with
its own textual history. Although Bickermann's statement that the
transmission of the LXX from its origins up to the 3rd century CE
provokes us to a confession of ignorance[20] seems exaggerated, it is
certain that only recently have we been able to glimpse some indications of the textual state at this stage of transmission.

We have already indicated the signs of revision in the text of the
LXX before the arrival of Christianity, some which are stylistic in
nature and others to make the Greek fit the current Hebrew text,
as well as the other changes that the LXX underwent to make it
into the official Bible of the Church. In terms of description, a large
number of Byzantine manuscripts are prefaced by the *Letter of Aristeas*
in the form of a prologue to the Octateuch and as an epilogue the
copyists insert three works on:

1. the various editions of the Greek Bible (LXX, Aquila, Symmachus,
   Theodotion, *quinta, sexta* and *septima*);
2. the successive deportations from Israel (nine in all from the invasion of pharaoh Shishak I to the Roman conquest by Vespasian);
3. the divine names among the Hebrews (ten in all, followed by an
   excursus on the Tetragrammaton).

From Origen's reaction to attempting the work of the Hexapla we
sense to what extent the transmission of the Bible among the Jews
had become separated from the transmission of the LXX in the
hands of Christians. However, even the Church tradition represented
by the common LXX did not provide a unified text. The pre-
Hexaplaric papyri, increasingly more numerous, are witnesses to this
disagreement. It is enough to mention here the most important of
the biblical papyri earlier than Origen, the Chester–Beatty Papyri,

---

[18] G. Cavallo, *Richerche sulla maiuscola biblica*, and A. Leone, *L'evoluzione della Scrittura*.
[19] See *CB* 68–80 and *BS* 88–102.
[20] E. J. Bickerman, "Some Notes on the Transmission of the LXX", 178.

written between the 2nd and 4th centuries CE, and Papyrus 967 from the close of the 2nd or the beginning of the 3rd century CE.

Besides this already multiple LXX, Origen came across the Jewish texts of "the three", Aquila, Symmachus, Theodotion, and probably other Jewish translation or revisions that were in circulation, the remains of which have left traces in the whole channel of Hexaplaric transmission. At this moment the preparation of the Hexapla comes on stage, to which I will devote the next chapter, to complicate even further the already entangled transmission of the LXX owing to Origen's linguistic criteria, predominantly synchronic, which governed his redaction.

Towards the end of the 4th century, according to Jerome's testimony,[21] exemplars of the Greek Bible were circulating under the name or patronage of Lucian. They were put into circulation in competition with the scientific edition of Caesarea spread by Eusebius and Pamphilus.[22] However, the Antiochene teachers of exegesis kept silent about the founder of their school and one of its most significant personalities.

The edict of Diocletian on 23 February 303, which commanded churches to be destroyed and the Scriptures to be thrown into the fire, did not affect the library of Caesarea, at least not fully, since several colophons of manuscripts such as the Sinaiticus to Esther and 2 Ezra, the *Codex Marchalianus* at the end of Isaiah and Ezekiel as well as various passages of the Syro-Hexapla, have subscriptions that go back to copies of exemplars from the sacred library of Caesarea, corrected according to the Hexaplaric edition.[23]

---

[21] Jerome, *Praef. in Lib. Paralipomenon*, and R. Devreesse, *Introduction à l'étude des manuscrits grecs*, 118.

[22] See the passage of the Armenian Pseudo-Chrysostom at Is. 9:6 quoted by J. Ziegler (*Septuaginta XIV Isaias*, Göttingen 1939, 73): "Patet igitur sanctum martyrem (Lucianum) nihil addidisse vel detraxisse, sed ab Hebraeis et ab aliis interpretibus (ea) collegisse et in ordinem digessisse, et omnia in lucem prodidisse. Non est igitur contemnenda (interpretatio) Luciani, sed immo praestantior atque correctior est quam textus Palestinorum."

[23] R. Devreesse, *Introduction à l'étude des manuscrits grecs*, 122–28. Here, by way of example, is the colophon of the later corrector of Sinaiticus at 2 Ezra: ἀντεβλήθη πρὸς παλαιώτατον λίαν ἀντίγραφον δεδιορθωμένον χειρὶ τοῦ ἁγίου μάρτυρος Παμφίλου. ὅπερ ἀντίγραφον πρὸς τῷ τέλει ὑποσημείωσίς τις ἰδιόχειρος αὐτοῦ ὑπέκειτο ἔχουσα οὕτως· Μετελήμφθη καὶ διωρθώθη πρὸς τὰ Ἑξαπλᾶ Ὠριγένους. Ἀντωνῖνος ἀντέβαλεν· Πάμφιλος διόρθωσα ("It was collated with a very ancient manuscript corrected by the hand of the holy martyr Pamphilus. At the end of this manuscript there was a note in his hand and writing which ran as follows: 'it was copied and

When Constantine came to power, he was concerned with spreading Bibles corrected according to Origen's recension.[24] The suspicions and hostility towards Origen's doctrine started in 400 and in 543 Justinian condemned nine of its sentences. This reaction against Origen favoured the spread of the *koiné* or Antiochene Vulgate.

Independently of the existence of the Hesychian recension, as yet not identified, Cyril of Alexandria, in his Commentary on the Twelve Prophets, reproduces an Egyptian local text of the LXX in the same way that Theodoret of Cyr reflects an Antiochene text. Cyril rarely mentions Aquila, Symmachus and Theodotion, but instead he often quotes another Jewish edition ἡ τῶν ἑβραίων ἔκδοσις, and according to Barthélemy its initial siglum ε' was confused in the Twelve Prophets with the siglum for the *quinta* (ε').[25]

The fact is that the Bible of the Fathers in the 4th/5th centuries does not present a uniform text. It has been proved that the pre-Origen *koiné* did not exist as such, but the pre-Hexaplaric papyri are witnesses to extreme variety. With the help of "the three", this text was adapted by Theodotion to the sequence and arrangement of the Hebrew text in circulation at his time. The Hexapla is a source of continual confusion, especially in positioning the Aristarchic signs when their true meaning was not perceived by copyists. It is much more difficult to ascertain their precise position since the asterisk sometimes also referred to a marginal gloss.

The principal uncials we preserve already belong to the 4th and 5th centuries: Vatican, Alexandrian and Sinaiticus, which in Judges, Tobias and often in 1 Kings have very divergent texts. To this period belong the Eastern *koiné* and the Egyptian *koiné* mentioned by Jerome in the prologue to his translation of the book of Chronicles. The first has been identified as the Lucianic recension, discovered in almost all the books of the Greek Bible except for the Pentateuch, and reproduces the ancient LXX with some stylistic corrections and a large number of additions taken from the Hexaplaric recension. It has not been possible to identify the Egyptian *koiné* as the

---

corrected according to Origen's Hexapla; Antoninus collated it; Pamphilus corrected it'"). Antoninus died a martyr on the 13 November 308, see G. Mercati, *Nuove note di letteratura biblica e cristiana antica*, Rome 1941, 14–15.

[24] Eusebius, *Vita Constantini* IV, 34–37, and H. Dörrie, "Zur Geschichte der Septuaginta", on information from ancient sources and the real history of the Lucianic recension.

[25] See chapter 10, pp. 157–58.

recension of Hesychius; however, there are witnesses of an Alexandrian text that agrees especially with the quotations from the Egyptian Fathers, particularly Cyril of Alexandria and Didymus the Blind.

To this varied spectrum have to be added other editions often cited by the Fathers such as the Syriac, Hebrew, Samariticon, Josephus. The LXX that the Fathers of the Church knew and used was very far from presenting a unified text.

From the 10th to the 15th centuries the texts continued to be copied, accumulating new risks of confusion due to the use of the *minuscule* script. However, the minuscule manuscripts also preserve precious variants (*recentiores non deteriores*) often vouched for by much older witnesses. Several of these readings have found, in recently discovered papyri, confirmation of their textual worth and their antiquity.

Another determining factor in the external history of the LXX is that the sequence of books in Greek is not the same as in Hebrew; that this sequence is not even kept uniform in the various Greek manuscripts; and that the lists of books in the Fathers of the Church and in the Councils are not always the same. The titles of the books are sometimes different in Greek and in Hebrew; for example, the books of the Pentateuch, cited in Hebrew according to the first word or words of each, adopt in the LXX descriptive names almost always suggested by one word of a version. And besides the books exclusive to the Alexandrian text (1 Ezra, Wisdom, Sira, Judith, Tobit, Baruch, Letter of Jeremiah, 1–4 Maccabees, Psalms of Solomon) differences from the Hebrew in content and sequence are not rare.[26]

The beginning of the 16th century ushered in the period of printed editions, still with primitive textual criteria. Then came the polyglot and the scientific editions, some of them, as yet incomplete, proposing as their goal the restoration of a text as close as possible to what the original LXX might have been.[27]

---

[26] See H. B. Swete, *An Introduction to the Old Testament in Greek*, Cambridge 1914, 197–210.

[27] For printed editions from the Renaissance to the 19th century, H. B. Swete, *An Introduction to the Old Testament in Greek*, 171–94, and N. Fernández Marcos, "Los estudios de 'Septuaginta'. Visión retrospectiva y problemática más reciente", *CFC* 11 (1976), 413–168, esp. 419ff., and O. Munnich, "Le texte de la Septante", 194–200, can be consulted.

c) *Internal Transmission*

As for the internal history of the LXX, it can be stated with Margolis that the more a book is copied the more the influences of one text on another multiply, as do the possibilities of palaeographic mistakes.[28] Hence no manuscript is valueless and none is free of serious corruptions. In the Greek Bible it seems impossible to establish a *stemma* of manuscripts in imitation of the ideal presented by P. Maas for the restoration of classical texts.[29] Nevertheless, manuscripts can be grouped into families on the basis of common additions and omissions as well as the corruptions shared by several witnesses. With this procedure, Margolis identified four main recensions in the book of Joshua[30] and by the same method the different recensions of each book are determined in the critical editions of Göttingen. There is a whole range of variants with different typologies. Among the commonest palaeographic variants can be noted:

1. mistakes due to confusing the letters of the following groups in the first stage of uncial writing: ΑΔΛΜ // ΕΣΘΟ // ΓΤΥΙ // ΗΝΜΠ;
2. mistakes arising from the stage of transmission with minuscule writing: β/μ // ξ/ζ.

Confusion of sounds with close articulation due to internal dictation, such as ρ/λ // φ/β // φ/θ // χ/γ. Interchange of consonants at the end of a word like θ/β // λ/ρ // μ/ν, a problem aggravated by manuscripts that make use of abbreviations. Omissions through haplography, *homoioteleuton* or *homoioarcton*; transposed letters and words, dittography, etc.

Besides the studies by Margolis, the sections on *Grammatica* in the Göttingen edition of books already published illustrate new aspects of the internal history of transmission.[31] For the study of the

---

[28] M. L. Margolis, "The Textual Criticism of the Greek Old Testament", 187.

[29] P. Maas, *Textkritik*, Leipzig 1960, 7ff.

[30] M. L. Margolis, *The Book of Joshua in Greek According to the Critically Restored Text with an Apparatus Containing the Variants of the Principal Recensions and of the Individual Witnesses*, Paris 1931, which now has to be supplemented by the edition of *Part V: Joshua 19:39–24:33*, Philadelphia 1992, edited by E. Tov and L. Greenspoon, *Max Leopold Margolis: A Scholar's Scholar*, Atlanta, Ga. 1987. See also H. S. Gehman, "Some Types of Errors".

[31] R. Hanhart, *Septuaginta. VIII, 3 Esther*, Göttingen 1966, 99–123, and Hanhart, *Septuaginta. VIII, 1 Esdrae Liber 1*, Göttingen 1974, 33–51; Hanhart, *Septuaginta. VIII,*

manuscript material of the LXX and its classification, the principal existing editions and the problems they pose we have to refer you – as they exceed the limits of this introduction – to specialised studies that have treated more exhaustively the mass of data related to the topic.[32]

d) *Textual Restoration*

Due to the complex evolutionary development of the text of the LXX throughout history, the reverse process of restoration of a text that is as close as possible to the original is extremely difficult. Hence textual criticism also continues to occupy a prime position in LXX studies. The first attempts at restoration are the printed editions of the 16th century: the Complutensian (1517), Aldine (1518) and Sixtine (1587). They present the text in accordance with traditional pronunciation, a method which successive editions of the LXX adopted until the manual of F. Constantin von Tischendorf appeared.[33]

Another editorial procedure, followed by the great Brooke-McLean edition, consists in collecting all the material available in one critical apparatus and editing as a text the diplomatic reproduction of a standard manuscript, the *Codex Vaticanus*.[34] The scientific Göttingen edition, instead, still unfinished, is an eclectic edition and has the deliberate aim of preferring in the restoration of the text the Greek forms to be expected at the time and under the conditions of the translations, even at the cost of rejecting those of the manuscripts.

---

2 Esdrae Liber II, Göttingen 1993, 32–64, can be consulted, where he examines the data from the manuscript tradition of these books following the guidelines set out by H. St J. Thackeray, *A Grammar of the Old Testament in Greek According to the Septuaginta*, Cambridge 1909, and W. Crönert, *Memoria Graeca Herculanensis*, Leipzig 1903.

[32] See *CB* 66–74; *BS* 87–100, and A. Rahlfs, *Verzeichnis der griechischen Handschriften des Alten Testament*, Göttingen 1914, which includes papyri as well as manuscripts; to be supplemented for the field of papyri by K. Aland, *Repertorium der griechischen christlichen Papyri*. The main LXX manuscripts are described in H. B. Swete, *An Introduction to the Old Testament in Greek*, 122–70, and in S. Jellicoe, *SMS*, 176–224.

[33] F. Constantin von Tischendorf, *Vetus Testamentum Graece iuxta LXX Interpretes*, Leipzig 1850.

[34] A. E. Brooke, N. McLean and (from Samuel to Tobit) H. St J. Thackeray, *The Old Testament in Greek According to the Text of Codex Vaticanus, Supplemented from Other Uncial Manuscripts, with a Critical Apparatus Containing the Variants of the Chief Ancient Authorities for the Text of the Septuagint*, Cambridge 1906–40. Nine volumes have appeared with the following books: Genesis, Exodus–Leviticus, Numbers–Deuteronomy, Joshua–Judges–Ruth, 1–2 Samuel, 1–2 Kings, 1–2 Chronicles, 1–2 Ezra and Esther–Judith–Tobit.

This is how Rahlfs, Ziegler, Hanhart and Wevers proceeded[35] in their respective editions, according to the guidelines followed in modern editions of Greek texts. It is the procedure that P. Katz defends in his recent monograph on the text of the LXX edited by Gooding.[36] The books of the LXX that have not yet been edited in either the Cambridge or the Göttingen series are: 4 Maccabees, Song of Songs, Ecclesiastes, Proverbs and Psalms of Solomon. For these, the manual edition by Rahlfs[37] can be used, or else, with more extensive use of the manuscripts, the edition by Holmes–Parsons.[38] An eclectic edition of a particular recension, the Antiochene or Lucianic text, for the Historical books has been published by the Madrid team.[39]

Although our knowledge of Greek of the 3rd and 2nd centuries BCE is still very imperfect, especially of literary Greek, we can already count on a considerable number of inscriptions that run from archaic dialects to the Byzantine period, and on an increasing number of papyri that cover the period of formation of the LXX. Basing his work on this documentation and on the grammatical studies on the inscriptions and papyri, Katz is optimistic about the possibilities of restoring the LXX.[40] In his *Memoria Graeca Herculanensis* (Leipzig 1903), W. Crönert set out the basic lines separating the different ways of pronunciation that left traces in the manuscripts during the Ptolemaic, Imperial and Byzantine periods. All this has increasingly helped to clarify the complex transmission of the LXX, contaminated since the period of recensions as is reflected in a good number of mixed

---

[35] The list of books that have so far appeared in the *editio magna* de Göttingen, with their respective editors, in chronological order, is as follows: A. Rahlfs, *Psalms* (1931, 1979); W. Kappler, *1 Maccabees* (1936, 1990); J. Ziegler, *Isaiah* (1939, 1983); J. Ziegler, *Twelve Prophets* (1943, 1984); J. Ziegler, *Ezekiel* (1952, 1978); J. Ziegler, *Daniel, Susannah, Bel and the Dragon* (1954); J. Ziegler, *Jeremiah, Baruch, Lamentations, Letter of Jeremiah* (1957, 1976); R. Hanhart, *2 Maccabees* (1959, 1976); R. Hanhart, *3 Maccabees* (1960, 1980); J. Ziegler, *Wisdom* (1962, 1981); J. Ziegler, *Eclessiasticus* (1965, 1981); R. Hanhart, *Esther* (1967, 1983); R. Hanhart, *1 Ezra* (1974, 1991); J. W. Wevers, *Genesis* (1974); Wevers, *Deuteronomy* (1977); R. Hanhart, *Judith* (1979); J. Ziegler, *Job* (1982); J. W. Wevers, *Numbers* (1982); R. Hanhart, *Tobit* (1983); J. W. Wevers, *Leviticus* (1986); Wevers, *Exodus* (1991); R. Hanhart, *2 Ezra* (1993).

[36] P. Walters, *The Text of the Septuagint*, 10–14.

[37] A. Rahlfs, *Septuaginta, id est Vetus Testamentum Graece iuxta LXX interpretes*, Stuttgart 1935, and later reprints.

[38] R. Holmes and J. Parsons, *Vetus Testamentum Graecum cum variis lectionibus*, 5 vols, Oxford, 1798–1827.

[39] N. Fernández Marcos and J. R. Busto Saiz, *El texto autioqueno de la Biblia griega* I–III, Madrid, 1989–96.

[40] P. Walters, *The Text of the Septuagint*, 17–28.

manuscripts. For the pre-recensional period, with the help of older papyri, we can go back to a text that with great probability and in spite of multiple determining factors, is close to the original LXX. These are the presuppositions of the Göttingen edition. The results are being nuanced as the new critical edition of each book incorporates the most recent achievements of philology and other sciences of antiquity.

Select Bibliography

Aland, K., *Repertorium der griechischen christlichen Papyri. I Biblische Papyri. Altes Testament, Neues Testament, Varia, Apokryphen*, Berlin–New York 1976 (with the review by J. O'Callaghan in *Bib* 57 [1976], 560–67).

Ally, Z., and L. Koenen, *Three Rolls of the Early Septuagint: Genesis and Deuteronomy. A Photographic Edition*, PTA 27, Bonn 1980.

Barthélemy, D., "L'Ancien Testament a mûri à Alexandrie". *TZ* 21 (1965), 358–70.

Bickerman, E. J., "Some Notes on the Transmission of the LXX". *A. Marx Jubilee Volume*, New York 1950, 149–78.

Bogaert, P.-M., "Septante et versions grecques". *DBS* 12, 1993, 536–692, especially 650–64 and 666–72.

Cavallo, G., *Ricerche sulla maiuscola biblica*, Florence 1967.

Devreesse, R., *Introduction à l'étude des manuscrits grecs*, Paris 1954.

Dörrie, H., "Zur Geschichte der Septuaginta im Jahrhundert Konstantins". *ZNW* 39 (1940), 57–110.

Fernández Marcos, N., "Tipología de variantes en la transmisión de un texto patrístico". *Emerita* 45 (1977), 19–32.

Fritsch, Ch. T., "The Treatment of Hexaplaric Signs in the Syro-Hexaplar of Proverbs". *JBL* 72 (1953), 169–81.

Gehman, H. S., "Some Types of Errors of Transmission in the LXX". *VT* 3 (1953), 397–400.

Graetz, H., "Fälschungen in dem Texte der LXX von christlicher Hand zu dogmatischen Zwecken". *MGWJ* 2 (1853), 432–36; 3 (1854), 121–23.

Haelst, J. van, *Catalogue des papyrus littéraires juifs et chrétiens*, Paris 1976.

Irigoin, J., "Structure et évolution des écritures livresques de l'époque byzantine". *Polychronion. Festschrift für Franz Dölger*, Heidelberg 1966, 253–65.

Kenyon, F. G., *The Text of the Greek Bible*, London 1937 (3rd edn, London 1975).

Kilpatrick, G. D., "The Cairo Papyrus of Genesis and Deuteronomy (P. F. Inv. 266)". *Études de Papyrologie* 9 (1971), 221–26.

Kraft, R. A., "Christian Transmission of Greek Jewish Scriptures: A Methodological Probe". *Paganisme, Judaïsme, Christianisme. Mélanges offerts à Marcel Simon*, Paris 1978, 207–26.

Leone, A., *L'evoluzione della Scrittura nei papiri greci del Vecchio Testamento*, Barcelona 1975.

Margolis, M. L., "Scribal Errors in the LXX" (in Hebrew). *Fs. zu Ehren des Dr. A. Karkavy*, St Petersburg 1908, 112–16.

Margolis, M. L., "The Textual Criticism of the Greek Old Testament". *Transactions of the American Philosophical Society* 67 (1928), 187–97.

Metzger, B. M., *Manuscripts of the Greek Bible: An Introduction to Palaeography*, New York–Oxford 1981.

Munnich, O., "Le texte de la Septante". M. Harl *et al.*, *La Bible grecque des Septante*, 129–42 and 194–200.

O'Callaghan, J., "Lista de los papiros de los LXX". *Bib* 56 (1975), 74–93.

Roberts, C. H., *The Antinoopolis Papyri: Part I. Edited with Translations and Notes*, London 1950.

Seeligmann, J. L., "Indications of Editorial Alteration and Adaptation in the Masoretic Text and the Septuagint". *VT* 11 (1961), 201–21.

Skeat, T. C., "Early Christian Book-production: Papyri and Manuscripts". *The Cambridge History of the Bible* 2, Cambridge 1969, 54–80.

Stegmüller, O., "Überlieferungsgeschichte der Bibel". *Geschichte der Textüberlieferung der antiken und mittelalt. Literatur*, Zurich 1961, I, 152–64.

Turner, E. G., *Greek Papyri: An Introduction*, Oxford 1968 (I, Writings, Materials and Books).

Ulrich, E. C., "The Greek Manuscripts of the Pentateuch from Qumrân, Including Newly-Identified Fragments of Deuteronomy (4QLXXDeut)". *De Septuaginta*, 1984, 71–82.

Walters, P. (formerly Katz), *The Text of the Septuagint: Its Corruptions and their Emendation (ed. D. W. Gooding)*, Cambridge 1973 (with the reviews by S. P. Brock in *JTS* 25, 1 [1974], 148–52, and by J. Barr in *VT* 25, 2 [1975], 247–54).

Wendland, P., "Zur ältesten Geschichte der Bibel in der Kirche". *ZNW* 1 (1900), 267–90.

Wevers, J. W., "Text History and Text Criticism of the Septuagint". *VTS* 29, Leiden 1978, 392–402.

Ziegler, J., "Die Bedeutung des Chester–Beatty–Scheide Papyrus 967 für die Textüberlieferung der Ezechiel-LXX". *ZAW* 48 (1945), 76–94.

This list can be supplemented by the extensive bibliography of *BS* 87–107 concerning particular aspects of transmission.

CHAPTER THIRTEEN

ORIGEN'S HEXAPLA

a) *Origen and his Knowledge of Hebrew*

Origen, perhaps the most important and discussed theologian of the
Eastern Church, was born around 185, probably in Alexandria. He
was the disciple of the neo-Platonist Ammonius Sacas and a co-
disciple of Porphyrius. His hectic lifestyle, due to journeys and persecution, put him in contact with Rome (*c.* 215), Palestine (230) and
once again Alexandria (231/2). Although he moved around so much,
this did not prevent him from being one of the most productive
writers of his time. Director of the School of Catechetics in Alexandria,
in which he was professor of philosophy, theology and exegesis, after
234/5 he moved to Caesarea where he founded a school like the
one in Alexandria. He probably died in Tyre *c.* 253–54 as a result
of the torture he suffered in the persecution of Decius.[1]

Of the many aspects of his human life we are particularly interested in Origen as textual critic, as author of the Hexapla. In connection with the composition of the Hexapla, one of the most discussed
problems is his knowledge of Hebrew. To penetrate this area we
rely on two sources of information: one direct, reflected in the ancient
accounts regarding his studies, his contact with Jews and the method
he followed in the composition of the Hexapla; and the other indirect, from his works and in particular the knowledge of Hebrew
reflected in his biblical quotations and the exegesis of certain
passages.

According to Eusebius and Jerome, Origen was the first Christian
that we know of who learned Hebrew.[2] This evidence has been inter-

---

[1] See B. Altaner and A. Stuiber, *Patrologie. Leben, Schriften und Lehre der Kirchenväter*,
Freiburg–Basle–Vienna 1966, 197–209, and P. Nautin, *Origène*, 413–41.

[2] Eusebius, *Hist. Ecc.* VI, 16: τοσαύτη δὲ εἰσήγετο τῷ Ὠριγένει τῶν θείων λόγων
ἀπηκριβωμένη ἐξέτασις, ὡς καὶ τὴν Ἑβραΐδα γλῶτταν ἐκμαθεῖν τάς τε παρὰ τοῖς
Ἰουδαίοις ἐμφερομένας πρωτοτύπους αὐτοῖς Ἑβραίων στοιχείοις γραφὰς κτῆμα
ἴδιον ποιήσασθαι ("Origen's research on the divine Scriptures was so meticulous
that he even managed to learn Hebrew thoroughly and made his own the original
Scriptures which belong to the Jews in Hebrew characters"). And Jerome in *De vir.*

preted in various ways. Nevertheless, at the beginning of this century, the opinion of specialists is growing in favour of Origen's knowledge of Hebrew and thus in favour of Origen being the author of the second column of the Hexapla.

H. Lietzmann reached the conclusion that his learning of Hebrew hardly went beyond the alphabet, since in spite of the testimony of Eusebius and Jerome, his writings do not reveal a real knowledge of the language.[3] C. J. Elliott holds that the first two columns of the Hexapla must have been exclusively the work of his Jewish amanuenses.[4] In the second edition of *The Cairo Geniza*, P. Kahle is more optimistic than in the first in respect of Origen's Hebrew. According to Kahle, he knew Hebrew but not well enough to compose the whole Hexapla. In line with his targumic theory on the origins of the LXX, the second column, says Kahle, was not composed by Origen or entrusted to his co-workers but was taken from transliterated Hebrew texts that circulated previously among the Jews.[5]

Another group of specialists, particularly R. P. C. Hanson and G. Bardy, think that Origen did know Hebrew, but only superficially. As a result he resorted to Jewish teachers, as Jerome did later, to resolve the problems of the holy language. Hanson reaches these conclusions from interpretation of the proper names.[6]

On the other hand, Origen always talks of his great lack of confidence in his knowledge of Hebrew. His etymologies come from Christian compilations. Some Hebrew etymologies probably derive from rabbis during his stay in Caesarea.

Bardy also insists that when Origen speaks of his expertise in Hebrew, he is much more modest than Eusebius and Jerome claim. Sometimes he refers to numerous Jewish traditions but he never indicates the exact source, using instead such expressions as "the Hebrews", "the masters of the Jews", "the wise men among the Hebrews", "a tradition has reached me", etc. He seems to restrict himself to the interpretations and legends that come from Jewish traditions, many of them by word of mouth and others from reading apocryphal and

---

ill., 54: "quis autem ignorat quod tantum in scripturis divinis habuerit studii ut etiam Hebraeam linguam contra aetatis gentisque suae naturam edisceret?"

[3] H. Lietzmann, *The Founding of the Church Universal*, London 1953, 302.
[4] In "Hebrew Learning among the Fathers", *DCB* II, 859a.
[5] P. Kahle, *The Cairo Geniza*, London 1959, 158.
[6] R. P. C. Hanson, "Interpretation of Hebrew Names in Origen".

pseudepigraphical books.[7] De Lange maintains that Origen's contact with his Jewish teachers was frequent and intensive in Caesarea. This enabled him to know Jewish exegetical traditions and rabbinic hermeneutics.[8] Still according to De Lange, Origen was interested in Hebrew but could neither read nor write it easily, although he had the good fortune to have Jewish friends who helped him in his task.[9]

Recently, S. P. Brock has insisted that we cannot judge Origen's work from our modern criteria of textual criticism. Origen knew more Hebrew than appears at first glance, but his perspective is different from ours. He is more interested in a synchronic vision of the language for apologetic purposes; hence his work does not reflect all the Hebrew that he knows.[10] Nor can the absence of a historical perspective in his reflections on biblical Greek be cited as an indication of his lack of knowledge of Hebrew. M. Harl has noted how Origen comments on all the difficult passages of the Bible without relinquishing the Greek system and without resorting to all the possible Hebraisms or Aramaisms of translation Greek. The fact that he does not use Hebrew to explain these passages does not mean that he did not know it, but shows that he respects the obscurity of the text, probably because it favoured his tendency for allegorical and not literal explanation.[11]

b) *The Hexapla*

The Names

The *names* most used by Eusebius and Epiphanius for Origen's work are τὰ ἑξαπλᾶ, τὰ τετραπλᾶ. In later authors, the singular τὸ ἑξαπλοῦν, τετραπλοῦν is used with equal frequency. As it is composed of six columns (σελίδες), in Origen's writings it is also called τὸ ἑξασέλιδον, τὸ τετρασέλιδον.[12] Origen himself never speaks of Hexapla and Tetrapla, although these terms are used by Eusebius and Epiphanius.

---

[7] G. Bardy, "Les traditions juives", especially pp. 226–29.

[8] N. de Lange, *Origen and the Jews*, 29–37 and 133–35.

[9] N. de Lange, *Origen and the Jews*, 22: "We shall not be far from the truth if we conclude that Origen could not speak or read Hebrew, but that he was fortunate in having acquaintances who did, and who gave him such help as he demanded."

[10] S. P. Brock, "Origen's Aims as a Textual Critic". G. Sgherri, "A proposito di Origene", also defends Origen's considerable but not profound knowledge of Hebrew.

[11] M. Harl, "Origène et la sémantique du langage biblique".

[12] F. Field, *Origenis Hexaplorum quae supersunt*, IX–XIII, as against the Hexaplaric manuscripts, which only contained the Septuagintal edition, which he called ἁπλᾶ.

For the latter the Tetrapla included an edition of the first two columns of Aquila, Symmachus, the LXX and Theodotion; when these were accompanied by the first two columns plus the Hebrew text, they formed the Hexapla.[13] However, against this is the testimony of Eusebius, according to whom they were called Hexapla because they contained six Greek translations as well as the two Hebrew columns.[14]

In fact the Tetrapla, mentioned frequently in *scholia* and by ecclesiastical writers, refers to the four best-known Greek versions cited by Epiphanius. However, Mercati insists that it was not simply a Hexapla without the first two columns but included many other changes, and for confirmation refers to the same passage of Eusebius according to whom after the first column (LXX) were placed the other three Jewish versions in a trial run, before the Hexapla was started, in order to assist Christians in studying the Old Testament.[15] Contrary to the common view, which considers the Tetrapla as a later, simplified edition of the Hexapla, Nautin maintains that Origen began his work on the text for the Tetrapla which he compiled in Alexandria before the production of the Hexapla in Caesarea.[16]

First Orlinsky and later Barthélemy have begun to doubt the very existence of the Tetrapla as a separate work from the Hexapla. In fact it is strange that no remains of them have been preserved, whereas fragments of the Hexapla and the LXX corrected against the Hexaplaric recension have survived.[17]

---

[13] Epiphanius, *De mens. et ponderibus*, 19: τετραπλᾶ γὰρ τὰ Ἑλληνικά, ὅταν αἱ τοῦ Ἀκύλα καὶ Συμμάχου καὶ τῶν οβ' καὶ Θεοδοτίωνος ἑρμενεῖαι συγτεταγμέναι ὦσι· τῶν τεσσάρων δὲ τούτων σελίδων ταῖς δυσὶ ταῖς Ἑβραϊκαῖς συναφθεισῶν ἑξαπλᾶ καλεῖται ("So that the Tetrapla are the Greek [columns] when the versions by Aquila, Symmachus, LXX [72] and Theodotion are placed together. When to these four are joined the two in Hebrew they are called the Hexapla").

[14] Eusebius, *Hist. Ecc.* VI, 16: ταύτας δὲ ἁπάσας [i.e. α' σ' θ' ο' ε' ς'] ἐπὶ ταὐτὸν συναγαγών, διελών τε πρὸς κῶλον καὶ ἀντιπαραθεὶς ἀλλήλαις μετὰ καὶ αὐτῆς τῆς Ἑβραίων σημειώσεως τὰ τῶν λεγομένων Ἑξαπλῶν ἡμῖν νἀντίγραφα καταλέλοιπεν ("Putting all these [versions] together in the same folio, dividing them up into clauses and comparing them with each other and even with the Hebrew signs, he bequeathed to us the manuscripts of what are known as the Hexapla").

[15] G. Mercati, "Il problema della Colonna seconda", 212ff.; see also Eusebius, *Hist. Ecc.* VI, 16, following on from the passage quoted in the previous note: ἰδίως τὴν Ἀκύλου καὶ Συμμάχου καὶ Θεοδοτίωνος ἔκδοσιν ἅμα τῇ τῶν Ἑβδομήκοντα ἐν τοῖς τετρασσοῖς ἐπισκευάσας ("Arranging the edition of Aquila, Symmachus and Theodotion in a special way, together with the Septuagint in the Tetrapla").

[16] P. Nautin, *Origène*, 342–43.

[17] H. M. Orlinsky, "Origen's Tetrapla: A Scholarly Fiction?", and D. Barthélemy, "Origène et le texte de l'Ancien Testament", who connected the term τετρασσοῖς in the quotation by Eusebius with the expression τρισσὰ καὶ τετρασσά by Eusebius,

The Pentapla is mentioned once in the *Codex Marchalianus* for Is. 3:24 (οὐκ ἔκειντο ἐν τῷ πεντασελίδῳ). Unless it has been confused with the Tetrapla, it would have to be understood as the four best-known Greek versions together with the Hebrew text, since no trace of the *quinta* is to be found in the book of Isaiah. The name Heptapla, which occurs in a superscription to the Syro-Hexaplaric version at 4 Kgs 16:2, seems to include the *quinta*, as its readings are common in these books. The Octapla is mentioned in the Syro-Hexapla of the book of Job and in some Greek *scholia* to the book of Psalms, but apparently it means the same as the Hexapla, given that the Psalms often have readings from the *quinta* and *sexta*.[18]

The composition of the Hexapla

In his commentary on the gospel of Matthew, Origen refers to the condition of the text of the Greek Bible as it reached him and the procedure he adopted to restore it. The text he inherited was corrupt in various ways due to the carelessness of some scribes, the bad intentions of others and the nonchalance of those who added or omitted as they felt inclined.[19] In fact, from very early on the LXX had been revised in various ways. Also, the LXX differed considerably from the Hebrew text in the titles and distribution of the books and in the length and arrangement of material in some of them, such as Samuel–Kings, Job, Jeremiah, Daniel, Esther, etc. Today, through the pre-Hexaplaric papyri, we can determine how different it was from the text that reached Origen's hands.[20]

The way Origen addressed these divergences from the Hebrew text and among the manuscripts themselves was to compare the text of the LXX with the text of the other Greek editions (Aquila, Symmachus, Theodotion and others) and to retain it where they agreed. To mark the divergences he placed some obeluses (÷ indicating spurious or not authentic) before those words or phrases of

---

Vit. Const. IV, 37 which refers to the Bibles in three or four volumes (or in triplicate, quadruplicate) but not "in three or four columns (or Tetrapla)".

[18] See chapter 10, pp. 157 and 159.

[19] Origen, *Comm. in Matth.* XV, 14: πολλὴ γέγονεν ἡ τῶν ἀντιγράφων διαφορά, εἴτε ἀπὸ ῥαθυμίας τινῶν τῶν γραφέων, εἴτε ἀπὸ τόλμης τινῶν μοχθηρᾶς ... εἴτε καὶ ἀπὸ τῶν τὰ ἑαυτοῖς δοκοῦντα ἐν τῇ διορθώσει ἢ προστιθέντων ἢ ἀφαιρούντων ("There was a large difference in the manuscripts, due to negligence by the scribes, to the perverse boldness of others ... or even to those who add or omit what they like when they correct").

[20] See chapter 12, pp. 195–96.

the LXX missing from the Hebrew text; and an asterisk (※) before
those words or phrases missing from the LXX but found in the other
Greek editions in agreement with the Hebrew.[21] In the Letter to
Africanus he expresses the primarily apologetic aim of his work: so
that in discussion with Jews, Christians do not quote passages not
to be found in their Scriptures and so that Christians, in turn, could
also use what was to be found in Jewish manuscripts even though
not in their own.[22]

We do not know for certain when he composed the Hexapla. It
is assumed that he began collecting material during his time in
Alexandria and had already finished it in Caesarea. In writing his
Commentary to Matthew (249) and in his Letter to Africanus (c.
240) as we have just seen, he already mentions his edition which
included asterisks and obeluses. From analysis of the biblical quotations in Origen's commentaries, Rahlfs draws the following conclusions regarding the chronology of the Hexapla: Hexaplaric quotations
occur in the Letter to Africanus, in *Contra Celsum* and in some un-
specified material. Non-Hexaplaric quotations occur in the Commentaries on John, Exodus, Isaiah and Matthew. Although critical studies
must have started much earlier, in Alexandria even, the mass of
Hexaplaric production must be dated between 235 and 245. The non-
Hexaplaric quotations in works from Origen's last years, such as

---

[21] Origen, *Comm. in Matth.* XV, 14: τὴν μὲν οὖν ἐν τοῖς ἀντιγράφοις τῆς παλαιᾶς
διαθήκης διαφωνίαν θεοῦ διδόντος εὕρομεν ἰάσασθαι, κριτηρίῳ χρησάμενοι ταῖς
λοιπαῖς ἐκδόσεσιν· τῶν γὰρ ἀμφιβαλλομένων παρὰ τοῖς Ἑβδομήκοντα διὰ τὴν τῶν
ἀντιγράφων διαφωνίαν τὴν κρίσιν ποιησάμενοι ἀπὸ τῶν λοιπῶν ἐκδόσεων τὸ συνᾷ-
δον ἐκείναις ἐφυλάξαμεν, καὶ τινὰ μὲν ὠβελίσαμεν <ὡς> ἐν τῷ Ἑβραϊκῷ μὴ
κείμενα (οὐ τολμήσαντες αὐτὰ πάντη περιελεῖν), τινὰ δὲ μετ' ἀστερίσκων
προσεθήκαμεν, ἵνα δῆλον ᾖ ὅτι μὴ κείμενα παρὰ τοῖς Ἑβδομήκοντα ἐκ τῶν λοιπῶν
ἐκδόσεων συμφώνως τῷ Ἑβραϊκῷ προσεθήκαμεν ("With divine help we eventually
overcame the discrepancy of the Old Testament in the manuscripts using the other
editions as a criterion. And we decided on the doubtful matters of the LXX by
means of the disagreement of the manuscripts from the other editions, retaining
what is in agreement with them. And some things we obelised because they do not
occur in Hebrew [not daring to remove them completely] and others we added
with an asterisk in order to make clear that, as they do not occur in the LXX, we
added them from the other editions in agreement with the Hebrew").

[22] Origen, *Ep. ad Afr.* 5.: Ἀσκοῦμεν δὲ μὴ ἀγνοεῖν καὶ τὰς παρ' ἐκείνοις· ἵνα
πρὸς Ἰουδαίους διαλεγόμενοι, μὴ προφέρωμεν αὐτοῖς τὰ μὴ κείμενα ἐν τοῖς ἀντιγράφοις αὐτῶν, καὶ ἵνα συγχρησώμεθα τοῖς φερομένοις παρ' ἐκείνοις· εἰ καὶ ἐν
τοῖς ἡμετέροις οὐ κεῖται βιβλίοις ("And we make an effort not to ignore the ones
belonging to them; so that when we converse with the Jews, we do not quote to
them what is not found in their manuscripts, and so that we can use what they
[in turn] show even though not found in our books").

those in the Commentary on Matthew, have to be interpreted in the light of his view, as expressed in the Letter to Africanus, that the Hexapla was only an instrument for disputes with the Jews and not for church use.

Ancient writers agree about the arrangement of the columns in the following sequence: Hebrew text, transliteration into Greek, Aquila, Symmachus, LXX and Theodotion. For the various forms of the asterisks and obeluses used in Hexaplaric manuscripts, see Field and Swete.[23]

However, the Aristarchian signs, taken from Alexandrian philology when the Homeric texts were edited, are far too simple to transmit accurately all the corrections that Origen inserted into the text. In fact they could only be used to mark additions and omissions. In the book of Proverbs he uses a combination of asterisk and obelus (÷ / ※ ÷) to mark a transposition for here, unlike the other books, he keeps to the LXX sequence. However, he had no suitable signs to indicate any other set of changes. It is therefore correct to consider as Origen's corrections all the specifically Hexaplaric readings even though not marked with asterisks and obeluses.

Later history and the impact of the Hexapla

The enormous work of the Hexapla was probably never copied out again completely given the sheer size of such a reference work and the cost it would entail.[24] However the successors of Origen, Eusebius and Pamphilus circulated copies of the corrected LXX, and Caesarea soon became a publishing centre that made multiple copies of the restored exemplars. Around 330, Constantine assigned fifty copies (σωμάτια) in parchment to Eusebius to distribute to his churches.[25]

---

[23] F. Field, *Origenis Hexaplorum quae supersunt*, LII–LX, and H. B. Swete, *An Introduction to the old Testament in Greek*, 69–73.

[24] It is estimated that they covered about fifty volumes or codices (see F. Field, *Origenis Hexaplorum quae supersunt*, XCVIII). Origen's way of working, surrounded by co-workers and many stenographers, is described by Eusebius in *Hist. Ecc.* VI, 23, 1ff. Barthélemy ("Origène et le texte de l'Ancien Testament", 255) even wonders whether Origen really was the author of the Hexapla and not instead the coordinator or supervisor of the work. According to Barthélemy this would comprise an enormous dossier of data collected by Origen's assistants, a dossier which he annotated as is indicated in several colophons to Hexaplaric manuscripts, which he used for reference in preparing his own critical edition of the LXX, with asterisks and obeluses, called the Origenic or Hexaplaric recension or Hexapla.

[25] Eusebius, *Vit. Const.* IV, 36.

Proof of this publishing activity and the early circulation of the fifth column (= LXX) separately, corrected and furnished with diacritic signs, i.e. Origen's recension, is provided by: ms. *Colbertinus-Sarravianus* (G, 4th/5th centuries) although with neither colophon nor marginal notes of "the three"; the colophons of *Codex Marchalianus* (Q, 6th century) at the beginning of Ezekiel and Isaiah; and the corrector of Sinaiticus (S^c, 7th century) at the end of the book of Esther. From comparison of these colophons it can be deduced that the work of textual criticism continued in Caesarea, along the lines begun by Origen, of restoring an eclectic text.[26]

Even fifty years after its composition, Jerome could study copies of the Hexapla in Caesarea.[27] And in 616, Paul of Tella translated into Syriac the LXX edition of the Hexapla, corrected and with Aristarchian signs.[28] Finally, in 638 Caesarea fell into the hands of the Arabs, not by sack or destruction but by the purchase of its citizens. From then on we have no further information about the Hexapla; furthermore, until the end of the 19th century it was thought that only the Hexaplaric recension had survived – i.e. the fifth column corrected and edited by Pamphilus and Eusebius, as reproduced in manuscripts of the Origen recension – and only sporadic variants from other columns.[29] Not until 1896, in palimpsest O.39 of the Ambrosian Library of Milan, were fragments of the Hexapla to the Psalms discovered by G. Mercati, and in 1897, Burkitt and Taylor published a manuscript that contains Aquila's version of 1 Kgs 20:7-17 and 2 Kgs 23:12-27. Finally, in 1900, among material from the Cairo Genizah, Taylor identified fragments of the Hexaplaric Psalm 22(21).[30]

---

[26] See E. Ulrich, "The Old Testament Text of Eusebius: The Heritage of Origen", *Eusebius, Christianity, and Judaism*, ed. H. W. Attridge and G. Hata, Leiden 1992, 543–62.

[27] F. Field, *Origenis Hexaplorum quae supersunt*, XCIX.

[28] For the history of the Syro-Hexaplar, see S. Jellicoe, *SMS*, 124–27. Recent discoveries and studies to be added are W. Baars, *New Syro-hexaplaric Texts*, Leiden 1968; A. Vööbus, *The Hexapla and the Syro-Hexapla: Very Important Discoveries for Septuagint Research*, Stockholm 1971; Vööbus, "The Discovery of the Pentateuch of the Syro-Hexapla", *JAOS* 93 (1973), 354–55; M. H. Goshen Gottstein, "Neue Syrohexapla-fragmente", *Bib* 37 (1956), 162–83. This can be supplemented by the most recent bibliography in *BS* 305–306.

[29] See E. Schwartz, "Zur Geschichte der Hexapla".

[30] For the work by Mercati, see Select Bibliography. F. C. Burkitt and C. Taylor, *Fragments of the Books of Kings According to the Translation of Aquila*, Cambridge 1987, and C. Taylor, *Hebrew–Greek Cairo Genizah Palimpsests from the Taylor–Schechter Collection Including a Fragment of the Twenty-second Psalm According to Origen's Hexapla*, Cambridge 1900.

With these surviving witnesses of the Hexapla, even if fragmentary, our information about them from ancient sources has been confirmed in some respects and corrected in others.

The fragment from the Cairo Genizah contains Ps. 22:15-18, 20–28; it does not preserve any remains of the first column (Hebrew text); instead it transmits some fragments of the *secunda*, the third and the fourth (Aquila and Symmachus) almost completely, part of the fifth (LXX) and none of the sixth. Perhaps the manuscript contained the whole Psalter; Aquila, Symmachus and Theodotion all have the *Tetragrammaton* written as ΠΙΠΙ.

The Milan palimpsest contains all the columns (five in all) except the Hebrew text; underneath, the continuous LXX text and then a catenary text.[31] It is made up of thirteen fragments with a total of 151 verses from different psalms, from 17 to 88. It is more likely to be a condensed Hexapla, with one column left out, than an extended Tetrapla.[32]

The importance of the details in this description of the manuscript is the repercussions they have on our knowledge of the Hexapla. In fact, before this find, we only knew it from information in Origen, Eusebius, Jerome, Epiphanius, etc.; from corrected manuscripts that contained the Origen recension (some of them supplied with colophons and Aristarchian signs) and from isolated readings of "the three" in the margins of manuscripts and quotations by the Fathers.[33]

Now for the first time we have at our disposal lengthy, continuous texts of "the three" and remains of the Hexapla as the ancient authors described it. The main results can be summarised as follows:

1. The traditional order of *secunda*, third (Aquila) and fourth (Symmachus) columns is confirmed.

---

[31] See G. Mercati, *Psalterii Hexapli reliquiae* in the introduction. For the *catenae*, see *infra*, chapter 19.

[32] For several reasons: first we can ask ourselves whether Tetrapla existed of which nothing has been preserved. If they did exist, it is doubtful whether columns would have been arranged in the same way as in the Hexapla. And finally, it is unlikely that the amanuensis would have used some Hexapla to attach the second transliterated column to the Tetrapla.

[33] For the new Hexaplaric material recovered after Field's edition through the publication of manuscripts, commentaries by the Fathers and *catenae*, see D. Barthélemy, *Critique textuelle de l'Ancien Testament. Tome 3*, Fribourg–Göttingen 1992, CLX–CLXI. On the projected new edition of the Hexaplaric fragments, see A. Salvesen (ed.), *Origen's Hexapla and Fragments*, 439–49.

2. The old supposition that the Hexapla was never copied out again has been corrected. We have at least witnesses of copies of a shorter Hexapla or perhaps complete copies in certain books.

3. In the fifth column of the Milan palimpsest there is no trace of any diacritical signs.

4. However, no doubt the biggest surprise is that the last column of the palimpsest does not contain Theodotion, as was thought, but the *quinta* (ε'). This fact gives ground for suspecting the authenticity of the attributions in other books: we do not know whether the anonymous author whom Origen placed in the sixth column of the Hexapla was always the same from Genesis until the end, or whether he really was Theodotion.[34]

Since the fragments cited by Theodoret of Cyr in Psalms as belonging to Theodotion are from the *quinta*, there is no doubt that already in the first half of the 5th century, perhaps earlier, schematic Hexaplaric psalters were known with the omission of one column, such as Theodotion, as in this case. There is also the possibility that the Hexapla circulated not only without the first two columns (which were enigmatic to Christian copyists who did not know Hebrew) but also without one or other of the versions.

c) *The Fifth Column of the Hexapla and the* secunda

The two most discussed problems in Hexaplaric research concern these two columns. As for the first, we are still asking ourselves which text Origen put in the LXX column. Was it corrected or uncorrected, with or without Aristarchian signs?

As there are no signs at all in the palimpsest, Mercati thinks that Theodotion inserted the common LXX in the fifth column, only slightly corrected according to the manuscripts he had available, and with neither asterisks nor obeluses.[35] Kahle, Lietzmann, Procksch,

---

[34] To prove this, Mercati analyses the readings in the last column, comparing them with the witnesses of the *quinta* and Theodotion known from other collections of variants in Hexaplaric manuscripts. The result was overwhelmingly positive in favour of the *quinta*. He examined three independent collections of readings: the marginal readings of ms. 264 of Holmes–Parsons; those in *Vat. Graec.* 754 and those of the Syro-Hexapla for the Psalter. The three controls used confirm that the readings of the last column of the palimpsest belong to the *quinta* (see G. Mercati, *Psalterii Hexapli reliquiae* I, XIXff.).

[35] There are several reasons: The Septuagintal text of the palimpsest is Alexandrian,

Pretzl and others agree with Mercati. However, in favour of the signs are such notable authorities in textual criticism of the LXX as Field, Brock, Soisalon-Soininen and Bo Johnson.[36] There are weighty reasons both for and against this supposition.[37] Those favouring the existence of signs refer to the witness of Origen himself in the Commentary on Mt. 15:14 and to Jerome's testimony in his prologue to the book of Chronicles.[38] Field, an expert in Hexaplaric readings, adds: "In scholiis graecis innumera exstant loca, quae contrarium aperte probent."[39] This means that the edition of the LXX-Hexaplaric column was no different from the text edited separately and with signs, like the one known from *Sarravianus*.[40] However, in view of the transpositions in Exodus 36–39 and Jeremiah 25–51, I do not see how Origen could have operated without great changes. The supporters of signs also insist that perhaps the Hexaplaric copy of the Ambrosian is late, is of a single book and does not really reflect the original Hexapla. S. Brock holds that the arguments against Field are not completely convincing.[41] Some of the reasons against the insertion of diacritic signs in the Hexapla are as follows: they have been found in the palimpsest from the Ambrosian; Mercati insists that the signs were not needed as the texts with their differences could be seen synoptically; and Field provides no actual examples to support his hypothesis. To this the supporters of the signs reply that, although specific quotations are missing, the long years of research by Field on Hexaplaric material give his statements great

---

nearly always in agreement with B, even though there is no good edition of the Psalms. The transpositions and signs would have created great confusion for the reader. Added to this is the actual difficulty of locating them and filling in the gaps and at the same time keeping in parallel with the other columns. Lastly, it seems more correct to use the inherited *koiné* of a mixed text for the comparison, (G. Mercati, *Psalterii Hexapli reliquiae* I, XXXIVff.).

[36] I. Soisalon-Soininen, *Der Charakter der asterisierten Zusätze in der Septuagitna*, Helsinki, 1959, 197, and B. Johnson, *Die hexaplarische Rezension des 1. Samuelbuches der Septuaginta*, Lund 1963, 144.

[37] Some of them can be consulted in H. B. Swete, *An Introduction to the Old Testament in Greek*, 77–78.

[38] Jerome, *Prologus ... in libro Paralipomenon*: "sed quod majoris audaciae est, in editione LXX Theodotionis editionem miscuit, asteriscis designans quae minus ante fuerant, et virgulis quae ex superfluo videbantur apposita".

[39] F. Field, *Origenis Hexaplorum quae supersunt*, LII.

[40] An example can be seen in H. B. Swete, *An Introduction to the Old Testament in Greek*, 73.

[41] See S. P. Brock, *The Recensions of the LXX Version of I Samuel*, Turin 1996, 39–42.

weight; and that the diacritic signs could have disappeared in the course of transmission, as happened in other cases.

The other problem that has attracted much attention is that of the Hexaplaric *secunda* because of the many questions of all kinds raised by this Hebrew text transliterated into Greek.[42] On the possibilities that Origen himself composed it we have already spoken above in connection with his knowledge of Hebrew. In the event that he took it from earlier Jewish synopses[43] and incorporated it later into the Hexapla, another problem arises: is it a text specially prepared for the Hexapla, which therefore reflects the pronunciation of Hebrew in the 3rd century CE, or did Hebrew texts transliterated into Greek for liturgical or didactic purposes circulate previously among the Jews? And connected with this, an additional problem: are the transcriptions of the *secunda* uniform throughout the Hexapla, as Mercati believes, or are they different precisely because they come from different layers, as Sperber has explained?

The transcriptions of the *secunda* are one of the pillars on which F. X. Wutz constructed his theory of the origins of the LXX from an intermediate text transliterated into Greek. We have already seen, when we explained his theory,[44] how the hypothesis of a change of script to Greek remains, in Mercati's opinion, a probable conjecture until the period of the *secunda* (around 235 CE). Even so, P. Kahle opposes Mercati and continues to defend the existence of transliterated Hebrew texts before Origen.[45] However, if these transliterations were so widespread among the Hellenistic Jews – Mercati argues – it is surprising that no fragment has been found apart from the

---

[42] There has been an increase in the number of studies since the Milan palimpsest was discovered; see O. Eissfeldt, "Zur Textkritischen Auswertung der Mercatischen Hexapla-Fragmente", *WO* 1 (1947–52), 93–97 = *KS* III, Tübingen 1966, 9–13.

[43] As P. Nautin, *Origène*, 339, thinks.

[44] See chapter 4. Besides F. X. Wutz, the following defended the existence of texts transliterated into Greek before the Hexapla: L. Blau, "La transcription de l'AT en charactères grecs", *REJ* 88 (1929), 18–22; A. Sperber, "Hebrew Based upon Greek and Latin Transliterations"; W. E. Staples, "The Hebrew of the Septuagint", *AJSL* 44 (1927–28), 6–30; J. Halévy, "L'origine de la transcription", and M. Ginsburger, "La transcription de l'AT".

[45] P. Kahle, "The Greek Bible Manuscripts Used by Origen". He bases this on the beginning of the homily on Easter by Melito of Sardis (*c.* 168 CE), which says: ἡ μὲν γραφὴ τῆς Ἑβραϊκῆς Ἐξόδου ἀνέγνωσται καὶ τὰ ῥήματα τοῦ μυστηρίου διασεσάφηται (The Scripture of the Hebrew Exodus is read and the words of the mystery are explained) (B. Lohse, *Die Passa-Homilie des Bischofs Meliton von Sardes*, Leiden 1958, 11). See also G. Zuntz, "On the Opening Sentence of Melito's Paschal Homily", *HTR* 36 (1943), 299–315.

Origen tradition, whereas codices of the Aramaic Targum from north and south Palestine, previously thought to be lost, are being recovered.[46] From the text of Melito of Sardis the most that can be deduced is that the first Christians, following synagogal usage in the reading from the Old Testament, had kept the reading of some pericopes in the original Hebrew for special events. Finally, Emerton, while not denying the possibility of this type of transcription before the Hexapla, says that the data provided by its defenders, especially the rabbinic passages quoted, do not prove that it existed.[47]

As for the *purpose* of the *secunda* – a topic closely related to the previous problems – it too has received no satisfactory explanation. For Orlinsky, the purpose of the Hexapla (including the *secunda*) was to provide Christians with a textbook for learning Hebrew, at a time when it was increasingly difficult to find rabbis as teachers, as it meant giving one's opponent the best weapon for theological debate.[48] However, it is difficult to think that such a lengthy work could have had any other purpose than the textual-apologetic originally attested by the sources.

Emerton's hypothesis about the *secunda* as a vocalisation system seems to be more likely and consistent:[49] in antiquity there were no vocalised Hebrew texts; however the fact that with time a system of pointing was devised shows that the need was felt for an aid to reading. The *secunda* would be a lengthier system than those traditionally known but it has the same purpose.[50] The Tiberian system became the final form that the manuscripts adopted, but it was preceded by a lengthy experimental history in Palestine and Babylonia. More like the *secunda* is the system adopted by the Jacobite Syrians who wrote Greek vowels above and below the Semitic consonants. Perhaps this procedure occurred to Origen or to one of his predecessors and was rejected in favour of transliteration as it was considered undignified

---

[46] G. Mercati, *Psalterii Hexapli reliquiae* I, XVIII.

[47] J. A. Emerton, "Were Greek Transliterations of the Hebrew?"

[48] H. M. Orlinsky, "The Columnar Order of the Hexapla".

[49] J. A. Emerton, "A Further Consideration of the Purpose of the Second Column".

[50] Prior to the *secunda*, an attempt had already been made to use *matres lectionis* (*'immôt ha-qeriah*), i.e. the use of certain consonants to indicate vowels. Their use in epigraphic Hebrew is very ancient; they occur, for example, in the 8th century BCE Siloam Inscription and in the 7th century BCE Lachish Ostraca. They are used very widely in biblical manuscripts from the period of textual fluidity and in the Dead Sea Scrolls; see F. Pérez Castro, "La transmisión del texto del Antiguo Testamento hebreo", in F. Cantera and M. Iglesias, *Sagrada Biblia. Versión crítica sobre los textos hebreo, arameo y griego.* Madrid 1979, XV–XXXVI.

to annotate the sacred text in this way. Emerton illustrates his hypothesis with various analogies in the non-Jewish ancient world of transliterated texts, always in relation to another text, i.e. as an indication that the transliterations were connected in some way with pronunciation. The *secunda* therefore claimed to make it possible for those who knew the Hebrew language and alphabet *to vocalise consonantal texts*.

The secunda *and the pronunciation of pre-Masoretic Hebrew.*[51]
For few matters is it so important as this to make a distinction between the facts and the theories built upon those facts. The facts basically derived from the *secunda* of the Hexapla to the psalms in the Milan palimpsests are as follows:

1. *bᵉgadkᵉfat*: for the double pronunciation (occlusive and fricative) of these Hebrew consonants, the *secunda* only transcribes χ/φ/θ for *k/p/t* with gemination, χχ/φφ/θθ, which is irregular in Greek, whereas the LXX preserves transliterations with κ/π/τ for the same phonemes and regular Greek gemination of κχ/πφ/τθ, according to the law of dissimilation of aspirates. The *secunda* instead uses /τ/ specifically for /t/ and /κ/ for /q/. However, precisely because of this specialisation of the different phonemes, the data from transliterations are in themselves not enough to prove that aspirates were fricative in 3rd century CE Hebrew.

2. The laryngeals א, ע, ה and ח are not indicated by Greek consonants. However the inadequacy of the Greek alphabet to reproduce these Hebrew sounds is even greater in this case than for the *bᵉgadkᵉfat* letters. Thus Origen's non-transliteration of these consonants in the *secunda* is not an indication that they were not pronounced in Hebrew in his time. It is not clear whether or nor they were indicated in the stage of language reproduced by the LXX. Although the laryngeals are not represented in Greek by

---

[51] The bibliography is enormous. Here are some of the main titles: E. A. Speiser, "The Pronunciation of Hebrew"; O. Pretzl, "Die Aussprache des Hebräischen"; A. Sperber, "Hebrew Based upon Greek"; P. Kahle, *The Cairo Geniza*, London 1959; F. X. Wutz, *Systematische Wege von der LXX zum hebräischen Urtext I*, Stuttgart 1937; F. Pérez Castro, "Problemas del hebreo premasorético"; E. Brønno, *Studien zur vormasoretischen Morphologie*; F. X. Wutz, *Die Transkriptionen von der Septuaginta bis zu Hieronymus*, Stuttgart I, 1925; II, 1933; J. Barr, "St Jerome and the Sounds of Hebrew", *JSS* 12 (1967), 1–36; G. Mercati, "Il problema della Colonna seconda"; E. Brønno, "Samaritan Hebrew and Origen's Secunda"; Mercati, "Zu den Theorien Paul Kahles von der Entstehung der Tiberischen Grammatik", *ZDMG* 100 (1950), 521–65, and G. Janssens, *Studies in Hebrew Historical Linguistics*.

consonants, nevertheless the accompanying vowels indicate their presence.

3. As for the *sibilants*, the incompatibility between the two languages is even greater. The ז is transcribed by the ζ, but for the four Hebrew phonemes ס צ שׂ and שׁ with differing pronunciations, Greek only uses σ.

4. The pronunciation of the vowels is more difficult to determine from the *secunda*, as in the Semitic languages the consonants form the skeleton of the spoken chain with a strong pronunciation whereas the vowels are more fluid. The beginnings of Hebrew vocalisation go back at most to the 6th century CE, and their crystallisation into the Tiberian system cannot be earlier than the end of the 8th century. The medium available to Origen in Greek for reproducing Hebrew vowels was weakened somewhat due to the shifts produced by iotacism within the system. However, in spite of the gradual disappearance of vowel quality and in spite of iotacism, the overall conclusion is that in the *secunda* the quality of vowels with an *e/o* timbre is indicated. The *qameṣ*, except for a few unimportant cases, can be accepted as long in the time of Origen. The *pataḥ* in stressed open syllables is not differentiated from *qameṣ*. Before semi-vowels and laryngeals it was short. The *segol* is transcribed by α/ε. For *ḥireq gadol* the transcription is predominantly ει. The *ḥolem* is transcribed as o. In other cases the system cannot be determined.

The theories

On the basis of these data from the *secunda*, together with the transcriptions of proper names in the LXX and in Jerome, theories have been constructed that try to draw the most pretentious conclusions. For example, A. Sperber compares the transcriptions in the Vatican Codex and Codex Alexandrinus: according to him the Vatican reflects an older pronunciation than the Hebrew. Codex Alexandrinus instead reflects the transition towards the stage of the language reproduced by the *secunda*. The *secunda* agrees in most of its transcriptions with the system of Codex Alexandrinus, but often goes with the Vatican Codex. From this Sperber deduces that the *secunda* does not have a uniform and contemporaneous text. On the basis of these transcriptions he tries to write a grammar and a dictionary of pre-Masoretic Hebrew. From the differences in pronunciation between the Masoretic and non-Masoretic forms he deduces that there were two schools of pronunciation of Hebrew in the kingdoms of Judah and Israel, the respective seats of these dialectal differences. The Tiberian system reflects the pronunciation of Judaea and the non-Tiberian sources reflects the Israelite pronunciation. Other differences emerge when comparing the Masoretic Pentateuch (Judaean) with the Samaritan Pentateuch (Israelite).[52] Kahle instead insists that in the *secunda* the laryngeals were not pronounced as consonants. However, in the LXX from the transcription of proper names we know that they were indicated by a helping vowel or by a prefixed ε/ι.[53] According to him, the Masoretes artificially restored the pronunciation of the gutturals due to the influence of Arabic and Syriac.

E. Brønno has severely criticised Kahle's thesis and indirectly Sperber's theories.[54] From the fact that the laryngeals *are not expressed* in the *secunda* it cannot be concluded that they did not exist or were not pronounced in its *Vorlage*, for account has to be taken of the unsuitability of the Greek alphabet for representing them. According to Brønno, laryngeals are not indicated in the LXX either. The examples proposed by Kahle are sporadic and could have been due to contamination. In any case it is suspicious that most of the examples with prothetic *iota* occur after a word ending in *iota*, as they could have arisen from inner-Greek corruption. Brønno places stress on vocalism: the *secunda* has a unique position in the history of Hebrew, for it uses different vowels for short and long *e/o* sounds. He criticises Sperber for completely ignoring vowel quality and for arranging the forms arbitrarily, especially the segholates.

In summary, in connection with the use in the *secunda* and in general of Greek transliterations to reconstruct the pronunciation of pre-Masoretic Hebrew, there has been a move from initial euphoria

---

[52] A. Sperber, "Hebrew Based upon Greek", and Sperber, *A Historical Grammar of Biblical Hebrew*, Leiden 1966.

[53] For example:

Αερνων	for 'arnôn	Jer. 31(48):20 A
Αηλαμ	for 'elām	1 Chron. 8:24 A
Ιαχειραν	for 'ahîrām	Num. 26:42(38) B
Ιασον	for 'āṣem	Josh. 19:3 B

Similarly, *ḥ* and ʿ had different pronunciations when the LXX was translated. See:

Γομορρα	for 'amorâ	Gen. 10:19ff.
Γαζα	for 'azzâ	Gen. 10:19ff.
Χορραιος	for ḥorî	Gen. 14:6 A

P. Kahle, *The Cairo Geniza*, 165.

[54] E. Brønno, "Zu den Theorien Paul Kahles von der Entstehung der tiberischen Grammatik".

(represented principally by Sperber, Wutz and Kahle) towards a position of complete reserve (reflected in the publications of Brønno, Mercati and Barr).[55] Applying a more modern linguistic approach, Barr insists that the transliterations do not open the way directly to the pronunciation of Hebrew but are at most an interpretation conditioned by the phonemic systems of Greek and Latin. Jerome, for example, probably transmitted to us at times a single graphic reproduction of two allophonic realisations. Contrary to the opinion of Kahle and particularly of Sperber, it seems that Jerome's material can be interpreted in a sense that is much closer to the Masoretic structure of Hebrew than had been thought until recently.[56] And the recent study by Brønno points in the same direction.[57]

Select Bibliography

Origen and the Hexapla

Bammel, C. P., "Die Hexapla des Origenes: die hebraica veritas im Streit der Meinungen". *Augustinianum* 28 (1988), 125–49.

Bardy, G., "Les citations bibliques d'Origène dans le 'De principiis'". *RB* 16 (1919), 106–35.

———, G., "Les traditions juives dans l'oeuvre d'Origène". *RB* 34 (1925), 217–52.

Barthélemy, D., "Origène et le texte de l'Ancien Testament". *Epektasis, Mélanges J. Daniélou* II, Paris 1972, 247–61.

Bietenhard, H., *Caesarea, Origenes und die Juden*, Stuttgart 1974.

Brock, S. P., "Origen's Aims as a Textual Critic of the Old Testament". *Studia Patristica* X, Berlin 1970, 215–18.

Caloz, M., *Études sur la LXX origènienne du Psautier*, Fribourg–Göttingen 1978.

Cox, C. E., *Hexaplaric Materials Preserved in the Armenian Version*, Atlanta, Ga. 1986.

Dorival, G., "L'apport des chaînes exégètiques grecques à une réédition des *Hexaples* d'Origène (à propos du Psaume 118)". *RHT* 4 (1974), 45–74.

Dorival, G., and A. Le Boulluec, *Origeniana Sexta*, Leuven 1995.

Field, F., *Origenis Hexaplorum quae supersunt I*, Oxford 1875, XLVII–LXXXIII.

Hanson, R. P. C., "Interpretations of Hebrew Names in Origen". *VC* 10 (1956), 103–23.

Harl, M., "Origène et la sémantique du langage biblique". *VC* 26 (1972), 161–87.

Jellicoe, S., *SMS*, 100–127.

Klostermann, E., "Formen der exegetischen Arbeiten des Origenes". *TLZ* 72 (1947), 203–208.

Lange, N. R. M. de, *Origen and the Jews: Studies in Jewish–Christian Relations in Third-century Palestine*, Cambridge 1978.

---

[55] G. Mercati ends his article on "Il problema della Colonna seconda" by noting that even if it was proved for certain that the transliteration in the *secunda* was faithful, he would not print it as a reconstruction of 3rd century CE Hebrew, being aware of the very many doubts and problems it would raise.

[56] J. Barr, "St Jerome and the Sounds of Hebrew".

[57] E. Brønno, *Die Aussprache der hebräischen Laryngale nach Zeugnissen des Hieronymus*, Århus 1970, with F. Corriente's review in *Sefarad* 33 (1973), 158–62.

Nautin, P., *Origène. Sa vie et son oeuvre*, Paris 1977, 303–61.

Neuschäfer, B., *Origenes als Philologe*, Basle 1987.

Norton, G. J., "Cautionary Reflections on a Re-edition of Fragments of Hexaplaric Material". *Tradition of the Text*, 1991, 129–55.

———, G. J., "Jews, Greeks, and the Hexapla of Origen". *The Aramaic Bible*, ed. D. R. G. Beattie and M. J. McNamara, Sheffield 1994, 400–419.

Preuschen, E., "Bibelcitate bei Origenes". *ZNW* 4 (1903), 67–74.

Rahls, A., "Origenes Zitate aus den Königsbüchern". *Septuaginta-Studien* I, Göttingen 1904, 47–87.

Salvesen, A. (ed.), *Origen's Hexapla and Fragments*, Tübingen 1998.

Schenker, A., *Hexaplarische Psalmenbruchstücke. Die hexaplarische Psalmenfragmente der Handschriften Vaticanus graecus 752 und Canonicianus graecus 62*, Fribourg–Göttingen 1975.

———, A., *Psalmen in der Hexapla. Erste kritische und vollständige Ausgabe der hexaplarischen Fragmente auf dem Rande der Handschrift Ottobonianus graecus 398 zu den Ps 24–32*, Rome (Vatican City) 1982.

Sgherri, G., "A proposito di Origene e la lingua ebraica". *Augustinianum* 14 (1974), 223–59.

———, G., "Sulla valutazione origeniana dei LXX". *Bib* 58 (1977), 1–28.

Swete, H. B., *An Introduction to the Old Testament in Greek*, Cambridge 1914, 59–86.

Ulrich, E. C., "Origen's Old Testament Text: The Transmission History of the Septuagint of the Third Century C. E." *Origen of Alexandria: His World and his Legacy*, ed. C. Kannengiesser and W. L. Petersen, Notre Dame, Ind. 1988, 3–33.

The *secunda*

Brønno, E., "Samaritan Hebrew and Origen's Secunda". *JSS* 13 (1968), 193–201.

———, E., *Studien zur vormasoretischen Morphologie und Vokalismus des Hebräischen auf Grundlage der Mercatischen Fragmente der zweiten Kolumne der Hexapla des Origenes*. 28, Leipzig 1943.

———, E., "The Isaiah Scroll DSIa and the Greek Transliterations of Hebrew". *ZDMG* nf 31 (1956), 252–58.

Eissfeldt, O., "Zur Textkritischen Auswertung der Mercatischen Hexapla Fragmente". *WO* 1 (1947), 93–97.

Emerton, J. A., "A Further Consideration of the Purpose of the Second Column of the Hexapla". *JTS* 22 (1971), 15–28.

———, J. A., "The Purpose of the Second Column of the Hexapla". *JTS* 7 (1956), 79–87.

———, J. A., "Were Greek Transliterations of the Hebrew Old Testament Used by Jews before the Time of Origen?". *JTS* 21 (1970), 17–31.

Ginsburger, M., "La transcription de l'AT en charactères grecs". *REJ* 87 (1929), 40–42; 88 (1929), 184–86.

Halevy, J., "L'origine de la transcription du texte hébreu en caractères grecs dans les Hexaples d'Origène". *JAS* IX, 17 (1901), 335–41; 18 (1902), 399–400.

Janssens, G., *Studies in Hebrew Historical Linguistics Based on Origen's secunda*, Leuven 1982.

Kahle, P., "The Greek Bible Manuscripts Used by Origen". *JBL* 79 (1960), 111–18.

Mercati, G., "Il problema della Colonna seconda dell'Esaplo". *Bib* 28 (1947), 1–30; 173–215.

———, G., *Psalterii Hexapli reliquiae*, I Rome 1958; II *Osservazioni*, Rome 1965.

Orlinsky, H. M., "Origen's Tetrapla: A Scholarly Fiction?". *Proceedings of the First World Congress of Jewish Studies*, I, Jerusalem 1952, 173–82.

———, H. M., "The Columnar Order of the Hexapla". *JQR* 27 (1936–37), 137–49.

Perez Castro, F., "Problemas del hebreo premasorético". *Sefarad* 8 (1948), 148–54.

Pretzl, O., "Die Aussprache des Hebräischen nach der zweiten Kolumne der Hexapla des Origenes". *BZ* 20 (1932), 4–22.

Sáenz-Badillos, A., *A History of the Hebrew Language*, translated by J. Elwolde, Cambridge 1993, 80–86.

———, A., "El hebreo del s. II d.C. a la luz de las transcripciones griegas de Aquila, Símmaco y Teodoción". *Sefarad* 35 (1975), 107–30.

Schwartz, E., "Zur Geschichte der Hexapla". *NGWGött* 6 (1903), 693–700.

Speiser, E. A., "The Pronunciation of Hebrew According to (Later: Based Chiefly on) the Transliterations in the Hexapla". *JQR* 16 (1925–26), 343–82; 23 (1933), 233–65; 24 (1934), 9–46.

Sperber, A., "Hebrew Based upon Greek and Latin Transliterations". *HUCA* 12/13 (1937–38), 103–274.

CHAPTER FOURTEEN

THE LUCIANIC RECENSION

a) *Ancient Witnesses*

Lucian was probably born in Samosata in Syria *c.* 250 CE. He studied in Edessa and Caesarea; then he went on to the famous school of Antioch, its chief representatives being Chrysostom, Diodorus, Theodoret of Cyr and Theodore of Mopsuestia.[1] A disciple of Paul of Samosata and of the presbyter Malchion, for reasons that are not quite clear he was for many years in the shade, cut off from Church communion.[2] Founder of the exegetical school of Antioch he took Arius as one of his disciples.[3] In his final years he returned to the Church and died a martyr in Nicomedia under the emperor Maximian (311–12).

Some have wondered whether the excommunicated Lucian is the same as the scripture scholar. However, in spite of certain discrepancies between the person and his literary work, it is not necessary to conclude that they are two different persons. Cases are not rare in antiquity where due to only part of their work being considered, certain authors have made us think they are two different persons.[4]

His contemporaries speak of him as a qualified biblical scholar: he knew Syriac as his mother tongue, Greek and perhaps some Hebrew in view of the important Jewish colony in Antioch.[5] However, they say nothing about his work of revising the Bible, his connection with the Hexapla, and other details connected with his philological work.

---

[1] Eusebius, *Hist. Ecc.* VII, 29–32; Jerome, *De vir. illustribus*, 71.

[2] Theodoret, *Hist. Ecc.* I,3: ἀποσυναγωγὸς ἔμεινε τριῶν ἐπισκόπων πολυετοῦς χρόνου ("He remained expelled during the long period of three bishops"). However, strictly speaking ἀποσυναγωγός means "expelled from the synagogue", see Jn 9:22.

[3] B. Altaner and A. Stuiber, *Patrologie. Leben, Schriften und Lehre der Kirchen-väter*, Freiburg–Basle–Vienna 1966, 214 and 190.

[4] B. M. Metzger, "The Lucianic Recension of the Greek Bible", 1ff., and N. Fernández Marcos, *Los 'Thaumata' de Sofronio. Contribución al estudio de la 'Incubatio' cristiana*, Madrid 1975, 5–11.

[5] K. Treu, "Die Bedeutung des griechischen für die Juden im römischen Reich", *Kairos* 17 (1975), 123–44.

Jerome's statements are too vague and contradictory for them to be believed. In the text of the prologue to the book of Chronicles he assigns the Lucianic exemplars to the region that extends from Constantinople to Antioch, in contrast to the recension of Hesychius and Origen.[6] In the Letter to Sunia and Fretela, he compares it with the Hexapla and calls it common, vulgate or Lucianic, "the old edition corrupted according to the places, times and fancy of the writers".[7] And in the prologue to the evangelists dedicated to Damasus he even despises the Lucianic codices, ignoring them since they lack importance.[8] The impression given is that Jerome's judgement on the Lucianic recension depends a great deal on whom he was writing to and is conditioned by an interest in praising his own Vulgate translation into Latin.

Pseudo-Athanasius confuses the edition by Lucian with the *septima* which we discussed above.[9] Suidas (Lexicographus) even considers his edition to have been a new translation from Hebrew.[10] Lastly, in the epilogue to several catenary manuscripts to the Octateuch, after listing the other editions of the Greek Bible, there is a reference to Lucian's edition, prepared for Christians and found in Nicomedia under Constantine in a whitewashed marble wall (πυργίσκῳ).[11]

---

[6] "Constantinopolis usque Antiochiam Luciani martyris exemplaria probat", *Prologus . . . in libro Paralipomenon.*

[7] *Ad Suniam et Fretelam*, 2: "In quo illud breviter admoneo, ut sciatis aliam esse editionem, quam Origenes et Caesariensis Eusebius, omnesque Graeciae tractatores κοινήν, id est "communem" appellant atque 'Vulgatam', et a plerisque nunc λουκιάνειος dicitur; aliam Septuaginta Interpretum, quae in ἑξαπλοῖς codicibus repperitur . . . Κοινή autem ista, hoc est communis editio ipsa est quae et Septuaginta. Sed hoc interest inter utramque, quod κοινή pro locis et temporibus, et pro voluntate scriptorum, vetus corrupta editio est."

[8] *In evangelistas ad Damasum praefatio*: "Praetermitto eos codices quos a Luciano et Hesychio nuncupatos, paucorum hominum asserit perversa contentio: quibus utique nec in toto Veteri instrumento emendare quid licuit, nec in Novo profuit emendasse: cum multarum gentium linguis scriptura ante translata, doceat falsa esse quae addita sunt" (*PL* 29, 527).

[9] See chapter 10: In the *Synopsis sacr. script.*: ἑβδόμη πάλιν καὶ τελευταία ἑρμηνεία τοῦ ἁγίου Λουκιανοῦ τοῦ μεγάλου ἀσκητοῦ καὶ μάρτυρος ("Finally, the seventh and last translation of St Lucian, the great ascetic and martyr", *PG* 28, 436).

[10] Suda, s.v. Λουκιανός· Λουκιανὸς ὁ μάρτυς . . . αὐτὸς ἁπάσας ἀναλαβὼν ἐκ τῆς Ἑβραΐδος ἐπανενεώσατο γλώττης ἣν καὶ αὐτὴν εἰς τὰ μάλιστα ἦν ἠκριβωκώς, πόνον τῇ ἐπανορθώσει πλεῖστον εἰσενεγκάμενος ("The martyr Lucian . . . returned personally to collect all [the Scriptures] in the Hebrew language in which he was quite an expert and he renewed them, making the best attempt at restoration").

[11] R. Devreesse, *Introduction à l'étude des manuscrits grecs*, Paris 1954, 119, n. 1: ἥτις ἔκδοσις μετὰ τὴν ἄθλησιν καὶ τὸ μαρτύριον τοῦ ἁγίου Λουκιανοῦ, τῆς τοῦ

According to Barthélemy, this is a process of idealising the Lucianic recension which even goes so far as to make it a new translation from Hebrew. A contributory factor is that at a certain moment the copyists began to interpret the sign *lambda omicron* (λ) as Λουκιανός, when in fact it refers to οἱ λοιποί ("the other interpreters").[12]

The key to interpreting this siglum is found in an editorial note that circulated after the 10th century in some manuscripts of Theodoret of Cyr in his Commentary on the Twelve Prophets, published by J. Phelipeau in 1630.[13] After mentioning various Hexaplaric sigla that appear in the manuscripts the copyist continued: ἐν οἷς δὲ τὸ λ, μέσον ἔχον τὸ ο', Λουκιανοῦ ("Those which have λ with an omicron in the middle, by Lucian"). Field speaks of Lucian in connection with the Hexapla as is apparent from the following words: "Luciani editio ad hexapla nostra non alio modo pertinet quam Hebraei, Syri et Samaritani selectae lectiones, quas omnes non in opere Origenis arquetypo per sex columnas descripto, sed in margine exemplarium versionis τῶν ο' hexaplaris inclusas fuisse credibile est."[14]

Montfaucon always interpreted the siglum λ as οἱ λοιποί. Field, instead, after suppressing the name Lucian in most of his edition, when he came across the siglum Ϫ of the Syro-Hexapla to 2 Kgs 9:9, understood its real meaning, i.e. Λουκιανός. This did not remove the ambiguity since by the working method of this exegete

---

Διοκλητιανοῦ καὶ Μαξιμιανοῦ καταληξάσης μανίας εὕρηται ἐξ ἰδιοχείρου γεγραμμένη ἐν Νικομηδείᾳ ἐπὶ Κωσταντίνου τοῦ Βασιλέως παρὰ Ἰουδαίοις ἐν πυργίσκῳ μαρμαρίνῳ καὶ κεκονιαμένῳ ("That edition after the combat and martyrdom of St Lucian, once the anger of Diocletian and Maximin had abated, was found written in his handwriting in Nicomedia under Constantine in Jewish circles in a wall of whitewashed marble"). The similarity of this account with the find of the *quinta* is suspicious, see chapter 10, p. 156.

[12] D. Barthélemy, (unpublished) conference at Oxford in 1970. Some of these ideas are included in D. Barthélemy, "'Les problèmes textuels de 2 Sam 11, 2–1 Rois 2, 11' reconsidérés à la lumière de certains critiques des 'Devanciers d'Aquila'", *1972 Proceedings IOSCS Pseudepigrapha*, Missoula, Mont. 1972, 16–88, reprinted in D. Barthélemy, *Études d'histoire du texte de'Ancien Testament*, Freiburg–Göttingen 1978, 218–55, especially pp. 243–54. See also Dörrie's reservations concerning the Lucianic recension in "Zur Geschichte der LXX im Jahrhundert Konstantins", *ZNW* 39 (1940), 57–110.

[13] J. Phelipeau, *Oseas primus inter Prophetas. Commentarius illustratus auctore Joanne Phellippaeo Societatis Iesu*, Paris 1630.

[14] F. Field, *Origenis Hexaplorum quae supersunt*, LXXXIV. It is based, therefore, on the prologue of two manuscripts of the Bodleian which contain the translation into Arabic of the Syro-Hexaplaric version of the Pentateuch, by Hârit ibn Sinan (10th century) and where the siglum Ϫ is included, meaning Λουκιανός.

in many passages the readings of "the three" and of Lucian could coincide.

Mercati, instead, reacted against Dörrie's over-scepticism on the possibility of transmitting Lucianic readings: all the readings preceded by this siglum without the article would have to be collected and compared with variants from the Lucianic group of manuscripts to obtain more exact results.[15] In his edition of the Twelve Prophets, Ziegler carried out this exhaustive study in respect of ms. 86 (= *Barb. gr. 549*): he distinguished twenty-two cases in which the siglum has to be interpreted as Lucian and twenty-three in which it definitely means the other interpreters.[16] Similarly in the book of Ezekiel, at least eight of the fourteen readings preceded by this siglum are backed up by Lucianic mss and the quotations by Chrysostom and Theodoret, so that in these cases it must be interpreted as Lucian.[17] After a study of this siglum in several manuscripts of 1–2 Kings, I have concluded that in these books it has to be understood as οἱ λοιποί (the other interpreters).[18] It seems clear therefore that the siglum λ can refer both to Lucian and to the other interpreters and that only a thorough analysis of its readings, comparing them with those from Lucianic manuscripts, can resolve the ambiguity in each case.[19]

Thus the siglum with the meaning of Λουκιανός is only found occasionally in the margins of some manuscripts. Accordingly his recensional work is to be found preferably in the groups of LXX manuscripts that have been revised with particular characteristics. And on this point research has focused since the close of the 19th century.

b) *History of Research*

One of the manuscripts that form the basis of the Complutensian Polyglot in the historical books is ms. 108 (*Vat. Graec.* 330). Therefore, this Polyglot exhibits, even if by accident, a Lucianic or Antiochene

---

[15] G. Mercati, "Di alcune testimonianze antiche".

[16] J. Ziegler, *Septuaginta XIII Duodecim Prophetae*, Göttingen 1967, 71–73.

[17] J. Ziegler, *Septuaginta XVI Ezechiel*, Göttingen 1952, 45.

[18] N. Fernández Marcos, "La sigla 'lambda omicron'".

[19] For example, the siglum *lambda omicron* also occurs in the Pentateuch in ms. *Athos Pantocrator* 24 (= Brooke–McLean's *v*, Wevers' 344). Wevers has decomposed this abbreviation into οι λ, i.e. "the other interpreters" in every case and perhaps with reason, as the Lucianic recension has not been identified in the Pentateuch. However, Brooke–McLean maintained the siglum *lambda omicron* to be different from

text in those books.[20] Ceriani and Field were the first to notice that
mss 19–82–93–108, in the historical books, coincide with quotations
from the Antiochene Fathers and with quotations preceded by the
siglum λ (*lamadh*) in the Syro-Hexapla.[21] In 1883, P. de Lagarde, in
an attempt to isolate and publish separately the Lucianic recension
as a first step towards going back to the edition of the original LXX,
extended the results of his research on the book of Ruth to the rest
of the Octateuch, assuming that the text of the manuscripts was uniform throughout all the books.[22] This methodological mistake by De
Lagarde was noted and corrected by Dahse, Hautsch and Rahlfs.
Dahse discovered the Lucianic recension for Genesis in the mss *fir*
(= 53–56–129 of Rahlfs).[23] Hautsch concludes that mss *gn* (= 54–75
of Rahlfs), are the ones that agree most with quotations in the
Antiochene Fathers Theodoret and Chrysostom.[24] Moore came to
the same conclusion for Judges, though he noted that the manuscripts change family or textual filiation from book to book and even
within the same book: thus *Codex Washingtonianus* in Deuteronomy
has many readings in common with mss 54–75, though this does
not apply to Judges. Furthermore, he insists that all analytical research
has to divest itself of the prejudice of looking for the three expected
recensions. If one group of manuscripts has a series of readings in
common this does not mean to say that it has the characteristics of
a recension in the strict sense. It could simply represent a local variety of a common text.[25]

Rahlfs distinguishes two groups of Lucianic manuscripts for the
books of Kings, one comprising the better quality mss 82–93, the
other mss 19–108.[26] And he establishes how in Psalms, the Lucianic
recension has become the official text of the Greek Church.[27] For

---

οι λ, as can be seen in their Hexaplar apparatus on Ex. 32:1; 34:29; Lev. 25:22;
26:44 and in Numbers and Deuteronomy *passim*.

[20] N. Fernández Marcos, "El texto griego de la Complutense", *Anejo a la edición
facsímile de la Biblia Políglota Complutense*, Valencia 1987, 33–42.

[21] B. M. Metzger, "The Lucianic Recension of the Greek Bible".

[22] P. de Lagarde, *Librorum Veteris Testamenti pars prior*, Göttingen 1883. In fact mss
19–108 are Lucianic from Ruth 4:11, but not in the Pentateuch.

[23] J. Dahse, "Zum Luciantext der Genesis".

[24] E. Hautsch, "Der Lukiantext des Oktateuchs".

[25] G. F. Moore, "The Antiochian Recension of the Septuagint".

[26] A. Rahlfs, *Lucians Rezension der Königsbücher*, 51–80. See also J. R. Busto Saiz,
"On the Lucianic Manuscripts in 1–2 Kings", *VI Congress of the IOSCS*, 1987, 305–10.

[27] A. Rahlfs, *Septuaginta-Studien 2. Der Text des Septuaginta-Psalters*, Göttingen 1907,
169ff.

Ruth, he agrees with Hautsch that the Lucianic text is transmitted to us in mss 54–75 and others, and from Ruth 4:11 also in mss 19–108 as well as in the books of Kings.[28] However, in his edition of Genesis he is much more cautious with respect to the possibility of isolating that recension and concludes that at most it occurs in ms. 75.[29]

When the critical editions of Göttingen began to stratify the manuscript material in a more complex and systematic way, the group of manuscripts of this recension in the prophetic books as well as their distinctive characteristics became much clearer. Up to now the Lucianic recension has been observed in all the prophetic books, in the books of Maccabees, in Judith and in 1–2 Ezra. In the Writings published so far it should be noted that in Wisdom and Sira it seems to be present in mss 248–493–637 but not so clearly as in the Prophets, for two reasons:

1. There are very few quotations from Theodoret and Chrysostom as a check on the recension of these books.
2. Many of these quotations have no Hebrew *Vorlage* to supply, through the Hexapla, a large number of the corrections of the Lucianic recension.[30]

In Job, instead, it occurs clearly in the Codex Alexandrinus, the *Codex Venetus* (V, from Job 30:8), in the minuscules 575–637 as well as in the commentaries on the book of Job by Julian the Arian and by Chrysostom.[31]

The debate remains open about the existence of this recension for the Octateuch. In a study of the lists of Canaanite nations, Thornhill concludes that although ms. *n* is on its own in Genesis and Exodus, as one progresses through the Octateuch it is supported by others together with which it forms a group. This group, which in Ruth covers mss glnowe₂ of Brooke–McLean, is related to the Old Latin and is Lucianic.[32]

The quotations by Chrysostom and Theodoret continue to be the weak point when identifying the Lucianic text. In a joint study of Genesis, A. Sáenz-Badillos and I concluded that no group of man-

---

[28] A. Rahlfs, *Das Buch Ruth griechisch als Probe einer kritischen Handausgabe der Septuaginta*, Stuttgart 1922, 4 and 16–17.

[29] A. Rahlfs, *Septuaginta. I Genesis*, Stuttgart 1926, 28–29.

[30] J. Ziegler, "Hat Lukian den griechischen Sirach rezensiert", 213ff.

[31] See J. Ziegler, *Septuaginta . . . IX,4 Iob*, Göttingen 1982, 86.124.

[32] See J. Ziegler, *Septuaginta . . . IX,4 Iob*, Göttingen 1982, 86.124.

uscripts contained systematically the text used by Theodoret of Cyr, but at most one could speak of an Antiochene text because a particular group of mss is closer to Theodoret's text.[33] In his recent history of the text of the various books of the Pentateuch, Wevers reaches a similar conclusion, i.e. that there are no proofs for the existence of a Lucianic text in Genesis, which agrees with Chrysostom and Theodoret. These authors follow a mixed text, and if there had been a Lucianic recension in Genesis they did not know it.[34]

It might be thought that the difficulty of determining the Lucianic recension in the Octateuch came from the fluctuation of Theodoret's text, since as it is not established by any modern critical edition it is not possible to derive objective conclusions. To remove this difficulty, we decided to edit critically Theodoret's *Quaestiones in Octateuchum*, an edition with many chapters missing. However, in connection with the problem of the Lucianic recension in the Octateuch we have reached much more nuanced conclusions, for even though it cannot be identified from Theodoret's text in the first books of the Octateuch, at least a typically Antiochene text emerges in the last three books.[35]

However, no-one has doubted the peculiar nature of the Lucianic or Antiochene text in the historical books (Samuel–Kings–Chronicles). No only that, but as the new documents from Qumran are being published and the plurality of texts around that change of era emerges, that text was at the forefront of most of the debate concerning the pluralism of the biblical text. Accordingly, once the critical text of Theodoret had been established as a control of the Antiochene text in those books,[36] it seemed convenient to us to edit critically the

---

[33] N. Fernández Marcos and A. Sáenz-Badillos, *Anotaciones críticas al texto griego del Génesis*, Madrid–Barcelona 1972, 73ff. and 125.

[34] Apart from the studies on this topic in successive histories of the Greek text of the Pentateuch published in the MSU of Göttingen between 1974 and 1992, see also J. W. Wevers, "A Lucianic Recension in Genesis?", *BIOSCS* 6 (1973), 22–35 and Wevers, "Theodoret's *Quaest.* and the Byzantine Text". Nor is there a Lucianic recension in the book of Esther, see R. Hanhart, *Septuaginta . . . VIII–3 Esther*, Göttingen 1967, 97, and J.-C. Haelewyck, "Le texte dit 'lucianique' du livre d'Esther. Son étendue et sa cohérence", *Le Muséon* 98 (1985), 5–44.

[35] N. Fernández Marcos and A. Sáenz-Badillos, *Theodoreti Cyrensis Quaestiones in Octateuchum*, LX–LXII, and N. Fernández Marcos, "Theodoret's Biblical Text in the Octateuch". For more nuanced conclusions concerning the book of Joshua, see S. Sipilä, "Theodoret of Cyrrhus and the Book of Joshua: Theodoret's *Quaestiones* Revisited", *Textus* 19 (1998), 157–70.

[36] N. Fernández Marcos and J. R. Busto Saiz, *Theodoreti Cyrensis Quaestiones in Reges et Paralipomena*, Madrid 1984.

Antiochene text from Samuel to Chronicles, a single, uniform text with very clear textual characteristics, unlike those in most of the text of the LXX.[37]

c) *Characteristics*

Although it is unlikely for all the characteristics of the Lucianic recension to appear in equal measure in the various books,[38] some of the more specific features can be noted which are of some guidance in those books where this recension has been studied best: Prophets, 1–3 Maccabees and 1 Ezra. In general, it can be stated that it tends to fill the gaps in the LXX in respect of the Hebrew text on the basis of additions taken from "the three", particularly from Symmachus. This procedure, combined with a certain freedom in handling the text, often gives rise to a series of doublets that are not in the LXX. It also inserts a series of interpolations (proper names instead of the corresponding pronoun, possessive pronouns, articles, conjunctions, making implicit subjects or objects explicit, etc.) which tend to clarify the sense or minimise incorrect grammar. It often resorts to changing a synonym, in most cases without it being possible to discover the reason for the change. At other times one notices a tendency to replace Hellenistic forms with Attic forms due to the influence of the grammarians of the time. There are also many grammatical and stylistic changes: of preposition, of simple to compound verbs, of person, number, etc.

The result is a full text with no omissions.[39] In his study on the history of the text in 1 Ezra, Hanhart agrees that the characteristics of this recension correspond to a large extent with those described in the Prophets and Maccabees.[40] The first recensional principle consists in correcting the text according to the corresponding Hebrew–Aramaic *Vorlage*; hence, Lucian supported most of the material from

---

[37] See Select Bibliography.

[38] Thus in books that have no Hebrew *Vorlage* the additions and omissions according to the *textus receptus*, generally taken from "the three", cannot be included, as is the case for the prophetic books.

[39] B. M. Metzger, "The Lucianic Recension of the Greek Bible", 24ff., and J. Ziegler, "Hat Lukian den griechischen Sirach rezensiert?" 219ff. And in general the section "Die Rezension des Lukians" in the introductions to the edition of the prophetic and wisdom books in the Göttingen series.

[40] R. Hanhart, *Text und Textgeschichte des 1. Esrabuches*, 20–28.

Origen's recension and therefore is late.[41] As a second principle of
the recension, subordinate to the first, especially noteworthy is the
tendency to make the text uniform and to explain it. This is particularly obvious where the Hebrew *Vorlage* is missing, as happens in
1 Esd. 3:1-5:6 (the episode of King Darius' three bodyguards) and
in the books of Maccabees. Here some mention must be made of
the correction of forms into Attic Greek, although never carried out
in a completely consistent way (restoration of the second aorist of
the 3rd person plural -ov instead of the Hellenistic -οσαν; replacing
the Hellenistic aorist passive of γίνεσθαι with the middle, etc.).
Prominent among these stylistic phenomena are the replacement of
a compound verb by a simple form, the insertion of a vocative, subject or pronoun, transpositions instead of the more classical hyperbaton, etc.

Together with these common features, which help to identify the
Lucianic recension in the various books, others have to be added of
a literary nature, valid at least for the historical books, where this
recension emerges more clearly. In these books the Antiochene text
completes what is unsaid or said only implicitly in the narrative
chain, often rewrites the phrase, adapting it stylistically to Greek
hyperbaton, and carries out another series of editorial interventions
that are theological, midrashic or simply cultic ("Gelehrtenkorrekturen").
In Samuel–Chronicles, then, it is an edited and revised text probably with a view to public reading.[42]

To summarise, it can be concluded from research over the last
few years that, whereas in the other books of the LXX the extent
and traits of the Lucianic recension have been nuanced in certain
ways and its existence has even been denied in some books,[43] in the
historical books it has been increasingly confirmed with more specific
characteristics.[44] This apparent paradox can be clarified by means

---

[41] For Joshua and Judges, see O. Pretzl, "Septuagintaprobleme im Buch der
Richter. Die griechischen Handschriftengruppen im Buch der Richter untersucht
nach ihrer Verhältnis zueinander", *Bib* 7 (1926), 233–69 and 353–83, especially for
the Lucianic recension 265–69; *Bib* 9 (1928), 377–427, especially 425–27.

[42] See N. Fernández Marcos, "Literary and Editorial Features".

[43] The existence of the Lucianic recension has been called into question, both
in the Pentateuch and in the book of Psalms, see A. Pietersma, "Proto-Lucian and
the Greek Psalter", *VT* 28 (1978), 66–72, and L. J. Perkins, "The So-called 'L'
Text of Psalms 72–82", *BIOSCS* 11 (1978), 44–63.

[44] See N. Fernández Marcos, "The Lucianic Text in the Book of Kingdoms".

of the following three statements, which can be used as guidelines for future research:

1. The Antioch recension of the LXX did not cover all the books of the Old Testament, or at least it has not been identified in all of them.
2. This recension was transmitted in a certain number of manuscripts. However, the manuscripts that transmit it change within the various groups of writings or even from book to book.
3. Although it has been possible to define some characteristics common to this extension as Antiochene, they are apparent in different degrees, depending on the book.

In other words, in terms of text, the Antiochene text of the Psalter is closer to the Byzantine text of the New Testament than to the Antiochene text of Samuel–Chronicles.[45]

From the earliest research it had already been noted that in the Lucianic recension there were two clearly differentiated components:

1. some late material, certainly post-Hexaplaric, included in the time of the historical Lucian;
2. an underlying layer of very ancient readings, earlier than the time of Lucian.

The hypothesis of the proto-Lucianic text has been used to explain this first layer of the recension and its insertion into the history of the LXX. This is perhaps, in Wevers' words, "the most difficult problem in modern Septuagint work",[46] which put the Lucianic recension to the forefront of debate in respect of the textual pluralism of the books of Samuel–Kings especially in the light of *Qumran Cave 4. Samuel.*

d) *Current Research and Future Prospects: The Proto-Lucianic Text*

By different paths the conclusion has been reached that several parts of the Old Latin (2nd century CE) contain Lucianic readings. Ceriani demonstrated this for Lamentations[47] and Vercellone for the mar-

---

[45] See N. Fernández Marcos, "Some Reflections on the Antiochian Text".
[46] J. W. Wevers, "Proto-Septuagint Studies", *The Seed of Wisdom; Fs. T. J. Meek*, Toronto 1964, 58–77, p. 69: "All in all, the so-called proto-Lucianic text is to my mind the most difficult problem in modern Septuagint work."
[47] A. M. Ceriani, *Monumenta sacra et profana* II, 2.

ginal glosses to the *Codex Legionensis* that do not agree with the common LXX but with mss 19–82–93–108, which are Lucianic in character, in Samuel–Kings.[48] Burkitt established that in the Prophets the Old Latin sometimes relied on the Lucianic text.[49]

The variety of data and their different origins do not make likely Dieu's thesis according to which the quotations from the Old Latin were subsequently retouched in the Lucianic sense.[50]

The same result is obtained from examining the quotations from Latin authors earlier than Lucian. Although Rahlfs concluded in his study on the books of Kings that no Latin author before Lucifer of Cagliari (d. 371) contained Lucianic readings, Cappelle's monograph on the Latin Psalter in Africa shows that Tertullian and Cyprian did know a proto-Lucianic recension.[51] According to Stockmayer, the Peshitta of 1 Samuel also contains Lucianic readings.[52] Although there are still many unexplained problems around the date of its composition, many think that the Peshitta comes from the 2nd/3rd centuries CE; in that case it would contain remains of the proto-Lucianic text.

Several Greek witnesses point in the same direction. In the first place, the text used by Josephus in his *Antiquities*, written towards the end of the 1st century CE, is Lucianic in type from Samuel to Maccabees, exactly as was noted by A. Mez and later corroborated by Thackeray.[53] With a few improvements, these results have been confirmed by more recent research by Ulrich and Spottorno.[54] Instead, there are serious doubts about other supposed witnesses of the proto-Lucianic text such as Pap. John Rylands 458 to Deuteronomy

---

[48] C. Vercellone, *Variae lectiones Vulgatae latinae bibliorum editionis*, Rome I, 1860; II, 1864.

[49] F. C. Burkitt, *The Rules of Tyconius*, Cambridge 1894.

[50] Dieu, "Retouches lucianiques".

[51] B. M. Metzger, "The Lucianic Recension of the Greek Bible", 38ff., and P. Capelle, *Le texte du Psautier latin en Afrique*, Rome 1913.

[52] T. Stockmayer, "Hat Lukian zu seiner Septuaginta-revision die Peschito benützt?" *ZAW* 12 (1892), 218–23.

[53] A. Mez, *Die bibel des Josephus untersucht für Buch V–VII der Archäologie*, Basle 1895, and H. St J. Thackeray, *Josephus: the Man and the Historian*, New York 1929, 85: "the Josephan Biblical Text is uniformly of this Lucianic type from I Samuel to I Maccabees", and on p. 86, "Next to 'Lucian', the Biblical text most nearly allied to the historian's is that of Symmachus."

[54] E. C. Ulrich, *The Qumran Text of Samuel and Josephus*, and Ulrich, "Josephus Biblical Text for the Books of Samuel", *Josephus*, 1989, 81–96, pp. 92–93; V. Spottorno, "Some Remarks on Josephus Biblical Text for 1–2 Kings", *VI Congress of the IOSCS*, Abbreviated titles 1987, 277–85.

(*c.* 150 BCE) or Pap. 2054 of Rahlfs (2nd/3rd century CE) which contains the text of Psalm 77:1-18.[55]

The other important witness of the proto-Lucianic continues to be the Old Latin, which in the historical books follows for preference a Greek text of Antiochene type. Of course, before being used as a witness of the proto-Lucianic text the material must be examined critically and what is original separated from what is recensional in that text.[56]

The hypothesis of the proto-Lucianic recension has been put forward chiefly on the basis of the historical books. The problem has become more acute with the discovery of Hebrew texts in Qumran differing from the *textus receptus* (especially 4QSamᵃ) which also agree in Samuel with the text of the Antiochene manuscripts 19–108–82–93–127.[57] On the other hand, Barthélemy's studies have set the proto-Lucianic recension within the frame of the Palestine καίγε revision, defining it as the old LXX "plus ou moins abâtardie et corrompue",[58] although later, besides the καίγε recension, he accepted in the book of Kings "une recension grécisante assez étendue subie par le texte de boc_2e_2".[59] In his dissertation on the recensions in the books of Samuel and later in a short study, S. P. Brock reacted against Barthélemy's over-simplification: the text of the mss boc_2e_2 did not contain the original LXX. That text had acquired its definitive form in a period very close to Lucian, but many of its distinctive traits were pre-Lucianic and in future the task will be to separate Lucianic from pre-Lucianic elements in that text.[60]

---

[55] The Lucianic character of these witnesses has been called into question by J. W. Wevers, "The Earliest Witness to the LXX Deuteronomy", *CBQ* 39 (1977), 240–44, and A. Pietersma, "Proto-Lucian and the Greek Psalter" 72.

[56] See R. Hanhart, "Ursprünglicher Septuagintatext und lukianische Rezension des 2. Esrabuches im Verhältnis zur Textform der Vetus Latina", 113–15, and N. Fernández Marcos, *Scribes and Translators: Septuagint and Old Latin in the Books of Kings*, Leiden 1994, 41–87.

[57] See S. Talmon, "Aspects of the Textual Transmission of the Bible in the Light of Qumran Manuscripts", *Textus* 4 (1964), 95–132; F. M. Cross, "The History of the Biblical Text in the Light of Discoveries in the Judaean Desert", *HTR* 57 (1964), 281–99; Cross, "The Evolution of a Theory of Local Texts", *Qumran and the History of the Biblical Text*, ed. F. M. Cross and S. Talmon, Cambridge, Mass.–London 1975, 306–20.

[58] D. Barthélemy, *Les Devanciers d'Aquila*. VTS 10, Leiden 1963, 127.

[59] D. Barthélemy, "Les problèmes textuels de 2 Sam 11,2–1 Rois 2,11", 28, reprinted in Barthélemy, *Études d'histoire du texte de l'Ancien Testament*, Fribourg–Göttingen 1978, 224.

[60] S. P. Brock, *The Recensions of the Septuaginta Version of I Samuel*, Turin 1996, 297–307, and Brock, "Lucian 'redivivus'", 180.

We are still far from having recovered the original LXX in this section of Samuel. In these five Antiochene manuscripts there are recensional elements of a stylistic nature with the aim of making the Greek text more readable. E. Tov returned to the topic, adopting an intermediate position between Barthélemy and Cross: for Tov the substrate of mss 19–108–82–93–127 contains either the ancient LXX or *an* ancient LXX, leaving the way open to other translations as different and as old as the claimed original LXX. In other words, there is not enough recensional foundation to sustain the proto-Lucianic hypothesis.[61]

There remains much work to be done in the historical books for a more precise definition of the proto-Lucianic recension. For a definitive reply we shall have to wait until the Hebrew texts from Qumran are published and the Greek material from these books is stratified in suitable critical editions. The publication of complete indexes to the Antiochene text would also enable the Lucianic material to be separated from the proto-Lucianic. Meanwhile, like E. Ulrich, I think that the proto-Lucianic is a fact,[62] although the component of a revision in favour of a Palestinian type of Hebrew text such as 4QSam^a is not proved, as Cross would wish. This is because there is no doubt that the relationship of 4QSam^a with the text of the LXX, a well-established kinship, is not at the same level as its relationship with the Antiochene text, which rests on a handful of weaker agreements.[63] However, what cannot be ignored is the stylistic component of this revision detected by Brock and already present in the early layer of these five manuscripts, the so-called proto-Lucianic.[64] The separation of the Antiochene tradition contained in these five manuscripts from the remainder of the LXX has in all likelihood to be dated to the 1st century CE. Now the geographic or historical conditions of Asia Minor do not justify a separate transmission of the Antiochene text against most of the LXX text. This is why I resorted to the hypothesis that the proto-Lucianic must have been a stylistic revision by the Jews of Alexandria in view of the

---

[61] E. Tov, "Lucian and Proto-Lucian".

[62] E. C. Ulrich, "4QSam^a and Septuagintal Research", *BIOSCS* 8 (1975), 26–27.

[63] See N. Fernández Marcos, "The Lucianic Text in the Books of Kingdoms", 170–72.

[64] S. P. Brock, "A Doublet and its Ramifications", *Bib* 56 (1975), 550–53, and Brock, "Bibelübersetzungen", *TRE* VI, 1980, 163–72 and 177–78.

important Jewish colony in Antioch in the 1st century CE.[65] It is difficult to prove when we are using such scant and fragmentary data – the lack of quotations from Antiochene Fathers before 300 CE, the fact that the tendencies of revision are the same in the proto-Lucianic as in the Lucianic, etc. – but at least there are plausible indications of that revision which would explain the traces that it in turn has left in the quotations by Josephus and in the Old Latin.

Beyond the books of Kings, where the debate has been more intense, we can conclude with Hanhart, on the basis of the tradition duly studied from Prophets and Maccabees:

1. that in these books there has been a post-Hexaplaric reworking of the text which must have taken place in Antioch and so can be called Lucianic;
2. that this recension, especially when it agrees with the Old Latin and/or Josephus, either in itself or through the Hexaplaric recension, bears an older pre-Hexaplar tradition;
3. that the pre-Hexaplaric character of this material is no criterion for originality, since to a large extent it is based on an older work of recension.[66]

SELECT BIBLIOGRAPHY

Bardy, G., *Recherches sur St. Lucien d'Antioche et son école*, Paris 1936, especially 164–77.
Brock, S. P., "Lucian 'redivivus': Some Reflections on Barthélemy's 'Les Devanciers d'Aquila'". *Studia Evangelica* V (1968) = TU 103, 176–81.
Busto Saiz, J. R., "The Antiochene Text in 2 Samuel 22". *VIII Congress of the IOSCS*, 1995, 131–43.
Cantera, J., "Puntos de contacto de la 'Vetus Latina' con la recensión de Luciano y con otras recensiones griegas". *Sefarad* 25 (1965), 69–72.

---

[65] N. Fernández Marcos, "El Protolucianico, ¿revisión griega de los judíos de Antioquía?"

[66] R. Hanhart, *Septuaginta VIII-3 Esther*, Göttingen 1966, 95 n. 1.

As for the later influence of the Lucianic recension, we have seen how in the Psalter it became the official text of the Orthodox Church. The Gothic Bible, translated by Ulfilas in the second half of the 4th century, is from a Lucianic text; and similarly, the translation into Slavonic by Cyril and Methodius was made from this recension. Finally, the Syriac version known as Philoxenian, the work of Philoxenus of Mabug (Hierapolis) in the patriarchate of Antioch, follows a Lucianic text, as is proved by the addition to Is. 9:6 that it includes. Its existence was unknown until 1868 when A. M. Ceriani edited part of Isaiah in *Monumenta sacra et profana*, V, see F. Kauffmann, "Beiträge zur Quellenkritik der gothischen Bibel Uebersetzung. Vorbemerkungen, I, Die alttestamentlichen Bruchstücke", *Zeitschrift für deutsche Philologie* 29 (1897), 306–37.

Dahse, J., "Zum Luciantext der Genesis". *ZAW* 30 (1910), 281–87.

Deconinck, J., *Essai sur la chaîne de l'Octateuque avec une édition des Commentaires de Diodore de Tarse*, Paris 1912.

Dieu, L., "Retouches lucianiques sur quelques textes de la vieille version latine (I et II Samuel)". *RB* ns 16 (1919), 372–403.

Fernández Marcos, N., "El Protoluciánico, ¿revisión griega de los judíos de Antioquía?". *Bib* 64 (1983), 423–27.

———, N., "La sigla 'lambda omicron' (λ) en I–II Reyes-LXX". *Sefarad* 38 (1978), 243–62.

———, N., "Literary and Editorial Features of the Antiochian Text in Kings". *VI Congress of the IOSCS*, 287–304.

———, N., "Some Reflections on the Antiochian Text of the Septuagint". *Studien zur Septuaginta*, 1990, 219–29.

———, N., "The Antiochian Text of I–II Chronicles". *VII Congress of the IOSCS*, 1991, 301–11.

———, N., "The Lucianic Text in the Books of Kingdoms: From Lagarde to the Textual Pluralism". *De Septuaginta*, 1984, 161–75.

Fernández Marcos, N., "Theodoret's Biblical Text in the Octateuch". *BIOSCS* 11 (1978), 27–43.

———, N., and A. Saenz-Badillos, *Theodoreti Cyrensis Quaestiones in Octateuchum. Editio critica*, Madrid 1979.

———, N., and J. R. Busto Saiz, *El texto antioqueno de la Biblia griega, I, 1–2 Samuel*, with the collaboration of V. Spottorno Díaz-Caro and S. P. Cowe, Madrid 1989; *II, 1–2 Reyes*, with the collaboration of V. Spottorno Díaz-Caro, Madrid 1992; *III, 1–2 Crónicas*, with the collaboration of V. Spottorno Díaz-Caro and S. P. Cowe, Madrid 1996.

Field, F., *Origenis Hexaplorum quae supersunt*, Oxford 1875, LXXXIV–XCIII.

Fischer, B., "Lukian-Lesarten in der 'Vetus Latina' der Vier Königsbücher". *Studia Anselmiana* 27–28 (1951), 169–77.

Hanhart, R., *Text und Textgeschichte des 1. Esrabuches*. MSU XII, Göttingen 1974.

———, R., "Ursprünglicher Septuagintatext und lukianische Rezension des 2. Esrabuches im Verhältnis zur Textform der Vetus Latina". *Philologia Sacra. Biblische und patristische Studien für Hermann J. Frede und Walter Thiele zu ihrem siebzigsten Geburtstag I*, ed. R. Gryson, Freiburg, 1993, 90–115.

Hautsch, E., "Der Lukiantext des Oktateuchs". MSU I = NGWGött (1909), 518–43.

Jellicoe, S., *SMS*, 157–76.

Mercati, G., "Di alcune testimonianze antiche sulle cure bibliche di San Luciano". *Bib* 24 (1943), 1–17.

Metzger, B. M., "The Lucianic Recension of the Greek Bible". *Chapters in the History of New Testament Textual Criticism*, Leiden 1963, 1–41.

Moore, G. F., "The Antiochian Recension of the Septuagint". *AJSL* 29 (1912–13), 37–62.

Pietersma, A., "Proto-Lucian and the Greek Psalter". *VT* 28 (1978), 66–72.

Rahlfs, A., *LXX-Studien III: Lucians Rezension der Königsbücher*, Göttingen 1911.

Spanneut, M., "La Bible d'Eustathe d'Antioche – Contribution à l'histoire de la 'version lucianique'". *Studia Patristica* 4 (1961) = TU 79, 171–90.

Swete, H. B., *An Introduction to the Old Testament in Greek*, Cambridge 1914.

Taylor, B. A., *The Lucianic Manuscripts of 1 Reigns. Vol. 1, Majority Text. Vol. 2, Analysis*, Atlanta, Ga. 1992 and 1993.

Thornhill, R., "Six or Seven Nations: A Pointer to the Lucianic Text in the Heptateuch with Special Reference to the Old Latin Version". *JTS* ns 10 (1959), 233–46.

Tisserant, E., "Notes sur la recension lucianique d'Ézéchiel". *RB* ns 8 (1911), 384–90.

Tov, E., "Lucian and Proto-Lucian". *RB* 79 (1972), 101–13.

————, E. (ed.), *The Hebrew and Greek Texts of Samuel*, Jerusalem 1980.

Ulrich, E. C., *The Qumran Text of Samuel and Josephus*, Missoula, Mont. 1978.

Vaccari, A., "Fragmentum Biblicum saeculi II ante Christum". *Bib* 17 (1936), 501–504.

Wevers, J. W., "Theodoret's *Quaest.* and the Byzantine Text". *Henoch* 13 (1991), 29–64.

Ziegler, J., "Hat Lukian den griechischen Sirach rezensiert?". *Bib* 40 (1959), 210–29.

CHAPTER FIFTEEN

HESYCHIAN RECENSION OR ALEXANDRIAN GROUP OF MANUSCRIPTS?

In 1975, J. W. Wevers stated that "the Hesychian recension still remains unidentified".[1] A century after the pioneering work of Lagarde with his programmatic declaration of separating out the three recensions mentioned by Jerome so as to attain the primitive LXX, the Göttingen project continues research in the direction begun by its founder, but distancing itself from the simplistic image of the three classical recensions. We have just seen how Lucian's recension has yet to be identified in the Pentateuch; and even the most-known, the Hexaplaric recension, is difficult to trace in certain books such as Chronicles. On the other hand, other textual families emerge that are different from these three, without any particular recensional base and they vary according to book. What happens with the Hesychian recension?

a) *Ancient Witnesses*

Our information about this recension is exclusively from two passages of Jerome that contradict each other: the well-known prologue to the book of Chronicles, "Alexandria et Aegyptus in Septuaginta suis Hesychium laudat auctorem,"[2] and the prologue to the evangelists, "Praetermitto eos codices quos a Luciano et Hesychio nuncupatos paucorum hominum adserit perversa contentio, quibus utique nec in Veteri instrumento post septuaginta interpretes emendare quid licuit nec in Novo profuit emendasse, cum multarum gentium linguis Scriptura ante translata doceat falsa esse quae addita sunt."[3]

---

[1] J. W. Wevers, "The Göttingen Septuagint", *BIOSCS* 8 (1975), 19–23, p. 22. See also P. de Lagarde, *Librorum Veteris Testamenti Canonicorum Pars Prior Graece*, Göttingen 1883 IIIff., and earlier, Wevers, *Ammerkungen zur griechischen Übersetzung der Proverbien*, Göttingen 1863, 3.

[2] Jerome, *Prologus . . . in libro Paralipomenon.*

[3] Jerome, *Praefatio . . . in Evangelio.*

Jerome's statements cannot be accepted unreservedly. According to Vaccari,[4] in the second paragraph the reference is only to the New Testament; Jellicoe instead thinks that his proposals concern both the Old and New Testaments.[5]

This reference, therefore, can serve as a *terminus ad quem* for the Hesychian recension. In the *Decretum Gelasianum* V, 3, 8–9, it says expressly: "evangelia quae falsavit Hesychius Apocrypha".[6] However today it is accepted that this condemnation is the result of a misunderstanding about Jerome's critical remarks on Hesychius.[7]

The difficulty in identifying the author of this recension is that Hesychius was a common name in early Christianity. In the *Dictionary of Christian Biography* there are twenty-seven different people with the same name. The best known is the lexicographer from the 5th century, whom some have claimed to identify as the biblical scholar. However, these two authors have nothing in common except their name. On the other hand, apparently the lexicographer was not a Christian and the Christian glosses and allusions to Christian writers come from a later hand. Finally, if he were a Christian he would not have lived before the 5th/6th century CE.[8]

Others have considered Hesychius to be an Egyptian bishop who died in the persecution of Diocletian, co-writer with two others of a letter to Meletios, schismatic bishop of Licopolis.[9] However, this identification is no more than mere conjecture and is not accepted uncritically by any scholar. Furthermore it would be difficult to connect him with the Alexandrian group of manuscripts represented by this recension since its characteristics already appear in Papyrus 965 from the first half of the 3rd century CE. In Ziegler's opinion, this papyrus is the chief witness against the Hesychian recension.[10] Are we perhaps looking for the author of a recension that never existed? As we shall see, this recension is barely tangible and impossible to pin down chronologically.

---

[4] A. Vaccari, "The Hesychian Recension of the Bible".

[5] S. Jellicoe, "The Hesychian Recension Reconsidered".

[6] In *De libris recipiendis et non recipiendis*, *PL* 59, 162.

[7] See E. von Dobschütz, *Das Decretum Gelasianum*. TU 38, 4, Leipzig 1912.

[8] K. Latte (ed.), *Hesychii Alexandrini Lexicon* I, Copenhagen 1953, VIII: "Sexto igitur quam quinto saeculo Hesychium potius adsignabis, nec scribae et auctoris officia coniuncta (αὐτὸς ἰδίᾳ χειρὶ γράφων) priori tempora pati videntur. Quamquam haec quidem omnia incerta sunt."

[9] Eusebius, *Hist. Ecc.* VIII, 13,7.

[10] J. Ziegler, *Septuaginta XIV. Isaias*, Göttingen 1939, 23.

b) *The History of Research*

Against the identification of this recension the Göttingen editors exhibit increasing uncertainty and scepticism. Grave was the first to expound the theory of identifying this recension as the Vatican Codex in his "Letter to Mill" (1705),[11] a theory accepted until very recently. De Lagarde,[12] Swete,[13] Nestle,[14] Cornill,[15] Ceriani,[16] McLean,[17] Ottley[18] and Rahlfs have maintained that a Hesychian text is reflected in some manuscripts, although the specialists did not agree on which. In his study of the text of the psalter, Rahlfs discovers it in Cyril of Alexandria, in the Vatican and Alexandrian codices (although here with Hexaplaric influence), in papyrus Amh VI (an Egyptian fragment from the 7th century), in certain minuscules (especially ms. 55) and in the Bohairic version, which in turn influenced the translations into Arabic and the Ethiopic Psalter.[19] However, in his 1931 edition of the Psalms, the same author does not mention the Hesychian recension. And in his manual edition of the LXX (1935) Rahlfs states categorically: "Es ist bisher noch nicht sicher gelungen diese dritte Rezension nachzuweisen."[20]

In the critical editions that have appeared so far in the Göttingen series, no group of manuscripts is labelled "recension of Hesychius". At most they speak of an Alexandrian group of manuscripts and it is described in very watered-down terms, falling short of an actual recension. The same type of scepticism is shown by H. Dörrie, who even calls it a "legendarische Rezension",[21] and F. G. Kenyon who

---

[11] *J. E. Grabii Epistola ad Clarissimum Virum Dn. Joannem Millium . . . qua ostenditur Libri Judicum Genuinam LXX. Interpretum Versionem eam esse quam Ms. Codex "Alexandrinus" exhibet. "Romenam" autem Editionem, quod ad dictum Librum ab illa prorsus diversam atque eandem cum "Hesychiana" esse*, Oxford 1705.

[12] P. de Lagarde, *Genesis Graece*, Leipzig 1868, 21.

[13] H. B. Swete, *An Introduction to the Old Testament in Greek*, 78ff. and 481ff.

[14] E. Nestle, in *A Dictionary of the Bible*, ed. J. Hastings, London–New York, 1898–1904, IV, 445b.

[15] C. H. Cornill, *Das Buch des Propheten Ezechiel*, Leipzig 1886, 66ff.

[16] A. Ceriani, *De Codice Marchaliano . . . Commentatio*, Rome 1890, 48ff. and 105ff.

[17] N. McLean, in *JTS* 2 (1901), 305–308, p. 306.

[18] R. R. Ottley, *The Book of Isaiah According to the LXX (Codex Alexandrinus)*, Cambridge 1904, I, 6ff. and 14ff.

[19] A. Rahlfs, *Septuaginta-Studien II*, 183–97 and 235–36.

[20] A. Rahlfs, *Septuaginta*, Stuttgart 1935, XIV.

[21] H. Dörrie, "Zur Geschichte der Septuaginta im Jahrhundert Konstantins", *ZNW* 39 (1940), 57–110.

maintains that the title "Hesychian" for B in the New Testament rests in fact on little more than "a shadow of shade".[22]

c) *Hesychian Recension or Alexandrian Revision?*

In more recent publications opinion continues to be divided. Some more positive judgements about this recension have emerged, as well as other indications that tend to revalorise it. However, at the same time the lack of criteria and of concrete characteristics to define it demand extreme caution. It is argued that the scant data we have on its author are not a reason for rejecting him from history if we remember that we know little more about Symmachus or Theodotion. In spite of such authoritative views as those of Ziegler or Rahlfs, who have denied the existence of this recension, Vaccari thinks that we can use the Coptic versions and the quotations of the Egyptian Fathers, especially the Alexandrian Fathers, from the 4th to the 5th centuries CE,[23] as a criterion for identifying it. For the historical books it would occur in mss M V 55 56 119 158 and those in its family. In Prophets, the Alexandrian group is principally made up of the mss A Q 26 86 106 198 and 233.[24] In his commentary on Is. 58:11, Jerome alludes to a passage that only occurs in the "Alexandrian copy" against B and S.[25] Therefore this passage, he insists, can be used as a key for further research on the recension. In examining the translations from Greek to Arabic and Coptic–Arabic, it is clear that ms. *ar.Vat.* 445 has this addition, in other words, that the Greek manuscript used by El 'Alam, a priest of Alexandria, belongs to this group. Similarly, the Arabic version of Daniel, also by El 'Alam, seems to follow Alexandrian manuscripts. This allows us to say, there-

---

[22] F. G. Kenyon, "Hesychius and the Text of the New Testament", 250. S. Jellicoe, *SMS*, 152.

[23] A. Vaccari, "The Hesychian Recension of the Bible".

[24] See, especially, J. Ziegler, *Septuaginta ... XIV. Isaias*, Göttingen 1967, 21–36, and Ziegler, *Septuaginta ... XIII Duodecim Prophetae*, Göttingen 1967, 39–53.

[25] καὶ τὰ ὀστᾶ σου ὡς βοτάνη ἀνατέλει καὶ πιανθήσεται (-σονται Cyr) καὶ κληρονομήσουσι(ν) γενεὰς γενεῶν ("And your bones shall sprout like a plant, they shall become fat and inherit many generations"), see J. Ziegler, *Isaias*, p. 339. And Jerome, *Comm. in Is.*, PL 24, 570: "Quod in Alexandrinis exemplaribus in principio huius capituli additum est: *Et adhuc in te erit laus mea semper*; et in fine: *et ossa tua quasi herba orientur, et pinguescent, et haereditate possidebunt in generationem et generationes*, in Hebraico non habetur, sed ne in Septuaginta quidem emendatis et veris exemplaribus: unde obelo praenotandum est."

fore, that there are indications of the Hesychian recension in the textual tradition of the Greek Old Testament.

So, as Jellicoe remarks, this addition could be even older than B and the exemplar of El 'Alam mentioned. This means that the text of B and S could be a revision of the Alexandrian text, i.e. the Hesychian recension, if B reproduces a revision based on the strictly Alexandrian principle of preference for the short reading.[26]

Groussouw concedes a place to this recension although he admits that it is the most problematic of all: the Bohairic version is a faithful representative of the Hesychian family.[27] Finally, in 1963 Jellicoe comes to the defence of the Hesychian recension using an old hypothesis formulated in a new perspective:[28] the Vatican Codex represents and relays a recension that it shortens, as can be seen in Judges, the text of Tobit and in Daniel-Theodotion. It has no textual uniformity. Its text is of inferior quality in Isaiah and corrupt in Chronicles–Ezra–Nehemiah. Its tendency to shorten is evident since the books of Maccabees are missing. Thus it would represent a recension begun in Alexandria for the churches of Egypt towards the end of the 3rd century CE, just as earlier Origen had made his recension for Palestine. Instead of being by one person it was a corporate enterprise in which the tendency to shorten was due more to necessity than to choice. The recension was interrupted by persecution, so that the books of Maccabees were excluded. In this hypothesis, B would be the work of a scribe who, following the Alexandrian principle initiated by Aristarchus and continued by his successors in editing the classics, adopted the shortest reading as the best. It should also not be forgotten that the number and sequence of Old and New Testament books in the Vatican Codex correspond exactly to those in the canon of scriptures set out by Athanasius of Alexandria in 367, in his festive letter number 39.[29]

However, this hypothesis, if we except a few incidental agreements, seems to ignore the researches of the Göttingen editors who

---

[26] S. Jellicoe, *SMS*, 155.

[27] W. Groussouw, *The Coptic Versions of the Minor Prophets*, Rome 1938, 101–103.

[28] S. Jellicoe, "The Hesychian Recension Reconsidered", and J. W. Wevers, "A Study in the Textual History of Codex Vaticanus in the Books of Kings", *ZAW* 64 (1952), 178–89. Wevers finds many passages marked by an asterisk in B. However, they do not go against the pre-Hexaplaric nature of the ms. but may be an indication of pre-Hexaplaric recensional traces according to the pre-Masoretic text, as happens in Papyrus 967.

[29] See *PG* 25, 1436–40.

precisely in books in which the manuscripts have been studied and classified, do not fit ms. B within the Alexandrian group. Also, if we take into account the results of Vaccari and Wevers, the same applies to the historical books and the Pentateuch.[30]

Since the quotations by the Alexandrian Fathers from the 2nd to 4th centuries (Clement, Origen and Didymus) follow text A and its group in Judges, whereas in the 5th century Cyril of Alexandria already uses text B and its group, G. F. Moore suspects that the Vatican text was translated in the 4th century CE.[31] However, Cox has shown that Cyril's quotations have to be used with the greatest reserve and cannot be related to Hesychius through the Vatican Codex since it is generally accepted today that this codex has a pre-recensional text.[32] We are, then, still very far from reaching definitive conclusions. Nowadays, comparison of isolated manuscripts is not acceptable; it has to be groups of manuscripts. And in Judges, B usually goes with mss $irua_2$. Furthermore, according to partial *sondages* in the Song of Deborah, its text has no connection with the alleged Hesychian recension, but instead contains a revision of the old LXX closely linked with the "three" and possibly identical with the καίγε revision.[33] In his monograph, Bodine reached the same conclusions recently when identifying the Vatican family in Judges with the καίγε recension.[34]

At the close of this analysis we can state that research on the Hesychian recension is in deadlock from which it is difficult to emerge without the help of new data from tradition or new methodological approaches.

---

[30] In fact, B in Isaiah belongs to the Hexaplaric group. On this point Jellicoe does not seem to be completely consistent since on page 155 of *SMS* he states: "In B, which we regard as pre-eminently *the representative of the Hesychian recension*, the text of Daniel is 'Theodotionic'". Against that, on page 156, n. 8 he affirms: "No grouping in the Göttingen LXX is classed as 'Hesychian'; cf. 'Alexandrian' in this edition." Nevertheless, the filiation of the Vatican ms. is not clear. It does not usually go with the "Alexandrian group" of manuscripts, but in several books its text is very close to some members of the group (for example, in Daniel, Ezekiel or Jeremiah).

[31] G. F. Moore, *Judges* in ICC. Moore thought that texts of A and B went back to two different translations, an hypothesis that has now been rejected.

[32] C. E. Cox, "Cyril of Alexandria's Text for Deuteronomy", 49–50.

[33] J. Schreiner, "Zum B-Text des griechischen Canticum Deborae", *Bib* 42 (1961), 333–58, and A. Sáenz-Badillos, "Transmisión griega y texto hebreo en el Canto de Débora (Ju 5)", *Sefarad* 33 (1973), 245–58.

[34] W. R. Bodine, *The Greek Text of Judges: Recensional Developments*, Chico, Calif. 1980.

New documents that can throw light on this period of textual history include the Tura Papyrus of Didymus the Blind, which contains a commentary on Psalms, Job, Ecclesiastes and Zachariah, discovered in 1941 and published recently.[35] Together with the quotations from Cyril of Alexandria, the biblical text of Didymus the Blind may help to locate this possible recension in Alexandria and Egypt. In the book of Zachariah, Didymus seems to be one of the most faithful witnesses of the Alexandrian group.[36] On the other hand, by extending the horizon of the LXX, it will be possible to obtain more precise results when monographs on the post-Ptolemaic papyri and other literary documents from the first centuries provide us with better knowledge of the Greek of Egypt.[37] The Alexandrian lexicographers merit particular attention. K. Latte insists on the special worth of a witness still ignored in studies on the Hesychian recension: the Cyrillian or Alexandrian glosses, especially when they agree with ms. A.[38] And finally, for the Octateuch and historical books, we will have to wait for modern critical editions to stratify the data and the filiation of the manuscripts in order to be able to reach a definitive solution.

Provisionally, the characteristics usually assigned to the Alexandrian group, both in the editions of the prophets and in other partial studies are as follows:

---

[35] N. Fernández Marcos, "El texto bíblico de Dídimo en el Comentario a Zacarías del Papiro de Tura", and L. Doutreleau, *Didyme l'Aveugle. Sur Zacharie. Texte inédit d'après un papyrus de Toura. Introduction, texte critique, traduction et notes*, I–III SC 83–85, Paris 1962. The commentaries by Didymus on Job, Psalms and Ecclesiastes have appeared in the collection "Papyrologische Texte und Abhandlungen" of Bonn from 1968 to 1972, edited by A. Henrichs, U. Hagedorn, D. Hagedorn, L. Koenen (Job); M. Gronewald, L. Doutreleau, A. Gesché (Psalms) and G. Binder, L. Liesenborghs, J. Kramer and B. Krebber (Ecclesiastes). However, as yet there is no overall systematic study on the biblical text of this writer.

[36] N. Fernández Marcos, "El texto bíblico de Dídimo", 281.

[37] See F. T. Gignac, *A Grammar of the Greek Papyri of the Roman and Byzantine Periods. 1: Phonology*, Milan 1976; *2: Morphology*, Milan 1981, and N. Fernández Marcos, "¿Rasgos dialectales en la κοινή tardía de Alejandría?".

[38] K. Latte, *Hesychii alexandrini Lexicon*, I Copenhagen 1953, XLV, n. 3: "Quaestionem de textu Scripturae in glossis illis et apud Cyrillum obvio tractare non meum est, sed cum horum documentorum per CL annos in investigandis Scripturae codicibus theologi plane obliti sint, monendi sunt hic testes exstare antiquissimis codicibus fere aequales, qui non solum Hexaplae lectiones exhibeant partim adhuc incognitas ... sed in universum adeo cum codicum A, interdum etiam B lectionibus conspirent, ut "Aegyptiae" quam vocant recensionis documenta pretiosissima habenda sint."

1. Most of this text is free from Hexaplaric additions.
2. Against the Hebrew text it often has a plus missing from the Hexaplaric recension.
3. It preserves the word order of the old LXX, whereas in the Hexaplaric recension the word order is as in Hebrew.
4. It contains free translation from the original text, translations which in the other recensions are adapted to the Hebrew.
5. However, these manuscripts have also undergone the influence of the Hexaplaric recension.

As can be seen, these characteristics are not recensional criteria that are maintained in a consistent way. This is why we have spoken of an Alexandrian group of manuscripts due to the difficulty of identifying them with one particular recension.

SELECT BIBLIOGRAPHY

Bauer, W., "Hesychius", in *RGG*, Tübingen 1959, III, 299.
Bousset, W., "Die Rezension des Hesychius". *Textkritische Studien zum Neuen Testament.* TU 11, 4 (1894), 74–110.
Cox, C. E., "Cyril of Alexandria's Text for Deuteronomy". *BIOSCS* 10 (1977), 31–51.
Fernández Marcos, N., "El texto bíblico de Dídimo en el Comentario a Zacarías del Papiro de Tura". *Sefarad* 36 (1976), 267–84.
———, "¿Rasgos dialectales en la κοινή tardía de Alejandría?". *Emerita* 39 (1971), 33–45.
Gehman, H. S., "The Hesychian Influence in the Versions of Daniel". *JBL* 48 (1929), 329–32.
Jellicoe, S., "The Hesychian Recension Reconsidered". *JBL* 82 (1963), 409–18.
———, *SMS*, 146–56.
Kenyon, F. G., "Hesychius and the Text of the New Testament". *Mémorial Lagrange*, Paris 1940, 245–50.
Rahlfs, "Alter und Heimat der vaticanischen Bibelhandschrift". NGWGött Phil.-Hist. Klasse 1899, I, 72–79.
———, *Septuaginta-Studien II. Der Text des Septuaginta Psalters*, Göttingen 1907.
Swete, H. B., *An Introduction to the Old Testament in Greek*, Cambridge 1914, 79–80.
Vaccari, A., "The Hesychian Recension of the Bible". *Bib* 46 (1965), 60–66.
Wevers, J. W., "Septuagint", in *IDB*, New York 1962, IV, 275.

CHAPTER SIXTEEN

OTHER REVISIONS

The three classic recensions noted by Jerome have been reduced to two, the Hexaplaric and the Lucianic in most books of the Greek Bible. Furthermore, in the Pentateuch, it has been possible to identify only the Hexaplaric recension together with a large group of catenary manuscripts and other new families or textual groups.[1] This means that the textual history of the LXX has become much more complex than was thought at the start of critical studies, and it also changes from book to book. For certainly, before these recensions, traces could be found of a varied work of revision that took place throughout the first stages of the transmission of the Greek Bible. Some of these revisions affect the LXX in the first stage of its history; they are therefore pre-Hexaplaric, and come to the fore in research after the finds at Qumran, as they directly affect the theory of a plural Hebrew text. Today we know that the work of revising the Greek Bible began, so to speak, the day after the translation of the Pentateuch.[2] These revisions are of primary importance for knowledge of the pre-Hexaplaric text, together with new Hebrew and Greek texts that have emerged among the documents from the Desert of Judah.

There are other revisions that affect a smaller or larger number of manuscripts and are difficult to fix chronologically, but they are all independent of the great recensions mentioned by ancient writers. We can set them out under the heading of para-Hexaplaric revisions.

a) *Pre-Hexaplaric Revisions*

There are two pre-Hexaplaric revisions that in recent years have been identified with certain systematic and consistent features: the καίγε revision which comprises a series of corrections to adapt the

---

[1] See J. W. Wevers, "Barthélemy and Proto-Septuagint Studies", 26.
[2] "There is a continuum from the Greek Pentateuch to Aquila in which approaches

original LXX to a proto-Masoretic type of Hebrew text in 1st century BCE Palestine;[3] and the proto-Lucianic revision which claims to
correct the original LXX in Palestine in the 2nd–1st centuries BCE,
according to a Hebrew text of the Palestinian type, remains of which
have been preserved in 4QSam[a]. It is present in the Antiochene
group of manuscripts as well as in the biblical quotations of Flavius
Josephus and in the Old Latin. This revision also has a stylistic component that tends to improve the Greek of the translation.[4]

It has not been possible to identify either of these two revisions
in the Pentateuch. Furthermore, recent studies have required slight
changes to certain points of view held by Barthélemy in his programmatic monograph on the predecessors of Aquila. Rather than
a uniform and monolithic work, today one prefers to speak of a
group of texts, all within the frame of a process of making the original LXX close to the proto-Masoretic Hebrew text, but with a range
of characteristics. Munnich has emphasised the influence that the
translation of the Psalter had on the choices of translation in this
group of texts.[5] And Gentry, in analysing the asterisked passages of
Job, finds similarities as well as dissimilarities with other members
of the group, especially the scroll of the Twelve Prophets from Naḥal
Ḥever and the Greek Psalter.[6] We find ourselves, therefore, before
a tradition that shares the same attitude towards the translation in
which a revision of a Hebraising type is carried out and to which
would belong the group of texts analysed by Barthélemy that stand
out for the consistent and systematic nature of the corrections and
the application of the hermeneutics of the Palestinian rabbinate.[7]

There are still many other indications of pre-Masoretic textual
pluralism,[8] but what interests us now is the relationship of these

---

and attitudes to translation are on the whole tending toward a closer alignment
between the Greek and the Hebrew," see P. Gentry, *The Asterisked Materials in the
Greek Job*, 497.

[3] See D. Barthélemy, "Redécouverte d'un chaînon manquant", and Barthélemy,
Les Devanciers d'Aquila.

[4] Not all specialists accept this second revision. The bibliography on these two
pre-Hexaplaric revisions is enormous. For a more detailed study see chapter 9,
pp. 148–53, and the section on the Proto-Lucianic in chapter 14, pp. 232–36.

[5] O. Munnich, "Contribution à l'étude de la première révision de la Septante".

[6] P. Gentry, *The Asterisked Materials in the Greek Job*, 495–99.

[7] J. W. Wevers, "Barthélemy and Proto-Septuagint Studies", has expressed himself on similar lines.

[8] See F. Pérez Castro, "Antiguo Testamento. Historia del texto hebreo", *Gran
Enciclopedia RIALP* 2 (1971), 359–66; and Pérez Castro, "La transmisión del texto

Greek revisions to the various Hebrew textual types. In fact, due to the discoveries of the Dead Sea, we have been able to determine how the various Hebrew textual families have left clear traces in the origin and transmission of the LXX. Following the theory of local texts developed by Cross,[9] which depends on the larger amount of material in the books of Samuel–Kings, three stages can be distinguished in the history of transmission:

1. The Egyptian textual type which served as the basis for the early LXX, *c.* 3rd century BCE, related to the Palestinian and from which perhaps it became independent in the 4th century BCE. In Qumran it is represented by 4QEx^a and 4QJer^b.

2. The proto-Lucianic revision made in the 2nd–1st centuries BCE in order to make the early LXX conform to the Hebrew text then current in Palestine, represented in Qumran by 4QSam^a, and within the LXX by the manuscripts boc$_2$e$_2$ in Samuel–Kings, the Hebrew text of Chronicles and biblical quotations in Josephus. It also occurs in the sixth column of the Hexapla (θ') throughout 2 Sam. 11:2–1 Kgs 2:11, probably due to confusion of this siglum for Theodotion with the one for Theodoret.[10]

We cannot determine exactly how long it was. It has not emerged in the Pentateuch. In Joshua–Judges–Ruth it is increasingly more defined in manuscripts *gln dpt* of Brooke–McLean. As we saw in another section,[11] it is very difficult to separate in the Antiochene text the material belonging to the proto-Lucianic revision of the old LXX on the one hand, from the late layer of the Lucianic recension on the other. On the other hand, apparently the proto-Lucianic revision was limited to corrections making the old LXX conform to the Palestinian Hebrew text of the 2nd–1st centuries BCE, but it also has an unavoidable component of stylistic and grammatical corrections.[12]

---

del Antiguo Testamento", *Sagrada Biblia. Versión crítica sobre los textos hebreo, arameo y griego*, ed. F. Cantera and M. Iglesias, Madrid 1975, XV–XXXVII.

[9] F. M. Cross, "The History of the Biblical Text", and Cross, "The Evolution of a Theory of Local Texts", 1975, 306–20.

[10] See chapter 9, p. 145.

[11] See chapter 14, p. 235 R. W. Klein, *Textual Criticism of the Old Testament*, 71–73, includes three criteria to identify proto-Lucianic readings already noted by Cross.

[12] S. P. Brock, "Lucian 'redivivus': Some Reflections on Barthélemy's 'Les Devanciers d'Aquila'", *Studia Evangelica* V, Berlin 1968, 176–81. Howard maintains that Josephus depended on at least two text types, preserved in the Antiochene text and in the καίγε revision, see G. Howard, "καίγε Readings in Josephus", *Textus* 8 (1973), 45–54, and Howard, "The 'Aberrant' Text of Philo's Quotations Reconsidered", *HUCA* 44 (1973), 197–211.

3. A text due to the second revision of the LXX (or parts of it) undertaken in Palestine from the 1st century BCE to make it fit a proto-Masoretic Hebrew text: it is the καίγε revision or Theodotionic.

This third text type is represented in Hebrew by 4QJer[a] and in the Twelve Prophets by the *Vorlage* of the Greek fragments from Naḥal Ḥever published by Barthélemy. It is also found in the *quinta* of the Psalter.[13] In Samuel–Kings-LXX it has displaced the original LXX in the βγ section (2 Sam. 11:2-1 Kgs 2:11) and γδ (2 Kings). The extent of this recension as well as on the main characteristics of this group can be judged from Barthélemy's work and later work on the topic.[14]

Thus there are three Hebrew text families: one Palestinian of an expansionist nature; another Egyptian, generally but not always complete, closely related to the Palestinian in its oldest phase of the Pentateuch (but not in Jeremiah where there are appreciable differences); and another Babylonian with a preference for a short text where it is preserved (Pentateuch and former Prophets).[15]

In spite of Howard's harsh criticism of this theory of local texts,[16] of Talmon's insistence on the sociological dimension of the texts,[17] and of the emphasis on textual diversity defended by Tov,[18] with some modifications it has proved to be valid for interpreting the new

---

[13] H. J. Venetz, *Die Quinta des Psalteriums. Ein Beitrag zur Septuaginta- und Hexaplaforschung*, Hildesheim 1974, 50–72.

[14] D. Barthélemy, *Les Devanciers d'Aquila*, 48–78. And also J. A. Grindel, "Another Characteristic"; M. Smith, "Another Criterion"; J. D. Shenkel, *Chronology and Recensional Development*, 113–16. Shenkel proposes a series of new characteristics of this recension, in particular the use of διώκειν for *rādaf* instead of the καταδιώκειν of the original LXX and of the proto-Lucianic; the use of words from the root σοφ- for *ḥākām* as against words from the root φρον- in the LXX and proto-Lucianic; σιωπᾶν for *ḥaraš* and *ḥašâ* against κωφεύειν of the LXX, etc. See also O. Munnich, "Contribution à l'étude de la première révision de la Septante", 205–17, and P. Gentry, *The Asterisked Materials in the Greek Job*, 389–402.

[15] R. W. Klein, *Textual Criticism of the Old Testament*, 70–71. In Samuel, for example, the Egyptian text would be found in the *Vorlage* of the old LXX; the Palestinian text would be reflected in the Hebrew text of Chronicles, in 4QSam[a-c], in the proto-Lucianic text of the Antiochene manuscripts and in the biblical text used in Josephus and translated by the Old Latin. Finally, the Babylonian text would be found in the Hebrew *Vorlage* of the καίγε revision.

[16] G. Howard, "Frank Cross and Recensional Criticism", *VT* 21 (1971), 440–51.

[17] S. Talmon, "The Textual Study of the Bible: A New Outlook", *Qumran and the History of the Biblical Text*, 321–400.

[18] E. Tov, "A Modern Textual Outlook Based on the Qumran Scrolls", *HUCA* 53 (1982), 11–27, and Tov, "Hebrew Biblical Manuscripts from the Judaean Desert: Their Contribution to Textual Criticism", *JJS* 39 (1988), 5–37.

information from Qumran.[19] Complete publication of this material and an exhaustive study of the manuscript tradition would help to clarify even more details and to determine the particular situation of each book. One thing seems clear in connection with the LXX: the appearance in Qumran of Hebrew texts similar to the *Vorlage* used by the translators of the LXX in books such as Jeremiah or Samuel should put us on our guard against interpreting the apparent discrepancies of that version from the Hebrew original. In fact, these discrepancies have become a very important tool for the critical restoration of the original in certain biblical books, and they even affect literary history when they reflect two different editions of those books.

Apart from these two early revisions of the LXX, which are more systematic and have helped to throw light on the history and development of the consonantal Hebrew text before it was finally fixed, two other lesser revisions have been identified from internal criticism. They reflect the intense activity of revision carried out before Origen, and they provide us with a revitalised image of a shadowy phase in the transmission of the LXX: the proto-Septuagint. They are revisions of a few books that at one time perhaps were longer and are attested in certain manuscripts of the LXX but not in the mainstream of its tradition. P. Katz refers to a series of pre-Hexaplaric rapprochements with the Hebrew text in the Coptic translations of the Twelve Prophets, in the text of Papyrus *Washingtonianus* (W), in Pap 967, and in Papyrus *Antinoopolitanus* on Ezekiel and Proverbs.[20]

---

[19] See E. Ulrich, "Pluriformity in the Biblical Text, Text Groups, and Questions of Canon", 25–29. Ulrich analyses the three theories of Cross, Talmon and Tov, not as contradictory but as complementary, since each stresses different aspects of the transmission. Despite accepting some corrections to the theory of local texts, to some extent contradicted by the data from Qumran, he continues to defend it as the only valid attempt at an overall explanation of the history of the biblical text in the first centuries of its transmission. See also F. M. Cross, "Some Notes on a Generation of Qumran Studies", 6–10.

[20] P. Katz, "Frühe hebraisierende Rezensionen der Septuaginta". See also J. Ziegler, *Septuaginta . . . XVI,2 Susanna, Daniel, Bel et Draco*, Göttingen 1954, 78, and Ziegler, "Die Bedeutung des Chester–Beatty–Scheide 967". Both Papyrus 967 and the Antinopolis papyrus are close to the Hebrew text, the second more than the first, see G. Zuntz, "Der Antinoe Papyrus der Proverbia", and E. Würthwein, *Der Text des Alten Testaments*, Stuttgart 1966, 172: "Die grösste Bedeutung hat der Pap 967 deshalb, weil er deutlich zeigt, dass bereits in vorhexaplarischer Zeit (vielleicht schon im 1. Jahrhundert n. Ch.) die Ez.-LXX nach dem hebräischen Text korrigiert wurde." For a description and commentary on the main features of this

Another fragment from Qumran Cave 7, 7Q1LXXEx, shows that already around 100 BCE the LXX was revised to bring it closer to the Hebrew text.[21]

Gooding has discovered about 235 variants in Deuteronomy that make the Greek text agree with the Hebrew. These corrections are the result of a conscious revision, independent of Origen and probably made before him.[22]

However, some of these witnesses, which earlier studies considered to be pre-Hexaplaric revisions, have had to be relinquished once the history of the text was correctly stratified for preparing critical editions. This is the case for Papyrus *Rylands gr.* 458 from the 2nd century BCE, considered to be Lucianic by Vaccari and placed by Wevers among witnesses of the old LXX.[23] Or 4QLXX Num, revised according to the Hebrew in Skehan's opinion,[24] in which the corrections are literary rather than Hebraising retouches.[25] This is an indication that, although there are clear signs of pre-Hexaplaric revisions, only an exhaustive study of the history of the text for each book will allow the real nature of these witnesses to be determined.

b) *Para-Hexaplaric Revisions*

These affect exclusively the Greek transmission of certain books. Due to being very late and to their special characteristics, they are of no interest for any question connected with the Hebrew *Vorlage*. They were discovered in studying the text for the critical editions of Göttingen.

The q *recension*

Hanhart discovered it for 2 and 3 Maccabees in mss 71, 74, 107, 102, 130, 370 and 371.[26] Unlike the Lucianic recension (L), the few

---

papyrus, see M. Fernández-Galiano, "Nuevas páginas del Códice 967 del A. T. griego (Ez. 28,19–43,9) [PMatr bibl 1]", *Studia Papyrologica* 10 (1971), 7–77.

[21] O. Munnich, "Le texte de la Septante", 157–58. On the Hebraising revision of 7Q1, see J. W. Wevers, "Pre-Origen Recensional Activity in the Greek Exodus", 122–23.

[22] D. W. Gooding, *Recensions of the Septuagint Pentateuch*, 8ff.

[23] J. W. Wevers, "The Use of the Versions for Text Criticism: The Septuagint", *La Septuaginta*, 20.

[24] P. W. Skehan, "4QLXX Num: A Pre-Christian Reworking of the Septuagint".

[25] O. Munnich, "Le texte de la Septante", 157.

[26] R. Hanhart, *Maccabaeorum Liber II*, 24ff.; *Maccabaeorum Liber III*, 28–32.

additions of this revision are not to ornament and explain the text
(except in 2 Mac. 11:13 and 15:18) but are exclusively grammatical
or stylistic in nature. The twenty cases in which an expression is
altered do not allow any particular tendency in the revision to be
recognised, since most are changes of synonym. Other deeper intru-
sions in the text are conditioned by the presence of difficult or corrupt passages (2 Mac. 8:33 and 13:15). The q recension is closer to
the original form of the LXX than the Lucianic recension; its textual changes are rare and superficial.

The a *recension*

For the book of Esther and 1 Ezra, their editor Hanhart has discovered this recension in minuscules 71, 74, 76, 106, 107, 120, 130,
236, 314, 370, 762[27] and with some variation in Tobit. In Esther it
represents a recension of the Septuagintal text (o') which sometimes
alone and sometimes together with other witnesses transmits 200
variants to us. No recensional principle can be found in it that is
followed consistently. It is related somewhat to the q recension of
Maccabees. Its grammatical forms are more Atticising than Hellenising.
As in q, the additions and omissions are based almost exclusively on
style; however there are also some ornamental and explanatory additions lacking in q. The contacts with the old tradition of adjusting
the Greek to the Hebrew text (preserved particularly in the Hexaplaric
and Lucianic recensions) cannot be due to chance.

The characteristics in 1–2 Ezra and in Judith are very like those
in the book of Esther: almost all the variants comprise changes of
synonym. The additions and transpositions are stylistic.

The b *recension*

It occurs in mss 46, 64, 98, 243, 248, 381, 728 and 731 of the book
of Esther and in the same minuscules of 1–2 Ezra and Judith[28] and,
with some variations, in Tobit. There are only about 100 variants
in Esther. The additions and omissions are of no importance; the
transpositions are more common than in the *a* recension. In the

---

[27] R. Hanhart, *Esther*, 81–84; Hanhart, *Septuaginta VIII/4 Judith*, Göttingen 1979,
23; Hanhart, *Text und Textgeschichte des 1. Esrabuches*, 28–30, and Hanhart, *Septuaginta . . .
VIII/2 Esdrae Liber II*, Göttingen 1993, 30–31.
[28] R. Hanhart, *Esther*, 84–87; Hanhart, *Iudith*, 23–25; Hanhart, *Text und Textgeschichte
des 1. Esrabuches*, 31–32, and Hanhart, *Esdrae Liber II*, 30–31.

grammatical forms, Atticisms occur and sporadically other formations from late Hellenism. It is not content with a few changes in
the Septuagintal text but also incorporates old recensional material
from Lucian and Origen. When accompanied by Vaticanus or a few
mixed codices or even when they agree with the Hexaplaric recension, both the *b* and the *a* recensions are witnesses of the original
text. However, *a* and *b* together, with no other accompanying manuscript, never represent the original text. In some variants of a secondary nature the *a* and *b* recensions are related to each other, a
fact which is due to late post-Hexaplaric tradition. In 1–2 Ezra, the
characteristics of the *b* recension are very like those of the book of
Esther; it has the same inconsistency with respect to the insertion of
Attic and Hellenistic forms.

The L-text of Esther

This text is not a recension of the LXX but comprises a new reworking of the Greek tradition of Esther supported to a large extent by
the Septuagintal text (o') of that book.[29] The o'-text and the L-text
of Esther are related to each other, to judge from the long passages
where divergence is minimal. Several passages show that in these
cases o' is the base and L is a reworking. On other occasions L is
so free in respect of the o'-text that it can only be understood as a
new arrangement or reworking of material from a tradition independent of the o'-text: this reworking is particularly evident in
periphrastic translations, many abbreviations and in small explanatory additions that only the L-text transmits. The Atticising tendency
is not applied systematically. Furthermore, L preserves many expressions that correspond to a later stage of Greek. Lexicographical examination leads to the same conclusions: when it diverges from the
o'-text it remains basically in the area of late Hellenistic Greek, very
close to the lexicon of Sira and Maccabees.

The L-text has no connection with the Lucianic recension, contrary to appearances at first glance. Its main feature, the conscious
shortening of the text, is not a principle of the Lucianic recension.
The Atticising tendency is not enough for identifying a recension

---

[29] R. Hanhart, *Esther*, 87–99. It was given the siglum L, to denote Lucian, because
it is transmitted by mss 19, 93, 108 and 319, the first three Lucianic or Antiochene
manuscripts in the historical books, even though in fact they have no connection
with that recension.

since Atticism is very widespread in late antiquity. Nor has it been possible to prove, for lack of witnesses, that the Antiochene Fathers knew only the L-text, nor that this text is due to the recensional work of that school.

Although it has contacts with Theodotion, as a whole the L-text is not at all Theodotionic. Nor are there criteria for classing it as proto-Lucianic. The confusion is due to de Lagarde that this text transmits mss 19, 93, 108 and 319, all of which, in the historical books, have a Lucianic text.[30] Tov considers text L to be a translation based on the LXX translation, but corrected in agreement with a Hebrew or Aramaic text that is different from the Masoretic text. The result is a midrashic type of reworking of biblical history.[31] Haelewyck, instead, postulates two stages for the origin of text L.[32] The textual history of the book of Esther tends to become complicated if we take into account the new Aramaic fragments of that book found in Qumran Cave 4, the relationship of which to the Hebrew and Greek texts of Esther are still far from being explained.[33] In addition, two recent monographs by Jobes and De Troyer have contributed, from different perspectives, to the renewal of interest in the L-text of Esther.[34]

The Greek text of Tobit has been transmitted in two different forms and partially in three. The relationship between them in terms of kinship is not easy to determine. Above all, the priority of one text over another still remains undetermined today.[35] However, here

---

[30] However an explanation would have been necessary since two of these manuscripts, 93 and 108, transmit both texts o' and L for Esther.

[31] E. Tov, "The 'Lucianic' Text of the Canonical and the Apocryphal Sections of Esther".

[32] J.-C. Haelewyck, "Le texte dit 'lucianique' du livre d'Esther".

[33] See J.-T. Milik, "Les modèles araméens du livre d'Esther dans la grotte 4 de Qumrân", *RQ* 15 (1992), 321–99.

[34] K. H. Jobes, *The Alpha-Text of Esther: Its Character and Relationship to the Masoretic Text*, Atlanta, Ga. 1996; Kristine de Troyer, *Het einde van de Alpha-tekst van Esther: Vertaal- en verhaal-techniek van MT 8, 1-17, LXX 8, 1-17 en AT 7, 14-41*, Leuven 1997.

[35] Cf. R. Hanhart, *Septuaginta VIII/5 Tobit*, Göttingen 1983, 31–36. Among the para-Hexaplaric recensions should be included also the recension called R ("Rezension unbekannter Herkunft") which Rahlfs detected for Ruth, Judges and Kings and the recension R which Katz identified in certain manuscripts of Philo for a series of conflicting quotations from the Pentateuch, see A. Rahlfs, *Das Buch Ruth griechisch als Probe einer kritischen Handausgabe der Septuaginta*, Stuttgart 1922, and P. Katz, *Philo's Bible: The Aberrant Text of Bible Quotations in some Philonic Writings and its Place in the Textual History of the Greek Bible*, Cambridge 1950, 98–103. See also E. Tov's review of S. Jellicoe, *SMS*.

we are probably leaving the field of para-Hexaplaric recensions to enter the problem of duplicate texts of the LXX, which we have discussed elsewhere.[36]

SELECT BIBLIOGRAPHY

Barthélemy, D., *Les Devanciers d'Aquila*. VTS 10, Leiden 1963.
———, "Redécouverte d'un chaînon manquant de l'histoire de la LXX". *RB* 60 (1953), 18–29.
Brock, S. P., "To Revise or not to Revise: Attitudes to Jewish Biblical Translations". *Septuagint, Scrolls and Cognate Writings*, 1992, 301–38.
Cross, F. M., "Some Notes on a Generation of Qumran Studies". *The Madrid Qumran Congress*, 1992, 1–14.
———, "The Contribution of the Qumran Discoveries to the Study of the Biblical Text". *IEJ* 16 (1966), 81–95.
———, "The Evolution of a Theory of Local Texts". *Qumran and the History of the Biblical Text*, ed. F. M. Cross and S. Talmon, Cambridge, Mass.–London 1975, 306–20.
———, "The History of the Biblical Text in the Light of Discoveries in the Judean Desert". *HTR* 57 (1964), 281–301.
Gentry, P. J., *The Asterisked Materials in the Greek Job*, Atlanta, Ga. 1995.
Gooding, D. W., *Recensions of the Septuagint Pentateuch*, London 1955.
Greenspoon, L., "Recensions, Revisions, Rabbinics: Dominique Barthélemy and Early Developments in the Greek Traditions". *Textus* 15 (1990), 153–67.
Grindel, J. M., "Another Characteristic of the καίγε Recension". *CBQ* 31 (1969), 499–513.
Haelewyck, J.-C., "Le text dit 'lucianique' du livre d'Esther. Son étendue et sa cohérence". *Le Muséon* 98 (1985), 5–44.
Hanhart, R., *Septuaginta VIII, 3 Esther*, Göttingen 1966, 81–95.
———, *Septuaginta IX, 2 Maccabaeorum Liber II*, Göttingen 1959, 24 ss.
———, *Septuaginta IX, 3 Maccabaeorum Liber III*, Göttingen 1960, 28–32.
———, *Text und Textgeschichte des 1. Esrabuches*. MSU XII, Göttingen 1974.
Katz, P., "Frühe hebraisierende Rezensionen der Septuaginta". *ZAW* 69 (1957), 77–84.
———, "The Recovery of the Original Septuagint: A Study in the History of Transmission and Textual Criticism". *Actes du Ier Congrès de la Fédération Internationale des Associations d'Études Classiques*, Paris 1951, 165–82.
Klein, R. W., *Textual Criticism of the Old Testament: From the Septuagint to Qumran*, Philadelphia 1974.
Leaney, A. R., "Greek Manuscripts from the Judaean Desert". *Studies in New Testament Language and Text*, ed. J. K. Elliot, Leiden 1976, 283–300.

I am not including other revisions that cover shorter sections within a book, such as the revision of chapter 66 of Isaiah-LXX. In Ziegler's opinion this chapter has so many new words compared to the rest of Isaiah that there must have been a recensional re-working of it, see J. Ziegler, *Untersuchungen zum LXX des Buches Isaias*, Münster 1934, chap. II. Similarly, in the review cited, p. 86, E. Tov mentions Ez. 28–39 as a late revision according to D. Barthélemy; Ez. 1–27 according to E. H. Kase, and Jer. 29–52 according to J. Ziegler.

[36] See chapter 6, p. 99.

Lifshitz, B., "The Greek Documents from the Cave of Horror". *IEJ* 12 (1962), 201–207.

Munnich, O., "Contribution à l'étude de la première révision de la Septante". *ANRW* II, 20, 1 (1987), 190–220.

———, "Le texte de la Septante". Harl *et al.*, *La Bible grecque des Septante*, 157–61.

O'Connell, K. G., *Greek Versions (Minor)*. IDBS, Abingdon 1976, 377–81.

———, *The Theodotionic Revision of the Book of Exodus*, Harvard 1972.

Schreiner, J., "Zum B-Text des griechischen Canticum Deborae". *Bib* 42 (1961), 333–58, especially 357–58.

Shenkel, J. D., *Chronology and Recensional Development in the Greek Text of Kings*, Harvard 1968.

Skehan, P. W., "4QLXX Num: A Pre-Christian Reworking of the Septuagint". *HTR* 70 (1970), 39–50.

Smith, M., "Another Criterion for the καίγε Recension". *Bib* 48 (1967), 443–45.

Tov, E., Review of *The Septuagint and Modern Study* by S. Jellicoe, in *RB* 77 (1970), 84–91.

———, "The 'Lucianic' Text of the Canonical and the Apocryphal Sections of Esther: A Rewritten Biblical Book". *Textus* 10 (1982), 1–25.

Ulrich, E. E., "Pluriformity in the Biblical Text, Text Groups and Questions of Canon". *The Madrid Qumran Congress*, 1992, 23–41.

Vermes, G., review of *Les Devanciers d'Aquila*, in *JSS* 11 (1966), 261–64.

Wevers, J. W., "Barthélemy and Proto-Septuagint Studies". *BIOSCS* 21 (1988), 23–34.

Ziegler, J., "Die Bedeutung des Chester–Beatty–Scheide Papyrus 967 für die Textüberlieferung der Ezechiel-LXX". *ZAW* 20 (1945–48), 76–94.

Zuntz, G., "Der Antinoe Papyrus der Proverbia und das prophetologion". *ZAW* 68 (1956), 124–84.

CHAPTER SEVENTEEN

INDIRECT TRANSMISSION: BIBLICAL QUOTATIONS

The breadth of this topic forces us to tackle some questions of methodology of particular interest for the history of the LXX, referring to other more specific publications for further details on aspects only mentioned here.

We can distinguish two blocks of quotations of the Greek Bible:

1. pre-recensional or pre-Hexaplaric quotations;
2. quotations from writers later than the mid-3rd century.

The first kind affect either the origins of the LXX, its initial unity or pluralism – Kahle bases his Targumic theory of the origins of the LXX on these – or at least they affect the textual pluralism of the pre-Hexaplaric LXX. In this chapter, quotations must be included that are preserved in inscriptions and papyri up to the 3rd century CE, quotations of or possible contact with LXX in the Jewish-Hellenistic historians, Philo, Josephus, pseudepigraphic writings preserved in Greek prior to the 3rd century CE, the New Testament, Qumran, some Gnostic writings, the Apostolic and Apologist Fathers.

From the 3rd century onwards, if we except some inscriptions and late papyri, we only come across biblical quotations from the LXX in the writings of the Fathers. Such quotations, could affect fundamentally the problem of recensions and act as an external criterion for identifying them.

Signs of caution and mistrust continually arise concerning this material and its use for critical purposes in editing the LXX.[1] In fact it can be stated that the question of biblical quotations is the weakest point of the Cambridge and Göttingen editions:[2] the absence

---

[1] An example of the critical attitude of an editor of the LXX towards Patristic quotations can be seen in J. Ziegler, "Jeremias-Zitate in Väter-Schriften".

[2] See the review by E. Hautsch of the Cambridge edition Vol. I, 1–2, in *Göttingische Gelehrte Anzeigen* 7 (1909), 563–80. The main defects to which he refers are: no distinction is made between authentic and false writings by Chrysostom; lemma and commentary are not discussed separately; all the quotations are given the same value without noting when they come from another context; and it is not taken into account that Theodoret and particularly Chrysostom, quote freely or simply

of critical editions of the Fathers, the process of quoting from memory, the adaptation to context, the mixed quotations due to assimilation of different passages, the influence of parallel passages, etc., all compel the deepest reserve when using them as witnesses of a genuine biblical text. Representatives of this position of maximum caution in respect of biblical quotations are Ziegler and Rahlfs and, in general, the Göttingen school, in spite of the importance accorded them by de Lagarde.[3]

Other scholars more familiar with patrology and the history of exegesis take a much more optimistic stance. Unlike Rahlfs, Boismard does not always give preference to manuscripts against the readings from the Fathers. He analyses a series of examples in which the tradition agrees against the main manuscripts to show that in many cases the reading in the Fathers is to be preferred. It is worth remembering that we only have four uncials from the 5th century from among the mass of manuscripts that the Fathers knew and used. There are pre-Hexaplaric papyri that provide variants that have disappeared from the rest of the manuscript tradition and yet have been preserved in the Fathers.[4] In other words, the quotations in the Fathers, used with due caution, comprise material that cannot be ignored. Projects under way at present, such as the compilation of a photographic record of all the patristic quotations,[5] are good proof of that. Although directed towards the history of exegesis, the

---

give the biblical narrative. An example in respect of the Göttingen edition is the witness by J. Ziegler for the Twelve Prophets: "Deshalb verdienen die Angaben im App. 'Cyr.' und 'Cyr.ᵖ' nicht unbedingtes Vertrauen. Die gerade in Beziegung auf die Bibeltexte ungenügende Ausgabe von Pusey ist schuld daran," see J. Ziegler, "Der Bibeltext des Cyrill von Alexandrien zu den zwölf kleinen Propheten in den Druck-Ausgaben", *Beiträge zum griechischen Dodekapropheton. Nachr. d. Akad. d. Wiss. zu Göttingen, Philol.-Hist. Klasse*, 1943 (= *Septuaginta Arbeiten*, Nr. 2, p. 412). See also N. Fernández Marcos, "El texto bíblico de Dídimo en el Comentario a Zacarías del Papiro de Tura", *Sefarad* 36 (1976), 267–84.

[3] J. Ziegler, "Jeremias-Zitate in Väter-Schriften", and A. Rahlfs, *Septuaginta-Studien I. Studien zu den Königsbüchern*, Göttingen 1904, p. 43: "Als Resultat unserer Untersuchung ergibt sich, dass Theodorets Zitate zur Herstellung eines ursprünglicheren L-Textes, als er uns in den Hss. vorliegt, nicht benutzt werden können. Sie sind sehr wertvoll für die Nachweisung der lucianischen Rezension in unsern Bibelhandschriften, aber wo sie von den Hss. abweichen, haben diese, trotz ihrer Jugend, doch das erste Wort su sprechen."

[4] M. E. Boismard, "Critique textuelle et citations patristiques", and G. Jouassard, "Requête d'un patrologue".

[5] Carried out by the Centre of Patristic Analysis and Documentation of the University of Strasbourg (CNRS) in France. For the publications by this team connected with the *Biblia Patristica*, see Select Bibliography.

critical editions of the Greek Old and New Testaments of Göttingen and Münster continue to benefit from them, as do the editors of the *Vetus Latina* in Beuron.

Without losing sight of our predominantly methodological approach we shall now survey the main stages or nuclei of interest in the biblical quotations in the various collections of writings of antiquity.

a) *The Septuagint in Hellenistic Jewish Historians*

Although only fragments of them have been preserved, several of the Hellenistic Jewish historians show clear indications that they knew the LXX. Rather than quotations, they represent contacts in lexicon and phrasing. Some of these fragments, such as the one of Eupolemos (2nd century BCE), comprise a *terminus ante quem* for the origin of the LXX. Similarly, Demetrius knows Genesis in Greek.[6] Eupolemos has bequeathed to us the longest remnant of a Jewish-Greek text earlier than Philo: the narrative of the reigns of Joshua, Samuel, Saul and David. His description of the dimensions of the temple agree neither with the Hebrew text nor with the LXX. Probably, following a procedure in use among Hellenistic Jewish historians, he rewrites the past in the light of present history.[7] He is dependent on the LXX for the Hexateuch, but – against Freudenthal – there are no proofs that he used the Greek version of Kings and Chronicles. He translates into Greek the technical terms transliterated in the LXX. Artapanus (2nd century BCE) generally follows the biblical account in the Exodus narrative, although he expands and embellishes it. His knowledge of the LXX is beyond doubt; he describes the miracles and plagues with the words of Ex-LXX, and there is hardly any indication that he knew the Hebrew Bible.[8]

From the historian Aristeas (2nd/1st century BCE), author of a περὶ ἰουδαίων, only a fragment of sixteen lines is preserved with narra-

---

[6] For the text of these fragments, see F. Jacoby (ed.), *Die Fragmente der griechischen Historiker*, III (1958), and A. M. Denis, *Fragmenta Pseudepigraphorum quae supersunt graeca una cum historicorum et auctorum judaeorum hellenistarum fragmentis* (published with M. Black, *Apocalypsis Henochi Graece*), Leiden 1970, 175–28. An important edition, with notes, is C. R. Holladay, *Fragments from Hellenistic Jewish Authors. Volume 1: Historians*, Chico, Calif. 1983; *Volume II: Poets*, 1989; *Volume III: Aristobulus*, 1995.

[7] N. Fernández Marcos, "Interpretaciones helenísticas del pasado de Israel", *CFC* 8 (1975), 157–86, and B.-Z. Wacholder, *Eupolemus: A Study of Judaeo-Greek Literature*, New York 1974.

[8] J. Freudenthal, *Hellenistische Studien* I and II, Breslau 1875, 215–16.

tive sections from the book of Job inserted into the Genesis 36 narrative. Aristeas is clearly dependent on the LXX of Job, but the epilogue of this version (Job 42:17b-e) is in turn dependent on Aristeas.[9]

The historian Demetrius, who lived during the reign of Ptolemy IV (221–204 BCE), knew at least Gen-LXX. Of this we have seven fragments which in the chronologies of the flood, the birth of Abraham and the Exodus agree with the LXX against the Hebrew text, so that perhaps he studied with the school that produced the LXX. Apart from the translators of the Greek Pentateuch, he is the first Jewish author known to write in Greek and the first to know the Greek translation of the Law.[10]

The lexicon and phraseology of the LXX also occur in Aristobulus and Ezekiel the Tragedian.[11]

These quotations and allusions to the LXX are very important for dating the translation. However, due to their scarcity, the unsystematic use of sources and the fragmentary nature of these writings (apart from proving contacts with the Greek Bible) they scarcely help to determine the actual text in the form known by these writers. This situation has not improved with the publication of the most recent studies.[12]

---

[9] Aristeas states that Bassara was Jobab's (Job's) mother due to a false interpretation of Gen. 36:33 (ἐκ Βοσόρρας) and from confusing her with Basemath (Gen. 36:3) who gave birth to Jobab (Job), Esau's son. Job-LXX in 42:17 corrects the slip by Aristeas, but perpetuates his original mistake (μητρὸς δὲ βοσόρρας 42:17c). The problem of the meaning of this epilogue in the LXX remains, which states that he took him ἐκ τῆς Συριακῆς βίβλου (42:17b). Perhaps he is alluding to a lost apocryphon of Job of which there are echoes in the Testament of Job, Bab. Batra 15b, Targum of Job 2:9 and Jerome in his commentary on Gen. 22:21. Aristeas was also able to use this Palestinian source, see B. Z. Wacholder, "Aristeas", *EJ* 3 (1971), 438–39.

[10] See J. Freudenthal, *Hellenistische Studien*, 40–41 and 50–51. See also A. M. Denis, *Introduction aux Pseudépigraphes Grecs de l'Ancien Testament*, Leiden 1970, 241ff., and E. J. Bickermann, "The Jewish Historian Demetrios", *Christianity, Judaism and Other Greco-Roman Cults*, 5 vols, J. Neusner (ed.), Leiden 1975, 3, 72–84.

[11] H. B. Swete, *An Introduction to the Old Testament in Greek*, 371. On the authenticity of the fragments of Aristobulus and their importance for determining the origins of the Greek translation of the Pentateuch, see N. Walter, *Der Thoraausleger Aristobulos. Untersuchungen zu seinen Fragmenten und zu pseudepigraphischen Resten der jüdisch-hellenistischen Litertur* (= TU 86), Berlin 1964, and D. Barthélemy, *Pourquoi la Torah a-t-elle été traduite en grec?*, 24ff. For Ezekiel the Tragedian, see H. Jacobson, *The Exagoge of Ezekiel*, Cambridge 1983.

[12] See B.-Z. Wacholder, *Eupolemus*, 292–93.

b) *The Septuagint in the Apocrypha and Pseudepigrapha*

Another area as yet little known and scarcely used for the textual criticism of the LXX comprises quotations in inter-testamental literature. This is due largely to a lack of critical editions of these books and to their literary form, since many of them develop the great biblical themes of the past in a midrashic way. Apart from two doctoral dissertations,[13] the remaining bibliography in respect of these writings does not come to grips with the problem of the biblical text used by their authors.

The *Letter of Pseudo-Aristeas* knows and cites at least the Greek Pentateuch. It cannot be proved with certainty that its author knew the books of Kings.[14]

The author of the book of Wisdom uses Exodus, Deuteronomy and Isaiah. When he uses Old Testament material he never follows the Hebrew text against the Greek. However, sometimes he departs from the Hebrew text to follow one of the Greek versions. Mostly he goes with the LXX but sometimes uses terms that we only know through Symmachus.[15]

---

[13] L. R. Hammill, "Biblical Interpretation in the Apocrypha and Pseudepigrapha", Diss. Chicago 1950, and J. K. Zink, "The Use of the Old Testament in the Apocrypha", Diss. Durham (North Carolina) 1963. See G. Delling, *Bibliographie zur jüdisch-hellenistischen und intertestamentarischen Literatur 1900–1965*, Berlin 1968, 73ff., and the second edition of G. Delling and M. Maser, *Bibliographie zur jüdisch-hellenistischen und intertestamentarischen Literatur 1900–1970*, TU 106, Berlin 1975.

[14] See the edition of the Letter in H. B. Swete, *An Introduction to the Old Testament in Greek*, 551–606, which prints the biblical quotations in capital letters, and H. G. Meecham, *The Letter of Aristeas: A Linguistic Study with Special Reference to the Greek Bible*, Manchester 1935, 316–24. J. W. Wevers actually says: "In my own comparison of the 3 Kingdoms, chapters 6–7, account of the temple and its furnishings with *Aristeas* 57–82, I could find no evidence of literary relation between the two accounts, whereas the correspondence between *Aristeas* and Ex. 25,23 f. seems completely convincing," see J. W. Wevers, "Proto-Septuagint Studies", *The Seed of Wisdom: Fs. T. J. Meek*, Toronto 1964, 63, n. 23.

[15] H. B. Swete, *An Introduction to the Old Testament in Greek*, 371–72, and J. Fichtner, "Der AT-Text der Sapientia Salomonis". It does not seem as if the relationship of the vocabulary of the book of Wisdom with that of Symmachus can be explained by its great nearness in time (since it would be even closer in time to Aquila or Theodotion!). Fichtner reflects as follows: "Denn auch Symmachus hat bei seiner Arbeit Vorlagen in älteren griechischen AT-Übersetzungen gehabt. Wir können also m. E. in der 'Zitierung' bei dem Verfasser der *Sap.* das Werden des griechischen AT-Textes beobachten und müssen feststellen, dass mancherlei Rezensionen lange Zeit nebeneinander her gelaufen sind. Dass wir in der *Sap.* Spüren der Übersetzungsweise treffen, die wir aus den späteren Symmachus-Fragmenten kennen, ist m. E. nicht unwichtig. Vielleicht lässt sich durch Untersuchungen ähnlicher Art wie

Sira not only knows of the existence of the Pentateuch, Prophets and 'other writings' but everywhere oozes the influence of LXX phraseology. Even so, there is no systematic study of Sira's attitude to the other books of the Greek Bible that he knows and uses.[16] Baruch rewrites the book of Jeremiah to fit his own time.[17]

Nor has there been a formal study of the use made of the LXX in the books of Maccabees in the Greek Old Testament. However we know that 2 Mac. 7:6 contains a quotation of Dt. 32:36, and that 4 Mac. 18:14ff. includes a *catena* of quotations – all according to the LXX – from Deuteronomy, Isaiah, Psalms, Proverbs, Ezekiel, etc.[18] The biblical text of the *Liber Antiquitatum Biblicarum* of Pseudo-Philo, a work probably written before 100 CE, is related to the Lucianic or proto-Lucianic manuscripts in Joshua–1 Samuel.[19] The author of the Testament of Job knows a text of the LXX that has already undergone recension, even though it is pre-Hexaplaric and comes from the region of Alexandria.[20]

Other pseudepigraphic writings have been studied more to throw light on New Testament passages in terms of the use their authors make of the Greek Old Testament.[21] And apart from rare exceptions, the excellent introductions by Charles to these books or the more recent editions of the Apocrypha and Pseudepigrapha of the Old Testament, published in German, French, English, Italian or Spanish, do not deal with the topic of which biblical text was used, except in notes to isolated passages at most. Specialists have focused primarily on fixing the text and the manuscript tradition and on determining what the original language could be.[22] However, it should

---

die hiermit vorgelegte noch manches Stück der Frühgeschichte der griechischen AT-Übersetzung und ihrer späteren Revisionen aufhellen" (*ibid.* 192). In the light of recent research on the early revisions of the LXX (see chapter 16), we are obliged to accept this conclusion made in 1939.

[16] See P. W. Skehan and A. A. di Lella, *The Wisdom of Ben Sira*, New York 1987, 40–46 and 55–56.

[17] See A. Kabasale Mukenge, "Les citations internes en *Ba.* 1,15–3,8. Un procédé rédactionnel et actualisant", *Le Muséon* 108 (1995), 211–37.

[18] See H. B. Swete, *An Introduction to the Old Testament in Greek*, 372.

[19] See D. J. Harrington, "The Biblical Text of Pseudo-Philo's".

[20] See B. Schaller, "Das Testament Hiobs", 405–406.

[21] See J. Jeremias, "Beobachtungen zu neutestamentlichen Stellen an Hand des neugefundenen griechischen Henoch-Buches", *ZNW* 38 (1939), 115–24, and M. Alberbach, "The Historical Allusions of Chapters IV, XI and XIII of the Psalms of Salomon", *JQR* 41 (1950–51), 379–96.

[22] R. H. Charles, *The Apocrypha and Pseudepigrapha of the Old Testament. II: Pseudepigrapha*, Oxford 1913, with the exception of the Book of Jubilees (*ibid*, pp. 4ff.) which agrees

not be forgotten that even parts of the Sibylline Oracles show the influence of the LXX.[23]

c) *The Septuagint in Philo and Josephus*

The quotations of these two Jewish writers have been studied particularly for their privileged position in history as both witness to and check on the pre-Hexaplaric LXX.[24] P. Katz, a disciple of Kahle, devoted a monograph to Philo,[25] which we considered in connection with the origins of the LXX. The text followed by Philo in some of his writings represents a lost recension of the Pentateuch – not a different translation – similar to recension *R* which Rahlfs discovered in the book of Ruth. Arnaldez has carefully studied how Philo uses the biblical text of the LXX and stresses the liberties that he takes with that text, not hesitating to change it for the needs of his argument or his exegesis. Philo approaches Scripture with a mind already trained in Greek philosophy, Platonism, the Stoics and other systems. His exegetical method allows him to draw the biblical text towards the meaning he wishes to make. Although it is possible that he consulted learned Jews who knew some Hebrew, it is preferable to attribute the divergences of his text from the LXX to his own exegesis.[26]

---

more often with the LXX or combinations of the LXX than any other version. The book of Enoch is also full of references and allusions to the Septuagintal text (*ibid*, 188ff. in the notes). The lack of an entry on the LXX in the Apocrypha and Pseudepigrapha in the recent bibliography by C. Dogniez, *Bibliography of the Septuagint*, Leiden 1995, is indicative. See also J. H. Charlesworth (ed.), *Old Testament Pseudepigrapha*, 1, New York, 1983; 2, London, 1985; the German series *Jüdische Schriften aus hellenistisch-römischer Zeit*, published in Gütersloh since 1973; A. Dupont-Sommer and M. Philonenko (eds.), *La Bible. Écrits intertestamentaires*, Paris 1987; P. Sacchi, *Apocrifi dell'Antico Testamento*, 1, Turin 1981; 2, 1989, and A. Díez Macho (ed.), *Apócrifos del Antiguo Testamento*, 1–5, Madrid 1983–87.

[23] See H. B. Swete, *An Introduction to the Old Testament in Greek*, 372: *Or. Sibyll.* III, 312 ἐξέχεας is reminiscent of Ps. 78:3; and III, 606 χειροποίητα σέβοντες, ἃ ῥίψουσιν βροτοὶ αὐτοί is taken from Is. 2:19ff., see J. Geffcken, *Die Oracula Sibyllina*, Leipzig 1902, *ad locum*.

[24] See *CB* 57–58 and *BS* 82–86.

[25] See also the section on the Targumic origin of the LXX in chapter 4 above and P. Katz, *Philo's Bible: The Aberrant Text*; G. Howard, "The 'Aberrant' Text of Philo's Quotations Reconsidered", *HUCA* 44 (1973), 197–211. *Contra* Katz, Howard states that the 'aberrant' text of mss UF sometimes represents the text type used by Philo. It would be like the text of the καίγε revision. In this supposition, Philo would have preserved one of the earliest remains of the καίγε revision in the Pentateuch unless this text type is not to be identified completely with that of the καίγε.

[26] R. Arnaldez, "L'influence de la traduction des Septante".

The biblical text used by Josephus in his writings has been studied in relation to the proto-Lucianic problem.[27] At least from 1 Samuel to 1 Maccabees he seems to follow a Lucianic or Antiochene type of text.[28]

d) *The Septuagint in the New Testament, Apostolic Fathers and Apologists*

For the complex problem of LXX quotations in the New Testament, refer to chapter 21 below.[29] It is sufficient to note in this context that these quotations belong to the process of early revisions that the LXX underwent from very early on, and that age-old problems such as the proto-Theodotionic question can be resolved within this framework.[30] On the other hand, every approach in the study of the quotations that ignores the condition of the text of the pre-Hexaplaric Septuagintal text seems to be mistaken. The important conclusion is that most of the Old Testament quotations in the New follow the text of the LXX in one of its known forms.[31]

There is some bibliography for the Apostolic Fathers and Apologists.[32] More work has been done on the quotations of Clement of Rome and there is increasing interest in those of Justin, as he preserves many readings of the καίγε recension.[33]

The advantage of the *Letter of Clement of Rome* is based on being able to date it to around 95/96 CE in Rome, and that it contains many quotations from the Old Testament. As happens in the New Testament, Psalms and Isaiah are the books most cited by Clement. In his monograph, Hagner prefers to consider clear quotations

---

[27] See chapter 14, p. 233.

[28] See H. St J. Thackeray, *Josephus: The Man and the Historian*, pp. 75–100: "Josephus and Judaism: His Biblical Text": "The Josephan Biblical text is uniformly of this Lucianic type from 1 Sam to 1 Mac" (*ibid.*, 85). Thackeray's opinion has been confirmed by recent research, see E. Ulrich, "Josephus' Biblical Text for the Books of Samuel". For the biblical text used in the Pentateuch, see E. Nodet, *Le Pentateuque de Flavius Josèphe*, and in Samuel–Kings, see V. Spottorno, "Flavio Josefo. Técnicals de adaptación", and C. Begg, *Josephus' Account*.

[29] See chapter 21, pp. 323–32.

[30] See N. Fernández Marcos, "La Biblia de los autores del Nuevo Testamento".

[31] See M. Harl, "La Septante et le Nouveau Testament: les citations", Harl *et al.*, *La Bible grecque des Septante*, 274–80, and G. J. Steyn, *Septuagint Quotations*.

[32] See *CB* 59–60.

[33] D. Barthélemy, *Les Devanciers d'Aquila*, 203–13; J. Smit Sibinga, *The OT Text of Justin Martyr: I The Pentateuch*, Leiden 1963; P. Katz, "Justin's OT Quotations and the Greek Dodekapropheton", *Studia Patristica* 1 (1957) = TU 63, 543–53; P. Prigent, *Justin et l'Ancien Testament*, Paris 1964.

provided with introductory formulae and deals only indirectly with allusions.[34] Most of the quotations by Clement agree with the LXX, although there are few strictly literal quotations. A small number differ considerably from the LXX and others are so different that of necessity they pose the problem of alternative quotations. In such cases – since most quotations are so exact – a source different from the LXX has to be postulated, before resorting to the respective options of quotations from memory, adaptations to context or use of collections of *testimonia*. Clement of Rome gives the impression that he uses a much more mixed text than the Palestinian writers of the New Testament had to hand.

In the case of Justin, although his work is only preserved in a single 14th century manuscript, it can be concluded that in the Twelve Prophets he often uses the καίγε recension in his quotations, to the extent that Barthélemy believes lost passages of this recension can be reconstructed on the basis of those quotations.[35]

Smit Sibinga cannot decide to draw conclusions about the Pentateuch until he has studied Justin's attitude in relation to the rest of the Greek Bible. However, it seems that the quotations from the Pentateuch do not diverge so much from the Septuagintal text as in the Twelve Prophets, although they contain much old and valuable material. Many of them, including the variants that can be called archaic, belong to a stage of the history of the LXX prior to the information from our codices.[36]

As far as the slight divergence from the LXX in the Pentateuch is concerned – even when Justin followed Palestinian texts in both the Pentateuch and Twelve Prophets – normally the first recensions of the Greek Bible deal first with books other than the Pentateuch, in which the LXX is not very different from the Hebrew text.[37]

---

[34] D. A. Hagner, *The Use of the Old and New Testaments*.

[35] D. Barthélemy, *Les Devanciers d'Aquila*, 203–12.

[36] J. Smit Sibinga, *The OT Text of Justin Martyr*, 162, and the review by D. W. Gooding in *JTS* 16 (1965), 187–92. A complete evaluation of Justin's text in connection with the oldest papyri, "the three", the recensions of the LXX, the Targumic traditions and the other Christian testimonies will only be possible when the quotations from the other books of the Old Testament have been studied.

[37] For the most exhaustive analysis of these quotations, see H. B. Swete, *An Introduction to the Old Testament in Greek*, 406–32, still valid with a few changes to take into account the new approaches from the καίγε recension. See also R. A. Kraft, *Épître de Barnabé*, Paris 1971, and A. B. Starrat, "The Use of the LXX in the Five Books against Heresies by Irenaeus of Lyon", Diss., University of Harvard 1952.

e) *The Septuagint in Inscriptions and Papyri*

There is an impressive number of biblical quotations in Greek inscriptions and those from the Old Testament are much more frequent than those from the New Testament.[38] The book cited most is the book of Psalms (143 quotations from 48 different psalms). The rest of the Old Testament only has 16 quotations. The distribution of finds by geographical area is as follows: 112 in Palestine and Syria (86 in Upper Syria); 18 in Egypt, 7 in Asia Minor, 8 in Europe and 2 in Greece. These facts provided by L. Jalabert at the beginning of the century need to be supplemented by those set out by D. Feissel in a more recent study.[39] They confirm the preference for quotations from the Psalter, and show that inscriptions, generally non-Christian, that are independent of the LXX, are rare. A Greek inscription from Thessalonica that contains Num. 6:22-27, is taken, apparently, from a Greek revision of the Pentateuch.[40] It is an exception for the LXX text to be seriously altered as in the case of the mosaic of Mopsuestia which reproduces the story of Samson (Jgs 16:1-4). Apparently, the retouches come either from the Jewish tradition of the Targum or from a rewritten text, Christian in origin but similar to a Jewish Targum.[41]

The point of interest of this geographical distribution is that it provides important information for areas which, like Syria, have no documentation in the form of papyri. Its real value is that they are pinpointed geographically, are dated and remain on the margin of the avatars of transmission by manuscript or papyrus with new copies and frequent revisions.[42] Some of these inscriptions contain the oldest witnesses of the LXX for these passages such as the lead scroll of

---

[38] See L. Jalabert and H. Leclercq, "Citations bibliques dans l'épigraphie". Compare this high number with the very few biblical quotations in the inscriptions and papyri that are quite clearly Jewish in origin, see J. B. Frey, *Corpus Inscriptionum Judaicarum I*, Rome 1952. The first volume was re-published in New York (Ktav Publishing House) 1975, with a *Prolegomenon* by B. Lifshitz. In this *corpus* it is more a case of biblical phraseology than direct quotations. See also V. A. Tcherikover, A. Fuks and (M. Stern), *Corpus Papyrorum Judaicarum*, I–III, Cambridge Mass., 1957–64.

[39] D. Feissel, "La Bible dans les inscriptions grecques", *Le monde grec ancien et la Bible*, BTT 1, Paris 1984, 223–31.

[40] See E. Tov, "Une inscription grecque d'origine samaritaine trouvée à Thessalonique", *RB* 81 (1974), 394–99.

[41] See D. Feissel, "La Bible dans les inscriptions grecques", 230, and R. Stichel, "Die Inschriften des Samson-Mosaiks in Mopsuestia".

[42] See L. Jalabert and H. Leclercq, "Citations bibliques dans l'épigraphie", 1746ff.

Rodas, an amulet with Psalm 79 from the 1st–3rd centuries CE,[43] the inscription of Lapethus in Cyprus with Psalm 14 from the 4th century CE or somewhat earlier,[44] or the ostracon of Judith 15:1-7 from the 3rd century CE, which is the oldest fragment for this book since the only papyrus known so far comes from the 5th century CE.[45]

Many of these quotations occur in a magical context and transmit to us an interesting page of the popular piety of that time; they are prophylactic formulae or ἀποτρόπαια, written on lintels, door frames and windows through which the evil spirits could slip. Others, instead, occur in liturgical context in churches, synagogues or tombs.[46] They often reproduce the text of the LXX with small variants. However, sometimes they preserve readings of great textual interest such as the Amulet of Acre which contains the word κάστυ, the reading of Aquila and Theodotion for Ez. 9:2.[47] At other times they confirm isolated and important variants of some Septuagintal manuscripts such as the reading τὴν μάχαιρα instead of τὴν χεῖρα of ms. 130 for Gen. 22:12 which continues to be a *hapax* in the edition of Genesis by Wevers and is confirmed by a painting with an inscription from the 10th century in Ballep Kilissé (Cappadocia).[48]

P. Collart distinguishes three groups of amulets with texts from the Psalms:

1. composite amulets in which the psalms occur together with other magical texts;
2. amulets with the continuous text of a psalm;
3. amulets in which isolated words from the psalms can be read.[49]

---

[43] See A. Rahlfs, *Septuaginta-Studien II*, Göttingen 1907, 14.

[44] See A. Rahlfs, *Septuaginta-Studien II*, 16.

[45] The AT 33 (= Rahlfs 968), see K. Aland, *Repertorium der griechischen christlichen Papyri. I*, Berlin–New York 1976, 98, and J. Schwartz, "Un fragment grec du livre de Judith".

[46] The inscription of Ps. 35:8-10 on the belly of a jar: μεθυσθήσονται ἀπὸ πιότητος τοῦ οἴκου σου (v. 9) is important and is probably a copy of the inscriptions that refer to Dionysius or to drink, common on such vases. Perhaps the jar was intended for liturgical use, see M. A. Steve and P. Benoît, "Une cruche avec inscription biblique".

[47] See E. Peterson, "Das Amulett von Acre".

[48] See G. de Jerphanion, "Une variante isolée d'un manuscrit", and J. W. Wevers, *Septuaginta . . . I Genesis*, Göttingen 1974, *ad. loc.*

[49] P. Collart, "Psaumes et amulettes". See also N. Fernández Marcos, "Motivos judíos en los Papiros Mágicos Griegos", *Religión, superstición y magia en la mundo Romano*, ed. J. Lomas, Cádiz 1985, 101–30, and A. Biondi, "Le citazioni bibliche nei papiri magici greci", *Studia Papyrologica* 20 (1981), 93–127, although the latter studies by preference quotations from the New Testament.

Without danger of exaggerating the importance of inscriptions for textual criticism, it can be stated that sometimes they are useful to delimit and specify geographically the sphere of influence of the recensions.

f) *Quotations from the Fathers and the Septuagint*

Also in connection with the biblical text followed by the Fathers, from the methodological point of view, the hypothesis of *testimonia* has to be considered since it could explain a large number of mixed quotations, incorrect attributions, texts of unknown origin and even *agrapha*.

The *testimonia* are collections of biblical texts without a commentary, correlated by a common theme. It is well attested that in late antiquity, collections and anthologies of quotations and maxims from famous authors were in circulation, called *florilegia*.[50] When these collections of texts comprise a chain of biblical quotations they are given the name *testimonia*. The discovery of collections of *testimonia* in the Qumran literature (4QT) requires us to go back to a pre-Christian origin for this literary form.[51] However, where it developed most was among Jewish Christians around central themes of the new religion such as messianism, eschatology, the Law, the cross, the rejection of Israel, the vocation of the gentiles.[52] This is what recent studies have shown.[53] The criteria for specialists concerning the characteristics of these collections and their use for establishing the biblical text vary a great deal. A. Méhat has analysed these collections in the text of Clement of Alexandria, and emphasises the problem of literary criticism that they pose when Clement does not take his texts directly

---

[50] See H. Chadwick, "Florilegium", *RAC* 7 (1969), 1131–59.

[51] See F. García Martínez, *The Dead Sea Scrolls Translated: The Qumran Texts in English*, Leiden 1996, 137–40.

[52] For the messianic interpretation of certain readings from the LXX in the New Testament, see M. Harl, "L'interprétation de la Septante dans le Nouveau Testament", Harl *et al.*, *La Bible grecque des Septante*, 282–88.

[53] See J. Daniélou, *Études d'exégèse judéo-chrétienne*, and P. Prigent, *Les testimonia dans le christianisme primitif*. In Prigent's opinion, the following facts work in favour of the *testimonia*: the recurrence of the same composite quotations; the recurrence of incorrect attributions in different contexts; the recurrence of the same textual variants; the recurrence of the same biblical sequences in authors presumed to be independent from each other; and lastly, cases where the author appeals to a set of quotations for a purpose which is not the same as the one which dictated the grouping of texts.

from the Bible but from other authors in which they circulated, already taken out of context. Probably the hypothesis of an *Urflorilegium* or book of *testimonia* on which all these quotations depend has to be abandoned in favour of a more fluctuating image, which incorporates the ebb and flow affecting these collections: from the original texts to the extracts edited separately, to be included once again in continuous commentaries by other authors.[54]

J. P. Audet, instead, is opposed to the concept of *testimonia* as a specific literary form. In any case they were reading notes or extracts from Scripture that circulated to assist memory and recitation but were never works intended for publication. To try to discover in them a purpose, an intention or even a particular theology, is futile and beyond our capabilities in the present state of documentation. Melito of Sardis (*c.* 170 CE) and Cyprian of Carthage (*c.* 250 CE) are the first two witnesses of biblical extracts intended for publication. These extracts had their proper place in the liturgy and were used as an introduction or guide in the reading of Scripture.[55]

If we have spent some time on the hypothesis of the *testimonia*, it is in order to illustrate an aspect of the serious problems posed by biblical quotations in the Fathers, especially when studied for textual reasons rather than only from the aspect of history of exegesis. It is further proof that before using them for the critical restoration of the LXX, the literary form in which they occur has to be determined as well as the context of lemma or commentary and other details that are indispensable for correctly evaluating the text of the quotation in question.

However, we would also like to insist that these quotations, duly restored, comprise an indispensable tool for determining the recensions of the Greek Bible. Without going into the enormous bibliography for the quotations of each Father here,[56] or into the new critical editions that have been published in the principal collections,[57] we shall restrict ourselves in what follows to listing the main conditions imposed by scholarly use of this quotation material before including it in textual criticism of the LXX.

---

[54] A. Méhat, "L'Hypothèse des 'Testimonia' à l'épreuve des Stromates. Remarques sur les citations de l'Ancien Testament chez Clément d'Alexandrie", *La Bible et les Pères*, ed. A. Benoît and P. Prigent, Strasbourg 1971, 229–42.

[55] J. P. Audet, "L'hypothèse des 'Testimonia'", 402ff.

[56] See *CB* 59–65 and the *Biblia Patristica* collection. See, also, Select Bibliography.

It is necessary to establish the chronology of these quotations, their places of origin and finally to establish their text in reliable critical editions. Later, the literary genre in which the quotation occurs has to be determined, since those transmitted in a collection of *testimonia* (with the additional literary problem of outlining the sources from which they have been taken) do not have the same value as those in an exegetical commentary or a homily.

Besides these requirements, it will have to be established whether the quotation occurs in a lemma or a commentary or in both at the same time; whether it is a quotation from memory, a conflation of parallel passages or an allusion that belongs to the biblical language of the author in question. Above all, it has to be seen whether the same author quotes the same passage in different ways; such quotations have special value, as Rahlfs and Ziegler have shown.[58] The resulting refined text is valid for the comparison of different groups of manuscripts that transmit the recensions and possibly local revisions of the text of the LXX.[59]

Select Bibliography

Arnaldez, R., "La Bible de Philon d'Alexandrie". *Le monde grec et la Bible*, ed. C. Mondesert, BTT 1, Paris 1984, 37–54.

———, R., "L'influence de la traduction des Septante sur le commentaire de Philon". *Études sur le Judaïsme hellénistique*, ed. R. Kuntzmann and J. Schlosser, Paris 1984, 255–66.

Audet, J. P., "L'hypothèse des 'Testimonia'. Remarque(s) autour d'un libre récent". *RB* 70 (1963), 381–405.

Begg, C., *Josephus' Account of the Early Divided Monarchy (AJ 8, 212–420): Rewriting the Bible*, Leuven 1993.

---

[57] The best known, such as *Sources Chrétiennes, Die griechischen christlichen Schrifsteller der ersten Jahrhunderte* or the *Corpus Christianorum. Series Graeca*, or other critical editions which have appeared in other series, see M. Geerard, *Clavis Patrum Graecorum*, vols 1–5, Brepols–Turnhout 1974–87; *Supplementum* by M. Geerard and J. Noret, Brepols–Turnhout 1998. See also *Das Korpus der griechischen christlichen Schriftsteller. Historie, Gegenwart, Zukunf*, ed. J. Irmscher and K. Treu, Berlin 1977.

[58] A. Rahlfs, *Septuaginta Studien* 1, Göttingen 1904, 16–87, and J. Ziegler, "Jeremias-Zitate in Väter-Schriften".

[59] It is the path that we have followed in our editions of *Quaestiones in Octateuchum*, and *Quaestiones in Reges et Paralipomena*, by Theodoret of Cyrus, before using his biblical quotations for the edition of the Antiochene text of the Greek Bible in the historical books, see N. Fernández Marcos and A. Sáenz-Badillos, *Theodoreti Cyrensis Quaestiones in Octateuchum*, Madrid 1979, XXXIX–LXII, and N. Fernández Marcos and J.-R. Busto Saiz, *Theodoreti Cyrensis Quaestiones in Reges et Paralipomena*, Madrid 1984, LI–LX.

Benoît, A., and P. Prigent, "Les citations de l'Écriture chez les Pères". *RHPhR* 2 (1966), 161–68.

Boehl, E., "Alte Christliche Inschriften nach dem Text der LXX". *TSK* 1881, 692–713.

Boismard, M. E., "Critique textuelle et citations patristiques". *RB* 57 (1953), 172–78.

Collart, P., "Psaumes et amulettes". *Aegyptus* 14 (1934), 463–67.

———, "Un papyrus Reinach inédit. Psaume 140 sur une amulette". *Aegyptus* 13 (1933), 208–12.

Daniélou, J., *Études d'exégèse judéo-chrétienne (Les 'Testimonia')*, Paris 1966.

Feissel, D., "La Bible dans les inscriptions grecques". *Le monde grec ancien et la Bible*, ed. C. Mondesert, BTT 1, Paris 1984, 223–31.

Fernández Marcos, N., "La Biblia de los autores del Nuevo Testamento". *II Simposio Bíblico Español*, ed. V. Collado-Bertomeu and V. Vilar-Hueso, Valencia–Córdoba 1987, 171–80.

Fichtner, J., "Der AT-Text der Sapientia Salomonis". *ZAW* 57 (1939), 155–92.

Hagner, D. A., *The Use of the Old and New Testaments in Clement of Rome*, Leiden 1973.

Hanhart, R., "Die Bedeutung der Septuaginta in neutestamentlicher Zeit". *ZTK* 81 (1984), 395–416.

Harl, M., "La Septante aux abords de l'ère chrétienne. Sa place dans le Nouveau Testament". Harl *et al.*, *La Bible grecque des Septante*, 1988, 269–88.

Harrinton, D. J., "The Biblical Text of Pseudo-Philo's 'Liber Antiquitatum Biblicarum'". *CBQ* 33 (1971), 1–11.

Hatch, E., *Essays in Biblical Greek*, Oxford 1989, 131–202 and 203–14.

Jalabert, L., and H. LECLERCQ, "Citations bibliques dans l'épigraphie grecque". *DACL* II, 2 (1914), 1731–79.

Jerphanion, G. de, "Une variante isolée d'un manuscrit confirmée par l'épigraphie". *Bib* 3 (1922), 444–45.

Jouassard, G., "Requête d'un patrologue aux biblistes touchant les Septante". *Studia Patristica* I (1957) = TU 63, 307–27.

Katz, P., *Philo's Bible: The Aberrant Text of Bible Quotations in some Philonic Writings and its Place in the Textual History of the Greek Bible*, Cambridge 1950.

Kraft, R. A., "The Epistle of Barnabas, its Quotations and their Sources". Diss., University of Harvard 1961.

Müller, M., "The Septuagint as the Bible of the New Testament Church: Some Reflections". *SJOT* 7 (1993), 194–207.

Nagel, P., "Die Septuaginta-Zitate in der Koptisch-Gnostischen 'Exegese über die Seele' (Nag Hammadi Codex II)". *Archiv für Papyrusforschung* 22/23 (1974), 249–69.

Nestle, E., "Alte Christliche Inschriften nach dem Text der LXX". *TSK* 1883, 153–54.

Nikiprowetzky, V., *Le Commentaire de l'Écriture chez Philon d'Alexandrie*, Leiden 1977.

Nodet, É., *Le Pentateuque de Flavius Josèphe*, Paris 1996.

Peterson, E., "Das Amulett von Acre". *Aegyptus* 33 (1953), 172–78.

Prigent, P., *Les testimonia dans le christianisme primitif. L'Épître de Barnabé I–XVI et ses sources*, Paris 1961.

Schaller, B., "Das Testament Hiobs und die Septuaginta-Übersetzung des Buches Hiobs". *Bib* 61 (1980), 377–406.

Schwartz, J., "Un fragment grec du livre de Judith (sur ostracon)". *RB* 53 (1946), 534–37.

Spottorno, V., "Flavio Josefo. Técnicas de adaptación del texto bíblico (1 Re 3, 16–28)". *Sefarad* 52 (1992), 227–34.

Steve, M. A. and P. Benoît, "Une cruche avec inscription biblique". *RB* 56 (1949), 433–42 (Ps. 35:8–10).

Steyn, G. J., *Septuagint Quotations in the Context of the Petrine and Pauline Speeches of the Acta Apostolorum*, Kampen 1995.

Stichel, R., "Die Inschriften des Samson-Mosaiks in Mopsuestia und ihre Beziehung zum biblischen Text". *ByZ* 71 (1978), 50–61, pl. 9–10 (Jgs 16:1-4).

Swete, H. B., *An Introduction to the Old Testament in Greek*, Cambridge 1914, 369–432.

Thackeray, H. St J., *Josephus: the Man and the Historian*, New York 1967, 75–100.

Ulrich, E. C., "Josephus' Biblical Text for the Books of Samuel". *Josephus, the Bible, and History*, 1989, 81–96.

Vermes, G., "Josephus' Treatment of the Book of Daniel". *JJS* 42 (1991), 149–66.

Wikgren, A., "Two Ostraca Fragments of the Septuagint Psalter". *JNES* 5 (1946), 181–84.

Wilcox, M., "On Investigating the Use of the Old Testament in the New Testament". *Text and Interpretation: Studies in the New Testament Presented to Matthew Black*, ed. E. Best and R. McL. Wilson, Cambridge 1979, 231–43.

Ziegler, J., "Jeremias-Zitate in Väter-Schriften. Zugleich grundsätzliche Betrachtungen über Schrift-Zitate in Väter-Ausgaben". *Hist. Jahrbuch* 77 (1958), 347–57.

For particular studies of Old Testament quotations in the New, see *BS*, 75–82, and for the text of the Old Testament in the Pseudepigrapha, see the bibliography by J. H. Charlesworth, *The Pseudepigrapha and Modern Research, with a Supplement*, Chico, Calif. 1981. For the biblical quotations and allusions of Nag Hammadi, see *Nag Hammadi Texts and the Bible*, ed. C. A. Evans, R. L. Webb and R. A. Wiebe, Leiden 1993. For quotations in the Fathers, J. Allenbach, A. Benoît, D. A. Bertrand, A. Hanriot-Couster, P. Maraval, A. Pautler, P. Prigent, (M. Scopello, F. Vinel, Th. Ziegler), *Biblia Patristica. Index des citations et allusions bibliques dans la littérature patristique*, 6 vols, with a supplement on Philo of Alexandria, Paris 1975–95, is indispensable.

CHAPTER EIGHTEEN

APORIAI AND BIBLICAL COMMENTARIES

Of the many literary forms of early Christian literature, we shall select two for their particular repercussions for the history of the Greek Bible: *erotapokriseis* literature and biblical commentaries.[1] It is useful to first note that the only Bible used for commentaries, questions, homilies and theological treatises for the Greek Fathers is the LXX, which means that in their works these authors attempt to resolve all the *Aporiai* of the biblical text and difficult passages (many of them due to the Greek of the translation), within the Greek language system.[2]

Before analysing these two genres with a view to using them for textual criticism of the LXX, we have to insist yet again on the lack of critical editions and on the false attributions that require clarification with the help of patristic literature,[3] especially if we compare the present neglect of Christian Greek literature with the attention that has been paid to classical Greek literature.

In what follows we shall trace out the path followed by these two literary forms, focusing particularly on their impact on the transmission and restoration of the Greek Bible.

---

[1] See H. Jordan, *Geschichte der altchristlichen Literatur*, 377 and 409–12.

[2] See M. Harl, "Origène et la sémantique du langage biblique", *VC* 26 (1972), 161–88; Harl, "Origène et les interprétations patristiques grecques de l'"obscurité' biblique", *VC* 36 (1982), 334–71; N. Fernández Marcos, "En torno al estudio del griego de los cristianos", *Emerita* 41 (1973), 45–56; M. Harl, "Y-a-t-il une influence du 'grec biblique' sur la langue spirituelle des chrétiens?. Exemples tirés du psaume 118 et de ses commentateurs d'Origène à Théodoret", *La Bible et les pères*, Strasbourg 1971, 243–62; A. Hilhorst, *Sémitismes et latinismes dans le "Pasteur" d'Hermas*, Nijmegen 1976.

Very few writers on the Fathers tackle the problem of biblical Greek from a linguistic standpoint as translation Greek, see G. J. M. Bartelink, "Observations de Saint Basile sur la langue biblique et théologique", *VC* 17 (1963), 85–105. Undoubtedly the most interesting treatise on biblical hermeneutics in antiquity is Hadrian's *Eisagoge*, from the first half of the 5th century, see O. Bardenhewer, *Geschichte der altkirchlichen Literatur IV*, 254–55, and for the text *PG* 98, 1273–312, and F. Goessling, *Adrians 'Eisagoge eis tas theias graphas'*, Berlin 1987. For philological studies by the Fathers on the Bible, G. Dorival, "Antiquité chrétienne et Bible", *Dictionnaire Encyclopédique de la Bible*, Turnhout 1987, can be consulted, especially 70–76.

[3] See J. B. Bauer, "Patrologie", and W. Speyer, "Fälschung".

a) Aporiai

The genre of *Aporiai* or *erotapokriseis* consists in the treatment of a topic by means of a series of questions and answers. Although the word is not ancient (it is used for the first time by Byzantine grammarians of the 13th century) the question-and-answer pattern for developing a topic goes back a long way in literature. Its beginnings are to be traced back to the beginnings of critical study on the Homeric poems. The first objections to be raised were concerned with morals. Later, the attacks focused on grammar and style and on the inconsistencies within the poems in respect of content. However, it was in the Hellenistic period that the genre ζητήματα καὶ λύσεις culminated.[4] The genre was particularly suited to biblical exegesis since, like the Homeric poems, many passages in the Old Testament posed problems of inconsistency, contradictions and passages offensive to morals. The genre was used particularly in writings of scientific content and in the literature of revelation. It is thus connected with the introductions (*Eisagogai*) to the sciences and apophantic literature in which a novice beginner comes before a deity or priest asking questions.[5] In antiquity they are usually treated unsystematically, in the form of explanations of difficult passages; the ζητήματα καὶ λύσεις of Philo of Alexandria comprise an exception as is evident from the Latin and Armenian fragments we possess. For each verse of the Pentateuch he formulates a question in order to answer it in a complete commentary.[6]

With the arrival of Christianity, this literary form took on a new dimension. For although Philo's attitude towards scripture is comparable to the attitude of Christian exegetes, his *quaestiones* are more a commentary, and in the fragments that have come down to us

---

[4] See A. Gudeman, Λύσεις. *PW* I.13.2 (1927), 2511–29, and O. Dreyer, "Lyseis", *KP* 3.16–17 (1968/9), 832–33. See also C. Schäublin, *Untersuchungen zu Methode und Herkunft*, 49–51, 55–65, and A. Kamesar, *Jerome, Greek Scholarship and the Hebrew Bible*, 82–96.

[5] Especially the Hermetic and Gnostic literature, see H. Dörrie and H. Dörries, "Erotapokriseis. A.-Nichtchristlich". In my opinion, an antecedent of this literary form is also to be found in passages in apocalyptic literature where the angel interpreter or mediator answers the initiate's questions on mysteries not explained to most mortals, such as where the supplies for the weather are kept or other secrets of the next world.

[6] See translation by R. Marcus, *Philo Supplement. I: Questions and Answers on Genesis; II: Questions and Answers on Exodus*, London–Cambridge, Mass. 1953; F. Petit, *Quaestiones in Genesim et Exodum. Fragmenta Graeca*, and J. Paramelle, *Philon d'Alexandrie*.

the basic *Aporiai* of Christian exegesis are missing. In Christian writers the ancient ζητήματα have new contents. Apparently the first questions correspond to inquiries about the infancy narratives and the resurrection: for example, the Περὶ τῶν ἐν Εὐαγγελίοις ζητημάτων καὶ λύσεων by Eusebius of Caesarea, of which we only have fragments.[7] Of the six books on Σύμμικτα ζητήματα by a successor Acacius of Caesarea, only fragments concerning 1 Corinthians 15 have been preserved. The questions on the Old Testament by Eusebius of Emessa that G. Bardy thought were lost, are probably extant in his Armenian Commentary on the Octateuch published by Hovhannessian.[8]

In the West, among the Latin Fathers, we have two recensions of the work *Quaestiones Veteris et Novi Testamenti* attributed to the author known as Ambrosiaster[9] and composed in Rome between 370 and 375; the *Quaestiones hebraicae in Genesim* by Jerome, the *De diversis quaestionibus ad Simplicianum* or *Quaestiones in Heptateuchum* by Augustine, and other treatises.[10] In Christian literature, eisagogic questions were studied intensively, as shown by the *Apophthegmata Patrum* and the *Gerontica*. In these collections the questions are very simple and refer to salvation (πῶς σωθῶ) and the answers are very short, a biblical *logion* easily applied to life.[11]

---

[7] See *PG* 22, 879ff.; H. Dörrie and H. Dörries, "Erotapokriseis. B. Christlich"; A. Kamesar, *Jerome, Greek Scholarship and the Hebrew Bible*, 85, and Chr. Schäublin, *Untersuchungen*, 49–55.

[8] G. Bardy, "La littérature patristique", 342. V. Hovhannessian, *Eusèbe d' Émèse 1. Commentaire de l'Octateuque*, Venice 1980, and R. B. ter Haar Romeny, *A Syrian in Greek Dress: The Use of Greek Hebrew, and Syriac Biblical Texts in Eusebius of Emesa's Commentary on Genesis*, Leuven 1997.

[9] See G. Bardy, "La littérature patristique", *RB* 41, 343–56.

[10] See G. Bardy, "La littérature patristique", *RB* 41, 356–69, 515–37; H. Dörrie and H. Dörries, "Erotapokriseis", and A. Kamesar, *Jerome, Greek Scholarship and the Hebrew Bible*, 86–96. In his *Quaestiones in Genesim* (a total 220) Jerome includes Jewish legends on the theme and in this way has transmitted ancient stories of Jewish origin, see M. Rahmer, *Die hebräischen Traditionen in den Werken des Hieronymus*, Breslau 1861, and D. Brown, *Vir Trilinguis: A Study in the Biblical Exegesis of Saint Jerome*, Kampen 1992, 55–87 and 167–93. The questions proposed by Jerome are the classic difficulties of certain passages; neither he nor his fictitious questioners invented them. He explains the *Aporiai* with a wide circle of readers in mind, not just particular individuals. And he is dependent on the Greek Fathers who had already provided solutions to the problems before him. It is strange that out of Jerome's 220 question on Genesis and Augustine's 170 on the same book (*Quaestiones in Heptateuchum*), no more than 30 are common to both.

[11] See D. Burton-Christie, *The Word in the Desert: Scripture and the Quest for Holiness in Early Christian Monasticism*, New York–Oxford 1993.

However, the most successful in the 4th and 5th centuries were the questions and answers concerning Scripture or difficult passages in it. There are two types:

1. Purely artificial questions that are no more than a pretext for a commentary. They are usually asked by the exegete in order to have an opportunity to resolve them (Philo, Augustine and Theodoret). If they follow the order of the biblical books we have a more or less continuous commentary.
2. Real difficulties that have been posed at a particular time to a famous interpreter, a wise bishop or a friend. This is the case for Eusebius of Caesarea, Jerome and some questions by Augustine.

However, there is great fluctuation between one genre and another. Several times the supposed questioner is imaginary and the exegete can pose real problems that interest or concern him.

When this genre first came into being, it was more interesting and personal than at its end. Little by little, the classic questions were crystallised and the collections tend to become anonymous or pseudepigraphical; they are open to new problems and it is difficult to identify the original author of successive questioners.

After the 5th–6th centuries there began the period of the *florilegia* and the *catenae*.[12] The collections of questions come very close to this other type of compilation and it is barely possible to identify them by more than their outward form. For although the *catena* is limited to juxtaposing several witnesses relating to the same biblical passage, there are *catenae* arranged around a nucleus formed by the *quaestiones* of Theodoret of Cyr.[13] This work by Theodoret became the most important of its kind among the Greek Fathers. Its title, quest, search (ζητήματα) into difficult passages of Sacred Scripture distinguishes two types of inquirer who ask questions about the Bible: the evil-minded who are trying to contradict the sacred text (οἱ μὲν δυσσεβῶς ἐρωτῶσι), and the ones who pose questions in order to learn (οἱ δὲ φιλομαθῶς ζητοῦσι). The edition by Schulze, printed by Migne (*PG* 80), includes sections from Origen, Diodorus, Didymus, Theodore

---

[12] See H. Chadwick, "Florilegium", *RAC* 7 (1969), 1131–59, and M. Richard, *Opera Minora I*, Turnhout–Leuven 1976, articles 1–4 and 6. On the *catenae*, see chapter 19.

[13] See chapter 19.

and other Fathers, fragments which both for content and scant representation in the manuscript tradition have to be excluded from a critical edition of the work.[14]

The questions are set by the author. However, sometimes allusion is made to other people and to older traditions. Only occasionally does Theodoret argue with Josephus, Marcion, Arius, Eunomius and Apollinaris. He attacks the heretics in their criticisms of the Old Testament[15] more than the pagans. The distribution of the questions in the books of the Octateuch and Kings can give us an idea of the problems that were of most interest to exegesis then. There are 111 questions on Genesis, 72 on Exodus, 38 on Leviticus, 51 on Numbers, 46 on Deuteronomy, 20 on Joshua, 28 on Judges and 2 on Ruth. This uneven distribution, which is found also in Augustine, gives the impression that the author is becoming increasingly tired as he goes through the biblical books. There follow 65 questions on 1 Samuel, 45 on 2 Samuel, 68 on 1 Kings and 57 on 2 Kings. Strangely, in the books of Chronicles the questions are replaced by a commentary.[16]

In line with the principles of the Antioch school, there is more literal and typological interpretation than allegorical. These *Aporiai* are by no means bookish or mere formalities, and there is much experience and use of information in the explanations. Question 33 on Exodus – which explains that, when fighting the Amalekites, the Hebrews used the weapons of the Egyptians whose corpses had been deposited by the waters on the shore of the Red Sea – occurs both here and in Hellenistic Jewish historians.[17] Although one of the sources

---

[14] See N. Fernández Marcos and A. Sáenz-Badillos, *Theodoreti Cyrensis Quaestiones in Octateuchum. Editio critica*, Madrid 1979, XI–XXIX. See the Prologue to the *quaestiones* on p. 3 of that edition, lines 14–17. The need for this edition was expressed by G. Bardy, "La littérature patristique", 42 (1933), 225, as follows: "Un autre problème, connexe au précédent, est celui du texte des *Quaestiones*. L'ouvrage a été édité d'après un manuscrit du XIIe siècle, le *Paris*. 842; et on peut lire, dans le texte imprimé quelques fragments de Diodore, de Théodore de Mopsueste et d'Origène ... Dans ces conditions on comprend, avec quelle urgence s'imposerait un examen sérieux de la tradition manuscrite."

[15] See J.-N. Guinot, *L'exégèse de Théodoret de Cyr*, 465–563.

[16] He only has one question on 1 Chron. 15:27 and after replying briefly with the interpretations of Aquila and Symmachus he continues with a sort of summary-commentary. The same thing happens with 2 Chronicles: he only has one question on 2 Chron. 10:15 and continues in the manner of a commentary, see N. Fernández Marcos and J. R. Busto Saiz, *Theodoreti Cyrensis Quaestiones in Reges et Paralipomena. Editio Critica*, Madrid 1984, 252 and 264.

[17] Used by Demetrius in order to exculpate the Hebrews to show that they were not armed when they fled from Egypt, see C. R. Holladay, *Fragments from Hellenistic*

used by Theodoret is indicated as Philo of Alexandria,[18] it seems that he was more influenced by Flavius Josephus, at least for questions on the Octateuch, Kings and Paralipomena, where he is often cited.[19] However, his main source, apparently, is Diodorus of Tarsus, to the extent that when editing his work he possibly had in front of him the *Quaestiones in Octateuchum* by that author, which we know only from fragments.[20] It would be extremely interesting for the history of exegesis to do research on Jewish haggadic material.[21]

The literature of *quaestiones et responsiones* is continued in the *Replies to the orthodox*, attributed to Justin, but actually dating to the time of Theodoret; in the *Aporiai of the gospel symphony* by Hesychius of Jerusalem, which is not of high quality and sometimes degenerates into mere curiosities; the *Quaestiones ad Antiochum* by Pseudo-Athanasius, dogmatic questions on dogma, exegesis and popular piety; the *Quaestiones ad Thalassium* by Maximus the Confessor, in which he replies to 65 questions on biblical *Aporiai* or passages that seem to be contradictory. And lastly, the *Quaestiones et responsiones* by Anthony of Sinai, in which biblical topics only occupy the nucleus from 21 to 81 and the appendix, from 142 to 1532.[22]

It is not easy to mark out the line dividing *Erotapokriseis* from related genres. The literature of the *Aporiai* stands out because the author himself asks the question and sometimes answers at great length. The *dialogue*, instead, is not satisfied with one answer but returns repeatedly to the same idea. The shift from *Erotapokriseis* to the *lexicon* of biblical concepts and words cannot have been difficult.

Jewish Authors. Volume I: Historians, Chico, Ca. 1983, 76–77. See also Josephus' *Antiquities*, II, 349.

[18] See P. Wendland, *Neu entdeckte Fragmente Philos*, Berlin 1891, 106–108.

[19] See N. Fernández Marcos and J. R. Busto Saiz, *Quaestiones in Reges et Parlipomena*, 314–15.

[20] See J.-N. Guinot, *L'exégèse de Théodoret de Cyr*, 234–52 and 748–99.

[21] An indication of how rich these works are can be found in the article by L. Ginzberg, "Die Haggada bei den Kirchenvätern und in der apokryphischen Litteratur" *MGWJ* 42 (1898), 537–50; 43 (1899), 17–22, 117–25, 149–59, 217–31, 293–303, 409–16, 461–70, 485–504, 529–47. Guinot in his important work on Theodoret's exegesis (*L'exégèse de Théodoret de Cyr*, 484–521) focuses rather on polemics than on the haggadic material.

[22] H. Dörrie and H. Dörries, "Erotapokriseis. B. Christlich", can be consulted for the path followed by this literary genre from apothegms up to its shift to *florilegia* and *catenae*. For Anastasius Sinaita, see M. Richard, "Les veritables 'Questions et réponses'". For Maximus Confessor, see *Maximus Confessor- quaestiones ad Thalassium*, I (QU. I–LV), una cum latina interpretatione Ioannis Scotti Eriugenae, edited by C. Laga and C. Steel, Turnhout 1980; II (QU. LVI–LXV) 1990.

All that was necessary was to put the questions into alphabetical order, as was done by Eucherius of Lyons in his two books of *Instructiones ad Salonium*.[23] In the final stage, the *Aporiai* become *florilegia* and *catenae*, where the interest lies neither in the questions nor in the name of compiler but in the witnesses of the great commentators of scripture in the golden age of the Fathers, set out like a chain.[24]

b) *Commentaries*

Although the history of Christian exegesis has yet to be written, some recent monographs open up a horizon of unsuspected possibilities. To retrace the ancestors of a particular book or biblical passage in the successive explanations by the Fathers is an adventure that not only provides us with unexpected new items but can even help in understanding the biblical text in question.[25]

Christian exegesis is as old as the gospels. Paul, the Letter to the Hebrews and James include midrashic techniques with continual references to the Old Testament. To trace the history of Christian exegesis we shall have to go as far back as Philo, even, for the enormous influence his exegesis of the Pentateuch has on Christian commentators, and even to the literature from Qumran because it largely inherits the problems and attitudes of Jewish exegesis.[26]

Among the Apostolic Fathers and Apologists, the work most like a commentary is the Letter of Barnabas (1st half of the 2nd century CE) in which an attempt is made to prove that the Church is the true heir of the synagogue. Justin's Dialogue with Tryphon is one of the oldest and most complete forms of Christian exegesis. However, according to Eusebius, Irenaeus and Clement, it is possi-

---

[23] *Sancti Eucherii Lugdunensis, Opera Omnia*, recensuit et comentario critico instruxit C. Wotke, CSEL 31, Vienna 1894.

[24] In spite of the theme of the *erotapokriseis* it retains its heuristic and pedagogical value and appears again in the famous *quaestiones disputatae* of the scholastics, although there is no direct connection with them.

[25] See Y.-M. Duval, *Le livre de Jonas dans la littérature chrétienne grecque et latine. Sources et influence du Commentaire sur Jonas de saint Jérôme*, I and II, Paris 1973.

[26] For biblical commentaries in Qumran, see G. Aranda Pérez, F. García Martínez and M. Pérez Fernández, *Literatura judía intertestamentaria*, Estella (Navarre) 1996, 92–119, and J. A. Fitzmyer, *The Dead Sea Scrolls: Major Publications and Tools for Study*, Atlanta, Ga. 1990, 160–61.

ble that commentaries in the strict sense appeared around 150 CE.[27] The oldest commentary known is the *Antithesis* by Marcion, mentioned by Tertullian in *Adversus Marcionem*; it is an explanation of Luke's gospel by Marcion on the basis of contrasts with and oppositions to the Jewish books.[28] The author of the first known commentary on the gospel of John in the 2nd century is a heretic, Herakleon, a disciple of Valentine. We know about him through Origen who tries to refute him in his *Commentarium in Joannem*. These facts may be due to chance or could indicate a greater scientific curiosity by the Gnostics, since we can count on a parallel in the origins of Christian poetry: our first information about it is through the Gnostic and Arian hymns.[29]

From the 3rd to the 4th centuries a wealth of commentaries, *scholia* and homilies on the holy books emerges; the literature is badly known because, generally, the summaries, *florilegia* and *catenae* have been more widespread, and after the 6th century they dominate the exegetical horizon.[30]

Although, in the prologues to his Commentaries, Jerome often speaks of commentators earlier than him such as Appolinaris, Origen and Didymus,[31] it is surprising how few fragments of them we have, especially when it is now accepted that a large part of Jerome's commentaries was composed on the basis of selections from Origen.

However, the most typical commentaries are connected with two great Christian centres in ancient times: Rome and Alexandria. Hippolytus and Origen are the two most productive writers of the 3rd century. Of the first we only have fragments in the works of other authors, especially in the *Eranistes* by Theodoret of Cyr.[32] Many of these exegetical works from the beginning only commented on

---

[27] W. Bousset, *Jüdisch-christlicher Schulbetrieb in Alexandria und Rom*, Göttingen 1915 = Hildesheim–New York 1975, 263–71.

[28] Fragments are preserved in the writings of Tertullian, Origen and Epiphanius. See A. von Harnack, *Marcion, das evangelium des fremden Gottes*. TU 45, Leipzig 1924.

[29] See W. Christ and M. Paranikas, *Anthologia graeca carminum christianorum*, Leipzig 1871; W. Meyer, *Anfang und Ursprung der lateinischen und griechischen rythmischen Dichtung*, Munich 1885; H. Follieri, *Initia Hymnorum Ecclesiae Graecae I–V*, ST 211–15bis, Vatican City 1960–66; K. Thraede, *Untersuchungen zum Ursprung und zur Geschichte der christlichen Poesie* I, JAC 1961, 108–27, and A. von Harnack, *Geschichte der altchristlichen Literatur bis Eusebius* I/1, Leipzig 1893 (reprint of the 2nd edn 1958), 795–97.

[30] See chapter 19 and A. G. Hamman, *Jacques-Paul Migne*, 22–35.

[31] For example, in the prologue to his commentary on Hosea, *PL* 25, 819–20.

[32] See the recent edition of the *Eranistes*: G. H. Ettlinger, *Theodoret of Cyrus Eranistes: Critical Text and Prolegomenon*, Oxford 1975.

short passages such as the *Hexameron*, paradise and the fall, the blessings of Isaac, Jacob, Balaam, Moses. The only commentaries by Hippolytus that survive today, and perhaps the only ones to exist as such in antiquity, are the commentaries on Song of Songs and Daniel. The one on Song of Songs is the first Christian example of allegorical interpretation; the commentary on Daniel, written under the persecution of 202, was intended to calm the faithful of Rome, notifying them that the end of the world was not near.[33]

However, the real creator of scientific exegesis in the Christian world is Origen. Through book IV of *De Principiis*, a true treatise on hermeneutics, and from the *Philocalia*, we can know his exegetical ideas, the principles of allegorical interpretation and the three meanings of Scripture. He is also the first author who feels the need to base his exegesis on a flawless biblical text for which he did not spare any means in the composition of the Hexapla.[34] In Jerome's prologues it is evident that Origen returned three times and in three different ways to the same biblical book: in the form of scholia or short notes on difficult passage, as homilies to the public and in complete commentaries on the biblical books. He has commentaries on Genesis, Psalms, Proverbs, Song of Songs, Isaiah, Jeremiah, Ezekiel and the Twelve Prophets.[35] Much by Origen is also to be found in the *Hexameron* by Ambrose, in the commentary on the Psalms by Hilary, and in Jerome. The importance of these last works is that they can be very useful for checking fragments attributed to Origen in the *catenae*.[36]

At the end of the 4th century there emerged a series of commentators from the school of Antioch openly opposed to the exegetes

---

[33] M. Richard, "Les difficultés d'une édition", and J. Ziegler, "Der Bibeltext im Daniel-Kommentar des Hipollyt von Rom", *Nachr. d. Akademie d. Wiss. zu Göttingen. Philolog.-Hist. Klasse*, 1952, 163–99.

[34] For the exegetical work and hermeneutics of Origen, see B. Altaner and A. Stuiber, *Patrologie*, Fribourg 1980, 200–205; P. Nautin, *Origène, sa vie et son oeuvre*, Paris 1977, 261–362, M. Harl, *Origène. Philocalie, 1–20, Sur les Écritures.* SC 302, Paris 1983, 42–157, and B. Neuschäfer, *Origenes als Philologe* I–II, Basle 1987, I, 139–246.

[35] G. Bardy, "Commentaires patristiques de la Bible", 91–94. The commentary on Genesis comprised thirteen books according to Jerome (*ep.* 33,4), but twelve according to Eusebius (*Hist. Ec.* VI, 24,2). For the fragments preserved, see *PG* 12, 46–146. Although Jerome used this work in his *Quaestiones Hebraicae in Genesim*, apparently he was critical of it, and sometimes had reservations about Origen's interpretation, see A. Kamesar, *Jerome, Greek Scholarship and the Hebrew Bible*, 98–103.

[36] R. Devreesse, *Les anciens commentateurs grecs de l'Octateuque*, 26–52, and Devreesse, *Les anciens commentateurs grecs des psaumes*, 1–88.

of Alexandria: they condemn the allegorical exegesis of Origen and his Alexandrian successors unreservedly and opt for literal and typological exegesis.[37] Behind both schools lie two different philosophical presuppositions which hinder mutual understanding: the Aristotelian philosophy of the Antiochenes and the neo-Platonism of the Alexandrians. However, recently the trend is to analyse the different interpretational methods of the two schools, insisting more on the different approaches that they contribute to the history of exegesis than on the supposed conflict of relations between Antioch and Alexandria or the radical opposition between typology and allegory.

The difficulty in studying the school of Antioch is that we only have fragments. The work by Diodorus of Tarsus, τίς διαφορὰ θεωρίας καὶ ἀλληγορίας, mentioned by Suidas, which would have been fundamental in understanding the differences between the two schools, has been lost. Diodorus is the teacher of the group, but only fragments of his works survive, taken from the *catenae* and the commentary on the Psalms.[38]

The theory of the exegetical school of Antioch is put together in Hadrian's Εἰσαγωγή, a work which, to judge from the fragments of the *catenae*, was much longer than is preserved in known manuscripts and printed editions.[39]

---

[37] See Chr. Schäublin, *Untersuchungen*; G. W. Ashby, *Theodoret of Cyrrhus as Exegete of the Old Testament*, Grahamstown 1972, 17–25; J.-N. Guinot, *L'exégèse de Théodoret de Cyr*, 71–76, and Guinot, "La typologie comme technique herméneutique", *Figures de l'Ancien Testament chez les Pères*, Cahiers de Biblia Patristica 2, Strasbourg 1989, 1–34.

[38] See J. Deconinck, *Essai sur la chaîne de l'Octateuque avec une édition des Commentaires de Diodore de Tarse*, Paris 1912, 84–169, where he published the fragments of Diodorus, dividing them into authentic, doubtful and false. It should be noted that Fragment 75 of Numbers (pp. 152–54) is not by Diodorus but by Theodoret, as we have shown from examining the manuscript tradition of the *Quaestiones in Octateuchum* by Theodoret of Cyr. See also R. Devreesse, *Les anciens commentateurs grecs de l'Octateuque*, 157–67; R. Abramowski, "Untersuchungen zu Diodor von Tarsus", *ZNW* 30 (1931), 234–62, and E. Schweizer, "Diodor von Tarsus als Exeget", *ZNW* 40 (1941), 33–75. And for his commentary on the psalms, *Diodorus Tarsensis-commentarii in psalmos*, I (Ps. I–L), ed., J.-M. Olivier, I vol., Turnhout 1980.

[39] See G. Mercati, "Pro Adriano", *RB* 11 (1914), 246–55. The most recent edition is by F. Goessling, *Adrians* Εἰσαγωγὴ εἰς τὰς θείας γραφάς, Leipzig 1887. On pp. 43–50 of the introduction Goessling analyses how Adrian agrees with the hermeneutics of Theodore of Mopsuestia, Theodoret, Chrysostom and with the Lucianic recension. See also A. Vaccari, "La *theoria* nella scuola esegetica di Antiochia", *Bib* 1 (1920), 3–36, and Vaccari, "La *theoria* esegetica antiochena", *Bib* 15 (1934), 94–101.

The two main representatives of the Antioch school are undoubtedly Theodore of Mopsuestia and Theodoret of Cyr. A list of Theodore's exegetical works is in Leontius of Byzantium.[40] The Commentaries on Psalms and on the Twelve Prophets come from the first exegetical period, before his bishopric; the commentaries on the gospels, epistles and possibly also the Commentary on Job and Ecclesiastes, the latter dedicated to Porphyrius, belong to the second period, probably after 400. He is the only Father of the Church to write a literal exegesis of the Song of Songs, he denies the charisma of inspiration to the author of Job, and his commentary on the Psalms was heavily criticised because it applied to the events of the people of Israel what, according to the Fathers, had to be understood of the Messiah. As a result, he argued for the exclusion of the book of Job and Song of Songs from the canon of inspired books and rejected the messianic interpretation of most of the Psalms.[41] The reduction of the number and extent of the messianic prophecies explains to a large extent why his commentaries disappeared[42] We now have a recent critical edition of his commentary on the Twelve Prophets.[43] And in general it is possible to state that some recent finds of parts of his works and other specialised monographs are helping to restore the image of this Antiochene Father, one of the greatest intellects in the Greek Church, who would have enjoyed much greater success in antiquity if his works had not been so popular among Nestorius' followers.[44] Theodoret of Cyr, a disciple of Theodore, has a continuous commentary on the Psalter[45] as well as commentaries on Isaiah, Jeremiah, Ezekiel, Daniel and the Twelve Prophets.[46]

And to close: there is a need to pay attention to the Commentaries by Eusebius of Caesarea, John Chrysostom, Apollinaris of Laodicea

---

[40] Leontius of Byzantium, *Contra Nestorium et Eutychium* III, 13–17 in *PG* 86, 1363–70.

[41] See L. Pirot, *L'oeuvre exégétique de Théodore de Mopsueste*, Rome 1913, 122–23.

[42] Some of them condemned, see Mansi IX, 249.

[43] H. N. Sprenger, *Theodori Mopsuesteni Commentarius in XII prophetas. Einleitung und Ausgabe*, Wiesbaden 1977, which replaces the one by Mai and von Wegnern printed in Migne, *PG* 66, 123–632.

[44] R. Bultmann's unpublished doctoral dissertation was on the exegesis of Theodore of Mopsuestia. See L. Pirot, *L'oeuvre exégétique de Théodore de Mopsueste*, especially the introduction, chap. VI and pp. 323–25, and R. Devreesse, *Essai sur Théodore de Mopsueste*, Vatican City 1948.

[45] *PG* 80, 857–1998.

[46] *PG* 81, 215–1988.

and Cyril of Alexandria for the East; and at least revise those by Hilary, Ambrose, Jerome and Augustine for the West. It is absolutely necessary to work on two fronts: by the production of modern critical editions that will reduce the great textual anarchy present in the field, and by monographs that trace the history of exegesis through the various schools and writers. It is many years since Rahlfs drew attention to the need for these editions in respect of the Greek Bible.[47]

SELECT BIBLIOGRAPHY

Alfonsi, L., "I generi letterari. Dall'antichità classica alla letteratura cristiana". *Augustinianum* 14 (1974), 451–59.

Altaner, B., "Der Stand der patrologischen Wissenschaft und das Problem einer neuen altchristlichen Literaturgeschichte". *Miscellanea Giovanni Mercati* I (= ST 121), Vatican City 1946, 483–520.

———, B., and A. Stuiber, *Patrologie. Leben, Schriften und Lehre der Kirchenväter*, Freiburg 1980.

Bardenhewer, O., *Geschichte der altkirchliche Literatur*, Freiburg I 1913, II 1914, III 1923, IV 1924, V 1962.

Bardy G., "Commentaires patristiques de la Bible". *DBS* 2 (1934), 73–103.

———, "La littérature patristique des 'Quaestiones et responsiones' sur l'Écriture Sainte". *RB* 41 (1932), 210–36; 341–69; 515–37; 42 (1933), 14–30; 211–29; 328–52.

---

[47] I shall only mention commentaries that require editions the most. In the commentaries on the psalms there is absolutely no order with respect to attributions. On these Rahlfs says that his remarks are completely provisional and precise research on the manuscripts is pressing, see A. Rahlfs, *Verzeichnis der griechischen Handschriften des Alten Testaments*, Berlin 1914, 402, n. 3. See also M. Richard, "Quelques manuscrits peu connus des chaînes exégétiques et de commentateurs grecs sur le Psautier", *BIRHT* 3 (1954), 87–107. Theodoret's Commentary on the Psalms is well worth editing for its wealth of Hexaplaric notes among other reasons.

On the commentary by Hesychius of Jerusalem on the Twelve Prophets (*PG* 93, 1339–86), Rahlfs, *Verzeichnis*, 432, n. 2 remarks: "Eine genauere Untersuchung ist erforderlich". Still unpublished are commentaries in Greek by unknown writers on the Twelve Prophets, such as the one preserved in ms. Ω-III-19 in the Royal Library of El Escorial and in another manuscript of the National Library of Madrid (*Bib. Nac.* 4698). Also required is a new edition of the Commentary on Twelve Prophets by Cyril of Alexandria. Ziegler apologises because the quotations from Cyril in his edition of *Dodekapropheton* are not reliable, see J. Ziegler, "Der Bibeltext des Cyrill von Alexandrien zu den zwölf kleinen Propheten in den Druck-Ausgaben", *Nachr. d. Akad. d. Wiss. zu Göttingen, Philol.-Hist. Klasse*, 1943, 345–412, especially 400–402.

And in the wisdom books, we are still expecting the edition of the Commentary by Malachias on the books of Wisdom, Ben Sira and Proverbs which is in the 14th century ms. Ω-I-7, in the Royal Library of El Escorial. Besides being one of the few commentaries on the wisdom books in existence, it has the attraction of providing a biblical text that is Lucianic, see J. R. Busto Saiz, "The Biblical Text of 'Malachias Monachus' to the Book of Wisdom", *La Septuaginta*, 1985, 257–69.

Baskin, J. R., "Rabbinic–Patristic Exegetical Contacts in Late Antiquity: A Biblio-graphical Reappraisal". *Approaches to Ancient Judaism* 5, Atlanta, Ga. 1985, 53–80.

Bauer, J. B., "Patrologie". *Was ist Theologie?*, ed., E. Neuhäussler and E. Gössmann, Munich 1966, 120–38.

Berardino, A. di (ed.), *Diccionario Patrístico y de la Antigüedad Cristiana*, I–II, Salamanca 1991–92.

Devreesse, R., *Le Commentaire de Théodore de Mopsueste sur les Psaumes (I–LXXX)*, Vatican City 1939.

———, R., *Les anciens commentateurs grecs de l'Octateuque et de Rois (Fragments tirés des chaînes)*, Vatican City 1959 (= ST 201).

———, R., *Les anciens commentateurs grecs des Psaumes*, Vatican City 1970 (= ST 264).

Dörrie, H., and H. Dörries, "Erotapokriseis". *RAC* 6 (1966), 342–70.

Ghellinck, J. de, "Diffusion, utilisation et transmission des écrits patristiques: guides de lectures, bibliothèques et pages choisis". *Gregorianum* 14 (1933), 356–400.

Guinot J. N., *L' exégèse de Théodoret de Cyr*, Paris 1995.

Hagedorn, D., *Der Hiobkommentar des Arianers Julian*, Berlin–New York 1973.

Hamman, A. G., *Jacques-Paul Migne. Le retour aux pères de l'Église*, Paris 1975.

Harl, M., *Origène. Philocalie, 1–20, Sur les Écritures*. SC 302, Paris 1983.

Harnack, A. von, *Geschichte der altchristlichen Literatur bis Eusebius I,1*, Leipzig 1958, XXI–LXI.

Jordan, H., *Geschichte der altchristlichen Literatur*, Leipzig 1911.

Kamessar A., *Jerome, Greek Scholarship, and the Hebrew Bible: A Study of the "Quaestiones Hebraicae in Genesim"*, Oxford 1993.

Kerrigan, A., *St Cyril of Alexandria Interpreter of the Old Testament*, Rome 1952.

Labriolle, P. de, *La réaction païenne*, Paris 1952, 487–508.

Margerie, B. de, *Introduction à l'histoire de l'exégèse: I. Les pères grecs et orientaux*, Paris 1980.

Musurillo, H., "Some Textual Problems in the Editing of the Greek Fathers". *Studia Patristica* 3, Berlin 1961, 85–97.

Nautin, P., *Origène. Sa vie et son oeuvre*, Paris 1977.

Nautin, P. and L. Doutreleau, *Didyme l'Aveugle. Sur la Genèse. Texte inédit d'après un papyrus de Toura* I–II. SC 233–34, Paris 1976–78.

Paramelle, J., avec la collaboration de Enzo Lucchesi, *Philon d'Alexandrie. Questions sur la Genèse II, 1–7. Texte grec, version arménienne, parallèles latins*, Geneva 1984.

Petit, F., *Quaestiones in Genesim et in Exodum. Fragmenta Graeca*, Paris 1978.

Richard, M., "Les difficultés d'une édition du commentaire de S. Hippolyte sur Daniel". *RHT* 12 (1972), 1–11.

———, "Les veritables 'Questions et réponses' d'Anastase le Sinaïte". *BIRHT* 15 (1967–68), 39–57.

———, "Quelques manuscrits peu connus des chaînes exégétiques et des com-mentateurs grecs sur le Psautier". *BIRHT* 3 (1954), 87–107.

Scäublin, C., *"Untersuchungen zu Methode und Herkunft der antiochenischen Exegese"*, Köln–Bonn 1974.

Speyer, W., "Büchervernichtung". *JAC* 13 (1970), 122–53.

———, "Fälschung". *RAC* 7 (1969), 236–77.

Treu, K., "Patristische Fragen. 1 Patristik und Spätantike. 2. Überlieferungs- und Editions- probleme der Patristik". *Svensk Exegetisk *rsbok* 34 (1969), 170–200.

Ulrich, E. C., "The Old Testament Text of Eusebius: The Heritage of Origen". *Eusebius, Christianity and Judaism*, ed. H. W. Attridge and G. Hata, Leiden 1992, 543–62.

CHAPTER NINETEEN

THE LITERATURE OF THE *CATENAE*

On the *catenae*, Swete stated that "Perhaps no corner of the field of
Biblical and patristic research offers so much virgin soil, with so good
a prospect of securing useful if not brilliant results."[1] In fact, even
today it continues to be barely explored territory where it is necessary to consult the actual manuscripts and mistrust some printed
material. Every attempt at classification must be considered provisional since as yet the catenary manuscripts have not been stripped
in a systematic way.

To be able to evaluate correctly the text of the *catenae* in order
to include them in the textual criticism of the Greek Bible, attention must be paid to the following aspects:

1. the genesis and development of this literary form,
2. the description of the catenary manuscripts from a formal aspect;
3. the textual content of the actual *catenae*.

The text of the *catenae* is interesting from two aspects:

1. for the possibility it provides of recovering, by means of these late
   compilations, lost texts of the Fathers, new Hexaplaric material
   of the most recent translators of the Bible or even ancient readings of the LXX;
2. for the type of biblical text that the mss classed as catenary (group
   C) in the critical editions of Göttingen can provide.

a) *Formation of the Literary Genre*

A *catena* is a collection of fragments taken from different works (commentaries, homilies, scholia) by ancient writers on texts from Scripture.
Usually these extracts are preceded by the name of the author to
whom they belong and follow the sequence of the biblical books in
the various books. As a result they comprise a sort of tacking together

---

[1] H. B. Swete, *An Introduction to the Old Testament in Greek*, Cambridge 1914, 363.

or sequence of exegetical commentaries by various authors, following the *catena* represented by the successive verses of a particular biblical book.

The name *florilegium* is usually reserved for dogmatic or ascetic-moral, not exegetical collections.

The genre is not specifically Christian but grew from imitation of the copious literature of *scholia* to classical authors, the ὑπομνήματα, real treatises that incorporated the author's text. There are 1st century papyri with commentaries on Homer in which the pericopes are threaded together into a continuous interpretation. As time went on, the explanations were subdivided into ἀπορήματα, ζητήματα and λύσεις. Later, they would be content with simple notes on the more difficult or stranger passages: the σχόλια.

In the Hellenistic period the works of medical doctors and famous philosophers were also annotated in this way. The same happens with juridical *scholia*, the collection of the Digest. The text is centre-page or in the inside of the page; the margins are kept for *scholia*.[2]

Originally the chains were called ἐξηγητικά, a term which includes both the continuous commentaries and homilies and the *scholia*. Later, the number was reduced to what was most significant and they were called ἐκλογαί or collections of selected texts.

They began to be formed at the beginning of the 6th century when original production of patristic literature was in decline. In this period new commentaries on the Old and New Testaments were no longer written but the commentaries by exegetes and men of the Church from the past were reworked and made into *catenae*. Procopius of Gaza was the first to start this type of compilation. As he notes in the prologue to the Octateuch, in a first stage he had tried to collect the ἐξηγήσεις of the Fathers, begging them from here and there.[3] He cited the selected portions as they were (αὐτολέξει). Soon he realised how large his work was becoming; consequently he decided make it shorter and revise it according to the following guidelines:

1. If several authors had the same text one quotation was enough.
2. If their opinions were different he was content to reproduce them in a sort of continuous explanation, including all their words in a single written format.[4]

---

[2] R. Devreesse, "Chaînes exégétiques grecques", 1085–87. The same formal parallel is to be noted in the arrangement of a page of rabbinic bibles.
[3] See the work by Theodoret of Cyr with precisely the title "the beggar" (ἐρανιστής).
[4] See *PG* 87, 21–24.

This second work is the one we have now; it is the commentary or epitome of the ἐκλογαί of Procopius.[5]

The aim of the catenarists was to present different types of exegesis in abbreviated form. And it is possible that the first attempts are to be looked for in the interpretations to be found in margins to the Syro-Hexaplaric version, where throughout the psalms the exegesis of Hesychius alternates with that by Athanasius, whereas in Job there are fragments of Chrysostom. However, there are many possible combinations from

1. the *catena* of two authors in which two commentaries alternate whose interpretations are followed from beginning to end;
2. the marginal *catena* around a commentary by someone famous (e.g. the *Quaestiones in Octateuchum* by Theodoret of Cyr or the commentary by John Chrysostom which comprises the pivot on which the *catena* to Job turns);
3. the *catena* by three authors;
4. a primitive *catena*, composed of sections chosen from different exegetes, that is later summarised and expanded with new commentaries from other authors.

One of the collections that has been studied most is the *catena* to the Psalms.

G. Dorival divides the history of these *catenae* into two phases. The first is centred in Palestine and represents the origins and first stage of the *catenae*; the second took place in Constantinople and its centres of influence, and is marked by the large number of collections and the appearance of new forms of *catenae*. In the Palestinian phase, three forms can be distinguished:

1. the form of Procopius, where the extracts are taken from commentaries or homilies by Palestinian writers and the page layout is set out as either one or two columns of text;
2. the *scholia-catenae*, marked by short discontinuous explanations. These *scholia* are set out in a column parallel to the corresponding biblical text;
3. the mixed model, a combination of the other two.

---

[5] See E. Lindl, *Die Octateuchcatene des Procop von Gaza*, 17ff. Other titles to be found in catenary manuscripts include συλλογὴ ἐξηγήσεων, ἐπιτομὴ ἑρμηνείων. The most recent name is the one retained until today: χρυσὴ ἄλυσις or *catena aurea*. The Greek word σειρά is no earlier than the end of Byzantine era. See also J. Deconinck, *Essai sur la chaîne de l'Octateuche*, 11ff.

In the second Constantinople phase several models also evolved:

1. the first makes systematic use of the works of Chrysostom and only when his commentary is missing is use made of the Theodoret's commentary on the Psalms;
2. the *catena* of two writers which gives the complete commentaries of two authors;
3. the mixed Constantinople model, which uses Chrysostom and Theodoret as the basic writers but also makes use of basic authors from Palestine.

The *catenae* to the Psalms evolved in a special way and ended up in turn to produce new forms of traditional exegesis from which they derived, i.e. homilies or *scholia*. This change is well attested from the 10th century, and can be said to have closed the circle of this literary form to produce new literary forms from those that nourished it.[6]

Another of the problems that interested specialists from the first was to know whether *catenae* can be found that reflect the concerns of a school. Against what had been believed, it seems instead that there were no collections that excluded heretical or suspect writers such as Origen, Theodore of Mopsuestia, Eusebius, Apollinaris, Severus or Diodorus. None of these is excluded beforehand. Orthodoxy was of so little concern to the catenarists that thanks to them we have many fragments, some lengthy, of the work of suspect writers or those condemned by the Church.

Valuable indications on the date of the formation of *catenae* are provided by the sequence in which the authors have entered the compilations.

b) *Formal Aspects of Catenary Manuscripts*

The technical terminology for various types of *catenae* is loose and thus both their description and the classification by external criteria can only be provisional. For a definitive classification, first all the manuscripts with *scholia*, all those that have continuous commentaries, and the imperfectly described manuscripts would have to be examined in a systematic way. Even so, Karo and Lietzmann and

---

[6] See G. Dorival, "La postérité littéraire de chaînes", especially 211–13. For a more exhaustive classification of the models of *catenae* to the Psalms, see M. Geerard, *Clavis Patrum Graecorum IV*, 188–212.

Deconinck propose the following division according to the outward form of the manuscript:[7]

1. Catenae *with columns*: with two or three columns per folio in which the commentaries of two or three famous authors are intertwined.
2. *Marginal* catenae ("Rahmencatene" or "Randcatene"): with the biblical text occupying centre-page, apart from about ten lines in semi-uncial or minuscule. The exegesis of the various Fathers surrounds this text on all sides in the form of a crown, about seventy lines in smaller cursive minuscule.
3. *Text* catena ("Breitcatene" or "Textcatene"), in which biblical text and commentary are not separated, although normally the biblical text stands out as it is written in uncial or semi-uncial, whereas the commentary is in minuscule.
4. *Marginal* catena, in which the manuscript originally only had the biblical text. The first scribe or a later one fills the margins with commentaries taken usually from other *catenae* and to the extent that these margins allow.

This formal description of the various page layouts in these catenary manuscripts can be completed today – thanks to the research of G. Dorival – with a diachronic approach that helps in understanding the development of various types of *catenae*. The page layout in the uncial manuscripts corresponds to the layout of marginal *catenae*: the biblical text is written on the central section of the page and the extracts from the Fathers are in the three margins. However, this was not the original layout of the *catenae*. It can be shown that initially the *catena* filled the whole page in a single column of text: the catenarist first set out the biblical text of a verse and then the extracts from the Fathers corresponding to that verse; next, the following verse, again with the appropriate commentaries of the Fathers, and so on. In other words, it is possible to state that the first *catenae* followed the model of biblical commentaries or ὑπομνήματα from the 3rd to the 5th centuries, which were used as a model for the page layout. This is the model followed by the first *catena* of Procopius of Gaza. However, after the 7th century, the *scholia* to scripture became a new source for the catenarists besides the exegetical commentaries and the homilies. This new source also influenced the page layout

---

[7] G. Karo and H. Lietzmann, *Catenarum graecarum catalogus*, 331, and J. Deconinck, *Essai sur la chaîne de l'Octateuche*, 25–26.

and explains the appearance of the *catenae* in two columns, and later of marginal *catenae* which became general from 750 up to the end of the 11th century in tandem with what happened to the content and again from the 11th century, the *catenae* turn to the commentary as a model even for the page layout. A parallel event can be noted in the commentary to the classics of Byzantine humanism.[8]

Within the text or in the margin of the manuscript, the name of the author to whom the fragment is attributed is usually indicated in abbreviated form and normally in a different ink. It goes without saying that these abbreviations very soon became a constant source of mistakes: the abbreviations for the two Gregories (of Nyssa and Nazianz) and for the two Eusebiuses (of Emessa and of Caesarea), for Didymus and Diodorus, Theodore and Theodoret, etc. The abbreviation for Origen (ωρ') can be confused with the one for ὡραῖον, the equivalent of our 'proper, fitting', the one for Chrysostom (χ') with the admiring exclamation of the copyist: χρυσοῦν.

When a fragment by the same author already cited follows, it is simply introduced by the note τοῦ αὐτοῦ. If the names of the authors of those texts have been lost in the transmission process, this is indicated simply by ἄλλος or ἀνωνύμου.

In the 10th century, the names begin to be removed from their positions and put in the margins, which becomes a source of new mistakes. It is not always easy to known where a fragment begins and ends. Faced with such a difficulty, many copyists left the fragments undivided and juxtaposed several names at the beginning of the whole paragraph, so that the problem of attribution became even more complicated.[9]

Finally, there is a series of illuminated *catenae* with scrolls and miniatures of the various passages of the Octateuch. Their textual interest – besides their artistic interest – is that they comprise a cri-

---

[8] For a detailed proof of this process, see G. Dorival, "Des commentaires de l'Écriture aux chaînes".

[9] Other useful signs, although not exclusive to the *catenae* (some of them inherited by the ancient scholiasts), are:

κείμενον	=	base text of the commentary
ἑρμ(ηνεία)	=	explanation proposed
σχό(λιον)	=	rapid note
γνώ(μη)	=	denotes a sort of sentence
ὑπ(όδειγμα)	=	introduces a comparison
ση(μαῖνον)	=	*nota bene*

See also H. B. Swete, *An Introduction to the Old Testament in Greek*, 364–65.

terion for determining the imitation writing, and thus are very important for dating the manuscript correctly.[10] Even the details of the miniatures can help to interpret the meaning of certain texts or words in difficult passages.

c) *Textual Contents of the* Catenae

In this section a distinction must be made between:

1. the type of biblical text that the catenary manuscripts transmit, i.e. the characteristics of what is called the *Catena*-group in the printed editions of the LXX;
2. the material of the extracts from exegetical commentaries included around the biblical text.

In the first case, in the three groups of writings published so far in the Göttingen series – Pentateuch, Prophetic Books and Writings (only in part) – the group C of catenary manuscripts occurs, sometimes divided into several subgroups, in all the books that have a Hebrew *Vorlage*. In the Pentateuch, the tendency for corrections that raise it to the level of a recension are not evident, but instead it is a mixed group that is very popular among catenarists. It should be noted, however, that not all the catenary manuscripts adopted a biblical text of this type C for their lemmata, and instead, there are some non-catenary manuscripts that do have the type C text. The group is distinguished by having a large number of singular readings which identify it as such.[11] In the prophetic books, the catenary group (C) is made up of the three minuscules 87–91–490 with a subgroup comprising mss 49–90–764. Most of the variants inserted by this group are grammatical and stylistic: changes of tense, mood and person, of compound verb to simple, changes due to contamination from parallel passages, etc. Sometimes it follows the Lucianic recension in its readings; in a very few cases it has a Hexaplaric addition agreeing with the Hebrew text, taken from Origen's or the Lucianic recension. In the catenary group of Isaiah it supports the text of the Complutensian for that book. In the Twelve Prophets it is closely

---

[10] See "Illustration of LXX" in *CB*, 195–201, and "Les illustrations de la LXX" in *BS*, 307–10.

[11] For the characteristic of this goup and its position in textual history *Septuaginta*, see J. W. Wevers, *Text History of the Greek Genesis*, Göttingen 1974, 82–100.

related to the Hexaplaric recension but it is not, as Procksch claimed, the most faithful representative of the Hexaplaric recension.[12] There are many omissions, some agreeing with the Hebrew text, others not conditioned by it but rather due to stylistic reasons or carelessness by the copyist. The additions are few and unimportant. It was subject to the influence of the Hexapla, but also underwent a revision that corrected another set of passages only in respect of their Greek and to some extent following Lucian. In his recent edition of the book of Job, Ziegler has studied the various groups of catenary manuscripts and their relationship to the types of *catenae* to that book.[13]

As regards the second aspect of the actual commentary that they include, the *catenae* have become one of the main sources of information about the thinking of ancient Christianity, a source which for the most part still remains hidden and unknown. Their special value is that they are the only means of rescuing fragments of authors whose works – due to having been condemned or declared suspect by a council – disappeared completely. Through them one can, to a large extent, follow the path of those writers in antiquity who fell under Church censure. This affects especially the principal writers of the school of Antioch who succumbed in the tensions of the Arian disputes and were collected by the catenarists in their compilations because they were only interested in the most complete dossier possible of a biblical passage, with no concern for schools.

In 1912, Deconinck[14] published important fragments of the lost commentary by Diodorus of Tarsus, extracted from the *catena* on the Octateuch, and later Devreesse edited catenary fragments belonging to Philo, Josephus, Origen, Eusebius of Emessa, Apollinaris of Laodicaea, Diodorus of Tarsus, Didymus, Severus of Antioch, etc.[15] In catenary manuscripts Mercati found fragments of the *Eisagoge* by

---

[12] See J. Ziegler, *Septuaginta XIII Duodecim Prophetae*, Göttingen 1967, 102, n. 1.

[13] J. Ziegler, *Septuaginta. XI, 4 Iob*, Göttingen 1982, 125–33.

[14] J. Deconinck, *Essai sur la chaîne de l'Octateuque*, 84–169.

[15] R. Devreesse, *Les anciens commentateurs grecs de l'Octateuque*. Sketched out previously in *RB* 44 (1935), 166–91; 45 (1936), 201–20 and 364–84. New fragments recovered can be found in F. Petit, *Catenae Graecae in Genesim et in Exodum. I. Catena Sinaitica; II. Collectio Coisliniana*, and Petit, *La chaîne sur la Genèse I, II*. For the catenary fragments in the books of Psalms, see R. Devreesse, *Les anciens commentateurs grecs des Psaumes*. ST 264, Vatican City 1970, and the editions by G. Dorival and E. Mühlenberg, cited in the Select Bibliography.

Adrian which are missing from the printed editions by Migne and Goessling.[16]

Of most interest for the Greek Bible is the new Hexaplaric material recovered. We should not forget that the Hexaplaric fragments to the psalms, discovered in palimpsest O.39 in Milan, appear in a catenary manuscript.[17] When providing a new edition of the Hexaplaric fragments which brings Field's up to date, it is important to examine all the sources that can provide us with new readings. And one of the richest for Hexaplaric readings is that of the catenary manuscripts,[18] as G. Dorival has proved recently.[19] He analyses which type of *catena* to the psalms is rich in Hexaplaric readings and therefore is deserving of study. He distinguishes four types of *catenae* to the psalms that provide Hexaplaric readings:

1. primary, ancient *catenae* of two or more authors;
2. recent primary *catenae* such as the one of Nicetas;
3. *catenae* of collections of Hexaplaric glosses;
4. recent *catenae*.

The principal one is the oldest *catena* to the psalms, the Palestinian (5th/6th century), both for the number and length of its Hexaplaric readings (many of them unpublished) and for the certain attribution and for the excellent condition of its text. The catenarist has arranged and made extracts from commentaries by authors who in general had direct access to the Hexapla in the Library of Caesarea, especially the commentary by Eusebius. The Monophysite *catena*, dated somewhat later (6th century), is less essential but puts us in contact with the better textual condition of the unpublished commentary by Hesychius of Jerusalem and transmits some Hexaplaric readings as

---

[16] G. Mercati, "Pro Adriano", *RB* 11 (1914), 251ff. New acquisitions from published *catenae* can be seen in R. Devreesse, *Introduction à l'étude des manuscrits grecs*, 176ff.: fragments of Eustace of Antioch on the Octateuch, Proverbs and Qoheleth, published by M. Spanneut in 1948; other fragments of Theophilus of Alexandria and Theophilus of Antioch, published by M. Richard in *RB* 47 (1938), 387–97; fragments of Philo edited by H. Lewy in *RB* 42 (1933), 136–38.

[17] See chapter 13 pp. 12–13.

[18] See the Hexaplaric fragments of indirect tradition published by A. Schenker, *Hexaplarische Psalmenbruchstücke. Die hexaplarischen Psalmenfragmente der Handschriften Vaticanus graecus 752 und Canonicianus graecus 62*, Freiburg–Göttingen 1975, and G. Mercati, *Alla ricerca dei nomi degli "altri" traduttori nelle omilie sui salmi di S. Giovanni Crisostomo e variazioni su alcune catene del Salterio*, Vatican City 1952 (ST 158).

[19] G. Dorival, "L'apport des chaînes exégétiques grecques". In the appendix he provides more than thirty unpublished Hexaplaric readings for Ps. 118.

yet unknown. The *catena* by Nicetas of Heraclea, in spite of coming from the 11th/12th century, is of interest because he had access to the lost commentary on the psalms by Eusebius and there are very many Hexaplaric readings.

Dorival prefers a distinction of a geographical or cultural nature to any other. The important thing is to discover the textual stage of very first original *catena*. Once this stage has been reached, either unpublished readings are acquired or readings of a textual condition that is more trustworthy than other sources, which reflect more recent secondary stages. Once this original phase is known it is superfluous to collate the more recent sources. Although ultimately only comparison among the different witnesses of the readings for each variant and knowledge of the translation techniques and the vocabulary of each of the translators recorded in the Hexapla allow access to the most certain stage of the text.

In their catalogue, Karo and Lietzmann provided a classification in terms of content into three groups for the Octateuch:[20]

1. The group comprising the ms. *Basileensis* I (10th century) which goes from Genesis to Ex. 14:31. It omits Justin, Isidore, Gennadius and almost all of Diodorus. Theodoret is abandoned early: from Gen. 48 the nucleus of the *catena* is made up of the *Glaphyra* by Cyril of Alexandria.
2. Groups represented by *Mosq.* 385 (10th century), *Barb. gr.* 569 and *Matr.* 4673 (both from the 15th to 16th centuries). This is closer to the next group than to the first. Theodoret forms the basis of the *catena* and has many quotations in it from Diodorus and Gennadius.
3. The group comprising about thirty mss to which the *Catena Lipsisensis* belongs, the only one for the Octateuch published.[21]

Devreesse proposes a new classification, but only provisionally, for he is aware that all the witnesses of interest have not yet been exam-

---

[20] G. Karo and H. Lietzmann, *Catenarum graecarum Catalogus 1*, 10ff.
[21] Also called the *Catena* of Nicephorus, printed in Leipzig in 2 volumes, 1772–73. It depends on an 11th century manuscript and on fragments from two other manuscripts. It inserts one asterisk whenever it seems that the author of the fragment has to be corrected in the manuscripts and two asterisks whenever he adds a *scholion* that is not in the manuscripts he uses. As is evident from this editorial procedure, it cannot be used to restore the original texts of the *catenae*.

ined to make that classification definitive.[22] Hence the importance of our edition of the *Quaestiones* by Theodoret of Cyr in order to clarify the origin and development of the *catenae* to Genesis–Kings, for they comprise the common basis not only of the *Catena Lipsiensis* but of all the other groups. As Devreesse already noted, and as we noticed in preparing our edition of Theodoret, ms. *Coisl.* 113 (9th century) is the oldest of the Genesis–Kings *catena* and comprises its earliest stage.[23]

Finally, F. Petit's accurate studies have resulted in the classification of the *catenae* of the Octateuch. Petit reduces Karo and Lietzmann's three types to two, combining their types I and II. The main material of the first group comprises a *catena* in the strict sense, with mixed contents, composed of short fragments and focused on the biblical text. The extracts come from different authors and are cited unchanged. The texture of the second group (= Karo and Lietzmann's III), is a collection of more homogenous content, representing above all the exegetical school of Antioch. This *catena* is made up of fairly long extracts and is based on Theodoret's *Quaestiones*. The *Coislinianus* 113 is the oldest manuscript of the group.

In all the witnesses of the first group, (Manuscripts from Leningrad [St Petersburg], Sinai, Moscow and Basle), Theodoret appears to be secondary. However, in the second group (= Karo and Lietzmann's III), the collection represented by *Coislinianus* 113 with Theodoret's *Quaestiones* as the nucleus of the *catena*. It is therefore a secondary *catena*, since all of its quotations are indirect and come from writings

---

[22] R. Devreesse, *Chaînes exégétiques grecques*, 1102: "Ce classement, on le pense bien, ne peut être que provisoire: il n'a été tenu compte que des mss qui ont été accessibles soit directement, soit par des analyses, soit par des reproductions partielles. Nous le répétons, tant qu'on n'aura pas examiné de près les manuscrits des *Quaestiones* de Théodoret, l'ordre de tous ces manuscrits cités comme représentant une IIIe famille des chaînes Genèse-Rois, sera impossible à établir définitivement."

[23] N. Fernández Marcos and A. Sáenz-Badillos, *Theodoreti Cyrensis Quaestiones in Octateuchum. Editio critica*, Madrid 1979, IXff. Within the third family of Karo and Lietzmann's catalogue we have found four separate groups, an indication of the many combinations that the catenarists produced. The first, comprising three manuscripts, is a *catena* of the text in terms of form, and preserves Theodoret's introduction to the *Quaestiones* and the names of the different authors. The second group of manuscripts does not preserve the names of the Fathers, but has many additions and abbreviations of the catenary type and mentions some Fathers at the end. And lastly, the third group is mixed: the manuscripts are catenary in the first part, even preserving the names of the Fathers. However, the second part has only Theodoret's *Quaestiones*, in discontinuous form but with several additions missing from most manuscripts of the *Quaestiones*.

that have already been reworked. Indirectly, this classification is confirmed by the fact that Procopius of Gaza, the first known compiler of *catenae*, completely ignores Theodoret's *Questiones*.[24]

d) *Methodology for Studying the* Catenae

As a first principle for future research on the *catenae* it should be noted that the catenary collections have to be studied for their own merits, without preconceived ideas or concern about the results they might bring. Before providing a formal classification such as the one by Karo and Lietzmann, which takes no account of the chronology of these compilations nor of their inter-relationships, it is better to try to reconstruct the genetic stages of these collections. In this perspective Deconinck's method is not free from criticism.[25] He divides the fragments of Diodorus recovered from the *catenae* into authentic, doubtful and false. They are authentic when, having compared the witness of the various groups of manuscripts, they agree on Diodorus as the author. Well, once it is established that nearly all the quotations come from the first stage of the *catena*, one has to look at the first representative of that stage, *Coisl.* 113, which is very important for Diodorus and to which preference has to be given for identification.

Even so, as of today it is difficult to replace the classification of the catalogue by Karo and Lietzmann with one that is more logical, for it has been shown that the medieval catenarists tried all possible combinations. The most logical way to define a *catena* is to determine its sources. The fragments themselves have to be studied without trusting the outward form and the arrangement, exposed to many shifts and changes, especially with regard to authorship. Nor are the *scholia* and philological notes that accompany many manuscripts always to be trusted. Instead, the fragments have to be examined in two ways:

1. comparing the commentaries of different types of *catenae* around a fragment of the text;
2. comparing the fragments attributed to a single author throughout the *catenae*. The touchstone for recognising the worth of the

---

[24] F. Petit, "Une chaîne exégétique grecque peu connue: Sinai gr. 2"; Petit, "La tradition de Théodoret de Cyr dans les chaînes sur la Genèse", and M. Geerard, *Clavis Patrum Graecorum IV*, 185–87.

[25] J. Deconinck, *Essai sur la chaîne de l'Octateuque*.

catena in question is the agreement of the fragments with the work of the exegete from which they have been taken (commentary, homily or *scholion*, if preserved) and with independent quotations by other catenarists. In cases where this comparison is possible, from Philo to Severus of Antioch, the reliability of the *catena* has survived the test.

e) *Catenary Manuscripts in Spanish Libraries*

At the beginning of the century, M. Faulhaber published a catalogue of catenary manuscripts in Spanish libraries.[26] He attempted this specifically because Karo and Lietzmann had taken no account of these documents in their catalogue. According to his study, Spain has 39 catenary manuscripts which include 53 *catenae* of 28 different types and run from the 10th to the 17th centuries, although most of them come from the 16th. Sixteen are in the Biblioteca of the Escorial; 11 in the Biblioteca Nacional of Madrid; 7 in the Biblioteca of the Palacio Real of Madrid; 3 in the Biblioteca Universitaria of Salamanca; 1 in the Biblioteca of the Cathedral of Toledo and 1 in the Biblioteca El Pilar of Zaragoza.

These manuscripts are of varying quality. Some are of no particular interest; others represent real finds in the field of patrology. Perhaps the most relevant are the El Escorial manuscripts, which include a *catena* to the book of Kings: undoubtedly the most interesting is manuscript Ψ.I.8, since, although it is late, it is of great value as it is an exact copy of manuscript, Σ.II.19 (13th century), which disappeared in the fire of 1671.[27]

---

[26] M. Faulhaber, "Katenenhandschriften in spanischen Bibliotheken".

[27] M. Faulhaber, *Katenenhandschriften der spanischen Bibliotheken*, 247ff., and A. Rahlfs, *Verzeichnis der griechischen Handschriften des Alten Testament*, Berlin 1914, 385. As has been noted by Faulhaber (*Katenenhandschriften*, 251, n. 1) ms. Ψ.I.8 displays in θεοδώρου the fragments from ms. Σ.II.19 marked by the signs θε' or θεοδω'. However, Faulhaber adds, "die katechetische Form des Scholions und die Parallelzitate würden aber eher für eine Auflösung in θεοδωρήτου sprechen. Nähere Untersuchung ist um so notwendiger, als dieses Lemma den Löwenanteil an der Kette hat. Sie hätte zu beachten, dass in 4 Rg in beiden Codices zur Unterscheidung von den zweifelhaften θε' -Scholien andere Zitate ausdrücklich mit θεοδώρου Ἡρακλείας lemmatisiert sind."

In addition there is the systematic search of catenary manuscripts being carried out in a project of the Institut Biblique of the University of Fribourg (Switzerland), in order to obtain new Hexaplaric material.

SELECT BIBLIOGRAPHY

Bertini, U., "La catena greca in Giobbe". *Bib* 4 (1923), 129–42.

Deconinck, J., *Essai sur la chaîne de l'Octateuque avec une édition des Commentaires de Diodore de Tarse*, Paris 1912.

Devreesse, R., "Chaînes exégétiques grecques". *DBS* 1 (1928), 1084–164.

———, *Introduction à l'étude des manuscrits grecs*, Paris 1954, 176–81.

———, *Les anciens commentateurs grecs de l'Octateuque et des Rois (Fragments tirés des chaînes)*, Vatican City 1959 (ST 201).

Dorival, G., "Des commentaires de l'Écriture aux chaînes". *Le monde grec ancien et la Bible*, ed. C. Mondesert. BTT 1, Paris 1984, 361–86.

———, "La postérité littéraire des chaînes exégétiques grecques". *REB* 43 (1985), 209–26.

———, "L'apport des chaînes exégétiques grecques à une réédition des *Hexaples* d'Origène (à propos du Psaume 118)". *RHT* 4 (1974), 45–75.

———, *Les chaînes exégétiques grecques sur les Psaumes. Contribution à l'étude d'une forme littéraire*, Leuven 1986, 1989 and 1992.

Faulhaber, M., *Die Prophetencatenen nach römischen Handschriften*, Freiburg 1899.

———, "Katenen-Handschriften in spanischen Bibliotheken". *BZ* 1 (1903), 151–59; 246–55; 351–71.

———, "Katenen und Katenenforschung". *ByZ* 18 (1909), 383–95.

Geerard, M., *Clavis Patrum Graecorum IV, Concilia. Catenae*, Turnhout–Leuven 1980.

Hagedorn, U., and D. Hagedorn, *Die älteren griechieschen Katenen zum Buch Hiob. I. Einleitung, Prologe und Epiloge, Fragmente zu Hiob 1, 1–8, 22*, Berlin–New York 1994.

Harl, M., *La chaîne palestinienne sur le psaume 118*, I and II, SC 190–91, Paris 1972.

Karo, G. and H. Lietzmann, *Catenarum graecarum Catalogus*. NGWGött (1902), 1, 3 and 5.

Labate, A., *Catena Hauniensis in Ecclesiasten in qua saepe exegesis servatur Dionysii Alexandrini*. CCSG 24, Turnhout–Leuven 1992.

Leanza, S., "Le catene esegetiche sull'Ecclesiaste". *Augustinianum* 17 (1977), 545–52.

———, *Procopii Gazaei catena in Ecclesiasten necnon Pseudochrysostomi commentarius in eundem Ecclesiasten*. CCSG 4, Turnhout–Leuven 1978.

Lietzmann, H., *Catenen: Mitteilungen über ihre Geschichte und handschriftliche Überlieferung*, Fribourg 1897.

Lindl, E., *Die Octateuchcatene des Prokop von Gaza und die Septuagintaforschung*, Munich 1902.

Luca, S., *Anonymus in Ecclesiasten commentarius qui dicitur Catena Trium Patrum*. CCSG 11, Turnhout–Leuven 1983.

Millet, G., "L'Octateuque byzantin d'après une publication de l'Institut russe à Constantinople". *Revue archéologique* 16 (1910), 71–80.

Mühlenberg, E., *Psalmenkommentare aus der Katenenüberlieferung I*, Berlin 1975; II and III, Berlin 1977 and 1978.

Petit, F., *Catenae graecae in Genesim et in Exodum. I. Catena Sinaitica*. CCSG 2, Turnhout–Leuven 1977; *II. Collectio Coisliniana, In Genesim*. CCSG 15, Turnhout–Leuven 1986.

———, *La chaîne sur la Genèse. Édition intégrale I. Chapitres 1 à 3: la création et la chute*, Leuven 1991; *II. Chapitres 4 à 11*, Leuven 1993; *III. Chapitres 12 à 28*, Leuven 1995; *IV Chapitres 29 à 50*, Leuven 1996.

———, "La tradition de Théodoret de Cyr dans les chaînes sur la Genèse. Vues nouvelles sur le classement de ces chaînes". *Le Muséon* 92 (1979), 281–86.

———, "L'édition des chaînes exégétiques grecques sur la Genèse et l'Exode". *Le Muséon* 91 (1978), 189–95.

————, "Le dossier origénien de la chaîne de Moscou sur la Genèse. Problèmes d'attribution et de double rédaction". *Le Muséon* 92 (1979), 71–105.

————, "Les "chaînes" exégétiques grecques sur la Genèse et l'Exode. Programme d'exploration et d'édition". *Studia Patristica* 12 (TU 115), ed. E. A. Livingstone, Berlin 1975, 46–50.

————, "Les fragments grecs du livre VI des Questions sur la Genèse de Philon d'Alexandrie". *Le Muséon* 89 (1971), 93–150.

————, "Une chaîne exégétique grecque peu connue: Sinai gr. 2. Description et analyse". *Studia codicologica. FS. Marcel Richard* 2 (TU 124), ed. K. Treu, Berlin 1977, 341–50.

Rahlfs, A., "Die Quellen der *Catena Nicephori*". *TLZ* 39 (1914), 92.

Richard, M., "Florilèges spirituels grecs". *Dictionnaire de spiritualité, ascétique et mystique* 33–34 (1962), 475–512.

————, "Les premiers chaînes sur le Psautier". *BIRHT* 5 (1956), 87–98.

————, "Quelques manuscrits peu connus des chaînes exégétiques et des commentaires grecs sur le Psautier". *BIRHT* 3 (1954), 87–106.

PART FIVE

THE SEPTUAGINT AND CHRISTIAN ORIGINS

CHAPTER TWENTY

THE RELIGION OF THE SEPTUAGINT AND HELLENISM

a) *Introduction*

The theology of the LXX as a stage of the religious history of Israel, and in relation to the religion of Hellenism, is a chapter that has not yet been examined in a systematic way. There is no reference to it in the manuals by Swete and Jellicoe. And it is only mentioned in passing in the classics by Frankel, Bousset and Gressmann, Nickelsburg or in the recent introduction to the LXX by the French team and other publications.[1] However, recently and in various contexts it has been mentioned as one of the most pressing tasks of Septuagintal research.

The topic has two clearly differentiated aspects:

1. On the one hand the study of the theology and exegesis of the LXX as an important moment in the history of Judaism and of the Hebrew Bible.[2] From this aspect the problem of whether or not an Alexandrian interpretation and an Alexandrian canon for the Hellenistic Jews of the diaspora existed, against the Palestinian canon and interpretation, is particularly important.

2. The influence of Hellenistic thought on the LXX, i.e. the degree of Hellenisation that the Hebrew Bible underwent in being translated into Greek as a concrete expression of a more complex phenomenon, which is the Hellenisation of the whole Middle East after the conquests by Alexander.

They are two points of view from the same approach, which considers the LXX to be the main manifestation of Hellenistic Judaism, and places the emphasis less on the textual stage it reflects than

---

[1] Z. Frankel, *Vorstudien zu der Septuaginta*, Leipzig 1841, and Frankel, *Über den Einfluss der palästinischen Exegese auf die alexandrinische Hermeneutik*, Leipzig 1851; W. Bousset and H. Gressmann, *Die Religion des Judentums*; G. W. E. Nickelsburg, *Resurrection, Immortality, and Eternal Life in Intertestamental Judaism*, Cambridge, Mass.–London 1972; M. Harl *et al.*, *La Bible grecque des Septante*, and M. Hengel and A. M. Schwemmer, *Die Septuaginta*.

[2] See. D. Barthélemy, "L'ancien Testament a mûri à Alexandrie", *TZ* 21 (1965), 358–70, and R. Hanhart, "Die Bedeutung der Septuagintaforschung", 63–64.

on the historical updating and religious thought reflected by the translation.

From the beginning of our century the idea spread, brilliantly formulated by A. Deissmann, that the LXX essentially embodied the Hellenisation of Jewish monotheism.[3] From then on only generic articles have appeared on the topic, such as those by Bertram, or oversimplifications, like those by Dodd,[4] which by over-generalisation emphasise the opposition between Semitic and Greek thought. The truth is that most of the articles of the theological dictionary of the New Testament edited by Kittel have a section on the LXX. However, the most significant contributions in this field, marking the path to follow in later research, lie in the sporadic commentaries we have on any book of the LXX as an independent literary work, such as the one by Seeligmann on Isaiah or those by Gerleman on Proverbs, Job or Chronicles.[5] They are an indication of the enormous possibilities provided, especially in certain books, by a philological and exegetical commentary on the LXX.

From the 1950s, several works began to appear on the redaction and theology of the LXX – not only on text criticism – in connection with translation techniques. However, before examining the influence of Hellenism on the Greek translation of the Bible, we shall briefly describe the cultural and religious background of Judaism in the Hellenistic period.

b) *The Hellenisation of the Jews*

The two concepts that determine the evolution of Greek religion in the Hellenistic period are Euhemerism and Theocrasy. After Alexander's conquest, supplantation of cult and the *interpretatio graeca* of foreign deities also reached Palestine. In most cases the new emperors gave Greek names to ancient Semitic divinities: Ashtarte of Ashkelon became Aphrodite Urania; Baʿal of Carmel became Zeus, the Baʿal of Tabor, Zeus Atabirios, Phoenician Resheph, Apollo, and Melqart, Heracles. The cult of Dionysus became amazingly popular.[6]

---

[3] A. Deissmann, "Die Hellenisierung des semitischen Monotheismus", *Neue Jahrbücher für das klassische Altertum*, (1903), 161–77.

[4] See Select Bibliography.

[5] See Select Bibliography.

[6] See "Baʿal" in *RAC* I, 1066–101; M. Hengel, *Judentum und Hellenismus*, 473–86,

However, it has to be stressed that before the arrival of Christianity, no Greek–Roman author was seriously concerned with the religion of Israel as it could be read in Greek from the 3rd century BCE in the LXX. Instead they criticised Jewish religion as *superstitio barbara*, even though, before anti-Semitism arose in Egypt, the Jewish people were considered to be a respectable race of philosophers, whose concept of God was usually equated with the monotheism of Stoic philosophy.[7]

Among educated Greeks of the Hellenistic period there was an increasing trend towards a universal piety in which the various religions were interpreted as manifestations of a single deity. Greek philosophy interested in religion was moving towards monotheism, as is evident in the Stoics, the Orphic groups and other philosophical movements. These circles soon aroused interest in the Jewish groups in Egypt and we have the example of Aristobulus and Artapanus who converted to Orpheus in witness to the Mosaic truth.

The tendency to equate the Jewish and Greek concepts of God is not only attested among the soldiers of a garrison in Upper Egypt (two Jewish inscriptions from a temple of Pan) but even in the learned circles that produced the *Letter of Aristeas*. The author of that letter explains to king Ptolemy this universal image of the Jewish God in the following words: . . . τὸν γὰρ πάντων ἐπόπτην καὶ κτίστην θεὸν οὗτοι σέβονται, ὃν καὶ πάντες, ἡμεῖς δέ, βασιλεῦ, προσονομάζοντες ἑτέρως Ζῆνα καὶ Δία ("They worship the creator of all things, who sees everything, the same one we all worship; except that we, Oh king, call them differently *Zeus* and *Dia*").[8] In Hellenistic society, therefore, Judaism is portrayed as a true philosophy of ethical monotheism.

---

and the thoughtful review of this book by A. Momigliano in *JTS* 21 (1970), 149–53. In ancient writers, Yahweh/Yao is often the equivalent of Dionysius. On the syncretistic union of Yao with pagan gods in the popular religion of the magical papyri, see N. Fernández Marcos, "Motivos judíos en los papiros mágicos griegos", *Religión, superstición y magia en el mundo romano*, ed. J. Lomas, Cadiz 1985, 101–30. On the cult of Dionysius at Beth Shean and the possible origin of this identification, cf. D. Flusser, "Paganism in Palestine", *The Jewish People in the First Century II*, eds. S. Safrai and M. Stern, Assen 1976, 1065–100, pp. 1068 and 1084.

[7] See N. Fernández Marcos, "Interpretaciones helenísticas del pasado de Israel", 175–77; A. Momigliano, *Alien Wisdom*, 91–96, and G. Delling, "Die Begegnung zwischen Hellenismus und Judentum".

[8] *Letter of Pseudo-Aristeas* 16, see A. Pelletier, *Lettre d'Aristée à Philocrate*, Paris 1962, 110; G. Delling, "Die Begegnung zwischen Hellenismus und Judentum", 10, and Y. Amir, "Die Begegnung des biblischen und des philosophischen Monotheismus als Grundthema des jüdischen Hellenisnus", *Evangelische Theologie* 38 (1978), 2–19.

However, this was not the predominant attitude in Judaism in respect of the images of God in the Greek cult. The negative trend of resistance to Hellenisation was much stronger, although even in this reaction they used the Hellenistic forms of criticism of religion, such as Euhemerism.[9] This attitude of resisting Hellenism and even of political and social separation from the Greeks is found in varying degrees both in Palestine and in the diaspora, in such diverse writers as the anonymous Samaritan, the Jewish Sibyll (*c.* 140 BCE), Artapanus, Philo, Josephus or the author of the 3rd book of Maccabees.[10]

These forms of criticism of religion as well as the equation of the gods of the philosophers with the god of the Bible were later adopted by Christian apologists.

The refusal by most of the Jewish people, even in the diaspora, to allow the names and images of non-Jewish deities to be transferred to the God of Israel – together with the withdrawal and gradual concealment of the original name of God, Yahweh/Yao – had a strange result:[11] since the abstract generic term used to name him in the Greek world – partly as κύριος, which initially had no religious meaning, or else as θεός – was too innocuous and depersonalised in Greek, the view spread that the god of the Jews could not be named, which indicated depravity. Apparently, against this portrayal by Greek and Roman writers, the Jews made virtue out of necessity and approved it to spread the idea that the true God had to be nameless.[12] The final consequence of this reduction, which also affected the early Christians, was the reproach of atheism which they had to bear.[13]

---

[9] See K. Thraede, "Euhemerismus" in *RAC*. R. Hanhart interprets the LXX translation as a reaction against Hellenism, not as a model of assimilation as Deissmann thought. The translation of the Bible into Greek is the means by which the Judaism of the diaspora defends itself against Hellenism, taking the war to its own land, in the same way that Palestine reacted by producing apocalyptic literature, see R. Hanhart, "Zum Wesen der makedonisch-hellenistischen Zeit Israels", *Wort, Lied und Gottesspruch I*, 49–59, p. 56.

[10] See A. Paul, "Le Troisième livre des Maccabées", *ANRW* II, 20.1, 298–336, pp. 331–33.

[11] W. Bousset and H. Gressmann, *Die Religion des Judentums*, 202–20: "Verschwinden des Yahvehnamens".

[12] E. Norden, *Agnostos Theos. Untersuchungen zur Formgeschichte religiöser Rede*, Stuttgart 1956, 52–62 and 115–24.

[13] The problem of assimilative theocracy not only emerged in the diaspora. In *Antiquities*, 12,261, Josephus alludes to a Samaritan temple without a name (τὸ ἀνώνυμον ἱερόν) in the letter from the Samaritan community to Antiochus IV (166 BCE).

The absence of images in the religion of Israel arouses the idea of pantheism in Greek and Roman writers, as can be seen in the preserved fragments of Hecate, Strabo and Dio Cassius.[14] Also to be noted is the assimilation of Yahweh ('Ιαώ in some transcriptions into Greek) to Dionysus, especially in the treatise Τίς ὁ παρ' 'Ιουδαίοις θεός by Plutarch of Queronea.[15]

The reasons for equating Dionysus with the god of the Hebrews are:

1. their greatest feast, Tabernacles, is celebrated at a time and a manner that are like the feasts of Dionysus;
2. they also have another feast in which they carry branches of fig and thyrsos, play the harp and trumpet in the manner of bacchanals;

And in Jerusalem the problem arose during the attempted reform by the Hellenistic Jews (175–163 BCE) of assimilation between the God of Zion and the images of god of the surrounding Greek and Oriental world.

[14] See M. Stern, *Greek and Latin Authors I*, 11,4: ἄγαλμα δὲ θεῶν τὸ σύνολον ʼοὐ κατεσκεύασε διὰ τὸ μὴ νομίζειν ἀνθρωπόμορφον εἶναι τὸν θεόν, ἀλλὰ τὸν περιέχοντα τὴν γῆν οὐρανὸν μόνον εἶναι θεὸν καὶ τῶν ὅλων κύριον ("It had absolutely no image of God so as to think that the deity does not have a human form but that the only god and lord of all things is the sky which surrounds the earth").

Strabo reacted against the Egyptian worship of animals, countering it with the pantheistic interpretation of the Jewish religion, induced perhaps by the absence of God's name in the LXX and by the ban of images in Israel, see M. Stern, *Greek and Latin Authors I*, 115,35: ἔφη γὰρ ἐκεῖνος καὶ ἐδίδασκεν, ὡς οὐκ ὀρθῶς φρονοῖεν οἱ Αἰγύπτιοι θηρίοις εἰ κάζοντες καὶ βοσκήμασι τὸ θεῖον οὐδ' οἱ Λίβυες· οὐκ εὖ δὲ οὐδ' οἱ Ἕλληνες, ἀνθρωπομόρφους τυποῦντες, εἴη γὰρ ἓν τοῦτο μόνον θεὸς τὸ περιέχον ἡμᾶς ἅπαντας καὶ γῆν καὶ θάλατταν, ὃ καλοῦμεν οὐρανὸν καὶ κόσμον καὶ τὴν τῶν ὄντων φύσιν ("Since he said and taught that neither the Egyptians nor the Libyans had the correct feelings in likening the divinity to wild animals and beasts; nor did the Greeks act well by sculpting them in human form. And that there was only one deity who contained us all and the land and the sea, whom we call sky and cosmos and the nature of beings").

The same idea recurs in Dio Cassius (160–230 CE), see M. Stern, *Greek and Latin Authors II*, 406,17.2: κεχωρίδαται δὲ ἀπὸ τῶν λοιπῶν ἀνθρώπων ἔς τε τἆλλα τὰ περὶ τὴν δίαιταν πάνθ' ὡς εἰπεῖν, καὶ μάλισθ' ὅτι τῶν μὲν ἄλλων θεῶν οὐδένα τιμῶσιν, ἕνα δέ τινα ἰσχυρῶς σέβουσιν. οὐδ' ἄγαλμα οὐδὲν <οὐδ'> ἐν αὐτοῖς ποτε τοῖς Ἱεροσολύμοις ἔσχον, ἄρρητον δὲ δὴ καὶ ἀειδῆ αὐτὸν νομίζοντες εἶναι περισσότατα ἀνθρώπων θρησκεύουσι ("They are separated from other men in everything related to the form of life, so to say, and especially in their not worshipping any of the other gods, but instead they worship one intensely. They never had at that time any image in Jerusalem itself, for they think that he is ineffable and has no shape and is above men and they worship him"), see N. Fernández Marcos, "La religión judía vista por los autores griegos y latinos".

[15] A historian who lived from 46 to 120 CE, see M. Stern, *Greek and Latin Authors I*, 258. The ancient Thracian–Phrygian god Sabazius, already assimilated to Dionysus or Zeus, came to be identified with Yahweh Sabaoth, god of the Jews, κύριος Sabazius or κύριος Sabaoth of the LXX, see F. Blanchetière, "Juifs et non Juifs".

3. even the Sabbath festival is not foreign to the cult of Dionysus, since many call the Bacchantes σαβοί or Sabazius's initiates.

4. the high priest wears many little bells which tinkle as he walks with a sound as in nocturnal feasts to Bacchus.

Unfortunate as the assimilation of Yahweh to Bacchus may seem, it was greatly approved among the harmonists of the 1st century CE.[16]

Finally, a striking item of information in Strabo is the practice of incubation among the Jews.[17] Certainly it is the only information we have that it was practised in the temple of Jerusalem. Nevertheless it merits better research in view of the many parallels Lieberman has discovered between the temple of Jerusalem and the pagan temples[18] and taking into account recent archaeological discoveries about the existence of healing sanctuaries in Palestine and even in the very grounds of the *Aelia Capitolina*.[19]

---

[16] For a discussion of the details, real or invented, in the paragraph from Plutarch, see M. Stern, *Greek and Latin Authors I*, pp. 559–62. For the description of the high priest with his solemn vestments, see Josephus, *Antiquities* III, 159ff.; *Jewish War* V, 230ff., and Ben Sira 50.

[17] See M. Stern, *Greek and Latin Authors I*, 115, 35: ἐγκοιμᾶσθαι δὲ καὶ αὐτοὺς ὑπὲρ ἑαυτῶν καὶ ὑπὲρ τῶν ἄλλων ἄλλους τοὺς εὐονείρους· καὶ προσδοκᾶν δεῖν ἀγαθὸν παρὰ τοῦ θεοῦ καὶ δῶρον ἀεί τι καὶ σημεῖον τοὺς σωφρόνως ζῶντας καὶ μετὰ δικαιοσύνης, τοὺς δ' ἄλλους μὴ προσδοκᾶν ("and it was important to spend the night in the sanctuary to intercede for themselves and to have other warning dreams on behalf of others; and it is appropriate that those living prudently and uprightly expect good things from the deity, continually expect some gift or sign, although the others do not expect it").

[18] S. Lieberman, *Hellenism in Jewish Palestine*, 164–79, "The Temple: Its Lay-out and Procedure".

[19] See A. Duprez, *Jésus et les dieux guérisseurs. À propos de Jean V*, Paris 1970, 85ff. On possible references to incubation in the Greek Bible, see N. Fernández Marcos, *Los 'Thaumata' de Sofronio. Contribución al estudio de la 'Incubatio' cristiana*, Madrid 1975, 24, n. 6. Perhaps in 1 Enoch 13:8 there is another allusion to the practice of incubation, or at least its formulae and technical terminology are preserved. Gnuse, instead, holds that Josephus is describing Jado's dream (*Antiquities* XI, 326–28) as an incubation dream, see R. Gnuse, "The Temple Experience of Jaddus in the 'Antiquities' of Josephus: A Report of Jewish Dream Incubation", *JQR* 83 (1993), 349–68.

For the attitude of the Jews towards dreams in the post-biblical period see S. Zeitlin, "Dreams and their Interpretation: From the Biblical Period to the Tannaitic Time. A Historical Study", *JQR* 66 (1975), 1–18, and B. Stemberger, "Der Traum in der rabbinischen Literatur", *Kairos* 18 (1976), 1–43, n. 2, where it is noted that they went to the pagan temples to practice incubation. The passage in Strabo on revelation through incubation has points in common with the view of Posidonius, but there is no conclusive proof of dependence on him, see M. Stern, *Greek and Latin Authors I*, 265. Some specialists think that Strabo depended on a Jewish source, *ibid.* 266.

c) *The Hellenisation of the Septuagint*

Bertram has stated that the LXX translation could make some contribution to the recent debate on demythologisation. In the Greek Bible he sees a spiritualisation of the religion of Israel which demythologises the Old Testament in a process parallel to what happened in Hellenism with the mythology of Homer and Hesiod. Hellenistic critical philosophy puts the ancient Hellenistic pantheon to the test and the LXX shares this critical philosophy.[20]

Bousset and Gressmann expounded the main novelties that the translation provided in the history of the religion of Israel. They consist in the Hellenisation of Jewish monotheism principally through the translation of God's names, the idea of the pre-existence of the Messiah and the presentation of a more developed eschatology which includes hope in an afterlife. Against the theocentrism of the Hebrew Bible, the LXX stands out for a predominance of anthropocentrism which emphasises the ethical attitude and the value of the individual.[21] These conclusions can scarcely be maintained today without several modifications.

The simplification of the names of God is evident when we compare the range of expressions in Hebrew to denote the deity[22] and the normal translation in the LXX using the common nouns κύριος and θεός. It is also evident in a tendency to remove any remnant of polytheism from the translation of God's names. The translators use circumlocutions to avoid the name of God, a tendency that would develop in late Judaism and in the rabbinic period. They translate ’*elohīm* as ἄγγελοι when it refers to the gods of the Canaanite pantheon and could cause difficulties if translated by θεοί. At other times, in the context of pagan deities, they intentionally translate the name of God as ἄρχων (Ez. 31:11), πάταχρον[23] (Is. 37:38), εἴδωλον, γλυπτός, βδέλυγμα.[24]

---

[20] G. Bertram, "Zur Bedeutung der Religion", and Bertram, "Vom Wesen der Septuaginta-Frömmigkeit", 275, n. 3.

[21] W. Bousset and H. Gressman, *Die Religion des Judentums*, 264ff.

[22] This range of expressions can be seen in F. Cantera and M. Iglesias, *Sagrada Biblia. Versión crítica sobre los textos hebreo, arameo y griego*, Madrid 1979. In this translation into Spanish, the variety of names in Hebrew for the names of God is followed so that this feature of the original is not lost; or see the recent French translation by A. Chouraqui, *La Bible*, Paris 1974–76.

[23] To denote the Assyrian god Nisrok. A tutelary god, who became πάτραρχον in most manuscripts and a *hapax legomenon* in LSJ, see I. L. Seeligmann, *The Septuagint Version of Isaiah*, 9–10.

[24] See C. H. Dodd, *The Bible and the Greeks*, 3–24, especially p. 23.

Isaiah is a good example of how the translators chose the word εἴδωλον, which has a great Greek tradition, to denote pagan deities, whereas they reserve δαιμόνιον to denote demons who prowl around ruins (Is. 13:21 and 34:14).[25] It is something similar to what is observed in the Masoretic text when it replaces the name of *Ba'al* with *bošet* = "ignominy, shame" (e.g. in Hos. 9:10; Jer. 3:14 and 11:13); by means of this linguistic practice, the judgement of a strict monotheistic religion is expressed against pagan deities. In the first two passages where it occurs, the LXX translates it as αἰσχύνη; in the third as βαάλ. However, usually the LXX considers βαάλ to be feminine, the same gender as αἰσχύνη.

Similarly, in Dan. 12:11 τὸ βδέλυγμα τῆς ἐρημώσεως (*šiqqûṣ šomēm*) is an ignominious parody of *ba'al šāmayîm*, the Ζεὺς Οὐράνιος.[26]

The translators of the LXX, who always translate *ṣur* as πέτρα when not used metaphorically to mean God, in this last case completely avoid a literal translation, in case it was interpreted as an image of God.[27] The warrior god in Ex. 15:3 and Is. 42:13 (*'îš milḥāmâ*) becomes a God who destroys wars, συντρίβων πολέμους; and the *wayithallēk ḥᵃnok 'et hā-'elohîm* of Gen. 5:22 ("Enoch walked with *hā-'elohîm*") is translated as εὐηρέστησεν δὲ Ἐνὼχ τῷ θεῷ ("Enoch pleased God").

It seems that the debate about the anti-anthropomorphic tendency of the Greek translation has to be resolved in a non-uniform way due to the non-uniform treatment of the text, depending on the book and in connection with the translation technique of each.[28] In some

---

[25] See I. L. Seeligmann, *The Septuagint Version of Isaiah*, 95–121: εἴδωλον, σκιά, ψεῦδος, βδέλυγμα, χειροποιητόν, for *'elil* (*ibid.* 99). See also H. Kampel, "Sirenen in der LXX", *BZ* 23 (1935), 158–65. Kampel thinks that σειρῆνες (Is. 13:21; 34, 13 and 43:29) is used in the LXX to denote demons of death and that they had a place in the popular belief of Hellenistic Jews.

[26] C. H. Dodd, *The Bible and the Greeks*, 23.

[27] See S. Olofsson, *God is my Rock*, Stockholm 1990, 35–45, p. 45: "The translator of the Book of Psalms always treated *ṣur* as a divine title differently from its literal and ordinary metaphorical meaning and the same is true of the translators of the other LXX books. A literal rendering of *ṣur* was consistently avoided when it referred to God."

[28] See Select Bibliography. Gard, for example, notes how the image of Job given by the Greek translator is not the same as in Hebrew. The translator of Job-LXX avoids the questions that Job addresses to God, does not reprove him, and tends to emphasise Job's humility in contrast to his presumptive character according to the Hebrew text. He also stresses Job's trust in divine justice, see D. H. Gard, "The Concept of Job's Character". Similarly, in Gard's opinion, Job-LXX has a more defined idea of the future life, an aspect missing from the Hebrew (Job 14:14), see D. H. Gard, "The Concept of the Future Life".

books the translation is strongly anti-anthropomorphic in nature; in others it is not so clear. However it is not possible to make a global judgement about the theology of the LXX on this point. Bertram, Fritsch, Gerleman and Gard defend the anti-anthropomorphic tendency of the LXX in their studies on Qoheleth, the Pentateuch and Job, whereas Orlinsky insists, perhaps too much, that the anthropomorphic Hebrew terms are reproduced accurately in the Greek translation of the Penateuch, as in Job and Isaiah.[29] And in his study on the book of Psalms, Soffer holds that this tendency does not have an important role in the translation since at times the terms in question are even translated more literally than necessary. Although in the translation of the psalms there must have been some models or exegetical exemplars, this anti-anthropomorphic tendency cannot be identified as one of them.

These nuances have to be extended to other concepts such as eschatology or messianism in the LXX. Lust concludes his study on messianism by stressing that the Greek Bible is not a single unit and as a result, each book or group of texts has to be studied separately.[30] However, recent monographs, such as the one by Schaper on Psalms or by Rösel on Genesis, recover an approach to the LXX that has proved to be fruitful since the studies by Z. Frankel in the previous century. They study it as an outstanding religious document, as the first Jewish interpretation known of the books in question and so as a source of historical and religious information for the exegesis and development of Jewish thought in the first three centuries before Christ. For ultimately, the LXX continues to be the main witness and first fruits of Jewish-Hellenistic thought.[31]

---

[29] H. M. Orlinsky, "Studies in the Septuagint of the Book of Job".

[30] J. Lust, "Messianism and Septuagint", 191: "At the present stage of the investigation we may conclude that the LXX certainly does not display a uniform picture of a developing royal messianism."

[31] J. Schaper, *Eschatology in the Greek Psalter*, 174–74, and M. Rösel, *Übersetzung als Vollendung und Auslegung*, 247–54. Against the Hellenistic interpretation of Genesis proposed by Schmitt (see Select Bibliography), M. Görg develops the thesis of Egyptian influence previously suggested by S. Morenz ("Ägyptische Spuren in der LXX", *JAC Engänzungsband* I [1964], 250–58). According to Görg, the Greek translation of the first chapters of Genesis shows contacts with Egyptian cosmogony and mythology; see M. Görg, "Ptolemäische Theologie in der Septuaginta". Certainly, contacts between the most famous Hellenistic Jews and Egyptian priests cannot be excluded, but no linguistic proofs are provided for such influences.

d) *The Formal Hellenisation of the Wisdom Writings*

In his monograph on the book of Proverbs, Gerleman discovers a series of Hellenising tendencies by the translator. Many passages are like an echo of literary Greek writers. He finds Homeric reminiscences in Prov. 30:19, καὶ τρίβους νηὸς ποντοπορούσης.[32] Other passages contain reminiscences of Plato, such as Prov. 19:15, δειλία κατέχει ἀνδρογύναιον.[33] In Gen. 2:21, the Hebrew word *tardēmâ* is used for the creation of the woman. However, the Greek translator, by association, has evoked not the biblical story of creation, but the account of Plato's Symposium (139/E).

The praise of the bee in Prov. 6:8*abc* has no equivalent in the Hebrew text; also it is unusual, as it goes against the attitude in the whole Old Testament which portrays the bee as an evil and dangerous species. Here, instead, the favourable and admiring attitude towards it probably comes from Greek writers: Aristotle calls it ἐργάτις as in this passage of Proverbs.[34] In Prov. 23:27, rather than Hebrew *kî-šûḥâ ᵃmuqqâ zônâ* "for the whore is a deep pit",[35] the LXX translates and interprets πίθος γὰρ τετρημένος ἐστὶν ἀλλότριος οἶκος ("another person's house is a jar full of holes"), words that evoke Plato's Gorgias (493/B), where πίθος τετρημένος represents uncontrolled excess and licence, although the second part of the verse leads us to Xenophon, *Oec.* VII, 40, where the same image is applied to a house where everyone behaves like a stranger and no-one bothers about ordinary chores.[36]

Perhaps Gerleman's conclusions require refining. To be specific, Cook considers that the Greek translation of Proverbs has to be dated to the beginning of the Hellenisation of Hellenistic-Jewish thought and it continued to retain, in Hellenistic guise, more Jewish

---

[32] For the Hebrew *derek ᵓoniyyâ beleb-yām* (= "the path of the ship in the midst of the sea"), see G. Gerleman, *Studies of the Septuagint. III: Proverbs*, 28. Note the same position of the participle in the verse from Odyssey, XI,11: τῆς δὲ πανημερίης τέταθ᾽ ἱστία ποντοπορούσης.

[33] For the Hebrew *ᶜaṣlâ taffîl tardēmâ* (= "laziness causes deep sleep"), see G. Gerleman, *Studies in the Septuaginta. III: Proverbs*, 29.

[34] Aristoteles, *Natural History*, 627/A. The passage from Proverbs runs as follows: ἢ πορεύθητι πρὸς τὴν μέλισσαν καὶ μάθε ὡς ἐργάτις ἐστίν, τήν τε ἐργασίαν ὡς σεμνὴν ποιεῖται ("or go to the bee and learn what kind of holy work it does"), see G. Gerleman, *Studies in the Septuagint. III: Proverbs*, 30–31.

[35] Unless the LXX reads *zarâ* ("foreign woman") instead of *zonâ*.

[36] G. Gerleman, *Studies in the Septuagint. III: Proverbs*, 33, and Gerleman, *The Septuagint of Proverbs*.

ideas than might appear.[37] However there is no doubt about the persistent evocations of Greek culture noted by Gerleman.

The translator of Proverbs was not the only one to be familiar with classical culture; it also applies to Job. The translator of Job tended to favour mythology and fable; by preference, the translator of Proverbs was inspired by poetry and philosophical literature.[38]

In any case, it is not an easy task to define the degree of Hellenisation of a biblical book of the LXX, whether a translation or composed originally in Greek, because it is not always easy to distinguish accurately between what is the result of actual translation techniques, determined by the different structures of the two languages, and the changes due to the translator's theology. These echoes of the Greek world that Gerleman detects in Proverbs, and which in the translation often provoke departures from the original, are explained by Bertram, Baumgartner and Wevers by the midrashic procedure of interpretation and by appealing to similar phenomena in Aramaic translations.[39]

In the books of the LXX that have no Hebrew *Vorlage*, the influence of Hellenism is more obvious, although is difficult to check since so little of Hellenistic literature has survived. Wisdom is not written in Septuagintal style; 335 words of this book are missing from the vocabulary of the LXX. Its lexicon and style, instead, are very close to the features of philosophical and rhetorical prose of late Hellenism.[40] Even so, the author of Wisdom was familiar with the Jewish Bible and the popular traditions of his people. Probably by editing the book he was attempting to prepare educated Jewish students to live in Hellenistic society. In any case, it is Hellenism, and not the classical Greek period, which influenced the book of Wisdom. Its author knows the popular piety of Hellenistic Egypt, as shown by the vocabulary which is related to that of the aretalogies of Isis, the critical philosophy of religion, and the polemics against idolatry (Wisdom 13–15). He borrows technical terms used

---

[37] J. Cook, "Hellenistic Influence in the Septuagint Book of Proverbs".

[38] See N. Fernández Marcos, "The Septuagint Reading of the Book of Job". In the Greek translation of the Song of Songs, instead, there are scarcely any traces of the influence of the surrounding Greek and Roman culture, see N. Fernández Marcos, "La lectura helenística del Cantar".

[39] See N. Fernández Marcos, "Los estudios de 'Septuaginta'. Visión retrospectiva y problemática más reciente", *CFC* 11 (1976), 413–68, p. 434.

[40] J. M. Reese, *Hellenistic Influence on the Book of Wisdom and its Consequences*, Rome 1970, 153–62.

by the Epicureans to explain the immortality of the gods. However, his use of Hellenism is primarily strategic, to build a bridge between the inherited biblical faith and the current situation of his readers.

The author of Ben Sira, instead, in the praise of the ancestors (Sira 44–49) intends to write a panegyric of the heroes and wise men of Israel in the form of an ἐγκώμιον, matching the heroes and wise men of the Greeks, and he sets them up for his contemporaries as ideals of behaviour for the difficult current situation. It marks something new in Old Testament literature, influenced probably by Hellenism as to genre, as the use of typical characters was a favourite practice among Hellenistic Greek writers. It also tries to build a bridge between Greek culture and the traditions of the ancestors by writing a book following models of the Greek school and shaping his wisdom material in line with Stoic behaviour. However, in his book a tension is noticeable between assimilation of Hellenism and resistance to it.[41]

If we have noted a series of facts that is by no means exhaustive – both in the translated books of the LXX and in those originally composed in Greek – pointing to the influence of Hellenistic thought and forms, it should be made clear, contrary to one-sided attitudes in the past, that this Hellenisation of the LXX is no more than external. The gestation period of the LXX continues to represent one moment in the religion of Israel. What is most surprising about this stage of Judaism in the diaspora is that it preserves its monotheism intact. Thus, the importance of the LXX for the religion of Israel and for theology does not lie in what has filtered in from the spirit of the age when it was translated, but in what marks it as a link between the religion of the Old Testament in its original language on the one hand, and the witness of the New Testament on the other.[42]

---

[41] See Th. Middendorp, *Die Stellung Jesu Ben Siras zwischen Judentum und Hellenismus*, 33–34 and 173–74, and N. Fernández Marcos, "Interpretaciones helenísticas", 164ff.

[42] See R. Hanhart, "Die Bedeutung der Septuaginta für die Definition des 'hellenistischen Judentums'". It is risky to put too much emphasis on the distinction between Palestinian Judaism and the Judaism of the diaspora to the point of seeing a radical opposition between them that never existed. For both Paul and Philo, wisdom literature through the LXX is one of the strongest links with Greek thought: "Il n'est guère douteux par ailleurs que le christianisme, à partir du moment où il s'adresse aux Gentils, s'est en quelque sorte placé dans le sillage du judaisme alexandrin," state M. Simon and A. Benoît in *Le Judaïsme et le Christianisme antique*, Paris 1968, 244.

The few monographs on the religious lexicon of the LXX show how the Greek words penetrate new semantic fields, introduce neologisms and are concerned about a selective lexicon which, as far as possible, avoids evoking the practices of Greek religion. By this means they try to affirm and delimit what is specific and original to the religion of Israel as against the religions of the Mediterranean area.[43] This process of stating its novelty would be continued by early Christianity in the first two centuries, following – as in so many other fields (different *topoi* of apologetics, allegorical exegesis, etc.) – the example of Hellenistic Judaism.[44]

However, this selective and peculiar nature of the religious vocabulary of the LXX must not be exaggerated, as happens sometimes in Kittel's Lexicon of the New Testament, in some entries on the use of certain words in Hellenistic Judaism.[45] In summary, the idea which was quite widespread until not many years ago, of the Greek moulding of Hebrew thought as a result of transferring a Semitic language to an Indo-European language, is no longer acceptable today. Two monographs have proved that both the binominations *nefeš*/ψυχή and *tôrâ*/νόμος have the same semantic range and underwent the same development and transformation of meaning in Hebrew and in Greek.[46] More recent research has shown that it is not possible to make a division between Palestinian and Alexandrian Judaism. Both in Palestinian circles and in those of the diaspora, Hellenism was accepted and rejected to various extents and in various ways. Perhaps the most remarkable element to stand out in such complex circumstances is that, apart from a few well-known exceptions, allegiance to the Law and to the ancestral religion was maintained in a world of many fascinating cultures and religions.[47]

---

[43] S. Daniel, *Recherches sur le vocabulaire du culte*, and J. A. L. Lee, *A Lexical Study of the Septuagint Version of the Pentateuch*. SCS 14, Chico, Calif. 1983.

[44] See N. Fernández Marcos, "En torno al estudio del griego de los cristianos", *Emerita* 41 (1973), 45–56.

[45] See J. Barr's remarks in *The Semantics of Biblical Language*, Oxford 1961, 282–87: "Detached Note on the non-use of certain words in the Greek Bible".

[46] N. P. Bratsiotis, "*Nepheš–psyché*", and L. M. Pasinya, *La notion de* νόμος. In these studies, which are somewhat philological, there is an obvious reaction against the inappropriate generalisations of T. Boman, *Das hebräische Denken im Vergleich mit dem griechischen*, Göttingen 1968, and C. Tresmontant, *Essai sur la pensée hébraïque*, Paris 1962 as well as some theologies of the Old Testament. Pasinya's study (pp. 25ff.) emphasises the defects of C. H. Dodd, *The Bible and the Greeks*, as well as the faults of the entry νόμος in *TWNT* and J. M. Flashar, "Exegetische Studien zum Septuagintapsalter".

[47] See G. Delling, "Die Begegnung zwischen Hellenismus und Judentum", 37–39.

As for the religion of the LXX, it must be stressed that as yet there is no theology of the Greek Bible that does justice to the great wealth of facts provided by that translation and the variety of opinions reflected by the various translators.

SELECT BIBLIOGRAPHY

Bertram, G., "Der Sprachschatz der Septuaginta und der des hebräischen Alten Testament". *ZAW* 57 (1939), 85–101.

———, "Die Bedeutung der LXX in der Geschichte des Diasporajudentums". *Klio* 21 (1927), 444–46.

———, "Die religiöse Umdeutung altorientalischer Lebensweisheit in der griechischen Übersetzung des Alten Testament". *ZAW* 54 (1936), 153–67.

———, "Vom Wesen der Septuaginta-Frömmigkeit". *WO* 2 (1956), 274–84.

———, "Zur Bedeutung der Religion der Septuaginta in der hellenistische Welt". *TLZ* 92 (1967), 245–50.

Blanchetière, F., "Juifs et non Juifs. Essai sur la Diaspora en Asie Mineure". *RHPhR* 54 (1974), 367–83.

Bousset, W., and H. Gressmann, *Die Religion des Judentums im späthellenistischen Zeitalter*, Tübingen 1966.

Bratsiotis, N. P., "*Nepheš–psyché*, ein Beitrag zur Erforschung der Sprache und der Theologie der Septuaginta", Leiden 1966, 58–89.

Cook, J., "Hellenistic Influence in the Septuagint Book of Proverbs". *VII Congress of the IOSCS*, 1991, 341–53.

———, *The Septuagint of Proverbs – Jewish and/or Hellenistic Proverbs? Concerning the Hellenistic Colouring of LXX Proverbs*, Leiden–New York–Köln, 1997.

Daniel, S., *Recherches sur le vocabulaire du culte dans la Septante*, Paris 1966.

Delling, G., "Die Begegnung zwischen Hellenismus und Judentum". *ANRW* II. 20.1, 1987, 3–39.

Dodd, C. H., *The Bible and the Greeks*, London 1954.

Feldman, L. H., "Hengel's 'Judaism and Hellenism' in Retrospect". *JBL* 96 (1977), 371–82.

Fernández Marcos, N., "Interpretaciones helenísticas del pasado de Israel". *CFC* 8 (1975), 157–86.

———, N., "La lectura helenística del Cantar de los Cantares". *Sefarad* 56 (1996), 265–88.

———, N., "La religión judía vista por los autores griegos y latinos". *Sefarad* 41 (1981), 3–25.

———, N., "The Septuagint Reading of the Book of Job". *The Book of Job*, ed. W. A. M. Beuken, Lovain 1994, 251–66.

Flashar M., "Exegetische Studien zum Septuagintapsalter". *ZAW* 32 (1912), 81–116; 161–89 and 24–68.

Fritsch, Ch. T., *The Antianthropomorphisms of the Greek Pentateuch*, Princeton 1943.

Gard, D. H., "The Concept of Job's Character According to the Greek Translator of the Hebrew Text". *JBL* 72 (1953), 182–86.

———, "The Concept of the Future Life According to the Greek Translator of the Book of Job". *JBL* 73 (1954), 137–43.

Gerleman, G., *Studies in the Septuagint. III: Proverbs*, Lund 1956.

Görg, M., "Ptolemäische Theologie in der Septuaginta". *Kairos* 20 (1978), 208–217.

Hanhart, R., "Die Bedeutung der Septuagintaforschung für die Theologie". *Theologische Existenz Heute*, 140 (1967), 38–64.

————, "Die Bedeutung der Septuaginta für die Definition des 'hellenistischen Judentums'". *VTS* 40 (1988), 67–80.

————, "The Translation of the Septuagint in Light of Earlier Tradition and Subsequent Influences". *Septuagint, Scrolls and Cognate Writings*, 1992, 339–79.

Hengel, M., *Juden, Griechen und Barbaren. Aspekte der Hellenisierung des Judentums in vorchristlicher Zeit*, Stuttgart 1976.

————, *Judentum und Hellenismus*, Tübingen 1973.

————, and A. M. Schwemmer, *Die Septuaginta zwischen Judentum and Christentum*, Tübingen 1994.

Kuntzmann, R., and J. Schlosser R eds., *Études sur le judaïsme hellénistique*, Paris 1984.

Lieberman, S., *Hellenism in Jewish Palestine*, New York 1962.

Lust, J., "Messianism and Septuagint". *VTS* 36 (1985), 174–91.

Marcus, R., "Divine Names and Attributes in Hellenistic Jewish Literature". *PAAJR* 3 (1931–32), 43–120.

————, "Jewish and Greek Elements in the LXX". *Louis Ginzberg Jubilee Volume*, New York 1945, 227–45.

McCasland, J. V., "The Asklepios-Cult in Palestine". *JBL* 58 (1939), 221–27.

Middendorp, Th., *Die Stellung Jesu Ben Siras zwischen Judentum und Hellenismus*, Leiden 1973.

Momigliano, A., *Alien Wisdom: The Limits of Hellenization*, Cambridge 1978.

Mussies, G., "Greek in Palestine and the Diaspora". *The Jewish People in the First Century II*, ed. S. Safrai and M. Stern, Assen 1976, 1040–64.

Neves, J. C. M. das, *A teologia da tradução grega dos Setenta no livro de Isaías (cap. 24 de Isaías)*, Coimbra 1973.

Nilsson, M. P., *Geschichte der griechischen Religion. II Die hellenistische und römische Zeit*, Munich 1961.

Orlinsky, H. M., "Studies in the Septuagint of the Book of Job". *HUCA* 28 (1957), 53–74; 29 (1958), 229–71; 30 (1959), 153–67; 32 (1961), 239–68.

Pasinya, L. M., *La notion de νόμος dans le Pentateuque Grec*, Rome 1973.

Pfeiffer, R. H., *History of New Testament Times with an Introduction to the Apocrypha*, New York 1949, 5–224.

Redpath, H. A., "Mythological Terms in the LXX". *AJT* 9 (1905), 34–35.

Rösel, M., *Übersetzung als Vollendung und Auslegung*. BZAW 223, Berlin–New York 1994.

Roussel, L., "Jéhova, βάκχος, Ίάκχος". *Mélanges offerts à M. le Professeur Victor Magnien*, Toulouse 1949, 75–76.

Sabugal, S., "La interpretación septuagintista del Antiguo Testamento". *Augustinianum* 19 (1979), 341–57.

Schaper, J., *Eschatology in the Greek Psalter*. WUNT 76, Tübingen 1995.

Schmitt, A., "Interpretation der Genesis aus hellenistischem Geist". *ZAW* 86 (1974), 138–63.

Seeligmann, I. L., *The Septuagint Version of Isaiah: A Discussion of its Problems*, Leiden 1948 (especially pp. 95–122: "The Translation as a Document of Jewish-Alexandrian Theology").

Simon, M., "Jupiter–Yahvé; sur un essai de théologie pagano-juive". *Numen* 23 (1975), 40–67.

Stern, M., *Greek and Latin Authors on Jews and Judaism*, 3 vols, Jerusalem 1974, 1980 and 1984.

Ziegler, J., *Dulcedo Dei. Ein Beitrag zur Theologie der griechischen Bibel*, Munich 1937.

CHAPTER TWENTY ONE

THE SEPTUAGINT AND THE NEW TESTAMENT

a) *Introduction*

In recent years, important discoveries have created successive centres of interest about Christian origins, displacing the academic
approaches of viewpoints adopted in the beginning of the century.
A glance at the New Testament bibliography shows the primacy that
Qumran studies have enjoyed in connection with the New Testament.
Although today publications on the Dead Sea Scrolls continue to
appear at a high rate, studies on Qumran and the New Testament
were concentrated especially in the 1950s and 1970s[1] (although a
new interest is arising in the kind of text used by the New Testament
authors).

Eclipsed by the sensationalism of Qumran, the discoveries of the
Gnostic library of Nag-Hammadi, contemporary with Qumran, are
gaining more importance as the facsimile editions of the various
codices have being published in Leiden (as well as translations into
modern languages). An excellent monograph on the relationship of
these writings with the Bible is now available.[2]

The growing interest provoked by this Jewish-Hellenistic and pseudepigraphic intertestamental literature, as the religious and cultural
background in which the New Testament was born, is apparent,
both in new text editions and in the translations of these works in

---

[1] See J. A. Fitzmyer, *The Dead Sea Scrolls: Major Publications and Tools for Study*,
Atlanta, Ga. 1990, 173–79. There are some schools of thought that once again
emphasise the importance of rabbinic literature for understanding the New Testament,
see G. Vermes, "The Impact of the Dead Sea Scrolls on the Study of the New
Testament", *JJS* 26 (1976), 107–17.

[2] C. A. Evans, R. L. Webb and R. A. Wiebe, *Nag Hammadi Texts and the Bible:
A Synopsis and Index*, Leiden 1993, and B. A. Pearson, "Biblical Exegesis in Gnostic
Literature", *Armenian and Biblical Studies*, ed. M. E. Stone, Jerusalem 1976, 70–80;
Pearson, "Use, Authority and Exegesis of Mikra in Gnostic Literature", *Mikra: Text,
Translation, Reading and Interpretation of the Hebrew Bible in Ancient Judaism and Early
Christianity*, ed. M. J. Mulder, Assen 1988, 635–52. D. M. Scholer, *Nag Hammadi
Bibliography: 1948–1969*, Leiden 1971, and the series of supplements by the same
scholar in *Novum Testamentum*. See also James M. Robinson (ed.), *The Nag Hammadi
Library in English*, 2nd edn, Leiden 1984.

modern languages and in studies throwing light on this little-known period of the history of Judaism.[3]

Finally, the discovery of the Palestinian Targum in ms. Neofiti by Professor Diez Macho has stimulated the study of the Aramaic spoken in Galilee at the time of Christ, giving rise to many studies in connection with the New Testament.[4] The approach to the New Testament in the light of rabbinic writings is the principal subject of Strack and Billerbeck's famous commentary and the theme of an important monograph by Daube.[5]

The common denominator of all these approaches to the New Testament consists in trying to understand and explain Christian origins from the linguistic and cultural background in which they emerged.

Without intending to monopolise the explanation of a phenomenon as complex as primitive Christianity, and being careful not to

---

[3] See G. Delling (ed.), *Bibliographie zur jüdisch-hellenistischen und intertestamentarischen Literatur 1900–1965*. TU 106, Berlin 1969, and the second edition by G. Delling and M. Maser, *Bibliographie zur jüdisch-hellenistischen und intertestamentarischen Literatur 1900–1970*. TU 106, Berlin 1975; J. H. Charlesworth, "A History of Pseudepigrapha Research: The Re-emerging Importance of the Pseudepigrapha", *ANRW* II, 19, 1, 1979, 54–88; Charlesworth, *The Pseudepigrapha and Modern Research, with a Supplement*. SCS 7, Missoula, Mont. 1981, Charlesworth, *The New Testament Apocrypha and Pseudepigrapha: A Guide to Publications, with Excursuses and Apocalypses*, Metuchen, N.J.–London 1987. R. Radice, D. T. Runia *et al.*, *Philo of Alexandria: An Annotated Bibliography 1937–1986*, Leiden 1988, 1992, and L. H. Feldman, *Josephus and Modern Scholarship (1937–1980)*, Berlin–New York 1984.

[4] See P. Nickels, *Targum and New Testament: A Bibliography with a New Testament Index*, Rome 1967; B. Grossfeld, *A Bibliography of Targum Literature I* and *II*, Cincinnati–New York 1972 and 1977, together with the comments and additions by W. Baars in his review of the first volume published in *VT* 25 (1975), 124–28; M. McNamara, *The New Testament and the Palestinian Targum to the Pentateuch*, Rome 1966; A. Díez Macho, *Ms Neophyti. IV Nœmeros*, Madrid 1974, 78^x–102^x; Díez Macho, "Derás y exégesis del Nuevo Testamento", *Sefarad* 35 (1975), 37–91; R. Le Déaut, "Targumic Literature and New Testament Interpretation", *Biblical Theology Bulletin* 4 (1974), 243–89; M. Black, *An Aramaic Approach to the Gospels and Acts*, 3rd edn, "with an Appendix on the Son of Man by G. Vermes", Oxford 1967.

[5] H. L. Strack and P. Billerbeck, *Kommentar zum Neuen Testament aus Talmud und Midrasch*, I–IV Munich 1969; V–VI, 1969; D. Daube, *The New Testament and Rabbinic Judaism*, London 1956. For an approach to the New Testament from the perspective of the Hellenistic world, the old edition J. J. Wetstein, *H KAINH ΔIAΘHKH. Novum Testamentum Graecum editionis receptae, cum lectionibus variantibus Codicum MSS., Editionum aliarum, Versionum et Patrum, necnon commentario pleniore Ex Scriptoribus veteribus Hebraeis, Graecis et Latinis et vim verborum illustrante opera et studio. Tomus I et II*, Amstelaedami, 1751–52 (reprinted in Graz 1962), can still be consulted, and the new collection intended as a continuation in the same line and still being published, "Studia ad Corpus Hellenisticum Novi Testamenti", see W. C. van Unnik, "Corpus Hellenisticum Novi Testamenti", *JBL* 83 (1964), 17–33, and G. Delling, "Zum Corpus Hellenisticum Novi Testamenti", *ZNW* 54 (1963), 1–15.

fall into a too facile "pan-Septuagintalism", I shall next set out the contribution made by the LXX for understanding the New Testament and the main problems posed by quotations of the Old Testament in the New.

First of all it should not be ignored that the New Testament is written entirely in Greek, whatever the early stages or oral transmission and earlier smaller collections before the final redaction of the text might have been.[6] The LXX therefore was the Bible of the New Testament writers in the same way that the Hebrew text (without for the moment considering the problem of a plurality of Masoretic texts) was the Bible for the writers of Qumran and the compilers of the Mishnah.[7] So far, Jellicoe's sentence, in turn modifying Deissmann, "He who would *read* the New Testament must know *Koiné*; but he who would *understand* the New Testament must know the LXX,"[8] can be accepted.

To this must be added that the LXX very soon became the Bible of the Church and was transmitted by manuscripts together with the New Testament and independently of the Hebrew text, as one more item of Greek literature. Thus, textual criticism of the LXX and of the New Testament poses many similar problems, as is shown by the fact that one of the recensions such as the Lucianic covered both the Old and the New Testaments, both considered by Christians as the *Corpus* of Scriptures.[9] However, in such a comparative study, two important differences have to be taken into account:

1. the fact that most of the LXX is a translation and the New Testament is not;

---

[6] See the comments by J. Kurzinger in *BZ* (1960), 19–30, who interprets the expression Ἑβραΐδι διαλέκτῳ used by Papias to describe Matthew's language (Eusebius, *Hist. Ecc.* III, 39,16), as referring to the Hebrew *style* which is very Semiticised in the first gospel *written in Greek*. See also J. H. Moulton, *A Grammar of New Testament Greek. IV: Style by N. Turner*, Edinburgh 1976, 2, 9 and 10 ("The Aramaisms are not all primitive survivals of the original teaching of Jesus, but they may rather be a part of the evangelists' Greek style") and the bibliography cited there on this aspect; C. J. Hemer, "Towards a New Moulton and Milligan", *NT* 24 (1982), 97–124, and W. D. Davies, "Reflections about the Use of the Old Testament in the New in its Historical Context", *JQR* 74 (1983), 105–37.

[7] See N. Fernández Marcos, "La Biblia de los autores del Nuevo Testamento", and M. Müller, *The First Bible of the Church*.

[8] S. Jellicoe, "Septuagint Studies in the Current Century", *JBL* 88 (1968), 191–99, p. 199

[9] S. Jellicoe, *SMS*, 354–58.

2. that the Greek of the LXX – except for some late books – is separated from New Testament Greek by three centuries.

The influence of the LXX on the New Testament can be observed at different levels:

1. in the shape of the language by means of which many lexical and syntactic Semitisms entered New Testament Greek;[10]
2. inasmuch as it comprises the main source for quotations from the Old Testament in the New Testament writings;
3. inasmuch as it is a source of inspiration for the redaction of many New Testament passages.

Finally, it should be noted that the LXX translation functioned as a *praeparatio evangelica* for the first mission and expansion of early Christianity. When Paul went round the synagogues of Asia Minor proclaiming the gospel, besides Jews he met among his listeners many proselytes (Acts 2:10; 6:5 and 13:43) already converted to Jewish monotheism, probably through reading the LXX in the synagogue.

b) *Quotations of the Old Testament in the New*

It is difficult to exaggerate the importance of Old Testament quotations in the New Testament since, together with Septuagintal quotations in Philo and Josephus, they reflect textual forms three centuries earlier than those of the principal uncials. Also, together with the pre-Hexaplaric papyri, they represent the only witnesses to the early history of the LXX before the Christian recensions. However, the data are in such a complex state that satisfactory conclusions cannot always be drawn.

At the beginning of the century, Dittmar collected Old Testament quotations in the New in two volumes.[11] More recent studies and specific monographs have completed this picture, as we shall see

---

[10] See M. Harl, "La Septante et le Nouveau Testament", 80–82; M. Wilcox, *The Semitisms of Acts*, Oxford 1965, and M. Silva, *Biblical Words and their Meaning: An Introduction to Lexical Semantics*, Grand Rapids, Mich. 1983, 53–73.

[11] W. Dittmar, *Vetus Testamentum in Novo. Die alttestamentliche Paralellen des NT in Wortlaut der Urtexte und der LXX*, 2 vols, Göttingen 1899 and 1903; now cf. H. Hübuer, *Vetus Testamentum in Novo.*; C. Smits, *Oudtestamentische citaten*, and G. L. Archer and G. Chirichigno, *Old Testament Quotations in the New Testament*. See also H. B. Swete, *An Introduction to the Old Testament in Greek*, Cambridge 1914, 381–405.

next. However, one must distinguish the data collected, however ambiguous they might seem, from the interpretation of the data. Only in this way can satisfactory conclusions be reached.

The books cited most in the New Testament are Psalms, Isaiah, Exodus and Deuteronomy, i.e. the most popular at the time, since they are also those cited most in the Qumran writings, Each part of the New Testament gives sufficient proof of knowing the LXX. These quotations diverge from the Masoretic text in 212 cases, whereas they differ from the Septuagintal text in only 185 cases. It can therefore be concluded that the LXX is the main source for quotations by the New Testament writers. This conclusion, as we shall see, will generally be confirmed by the most recent monographs that deal exhaustively with Old Testament quotations in the corpus of New Testament writings, although the problem of the Old Testament quotations in the New has become much more complex than was previously thought.

After a close examination of the passages preceded by an introductory formula,[12] or those that from context seem to be direct quotations or agree literally with the Greek Old Testament, the most acute problem is to interpret the many quotations that differ from the LXX.

The many explanations such as resorting to free quotation or quotation from memory, adaptation to fulfilment of prophecy, conflation of texts through collections of *testimonia*, or the influence of parallel passages, may explain some cases. However, at this point there is no avoiding modern theories about textual pluralism in the period when most of the New Testament was being formed,[13] the problems of the proto-Lucianic,[14] the proto-Theodotion or καίγε revision,[15] and even the possibility, as some believe, that these differences belong more to exegesis that to textual criticism.[16]

In any event, it seems that today Sperber's hypothesis about the existence of a Bible of the apostles, made up and defined negatively by all those quotations of the Old Testament that diverge from the

---

[12] Such as τοῦτο γέγονεν ἵνα πληρωθῇ τὸ ἐηθέν, οὕτως γέγραπται, καθὼς γέγραπται, εἶπεν ἡ γραφή.

[13] See chapter 6.

[14] See chapter 14.

[15] See chapter 9.

[16] See M. Wilcox, "Text Form", *It is Written*, 193–204.

LXX text[17] has to be rejected as not doing justice to the facts. In his study on this material in the gospel of Matthew, Gundry concludes that the layer composed of formal quotations is almost exclusively the LXX, whereas the parallels to Matthew are so to a lesser degree.[18] This study by Gundry is the first to take allusions or non-formal quotations into account. Matthew and Mark share 40 allusive quotations: of these, 11 are the same as the LXX, 12 are non-Septuagintal, and 8 contain a mixture of LXX and non-LXX. In other words, apart from the formal quotations from Marcan tradition, a mixed textual tradition is found in the other layers of synoptic material ranging over every literary form (narrative, didactic, apocalyptic). The most important element in this observation is that the original material of the quotation shows the same trilingual *milieu* as revealed by archaeology;[19] it also points towards Palestine of the 1st century as the point of departure of the gospel tradition.[20] However, the problems raised by Matthew's use of the Old Testament have not been resolved in this way. E. D. Freed, in his review of Gundry's book, points out one of the most significant defects of the monograph: it has not taken into account the pluralism of the Hebrew text as was made clear after the studies by Cross and Barthélemy, or of the problem of early revisions of the LXX.[21] Matthew usually

---

[17] Set out for the first time in *Tarbiz* 6 (1934), 1–29 (in Hebrew), and later in *JBL* 59 (1940), 193–293.

[18] R. H. Gundry, *The Use of the Old Testament*.

[19] J.-B. Frey, *Corpus Inscriptionum Judaicarum* II, Rome 1952, 114–322, W. Horbury and D. Noy, *Jewish Inscriptions of Graeco-Roman Egypt*, Cambridge 1992, and P. Trebilco, *Jewish Communities in Asia Minor*, Cambridge 1991. J. N. Sevenster, *Do you Know Greek? How much Greek could the Early Christians have Known?*, Leiden 1968, and J. H. Moulton, *A Grammar of New Testament Greek*, 6–9. See also J. A. Fitzmyer, "The Languages of Palestine in the First Century AD", *CBQ* 32 (1970), 501–31, and G. Mussies, "Greek in Palestine and the Diaspora", *The Jewish People in the First Century II*, ed. S. Safrai and M. Stern, Assen 1976, 1040–65.

[20] R. H. Gundry, *The Use of the Old Testament*, 177: "Apparently the explicit quotations in the Marcan tradition became hellenized exactly because they were explicit. They stood out, were recognized, and were assimilated to the LXX. The mass of allusive quotations escaped assimilation precisely because they were allusive. Beneath the surface, overlooked, and hard to be changed because they were grammatically tied to nonquotation material, the allusive quotations did not become hellenized."

[21] E. D. Freed in the review published in *Bib* 52 (1971), 588: "Gundry can be criticized for too easily evading the question of specific revisions of Greek texts on which Cross especially has been working along with Hebrew texts also now available." Previously A. Baumstark in "Die Zitate des Mt-Evangeliums", 313, had concluded that the many problems raised by Matthew's use of the Twelve Prophets had not yet been solved and tended towards the hypothesis that his quotations came

follows his sources closely, and consequently, with slight alterations, uses the Old Testament quotations that he finds in Mark or in the source Q. These quotations are chiefly from the LXX. However, it should not be forgotten that in many passages, Matthew condenses, expands or changes his sources in line with his own stylistic and theological concerns. These changes also affect the actual quotations. And very probably, Matthew is responsible for choosing and adapting many of them.[22]

Luke, instead, cites the minor prophets, Psalms and Isaiah, but gives no indication of knowing the LXX Pentateuch and he certainly did not know its legal sections. According to the study by Holtz, the text used by Luke is most like the Alexandrian group, proving yet again how old the readings from that group are.[23] The Acts of the Apostles are part of the Lucan work. The text used by Luke in his many quotations from the Old Testament throughout the speeches by Peter and Paul is basically the text of the LXX exactly as reconstructed in modern critical editions. The changes made are due to stylistic reasons or theological motives designed to prove that Jesus of Nazareth was the Messiah for whom the Jews hoped.[24]

A recent study of quotations in the three synoptic gospels, in order to test the hypothesis of the two documents in the composition of the gospels, confirms indirectly that the LXX is usually the basis for Old Testament quotations in the New.[25]

The importance of the Old Testament in the gospel of John supports the commonly accepted idea that this gospel was written in a sort of dialogue with the synagogue. John mainly quotes the original LXX and not the Hebrew. However, when the Greek version does not meet his needs, either he uses another translation or he

---

from an ancient lost Targum: "einem verschollenen ältesten Prophetentargum von wesentlich dem Charakter des altpalästinensischen Pentateuchtargums, dessen hebräische Vorlage dem von den Samaritanern festgehaltenen Vulgartext des Pentateuchs entsprach".

[22] See G. Stanton, "Matthew", *It is Written*, 205–19.

[23] T. Holtz, *Untersuchungen*, 166ff. And my review of that book in *Emerita* 37,1 (1968), 214–16. In fact, J. Ziegler frequently follows the Alexandrian in his edition of Isaiah and in the *Dodekapropheton*; see also R. Hanhart in his edition of II and III Maccabees.

[24] See C. K. Barret, "Luke/Acts", *It is Written*, 231–44, and G. J. Steyn, *Septuagint Quotations*, 230–48.

[25] D. S. New, *Old Testament Quotations in the Synoptic Gospels*.

alters the quotations to agree with the hermeneutics of contemporary Judaism, adapting the quotations to the context for christological reasons. His main concern was the reception of the Old Testament in the New. The Old Testament became a sort of vehicle not only for the fulfilment of the promises and prophecies in Jesus but also in largely replacing Jewish institutions with the sayings and actions of Jesus of Nazareth.[26]

The Letter to the Hebrews is an important document for checking the biblical text used since it includes very long quotations and it is likely that these seeped in from memory. K. J. Thomas has studied the use of the LXX in the letter to the Hebrews.[27] As the basis for comparison he used the Alexandrian and Vatican texts. Against the various hypotheses proposed in past studies (the author of Hebrews followed a recension close to the Alexandrian [F. Bleck]; his quotations are taken from a lost version of the Greek Old Testament [P. Padva], or from liturgical sources [Burch, Spicq, Dodd, Moule]; they are quotations from memory adapted by the author or are due to mistakes in copying the manuscript [Wete, Hastings, Stendahl]), Thomas concludes that they are closely related to the Alexandrian and Vatican texts. Six passages are quoted literally, in agreement with those texts. And of the 29 direct quotations from the Old Testament, there are only a total of 56 variants of every type in respect of Alexandrian and Vatican. Four of these are perhaps taken from Philo of Alexandria, one from the Letter to the Romans and another from a liturgical formula. Of the 48 remaining variants, 26 have no known textual parallels and 22 occur elsewhere. Those that have no textual parallel seem to be explained and owe their origin to the author of Hebrews, since as they fit his interpretation so well it is unlikely that these variants occur in Septuagintal texts.

In analysing this type of continuous text Thomas only distinguishes between original readings and edited readings. Among the latter,

1. some are due to more literal translations from the Hebrew,
2. some to grammatical and stylistic alterations to resolve certain language questions

---

[26] See D. A. Carson, "John and the Johannine Epistles", *It is Written*, 245–64; B. G. Schuchard, *Scripture within Scripture*, and M. J. J. Menken, *Old Testament Quotations in the Fourth Gospel*.

[27] K. J. Thomas, "The Old Testament Citations in Hebrews", 319–25.

3. some to textual changes to adapt the passage to particular exegetical trends.

There are overwhelming proofs that the author of Hebrews generally used an old LXX text. These conclusions are particularly against Sperber's hypothesis, who saw Alexandrian and Vatican as representatives of the two different translations of the Greek Bible, the first closely related to the asterisked readings of Origen's Hexapla and the second in connection with the obelised readings, again of the Hexapla.[28] The results of Thomas' study show it is highly unlikely that Alexandrian and Vatican represent two different traditions. In Prophets and Writings (the books cited most in Hebrews) these two uncials seem to be the descendants of a translation of which an early form was used by the author of Hebrews.

Hanson, instead, notes that the author of Hebrews should not be judged with the exegetical categories of our time. On the contrary, we have to accept that he did not take seriously the text that he quoted, and he modified it to suit himself. Hanson analyses the type of hermeneutics used, comparing it with the hermeneutics of Philo, Qumran, Paul and John. He shows that the exegesis of Hebrews is closer to Qumran than to Philo since he places stress on the eschatological viewpoint. Even so, he agrees most with Paul because both authors accept the Christocentric interpretation of the Old Testament. The author of the Letter to the Hebrews interprets Christ's work with cultic terms exactly as found in the Old Testament.[29]

Paul cites the Old Testament 93 times: the Pentateuch 33 times, Isaiah 25, and the Psalms 19.[30] Of these quotations, 51 agree completely or virtually with the LXX, 22 even against the Masoretic

---

[28] A. Sperber, "New Testament and LXX".

[29] A. T. Hanson, "Hebrews", It is Written, 292–302.

[30] E. E. Ellis, Paul's Use of the Old Testament 16ff. and 146ff., and D. M. Smith, "The Pauline Literature", It is Written, 265–91. The quotation from Rom. 9:33 is probably taken from Is. 8:14 according to Symmachus, since, if we follow the statement of Eusebius, he agrees most with this translator, see J. Ziegler, Septuaginta . . . XIV Isaias, Göttingen 1939, in the Hexaplaric apparatus. In Rom. 10:15 it is closer to Is. 52:7 according to "the three" (actually Theodotion) than to the LXX. In Rom. 11:4, the quotation is closer to the testimony of Aquila and Theodotion for 1 Kgs 19:18 than to the LXX. Many other quotations by Paul tell us about the textual fluctuation of LXX, the first revisions of which were accessible to the New Testament authors and, since they agree with the readings that we only know from Aquila, Symmachus or Theodotion, present serious problems – solved only partly by the καίγε recension; on the prehistory of these three Greek translators, see N. Fernández Marcos, "La Biblia de los autores del Nuevo Testamento", 176–77.

text; 4 follow the Hebrew text against the LXX, and 38 differ from both the Hebrew text and the LXX. In other words, it can be stated that Paul's use of the Old Testament in the letters accepted as authentic by modern criticism (Romans, 1 and 2 Corinthians, Galatians, Philippians, 1 Thessalonians and Philemon) is Septuagintal, taking into account that the textual condition of the LXX in the 1st century CE is not the same as the one transmitted by the great uncials of the 4th and 5th centuries. Barr has criticised the work of Ellis for treating with too little rigour the facts of the textual history of the LXX, in particular for not knowing that Kahle's theories are quite discredited among modern specialists of the LXX. Closer attention to the critical editions from Göttingen, concerned with restoring a text earlier than the Christian recensions and earliest revisions of the Greek Bible, has helped to focus the problem better. Although he admits progress in the monographs by Koch and Stanley, he insists that the last word has not been said on the treatment of Old Testament quotations in Paul's writings.[31]

Even so, I think that textual research alone does not resolve all the problems of Paul's quotations, as the influence of exegesis also has to be looked at. In many cases, Paul's text is closely connected with the application of that text to the present moment. These applications use common interpretations, oral or targumic traditions and the Targum method of exegesis. Paul uses the technique of *midraš pešer*. In this method, the explanation of the text determines the text form of the quotation. This occurs in several ways:

1. by mixing relevant verses within an express proof text;
2. by adapting the grammar to the context and application of the New Testament;
3. by choosing suitable translations of known texts or Targums;
4. by creating interpretations to fit the moment.

All in all, Paul was capable of applying scripture to the demands of every particular situation of the Christian community like any rabbi or sage of his time.[32]

Traditionally, it was accepted that the book of the Apocalypse cited Daniel according to "text θ'"; these quotations from Daniel in the Apocalypse comprised one of the main reasons to postulate a

---

[31] J. Barr, "Paul and the LXX", *JTS* 45 (1994), 593–601.
[32] See D. M. Smith, "The Pauline Literature", 276–83.

proto-Theodotion in circulation at least in the 1st century CE.[33] However, the study by Trudinger concludes that it cannot be held that the Apocalypse follows "text θ'" of Daniel, for it contains nine quotations contrary to that text.[34] Instead, the Greek version of Symmachus seems to underlie the wording of the Old Testament material used by the author of the Apocalypse.

Of the 120 references to the Old Testament in the Apocalypse, 53 can be considered quotations and the rest are allusions. In a wide sense, Trudinger concludes that the author of the Apocalypse takes his information primarily from Semitic sources. Although familiar with phrases from the Greek Old Testament, he could have learned them from collections of *testimonia*. In 39 quotations and at least as many allusions, the Apocalypse reading is against the LXX in any of its preserved versions. And a substantial number of quotations and allusions come from the text of the Aramaic Targums. Dependence on these Targums cannot be demonstrated conclusively, but the mere fact that there was a connection with the tradition represented by the Targums is already an interesting result, especially in view of the disputed problem of their dating. However, the forms of quotation and allusion to the Old Testament in Apocalypse are better explained if it is accepted that the author knew the *midrašim* of the respective passages quoted. There are also indications that the author knew a Hebrew textual tradition different from the Masoretic, related sometimes to one of the Qumran texts.

However, very recent studies have insisted on the familiarity of the author of the Apocalypse with the text of the Old Testament and in particular the influence of the LXX.[35] Furthermore, there is insistence on the different uses made of the Old Testament in that book: thematic, contextual, analogical, of combined allusions, of universalisation and fulfilment, and on the phenomenon of intertextuality.[36]

---

[33] See chapter 9.

[34] L. P. Trudinger, "Some Observations Concerning the Text". The quotations against Theodotion are: Ap. 1:13a; 4:9 and 20:12 as well as the allusions 1:13b, 15; 5:11; 12:4, 7 and 13:2.

[35] See G. K. Beale, "A Reconsideration of the Text of Daniel", and D. Schmidt, "Semiticisms and Septuagintalisms in the Book of Revelation".

[36] G. K. Beale, "Revelation", *It is Written*, 318–36; S. Moyise, *The Old Testament and the Book of Revelation*, Sheffield 1995, and J. van Ruiten, "The Intertextual Relationship between Isaiah 65, 17–20 and Revelation 21, 1–5b", *EstBib* 51 (1993), 473–510.

Perhaps the difficulty of identifying the source of the quotations in the Apocalypse results from the approach used. Callahan holds that when conventional critical research asks about the original language of the Apocalypse, it is asking the wrong question.[37] For Callahan, the language of the Apocalypse is a calque of the LXX. However, the visionary author took over material from the LXX in a poetic and not a narrative form, but at no time does he cite it. It is the language of a subordinate who consciously writes in the language of the dominant power. He deliberately breaks the rules of grammar to exercise his own discursive power.[38] The language of the Apocalypse is not narrative but provocative and political. However, it intentionally uses the LXX and from the distortion of language it cannot be concluded that the author knew Hebrew or Aramaic.[39]

Study of Old Testament quotations in Qumran literature and in the New Testament has caused Fitzmyer to observe some very similar quotation techniques and exegetical practices in both bodies of writing. This is an obvious result, however, if we remember that they are authors who apply current Jewish hermenutics to scripture.[40] And some New Testament writers, as Ellis has noted, use midrash to establish a Christian interpretation of the Old Testament, an interpretation included in the use of *testimonia* of these texts. Some independent quotations of the New Testament have been extracted from an earlier context of Christian midrash. Some Old Testament texts appear in the New Testament in an explicit midrash and as an independent quotation at the same time.[41] In these and similar contexts, some passages are closer in structure to the homiletic midrash and others to the pesher of Qumran. Sometimes they alter the Old

---

[37] "When one retroverts suspected Hebraisms or Aramaisms in the text, one creates the wrong answers," see A. D. Callahan, "The Language of Apocalypse", *HTR* 88 (1995), 453–70, p. 469.

[38] A. D. Callahan, "The Language of Apocalypse", 465.

[39] A. D. Callahan, "The Language of Apocalypse", 463: "His language hails neither from Palestine nor from Babylonia, but from the Septuagint. The author not only quarried the Septuagint for code names, but also used the language of the Septuagint to weave a biblical texture for his text. He did not quote the Septuagint at any point, however, because such a use of biblical material would invite an expositional reading."

[40] See J. de Waard, *A Comparative Study of the Old Testament Text*; J. A. Fitzmyer, "The Use of Explicit Old Testament Quotations", and Fitzmyer, "The Qumran Scrolls and the New Testament after Forty Years", *RQ* 13 (1988), 609–20.

[41] For example, Hab. 2:3-4; Pss 8:6; 110:1; 118:22ff.; 2 Sam. 7:12-14, see E. E. Ellis, "Midrash, Targum and New Testament Quotations", 65ff.

Testament text to fit the explanation that follows. Independent quotations may represent text-lemmata which have been taken from a
midrash. Thus, different types of midrash, targum, pesher and synagogal homily are probably represented in the way the Old Testament
is used in the New Testament.

All this is an indication of how, when evaluating the complex
problem of Old Testament quotations in the New, account must be
taken not only of the fluctuation and the textual pluralism of the
proto-Masoretic Hebrew text and the process of successive revisions
that the LXX text underwent from very early on, but also of the
frequent recourse to rabbinic exegesis, with direct repercussions on
the use of the Old Testament text by the authors of the New Testament (not to mention the various forms of inter-textuality rightly
emphasised in the monograph by Tuckett[42]).

c) *Other Areas of Influence*

The world of biblical quotations is not the only area of influence by
the LXX on the New Testament. In fact the background of the
Greek Bible emerges in many other ways. We have seen how in the
Apocalypse multiple and subtle use was made of the Old Testament:
contextual, thematic, literary, stylistic, analogical and even political.
This opens new avenues of research, not specifically textual, to the
influence of the Greek Bible on the New Testament.

The canticles of Luke 1–2, Stephen's speech and other speeches
in the book of Acts, the Epistle of James, the First Epistle of Peter,
the Letter to the Hebrews, and the Apocalypse are constructed and
strung together by a chain of quotations from the Greek Old Testament. Even books that are not specifically mentioned, such as
Wisdom, Ecclesiastes and 1–2 Maccabees – not to mention pseudepigraphical writings such as 1 Enoch[43] – find an echo in the New
Testament writings.

The authors of the New Testament searched the LXX for linguistic inspiration in the same way that the authors of the Qumran

---

[42] C. M. Tuckett, *The Scriptures in the Gospels*.
[43] Compare, for example, 1 Enoch 2–5:4 with Mt. 6:25-34/Lk. 12:22-31 and it
will be evident that they have the same literary structure and the same form of
argument. See also A. M. Dubarle, "Note conjointe sur l'inspiration de la Septante",
RSPhTh 49 (1965), 221–29, p. 222.

writings used the Hebrew Bible.[44] Although the word, considered on its own in the New Testament is Hellenistic, the style is conditioned by the biblical Greek of the LXX.[45] At the beginning of the century, the various aspects of the New Testament were studied from the supposition that Aramaic was the language spoken in the time of Christ.[46] Today, thanks to the study of both inscriptions and archaeological data, as well as to other linguistic studies, it is accepted that in 1st century Palestine there was trilingualism.[47]

Nowhere in the New Testament is the need for a Semitic *Vorlage* demanded by the evidence,[48] and most of the Hebraisms invoked by philologists are more easily explained as indirect Hebraisms or Septuagintalisms through the sub-language that was created for the Scriptures by the translation of the Bible into Greek. In the evangelists, especially in Luke, an express desire to imitate the LXX is evident in the use of pleonastic participles such as ἀφείς, καταλιπών, ἐλθών, πορευθείς, καθίσας, ἀναβλέψας; in the expletive ἤρξατο followed by infinitive and in other forms of expression.[49]

The study by Tabachovitz confirms the results obtained in other ways: that the Greek translation of the Old Testament that the authors of the New Testament followed differed in many details from the known text of the LXX as preserved in the extant manuscripts.

---

[44] Ch. Rabin, "The Translation Process and the Character of the Septuagint", 22, n. 80, and A. Pelletier, "Valeur évocatrice d'un démarquage chrétien de la Septante, [μοσχοποιεῖν, *Act* 7, 41]", *Bib* 48 (1967), 388–94. It is the term ἐμοσχοποίησαν in Acts 7:41, a biting allusion to the episode of the adoration of the calf in the desert (Ex. 32:4 ἐποίησε μόσχον) coined by this neologism.

[45] D. Tabachovitz, *Die LXX und das Neue Testament*, 18, and H. F. D. Sparks, "The Semitisms of St. Luke's Gospel", 134: "The bulk of his Semitisms are to be ascribed to his reverence for, and imitation of, the LXX. They are, in fact, not 'semitisms' at all, but 'Septuagintalisms'; and St. Luke himself was not a 'Semitizer' but an habitual, conscious, and deliberate 'Septuagintalizer'." See also E. Richard, "The Old Testament in Acts: Wilcox's Semitisms in Retrospect", *CBQ* 42 (1980), 330–41, p. 340: "Wilcox consistently overlooks the LXX's rich proto-history and manuscript tradition," and p. 341: "Indeed, the author's (of Acts) acquaintance with and creative use of the LXX and contemporary tradition in composing Acts hold many revelations for future scholarship."

[46] G. Dalman, *Die Worte Jesu*, Leipzig 1930, and the studies by F. Blass, C. C. Torrey, J. Jeremias and especially the influential book by M. Black, *An Aramaic Approach to the Gospels and Acts*, Oxford 1967.

[47] See J. N. Sevenster, *Do you Know Greek?*, and the bibliography mentioned in note 19.

[48] D. Tabachovitz, *Die Septuaginta und das Neue Testament*, 76.

[49] Linguistic usages which Dalman attributed to the influence of Aramaic, see D. Tabachovitz, *Die Septuaginta und das Neue Testament*, 24–40, and E. Plümacher, *Lukas als hellenistischer Schriftsteller. Studien zur Apostelgeschichte*, Göttingen 1972, 38–72.

For example, the ἴστε γινώσκοντες of Eph. 5:5 is a Hebraism that has been introduced through the Greek versions of the Bible; it exactly translates the Hebrew cliché of an infinite absolute and a finite verb, but not according to the LXX – which, after several attempts at this Hebrew syntagm, used specially the participle plus finite verb of the same root – but according to Symmachus, as is shown by Jer. 49:22.[50] Similarly, the special use of καὶ εὐθύς in Mark probably goes back to a Greek translation by Symmachus who uses that expression for wᵉhinnê in 2 Sam. 3:22. In Mark, καὶ ἰδού is missing but καὶ εὐθύς occurs many times including passages in which the translation "and then" does not fit. Thus rather than an Aramaism based on the construction miyad proposed by Dalman, one has to think of the influence of the translation techniques of one of the Greek versions.[51]

Other traces of the LXX continue to be found in many other gospel passages in which the evocative power of a word or Septuagintal construction makes the redactor automatically construct it on the linguistic framework of these Old Testament passages with which he particularly wants to associate them. This happens, for example, with the parable of vineyard (Lk. 20:9 and parallels) structured around Gen. 37:18ff. (the attack by Joseph's brothers) in combination with the song of the vineyard of Is. 5:5. Or the passage about the prayer in the garden (Mk. 14:32ff. and parallels) which has expressions evoking the story of the sacrifice of Isaac (Genesis 22); or the strange rhetorical imitation of sources that Brodie's studies have discovered in the work of Luke.[52] The redaction history of more than one New

---

[50] J. Ziegler, Septuaginta . . . XV Jeremias, Göttingen 1957, 429, in the Hexaplaric apparatus to Jer. 49:22, corresponding to the γνόντες γνώσεσθε of the LXX in Jer. 49:19, see D. Tabachovitz, Die Septuaginta und das Neue Testament, 91–92.

[51] See D. Tabachovitz, Die Septuaginta und das Neue Testament, 29–32. Twice LXX translates wᵉhinnê by καὶ εὐθύς (Gen. 15:4 and 38:29) although it is usually translated by καὶ ἰδού, see P. Fiedler, Die Formel 'und siehe' im Neuen Testament; M. Johannessohn, "Das biblische καὶ ἰδού in der Erzählung samt seiner hebräischen Vorlage", ZVS 66 (1939), 145–95; 67 (1940), 30–84, p. 182; A. Vargas-Machuca, "(Καὶ) ἰδού en el estilo de Mateo", Bib 50 (1969), 233–44; P. Katz, "Die Wiedergabe des biblischen 'und siehe' (והנה – wᵉhinnê) im Markusevangelium als theologisches Problem", TZ 55 (1999), 57–76.

[52] T. L. Brodie, "Towards Unraveling the Rhetorical Imitation", and N. Fernández Marcos, "La unción de Salomón y la entrada de Jesús en Jerusalén", as well as other recent works by Brodie and other authors mentioned in BS 75–82. To these can be added for the Apocalypse the article by A. D. Callahan, "The Language of Apocalypse", cited previously, and for the meeting of Jesus with the Samaritan

Testament pericope is revealed in this method of pivoting on a key-word from the LXX used by the redactor as inspiration and model for the woven text of his pericope.

Finally there is a strong linguistic argument for detecting a Septuagintalism in the periphrastic constructions of the New Testament: Tabachovitz has shown this in the construction from Mk. 10:22, ἦν γὰρ ἔχων κτήματα πολλά . The expression ἦν γὰρ ἔχων does not exist, nor can it exist, in Hebrew or Aramaic, as in both languages the suitable underlying word ἔχων (the verb "to hold") is missing. This expression does not occur in the LXX and thus it has to be explained as an analogical construction from similarity with many other periphrastic constructions of the LXX (although not with ἔχων) typi-cal of translation Greek. By analogy with many other parallels of the LXX, this periphrastic construction has been extended to a verb of which the equivalent is missing from the Semitic languages.[53]

Select Bibliography

Archer, G. L., and G. Chirichigno, *Old Testament Quotations in the New Testament: A Complete Survey*, Chicago 1983.

Barr, J., "Paul and the Septuagint: A Note on Some Recent Work". *JTS* 45 (1994), 593–601.

Barret, C. K., "The Interpretation of the Old Testament in the New". *Cambridge History of the Bible* I, 1970, 377–412.

Baumstark, A., "Die Zitate des Mt-Evangeliums aus dem Zwölfprophetenbuch". *Bib* 37 (1956), 296–313.

Beale, G. K., "A Reconsideration of the Text of Daniel in the Apocalypse". *Bib* 67 (1986), 539–43.

Bertram, G., "*Praeparatio evangelica* und die LXX". *VT* 7 (1957), 225–49.

Bludau, A., "Die Apocalypse und Theodotions Danielübersetzung". *Theologische Quartalschrift* 79 (1897), 1–26.

Brodie, T. L., "Towards Unraveling the Rhetorical Imitation of Sources in Acts: 2 Kgs 5 as One Component of Acts 8, 9–40". *Bib* 67 (1986), 41–67.

Callahan, A. D., "The Language of Apocalypse". *HTR* 88 (1995), 453–70.

Carson, D. A., and H. G. M. Williamson (eds.), *It is Written*, 1988, 193–336.

Clarke, W. K. L., "The Use of the LXX in Acts". *The Beginnings of Christianity*, ed. F. J. F. Jackson and K. Lake, London 1922, I.ii, 66–105.

Davies, W. D., "Reflections about the Use of the Old Testament in the New in its Historical Context". *JQR* 74 (1983), 105–37.

Dittmar, W., *Vetus Testamentum in Novo. Die alttestamentliche Paralellen des Neuen Testaments in Wortlaut der Urtexte und der LXX*, 2 vols, Göttingen 1899 and 1903.

woman (John 4) and for the episodes at the well (Genesis 24; 29 and Exodus 2), the article E. Nielsen, "Mødet vet Brønden".

[53] D. Tabachovitz, *Die Septuaginta und das Neue Testament*, 41–47.

Ellis, E. E., "Midrasch, Targum and New Testament Quotations". *Neotestamentica et Semitica: Studies in Honor of P. Matthew Black*, Edinburgh 1969, 61–69.

———, *Paul's Use of the Old Testament*, London 1957 (reprinted 1981).

Fernández Marcos, N., "La Biblia de los autores del Nuevo Testamento". *II Simposio Bíblico Español*, ed. V. Collado-Bertomeu and V. Vilar-Hueso, Valencia–Córdoba 1987, 171–80.

———, N., "La unción de Salomón y la entrada de Jesús en Jerusalén: I Re 1, 33–40/Lc 19, 35–40". *Bib* 68 (1987), 89–97.

Festugière, A. J., *Observations stylistiques sur l'Évangile de S. Jean*, Paris 1974.

Fiedler, P., *Die Formel 'und siehe' im Neuen Testament*, Munich 1969.

Fitzmyer, J. A., "The Use of Explicit Old Testament Quotations in Qumran Literature and in the New Testament". *NTS* 7 (1960–61), 297–333 (= J. A. Fitzmyer, *Essays on the Semitic Background of the New Testament*, London 1971, 3–59).

Freed, E. D., "Old Testament Quotations in the Gospel of John". *NTSuppl* 11, Leiden 1965.

Gundry, R. H., *The Use of the Old Testament in St. Matthew's Gospel*, Leiden 1967.

Hanhart, R., "Das Neue Testament und die griechische Überlieferung des Judentums". *Überlieferungsgeschichtliche Untersuchungen*, ed. F. Paschke. TU 125, Berlin 1981, 293–303.

———, "Die Bedeutung der Septuaginta in neutestamentlicher Zeit". *ZTK* 81 (1984), 395–416.

Harl, M., "La Septante et le Nouveau Testament: les citations". Harl *et al.*, *La Bible grecque des Septante*, 1998, 274–88.

Hemer, C. J., "Towards a New Moulton and Milligan". *NT* 24 (1982), 97–124.

Holtz, T., *Untersuchungen über die alttestamentliche Zitate bei Lukas*, Berlin 1968.

Howard, G., "The Septuagint: A Review of Recent Studies". *Restoration Quarterly* 13 (1970), 154–64.

———, "The Tetragram and the New Testament". *JBL* 96 (1977), 63–83.

Hübner, H., *Vetus Testamentum – in Novo. Band 2: Corpus Paulinum*, Göttingen 1997.

Johnson, S. E., "The LXX and the New Testament". *JBL* 56 (1937), 231–45.

Kahle, P., "The Greek Bible and the Gospels". *TU* 73 (1959), 613–21.

Kennedy, H. A. A., *Sources of New Testament Greek: or the Influence of the Septuagint on the Vocabulary of the New Testament*, Edinburgh 1895.

Koch, D.-A., *Die Schrift als Zeuge des Evangeliums: Untersuchungen zur Verwendung und zur Verständnis der Schrift bei Paulus*, Tübingen 1986.

McCullough, J. C., "The Old Testament Quotations in Hebrews". *NTS* 26 (1980), 363–79.

Menken, M. J. J., *Old Testament Quotations in the Fourth Gospel*, Kampen 1996.

Müller, M., *The First Bible of the Church: A Plea for the Septuagint*, Sheffield 1996.

———, "The Septuagint as the Bible of the New Testament Church: Some Reflections". *SJOT* 7 (1993), 194–217.

New, D. S., *Old Testament Quotations in the Synoptic Gospels and the Two Document Hypothesis*. SCS 37, Atlanta, Ga. 1993.

Nielsen, E., "Mødet vet brønden". *Dansk Teologisk Tidsskrift* 53 (1990), 243–59.

Rabin, Ch., "The Translation Process and the Character of the Septuagint". *Textus* 6 (1968), 1–27.

Richard, E., "Acts 7: An Investigation of the Samaritan Evidence". *CBQ* 39 (1977), 190–208.

Ruiten, J. van, "The Intertextual Relationship between Isaiah 65, 17–20 and Revelation 21, 1–5b". *EstBib* 51 (1993), 473–510.

Rydbeck, L., *Fachprosa, vermeintliche Volksprache und Neues Testament. Zur Beurteilung der sprachlichen Niveauunterschiede in nachklassischen Griechisch*, Uppsala 1967.

Schmidt, D., "Semitisms and Septuagintalisms in the Book of Revelation". *NTS* 37 (1991), 592–603.

Schuchard, B. G., *Scripture within Scripture: The Interrelationship of Form and Function in the Explicit Old Testament Citations in the Gospel of John*, Atlanta, Ga. 1992.

Smits, C., *Oud-testamentische citaten in het NT*, I and II, The Hague 1952 and 1955.

Sparks, H. F. D., "The Semitisms of St. Luke's Gospel". *JTS* 44 (1943), 129–38.

Sperber, A., "New Testament and LXX". *JBL* 69 (1940), 193–293.

Stanley, C. D., *Paul and the Language of Scripture: Citation Technique in the Pauline Epistles and Contemporary Literature*, Cambridge 1992.

Stendahl, K., *The School of St. Matthew and its Use of the Old Testament*, Uppsala 1954.

Steyn, G. J., *Septuagint Quotations in the Context of the Petrine and Pauline Speeches of the Acta Apostolorum*, Kampen 1995.

Tabachovitz, D., *Die Septuaginta und das Neue Testament. Stilstudien*, Lund 1956.

Thomas, K. J., "The Old Testament Citations in Hebrews". *NTS* 11 (1965), 303–25.

Trudinger, L. P., "Some Observations Concerning the Text of the Old Testament in the Book of Revelation". *JTS* 17 (1966), 82–88.

Tuckett, C. M. (ed.), *The Scriptures in the Gospels*, Leuven 1997.

Venard, L., "Citations de l'Ancien Testament dans le Nouveau Testament". *DBS* 2 (1934), 23–51.

Vogels, H. J., "Alttestamentliches im Codex Bezae". *BZ* 9 (1911), 149–58.

Waard, J. de, *A Comparative Study of the Old Testament Text in the Dead Sea Scrolls and in the New Testament*, Leiden 1965.

Wifstrand, A., "Lukas och Septuaginta". *Svensk Teologisk Kvartalskrift* 16 (1940), 243–62.

CHAPTER TWENTY TWO

THE SEPTUAGINT AND EARLY CHRISTIAN LITERATURE

a) *The Bible of the Fathers*

The LXX was the Bible of the authors of the New Testament. Its ubiquity can be seen not only in the quotations from the Old Testament in the New but also in the hermeneutic techniques and in many other forms of influence. There are certain Old Testament passages that following a sequence of keywords from the LXX are used as an inspiration and a model for the redaction of certain chapters in the gospels, the Acts of the Apostles and the Apocalypse of John.

The LXX was transmitted in Christian circles once it was adopted as the official Bible of the Church. This fact was of tremendous importance for the history of the Greek version.

The time has come for us to consider at length another aspect that emphasises the cultural importance of this translation for the history of Christianity. In fact, the LXX was also the Bible of early Christian writers and the Fathers of the Church, and even today continues to be the Bible of the Eastern Orthodox Church. To a large extent it was also the Bible of the western Fathers through the Old Latin, which continued in force until it was replaced by the Vulgate in the Carolingian period (end of the 8th century) or later, even in some peripheral regions of eastern Europe.[1]

As the Bible of the Fathers, it is worth pointing out that from the beginning they use it as an autonomous literary work, forget in practice that it is a translation, and try to find a meaning for difficult passages within the Greek language system.[2] It is the Bible to which, in polemics with Jews, Christians continually refer. Only in the Hex-

---

[1] See S. Berger, *Histoire de la Vulgate pendant les premiers siècles du Moyen Age*, Paris 1895; D. Debruyne, "Études sur les origines de la Vulgate en Espagne", *RBén* 31 (1914–19), 373–401, and B. Kedar, "The Latin Translations", *Mikra. Texts, Translations, Reading and Interpretation of the Hebrew Bible in Ancient Judaism and Early Christianity*, ed. M. J. Mulder, Assen–Maastricht 1988, 299–338.

[2] M. Harl, "Y a-t-il une influence", 188.

apla does Origen present the complete text of the Bible, the Bible of Jewish tradition and the Bible of Christian tradition, for study and academic debate, although continuing to cite the text according to the inherited LXX.[3]

The Greek version, either directly or through the Old Latin, provided the basis for Christian interpretation of the Old Testament, an interpretation which regulated the religious and social life of early Christianity. Even the Vulgate preserves much material from the Old Latin and consequently it can be said that the LXX extends its influence in the west through this version.[4]

Leaving aside the quotations that I have considered elsewhere,[5] the language of the Fathers is biblical because the wording of the Greek version surfaces everywhere. An important moment is the origin of monasticism where the relevance of the language and models of scripture is evident.[6]

The messianic interpretations and the various forms of Christological exegesis, like the theological language of Christianity, depend on the LXX. In the hermeneutics of the Fathers, the ambiguities of the translation emerge brilliantly, as do the various semantic fields of many Greek words, the divisions of verses and whole chapters – sometimes very different from those in the Hebrew text – the new theological interpretations of the LXX and the supplements to the books which are only found in this version.[7]

The philological work of the Fathers on the Greek Bible gave rise to many *scholia, aporiai*, commentaries, homilies and the literature of the *catenae*. This has been discussed elsewhere.[8] However, little has been written about the LXX as the point of departure of certain Christian literary genres. It seems that the psalter influenced devotional prayer and the hymns of Christian liturgy,[9] and there are indications that several Old Testament stories served as models for the

---

[3] See chapter 13.

[4] See H. B. Swete, *An Introduction to the Old Testament in Greek*, 474–76.

[5] See chapter 17.

[6] See N. Fernández Marcos, "La Biblia y los orígenes del monaquismo", *Palabra y Vida. Homenaje al Profesor José Alonso Díaz*, Madrid 1984, 383–97, and D. Burton-Christie, *The Word in the Desert*.

[7] See G. Dorival, "La Septante chez les Pères grecs", 307–11.

[8] See chapters 18 and 19. See also B. M. Metzger, "The Practice of Textual Criticism among the Church Fathers", *Studia Patristica XII* (= TU 114), ed. E. A. Livingstone, Berlin 1975, 340–49.

[9] See H. B. Swete, *An Introduction to the Old Testament in Greek*, 471–73.

editing of the *Life of Anthony* by Athanasius of Alexandria, and the
martyrdom of the Maccabees was the basis for the composition of
the Acts of the martyrs and other Christian writings.[10]

Two areas of influence deserve particular mention because they
have gone almost unnoticed: the chapter of introductions to Scripture
and the chapter of rewritings of the Bible.

Among the former we can include two *Synopsis scripturae sacrae*, one
attributed to Athanasius of Alexandria (295–373) and the other to
John Chrysostom,[11] both requiring modern editions and studies to
determine their true authorship, their chronology and their length;
the *Liber Regularum* of the African Donatist Tyconius (*c.* 380), the first
Latin compendium of biblical hermeneutics;[12] Hadrian's *Eisagoge in
sacras scripturas* (beginning of the 5th century), which systematised the
exegetical principles of the Antioch School; and the treatise *De Mensuris
et Ponderibus* by Epiphanius (*c.* 392), a veritable encyclopaedic introduction, preserved completely in Syriac and partially in Greek, which
deals with biblical books, biblical translations, weights and measures
and the geography of Palestine.[13] In about 542, Junilius the African
translated into Latin and re-edited in Constantinople a work written in Greek by the Persian Paul of Nisibis. It has the title *Instituta
regularia divinae legis*, and it is an introduction to the study of the Bible
which deals with important topics and includes faithfully Theodore
of Mopsuestia's points of view.

The other chapter is about rewritings of the Bible, either through
the use of paraphrase to adapt the language of Scripture to the usage

---

[10] See G. Dorival, "La Septante chez les Pères grecs", 318–20; H. Musurillo, *The
Acts of the Christian Martyrs*, Oxford 1979, L–LVII, and J. Rougé, "Le *de mortibus per-
secutorum*, 5e livre des Macchabées", *Studia Patristica XII*, 135–43.

[11] See *PG* 28, 284–437, and *PG* 56, 313–86 (incomplete). See *CPG* II, 3746, and
E. Klosterman, *Analecta zur Septuaginta, Hexapla und Patristik*, Leipzig 1895.

[12] See H. Jordan, *Geschichte der altchristlichen Literatur*, Leipzig 1911, 423–27; F. C.
Burkitt, *The Rules of Tyconius*, Cambridge 1894, and W. S. Babcock, *Tyconius: The
Book of Rules*, Atlanta, Ga. 1989. Augustine depends on these rules in writing the
first three books of his *De doctrina Christiana*, on biblical hermeneutics. Through
Augustine's work these rules by Tyconius were to have a decisive influence in the
Middle Ages and on the main biblical introductions of the Renaissance: P. A.
Beuter, M. Martínez of Cantalapiedra, Sixto of Siena and Flacius Illyricus.

[13] In spite of the importance of Hadrian's *Eisagoge*, the most recent edition is still
the one by F. Goessling, *Adrians Eisagoge eis tas theias graphas*, Berlin 1887. Furthermore,
the edited text, apparently, only contains a summary of Hadrian's work, as can be
shown from some fragments transmitted by the *catenae*, see *CPG* III, 6527. The
urgent need for a complete examination of the manuscript tradition, a critical edition and a more detailed analysis of this writing are therefore evident.

of the period, or by the use of versification to adapt it to the pedagogical needs required by the legislation of the empire. An example
of the former has come down to us in the Paraphrase of Ecclesiastes
by Gregory Thaumaturgos.[14] Towards the end of the 3rd century,
this writer, a disciple of Origen, wrote a paraphrase of Qoheleth
adapting it to the language of his century. In this way, not only did
he bring about a linguistic transformation of the book, improving
the style of the Greek and removing the Semitisms of a literal translation which makes it one of the predecessors of Aquila, but at the
same time he eliminated the more shocking elements of Qoheleth's
thought, harmonising them with Christian theology. Gregory Chris-
tianised the book to such an extreme that sometimes he makes
it say things different from the original Greek, such as that the
wise man will never have the same fate as the wicked. To preserve
the Salomonic authorship of the book, some of its more daring
opinions are attributed to young Solomon at the same time that
it has to be admitted that on reaching old age he really knows that
these points of view are false. In this way, the original book is turned
into a moralising sermon preached to the assembly of God for
the wisest of his chosen messengers. With this work Gregory does
the same service for the assembly of God that the Aramaic paraphrase did for the Jewish community, in presenting Qoheleth's words
in harmony with Jewish tradition. He turned the book of Ecclesiastes into a pious book of the Church and opened the way to
allegorical interpretation, which was to predominate after Jerome's
commentary.[15]

There must have been several attempts at the versification of the
Bible with the aim of 'Homerising' it. However, we only know of
one epic poem with a biblical theme, attributed to Apollinaris of
Laodicea, which continued the tradition begun by Hellenistic Judaism
of putting biblical history into hexameters with works such as those
by Theodotus on Shechem or Ezekiel the Tragedian on Exodus

---

[14] See the edition in *PG* 10, 963/1232. This work has merited the attention of
several recent studies such as K. W. Noakes, "The Metaphrase on Ecclesiastes of
Gregory Thaumaturgus", *Studia Patristica* 15 (= TU 128), ed. E. A. Livingstone,
Berlin 1984, 196–99; F. Vinel, "La *Metaphrasis in Ecclesiasten* de Grégoire le Thau-
maturge: entre traduction et interprétation, une explication de texte", *Cahiers de
Biblia Patristica 1*, Strasbourg 1987, 191–215, and J. Jarick, *Gregory Thaumaturgos'
Paraphrase of Ecclesiastes*. SCS 29, Atlanta, Ga. 1990.

[15] See C. Jarick, *Gregory Thaumaturgos' Paraphrase of Ecclesiastes*, 311–16.

(*Exagoge*).[16] As Sozomenus tells us, the decree of the emperor Julian (362) which forbade Christians from teaching the Greek poets in school, made Apollinaris compose an epic of twenty-four poems in hexameters on biblical history up to the reign of Saul, of which nothing has survived.[17]

The decree was abrogated two years later and Christians did not wish to deprive themselves of the legacy of pagan Greek literature in teaching in schools. However, a century later, an anonymous writer, probably from Alexandria, composed a paraphrase of the Greek psalter in Homeric verses, which fortunately does survive.[18]

The Fathers of the Church did not formulate specific exegetical rules as did the rabbis,[19] however they relied on a few principles or criteria of interpretation common to them all: the principle of the unity of the biblical text of the two Testaments, the interpretation of the Old in the light of the New, and the conviction that all the texts of the Old Testament spoke of Christ and of Christian mysteries.[20] The various schools adopted these principles, modifying them with various refinements, either preferring to stress allegory (Alexandria) or insisting instead on typology (Antioch).[21]

---

[16] See S. Brock, "Bibelübersetzungen I", 170.

[17] Sozomenus, *Hist. Ecc. V, 18*, in *Sozomenus Kirchengeschichte*, ed. J. Bidez, G. C. Hansen, Berlin 1960, p. 222: ἡνίκα δὴ Ἀπολινάριος οὗτος εἰς καιρὸν τῇ πολυμαθείᾳ καὶ τῇ φύσει χρησάμενος, ἀντὶ μὲν τῆς Ὁμήρου ποιήσεως ἐν ἔπεσιν ἡρῴοις τὴν Ἑβραϊκὴν ἀρχαιολογίαν συνεγράψατο μέχρι τῆς Σαοὺλ βασιλείας καὶ εἰς εἰκοσιτέσσαρα μέρη τὴν πᾶσαν πραγματείαν διεῖλεν, ἑκάστῳ τόμῳ προσηγορίαν θέμενος ὁμώνυμον τοῖς παρ᾽ Ἕλλησι στοιχείοις κατὰ τῶν τούτων ἀριθμὸν καὶ τάξιν ("When this certain Apollinaris, thanks to his capabilities and his education, had the opportunity, he composed, as a counterpart to the poetry of Homer, the ancient Hebrew history in heroic epic until the kingdom of Saul; and he divided the material into 24 parts, giving each volume a title similar to the Greek poems, using the same numbering and distribution").

Sozomenus then adds that for the same purpose Apollinaris composed comedies, tragedies and lyric poems like those by Menander, Euripides and Pindar.

[18] See G. Dorival, "Antiquité chrétienne et Bible", 75; J. Golega, *Der homerische Psalter*, Ettal 1960; A. Ludwig, *Apollinari metaphrasis Psalmorum*, Leipzig 1912, and K. Thraede, "Ps.-Apollinarios", *RAC* 5 (1962), 1003–1006. For similar versification in Latin, see K. Smolak, "Lateinische Umdichtungen des biblischen Schöpfungsberichtes", *Studia Patristica* XII, 350–60.

[19] See J. Trebolle, *The Jewish Bible and the Christian Bible*, 479–81.

[20] See H. F. von Campenhausen, *Die Entstehung der christlichen Bibel*, Tübingen 1969, 378: "Die christliche Bibel – das ist die erste und durch nichts zu erschütternde Erkenntnis – entsteht und gilt als das *Christusbuch*. Die 'Herrenschriften' bezeugen den Herrn, das Alte Testament prophetisch, das Neue Testament historisch. Christus spricht in beiden Testamenten und ist ihr eigentlicher Inhalt. Dies allein macht sie zur christlichen Bibel, zum Buch der christlichen Kirche."

[21] See G. Dorival, "La Septante chez les Pères grecs", 297–99, and J. Trebolle, *The Jewish Bible and the Christian Bible*, 528–31.

The Fathers used the various texts attested by the different Christian recensions depending on the area from which the authors came. They often used variants from the other Greek versions to explain the passage on which they are commenting. That is to say, they used the various textual forms for their exegesis and took advantage of the different variants as stages of the text that have normative value. In addition, according to Origen's theory, words are incapable of fully expressing the meaning or exhausting all the meanings of the original. This type of exegesis caused them to defend a plurality of meanings in Scripture, meanings which sometimes were contradictory, which have been transmitted as a reflection of the various re-readings of scripture throughout the centuries.[22]

b) *The Septuagint and Christian Greek*

There is an aspect of the survival of the LXX that is not without interest for the history of the Greek language: the question as to whether or not the language of the LXX influenced the Greek used by Christians. The difficulties emerge as soon as the question is posed, i.e. whether one can really speak about Christian Greek. In this respect it is worth remembering the criticisms made by M. Harl when G. W. H. Lampe's *Patristic Greek Lexicon* was published.[23] It is difficult to separate elements dependent upon the general evolution of a language from those produced by the effect of external agents, such as the influence of translation Greek or biblical Greek. M. Harl criticised the approach used in preparing that dictionary, which focuses one-sidedly on new words of the Christian lexicon and on words that are important for the history of ideas and institutions. Lampe's dictionary, instead, leaves out the vocabulary of the common everyday language of Christians, which was probably close to profane Greek of the period, of the Stoics, of average Platonism or the moralists and popular philosophers. Christian Greek has to be studied as an extension of classical Greek on the one hand, and of biblical and Jewish-Hellenistic Greek on the other. Generally, it seems clear that it has fewer neologisms than Christian Latin.[24] In any case

---

[22] See M. Harl, "La Septante et la pluralité textuelle"; Harl, "Le renouvellement du lexique des Septante", and G. Dorival, "Antiquité chrétiennne et Bible", 79.

[23] M. Harl, "Remarques de la langue des chrétiens".

[24] See Ch. Mohrmann's studies on the Latin used by Christians especially "Linguistic Problems of the Early Christian Church", *VC* 11 (1957), 11–37.

it would be necessary, as Deissmann and Moulton did for the New Testament Greek in relation to the papyri,[25] for Christian Greek to be submitted to a similar comparison with the language of the philosophers and moralists of late antiquity. We can only determine what is peculiar to Christian Greek if we have available a lexicon of postclassical Greek philosophy where the many philosophical and moral movements adopt a religious tone.[26] M. Harl has followed this phenomenon, analysing closely the commentaries on Psalm 118 and concludes that the number of words from the LXX directly adopted by Christians and not through the New Testament, is very small. She only records three words from the psalm adopted by Christians with a new meaning: ἀδολεσχία as "meditation" on the divine Law; ταπείνωσις as "probation, ascetic testing"; and ἀκηδία as a "state of worry and distress".[27] In short, the influence remains restricted to a handful of words belonging to the semantic field of spiritual or monastic life. However, what is most surprising is that one cannot speak of a linear process that considers the Greek of Christians as a continuation of biblical Greek *tout court*. Together with the assimilation of part of the biblical vocabulary there is also in the Fathers a parallel process of estrangement with respect to the language of the LXX. Perhaps, as it is translation Greek, once it lost contact with Hebrew, it continued to be difficult Greek for these writers, a Greek that needed interpretation. Hence they continually refer in their writings to a series of *voces biblicae* or words peculiar to Scripture.

In addition, the various forerunners of Christianity and in particular, the process of coming towards or away from Greek culture had repercussions on the development of the Greek of the Christians. The first generations of the Apostolic Fathers went through a new experience which left its mark on the language. They considered themselves to be a group of people apart, different from the Jews and the other worshippers of many gods, whether they were Greeks, Egyptians or Syrians.[28] Bartelink has analysed the language of the Apostolic Fathers as the language of a group, concluding that its reaching the conclusion that its specific vocabulary went beyond the

---

[25] See chapter 1.
[26] M. Harl, "Remarques sur la langue des chrétiens", 181–82.
[27] M. Harl, "Y-a-t-il une influence", 200–202.
[28] See Aristides, *Apology*, 2.

vocabulary of other special languages.[29] The Apologists, instead, systematically and by design, avoid specifically Christian words and shun certain topics of the new religion, since the aim of their writings is to introduce Christianity to society with patterns that are familiar to their readers.[30]

Another important event, the transition of Christianity to the state religion under Constantine, also has repercussions on the language. In the 4th and 5th centuries, the religious terminology of the mystery religions, which was carefully avoided in the earliest writings, emerges comprehensively in the vocabulary of the cult. One can even speak in some sense of a supplantation of the language by which the terms used for the mysteries of Eleusis, Isis or Sabazius come to denote the sacraments of Christian initiation.[31] The writers of the golden age of the Fathers, Basil of Caesarea, Gregory of Nazianz, Gregory of Nyssa or John Chrysostom, begin to form the best universities of the time, in Athens or Alexandria, together with their pagan colleagues. They follow the classical models and set themselves up as continuing literary *koiné*. Some of them even artificially revive the ancient dialects (Sinesius of Cyrene writes his hymns in Doric, several poems of Gregory of Nazianz are in Aeolic) or ancient metre (the iambic trimeters of Gregory of Nazianz or the anacreontics of Sophronius of Jerusalem). Accordingly, the survival of biblical Greek has to be sought, as M. Harl had already insisted, in the vocabulary of the spiritual and monastic life and in secondary literature: gospels and apocryphal acts of the Apostles, acts of the martyrs, hagiographical writings, accounts of miracles and monastic legends.[32]

In sum, the study of the Greek of the Christians can only be begun as a continuation of classical and Hellenistic Greek and within the general evolution that Greek underwent in the Byzantine period. The historical changes or the successive dominant cultural periods influenced the development of the language, but on its own this influence does not justify the spoken language of a particular language group. In fact, no-one speaks the language of the Stoics, of

---

[29] G. J. M. Bartelink, *Lexicologisch-semantische Studie over de Taal van de apostolische Vaders. Bijdrage tot de Studie van de groeptaal der griekse Christenen*, Utrecht 1952.

[30] G. J. M. Bartelink, "Die Meidung heidnischer oder christlicher Termini in dem frühchristlichen Sprachgebrauch", *VC* 19 (1965), 193–210.

[31] See N. Fernández Marcos, "En torno al estudio del griego de los cristianos", 52–55.

[32] N. Fernández Marcos, "En torno al estudio del griego de los cristianos", 54.

Pythagorism or of neo-Platonism. However, the component of biblical Greek brings to the language of the Christians, and in particular of the spiritual life, the baggage of neologisms which must be taken into account in the historical study of the language.

c) *The Septuagint Translated*

Perhaps the most important cultural impact of the LXX in early Christian literature is due to the many translations of it into the main languages of late antiquity.

Not only did Christianity adopt a translated Bible as the official Bible, but from its beginnings it was a religion that favoured translation of the Bible into vernacular languages. Unlike Jewish communities, the Christian communities did not feel themselves to be chained to the Hebrew text as such but only to its contents, nor were they tied to the Greek text of the LXX. The new translations, as distinct from happened with the Aramaic *Targumim*, became independent and took the place of the original in the life of the communities. This attitude conferred on the new versions of a Bible a status unlike that of the Jewish translations. They were not merely an aid to understanding the text but they replaced the original with authority. Hence, biblical translation is spoken of as a specifically Christian activity.[33]

It is appropriate to note that, with the exception of the Aramaic translations, most of the ancient versions of the Bible were made from the LXX and not from the Hebrew. Not even the Peshitta or the Vulgate, most of which was translated from Hebrew, are immune to the influence of the LXX.

These versions accompanied Christianity in its expansion to the limits of the Roman Empire,[34] echo the social movements and theological conflicts of antiquity,[35] and have an appreciable cultural importance. In fact, in some cases, such as the versions into Armenian, Georgian, Gothic or ancient Slavonic, they coincide with the invention of the alphabet in those languages and with the beginning of

---

[33] See Ch. Rabin, "Cultural Aspects of Bible Translation", 43. Christianity was polyglot from its beginnings and to this tradition belong Origen's Hexapla and the 16th- and 17th-century polyglot bibles.

[34] H. Koester, *History and Literature of Early Christianity*.

[35] See G. Bardy, *La question des langues dans l'Église ancienne*, 1–79.

the vernacular literature of those peoples. They are pioneer works of enormous linguistic interest, as they represent the oldest documents we have for the study of these languages and literatures.

The new traditions also became a vehicle for the spread of biblical and para-biblical literature to new cultures. For it should not be forgotten that most pseudepigraphical literature, which grew in the shadow of the Bible between the 3rd century BCE and the 3rd century CE, has reached us through these versions.[36] They also throw light on areas of the history of the canon that were in shadow: the late translation of the Apocalypse into Georgian shows the doubts about the canonicity of this book which some Eastern Churches maintained; and the presence of the book of Enoch or the book of Jubilees in the Ethiopic Bible shows us that these books were venerated as canonical in that community.

In what follows, I provide a short survey of the main ancient versions of the LXX, which may serve as a guide to further study. I shall indicate the cultural importance and the methodological criteria required for using it in textual criticism of the Bible. Since each language codifies reality, shaping it in its own image, it is first necessary to know the structures of the various languages in order to evaluate correctly the various translation techniques and the limitations of each translation.[37]

1. *The Oriental versions*

The Coptic versions

In the latest publications it has been topical to speak of the obscure origins of Christianity in Egypt, its relation with the brilliant tradition of Hellenistic Judaism, with Gnosis and other unorthodox forms of Christianity. There is a certain consensus that Egyptian Christianity was based on a wider literary tradition and on a less defined ecclesiastical tradition than the Christianity of Syria or Rome.[38] Also the

---

[36] See A.-M. Denis, *Introduction aux pseudépigraphes grecs d'Ancien Testament*; J. H. Charlesworth, *The Pseudepigrapha and Modern Research*; H. Jordan, *Geschichte der altchristlichen Literatur*, 430–44; M. E. Stone, *Armenian Apocrypha Relating to the Patriarchs and Prophets*, Jerusalem 1982; Stone, *Selected Studies in Pseudepigrapha and Apocrypha, with Special Reference to the Armenian Tradition*, Leiden 1991, and A. de Santos Otero, *Die handschriftliche Überlieferung der altslavischen Apokryphen*, Berlin–New York 1978.

[37] See *La Septuaginta*, 15–82 for a more detailed study of these aspects as applied to Greek, Armenian, Syriac, Coptic and Latin.

[38] See C. H. Roberts, *Manuscript, Society, and Belief in Early Christian Egypt*, Oxford 1979, and C. W. Griggs, *Early Egyptian Christianity: From its Origins to 451 CE*, Leiden 1990.

origins of the Coptic versions of the Old and New Testaments remain in the shade. Christianity first set root in Alexandria, a Greek-speaking city which needed no other translation than the LXX. Only when the Christian mission penetrated Egypt's interior were translations into the Egyptian vernacular, i.e. Coptic, necessary. The *Vita Antonii* opens with Athanasius relating how Anthony felt the call of the desert on hearing Matthew's gospel in the liturgy. Anthony knew Coptic and not Greek, as is repeated once or twice in his biography. Thus it can be concluded that in the second half of the 3rd century, the gospels had already been translated into Coptic. In fact, the oldest biblical manuscript in Coptic that we have, Papyrus Bodmer VI with the book of Proverbs, comes from the close of the 3rd century.

The translation of the bible into Coptic is not uniform because the language is divided into three dialects based on differences in location and text: Akhmimic, Sahidic and Bohairic. There was only one complete translation of the Old Testament into Sahidic but we do not have any manuscripts that contain the whole Old Testament. The tradition varies from book to book, from the existence of several witnesses of the same document to mere fragments.

Three stages can be distinguished in the Coptic versions of the bible:

1. from the 2nd to the 4th centuries, when translators worked separately in the various dialects using different methods;
2. during the 4th and 5th centuries, the canonisation and standardisation of the Sahidic translation took place;
3. a third stage that presupposes the standardisation of the translation into Bohairic which was completed probably in the 9th century.

In other words, at the beginning there was a variety of biblical translations into different dialects. These were replaced, around the 7th century, by translations into the two main dialects, Sahidic and Bohairic. The standard translation in Bohairic was not completed until the 9th century.

There are codices and fragments from the first stage, but there is no edition of the Coptic Bible of the Old Testament comparable to Horner's for the New.[39] Nor is there a diachronic study on the Coptic versions that takes into account the different dialects. In the light of

---

[39] The standard edition for the New Testament is G. W. Horner, *The Coptic*

new texts published, the main problems to be resolved concern the date of the versions, the matter of dialectal priority, the relationships between private and official versions, the reconstruction of the Greek exemplar used for translation and the insertion of the various translations into the different recensions or textual families of the LXX.[40] In spite of the tasks that remain (in the production of true critical editions in the different dialects and in the correct assessment of the textual variants), there are some points where scholars are in agreement, i.e. that the Coptic Bible is based on Greek models that transmit the LXX, not the Hebrew text, and that the Sahidic and Bohairic versions are different and independent translations of the Greek. The Akhmimic version, instead, is an interlinear translation of the Sahidic.

The Sahidic version of the Minor Prophets is closer to the Hebrew than to the LXX. However it was not revised according to the Hebrew but is based on a Greek Hebraising revision related to the καίγε revision, to which belong also the *quinta* of the Hexapla and the oldest link of which is to be found in the fragments of the Twelve Prophets found in Naḥal Ḥever.[41]

The bilingual codices are a peculiar form of textual transmission in the Coptic Bible. Those from the first millennium are Greek–Sahidic bilinguals which later would be replaced by Bohairic–Arabic bilinguals.[42]

Version of the New Testament in the Northern Dialect, 4 vols, London 1898–1905, and Horner, *The Coptic Version of the New Testament in the Southern Dialect*, 7 vols, Oxford 1911–24.

Coptic scholars have chosen to edit individual manuscripts, see H. Quecke, *Das Markusevangelium saïdisch. Text der Handschrift PPalau Rib. Inv.-Nr. 182 mit den Varianten der Handschrift M 569*, Barcelona 1972; Quecke, *Das Lukasevangelium sahidisch*, Barcelona 1977; H.-M. Schenke, *Das Matthäus-Evangelium im mittelägyptischen Dialekt des Koptischen, Codex Scheide*, Berlin 1981; G. Aranda Pérez, *El evangelio de San Mateo en copto sahídico*, Texto de M 569, Madrid 1984, and Aranda Pérez, *El evangelio de San Marcos en copto sahídico*, Madrid 1988.

For the Old Testament, the edition of the Pentateuch is at an advanced stage of preparation, see M. K. H. Peeters, *A Critical Edition of the Coptic (Bohairic) Pentateuch. Vol. 5: Deuteronomy*, Chico, Calif. 1983; *Vol. 1: Genesis*, Atlanta, Ga. 1985; *Vol. 2: Exodus*, Atlanta, Ga. 1986.

[40] See T. Orlandi, "Coptic Literature", *The Roots of Egyptian Christianity*, ed. B. A. Pearson and J. E. Goehring, Philadelphia 1986, 51–81, pp. 53–55.

[41] See chapter 10.

[42] See P. Nagel, "Old Testament, Coptic Translations of", *The Coptic Encyclopedia*. Vol. 6, ed. A. S. Atiya, New York 1991, 1836–40, and B. J. Diebner and R. Kasser, *Hamburger Papyrus Bil. 1*, Geneva 1989 with Song of Songs (Coptic), Lamentations (Coptic) and Ecclesiastes (Greek and Coptic).

On the limitations of Coptic for reproducing Greek we can refer to the perceptive studies by J. M. Plumley and M. K. H. Peters, which are indispensable for correct use of these versions in the textual criticism of the LXX.[43]

The Armenian Version

Armenia was the first kingdom to accept Christianity as the official religion, in 304, under Tiridates III. The translation of the Bible into Armenian dates to the beginning of the 5th century. It was the work of the *Catholikos* or chief of the Church Sahak, of the monk and missionary Mesrop and of his disciples. With the support of the king, Mesrop invented the Armenian alphabet of 36 letters which gave rise to a cultural renaissance and the beginnings of literature in Armenia precisely with the translation of the Bible, which ended between 410 and 414.

This translation includes books held as apocryphal in other traditions, such as Joseph and Aseneth, the Testament of the Twelve Patriarchs and the Letter of the Corinthians to Paul and Paul's third letter to the Corinthians.

From internal study of this version it can be concluded that it went through at least two stages: an initial translation (Arm 1), perhaps followed by a preliminary revision, and a complete later revision or new translation (Arm 2). Although in its various stages the translation was under the influence of the Greek and Syriac, it was made principally from the Greek in the Lucianic and Hexaplaric recensions. Ruth, 1 Samuel, Daniel and Sira were translated, apparently from a Lucianic type of text influenced by Syriac. Text Arm 1 of Chronicles followed a Greek exemplar of Lucianic type for its translation, whereas Arm 2 had a Hexaplaric-type text as its *Vorlage*.[44] The version of Genesis is based on the Hexaplaric recension; the versions of Deuteronomy and 1 Samuel are strongly influenced by

---

[43] J. M. Plumley, "Limitations of Coptic (Sahidic) in Representing Greek", *The Early Versions*, 141–52, and M. K. H. Peters, "The Use of Coptic for Textual Criticism of the Septuagint", *La Septuaginta*, 55–66.

[44] See S. P. Cowe, "The Armenian Version", N. Fernández Marcos and J. R. Busto Saiz, *El texto antioqueno de la Biblia griega III. 1–2 Crónicas*, Madrid 1996, XLVIII–LV, and S. P. Cowe, "The Two Armenian Versions of Chronicles: Their Origin and Translation Technique", *Revue des Études Armeniens* 22 (1990–91), 53–96.

the Hexaplaric recension.[45] In the book of Job this version is an excellent testimony of the Origen recension.[46]

Between the 5th and 8th centuries, Arm 2 underwent a gradual revision to make it agree more closely with the Greek text of the LXX.

The main collections of Armenian manuscripts are in the Matenadaran library of Yerevan, in the Armenian Patriarchate of Jerusalem, and with the Mekitarist Fathers of Venice and Vienna. The only complete edition of the Armenian Bible continues to be the one by Y. Zohrab (Venice 1805) which became the standard Bible of the Armenian Church. The Academy of Sciences of Yerevan and the Matenadaran Library are preparing a critical edition of the Old and New Testaments in Armenian.[47]

The Armenian version tends to be more literal and of high quality; hence its interest for textual criticism is increasing as the new manuscripts are studied. On the phonetic, morphological and syntactic limitations of Armenian for reproducing Greek and the appropriate use of Armenian in textual criticism of the LXX, the works by E. F. Rhodes and C. Cox are indispensable.[48]

The Georgian Version

The ancient name of Georgia is Iberia, and from it is derived the name *Iveron* of the monastery on Mount Athos, at one time a Georgian monastery. The Georgian language has no other cognate language outside the Caucasus. It has neither the article nor different genders. The verb is polypersonal, i.e. within the same verbal form the

---

[45] See C. E. Cox, *The Armenian Translation of Deuteronomy*, Chico, Calif. 1981, 250, and B. Johnson, *Die armenische Bibelübersetzung als hexaplarischer Zeuge im 1. Samuelbuch*, Lund 1968. According to S. P. Cowe, Johnson's conclusions are valid for the second layer of the Armenian version (Arm 2), but for the first layer (Arm 1), represented by a small group of manuscripts, in 1 Samuel this version also follows a Lucianic or Antiochene type of text, see S. P. Cowe, "The Armenian Version", N. Fernández Marcos and J. R. Busto Saiz, *El texto antioqueno de la Biblia griega. I, 1–2 Samuel*, Madrid 1989, LXXI–LXXIX.

[46] For the Hexaplaric material of this version which has been preserved, see C. E. Cox, *Hexaplaric Materials Preserved in the Armenian Version*. SCS 21, Atlanta, Ga. 1986, and Cox, *Aquila, Symmachus and Theodotion in Armenia*. SCS 42, Atlanta, Ga. 1996.

[47] See J. M. Alexanian, "Armenian Versions", *ABD* 6, 805–808.

[48] E. F. Rhodes, "Limitations of Armenian in Representing Greek", *The Early Versions*, 171–81, and C. E. Cox, "The Use of the Armenian Version for the Textual Criticism of the Septuagint", *La Septuaginta*, 25–35.

morphemes can indicate the subject and the direct or indirect object of the verb.

The oldest texts in Georgian are Christian. The oldest manuscripts we have of the biblical version come from the 5th to 10th centuries. Most of them are in fragments and transmitted on palimpsests. Of the Old Testament, fragments of Genesis, Proverbs and Jeremiah are preserved, all published, as well as fragments of Deuteronomy and Judges, as yet unpublished. We do not know whether the translation covered the whole Old Testament. Of the pseudepigrapha, the 4th book of Ezra is preserved in Georgian.

The translations were probably made from Armenian, but were revised very soon according to a Greek text of Lucianic type, although there are also traces of Hexaplaric influence. The fragments of gospels were translated sometimes from Armenian and sometimes from Greek. As yet we do not have a complete edition of the Old Testament.[49]

The contribution of M. Brière[50] can be consulted for the limitations of Georgian for reflecting Greek.

The Ethiopic Version

The version into Ethiopic or *ge'ez* was made from Greek between the 4th and 6th centuries. The whole Old Testament has been preserved, although the books of Maccabees were translated later from Latin. Ethiopic tradition does not distinguish between canonical and extra-canonical books, since the biblical manuscripts contain various pseudepigrapha such as the book of Enoch, the book of Jubilees, the Ascension of Isaiah or the book of Paralipomena of Jeremiah (4 Baruch). It is certain that the earliest translation into Ethiopic was made from Greek. In most of the books it took as the base text a text type very close to the Vatican manuscript and thus it is relatively free of Hexaplaric influences. However, this ancient translation was revised later according to other Greek manuscripts or following Arabic manuscripts. On this point there is no agreement among specialists.[51]

---

[49] See S. P. Brock, "Bibelübersetzungen. I", 204–205, and J. N. Birdsall, "Georgian Versions", *ABD* 6, 810–13.

[50] M. Brière, "Limitations of Georgian in Representing Greek", *The Early Versions*, 199–214.

[51] See S. P. Brock, "Bibelübersetzungen. I", 206–207, and R. Zuurmond, "Ethiopic Versions", *ABD* 6, 808–10.

There are no manuscripts of the Ethiopic Bible earlier than the 13th/14th centuries, and most of them are later than the 16th century. A large part of the books of the Old Testament was edited by A. Dillmann in the second half of the 19th century. In the same century some critical editions of great value were published, such as the ones by O. Löfgren for Daniel and the Twelve Prophets.[52]

For the phonetic, morphological and syntactic limitations of Ethiopic for adequately reproducing Greek, the article by J. Hofmann is instructive.[53]

The appearance of various Aramaic fragments of the book of Enoch and of some Hebrew fragments of the book of Jubilees among the documents from Qumran has led to new editions in Ethiopic of these pseudepigrapha.[54]

The Syro-Hexaplaric Version

It is the translation into Syriac of the fifth column of Origen's Hexapla, the LXX corrected according to the Hebrew text from other Jewish traditions and marked by obeluses, asterisks and other diacritical signs.[55] As the colophons of the manuscripts indicate, this version was completed by bishops Paul of Tella (Mesopotamia) and Thomas of Harkel (Syria) in the monastery of *Enaton*, near Alexandria, where they had fled from the Arab invasion. The colophons to the books of Kings, Twelve Prophets and Daniel show that the translation was made between 615 and 617.[56]

Due to its uniform character and the literal nature of the translation, as Rørdam's study showed,[57] it is a first-class tool for recovering Origen's Hexaplaric recension of the LXX and one of its principal witnesses. It also contains several marginal notes with readings from Aquila, Symmachus and Theodotion. In his classic work on Hexaplaric

---

[52] O. Löfgren, *Die äthiopische Übersetzung des Propheten Daniel*, Paris 1927, and Löfgren, *Jona, Nahum . . . Maleachi äthiopisch*, Uppsala 1930.

[53] J. Hofmann, "Limitations of Ethiopic in Representing Greek", *The Early Versions*, 240–56.

[54] See M. A. Knibb, *The Ethiopic Book of Enoch*, 2 vols, Oxford 1978 and J. C. Vanderkam, *The Book of Jubilees: Critical Text and Translation*, 2 vols, CSCO 510 and 511, Leuven 1989.

[55] See chapter 13.

[56] See S. P. Brock, "Bibelübersetzungen. I", 185–89.

[57] S. Rørdam, *Dissertatio de regulis grammaticis quas secutus est Paulus Tellensis in veteri testamento ex graeco syriace vertendo: Libri Judicum et Ruth secundum versionem syro-Hexaplarem*, Copenhagen 1859–61.

fragments,[58] Field provides retranslations into Greek of this material from "the three". The publication of new Hexaplaric material has in general confirmed the correctness of F. Field's retranslations.

There are many important manuscripts of this version. Apparently there was an edition of the whole work in two volumes. Even in the Renaissance period a manuscript with the first part of the Old Testament was in circulation, the property of Andrés Masius, but it disappeared after his death. In the 18th century, the second part of this manuscript, with the rest of the Old Testament, came into the possession of the Ambrosian Library of Milan, and A. M. Ceriani published a photographic edition of it.[59] Since then new manuscripts have appeared, some of which have been published.[60]

The studies by S. P. Brock and M. J. Mulder[61] are indispensable for the limitations of Syriac to represent the Greek and the strange translation techniques of the various books.

The Syro-Palestinian Version

It is a translation into the Aramaic of the Palestine Christians, which uses the Syriac script known as Estrangela. All the literature preserved in this dialect is completed by translations from Greek made by the Aramaic-speaking Christian community of Palestine. This community belonged to the Melchites who did not wish to follow the doctrines of Nestorians or Monophysites.

---

[58] F. Field, *Origenis Hexaplorum quae supersunt*, Oxford 1875.

[59] A. M. Ceriani, *Codex Syro-Hexaplaris photolithographice editus. Monumenta Sacra et prophana VII*, Milan 1874.

[60] W. Baars, *New Syro-Hexaplaric Texts. Ed. Commented upon and Compared with the LXX*, Leiden 1968; A. Vööbus, *Discoveries of Very Important Manuscript Sources for the Syro-Hexapla: Contributions to the Research on the Septuagint*, Stockholm 1970; Vööbus, *The Hexapla and the Syro-Hexapla: Very Important Discoveries for Septuagint Research*, Estocolmo 1971, and Vööbus, *The Pentateuch in the Version of the Syro-Hexapla: A Facsimile Edition of a Midyat Ms. Discovered in 1964*, CSCO 369, Leuven 1975; Vööbus, *The Book of Isaiah in the Version of the Syro-Hexapla. A Facsimile Edition of Ms. St. Mark 1 in Jerusalem with an Introduction*, CSOC 449, Leuven 1983, and R. J. V. Hiebert, *The "Syrohexaplaric" Psalter*. SCS 27, Atlanta, Ga. 1989.

[61] S. P. Brock, "Limitations of Syriac in Representing Greek", *The Early Versions*, 83–98, and M. J. Mulder, "The Use of the Peshitta in Textual Criticism", *La Septuaginta*, 37–53.

On the Peshitta there is an extensive and excellent bibliography. See the critical edition being prepared by the Peshitta Institute in Leiden, the bibliography by P. B. Dirksen, *An Annotated Bibliography of the Peshitta of the Old Testament*, Leiden 1989, and the following monographs: P. B. Dirksen and M. J. Mulder (eds), *The*

The manuscripts preserved of this version only contain fragments of biblical books or extracts from lectionaries or other liturgical texts. Most of them come from Sinai or the Cairo Genizah. The oldest are palimpsests. The translation is usually dated to the 6th century.[62]

It has not seemed appropriate to include here the Arabic versions of the Bible, in spite of their importance, as they are of mediaeval origin and only a very small part of them, in use among the Copts, was made directly from the LXX, although others are influenced indirectly by Greek through Coptic. For an excellent study of current research we refer to the article by K. Samir.[63]

2. Western Versions

The Latin Versions

In the initial stages of the expansion of Christianity to the West, the usual language in the Mediterranean basin was Greek. However, very soon it was replaced by Latin; in North Africa already by the 2nd century, the LXX and the New Testament were translated into that language. Tertullian (160–220) was able to use a Latin version, and in the mid-3rd century, Cyprian, bishop of Carthage, quotes extensively in his works from a Latin version which had already been revised and thus has a complex history behind it. The process of successive revisions according to the various text forms in Greek that were in circulation continued into the following centuries and is one of the more specific characteristics of Latin translations before Jerome's translation. In some of these revisions there are even traces of a tendency to bring it close to Hebrew. These Hebraisms of the Old Latin led some specialists[64] to think that the translators might

Peshitta: Its Early Text and History, Leiden 1988, and P. B. Dirksen and A. van der Kooij (eds), *The Peshitta as a Translation*, Leiden 1995.

[62] See S. P. Brock, "Bibelübersetzungen. I", 187–89; Brock, "The Palestinian Syriac Version", *The Early Versions*, 75–82; F. Schulthess, *Lexicon Syropalaestinum*, Berlin 1903; H. Duensing, *Christlich-palästinisch-aramäische Texte und Fragmente nebst einer Abhandlung über den Wert der palästinischen Septuaginta*, Göttingen 1906; M. H. Goshen-Gottstein and H. Shirun, *The Bible in the Syropalestinian Version. I: Pentateuch and Prophets*, Jerusalem 1973, and M. Sokoloff and J. Yahalom, "Christian Palimpsests from the Cairo Geniza", *RHT* 8 (1978), 109–32.

[63] K. Samir, "Old Testament, Arabic Versions of the", *The Coptic Encyclopedia* 6, 1827–36, pp. 1833–34.

[64] See D. S. Blondheim, *Les parlers judéo-romans et la Vetus Latina. Études sur les rapports entre les traductions bibliques en langue romane des Juifs au moyen âge et les anciennes*

have been Jews. However, this theory has not been supported by more recent research.[65]

Both for existing manuscripts and for quotations from the Fathers it is clear that the text of this version is not a uniform text, but has a large number of differing texts. Even so, it does not seem that these are due to different translations of the same book since the similarities are very numerous and very strange. Rather, these divergences must be attributed to the constant process of revision that it underwent following different Greek models, and to variations in vocabulary due to the evolution of Latin in a very creative period. Hence the witnesses of the Old Latin contain material from different origins and of unequal value. In consequence, they should not be used for textual criticism of the Bible without rigorous internal criticism.[66]

The term "Old Latin" is used correctly for translations and revisions before Jerome. Two text types are usually distinguished, one African and the other European, with variations depending on where the manuscripts came from. From its chronology, this version was made from pre-Hexaplaric Greek models which differ markedly from the text transmitted by the great uncials of the 4th and 5th centuries. In the New Testament it is based on the Greek text of a Western type, and in the Old Testament it follows a Greek text closely related to the Antiochene text and earlier than the historical Lucian, called the proto-Lucianic.[67]

This version had enormous influence on the development of western Latin Christian vocabulary. Until the 7th century it was not replaced by Jerome's translation and also it was kept in those books of the Vulgate for which Jerome had no Hebrew text available for his translation (Wisdom, Sira, Baruch, Maccabees). In the book of Psalms the situation is more complex. Together with Jerome's translation (*Psalterium iuxta Hebraeos*), the Vulgate also transmits the *Psalterium*

---

versions, Paris 1925, and U. Cassuto, "The Jewish Translations of the Bible into Latin and its Importance for the Study of the Greek and Aramaic Versions", *Biblical and Oriental Studies* 1, Jerusalem 1973, 285–99.

[65] See S. P. Brock, "Bibelübersetzungen. I", 177–78; P.-M. Bogaert, "Latin Versions", *ABD* 6, 799–803, and J. Gribomont, "Les plus anciennes traductions latines", *BTT* 2, 44–65.

[66] See N. Fernández Marcos, *Scribes and Translators: Septuagint and Old Latin in the Books of Kings*, Leiden 1994, 41–87.

[67] See chapter 14, pp. 233–36.

Gallicanum, a revision of the ancient Latin versions on the basis of the Hexaplaric recension of the LXX.[68]

The main sources for study of the Old Latin are:

1. the oldest biblical manuscripts, some of them from the 5th century;[69]
2. the quotations in patristic literature stored in the card indices of the Vetus Latina Institut of Beuron (Germany);[70]
3. the Vulgate bibles with a large amount of material from the Old Latin;[71]
4. the glosses or additions to Jerome's translation in books such as Samuel or Proverbs, in which the Vulgate is shorter that the LXX and the Old Latin.[72]

The oldest layers of the Latin versions can attest text forms of great value for restoring the LXX and can even be used to recover some readings that have disappeared from Greek manuscripts and go back to a Hebrew text that is different from the Masoretic.[73]

The editions of the Old Latin are scattered in a range of publications, and Sabatier's edition is still useful.[74] In 1949, the Vetus

---

[68] See C. Estin, *Les Psautiers de Jérôme à la lumière des traductions juives antérieures*, Rome 1984.

[69] See B. Fischer, *Vetus Latina I. Verzeichnis der Sigel für Handschriften und Kirchenschriftsteller*, Fribourg Br. 1949, and P. Petitmengin, "Les plus anciens manuscrits de la Bible latine", *BTT* 2, 89–127.

[70] See H.-J. Frede, *Kirchenschriftsteller. Verzeichnis und Sigel*, 4th edn, Fribourg Br. 1995.

[71] Like the first Alcalá Bible (Madrid, *Univ. Complutense ms. 31*), from the 10th century, which transmits Old Latin texts for the books of Tobit, Judith, Esther, Maccabees, 2 Chronicles and Ruth, see R. Weber, *Les anciennes versions latines du deuxième livre des Paralipomènes*, Rome 1945, VII–VIII.

[72] See J. Schildenberger, *Die altlateinischen Texte des Proverbien-Buches. Erster Teil: Die alte Afrikanische Textgestalt*, Beuron 1941.
For the glosses of the Old Latin transmitted in a family of Spanish manuscripts of the Vulgate, see T. Ayuso Marazuela, *La Vetus Latina Hispana. 2 El Octateuco*, Madrid 1967; J. Ziegler, *Randnoten aus der Vetus Latina des Buches Iob in spanischen Vulgatabibeln*, Munich 1980; C. Morano Rodríguez, *Glosas marginales de Vetus Latina en las Biblias Vulgatas españolas. 1–2 Samuel*, Madrid 1989; A. Moreno Hernández, *Las glosas marginales de Vetus Latina en las Biblias Vulgatas españolas. 1–2 Reyes*, Madrid 1992, and J. M. Cañas Reíllo, *Glosas marginales de Vetus Latina en las Biblias Vulgatas españolas: 1–2 Macabeos*, Madrid 2000. The edition and analysis of the remaining marginal notes for the Old Testament in Spanish Vulgate Bibles will soon be completed.

[73] See J. Trebolle Barrera, "From the 'Old Latin' through the 'Old Greek' to the 'Old Hebrew' (2 Kgs 10.23-25)", *Textus* 11 (1984), 17–36.

[74] P. Sabatier, *Bibliorum Sacrorum Latinae Versiones antiquae seu Vetus Italica*, 3 vols, Rheims 1743–49 (Reprint [Brepols], Turnhout 1991).

Latina Institut of Beuron began the critical edition of this version, which in recent years has been revitalised under the direction of H.-J. Frede. In the Old Testament, complete editions of Genesis (B. Fischer), Wisdom (W. Thiele), several fascicles of Sira (W. Thiele), and the Song of Songs (E. Schulz-Flügel) have appeared and Isaiah (R. Gryson) is on the point of completion. Most of the New Testament epistles have also been published, thanks to the work of H.-J. Frede, W. Thiele, H. S. Eymann and U. Fröhlich. As well as this editorial work the Institute of Beuron has produced thirty-five monographs on the history of the Latin Bible.[75]

For a critical appraisal of publications on the Latin versions the bulletin that P.-M. Bogaert[76] periodically issues can be consulted. On the linguistic limitations of Latin for reproducing Greek and the correct use of this version in text criticism, the comments by B. Fischer and E. Ulrich[77] are very helpful.

The Gothic version

Philostorgius narrates that bishop Ulfilas (or Wulfila) translated the whole bible into Gothic, including the Old Testament, except for the books of Kings, since it would be unsuitable for the Goths, a warrior people, whose warlike instincts needed to be restrained rather than stimulated, to recount these battle stories.[78] However, most of the texts preserved in this language belong to the New Testament, and more than half of them to the gospels, the text of which has been transmitted essentially in a single source, the famous *Codex Argenteus* in the library of the university of Uppsala.

Of the Old Testament a scant ten pages, some words and numbers in Genesis and fragments of Nehemiah 5–7, have reached us.[79]

---

[75] See *42. Arbeitsbericht der Stiftung. 28. Bericht des Instituts*, Beuron 1998.

[76] P.-M. Bogaert, "Bulletin de la Bible Latine (1955–73)", supplement to *RBén* 74–78 (1964–74), and supplement to *RBén* 85–108 (1975–98).

[77] See B. Fischer, "Limitations of Latin in Representing Greek", *The Early Versions*, 262–374, and E. Ulrich, "Characteristics and Limitations of the Old Latin Translation of the Septuagint", *La Septuaginta*, 67–80.

[78] *Hist. Ecc.* II, 5, in *Philostorgius Kirchengeschichte*, ed. J. Bidez, 2nd edn by F. Winkelmann, Berlin 1922, p. 18: καὶ τά τε ἄλλα αὐτῶν ἐπεμελεῖτο καὶ γραμμάτων αὐτοῖς οἰκείων εὑρετὴς καταστάς, μετέφρασεν εἰς τὴν αὐτῶν φωνὴν τὰς γραφὰς ἁπάσας, πλήν γε δὴ τῶν Βασιλειῶν, ἅτε τῶν μὲν πολέμων ἱστορίαν ἐχουσῶν, τοῦ δὲ ἔθνους ὄντος φιλοπολέμου καὶ δεομένου μᾶλλον χαλινοῦ τῆς ἐπὶ τῆς μάχας ὁρμῆς, ἀλλ᾽ οὐχὶ τοῦ πρὸς ταῦτα παροξύνοντος.

[79] See W. Streitberg, *Die gotische Bibel*, Heidelberg 1971.

The references to a translation of the Psalms and of Ezra in ancient documents is due, apparently to false interpretation.[80]

Our knowledge of Gothic, an Indo-European language no longer used today and belonging to the Germanic group, derives almost exclusively from biblical translations. Hence its importance as the oldest cultural record we have of this language. Ulfilas created a new alphabet using characters taken from the Greek, Latin and Runic alphabets. The translation is very literal and uniform and reflects a high degree of competence on the part of the translator and his co-workers, who take great care in their choice of vocabulary. It was made in about 383, based on the Greek text of an Antiochene or Lucianic type, although in the New Testament it is also influenced by the Old Latin. In fact, the preserved fragments of Nehemiah correspond systematically to manuscripts 19 108 and 93, which in the books of Samuel, Kings and Chronicles have an Antiochene text. Accordingly it is one of the oldest witnesses to the Antiochene text.

On the limitations of Gothic to translate Greek and its correct use in text criticism, the work G. W. S. Friedrichsen[81] can be consulted.

The Slavonic Version

Like all beginnings, the arrival of Christianity to the Slav peoples is surrounded by legends and immersed in shadow. Apparently, it was the emperor Heracleus (575–641) who, without much success, made the first efforts to evangelise these peoples in the first half of the 7th century. In the 9th century there was another Byzantine mission to these peoples of which we are better informed and it produced surprising results among the Bulgarians, Serbs, Croats and Eastern Slavs. The evangelisation affected the bases of the oldest Slavonic-Christian culture. The account of these facts has been transmitted in two Slavonic sources, the *Vita Constantini* and the *Vita Methodii*, which, in spite of defective transmission, contain reliable historical data.[82] According to these sources, these two brothers, born in Thessalonica, were responsible for the mission to the Slavs. Before leaving for

---

[80] See J. N. Birdsall, "Gothic Versions", *ABD* 6, 803–805, p. 804. See, for example, the edition by H. C. de Gabelentz and J. Loebe, *Ulfilas. Veteris et Novi Testamenti Versionis Gothicae Fragmenta quae supersunt* I, Leipzig 1843, 353–56.

[81] G. W. S. Friedrichsen, "Limitations of Gothic in Representing Greek", *The Early Versions*, 388–93.

[82] See B. M. Metzger, *The Early Versions of the New Testament*, 395–96.

Moravia, Constantine, who later took the name of Cyril, designed a thirty-eight-letter alphabet for the Slav script and began to translate the gospels.[83] The translation of the Psalter is also attributed to Cyril. After the death of Cyril (869), Methodius, with the help of two or three priest-scribes, towards the end of the 9th century, completed the translation of the Old Testament, with the exception of Maccabees, since Methodius died in 885.

It is not certain that they translated all the books of the Old Testament. Besides, these original versions underwent many later revisions and in some 15th century manuscripts which include the whole bible, there are books that have been translated from the Vulgate, not from the Greek.

Most of the version by Cyril and Methodius was lost early on and only incomplete Psalters and fragments of gospels have reached us in relatively ancient manuscripts of around 1000 CE.[84] Some of these older manuscripts use the Glagolithic script and not the Cyrillic.

The Greek text used as the basis for the translation of the Old Testament was like the text of the Lucianic recension. Some agreements with Hebrew against Greek are to be attributed to the influence of the Hexaplaric recension of the LXX rather than to the translators knowing Hebrew.[85] A large amount of apocryphal and parabiblical literature has been preserved in ancient Slavonic in a rich manuscript tradition.[86]

On the limitations of ancient Slavonic for correctly translating Greek, the contribution by H. G. Lunt[87] is basic.

---

[83] There is no agreement among specialists on which type of alphabet Cyril invented, the Glagolithic or the Cyrillic. The relationship between the alphabets is also disputed. Today it is thought that the Glagolithic was the first alphabet of ancient Slavonic and that the Cyrillic alphabet is based on the Greek uncial script of the 9th–10th centuries. Towards the end of the 9th century, the Cyrillic alphabet was made official for ecclesiastical and secular use, see B. M. Metzger, *The Early Versions of the New Testament*, 401–403.

[84] The most important is the Psalter of Sinai, from the 9th century, in the Glagolithic script, which contains Psalms 1–137, see M. Altbauer, *Psalterium Sinaiticum: An 11th Century Glagolithic Manuscript from St Catherine's Monastery, Mount Sinai*, Skopje 1971. See also J. C. Tardanides, *The Slavonic Manuscripts Discovered in 1975 at St Catherines Monastery on Mount Sinai*, Thessalonica 1988.

[85] S. P. Brock, "Bibelübersetzungen. I", 215–16.

[86] See the monograph by A. de Santos Otero cited in note 36, and É. Turdeanu, *Apocryphes slaves et roumains de l'Ancien Testament*, Leiden 1981.

[87] H. G. Lunt, "Limitations of Old Church Slavonic in Representing Greek", *The Early Versions*, 431–42.

A table of these versions of the LXX follows with an approximate date for each version. Note that I indicate the date of the oldest translation known for the language in question, not the date of later revisions or translations.

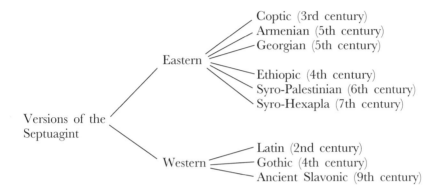

Versions of the Septuagint

Eastern
- Coptic (3rd century)
- Armenian (5th century)
- Georgian (5th century)
- Ethiopic (4th century)
- Syro-Palestinian (6th century)
- Syro-Hexapla (7th century)

Western
- Latin (2nd century)
- Gothic (4th century)
- Ancient Slavonic (9th century)

SELECT BIBLIOGRAPHY

Albert, M., *et al.*, *Cristianismes orientaux. Introduction à l'étude des langues et des littératures*, Paris 1993.

Altaner, B., and A. Stuiber, *Patrologie. Leben, Schriften und Lehre der Kirchenväter*, Fribourg Br. 1980, 10–13.

Assfalg, J., and P. Krüger, *Petit Dictionnaire de l'Orient Chrétien*, Brepols 1991 (especially, the articles "langue" and "littérature").

Bardy, G., *La question des langues dans l'Église ancienne. Tome I*, Paris 1948.

Beckwith, R. T., *The Old Testament Canon of the New Testament Church and its Background in Early Judaism*, London 1985.

Brock, S. P., "Bibelübersetzungen I. Altes Testament". *TRE* 6, 1980, 172–216.

Burton-Christie, D., *The Word in the Desert: Scripture and the Quest for Holiness in Early Christian Monasticism*, Oxford 1993.

Charlesworth, J. H., *The Pseudepigrapha and Modern Research with a Supplement*, Chico, Calif. 1981.

Denis, A.-M., *Introduction aux Pseudépigraphes grecs d'Ancien Testament*, Leiden 1970.

Dorival, G., "La Septante dans le monde chrétien. Canon et versions". Harl *et al.*, *La Bible grecque des Septante*, 1988, 321–34.

———— *et al.*, "Versions anciennes de la Bible". *Dictionnaire Encyclopédique de la Bible*, Turnhout 1987, 1302–25.

Fernández Marcos, N., "En torno al estudio del griego de los critianos". *Emerita* 41 (1973), 45–56.

————, (ed.), *La Septuaginta*, 1984, 15–80.

Gribomont, J., "Las traducciones bíblicas". *Patrología III. La edad de oro de la literatura patrística latina*, ed. J. Quasten and A. di Berardino, Madrid 1981, 231–37.

Hanson, R. P. C., "Biblical Exegesis in the Early Church". *Cambridge History of the Bible I*, 412–53.

Harl, M., "La Septante chez les Pères grecs et dans la vie des Chrétiens". Harl *et al.*, *La Bible grecque des Septante*, 1988, 290–320.

————, "La Septante et la pluralité textuelle des Écritures. Le témoignage des Pères Grecs". *Naissance de la méthode critique. Colloque du centenaire de l'École Biblique et archéologie française de Jérusalem*, Paris 1992, 231–43 (= *La langue de Japhet* 253–66).

————, "Le renouvellement du lexique des Septante d'après le témoignage des recensions, révisions et commentaires grecs anciens". *VI Congress of the IOSCS*, 1991, 239–59 (= *La langue de Japhet* 145–65).

————, "Origène et les interprétations patristiques grecques de l'obscurité biblique". *VC* 36 (1982), 334–71.

————, "Remarques sur la langue des chrétiens, à propos du *Patristic Greek Lexicon*". *JTS* 14 (1963), 406–20 (= *La langue de Japhet* 169–82).

————, "Y-a-t-il une influence du 'grec biblique' sur la langue spirituelle des chrétiens?". *La Bible et les Pères*, Strasbourg 1971, 243–63 (= *La langue de Japhet*, 183–202).

Kaestli, J.-D., and O. Wermilinger (eds), *Le Canon de l'Ancien Testament. Sa formation et son histoire*, Geneva 1984, 103–211.

Koester, H., *Introduction to the New Testament. Volume 2: History and Literature of Early Christianity*, Berlin–New York 1987.

Lamb, J. A., "The Place of the Bible in the Liturgy". *Cambridge History of the Bible I*, 563–86.

Metzger, B. M., *The Early Versions of the New Testament: Their Origin, Transmission and Limitation*, Oxford 1977.

Rabin, Ch., "Cultural Aspects of Bible Translation". *Armenian and Biblical Studies*, ed. M. E. Stone, Jerusalem 1976, 35–49.

Simonetti, M., *La letteratura cristiana antica greca e latina*, Florence–Milan 1969.

Swete, H. B., *An Introduction to the Old Testament in Greek*, Cambridge 1914, 462–77.

Trebolle, J., *The Jewish Bible and the Christian Bible*, Leiden–New York–Köln 1998, 348–65 and 513–44.

Various Authors, "Versions, Ancient". *ABD* 6, New York 1992, 787–813.

Vielhauer, P., *Geschichte der urchristlichen Literatur*, Berlin–New York 1975.

Wigtil, D. N., "The Independent Value of Ancient Religious Translations". *ANRW* II.16, 3, 1986, 2052–66.

More information about the various versions of the Septuagint can be found in *SMS* 243–68, *CB* 144–94 and *BS* 281–306.

GLOSSARY OF TECHNICAL TERMS

apocrypha — in Catholic terminology it denotes books of the Old and New Testaments not included in the canon of inspired books. For Protestants instead it refers to the biblical books not included in the Hebrew canon, although they are in the Septuagint. The latter are called deuterocanonical by Catholics.

Aramaism — cf. Semitism.

Aristarchian (signs) — diacritical signs used in Alexandrian philology (i.e. by Aristarchus) in the editions of the Greek classics. Adopted by Origen in editing his Hexapla; cf. asterisk and obelus.

asterisk — a sign used in the Hexapla to mark passages found in Hebrew but missing from the Septuagint translation. Origen included them in the text, taking them from other translators.

begadkefat — a siglum formed from the six Hebrew consonants that can be either occlusive or fricative.

Caraites — or followers of the Bible, a Jewish sect founded in the 9th century CE. Their aim was to follow the Bible in its teachings and religious opinions with the exclusion of traditional rabbinic laws.

catena — a literary form of early Christianity which consists in tacking together testimonies from the Fathers of the Church around a particular book or biblical passage; see chapter 19.

deuterocanonical — see apocrypha.

Dodekapropheton — Greek title of the book of the Twelve Minor Prophets.

Estrangela — the name of an early form of Syriac script. Later it would develop into two different forms Nestorian, from the school of Nisibe and serta, belonging to the school of Edessa and the Western Syrians.

Euhemerism — historical explanation of the origin of religion according to which the gods were famous men of the past elevated to divine status for their acts and inventions on behalf of humankind.

Gaonic	related to the gĕ'ônîm, a title given to heads of the Babylonian academies of Sura and Pumbedita. By means of their interpretation of the Mishnah the Amra'm produced the Talmud and the gĕ'ônîm undertook to interpret it.
Genizah	store, graveyard or repository of books withdrawn from liturgical use in the synagogue. So far the most important known is the one in Old Cairo, discovered in the 19th century which held large quantities of Hebrew manuscripts.
Ḥaftarâ	second reading in the synagogue liturgy after the Law, taken from the prophetic books.
Haggadâ	every type of exegesis of the scriptures that is not Halakâ. It includes all parts of ancient rabbinic literature that are not strictly legal.
Halakâ	set of doctrines or rules that Jews follow in daily life. Sometimes it denotes legal parts of Jewish tradition.
haplography	a mistake made by not writing a letter or group of similar letters which should be repeated.
Hebraism	see Semitism.
hifîl	the causative form of the Hebrew verb.
ḥireq	Hebrew vowel with an *i* sound.
hofâl	the causative–passive form of the Hebrew verb.
ḥôlem	Hebrew vowel with an *o* sound.
homoioteleuton	similarity between the ends of two words close together in a text, or of two sentences or clauses.
Indo-European	a linguistic stock or trunk from which comes the group comprising the following languages and language groups: Hittite, Tokharian, Indo-Iranian, Armenian, Baltic, Slavonic, Albanian, Greek, Italic (Latin and Osco-Umbrian) and Celtic.
iotacism	characteristic process of the vocalic system of late Greek which has combined in the i-sound (iota) several vowels and diphthongs of classical Greek (η, υ, ει, οι).
(revision)	revision of the Septuagint text to make it closer to the Hebrew text current in 1st century CE Palestine. The name comes from the peculiar translation of Hebrew *gam* = "also" by the Greek particle. Cf. proto-Theodotion.
Masoretic (text)	see *textus receptus*.
Midrash	type of exegesis of scripture opposed to pešat or literal interpretation, which tries to examine all aspects of the

	sacred text and to extract the corresponding interpretation. When applied to the legal sections of scripture it is called halakhic midrash. When applied to the rest of the Bible to interpret it or explain it in a moralising or edifying way it is called haggadic midrash.
Mishnah	denotes both the instruction, teaching and learning of tradition and the content of such instruction, i.e. traditional Jewish doctrine as it developed up to the beginning of the 3rd century CE. It is frequently applied to orally transmitted law as against the Miqra', the Law both written and read.
obelus	sign of something spurious. Origen used it to mark words or passages that were in the Septuagint but missing from the corresponding Hebrew text.
Old Latin	translation of the Septuagint into Latin, 2nd century CE.
palaeo-Hebrew	the oldest form we have of the Hebrew script before the square script. The shift from the palaeo-Hebrew script to the square script occurred from the 4th to 2nd centuries BCE although we cannot be more precise about the date.
palimpsest	ancient manuscript that has been erased and re-used and so preserves traces of previous writing.
pataḥ	Hebrew vowel with an *a* sound
pešer	exegetical technique used in the Qumran writings and the New Testament, which consists of applying individual sayings of the past to contemporary events.
piel	intensive form of the Hebrew verb.
Pre-Masoretic	Hebrew text before the period of vocalisation carried out by the Masoretes or transmitters from the 6th century CE.
pre-recensional	normally applied to the text of the Septuagint before the 3rd century CE, i.e. before it was revised by the three recensions mentioned by Jerome, namely, those by Origen, Lucian and Hesychius.
Prophets	in the Hebrew Bible denotes a collection of writings that includes Former Prophets (Joshua, Judges, Samuel and Kings) and Latter Prophets (Isaiah, Jeremiah, Ezekiel and the Twelve Minor Prophets).
proto-Lucianic	revision of the Old Septuagint to conform to the Hebrew text current in 1st century BCE Palestine, probably together with a stylistic revision. In Samuel–Kings it corresponds to one of the oldest layers, even though already revised, of the Antiochene text.

proto-Masoretic   Hebrew text that is a forerunner or predecessor of the Masoretic text but in the period of textual pluralism, *c.* 300 BCE–100 CE.

Proto-Theodotion   an early revision of the Septuagint equated by many specialists with the καίγε revision. Some accept that it was used later by the historical Theodotion.

Pseudepigraphic   a writing with a theme more or less related to the Old Testament, excluded from the canon of inspired books and chronologically set generally between the two Testaments.

qāmeṣ   Hebrew vowel with an *a/o* sound.

runic   the name of characters used for writing by the ancient Scandinavians.

segôl   Hebrew vowel with an *e* sound.

segholate   triliteral Hebrew noun generally vocalized with a double *segôl*.

Semitism   form of biblical Greek that is only explained by the influence of the underlying Semitic text. It can be a Hebraism or an Aramaism, depending on whether Hebrew or Aramaic is the original language being translated.

Septuagint(al)ism   form of biblical Greek caused by the influence of the Septuagint on later biblical writings and in particular on the New Testament.

Syro-Hexapla   translation into Syriac of the fifth column of the Hexapla carried out in the 7th century CE. It preserves the Hexaplaric diacritic signs and marginal notes from other Jewish translators.

Talmud   name of one of two Jewish works prepared by the schools of Palestine (Jerusalem Talmud) and of Babylonia (Babylonian Talmud) from the 3rd to the 5th centuries CE. It is generally used for the whole corpus of this literature and marks the culmination of the writings of Jewish tradition. It includes the Mishnah and the commentary on it called Gemarâ.

Targum   although literally it means 'translation, interpretation', it has been restricted to denote translation of the Bible into Aramaic. The plural is Targumim or Targums.

Tetragrammaton   God's name in Hebrew, so called because it comprises four letters (YHWH).

textual pluralism	variety of Hebrew texts which circulated before the unifying tendency that is evident towards the end of the 1st century CE (Synod of Yamnia).
textus receptus	text transmitted as official by the Masoretes and printed in the Hebrew Bibles until the Leningrad manuscript B19a began to be published.
the three	conventional name for the more recent translators of the Bible into Greek, i.e. Aquila, Symmachus and Theodotion
Theocrasia	another name for syncretism, a kind of universal religiosity which arose in the Hellenistic period from confusing or equating various deities as manifestations of a single numen.
Tiqqûnê sôferîm	corrections by the Hebrew scribes traditionally applied to eighteen passages, modified, apparently, to remove bad-sounding expressions from the biblical text.
Torah	Hebrew name for the Pentateuch or the five books of the Law.
Tosefta'	collection of treatises on topics of traditional Jewish Law studied more extensively than in the Mishnah.
Vetus Latina	See Old Latin.
Vorlage	said of any text used as the basis for a translation. It is generally used for the Hebrew text underlying the translation of the Septuagint.
Writings, the	Heb. *kᵉtûbîm*, the title used to denote in the Hebrew Bible books not included in the Law and the Prophets.
Yôm kippûr	day of atonement, an important feast in the Jewish calendar celebrated on the 10th of Tishri (September–October) and dedicated to begging reconciliation and pardon from God and one's fellow. Among other practices and rites on this day, the book of Jonah is read as the *Ḥaftarâ* in the synagogue.

INDEX OF MODERN AUTHORS

INDEX OF BIBLICAL QUOTATIONS

OLD TESTAMENT[1]

---

[1] Quotations according to the septuagint. If there are significant differences, as in the book of Jeremiah, the numbers in brackets refer to the Hebrew text.

NEW TESTAMENT

ABBREVIATIONS

Periodicals and Collections

AB	*Analecta Biblica*. Rome
ABD	*The Anchor Bible Dictionary*. New York
AbhKM	*Abhandlungen für die Kunde des Morgenlandes*
AION	*Annali dell'Istituto Orientale di Napoli*. Naples
AJSL	*American Journal of Semitic Languages and Literatures*. Chicago
AJT	*American Journal of Theology*. Chicago
AKM	*Abhandlungen für die Kunde des Morgenlandes*. Leipzig
ANRW	*Aufstieg und Niedergang des römischen Welt*. Berlin–New York
ASNP	*Annali della Scuola Normale Superiore di Pisa*
ATA	*Alttestamentliche Abhandlungen*. Münster
ATANT	*Abhandlungen zur Theologie des Alten und Neuen Testaments*. Zürich
BASOR	*Bulletin of the American Schools of Oriental Research*. New Haven
Bib	*Biblica*. Rome
BIOSCS	*Bulletin of the International Organization for Septuagint and Cognate Studies*.
BIRHT	*Bulletin d'information de l'Institut de recherche et d'histoire des textes*. Paris (cf. *RHT*)
BJGS	*Bulletin of Judaeo-Greek Studies*. Cambridge
BJRL	*Bulletin of the John Rylands Library*. Manchester
BTT	*La Bible de Tous les Temps*. Paris
BWAT	*Beiträge zur Wissenschaft vom Alten Testament*. Leipzig–Stuttgart
ByZ	*Byzantinische Zeitschrift*. Leipzig–Berlin–Munich
BZ	*Biblische Zeitschrift*. Freiburg–Paderborn
BZAW	*Beihefte zur Zeitschrift für die alttestamentliche Wissenschaft*. Giessen–Berlin
CBQ	*Catholic Biblical Quarterly*. Washington
CCSG	*Corpus Christianorum. Series Graeca*. Turnhout–Leuven
CFC	*Cuadernos de Filología Clásica*. Madrid
CIJ	*Corpus Inscriptionum Judaicarum*. Rome
CPG	*Clavis Patrum Graecorum I–V*, Turnhout–Leuven 1983–87
CQ	*Classical Quarterly*. Oxford
CSCO	*Corpus Scriptorum Christianorum Orientalium*. Leuven
CSEL	*Corpus Scriptorum Ecclesiasticorum Latinorum*. Vienna
CSIC	*Consejo Superior de Investigaciones Científicas*. Madrid
DACL	*Dictionnaire d'Archéologie chrétienne et de Liturgie*. Paris
DB	*Dictionnaire de la Bible*. Paris
DBS	Supplement to *Dictionnaire de la Bible*. Paris
DCB	*A Dictionary of Christian Biography*. London
DJD	*Discoveries in the Judean Desert*. Oxford
DSD	*Dead Sea Discoveries*. Leiden
EJ	*Encyclopaedia Judaica*. Jerusalem
EncBibl	*Enciclopedia Bíblica*. Barcelona
EstBib	*Estudios Bíblicos*. Madrid
ET	*The Expository Times*. Edinburgh
ETL	*Ephemerides Theologicae Lovanienses*. Leuven
FRLANT	*Forschungen zur Religion und Literatur des Alten und Neuen Testaments*. Göttingen
GRBS	*Greek, Roman and Byzantine Studies*. Cambridge Mass.

HTR	*Harvard Theological Review.* Cambridge Mass.
HUCA	*Hebrew Union College Annual.* Cincinnati
ICC	*International Critical Commentary.* Edinburgh–New York
IDB	*The Interpreter's Dictionary of the Bible.* New York–Nashville
IDBS	Supplement to *Interpreter's Dictionary of the Bible.* New York–Nashville
IEJ	*Israel Exploration Journal.* Jerusalem
ISBE	*International Standard Bible Encyclopaedia.* Chicago
JAC	*Jahrbuch für Antike und Christentum.* Münster
JAOS	*Journal of the American Oriental Society.* Baltimore
JAs	*Journal Asiatique.* Paris
JBL	*Journal of Biblical Literature.* Philadelphia
JE	*The Jewish Encyclopaedia.* New York–London
JJS	*Journal of Jewish Studies.* Oxford
JNES	*Journal of Near Eastern Studies.* Chicago
JNSL	*Journal of Northwest Semitic Languages.* Stellenbosch
JQR	*Jewish Quarterly Review.* London–Philadelphia
JSHRZ	*Jüdische Schriften aus hellenistisch-römischer Zeit.* Gütersloh
JSJ	*Journal for the Study of Judaism.* Leiden
JSOT	*Journal for the Study of the Old Testament.* Sheffield
JSS	*Journal of Semitic Studies.* Manchester
JTS	*The Journal of Theological Studies.* Oxford
KP	*Der Kleine Pauly Lexikon der Antike.* Stuttgart
KS	*Kleine Schriften.*
KT	*Kleine Texte für Vorlesungen und Übungen.* Berlin
Mansi	J.D. Mansi, *Sacrorum Conciliorum Nova et Amplissima Collectio.* Florence–Paris–Leipzig
MGWJ	*Monatsschrift für Geschichte und Wissenschaft des Judentums.* Breslau
MIOF	*Mitteilungen des Instituts für Orientforschung.* Berlin
MSU	*Mitteilungen des Septuaginta-Unternehmens.* Berlin–Göttingen
NGWGött	*Nachrichten von der (Kgl.) Gesellschaft der Wissenschaften zu Göttingen.* Göttingen
NKZ	*Neue kirchliche Zeitschrift.* Leipzig, Erlangen
NT	*Novum Testamentum.* Leiden
NTS	*New Testament Studies.* Cambridge
NTSuppl	Supplement to *Novum Testamentum.* Leiden
OBO	*Orbis Biblicus et Orientalis.* Fribourg–Göttingen
OLZ	*Orientalische Literaturzeitung.* Berlin
OS	*Orientalia Suecana.* Uppsala
OTS	*Oudtestamentische Studiën.* Leiden
PAAJR	*Proceedings of the American Academy for Jewish Research.* Philadelphia
PG	*Patrologiae Cursus Completus. Series Graeca.* Paris
PL	*Patrologiae Cursus Completus. Series Latina.* Paris
PSBA	*Proceedings of the Society of Biblical Archaeology.* London
PTA	*Papyrologische Texte und Abhandlungen.* Bonn
PW	*Paulys-Wissowa Real Encyclopädie der Classischen Altertumswissenschaft.* Stuttgart
RAC	*Reallexikon für Antike und Christentum.* Stuttgart
RB	*Revue Biblique.* Paris
RBén	*Revue Bénédictine.* Maredsous
REB	*Revue des Études Byzantines.* Paris
REG	*Revue des Études Grecques.* Paris
REJ	*Revue des Études Juives.* Paris
RGG	*Die Religion in Geschichte und Gegenwart.* Tübingen
RHPhR	*Revue d'Histoire et de Philosophie Religieuses.* Strasbourg–Paris
RHR	*Revue de l'Histoire des Religions.* Paris
RHT	*Revue d'Histoire de Textes.* Paris (previously *BIRHT*)

RivB   *Rivista Biblica Italiana.* Bologna
RQ   *Revue de Qumran.* Paris
RSPhTh   *Revue des Sciences Philosophiques et Théologiques.* Paris
RSR   *Revue des Sciences Religieuses.* Strasbourg
SBFLA   *Studii biblici Franciscani Liber Annuus.* Jerusalem
SC   *Sources Chrétiennes.* Paris
SCS   *Septuagint and Cognate Studies.* Missoula Mont.
SJOT   *Scandinavian Journal for the Old Testament.* Århus
ST   *Studi e Testi.* Rome
TECC   *Textos y Estudios Cardenal Cisneros.* Madrid
TLZ   *Theologische Literaturzeitung.* Leipzig–Berlin
TR   *Theologische Rundschau.* Tübingen
TRE   *Theologische Realenkyklopädie.* Berlin
TRev   *Theologische Revue.* Münster
TSK   *Theologische Studien und Kritiken.* Hamburg–Gotha–Leipzig–Berlin
TU   *Texte und Untersuchungen.* Leipzig–Berlin
TWNT   *Theologisches Wörterbuch zum Neuen Testament.* Stuttgart
TZ   *Theologische Zeitschrift.* Basle
VC   *Vigiliae Christianae.* Amsterdam
VT   *Vetus Testamentum.* Leiden
VTS   Supplement to *Vetus Testamentum.* Leiden
WO   *Die Welt des Orients.* Wuppertal–Stuttgart–Göttingen
WS   *Wiener Studien.* Vienna
WUNT   *Wissenschaftliche Untersuchungen zum Neuen Testament.* Tübingen
ZAH   *Zeitschrift für Althebraistik.* Stuttgart
ZAW   *Zeitschrift für die Alttestamentliche Wissenschaft.* Giessen–Berlin
ZDMG   *Zeitschrift der Deutschen Morgenländischen Gesellschaft.* Leipzig–Wiesbaden
ZNW   *Zeitschrift für die Neutestamentliche Wissenschaft.* Giessen–Berlin
ZTK   *Zeitschrift für Theologie und Kirche.* Tübingen
ZVS   *Zeitschrift für Vergleichende Sprachforschung.* Göttingen

Titles of Books Cited

P. R. Ackoyd and C. F. Evans (eds), *The Cambridge History of the Bible. Volume 1: From the Beginnings to Jerome*, Cambridge 1970 = *Cambridge History of the Bible I.*

G. J. Brooke and B. Lindars (eds), *Septuagint, Scrolls and Cognate Writings: Papers Presented to the International Symposium on the Septuagint and its Relations to the Dead Sea Scrolls and Other Writings (Manchester, 1990)*, SCS 33, Atlanta, Ga. 1992 = *Septuagint, Scrolls and Cognate Writings.*

D. A. Carson and H. G. M. Williamson (eds), *It is Written: Scripture Citing Scripture. Essays in Honour of Barnabas Lindars*, Cambridge 1988 = *It is Written.*

P. Casetti, O. Keel and A. Schenker (eds.), *Mélanges Dominique Barthélemy. Études bibliques offertes à l'occasion de son 60ᵉ anniversaire.* OBO 38, Fribourg–Göttingen 1981 = *Mélanges Dominique Barthélemy.*

C. E. Cox (ed.), *VI Congress of the International Organization for Septuagint and Cognate Studies, Jerusalem 1986.* SCS 23, Atlanta, Ga. 1987 = *VI Congress of the IOSCS.*

C. E. Cox (ed.), *VII Congress of the International Organization for Septuagint and Cognate Studies, Leuven 1989.* SCS 31, Atlanta, Ga. 1991 = *VII Congress of the IOSCS.*

W. D. Davies and L. Finkelstein (eds), *The Cambridge History of Judaism. 2: The Hellenistic Age*, London 1989 = *The Cambridge History of Judaism.*

G. Dorival and O. Munnich (eds), *"Selon les Septante"*. *Hommage à Marguerite Harl*, Paris 1995 = *Selon les Septante*.

L. H. Feldman and G. Hata (eds), *Josephus, the Bible, and History*, Leiden 1989 = *Josephus*.

N. Fernández Marcos (ed.), *La Septuaginta en la investigación contemporánea (V Congreso de la IOSCS)*. TECC 34, Madrid 1985 = *La Septuaginta*.

N. Fernández Marcos, J. C. Trebolle Barrera and J. Fernández Vallina (eds), *Simposio Bíblico Español, Salamanca 1982*, Madrid 1984 = *Simposio Bíblico Español*.

D. Fraenkel, U. Quast and J. W. Wevers (eds), *Studien zur Septuaginta-Robert Hanhart zu Ehren. Aus Anlass seines 65. Geburtstages*. MSU XX, Göttingen 1990 = *Studien zur Septuaginta*.

L. Greenspoon and O. Munnich (eds), *VIII Congress of the International Organization for Septuagint and Cognate Studies, Paris 1992*. SCS 41, Atlanta, Ga. 1995 = *VIII Congress of the IOSCS*.

M. Harl, G. Dorival and O. Munnich, *La Bible grecque des Septante. Du judaïsme hellénistique au christianisme ancien*, Paris 1988 = *La Bible grecque des Septante*.

M. Harl, *La langue de Japhet. Quinze études sur la Septante et le grec des chrétiens*, Paris 1992 = *La langue de Japhet*.

B. M. Metzger, *The Early Versions of the New Testament: Their Origin, Transmission and Limitations*, Oxford 1977 = *The Early Versions*.

M. J. Mulder and H. Sysling (eds), *Mikra: Text, Translation, Reading and Interpretation of the Hebrew Bible in Ancient Judaism and Early Christianity*, Assen–Maastricht 1988 = *Mikra*.

D. Muñoz León (ed.), *Salvación en la Palabra. Targum-Derash-Berith. En memoria del profesor Alejandro Díez Macho*, Madrid 1986 = *Salvación en la Palabra*.

G. J. Norton and S. Pisano (eds), *Tradition of the Text: Studies Offered to Dominique Barthélemy in Celebration of his 70th Birthday*. OBO 109, Fribourg–Göttingen 1991 = *Tradition of the Text*.

A. Pietersma and C. Cox (eds), *De Septuaginta: Studies in Honour of John William Wevers on his Sixty-fifth birthay*. Mississauga, Ontario 1984 = *De Septuaginta*.

J. Schreiner (ed.), *Wort, Lied und Gottesspruch. Festschrift für Joseph Ziegler*. Vol. 1: *Beiträge zur Septuaginta*, Vol. 2: *Beiträge zu Psalmen und Propheten*, Würzburg 1972 = *Wort, Lied und Gottesspruch*.

E. Schürer, *The History of the Jewish People in the Age of Jesus Christ*, G. Vermes, F. Millar and M. Goodman (eds), Edinburgh III.1, 1986; III.2, 1987 = *The History of the Jewish People*.

J. Trebolle Barrera and L. Vegas Montaner (eds), *The Madrid Qumran Congress: Proceedings of the International Congress on the Dead Sea Scrolls, Madrid 18–21 March 1991*, Leiden–Madrid 1992 = *The Madrid Qumran Congress*.

General Abbreviations

o'	The Septuagint
α'	Aquila
σ'	Symmachus
θ'	Theodotion

ε'	*Quinta*
ς'	*Sexta*
A	Alexandrian Codex
B	Vatican Codex
BCE	Before the Common Era
Brooke–McLean	A. E. Brooke, N. McLean, H.St J. Thackeray, *The Old Testament in Greek According to the Text of Codex Vaticanus . . .* 1–9 Cambridge 1906–40.
BS	C. Dogniez, *Bibliography of the Septuagint. Bibliographie de la Septante 1970–1993*, Leiden 1995.
c.	*circa*
CB	S. P. Brock, Ch. T. Fritsch, S. Jellicoe, *A Classified Bibliography of the Septuagint*, Leiden 1973.
CE	Common Era
cf.	*confer*
d.	died
deş	*desinit*
Diss.	Dissertation, doctoral thesis
ed./eds	edited by/editors
esp.	especially
Fs.	*Festschrift*
ibid.	*ibidem*
inc.	*incipit*
IOSCS	*International Organization for Septuagint and Cognate Studies*. Missoula, Mont.
LSJ	H. G. Liddell, R. Scott, H. S. Jones, *A Greek-English Lexicon*, Oxford, 1968.
LXX	The Septuagint
ms./mss	manuscript/manuscripts
NF(nf)	Neue Folge
NS(ns)	New Series
NT	New Testament
op. cit.	*opus citatum*
OT	Old Testament
p./pp.	page/pages
Pap.	papyrus
S	Codex Sinaiticus
SBL	Society of Biblical Literature, Philadelphia
SMS	S. Jellicoe, *The Septuagint and Modern Study*, Oxford 1968.
vol.	volume

Abbreviations of the Biblical Books

OLD TESTAMENT

Gen.	Genesis		1 Kgs	1 Kings
Ex.	Exodus		2 Kgs	2 Kings
Lev.	Leviticus		1 Chron.	1 Chronicles
Num.	Numbers		2 Chron.	2 Chronicles
Dt.	Deuteronomy		Ezra	Ezra
Josh.	Joshua		Neh.	Nehemiah
Jgs	Judges		Tob.	Tobit
1 Sam.	Samuel		Jud.	Judith
2 Sam.	Samuel		Est.	Esther

1 Mac.	1 Maccabees	Ez.	Ezekiel
2 Mac.	2 Maccabees	Dan.	Daniel
Job	Job	Hos.	Hosea
Ps./Pss	Psalm/Psalms	Jl	Joel
Prov.	Proverbs	Am.	Amos
Ruth	Ruth	Obd.	Obadiah
Qoh.	Qoheleth (Ecclesiastes)	Jon.	Jonah
Song	Song of Songs	Mic.	Micah
Wis.	Wisdom	Nah.	Nahum
Sira	Sira (Ecclesiasticus)	Hab.	Habakkuk
Is.	Isaiah	Zeph.	Zephaniah
Jer.	Jeremiah	Hag.	Haggai
Lam.	Lamentations	Zac.	Zachariah
Bar.	Baruch	Mal.	Malachi

NEW TESTAMENT

Mt.	Matthew	1 Tim.	1 Timothy
Mk	Mark	2 Tim.	2 Timothy
Lk.	Luke	Tit.	Titus
Jn	John	Phm.	Philemon
Acts	Acts	Heb.	Hebrews
Rom.	Romans	Jam.	James
1 Cor.	1 Corinthians	1 Pe.	1 Peter
2 Cor.	2 Corinthians	2 Pe.	2 Peter
Gal.	Galatians	1 Jn	1 John
Eph.	Ephesians	2 Jn	2 John
Phil.	Philippians	3 Jn	3 John
Col.	Colossians	Jude	Jude
1 Thess.	1 Thessalonians	Ap.	Apocalypse/Revelation
2 Thess.	2 Thessalonians